MACRO-ECONOMICS

RUDIGER DORNBUSCH

STANLEY FISCHER

Department of Economics
Massachusetts Institute of Technology

McGRAW-HILL BOOK COMPANY

New York   St. Louis   San Francisco   Auckland   Bogotá   Düsseldorf
Johannesburg   London   Madrid   Mexico   Montreal   New Delhi
Panama   Paris   São Paulo   Singapore   Sydney   Tokyo   Toronto

To Taeko and Rhoda

This book was set in Caledonia by Black Dot, Inc.
The editors were J. S. Dietrich and Madelaine Eichberg;
the designer was Joan E. O'Connor;
the production supervisor was Leroy A. Young.
The drawings were done by J & R Services, Inc.
Von Hoffmann Press, Inc., was printer and binder.

MACROECONOMICS

67890 VHVH 83210

Library of Congress Cataloging in Publication Data

Dornbusch, Rudiger.
Macroeconomics.

Includes index.
1. Macroeconomics. I. Fischer, Stanley, joint
author.
HB171.5.D618   339   77-22683
ISBN 0-07-017751-1

Contents

Preface

Our aim in writing this book has been to explain how modern macroeconomics is used in understanding important economic issues, and to help the reader analyze macroeconomic problems for her or himself. The book provides full coverage of basic macroeconomics, such as national income accounting, aggregate demand, and IS-LM analysis. It goes beyond the standard coverage in presenting also the theory of aggregate supply, the interesting and vitally important topics of inflation and unemployment, and a detailed treatment of basic open-economy macroeconomics. No important topic has been omitted because it is too difficult, but we have taken great pains to make nothing more difficult than it need be.

The book is policy- and issue-oriented, and this orientation is emphasized in a number of ways. Any presentation of macroeconomics and economic policy has to ask why, with all the theory we have at our disposal, recent economic performance has been so poor. We discuss problems of economic policy making directly in Chapters 9 and 15. Then in Chapters 10 and 16 we apply our basic macro theory to study the behavior of the economy in the 1960's and 1970's, respectively. Policy making and its problems are also emphasized by our continual references to economic events, issues, and dilemmas in the postwar United States economy, as we elucidate the relevance of the theoretical material. Finally, policy considerations are emphasized in that a full chapter is devoted to a discussion of the public sector budget and its financing. That chapter discusses not only the facts about government spending, taxes, and the national debt but also considers how the debt is financed, the meaning of the burden of the national debt, and the relationship between government budget deficits and inflation.

Macroeconomics is less cut-and-dried than microeconomics. That makes it unsatisfying if you are looking for definite answers to all economic problems, but should also make it more interesting because you have to think hard and critically about the material being presented. We have not hesitated to indicate where we think theories are incomplete. We unfortunately cannot guarantee that you will not at some future time have to unlearn something you learned from this book, but we hope you will have been warned.

Because the state of macroeconomics is not settled, and because it is so intimately tied up with policy making, the field is often seen as one in which anything goes and in which opposing Monetarist and Keynesian schools contend on almost every point. That is simply untrue. There are substantial areas of agreement among almost all macroeconomists—but it is less interesting to discuss points of agreement once you have understood them than to argue about disagreements. However, we do not emphasize the Keynesian-Monetarist debate in this book, preferring to discuss substantive matters and mentioning alternative views where relevant. Some prepublication reviewers of the book labeled us Keynesians and others called us Monetarists. We are quite happy to be known as neither or both.

HOW TO USE THE BOOK

To the Student:

Because we have not shied away from important topics even if they are difficult, parts of the book require careful reading. There is no mathematics except simple algebra. Some of the analysis, however, involves sustained reasoning. Careful reading should therefore pay off in enhanced understanding. Chapter 1 gives you suggestions on how to learn from this book. The single most important suggestion is that you learn actively. Some of the chapters (such as Chapter 9) are suitable for bedtime reading, but most are not. Use pencil and paper to be sure you are following the argument. See if you can find reasons to disagree with arguments we make. Work the problem sets! Be sure you understand the points contained in the summaries to each chapter. Follow the economic news in the press, and see how that relates to what you are learning. Try to follow the logic of the budget or any economic packages the administration may present. Occasionally, the chairpersons of the Federal Reserve Board or the Council of Economic Advisers testify before the Congress. Read what they have to say, and see if it makes sense to you.

To the Instructor:

An *Instructor's Manual*, written by Steven Sheffrin of the University of California at Davis, is available. It includes suggestions for different ways of using the book, particularly for organizing a one-semester or quarter course. Beyond suggestions for organizing different course requirements around this book, the manual contains further bibliographic indications and other course material.

ACKNOWLEDGMENTS

The debts incurred by authors are among the nicest there are, and we are fortunate to have acquired many in a short time. We want first to thank colleagues and present or former students who used the book and/or advised us about it: Richard Anderson, Yves Balcer, Olivier Blanchard, Cary Brown, Robert Bishop, Jacques Cremer, Allan Drazen, Jeffrey Frankel, Paul Joskow, Roger Kaufman, Charles Kindleberger, Mark Kuperberg, Frederic Mishkin, Mary Kay Plantes, Paul Samuelson, Steven Sheffrin, Robert Solow, Charles Steindel, and Hal Varian.

We were fortunate to receive detailed comments on the book from Professors Lloyd Atkinson (American University), Alan Deardorff (University of Michigan), Don Heckerman (University of Arizona), Thomas Mayer (University of California at Davis), William Poole (Brown University), and Steven Shapiro (University of Florida). Their suggestions have led us to make extensive revisions that have clarified, simplified, and sharpened the exposition, and we are very grateful for the encouragement and enthusiasm they have shown. We appreciate also the critical comments on early portions of the manuscript that we received from Professors Michael Babcock (Kansas State University), Arnold Collery (Amherst College), William Hosek (University of New Hampshire), Timothy Kersten (California Polytechnic State University), Charles Knapp (Department of Labor), Charles Lieberman (University of Maryland), Andrew Policano (University of Iowa), and from some anonymous reviewers.

We have not hesitated to impose on our friends and wish to acknowledge helpful suggestions from Jacob Frenkel (University of Chicago), Ronald Jones (University of Rochester), Edi Karni (Tel Aviv University), David Levhari and Don Patinkin (The Hebrew University), Don Richter (Boston College), and Michael Rothschild (University of Wisconsin).

Stephen Dietrich, McGraw-Hill economics editor, provided us with unfailing support and assistance. It has been a pleasure to work with him and the other members of the McGraw-Hill staff. Carl Shapiro, research assistant extraordinary, Nancy Johnson, and Barbara Ventresco were indispensable in the production of the manuscript(s). Their efficiency, cheerfulness, and willingness to work long hours helped keep us going and are deeply appreciated.

Rudiger Dornbusch
Stanley Fischer

PART

I

1

Introduction

Macroeconomics is concerned with the behavior of the economy as a whole—with booms and recessions, the economy's total output of goods and services and the growth of output, the rates of inflation and unemployment, the balance of payments, and exchange rates. To study the overall performance of the economy, macroeconomics focuses on the economic policies and policy variables which affect that performance—on monetary and fiscal policies, the money stock and interest rates, the public debt, and the federal government budget. In brief, macroeconomics deals with the major economic issues and problems of the day.

Macroeconomics is interesting because it deals with important issues. But it is interesting, too, because it is fascinating and challenging to reduce the complicated details of the economy to manageable essentials. *Those essentials lie in the interactions among the goods, labor, and assets markets of the economy.*

In dealing with the essentials, we have to disregard details of the behavior of individual economic units, such as households and firms, or the determination of prices in particular markets, or the effects of monopoly on individual markets. These are the subject matter of microeconomics. In macroeconomics we deal with the market for goods as a whole, treating all the markets for different goods—such as the markets for agricultural products and for medical services—as a single market. Similarly, we deal with the labor market as a whole, abstracting from differences between the markets for migrant labor and doctors. We deal with the assets markets as a whole, abstracting from the differences between the markets for AT&T bonds and Rembrandt paintings. The cost of the abstraction is that omitted details sometimes matter. For instance, agricultural price rises in early 1973 had a significant effect on inflation and unemployment, but few macroeconomists paid attention to the details of agricultural developments before that time. (But they have since!) The benefit of the abstraction is increased understanding of the vital interactions among the goods, labor, and assets markets.

Despite the contrast between macroeconomics and microeconomics, there is no basic conflict between them. After all, the economy in the aggregate is nothing but the sum of its submarkets. The difference between micro- and macroeconomics is therefore primarily one of emphasis and exposition. In studying price determination in a single industry, it is convenient for microeconomists to assume that prices in other industries are given. In macroeconomics, where we study *the* price level, it is for the most part sensible to ignore changes in relative prices of goods among different industries. In microeconomics it is convenient to assume the total income of all consumers is given and to ask how consumers divide their spending out of that income among different goods. In macroeconomics, by contrast, the aggregate level of income or spending is among the key variables to be studied.

The great macroeconomists, including Keynes, and modern American leaders in the field, like Milton Friedman of Chicago, Franco Modigliani of

MIT, and James Tobin of Yale, have all had a keen interest in the applications of macrotheory, especially to problems of policy making. Developments in macrotheory are closely related to the economic problems of the day. Indeed, the study of macroeconomics does not yield its greatest rewards to those whose primary interest is theoretical. The need for compromise between the comprehensiveness of the theory and its manageability inevitably makes macrotheory a little untidy at the edges. And the emphasis in macro is on the manageability of the theory, and on its applications. To demonstrate that emphasis, this book uses the theories we present to illuminate recent economic events, from the early 1960s through the 1970s. We also refer continuously to recent economic events to elucidate the meaning and the relevance of the theoretical material.

Modern macroeconomics is often seen as the battleground for conflict between two implacably opposed schools of thought—monetarism, represented by its champion, Milton Friedman, and "keynesianism," or nonmonetarism, or fiscalism, represented by economists such as Franco Modigliani and James Tobin. This view is seriously misleading. There are indeed conflicts of opinion and even theory between monetarists and nonmonetarists, but much more there are major areas of agreement: there is far more to macroeconomics than the topics on which monetarists and fiscalists disagree. We do not emphasize the monetarist-fiscalist debate in this book, preferring to discuss substantive matters, while mentioning alternative views where relevant.

We shall now in Sec. 1-1 present an overview of the key concepts with which macroeconomics deals. Section 1-2 presents a diagrammatic introduction to aggregate demand and supply, and their interaction; it gives a very general perspective on the fundamentals of macroeconomics and the organization of this book. Then, in Sec. 1-3, we outline the approach of the book to the study of macroeconomics and macropolicy making, and present a preview of the order in which topics are taken up. Section 1-4 contains brief remarks on how to use the book.

1-1 KEY CONCEPTS

Gross National Product

Gross national product (GNP) is the value of all goods and services produced in the economy in a given time period. In 1975, GNP in the United States economy was $1,516 billion, or a little over $7,000 per person. In 1955, GNP was $399 billion, or about $2,400 per person (per capita, or per head, is the usual expression). The primary task of macroeconomics is to explain what determines the level of GNP and its growth over time. Why did GNP grow by over 275 percent over those twenty years, or at an average annual rate of growth of 6.9 percent?

There are three factors making up GNP growth. First, GNP can increase because prices rise. The prices of most goods produced in the economy were higher in 1975 than the prices of the same goods in 1955. For most purposes we are interested in the physical production of goods and services, rather than the dollar value of the production. For that reason we distinguish between *nominal* GNP, which measures GNP in the prices of the year in which the goods are produced, and *real* GNP. Real GNP measures the value of output in different years using the prices of a common *base* year. At present the base year for measuring real GNP is 1972. The choice of the base year is a matter of convention, and no particular significance attaches to 1972. We refer to nominal GNP alternatively as GNP at current prices or *GNP in current dollars*. We refer to real GNP as GNP at 1972 prices (if 1972 is the base year) or *GNP in constant dollars*. The term *constant dollars* signifies that we measure GNP in dollars with constant purchasing power.

Table 1-1 shows real and nominal GNP in 1955 and 1976. The 1955 real GNP of $655 billion is higher than the nominal GNP of $399 billion. But the 1976 real GNP of $1,265 billion is lower than nominal GNP of $1,692 billion. Is there a puzzle? No, the table simply reflects the continuing rise in the price level from 1955 to 1976. Thus using the (higher) 1972 prices to value 1955 output gives us a larger GNP than we obtain from using 1955 prices. It follows that 1955 real GNP exceeds 1955 nominal GNP. Furthermore, because prices rose between 1972 and 1976, using 1972 prices to value 1976 output gives a real GNP number that is less than 1976 GNP measured at current 1976 prices.

Real GNP in 1976 is 93 percent higher than real GNP in 1955. The average annual growth rate of real GNP over that twenty-year period is 3.2 percent. Nominal GNP over the period grew at an annual average rate of 7.1 percent. The difference between growth in nominal and real GNP is purely a result of price level changes. We can conclude therefore that, over the period, prices increased at an average annual rate of 3.9 percent (= 7.1 percent − 3.2 percent). Thus over half the growth in nominal GNP from 1955 to 1976 was the result of price increases or *inflation*.

The second reason GNP changes over time is that the amount of resources available in the economy for production changes. The resources are conveniently split into labor and capital. The labor force, the number of people either working or looking for work, grew from 68 million in 1955

TABLE 1-1 REAL AND NOMINAL GNP

	1955 $	1976 $	Average annual percentage change, %
Nominal GNP	399	1,692	7.1
Real GNP (1972 prices)	655	1,265	3.2

Source: *Economic Report of the President*, 1977 and *Economic Indicators*, March 1977.

to nearly 97 million in 1976. The capital stock, the buildings and machines available for use in production, also grew over the period. Increases in the availability of *factors of production*—the labor and capital used in producing goods and services—account for part of the increase in real GNP.

The third reason GNP changes is that the employment of the resources available for production changes. Not all the labor and capital available in the economy is actually used in production. The *unemployment rate* (of labor) in 1955 was 4.4 percent, meaning that 4.4 percent of the then available 68 million workers were not working. In 1976 the unemployment rate was 7.7 percent—among the highest since the thirties. Given the total availability of factors of production, GNP changes when the employment of those factors changes.

Potential Output

One of the key macroeconomic policy concepts that we shall be using repeatedly is *potential real GNP*, or *potential output*. Potential output is shown along with actual output in Chart 1-1. It represents a measure of the level at which real GNP would be if there were full employment. The official measure of full employment underlying the potential output series shown in Chart 1-1 is an employment level of 96 percent of the labor force or 4 percent unemployment. Thus, potential output is a measure of what real GNP would be if unemployment was 4 percent.

An unemployment rate of 4 percent served as a bench mark for measuring potential output throughout the sixties and early seventies. That number has, however, been increasingly questioned and it is believed that a figure of about 5 percent is now more realistic. Indeed, this view has been taken in the 1977 *Economic Report of the President*. The exact concept and measurement of potential output remains a live issue of debate and research.[1] It is an important issue because, as we shall see, it defines the target that policy makers should set for the performance of the economy.

This point is brought out by comparing the *GNP gap*, that is, the difference between actual and potential output, under the old and new measures of potential output. In Table 1-2 we show actual output and the old and new measures of potential output for the 1968–1976 period. It is immediately apparent that the new measure—based on about 5 percent unemployment—shows a consistently smaller GNP gap. It thus suggests that policy performed better than the alternative measure would lead us to believe. In this book we generally use the old measure of potential output (at 4 percent unemployment) primarily because data are more conveniently available on that basis, but also because a new consensus has not yet developed.

---

[1]For details on the construction of potential output series, see *Economic Report of the President*, 1977.

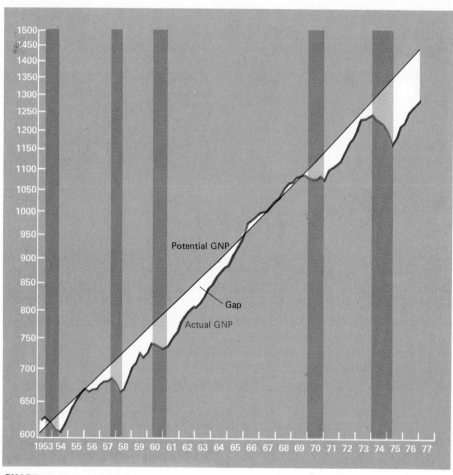

CHART 1-1 ACTUAL AND POTENTIAL
GNP. (Source: *Current Business
Conditions,* September 1976)

Potential output, or potential GNP, changes over time because the
labor force grows and also because the average output of an employed
person grows over time. The typical American worker today produces
more, in the same amount of time, than the typical worker of twenty years
ago. This increase in output per worker is called *productivity increase*.
There are two reasons for the increase in productivity. The first is that the
typical workers have more capital—machines and factory space—with
which to work now than they did then. The second is that there is *technical progress*—workers are better educated and machines are more sophisticated. (Think of pocket calculators!) As a result of productivity in-

TABLE 1-2 ACTUAL AND POTENTIAL OUTPUT, 1968–1976 (*In billions of 1972 dollars*)

	Potential GNP		Actual GNP
	Old	New	
1968	1,040.9	1,031.7	1,051.8
1969	1,081.6	1,068.3	1,078.8
1970	1,124.9	1,106.2	1,075.3
1971	1,169.9	1,145.5	1,107.5
1972	1,216.7	1,186.1	1,171.1
1973	1,265.4	1,228.2	1,233.4
1974	1,315.9	1,271.7	1,210.7
1975	1,368.6	1,316.9	1,191.7
1976	1,419.9	1,363.6	1,265.0

Source: *Economic Report of the President*, 1977.

creases and growth of the labor force, potential GNP is assumed to grow at a rate of about 4 percent per year.

The official estimate shows potential output in Chart 1-1 growing in almost a straight-line fashion, while actual GNP fluctuates around the level of potential output.[2] Actual real GNP fell short of potential GNP in the fifties and remained below potential output all the way through 1965. From about 1961, though, actual GNP began to grow more rapidly than potential output. Actual GNP stayed above potential output from 1965 until 1969, remaining below it since then. The depth of the 1973–1975 recession is shown by the gap of nearly 12 percent between actual and potential output that existed in 1975.

How is it possible for actual GNP to exceed potential GNP, as it did from 1965 to 1969? Remember that potential output is defined as the level of output that can be achieved if the unemployment rate is as low as 4 percent. In 1965–1969, the unemployment rate was even lower than 4 percent. The economy was operating at "high pressure" and produced in excess of the estimate of potential output. This suggests once more that potential output is only a bench mark for the economy's capacity. It is certainly neither a very accurate estimate nor a very rigid constraint.

Much of the recent history of the economy can be read from Chart 1-1. The economic performance of the Eisenhower years increased the GNP gap, as that administration concentrated its attention on fighting inflation.

[2]Notice that the scale for GNP in Chart 1-1 is not linear. For example, the distance from 600 to 650 is bigger than the distance from 1,450 to 1,500. The scale is logarithmic, which means that equal ratios are represented by equal distances. For instance, the distance from 600 to 1,200 is the same as the distance from 750 to 1,500, since GNP doubles in both cases. On a logarithmic scale, a variable growing at a constant rate (e.g., 4 percent per annum) is represented by a straight line.

Actual GNP shows clearly the 1957–1958 and 1960–1961 recessions. The Kennedy and Johnson administrations undertook economic policies to increase GNP rapidly, and reduce the gap, and they were successful in doing so. That success, however, came at the cost of increasing inflation over the period. The Nixon administration inherited the inflation of the last Johnson years and produced the recession of 1970–1971 in fighting that inflation. Then in 1972 and 1973, real GNP expanded rapidly, under the impetus of expansionary monetary policies of the Federal Reserve. And from 1973 to 1975, we see the seriousness of the recent recession.

Recessions are shown in Chart 1-1 by the vertical shaded lines, as for instance from August 1957 to April 1958. Each recession is a period of falling real GNP. The National Bureau of Economic Research, a private research organization in New York, provides definitions of periods of recession based on a number of criteria, including the behavior of real GNP. The latest recession is indicated by the period November 1973 to March 1975. The recovery started in March 1975.

Growth and Unemployment

Chart 1-2 shows the *growth rate* of real GNP since 1953. The growth rate is simply the rate of increase of GNP. Real GNP in 1973 was $1,235 billion and it was $1,171 in 1972. Real GNP in 1973 was, accordingly, 1.055 (= $1,235 ÷ $1,171) times as large as it was in 1972—or real GNP grew by 5.5 percent from 1972 to 1973. Recent economic events can be read off Chart 1-2 just as off Chart 1-1. For instance, we see the long period from 1961 through 1969 during which growth was positive, and for most of the period, in excess of 4 percent. And we can also see the negative growth of the economy starting at the end of 1973 and ending only in mid-1975. But note how erratic the growth rate of real GNP is, fluctuating between plus 7 percent and minus 3 percent.

Chart 1-2 also shows the behavior of the unemployment rate. The unemployment rate is widely watched as an indicator of the performance of the economy and as a matter of concern in its own right. High rates of unemployment mean that the economy is wasting output by not putting labor to work, and mean economic and psychic discomfort and distress to the unemployed themselves. We shall explore the anatomy of unemployment in great detail in Chap. 15.

From the viewpoint of understanding the behavior of unemployment, the interesting feature of Chart 1-2 is that the unemployment rate and the growth rate of real output are clearly related. Periods of high growth are reflected in reduction in unemployment, as through the sixties, and periods of low growth are reflected in rising unemployment, as in 1974.

A relationship between real growth and changes in the unemployment rate is known as *Okun's law*, named after its discoverer, Arthur Okun of the Brookings Institution, and formerly chairperson of the Council of Eco-

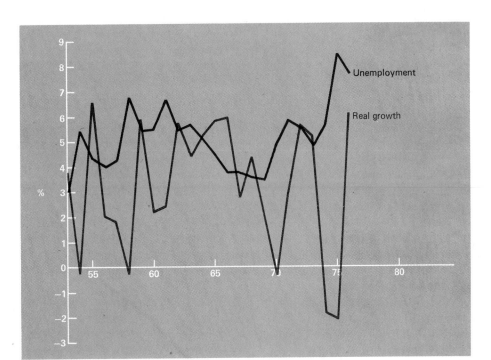

CHART 1-2 THE GROWTH RATE OF REAL
OUTPUT AND THE RATE OF
UNEMPLOYMENT. (Source: *Economic
Report of the President,* 1977)

nomic Advisers (CEA). Okun's law says that for every three percentage
points growth in real GNP above the trend rate of 4 percent that is sustained for a year, the unemployment rate declines by one percentage point.
This 3:1 relationship, the status of which is somewhat exaggerated by calling it a law rather than an empirical regularity, provides a rule of thumb for
assessing the implications of real growth for unemployment.

To provide an example of the way Okun's law is used in policy discussions, consider the rates of GNP growth that are needed to reduce unemployment by the end of 1980 to 5.0 percent, from the early 1977 level of 7.5
percent. To get the unemployment rate down by 2.5 percent, real growth
has to total 7.5 percent more than trend growth over the period. That
implies an average of growth above trend of nearly 2.0 percent over the
next four years. Given the trend growth rate of output of 4 percent, we
need an average growth rate of output of about 6.0 percent for the period
1977–1980.

Alternatively, to achieve the 5.0 percent unemployment level by early
1979, it would again be necessary to have real growth of 7.5 percent more
than trend, this time within two years. Real output would have to grow at

7.8 percent for two years to reduce[3] the unemployment rate by 2.5 percent. Chart 1-2 shows that since 1955 there has not been real growth of 7 percent for a two-year period in the United States economy. Thus, we should regard it as unlikely that real growth will be at a sufficient rate to reduce the unemployment rate back to around 5.0 percent by early 1979.

Okun's law can also be used to estimate the loss of real output due to unemployment. Using the 3:1 rule, we obtain a 3 percent increase in real output for every 1 percent reduction in the unemployment rate. Taking a 5.0 percent level of unemployment as normal, in early 1977 the economy is 7.5 percent short of potential output. With real GNP (in 1972 dollars) equal to about $1,300 billion, $98 billion in real output is lost owing to the unemployment of resources.

The importance of the rate of unemployment taken to be full employment should be clear from this section. Suppose we took 4 percent to be full employment; then we would currently be 10.5 percent short of potential output, giving an income loss of about $140 billion, which is closer to the number shown in Chart 1-1.

The Okun's law estimate of the loss of real output due to unemployment is a dramatic way of presenting the issue of why such high rates of unemployment occur, and what can be done about them. To answer those questions, we turn to the concept of aggregate demand.

Aggregate Demand

Aggregate demand, or spending, is the total demand for the goods and services produced in the economy, and is one of the key determinants of the demand for factors of production to produce goods and services. To reduce unemployment, it is necessary to increase aggregate demand. That immediately raises a number of questions, which are at the heart of macroeconomics and policy problems.

First, what determines aggregate demand? Second, what is the relationship between aggregate demand and the level of real output? Third, is there any way of increasing aggregate demand? And fourth, if it is possible to increase aggregate demand, is there any reason *not* to do so when there is unemployment?

These questions provide the main themes of this book. Chapters 3 through 9 discuss the determinants of aggregate demand, and particularly the roles of monetary and fiscal policy in affecting aggregate demand. The relationship between aggregate demand and output involves questions of aggregate supply, which are the subject of Chaps. 11 through 13. Aggregate supply specifies the relationship between the amount of output firms produce and the aggregate price level. The interaction between aggregate supply and aggregate demand determines the proportions in which a given

---

[3]Be sure you know how we got from the 7.5 percent excess of real growth above the trend rate to the 7.8 percent rates of growth.

change in aggregate demand results in an increase in prices and an increase in physical output. Stimulating aggregate demand may raise prices, and produce *inflation*, rather than reduce unemployment. And that is the reason why it may not be desirable to expand aggregate demand when there is unemployment.

Inflation

Inflation is the rate of increase of prices. Expansionary aggregate demand policies tend to produce inflation, unless they occur when the economy is at high levels of unemployment. Protracted periods of low aggregate demand tend to reduce the inflation rate. Chart 1-3 shows one measure of inflation for the United States economy for the period since 1953. The inflation measure in the chart is the rate of change of the consumer price index, the cost of a given basket of goods, representing the purchases of a typical urban wage earner.

The rate of inflation shown in Chart 1-3 fluctuates considerably. Just

CHART 1-3 THE RATE OF INFLATION, 1951–1976. (Source: *Economic Report of the President,* 1977)

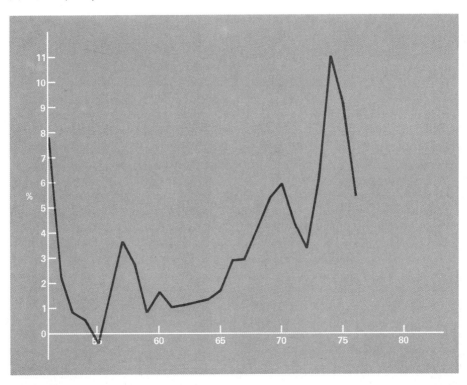

as we could tell much about the recent history of the economy from looking at Chart 1-1's picture of the course of GNP, we can likewise see much of recent economic history in Chart 1-3. In particular, there is the long period of steady inflation from 1960 through 1964 when the inflation rate hovered around the 2 percent level. Then there is a slow climb in the inflation rate from 1965 to 1970, followed by a slowing down of inflation till mid-1972. And finally there is the inflationary burst from 1972 through 1974—unprecedented in the last fifty years—as the inflation rate climbed to 12 percent.

Chart 1-3 presents the percentage *rate of change* of the consumer price index. It is interesting to ask how all those changes add up. Since 1952, consumer prices have more than doubled; in other words, the total increase in the price index since 1952 is over 100 percent. Much of that increase took place in the last few years.

Inflation, like unemployment, is a major macroeconomic problem. However, the costs of inflation are much less obvious than those of unemployment. In the case of unemployment, it is clear that potential output is going to waste, and therefore it is clear why it is desirable to reduce the unemployment. In the case of inflation, there is no obvious loss of output. Nonetheless, policy makers have been willing to increase unemployment in an effort to reduce inflation—that is, to *trade off* some unemployment for less inflation.

Inflation-Unemployment Tradeoffs

The *Phillips curve* is a relationship between the rates of inflation and unemployment that has played a key role in macroeconomic policy discussions since its publication in 1958. Figure 1-1 presents a typical Phillips curve, showing that high rates of inflation are accompanied by low rates of unemployment and vice versa. The curve suggests that less unemployment can always be attained by incurring more inflation and that the inflation rate can always be reduced by incurring the costs of more unemployment. In other words, the curve suggests there is a *tradeoff* between inflation and unemployment.

Economic events of the last decade, particularly the combination of high inflation and high unemployment in 1974, have led to considerable skepticism about the unemployment-inflation relation shown in Fig. 1-1. Chart 1-4 presents the inflation and unemployment rate combinations for the years 1963 to 1976. There is clearly no simple relationship of the form shown in Fig. 1-1.

Nonetheless, there remains a tradeoff between inflation and unemployment which is more sophisticated than a glance at Fig. 1-1 would suggest, and which will enable us to make sense of Chart 1-4. In the short run, of say two years, there is a relation between inflation and unemployment of the type shown in Fig. 1-1. That *short-run Phillips curve*, how-

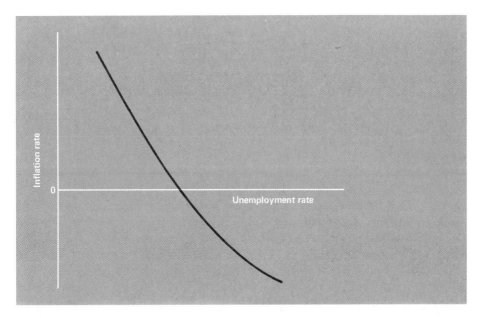

FIGURE 1-1 A PHILLIPS CURVE

ever, does not remain stable. It shifts as expectations of inflation change. In the long run, there is no tradeoff worth speaking about between inflation and unemployment. In the long run, the unemployment rate is basically independent of the long-run inflation rate.

The short- and long-run tradeoffs between inflation and unemployment are obviously a major concern of policy making and are the basic determinants of the potential success of stabilization policies.

Stabilization Policy

Policy makers have at their command two broad classes of policies with which to affect the economy. The first is *monetary policy*, which is controlled by the Federal Reserve System (the Fed). The instruments of monetary policy are changes in the stock of money, changes in the interest rate—the discount rate—at which the Fed lends money to banks, and some controls over the banking system. The second class of policies is *fiscal policy* under the control of the Congress, usually initiated by the executive. The instruments of fiscal policy are tax rates and government spending.

Monetary and fiscal policies affect the economy mainly through their effects on aggregate demand—these are *demand management* policies. Fiscal policy can also be used to some extent to affect aggregate supply, through policies known as *supply management*.

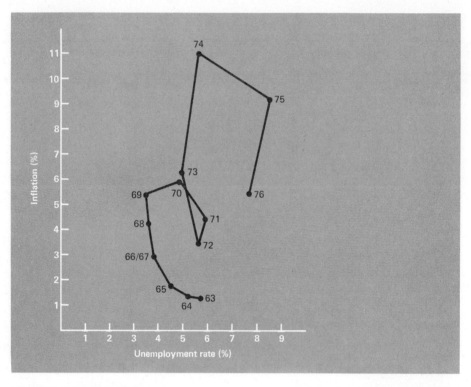

CHART 1-4 INFLATION AND
UNEMPLOYMENT. (Source: *Economic
Report of the President,* 1977)

One of the central facts of policy is that the effects of monetary and fiscal policy on the economy are not fully predictable, both in their *timing* and in the *extent* to which they affect demand. These two uncertainties are at the heart of the problems of *stabilization policy*—policies designed to moderate the fluctuations of the economy, and particularly the fluctuations of the rates of inflation, output, and unemployment. Chart 1-4 above shows the recent fluctuations of the rates of inflation and unemployment, and suggests strongly that stabilization policy has not been fully successful in keeping them within reasonable bounds. The failures of stabilization policy are due mostly to uncertainty about the way it works.

However, there are also questions of political economy involved in the way stabilization policy has been operated. The speed at which to proceed in trying to eliminate unemployment, at the risk of increasing inflation, is a matter of judgment both about the economy and about the costs of mistakes. Those who regard the costs of unemployment as high, relative to the costs of inflation, will run higher risks of inflation to reduce unemployment than will those who regard the costs of inflation as primary and unemployment as a relatively minor misfortune.

Political economy affects stabilization policy in more ways than through the costs which policy makers of different political persuasions attach to inflation and unemployment, and the risks they are willing to undertake in trying to improve the economic situation. There is also the so-called *political cycle*, which is based on the observation that election results are affected by economic conditions. Election results are affected not so much by the actual condition of the economy as by the way in which the economic situation is changing. When the economic situation is improving, and the unemployment rate is falling, incumbent presidents tend to be reelected. There is thus the incentive to policy makers running for reelection, or who wish to affect the election results, to use stabilization policy to produce booming economic conditions before elections. There is no question, for instance, that economic policy in 1971 was seriously affected by the knowledge that there would be an election the next year.

Stabilization policy is also known as *countercyclical* policy, that is, policy to moderate the trade cycle or *business cycle*, consisting of fairly regular cycles of booms, declines, recessions, and recoveries.[4] Chart 1-1 shows that cycles in the last fifteen years have been far from regular. The behavior, and even the existence, of the trade cycle is substantially affected by the conduct of stabilization policy. Successful stabilization policy smoothes out the cycle, while unsuccessful stabilization policy may worsen the fluctuations of the economy. Indeed, one of the tenets of monetarism is that the major fluctuations of the economy are a result of government actions rather than the inherent instability of the economy's private sector.

Monetarism, Nonmonetarism, and Activism

We noted above that there is some controversy over the existence of the tradeoff between inflation and unemployment. That controversy arose around 1967–1968 in part in the context of the debate in macroeconomics between monetarists and nonmonetarists, or fiscalists. We have already identified some of the major participants in the debate as Milton Friedman on the monetarist side and Franco Modigliani and James Tobin on the nonmonetarist side. But macroeconomists cannot be neatly classified into one camp or the other. Instead there is a spectrum of views. There are monetarists who make Friedman look like a fiscalist or keynesian, and keynesians who make Modigliani look like a monetarist. Not only that, there is no compelling unity to the views that are identified with monetarism, and the balanced economist is likely to accept some monetarist arguments and reject others. Nor is the debate one in which there is no progress. For instance, both theory and empirical evidence

[4]See, for instance, Paul A. Samuelson, *Economics*, 10th ed., McGraw-Hill, Chap. 14, 1976.

have been brought to bear on the issue of the inflation-unemployment tradeoff, and it is no longer central to the monetarist-fiscalist debate.

Another major point of contention is the relation between *money and inflation*. Monetarists tend to argue that the quantity of money is the prime determinant of the level of prices and economic activity, and that excessive monetary growth is responsible for inflation, and unstable monetary growth for economic fluctuations. Since they argue that variability in the growth rate of money accounts for variability of real growth, they are naturally led to argue for a monetary policy of low and constant growth in the money supply—a monetary growth rule. *Activists*, by contrast, point out that there is no close relationship between monetary growth and inflation in the short run and that monetary growth is only one of the factors affecting aggregate demand. They argue that policy makers are—or at least can be—sufficiently careful and skillful to be able to use monetary and fiscal policy to control the economy effectively.

The skill and care of the policy makers is important because monetarists raise the issue of whether aggregate demand policies might not worsen the performance of the economy. Monetarists point to episodes such as the overexpansionary policies followed by the Fed in 1972, to argue that policy makers cannot and do not exercise sufficient caution in the conduct of policy to justify using activist policy. Here the activists are optimists, suggesting that we can learn from our past mistakes.

A further issue that divides the two camps concerns the proper role of government in the economy. This is not really an issue that can be analyzed using macroeconomic theory, but it is difficult to follow some of the debate without being aware that the issue exists. Monetarists tend to be conservatives who favor small government and abhor budget deficits and a large public debt. They would favor tax cuts during recessions and cuts in public spending during booms with the net effect of winding up with a smaller share of government in the economy. Activists, by contrast, tend to favor an important and large role for government and are therefore not disinclined to use increased government spending and transfers as tools of stabilization policy. Differences between monetarists and activists must, therefore, be seen in a much broader perspective than their particular disagreements about the exact role of money in the short run.

1-2 AGGREGATE DEMAND AND SUPPLY

We have sketched the major issues and concepts we shall be discussing and using in the book. The key overall concepts are aggregate demand and aggregate supply. In this section we provide a brief preview of those concepts and of their interaction, with the aim of showing where we are heading, and to keep the material of Chaps. 3 through 10 in perspective.

Figure 1-2 shows aggregate demand and supply curves. The vertical axis P is the price level, and the horizontal axis Y is the level of real output

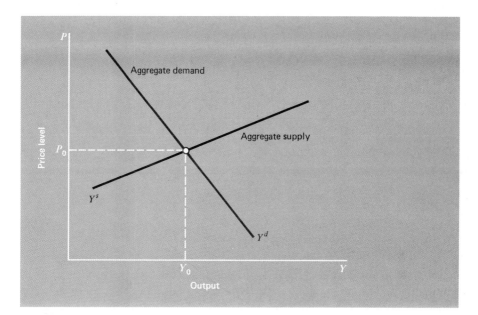

FIGURE 1-2 AGGREGATE DEMAND AND
SUPPLY

or income. Although the curves look like the ordinary supply and demand
curves of microeconomics, a full understanding of the curves will not be
reached until Chap. 12.

Aggregate demand is the total demand for goods and services in the
economy. It depends on the aggregate price level, as shown in Fig. 1-2. It
can be shifted through monetary and fiscal policy. The aggregate supply
curve shows the price level associated with each level of output. It can, to
some extent, be shifted by fiscal policy. Aggregate supply and demand
interact to determine the price level and output level. In Fig. 1-2, P_0 is the
equilibrium price level and Y_0 the equilibrium level of output. If the Y^d
curve of Fig. 1-2 shifts up to the right, then the extent to which output and
prices respectively are changed depends on the steepness of the aggregate
supply curve.[5] If the Y^s curve is very steep, then a given change in aggregate demand mainly causes prices to rise and has very little effect on the
level of output. If the Y^s curve is flat, a given change in aggregate demand
will be translated mainly into an increase in output and very little into an
increase in the price level.

Now, one of the crucial points about macroeconomic adjustment is that
the aggregate supply curve is not a straight line. Figure 1-3 shows that at
low levels of output, below potential output Y_p, the aggregate supply curve
is quite flat. When output is below potential, there is very little tendency

[5]Experiment with graphs like Fig. 1-2 to be sure you understand this.

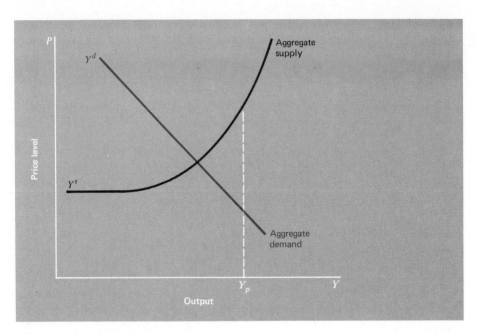

FIGURE 1-3 AGGREGATE DEMAND AND
NONLINEAR AGGREGATE SUPPLY

---

for prices of goods and factors (wages) to fall. Conversely, when output is above potential, the aggregate supply curve is steep, and prices tend to rise continuously. The effects of changes in aggregate demand on output and prices therefore depend on the level of output relative to potential.

All this is by way of a very important warning. In Chaps. 3 through 10 we focus on aggregate demand as the determinant of the level of output. We shall assume that prices are given and constant, and that output is determined by the level of demand—that there are no supply limitations. We are thus talking about the very flat part of the aggregate supply curve, at levels of output below potential.

The suggestion that output rises to meet the level of demand, without prices rising, leads to a very activist conception of policy. Under these circumstances, without any obvious tradeoffs, policy makers would favor very expansionary policies to raise demand and thereby cause the economy to move to a high level of employment and output. There are circumstances where such a policy view is altogether correct. The early 1960s are a case in point. Chart 1-1 shows that in these years output was substantially below potential. There were unused resources and the problem was a deficiency of demand. By contrast in the late 1960s and early 1970s, the economy was operating at full employment. There was no significant GNP gap. An attempt to further expand output or real GNP would run into supply limitations and force up prices rather than the production of goods.

In these circumstances a model that assumes that output is demand-determined and that increased demand raises output and *not* prices is simply inappropriate.

Should we think that the model with fixed prices and demand-determined output is very restricted and perhaps artificial? The answer is no. There are two reasons for this. First, the circumstances under which the model is appropriate—those of high unemployment—are neigher unknown nor unimportant. Unemployment and downward price rigidity are continuing features of the United States economy. Second, even when we come to study the interactions of aggregate supply and demand in Chap. 12 and later, we need to know how given policy actions *shift* the aggregate demand curve at a given level of prices. Thus all the material of Chaps. 3 through 10 on aggregate demand retains a vital part in the understanding of the effects of monetary and fiscal policy on the price level as well as output in circumstances where the aggregate supply curve is upward-sloping.

What then is the warning of this section? The warning is simply that the very activist spirit of macroeconomic policy under conditions of unemployment must not cause us to overlook the existence of supply limitations and price adjustment when the economy is near full employment.

1-3 OUTLINE AND PREVIEW OF THIS TEXT

We have sketched the major issues we shall be discussing and using in the book. We can now outline our approach to macroeconomics and the order in which the material will be presented. The key overall concepts, as already noted, are aggregate demand and aggregate supply. Aggregate demand is influenced by monetary policy, primarily via interest rates, and by fiscal policy. Aggregate supply is to some extent affected by fiscal policy.

Figure 1-4 presents a schematic view of the approach of the book to macroeconomics. Being schematic, the diagram is not comprehensive, but it does show the most important relationships we shall examine.

In broad outline, Chaps. 3 and 4 are concerned with aggregate demand, Chap. 11 with aggregate supply, and Chaps. 12 and 13 with the interactions between aggregate supply and demand. Chapters 5 through 10 present material which clarifies and deepens understanding of aggregate demand and of the ways in which monetary and fiscal policies affect the economy. Chapters 14 through 17 perform a similar service for aggregate supply and the interactions of aggregate supply and demand. Chapters 18 and 19 examine effects of international trade in goods and assets on the economy.

We now proceed to a chapter-by-chapter outline of the book. Chapter 2 is concerned with some definitions and relationships that arise in national income accounting. Many of these relationships, such as that between savings and investment, are used repeatedly in the rest of the book. Chapter 3 is the first, rudimentary model of aggregate demand and the determination of real output. This simple model shows how aggregate demand

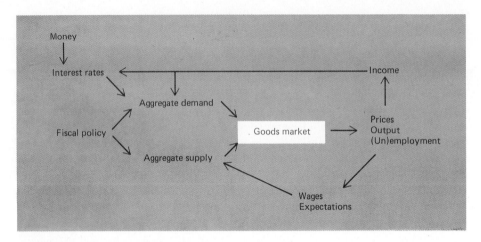

FIGURE 1-4 BASIC APPROACH TO
MACROECONOMICS

determines the level of output. While it is decidedly simple, it nevertheless contains some of the essential elements of modern macroeconomics,
and it is the backbone for some of the subsequent and more-developed
models. This rudimentary model enables us to give preliminary answers
to questions about fiscal policy, such as: What is the effect on output of a 10
percent cut in taxes? What is the effect on output of an increase in government spending matched by an equal increase in taxes?

Chapter 3 abstracts entirely from monetary considerations in discussing income determination. Chapter 4 introduces those considerations.
In that chapter, the simultaneous determination of output and interest rates
is studied and emphasis is given to the interaction between the goods
market—the market for goods and services—and assets or financial markets. A main point of that chapter is to study the role of money in the
economy, and to show how variations in the quantity of money, by changing interest rates, exert an effect on aggregate demand and thereby on the
level of output.

Chapters 5 through 8 put flesh on the skeleton model which is used in
Chap. 4 to study output determination and the channels through which
monetary and fiscal policy affect the economy. Chapter 5 examines the
determinants of consumption spending, which is the major component of
aggregate demand. Chapter 6 discusses investment spending, which is
important because it fluctuates a good deal and is significantly affected by
monetary and fiscal policies. Chapter 7 examines the determinants of the
demand for money, and Chap. 8 discusses the money supply process.
Chapter 8 clarifies the role of the Federal Reserve System in affecting and
controlling the money supply, and explains the mechanics of the way in
which the Fed conducts monetary policy.

Chapters 9 and 10 are the first chapters discussing stabilization policy.

Chapter 9 examines the problems of stabilization policy. It asks why it is not easier to apply the lessons of Chaps. 3 through 8 to the control of the economy than the performance of the economy in recent years suggests it is. Chapter 10 reviews economic policy made in the Kennedy and Johnson years, presenting the history of policy in the sixties and illustrating the use of the tools acquired in earlier chapters. There is, for instance, a detailed examination of the effects of the successful 1964 tax cut.

Chapter 11 begins the move over from the aggregate demand approach of the earlier chapters, which are of major relevance when the economy is operating at less than full capacity and prices can be taken to be more or less constant, to examine aggregate supply. Chapter 12 then combines the aggregate supply relationship with the aggregate demand apparatus developed in Chap. 4, to study the joint determination of the levels of real output, interest rates, and prices.

Chapter 13 moves on from the determination of the price *level* and *level* of output to discuss inflation, output, and unemployment. The apparatus of Chap. 12 is useful in examining the effect of one-time changes in the money supply and fiscal policy on the economy, but quite unwieldy for the study of ongoing processes of inflation and changes in output over time. The model of Chap. 13 is well suited to discuss ongoing inflation along with output and unemployment.

Chapter 14 returns to fiscal policy and the role of government spending in the economy. We are particularly concerned in that chapter with the financing of government spending, and the effects of budget deficits on inflation. The chapter discusses too the components of government spending and the way in which taxes are raised.

Chapter 15 returns to the inflation-unemployment tradeoff and the costs of inflation and unemployment. It examines the anatomy of unemployment in detail, and draws the important distinction between anticipated and unanticipated inflation in discussing the costs of inflation. Chapter 16 then examines the record of the economy over the 1969–1976 period, using the apparatus of Chap. 13 to illuminate recent economic developments. It also draws on the discussion of Chap. 15 in trying to understand why policy makers made the policy choices they did.

Chapter 17 turns aside from the primarily short- and intermediate-run orientation of the book to examine long-term economic growth and the explanations for United States growth over the past century. In so doing, it essentially provides a detailed accounting of the development of potential output that has, up to that point, not been carefully examined.

Chapters 18 and 19 are devoted to international trade in goods and in assets. Although international trade is less important for the American economy than for most others, trade has been increasing as a fraction of GNP since World War II, and the major economic shock of the recent recession—the oil price increase—was trade-connected. Chapter 18 examines the ways in which trade affects GNP determination and the roles of monetary and fiscal policy under a system of fixed exchange rates. The fixed exchange rate system of the post-World War II world economy came under increasing pressure in the late sixties and early seventies and finally dissolved in 1973. From 1973, exchange rates have been *flexible* in that they change from day to day. Chapter 19 discusses trade and capital flows under flexible exchange rates, as well as the appropriate uses of monetary and fiscal policy in stabilizing an open economy.

1-4 PREREQUISITES AND RECIPES

In concluding this introductory chapter a few words on how to use this book will be helpful. First, we note that there is no mathematical prerequisite beyond high school algebra. We do use equations whenever they appear helpful, but they are not an indispensable part of the exposition. Nevertheless, they can and should be mastered by any serious student of macroeconomics.

The technically harder chapters or sections are marked by an asterisk (*). These parts can be skipped or dipped into. Either they represent supplementary material, or else we have provided sufficient nontechnical coverage to help the reader get on without them later in the book. The only reason we do present more advanced material or treatment is to afford a complete and up-to-date coverage of the main ideas and techniques in macroeconomics. Even though you may not be able to grasp every point of a section marked by an asterisk on first reading—and should not even try to—these sections should certainly be read to get the main message and an intuitive appreciation of the issues that are raised.

The main problem you will encounter comes from the interaction of several markets and many variables. As Fig. 1-4 already suggests, the direct and feedback effects in the economy constitute a quite formidable system. How can you be certain to progress efficiently and with some ease? The most important point is to ask questions. Ask yourself, as you follow the argument, why is it this or that variable should affect, say, aggregate demand? What would happen if it did not? What is the critical link?

There is no substitute whatsoever for an *active form of learning*. Reading sticks at best for seven weeks. Are there simple rules for active study? The best way to study is to use pencil and paper and work the argument by drawing diagrams, experimenting with flowcharts, writing out the logic of an argument, and working out the problems at the end of each chapter. Another valuable exercise is to take issue with an argument or position, or to spell out the defense for a particular view on policy questions. Beyond that, if you get stuck, read on for half a page. If you are still stuck, go back five pages.

As a final word, this chapter is designed for reference purposes. You should return to it whenever you want to check where a particular problem fits or where a particular subject matter fits. The best way to see the forest is from Chap. 1.

2

National Income Accounting

M acroeconomics is ultimately concerned with the determination of the economy's total output, the price level, the level of employment, interest rates, and other variables which we discussed in Chap. 1. A necessary step in understanding how these variables are determined is *national income accounting*. The national income accounts provide both the actual measures of such macroeconomic variables as output and income and a conceptual framework for relating the various measures to one another.

We study national income accounting not only because it provides us with our basic measure of the performance of the economy in producing goods and services, but also because it highlights the relationships among three key macroeconomic variables: output, income, and spending. This chapter will introduce a few accounting relationships among output, income, spending, and components of spending, and in so doing will advance us right into the subject of macroeconomics—because those accounting relationships involve some of the chief concepts with which we deal throughout the book.

Before we delve into the details of national income accounting, we can briefly indicate the main relationships among the key variables. The central concept is gross national product (GNP), which measures the value of all final goods and services currently produced in the economy and valued at market prices. GNP is thus a measure, indeed the basic measure, of the total output produced in the economy in a given year.[1] GNP includes the value of goods, such as automobiles and eggs, produced, along with the value of services such as haircuts or medical services.

Starting from the concept of GNP it will be shown, first, that the value of output produced gives rise to the total income received by wage earners and the recipients of interest, profits, and dividends. Second, total spending on goods and services in the economy is equal to the value of output. And third, total spending is therefore also related to the value of all incomes received. The relationship between total spending and total income suggests, correctly, that spending on goods and services plays a role in determining the levels of income and production in the economy. The economics of the interactions between spending and the level of output constitutes the main theme of Chap. 3.

Although these three relationships we have described appear simple, there is considerable complexity in the actual national income accounts in relating GNP to national income and to total spending. Those complexities arise in large part from the way in which indirect and direct taxes affect national income relative to GNP, but also involve the role of foreign trade. We investigate the details of the relationships among output, in-

---

[1]GNP suffers from some defects as a measure of the performance of the economy because it does not value certain economic activities that are hard to measure, such as the value of housepersons' services, or the work of volunteers, and also because it does not deduct the costs of nuisance outputs, such as pollution, from the value of output. For a discussion of a measure that attempts to remedy those defects, NEW or Net Economic Welfare, see Paul A. Samuelson, *Economics*, 10th ed., McGraw-Hill, 1976.

come, and spending in Sec. 2-1 through 2-3, starting in Sec. 2-1 with a description of GNP.

In Sec. 2-4 we further expand on the distinction between *nominal* GNP or output measured in current prices, and *real* GNP. The discussion is followed in Sec. 2-5, with a brief look at different price indexes. Here we distinguish the consumer price index from wholesale prices and the GNP deflator. In Sec. 2-6 we set out the national income relations formally, as a prelude to the economic analysis that begins in Chap. 3.

2-1 GROSS NATIONAL PRODUCT AND NET NATIONAL PRODUCT

Our aim in this section is to describe some important aspects of the measurements of GNP. This will set the scene for the discussion of the important relationships among GNP, income, and spending, which were emphasized in the introduction and which will be examined in Sec. 2-2 and 2-3.

As we noted above, GNP measures the value of all final goods and services produced in the economy during a given period. It includes the value of such goods produced as houses and bourbon, and the value of services, like brokers' services and economists' lectures. Each of these is valued at its market price and the total is added together to give GNP. In a simple economy that produces twenty bananas, each valued at 30 cents, and sixty oranges, each valued at 20 cents, GNP is equal to $18 (= 30 cents $\times$ 20 + 20 cents $\times$ 60). In the United States economy in 1976, the value of GNP was $1,692 billion.

There are a number of subtleties in the calculation of GNP that are important to keep in mind. First, we are talking about *final* goods and services. The insistence on final goods and services is simply to make sure that we do not double-count. For example, we would not want to include the full price of an automobile in GNP, and then also include the value of the tires which were sold to the automobile producer as part of GNP. The components of the car, sold to the manufacturers, are called *intermediate* goods, and their value should not be included in GNP. Similarly, the wheat that goes into bread is an intermediate good, and we do not count the value of the wheat sold the miller, and the value of the flour sold the baker, as well as the value of the bread, as part of GNP.

In practice, double-counting is avoided by working with *value added*. At each stage of the manufacture of a good, only the value added to the good at that stage of manufacture is counted as part of GNP. The value of the wheat produced by the farmer is counted as part of GNP. Then the value of the flour sold by the miller *minus* the cost of the wheat is the miller's value added. If we follow this process along, we will see that the sum of value added at each stage of processing will be equal to the final value of the bread sold.[2]

---

[2]How about the flour that is directly purchased by households for baking in the home? It is counted as a contribution toward GNP since it represents a final sale.

The second point is that GNP consists of the value of output *currently* produced. It thus excludes transactions in existing commodities such as old masters or existing houses. We count the construction of new houses as part of GNP, but we do not add trade in existing houses. We do, however, count the value of realtor's fees in the sale of existing houses as part of GNP. The realtor provides a current service in bringing buyer and seller together, and that is appropriately part of current output.

Third, GNP values goods at *market prices*. It is important to recognize that the market price of many goods includes indirect taxes such as the sales tax and various excise taxes, and thus the market price of goods is not the same as the price the seller of the good receives or the cost of production. We refer to the price net of indirect taxes as the *factor cost*, meaning that is what is received by the factors of production that manufactured the good. GNP is valued at market prices, and not at factor cost. This point becomes important when we relate GNP to the incomes received by the factors of production.

Valuation at market prices is a principle that is not uniformly applied because there are some components of GNP that are difficult to value. There is no very good way of valuing the services of housespouses, or a self-administered haircut, or, for that matter, the services of the police force or the government bureaucracy. Some of these activities are simply omitted from currently measured GNP, as, for instance, housespouses' services. Government services are valued at cost, so that the wages of government employees are taken to represent their contribution to GNP. There is no unifying principle in the treatment of these awkward cases, but rather a host of conventions is used, which we will not detail here.

Net national product (NNP) as distinct from GNP deducts from GNP the *depreciation* of the existing capital stock over the course of the period. The production of GNP causes wear and tear on the existing capital stock; for instance, a house depreciates over the course of time, or machines wear out as they are used. If resources were not used to maintain or replace the existing capital, GNP could not be kept at the current level. Accordingly, we use NNP as a better measure of the rate of economic activity that could be maintained over long periods, given the existing capital stock and labor force. Depreciation is a measure of the part of GNP that has to be set aside to maintain the productive capacity of the economy, and we deduct that from GNP to obtain NNP. In 1976, depreciation was $180 billion, or about 10 percent of GNP. We tend to work with the GNP rather than the NNP data because depreciation estimates are quite inaccurate, and also are not quickly available, whereas the GNP estimate for each calendar quarter is available in preliminary form about a month and a half after the end of the quarter.[3]

---

[3]National income accounts are regularly reported in the *Survey of Current Business*. Historical data are available in *Business Statistics*, a biennial edition, and the *Economic Report of the President*.

Now that we have developed the basic concept of the value of output or GNP in the economy, we shall proceed to develop the relationships described earlier, which center around GNP. In particular, we will focus on the following three areas:

1 The production of GNP has as its counterpart the income of the factors of production. We will want to know what the breakdown of income is among wages and salaries, rents, interest, and profits.
2 Cutting across the categories of income described in point 1, we shall want to examine what part of GNP accrues to households, whether in the form of wages, or interest, or rental income, or profits. We are led to the concept of *personal disposable income,* the amount of income households have available for spending or saving. We shall want to see how that is related to GNP.
3 The production of GNP gives rise to a supply of goods and services that is sold. We will want to know how GNP is divided among the types of goods sold and what sectors of the economy buy the ouput. Here we will examine the breakdown of GNP into consumption, investment, government spending on goods and services, and net exports, as components of the aggregate demand for output.

Points 1 and 2 are taken up in Sec. 2-2, and point 3 is analyzed in Sec. 2-3.

2-2 GNP AND INCOME

We now consider the relation between the value of output or GNP and the incomes that are generated in the production process. In this section we show that *income is equal to the value of output* because the receipts from the sale of output must accrue to someone as income. The purchaser of bread is indirectly paying the farmer, the miller, the baker, and the supermarket operator, for the labor and capital used in production and is also contributing to their profits.

GNP and National Income

Our statement above equating the value of output and income is correct with two qualifications:

1 Indirect taxes, in particular sales taxes, that introduce a discrepancy between market price and prices received by producers. GNP is valued at market price, but the income accruing to producers does not include the sales taxes that are part of market price, and thus falls short of GNP. Indirect taxes, along with some other items of the same nature, account for about 10 percent of GNP.

2　The second correction arises from depreciation.　As already noted, part of GNP has to be set aside to maintain the productive capacity of the economy.　Depreciation should not be counted as part of income, since it is a cost of production.　As a rule, depreciation amounts to about 10 percent of GNP.　Depreciation is usually referred to in the national income accounts as the *capital consumption allowance.*

With these two deductions we can derive *national income* from GNP, as shown in Table 2-1, which gives the dollar figures for 1976.[4]　National income gives us the value of output at *factor cost* rather than market prices, which is GNP.　It tells us what factors of production actually receive as income before direct taxes and transfers.

Factor Shares in National Income

We next ask how national income is split between different types of incomes, as shown in Table 2-2.

The most striking fact of Table 2-2 is the very large share of wages and salaries—compensation of employees—in national income.　This accounts for 76 percent of national income.　Proprietors' income is income from unincorporated businesses.　Rental income of persons includes the *imputed* income of owner-occupied housing[5] and income from ownership in patents, royalties, etc.　The net interest category includes interest pay-

---

[4]The item "Other (net)" in Table 2-1 includes a statistical discrepancy.　In addition, it subtracts from NNP government transfer payments but adds subsidies to, less current surpluses of, government enterprises.　The adjustment for government enterprises is required because, in the case of subsidies, market price understates the factor cost.　In the case of deficits, similarly the value of output measured at market prices falls short of the factor cost.

[5]GNP includes an estimate of the services homeowners receive by living in their homes.　This is estimated by calculating the rent on an equivalent house.　Thus the homeowner is treated as if she pays herself rent for living in her house.

TABLE 2-1　GNP AND NATIONAL INCOME, 1976 (*In billions of dollars*)

Gross national product (GNP)		$1,692
Less:		
Depreciation	$180	
Equals:		
Net national product (NNP)		$1,512
Less:		
Indirect taxes	$150	
Other (net)	$ 14	
Equals:		
National income		$1,349

Note: Numbers do not add because of rounding.
Source: Survey of Current Business, March 1977.

TABLE 2-2   NATIONAL INCOME AND ITS DISTRIBUTION, 1976 *(In billions of dollars)*

National income	$1,349	100%
Compensation of employees	$1,028	76%
Proprietors' income	$ 97	7%
Rental income of persons	$ 24	2%
Corporate profits	$ 118	9%
Net interest	$ 82	6%

Source: *Survey of Current Business*, March 1977.

ments by domestic businesses and the rest of the world to individuals and firms who have lent to them.

The division of national income into various classes is not too important for our macroeconomic purposes. It reflects, in part, such questions as whether corporations are financed by debt or equity, whether a business is or is not incorporated, and whether the housing stock is owned by persons or corporations—which, in turn, are owned by persons.[6]

National Income and Disposable Income

A considerably more important question from the macroeconomic viewpoint is how much the private sector—corporations and households—actually receive as income after all taxes but inclusive of transfers. As a matter of terminology, we refer to *transfers* as all those payments that do *not* arise out of current productive activity. Thus, welfare payments or unemployment benefits are examples of transfer payments. The level of *disposable* income available to the private sector is very important because that income, as we shall see in later chapters, influences spending decisions and thereby income and employment.

In moving from GNP to national income, we already have taken account of indirect taxes. To arrive at disposable income, we have to make the further adjustment of subtracting all *direct* taxes and adding transfers and interest payments by the government.

Three kinds of direct taxes have to be subtracted from national income:

1 Social insurance contributions, which are treated as a tax on wage income, levied in part on employers and in part on workers.
2 Personal income taxes and nontax payments. Nontax payments include such items as license fees, traffic tickets, and any other payment that is not a direct tax.
3 Corporate profit taxes.

[6]You might want to work out how Table 2-2 would be modified for each of the possibilities described in this sentence.

TABLE 2-3 NATIONAL INCOME AND DISPOSABLE INCOME IN 1976 *(In billions of dollars)*

National income	$1,349
Less:	
Corporate profits tax	$ 64
Personal tax and nontax payments	$ 194
Contributions for social insurance	$ 123
Plus:	
Government transfer payments	$ 184
Net government interest payments	$ 17
Equals:	
Disposable income	$1,169

Source: Survey of Current Business, March 1977.

Table 2-3 shows that of these taxes the personal income tax is the most important in terms of revenue. The corporate profit tax yields a relatively small revenue.

Transfer and interest payments by the government have to be added to national income in order to arrive at disposable income. These payments do not arise as a compensation for productive activity and, accordingly, are not included in GNP or national income. Clearly, however, they represent income to the recipients and thus have to be introduced on the way from national income to disposable income. We observe that of the two items, interest payments on the public debt are only $17 billion and thus are quite small. Transfer payments, by contrast, have become very large and, as shown in Table 2-3, by now almost match the revenue from the personal income tax. Government transfer payments have become a very controversial issue, to which we return in more detail in Chap. 14.

Table 2-3 establishes the link between national income and disposable income. It is worth observing that they are two quite distinct concepts. National income is a measure of the value of output produced, properly adjusted for excise or indirect taxes and depreciation. Disposable income, by contrast, is a measure of the income ultimately received by the private sector after *all* taxes are subtracted from the income generated by production and after transfers and interest payments are added. After all is said and done, however, these two numbers are not very different. As the table shows, disposable income falls short of national income by about 13 percent.

The table further suggests the interesting question of whether disposable income could possibly exceed national income. If transfer payments further increased, as they have done in the recent past, and if further increases in the public debt caused the interest bill of the government to rise, perhaps we would encounter a case where there is more income to spend than is produced. This question is clearly intriguing. It obviously has to do with how the government finances its outlays. We will not provide an answer here but note that we will return to this important question at various points in the book and, in particular, in the discussion on the budget in Chap. 14.

Personal Disposable Income

For some purposes it is useful to split up disposable income—the measure that we have just arrived at—into the part that accrues to households and the part that is retained by corporations as undistributed profits. In Table 2-4 we show that disposable income can be split into personal disposable income and corporate undistributed profits along with a valuation adjustment. In Table 2-4 we have introduced the notion of the *personal or household sector* as distinguished from the business and government sectors. We can think of the personal sector simply as households. Table 2-4 answers the question: What is personal disposable income? Personal disposable income, as the table shows, is closely related to disposable income with some adjustments required for undistributed corporate profits, business transfer payments—such as bad debts—which businesses make to the personal sector, and valuation adjustments. The latter arise with respect to inventories and depreciation and are primarily the consequence of price changes. The valuation adjustments are introduced into the national income accounts in an attempt to adjust the value of profits and to take correct account of inflation,[7] but the adjustments are not available for spending by households and are thus excluded from personal disposable income.

In summary, this section has shown the relation between GNP, which is a measure of productive activity in the economy, and income receipts that accrue to the private sector. The main steps in the long chain we have followed arise from taxes, transfers between sectors, and depreciation and

[7]Computed profits are affected by the value firms place on the goods they sell. In inflationary times, typical ways of valuing inventories *understate* the cost of goods sold, and thus lead to an *overstatment* of profits. The inventory valuation adjustment is an attempt to correct that error.

TABLE 2-4   DISPOSABLE INCOME AND PERSONAL DISPOSABLE INCOME, 1976 *(In billions of dollars)*

Disposable income	$1,169
Less:	
Undistributed corporate profits	$ 49
Valuation adjustment (inventory and depreciation)	$ −30
Plus:	
Business transfer payments	$ 7
Equals:	
Personal disposable income	$1,157

Source: Survey of Current Business, March 1977.

valuation adjustments. These intermediate steps remind us that there is an important difference between GNP as the value of output at market prices and the spendable receipts of the private sector. We could have a positive personal disposable income even if GNP were zero provided there was someone to make the necessary transfer payments. Likewise, GNP could be large and disposable income small if the government sector took in a lot of taxes. The larger taxes are, relative to government transfers, the smaller is disposable income relative to GNP.

Allocation of Personal Disposable Income

In concluding this section we can briefly ask how the personal sector allocates its personal disposable income. Table 2-5 answers that question. We observe from Table 2-5 that about 7 percent of personal disposable income is saved. The remainder is spent. Personal consumption spending absorbs most of personal disposable income. The remainder is taken up by transfers to the rest of the world.[8]

Tables 2-4 and 2-5 emphasize the personal sector of the economy as distinguished from the business sector. That distinction becomes important when one studies the detailed adjustment of the economy to fiscal policy such as an income tax change. In Chap. 10 we will draw on that distinction. For the major part of the book, however, we will not emphasize the difference between the household and business sector. We will be primarily concerned with the distinction between the government sector and the private sector, thus lumping together businesses and households and individuals. Furthermore, in most of the book we will not make the distinction between disposable and personal disposable income that arises largely from undistributed profits. We will pretend either that all

---

[8]In Tables 2-4 and 2-5 we have departed from standard national income accounting practices by excluding on the income and outlay side of the personal sector the interest payments made by households to businesses. These amount to $24 billion. They are not included in GNP, NNP, or national income because they do not represent payment for a current, productive contribution. Since, however, they are made as part of personal outlays, the current convention is to add them in on the way from national income to personal disposable income and, correspondingly, include them among consumer outlays. Since we will not be using the concept of consumer interest anywhere in the book, we dispose of the issue in this footnote.

TABLE 2-5 ALLOCATION OF PERSONAL DISPOSABLE INCOME, 1976 *(In billions of dollars)*

Personal disposable income		$1,157	100%
Personal outlays:		$1,081	93%
Personal consumption expenditures	$1,080		
Personal transfers to foreigners	$ 1		
Personal saving		$ 77	7%

Source: Survey of Current Business, March 1977.

profits are distributed or else that households think of undistributed profits as income, since after all, they own the corporations.

Summary

We summarize here in a few identities (and in the accompanying Chart 2-1) the relationships reviewed in each table:

$$\text{GNP} - \text{capital consumption allowance} \equiv \text{NNP (Table 2-1)} \qquad (1)$$

$$\text{NNP} - \text{indirect taxes} \equiv \text{national income (Table 2-1)} \qquad (2)$$

$$\text{National income} \equiv \text{wages and salaries} + \text{proprietors' income}$$
$$+ \text{rental income of persons} + \text{corporate profits} + \text{net interest}$$
$$\text{(Table 2-2)} \quad (3)$$

CHART 2-1 THE RELATION BETWEEN
GNP AND DISPOSABLE INCOME

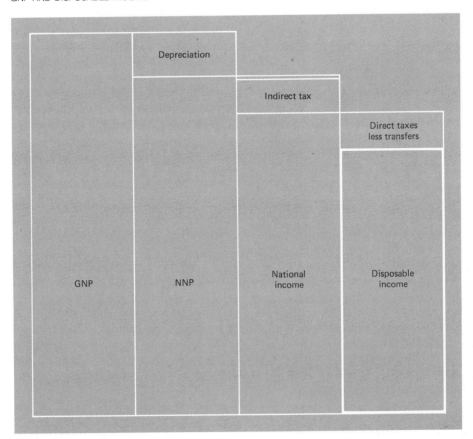

$$\text{National income} - \text{direct taxes} + \text{government interest and transfer}$$
$$\text{payments} \equiv \text{disposable income (Table 2-3)} \quad (4)$$

$$\text{Disposable income} - \text{undistributed corporate profits} - \text{valuation}$$
$$\text{adjustments} + \text{business transfer payments} \equiv \text{personal disposable}$$
$$\text{income (Table 2-4)} \quad (5)$$

$$\text{Personal disposable income} \equiv \text{personal outlays} + \text{personal savings}$$
$$\text{(Table 2-5)} \quad (6)$$

2-3 OUTPUT AND COMPONENTS OF DEMAND

In the previous section we started with GNP and asked how much of the value of goods and services produced actually gets into the hands of households. In this section we present a different perspective on GNP by asking who buys the output, rather than who receives the income. More technically we look at the demand for output and speak of the *components* of the aggregate demand for goods and services. Total demand for domestic output is made up of four components: (1) consumption spending by households; (2) investment spending by businesses or households; (3) government (federal, state, and local) purchases of goods and services; and (4) net foreign demand. We shall now look more closely at each of these components.

Table 2-6 presents a breakdown of the demand for goods and services in 1976 by components of demand. The table illustrates that the chief component of demand is consumption spending by the personal sector. This includes anything from food to golf lessons but includes also, as we shall see in discussing investment, consumer spending on durable goods such as automobiles, spending which might be regarded as investment rather than consumption.

Next in importance we have government purchases of goods and services. Here we have such items as national defense expenditures, road paving by state and local governments, and salaries of government employees.

TABLE 2-6 GNP AND COMPONENTS OF DEMAND, 1976 *(In billions of dollars)*

Personal consumption expenditures	$1,080	64%
Gross private domestic investment	$ 240	14%
Government purchases of goods and services	$ 366	22%
Net exports of goods and services	$ 7	
Gross national product (GNP)	$1,692	100%

Note: Numbers do not add because of rounding.
Source: Survey of Current Business, March 1977.

Gross private domestic investment is an item that requires some definitions. First, throughout this book, we will mean by investment additions to
the physical stock of capital. As we use the term, investment does *not*
include buying a bond or purchasing stocks in General Motors. Practically, investment includes housing construction, building of machinery,
business construction, and additions to a firms's or store's inventories of
goods. Recently, additions to the stock of mobile homes made the transition from consumption spending to being included in investment. This
illustrates that the classification of spending as consumption or investment
remains to a significant extent a matter of convention. From the economic
point of view there is little difference between a household building up an
inventory of peanut butter and a grocery store doing the same. Nevertheless, in the national income accounts, the individual's purchase is treated as
a personal consumption expenditure, whereas the store's purchase is
treated as investment in the form of inventory investment. Although these
borderline cases clearly exist, we can retain as a simple rule of thumb that
investment is associated with the business sector adding to the physical
stock of capital, including inventories.

It is worth emphasizing that much of the classification of expenditures
is a matter of convention rather than logic. For instance, how should we
treat purchases of automobiles by households? Since automobiles usually
last for several years, it would seem sensible to classify household purchases of automobiles as investment. We would then treat the *use* of
automobiles as providing consumption services. (We could think of imput-
ing a rental income to owner-occupied automobiles.) However, the convention is to treat all household expenditures as consumption spending.
This is not quite as bad as it might seem, since the accounts do separate out
household purchases of durable goods like cars and refrigerators from their
other purchases. There is thus information in the accounts on those parts
of household spending that with considerable justification could be
categorized as investment spending. When consumer spending decisions
are studied in detail, expenditures on consumer durables are usually
treated separately.

The convention that is adopted with respect to the household sector's
purchases of houses also deserves comment. The accounts treat the building of a house as investment by the business sector. When the house is
sold to a private individual, that is treated as the transfer of an asset, and not
then an act of investment. Even if a house is custom-built by the owner,
the accounts treat the builder who is employed by the owner as undertaking the act of investment in building the house. The investment is thus
attributed to the business sector.

In passing, we note that in Table 2-6 investment is defined as "gross"
and "domestic." It is gross in the sense that depreciation is not deducted
from investment. Net investment is gross investment minus depreciation.
Thus NNP is equal to net investment plus the other categories of spending
in Table 2-6.

The term *domestic* means that this is investment spending by domestic residents but is not necessarily spending on goods produced by us. It may well be an expenditure that falls on foreign goods. Similarly, consumption and government spending may also be partly for imported goods. On the other hand, some of domestic output is sold to foreigners.

The item "Net exports" appears in Table 2-6 to show the effects of domestic spending on foreign goods and foreign spending on domestic goods on the aggregate demand for domestic output. The total demand for the goods we produce includes exports, the demand from foreigners for our goods. It excludes imports, the part of our domestic spending that is not for our own goods. Accordingly, the difference between exports and imports, called *net exports*, or net foreign demand, is a component of the total demand for our goods.

The point can be illustrated with an example. Assume that instead of having spent $1,080 billion, the personal sector had spent $20 billion more. What would GNP have been? If we assume that government and investment spending had been the same as in Table 2-6, we might be tempted to say that GNP would have been $20 billion higher. That is correct if all the additional spending had fallen on our goods. The other extreme, however, is the case where all the additional spending falls on imports. In that case, consumption would be up $20 billion *and* net exports would be down $20 billion with no net effect on GNP.

2-4 REAL AND NOMINAL GNP

Nominal GNP measures the value of output in a given period in the prices of that period or, as it is sometimes put, in *current dollars*. Thus 1976 nominal GNP measures the value of the goods produced in 1976 at the market prices that prevailed in 1976, and 1974 GNP measures the value of goods produced in 1974 at the market prices that prevailed in 1974. Nominal GNP changes from year to year for two reasons. The first is that the physical output of goods changes. The second is that market prices change. As an extreme and unrealistic example, one could imagine the economy producing exactly the same output in two years, between which all prices have doubled. Nominal GNP in the second year would be double nominal GNP in the first year, even though the physical output of the economy has not changed at all.

Real GNP is a measure that attempts to isolate changes in physical output in the economy between different time periods, by valuing all goods produced in the two periods *at the same prices*, or in *constant dollars*. Real GNP is now measured in the national income accounts in the prices of 1972. That means that, in calculating real GNP, today's physical output is multiplied by the prices that prevailed in 1972 to obtain a measure of what today's output would have been worth had it been sold at the prices of 1972. We can return to the extremely simple example we used at the

TABLE 2-7 REAL AND NOMINAL GNP: AN ILLUSTRATION

1972 nominal GNP	1978 nominal GNP	1978 real GNP*
15 bananas @ 15¢: $2.25	20 bananas @ 30¢: $6.00	20 bananas @ 15¢: $3.00
50 oranges @ 18¢: $9.00	60 oranges @ 20¢: $12.00	60 oranges @ 18¢: 10.80
$11.25	$18.00	$13.80

*Measured in 1972 prices.

beginning of the chapter of an economy which produces only bananas and oranges, to illustrate the calculation of real GNP. The hypothetical outputs and prices of bananas and oranges in the two years are shown in the first two columns of Table 2-7. Nominal GNP in 1972 was $11.25 and nominal GNP in 1978 was $18.00, or an increase in nominal GNP of 60 percent. However, much of the increase in nominal GNP is purely a result of the increase in prices between the two years, and does not reflect an increase in physical output. When we calculate real GNP in 1978 by valuing 1978 output in the prices of 1972, we find real GNP equal to $13.80, which is an increase of 23 percent rather than 60 percent. The 23 percent increase is a better measure of the increase in physical output of the economy than the 60 percent increase.

We see from the table that the output of bananas rose by 33 percent, while the output of oranges increased by 20 percent from 1972 to 1978. We should thus expect our measure of the increase in real output to be somewhere between 20 percent and 33 percent, as it is. You will realize that the increase in real GNP that is calculated depends on the prices that are used in the calculation. If you have a calculator, you might want to compare the increase in real GNP between 1972 and 1978 if the prices of 1978 are used to make the comparison. The ambiguities that arise in comparisons using different prices to calculate real GNP are an inevitable result of the attempt to use a single number to capture the increase in output of both bananas and oranges when those two components did not increase in the same proportion. However, the ambiguity is not a major concern when there is inflation at any substantial rate and that is precisely when we most want to use real (rather than nominal) GNP to study the performance of the economy.

Chart 2-2 shows the behavior of real and nominal GNP over the past few years. It is particularly noteworthy that nominal GNP fell only once (from 1974/IV to 1975/I) during the period, even while real GNP fell in two consecutive years from 1973 to 1975. It would clearly be a mistake to regard the increases in nominal GNP as indicating that the performance of the economy was improving from 1973 to 1975, even as physical output fell. Real GNP is the better measure of the performance of the economy in producing goods and services, and it is the measure we should and do use in comparing output in different years.

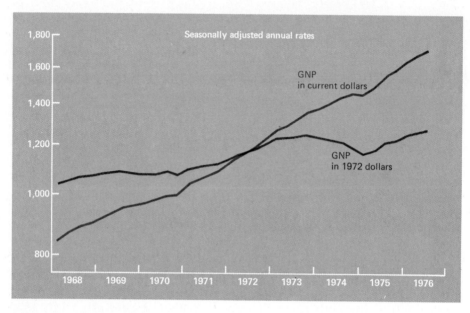

CHART 2-2   REAL AND NOMINAL GNP
(BILLIONS OF DOLLARS). (Source:
Economic Indicators, October 1976)

2-5 PRICE INDEXES

The calculation of real GNP gives us a useful measure of inflation, known as the *GNP deflator*.   Returning to Table 2-7, we can get a measure of inflation between 1972 and 1978 by comparing the value of 1978 GNP in 1978 prices and 1972 prices. The ratio of nominal to real GNP in 1978 is 1.30 (= 18 ÷ 13.80). In other words, output is 30 percent higher in 1978 when it is valued using the higher prices of 1978, than when it is valued in the lower 1972 prices. We ascribe, accordingly, the 30 percent increase to price changes, or inflation, over the period 1972–1978. The GNP deflator is the ratio of nominal GNP in a given year to real GNP, and it is a measure of inflation from the period from which the base prices for calculating real GNP are taken, to the current period.

Since the deflator is based on a calculation involving all the goods produced in the economy, it is a very widely based price index that is frequently used to measure inflation. It differs in two major ways from the other major index, the *consumer price index* (CPI), or cost of living index. First, it measures the price changes of a much wider group of goods than the CPI, which is based on the market basket of goods consumed by an urban wage earner. Second, the CPI measures the cost of a given basket of goods, which is the same from year to year. The basket of goods included in the GNP deflator, however, differs from year to year, depending on what is produced in the economy in each year. The goods valued in the deflator in a given year are the goods that are produced in the economy in that year. When corn crops are high, corn receives a relatively large weight in the computation of the GNP deflator. By contrast, the CPI measures the cost of a fixed bundle of goods that does not vary over time.[9] The behaviors of the two main indexes used to compute inflation, the GNP deflator and the CPI, accordingly, differ from time to time.

A third important price index is the *wholesale price index* (WPI). Like the CPI, this is a measure of the cost of a given basket of goods. It differs from the CPI partly in its coverage, which includes, for example, raw materials and semifinished goods. It differs, too, in that it is designed to measure prices at an early stage of the distribution system. Whereas the CPI measures prices where urban households actually do their spending—that is, at the retail level—the WPI is constructed from prices at the level of the first significant commercial transaction. This difference is important because it makes the WPI a relatively flexible price index and one that signals upturns in the general price level, or the CPI, some time before they actually materialize. For this reason the WPI, and, more particularly, some of its subindexes, such as the index of "sensitive materials," serves as one of the business cycle indicators that are closely watched by policy makers.

Table 2-8 shows the CPI, the WPI, and the GNP deflator for the last twenty-five years. Both the CPI and WPI use 1967 as their base. This means that the weights in the standard basket that is priced are those of 1967. For the GNP deflator, the base now is 1972. We note from the table that all three indexes have been increasing throughout the period. This is a reflection of the fact that the average price of goods has been rising, whatever basket we look at. We note, too, that the cumulative increase

[9]Price indexes are, however, occasionally revised to change weights to reflect current expenditure patterns.

TABLE 2-8 IMPORTANT PRICE INDEXES

	CPI (1967 = 100)	WPI (1967 = 100)	GNP deflator (1972 = 100)
1950	72.1	81.8	53.6
1960	88.7	94.9	68.7
1967	100.0	100.0	79.0
1970	116.3	110.4	91.4
1972	125.3	119.1	100.0
1976	170.5	182.9	133.8
Increase: price 1976/price 1950	136.5%	123.6%	149.6%

Source: Economic Report of the President, 1976, and *Economic Indicators,* March 1977.

(price 1976/price 1950) differs across indexes. This difference occurs because the indexes represent the prices of different commodity baskets.

The mechanics of price indexes are illustrated with the help of the price index formula.[10] Both the WPI and CPI are price indexes which compare the current and base year cost of a basket of goods of *fixed* composition. If we denote the base year quantities of the various goods by $q_0{}^i$ and their base year prices by $p_0{}^i$, the cost of the basket in the base year is $\Sigma p_0{}^i q_0{}^i$, where the summation (Σ) is over all the goods in the basket. The cost of a basket of the *same* quantities but at today's prices is $\Sigma p_t{}^i q_0{}^i$, where $p_t{}^i$ is today's price. The CPI or WPI, is the ratio of today's cost to the base year cost, or

$$\text{Price index} = \frac{\Sigma p_t{}^i q_0{}^i}{\Sigma p_0{}^i q_0{}^i} \times 100$$

multiplied, as a matter of convention, by 100.[11] Table 2-8 thus shows that in 1976 the cost of the standard (1967) consumer basket had increased relative to 1967 by 71 percent. Similarly, the WPI had risen relative to the base year by almost 83 percent.

2-6 SOME IMPORTANT IDENTITIES

In this section we formalize the discussion of Sec. 2-1 through 2-3 by writing down a set of relationships which will be used extensively in Chap. 3. We introduce here some notation and conventions that we will follow throughout the book.

For analytical work in the following chapters we will not use all the detail that comes up in national income accounting. Specifically, we will simplify our analysis by omitting the distinction between GNP and national income. For the most part we will disregard depreciation and thus the difference between GNP and NNP as well as the difference between gross and net investment. We shall refer simply to investment spending. We will also disregard indirect taxes and business transfer payments. With these conventions in mind *we refer to national income and GNP interchangeably as income or output.* These simplifications have no serious consequence and are made only for expositional convenience. Finally, and only for a brief while, we omit both the government and the foreign sector.

[10]Detailed discussion of the various price indexes can be found in the Bureau of Labor Statistics, *Handbook of Methods*, and in the Commerce Department biennial edition of *Business Statistics*. See, too, prob. 7 at the end of this chapter.

[11]The price index defined here is called a Laspeyres index. A Laspeyres index uses base year weights and in that respect differs from a Paasche index, which uses current year quantities as weights. See prob. 7.

A Simple Economy

We denote the value of output in our simple economy, which has neither a government nor foreign trade, by Y. Consumption is denoted by C and investment spending by I. The first key identity we want to establish is that between output produced and output sold. Output produced is Y, which can be written in terms of the components of demand as the sum of consumption and investment spending. (Remember, we have assumed away the government and foreign sector.) Accordingly, we can write the identity of output sold and output produced as:[12]

$$Y \equiv C + I \tag{7}$$

Now the question is whether Eq. (7) is really an identity. Is it inevitably true that all output produced is either consumed or invested? After all, do not firms sometimes make goods that they are unable to sell? The answer to each of the questions is yes. Firms do sometimes make output that they cannot sell, and that accumulates on their shelves. However, we count that accumulation of inventories as part of investment (as if the firms sold it to themselves), and, therefore, all output is either consumed or invested. Note that we are talking here about *actual* investment, which includes investment in inventories that firms might be very unhappy to make. Because of the way investment is defined, output produced is identically equal to output sold.

Identity (7) formalizes the basis of Table 2-6 (we are still assuming away the government and external sector). The next step is to draw up a corresponding identity for Table 2-5 and identity (6), which examined the disposition of income. For that purpose, it is convenient to ignore the existence of corporations and consolidate or add together the entire private sector. Using this convention, we know that private sector income is Y, since the private sector receives as income the value of goods and services produced. Why? Because who else would get it?—there is no government or external sector yet. Now the private sector receives, as personal disposable income, the whole of income Y. How will that income be allocated? Part will be spent on consumption and part will be saved. Thus we can write[13]

$$Y \equiv S + C \tag{8}$$

---

[12]Throughout the book we will be careful to distinguish identities from equations. Identities are statements that are *always* true because they are directly implied by definitions of variables or accounting relationships. They do not reflect any economic behavior but are extremely useful in organizing our thinking. Identities, or definitions, will be shown with the sign $\equiv$, and equations with the usual equality sign $=$.

[13]Again ask yourself why Eq. (8) should be identically true? What could you do with your income other than consume or save it? There is no alternative.

where S denotes private sector saving. Identity (8) tells us that the whole of income is allocated to either consumption or saving.

Next, identities (7) and (8) can be combined to read:

$$C + I \equiv Y \equiv C + S \tag{9}$$

The left-hand side of Eq. (9) shows the components of demand, and the right-hand side shows the allocation of income. The identity emphasizes that output produced is equal to output sold. The value of output produced is equal to income received, and income received, in turn, is spent on goods or saved.

The identity in Eq. (9) can be slightly reformulated to look at the relation between saving and investment. Subtracting consumption from each part of Eq. (9), we have:

$$I \equiv Y - C \equiv S \tag{10}$$

Identity (10) is an important result. It shows first that saving is identically equal to income less consumption. This result is not new, since we have already seen it in Eq. (8). The new part concerns the identity of the left and right sides: Investment is identically equal to saving. One can think of what lies behind this relationship in a variety of ways. In a very simple economy, the only way of saving for the individual is by undertaking an act of physical investment—by storing grain or building an irrigation channel. In a slightly more sophisticated economy, one could think of investors financing their investing by borrowing from individuals who save. However, it is important to recognize that Eq. (10) expresses the identity between investment and saving, and that some of the investment might well be undesired inventory investment, occurring as a result of mistakes by producers who expected to sell more than they actually do. The identity is really only a reflection of our definitions—output less consumption is investment, output is income, and income less consumption is saving. Even so, we will find that identity (10) will play a key role in Chap. 3.

Reintroducing the Government and Foreign Trade

We can now reintroduce the government sector and the external sector. First, for the government we shall denote expenditures by G and all taxes by T. Transfers to the private sector (including interest) are denoted by R. Net exports (exports minus imports) are denoted by NX.

We return to the identity between output produced and sold, taking account now of the additional components of demand, G, and NX. Accordingly, we restate the content of Table 2-6 by writing

$$Y \equiv C + I + G + NX \tag{11}$$

Once more we emphasize that in Eq. (11) we use actual investment in the identity and thus do not preclude the possibility that firms might not at all be content with the investment. Still, as an accounting identity, Eq. (11) will hold.

Next we turn to the derivation of the very important relation between output and disposable income. Now we have to recognize that part of income is spent on taxes, and that the private sector receives net transfers R in addition to national income. Disposable income is thus equal to income less taxes plus transfers:

$$Y_d \equiv Y + R - T \tag{12}$$

We have written Y_d to denote disposable income. Disposable income, in turn, is allocated to consumption and saving so that we can write

$$Y_d \equiv C + S \tag{13}$$

Combining Eqs. (12) and (13) allows us to write consumption as the difference between income plus transfers and taxes and saving:

$$C + S \equiv Y_d \equiv Y + R - T \tag{14}$$

or

$$C \equiv Y_d - S \equiv Y + R - T - S \tag{14a}$$

Identity (14a) states that consumption is disposable income less saving, or alternatively, that consumption is equal to income plus transfers less taxes and saving. Now we use the right-hand side of Eq. (14a) to substitute for C in identity (11). With some rearrangement we obtain:

$$S - I \equiv (G + R - T) + NX \tag{15}$$

Identity (15) cannot be overemphasized. What it states is that the excess of saving over investment of the private sector $(S - I)$ is equal to the *budget deficit* $(G + R - T)$ plus the *trade surplus* (NX). On the right-hand side of Eq. (15) the first term is the budget deficit of the government—government spending plus transfers (including interest payments) less tax collection. The second term on the right-hand side of Eq. (15) shows net exports. Even without any behavioral content, Eq. (15) is already useful because it suggests that there are important relations between the accounts of the domestic private sector $S - I$, the government budget $G + R - T$, and the external sector. Identity (15) states that if the private sector is in balance in the sense that saving equals investment, then any government budget deficit (surplus) is reflected in an equal external deficit (surplus).

Another perspective on this key identity is gained by singling out the government budget:[14]

---

[14]*Government* throughout this chapter means the federal government plus state and local governments. A breakdown between these entities can be found in the *Economic Report of the President*. There one would see, for example, that state and local governments run surpluses in their public enterprises and are net recipients of interest payments.

$$T - R - G \equiv (I - S) + NX \qquad (15a)$$

If the government has a budget surplus because spending and transfers are smaller than tax collection, then the counterpart is either an external surplus, or an excess of private investment over saving. The principle can be generalized by noting that any imbalance in the budget or the balance between saving and investment must be reflected in a matching external deficit. If the domestic economy absorbs more resources than it produces—investment exceeds savings and/or the budget is in deficit— then there is an external deficit. Conversely, if a country spends less than its income, there will be an external surplus. An individual spending less than her income will build up assets or claims on other people. For example, these assets could be money, or bonds, or stocks. A sector that spends less than its income accumulates claims on other sectors. Thus, if we have an excess of saving over investment, then the domestic private sector will be accumulating claims on either the government—if there is a budget deficit—or on the rest of the world—if there is an external surplus. One sector's deficit is always equal to another's surplus simply because one person's receipts are another person's expenditures.

2-7 SUMMARY

We conclude with a brief summary of the major points of this chapter.

1 Nominal GNP is the value of the economy's output of final goods and services measured at market prices.
2 Real GNP is the value of the economy's output measured in the prices of some base year. Real GNP comparisons, based on the same set of prices for valuing output, provide a better measure of the change in the economy's physical output than nominal GNP comparisons which also reflect inflation.
3 National income is equal to GNP minus depreciation and indirect taxes.
4 National income is equal to the incomes received in the economy, valued at factor cost.
5 Spending on GNP is conveniently divided into consumption, investment, government spending on goods and services, and net exports. The division between consumption and investment in the national income accounts is somewhat arbitrary at the edges.
6 One sector's surplus is another sector's deficit. For instance, the excess of the private sector's savings over investment is equal to the sum of the budget deficit and the foreign trade surplus.
7 For the remainder of the book we use a simplified model for expositional convenience. We assume away depreciation, indirect taxes, business transfer payments, and the difference between households and

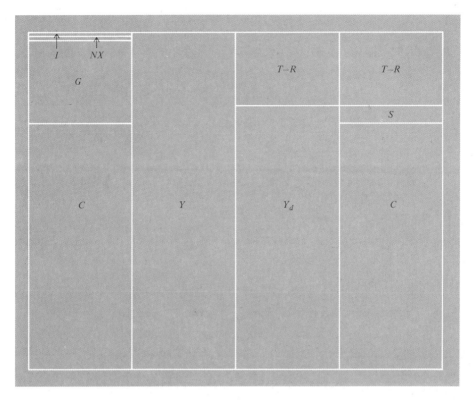

CHART 2-3 THE BASIC
MACROECONOMIC IDENTITY

corporations. For this simplified model, Chart 2-3 and Eq. (16) review
the *basic macroeconomic identity:*

$$C + G + I + NX \equiv Y \equiv Y_d + (T - R) \equiv (T - R) + S + C \qquad (16)$$

The left-hand side is the the demand for output by components which is
identically equal to output supplied. Output supplied is equal to income.
Disposable income is equal to income plus transfers less taxes. Disposable income is allocated to saving and consumption.

PROBLEMS

1 Show from national income accounting that:
   (a) An increase in taxes must imply a change in the trade balance, government
         spending, or the saving-investment balance.
   (b) An increase in disposable income must imply an increase in consumption
         or an increase in savings.

   (c) An increase in both consumption and saving must imply an increase in disposable income.

2 The following is information from the national income accounts for a hypothetical country:

GNP	1,500
Gross investment	200
Net investment	60
Consumption	1,000
Government spending on goods and Services	330
National income	1,200
Wages and salaries	900
Proprietors' income + rental income of persons	110
Net interest	60
Government budget surplus	− 20
Personal interest payments	0
Undistributed corporate profits	− 20
Valuation adjustments	− 20
Business transfer payments	0
Personal transfers to foreigners	0

What is:
(a) NNP?
(b) Net exports?
(c) Indirect taxes?
(d) Corporate profits?
(e) Net taxes–transfers?
(f) Disposable income?
(g) Personal disposable income?
(h) Personal saving?
(i) Total private saving?

3 What would happen to GNP if the government took unemployed workers who had been getting R in unemployment benefits and hired them as government employees to do nothing, still giving them R? Explain.

4 What is the difference in the national income accounts between:
(a) A firm buying an auto for an executive and the firm paying the executive additional income to purchase himself a car?
(b) You hiring your spouse (who takes care of the house) rather than just having him or her do the work without pay?
(c) You deciding to buy an American car rather than a German car?

5 Explain the following terms:
(a) Value-added   *(c)* Inventory investment
(b) Factor cost   *(d)* GNP deflator

6 Use the information in the various tables to construct a table showing the government receipts and outlays as well as the government budget deficit.

7 This question deals with price index numbers. Consider a simple economy where there are only three items in the CPI: food, housing, and entertainment (fun). Assume in the base period, say 1967, the household consumed the following quantities at the then prevailing prices:

	Quantities	Prices per unit, dollars	Expenditure, dollars
Food	5	14	70
Housing	3	10	30
Fun	4	5	20
Total			120

(a) Consider what the CPI will be in 1977 if the prevailing prices have changed as follows: food, $17 per unit; housing, $12 per unit; and fun, $4 per unit. In making your calculations, use the formula for the CPI given in the text.

*(b) Show that the change in the CPI relative to the base year is a weighted average of the individual price changes where the weights are given by the base year expenditure shares of the various goods.

(c) Price indexes that use base year quantities are called Laspeyres indexes. By contrast, an index that uses current year quantities is called a Paasche index. A Paasche index, therefore, is defined by the formula:

$$\text{Price index} = \frac{\Sigma q_t^i p_t^i}{\Sigma q_t^i p_0^i} \times 100$$

You are asked to calculate both the Laspeyres and Paasche indexes for the information provided in Table 2-7. In addition, find the GNP deflator (base year 1972) appropriate for that table. How do the three indexes compare?

8 This question is a national income accounting puzzle. Consider an economy where personal disposable income is $1,000. Undistributed profits are $65. Gross investment is $180, and net investment is $140. There are no valuation adjustments. The government makes transfer payments of $100 and interest payments of $30. The corporate profits tax amounts to $50. Indirect business taxes are $190. The government collects $150 in personal income taxes and Social Security contributions. Government enterprises make a deficit of $4. Business transfer payments are $9. Given this information, what is GNP?

9 Discuss the implications of the following events for national income and personal disposable income:
(a) The government increases the corporate income tax rate from 48 percent to 60 percent.
(b) The state of Pennsylvania liquor stores (part of "government enterprises") make a profit on their operation.
(c) Social Security taxes are increased.
(d) There is an increase in veteran benefit payments.
In all these questions assume that GNP remains unchanged.

10 Assume GNP is $1,200 and disposable income is $1,000 and that the government budget deficit is $70. Consumption is $850, the trade surplus is $20.
(a) How large is savings S?
(b) What is the size of investment I?
(c) How large is government spending?

3

Aggregate Demand
and Equilibrium
Income and Output

n Chap. 2 we studied the measurement of national income and output
(GNP). Now that we know how to measure these fundamental concepts,
we are able to begin our study of the factors that determine the level of
national income and product. Ultimately, we want to know why national
income sometimes falls (and the rate of unemployment rises), as it did in
1974–1975, and why at other times the level of income rises very rapidly
(and the unemployment rate falls), as it did early in 1976. We also want to
know what determines the rate of inflation. Why was it so high in 1974?
Why did it fall in 1976 as compared with 1975? We want to know whether
and how public policies, such as changes in government spending and tax
rates, or changes in the growth rate of the money supply, or changes in
interest rates, can affect the behavior of the level of income and the rates of
inflation and unemployment.

The study of those questions occupies the rest of the book. But we
will proceed slowly. We begin in this chapter with a simplified model of
the economy that isolates the crucial concept of *aggregate demand*, while
omitting both some factors that affect aggregate demand and considerations
of aggregate supply. In later chapters we gradually reintroduce those
other factors. By the time we have completed Chap. 13, we will be able to
understand the behavior of the key macroeconomic variables—the rates of
unemployment and inflation, and the level of GNP.

Our discussion of the determination of the level of output in this chapter starts from the basic macroeconomic identity that was expressed as Eq.
(16) of Chap. 2, and that can also be seen clearly in Chart 2-3. The identity
is based on two equalities. First, net national product (NNP) is equal to
total spending on goods and services, consisting of consumption C, net
investment I, government spending on goods and services G, and net exports NX. Second, net national product is also equal to net income received in the economy.[1] Income, in turn, increased by transfers R and
reduced by taxes T, is allocated to consumption C and saving S. Thus:

$$C + I + G + NX \equiv Y \equiv S + (T - R) + C$$

In this chapter we go beyond that accounting identity to begin our
study of the factors that determine the level of national product or output.
In particular, we focus on the interactions between the level of output and
aggregate demand. We shall see that there is a single level of *equilibrium*
output at which the aggregate (total) demand for goods and services is equal
to the level of output. To begin with, we simplify our task by discussing a
hypothetical world without a government ($G \equiv T \equiv R \equiv 0$) and without
foreign trade ($NX \equiv 0$). In such a world, the accounting identity simplifies
to:

---

[1]Because net national product (or output) is equal to net income received in the economy,
economists tend to use the terms *income* and *output* interchangeably when discussing the
level of economic activity.

$$C + I \equiv Y \equiv S + C \tag{1}$$

where Y denotes the real value of output and income. Further, we will remember that throughout this chapter a change in a macroeconomic aggregate is a change in its *real* value at constant prices. Thus, when we speak of a change in income, or a change in consumption spending, we mean a change in real income, or a change in real consumption spending.

With this convention in mind, we shall study in Sec. 3-1 the important concepts of *goods market equilibrium* and *equilibrium output*. In Sec. 3-1 we assume, for expositional purposes, that aggregate demand is *autonomous*—that is, independent of the level of income. In fact, however, consumption spending is related to the level of income—that is, changes in consumption spending are *induced* by changes in income.[2] Accordingly, in Sec. 3-2 we recognize this point and discuss the factors that affect the level of consumption by introducing the *consumption function*. We derive an explicit formula for the equilibrium level of income and output. Section 3-3 studies the effects of changes in autonomous spending on the equilibrium level of output. The effects of those changes are summarized by the *multiplier*, which is examined in some detail in Sec. 3-3. The government sector is introduced in Sec. 3-4, which includes a first discussion of fiscal policy. The discussion of fiscal policy is extended to the government budget in Sec. 3-5.

3-1 EQUILIBRIUM OUTPUT

In this chapter and the next we shall assume a world where all prices are given and constant. Such a world would exist if a sufficient level of unemployment of resources allowed firms, within the relevant range, to supply any amount of output without significantly affecting their unit costs.[3] In terms of Fig. 1-2, we are dealing with a situation in which the aggregate supply curve is horizontal.

If firms could supply any amount of output at the prevailing level of prices, what would determine the level of output actually produced? Demand must enter the picture. We would expect firms to produce at a level just sufficient to meet demand. If output produced was in excess of demand, firms would find their inventories piling up, and conversely, if production fell short of demand, inventories would be running down or

---

[2] The terms *autonomous* and *induced* are traditionally used to indicate spending that is independent of the level of income and dependent on the level of income, respectively. More generally, autonomous spending is spending that is independent of the other variables that are explained in a given theory.

[3] It is important to note that the assumption that prices are constant is made to simplify the exposition of Chaps. 3 and 4. In later chapters, we use the theories developed in Chaps. 3 and 4 to study the factors that determine the price level and cause it to change over time.

households would be unable to make the consumption purchases they had planned.

The preceding paragraph suggests a notion of equilibrium output as that level where demand equals supply, so that unintended changes in inventories are zero, and households' actual consumption is equal to their planned consumption. Before exploring that notion further, we have to dispose of an unsettling issue that arises from the accounting identity in Eq. (1), derived from our study of national income accounting. The identity in Eq. (1) states that demand, $C + I$, is *identically* equal to supply Y, whatever the level of output. That seems to mean that demand equals supply at *any* level of output, so that any level of output could be the equilibrium level.

The issue is resolved by remembering that in Eq. (1) investment is *actual* investment and consumption is *actual* consumption. The investment measured in Eq. (1) includes involuntary, or unintended, inventory changes, which occur when firms find themselves selling more or less goods than they had anticipated they would sell. Similarly, if households cannot buy all the goods they want, the consumption measured in Eq. (1) would be different from planned consumption. By contrast, our concept of equilibrium output suggests a situation where unintended inventory changes are zero and consumption is equal to planned consumption. We clearly have to make a distinction between the *actual* aggregate demand that is measured in an accounting context, and the relevant economic concept of *planned* (desired, intended) aggregate demand.

Actual aggregate demand $(C + I)$ is, by the accounting identity in Eq. (1), equal to the level of output (Y). The output level is determined by firms. In deciding how much to produce, firms calculate how much investment, including inventory investment, they want to undertake. They also produce to meet the demand for consumption they forecast will be forthcoming from households. *Planned* aggregate demand consists of the amount of consumption households plan to carry out plus the amount of investment planned by firms.[4] If firms miscalculate households' consumption demands, planned aggregate demand does not equal actual aggregate demand. Suppose first that firms overestimate consumption demand. The firms find their inventories increasing by more than they had planned, because some of the goods they had planned to sell are not bought by consumers and have instead to be added to inventories. In that case, actual aggregate demand or output exceeds planned aggregate demand, and firms have unanticipated or unintended inventory investment. Similarly, if firms underestimate households' consumption demand, there is unintended inventory decumulation, and actual aggregate demand is less than planned aggregate demand. If we denote aggregate demand by A, the above discussion implies

[4]From now on we shall assume that actual consumption is equal to planned consumption, so that all differences between actual and planned aggregate demand are reflected in unintended inventory changes. In practical terms, this means we are not considering situations where firms put "Sold Out" signs in their windows and customers cannot buy what they want.

$$I_{\text{unintended}} \equiv A_{\text{actual}} - A_{\text{planned}} \qquad (2)$$

Now actual aggregate demand (A_{actual}) is equal to the level of output Y, and planned aggregate demand (A_{planned}) is the sum of consumption and intended investment $C + I_{\text{int}}$.[5] Thus, using Eq. (2), we find

$$I_{\text{unint}} \equiv A_{\text{actual}} - A_{\text{planned}}$$
$$\equiv Y - (C + I_{\text{int}}) \qquad (3)$$

The identity in Eq. (3) can now be linked with the discussion of equilibrium output. We defined equilibrium output as the level of production such that actual aggregate demand is equal to planned aggregate demand. By Eq. (3), this implies that unintended inventory accumulation is zero when output is at its equilibrium level.

Now that we have distinguished between planned and actual aggregate demand, we shall adopt the convention of using the term *aggregate demand* only in the sense of "planned" and reserve for it the notation A. Similarly, we shall use the term *investment demand* exclusively for planned investment spending—the amount firms plan to spend for investment—and denote it by I. Unintended inventory changes will be denoted by I_u. With these conventions, we can rewrite Eq. (3) as

$$I_u \equiv Y - A \equiv Y - C - I \qquad (3a)$$

where we have used the fact that $A \equiv C + I$ (aggregate demand is the sum of consumption and investment demands).

So far we have isolated a *concept* of equilibrium output. We have said that there is equilibrium when output supplied is equal to aggregate demand. We define that as equilibrium because in that situation households find themselves consuming at the rate they planned, and firms find themselves investing at the rate they planned. We have also defined aggregate demand in terms of planned spending. To repeat, aggregate demand is the sum of the amounts households plan to spend on consumption goods and firms plan to spend on investment.

Now we want to go beyond the mere concept of equilibrium output and find out what the equilibrium level of output actually is. For that purpose we need to make an assumption about aggregate demand. The simplest assumption we can make is that aggregate demand is some constant level $\overline{A}$. That is, our simplest assumption makes the demands for consumption and investment independent of the level of income (or autonomous). With this aggregate demand function, it is easy to determine the equilibrium level of output. Recalling that the equilibrium condition is that output supplied equals aggregate demand, we have

---

[5]Recall that we are assuming actual consumption is equal to planned consumption.

$$Y = \overline{A} \qquad\qquad (4)$$

There are some insights to be gained even from this simple model. For that purpose we turn to Fig. 3-1, where we have plotted on the horizontal axis output Y and, on the vertical axis, aggregate demand A. The aggregate demand function $A = \overline{A}$ is shown as the horizontal line with intercept $\overline{A}$. We have drawn, too, a 45° line that serves as a reference line in that it translates any horizontal distance into an equal vertical distance. In other words, for any given level of Y on the horizontal axis, the 45° line gives the level of A on the vertical axis such that $Y = A$. Clearly, from Eq. (4) and Fig. 3-1, the equilibrium level of output is Y_0.

Consider now a level of output below Y_0, corresponding to a situation in which firms produce less than the equilibrium level of output. At any level of output below Y_0, aggregate demand $\overline{A}$ exceeds the level of output so that there is an *excess demand*—aggregate demand exceeds output. Consequently, inventories are run down, or unintended inventory reductions take place. The magnitude of unintended inventory changes is given by the vertical distance between the aggregate demand schedule $\overline{A}$ and the 45° line at each level of income, since, using Eq. (3a), $I_u \equiv Y - \overline{A}$. At a level of income above Y_0, by contrast, output exceeds aggregate demand, and inventories consequently pile up at a rate equal to the difference between the 45° line and the aggregate demand schedule. At Y_0 output exactly equals

FIGURE 3-1 EQUILIBRIUM WITH
CONSTANT AGGREGATE DEMAND

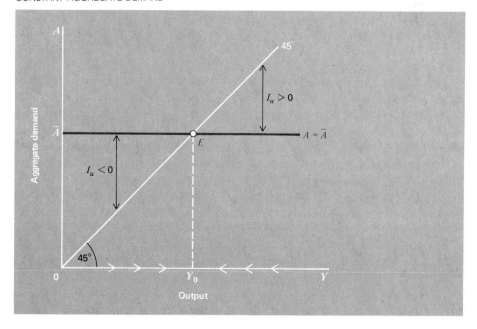

aggregate demand, and correspondingly there are no unintended inventory changes.

Next we can ask whether the economy would actually reach the equilibrium output level Y_0. It is reasonable to assume that firms cut production whenever an excess of output over aggregate demand causes inventories to pile up. Thus suppose that output initially exceeds the equilibrium level Y_0. Then firms are unable to sell all the goods they produce and find themselves with increasing inventories. As they find their inventories increasing, it is reasonable for them to reduce the level of production so as to prevent a further buildup of inventories. Conversely, suppose that the level of output is below the equilibrium level Y_0. Then firms find their inventories decreasing because demand exceeds their production.[6] Under those circumstances, they should be expected to increase output to meet the demand for goods. The arrows on the horizontal axis in Fig. 3-1 are a convenient way of describing the behavior of firms that we have discussed. The arrows show that the level of output is decreasing whenever output is above Y_0 and increasing whenever Y is less than Y_0. Accordingly, Y will move to the equilibrium level Y_0, which is precisely what our verbal discussion leads us to believe.[7]

We have now mastered both the concept and the mechanics of the determination of equilibrium output. There are three essential notions:

1 Aggregate demand determines the equilibrium level of output.
2 At equilibrium, unintended changes in inventories are zero, and households consume the amount they plan to consume.
3 An adjustment process for output based on unintended inventory changes will actually move the level of output to its equilibrium level.

Note, too, that the definition of equilibrium implies that actual spending on consumption and investment equals planned spending. In equilibrium, aggregate demand, which is planned spending, equals output. Since output identically equals income, we see also that in equilibrium planned spending equals income.

---

[6]Alternatively, if inventories are zero, firms find themselves having to turn away customers because goods are out of stock. This too would lead firms to increase their output.

[7]You may have noticed that the adjustment process we describe raises the possibility that output will temporarily exceed its new equilibrium level during the adjustment to an increase in aggregate demand. This is the *inventory cycle*. Suppose firms desire to keep on hand inventories which are proportional to the level of demand. When demand unexpectedly rises, inventories are depleted. In subsequent periods, the firms have to produce not only to meet the new higher level of aggregate demand, but also to restore their depleted inventories and to raise them to a higher level. While they are rebuilding their inventories and also producing to meet the higher level of demand, their total production will exceed the new level of aggregate demand.

3-2 THE CONSUMPTION FUNCTION AND AGGREGATE DEMAND

The preceding section studied the equilibrium level of output (and income) on the assumption that aggregate demand was simply a constant $\overline{A}$. In this section, we extend the discussion to a more realistic specification of aggregate demand and begin to examine the economic variables that determine aggregate demand. For that purpose we separate aggregate demand into its components, consumption and investment demand, and assume an explicit *consumption function*. The consumption function we shall assume relates consumption spending by households to the level of income. For the present we shall treat planned investment as constant at the level $\overline{I}$. Because consumption demand depends on the level of income, so too does aggregate demand. Aggregate demand is no longer constant as in Sec. 3-1, and we shall have to modify Fig. 3-1 accordingly. First, though, we examine the consumption function.

The Consumption Function

We shall assume that consumption spending is a simple linear function of income:[8]

$$C = \overline{C} + cY \tag{5}$$

where

$$\overline{C} > 0 \quad \text{and} \quad 0 < c < 1$$

This consumption function is shown in Fig. 3-2a. The *intercept is* $\overline{C}$ and the *slope* is c.

The fundamental notion underlying this consumption function is that an individual's level of consumption is primarily determined by his income. The higher the income, the higher the level of consumption.

The consumption function Eq. (5) further states that at low levels of income, consumption exceeds income, while at high levels of income, consumption falls short of income. This feature can be seen in Fig. 3-2a, which includes a 45° line, along which income is equal to consumption. At low levels of income, the consumption function lies above the 45° line, and consumption therefore exceeds income. As we shall see below, that means that at low levels of income, the individual or household is dissaving. At high levels of income, the household saves, since consumption is less than income.

These relationships between income and consumption arise from the positive intercept, $\overline{C}$ in Eq. (5), and the fact that the coefficient c is less than

---

[8]Note that because income is equal to output, we use the same symbol, Y, for both income and output.

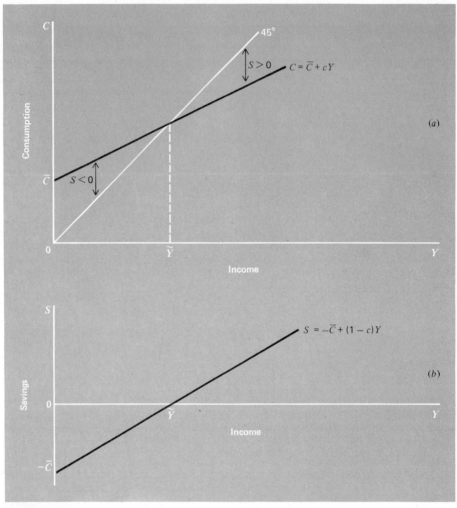

FIGURE 3-2a THE CONSUMPTION
FUNCTION
FIGURE 3-2b THE SAVING FUNCTION

unity. The coefficient c is sufficiently important for us to have a special name for it. The coefficient c is called the *marginal propensity to consume*: it is the increase in consumption per unit increase in income. In our case, the marginal propensity to consume is less than unity, which implies that out of a dollar increase in income, only a fraction c is spent on consumption. For instance, if c is 0.9, then when income rises by $1, consumption increases by 90 cents.

Consumption and Saving

What happens to the rest, the fraction $1 - c$ that is not spent on consumption? Looking at the right-hand side of Eq. (1) above (namely, $Y \equiv S + C$), we recognize that there is a relationship among income, consumption, and saving. Specifically, Eq. (1) tells us that income that is not spent on consumption is saved, or

$$S \equiv Y - C \tag{6}$$

What Eq. (6) tells us is that by definition, *saving is equal to income minus consumption*. This means that we cannot, in addition to the consumption function, postulate an independent saving function and expect consumption and saving to add up to income.

The consumption function in Eq. (5) together with Eq. (6), which we call the *budget constraint*, implies a saving function. The saving function is the function that relates the level of saving to the level of income. Substituting the consumption function in Eq. (5) into the budget constraint in Eq. (6) yields the saving function

$$\begin{aligned} S &\equiv Y - C \\ &= Y - (\overline{C} + cY) \\ &= -\overline{C} + (1 - c)Y \end{aligned} \tag{7}$$

From Eq. (7) saving is an increasing function of the level of income because the *marginal propensity to save*, $s = 1 - c$, is positive. Furthermore, the saving function is the mirror image of the consumption function. At low levels of income, saving is negative, thus reflecting the fact that consumption exceeds income. Conversely, at sufficiently high levels of income, saving becomes positive and thus reflects the fact that not all income is spent on consumption.

The interrelationship between the consumption and saving function examined in Eq. (7) can also be seen graphically in Fig. 3-2, where the vertical distance between the consumption function and the 45° line at each level of income measures saving. Figure 3-2*b* shows the saving function that is derived from the consumption function in Fig. 3-2*a* by plotting the vertical distance between income and consumption spending at each level of income. Of course, as noted above, we can also obtain the saving function directly from Eq. (7). Note that the slope of the saving function in Fig. 3-2*b* is the marginal propensity to save, $s = 1 - c$, as defined above.

Planned Investment and Aggregate Demand

We have now specified one component of aggregate demand, consumption spending. To complete the specification of aggregate demand, we must also consider the determinants of investment spending, or an *investment function*. We shall cut short the discussion for the present by simply assuming that planned investment spending is at a constant level $\bar{I}$.[9] Having specified each of the components of aggregate demand, we can now write down the aggregate demand function as their sum:

$$A \equiv C + I_{\text{intended}}$$
$$\equiv \bar{C} + cY + \bar{I} \tag{8}$$

Equilibrium Income and Output

The next step is to use this aggregate demand function to determine the equilibrium level of income and output. For that purpose we return to the *equilibrium condition* in the goods market:

$$Y = A \tag{9}$$

which states that in equilibrium, output supplied, or income, equals output demanded, or planned aggregate spending. The level of aggregate demand is specified in Eq. (8), so that substituting for A in Eq. (9), we have the equilibrium condition as

$$Y = \bar{C} + cY + \bar{I} \tag{10}$$

Since we have Y on both sides of the equilibrium condition in Eq. (10), we can solve for the equilibrium level of income and output, denoted by Y_0, in terms of the parameters of the aggregate demand function $(\bar{C}, \bar{I}, c)$. From Eq. (10), we can write

$$Y - cY = \bar{C} + \bar{I}$$

or

$$Y(1 - c) = \bar{C} + \bar{I}$$

Thus the equilibrium level of income, at which aggregate demand equals output, is[10]

$$Y_0 = \frac{1}{1 - c} (\bar{C} + \bar{I}) \tag{11}$$

---

[9]In Chaps. 4 and 6, investment spending will become a function of the rate of interest and will gain an important place in the transmission of monetary policy.

[10]As a convention we use the subscript $_0$ to denote the equilibrium level of a variable.

We have arrived rather quickly at Eq. (11) for the equilibrium level of income and output. It is therefore worthwhile retracing our steps and using Fig. 3-3 to gain understanding of what is involved in the derivation of Eq. (11). In Fig. 3-3 we plot the aggregate demand function shown in Eq. (8). The intercept $\overline{A}$—autonomous spending—is equal to $\overline{C} + \overline{I}$, and the slope is given by the marginal propensity to consume, c. This aggregate demand schedule shows the planned level of spending in the economy (consumption plus investment spending), associated with each level of income. As is apparent from the figure, aggregate demand increases as the level of income rises. In fact, Fig. 3-3 differs from Fig. 3-1 only in that the aggregate demand function of Fig. 3-3 is upward-sloping rather than horizontal. This relation arises because consumption spending, a component of aggregate demand, increases as income increases.

Consider now the determination of the equilibrium level of income. Remember that the equilibrium level of income is such that aggregate demand equals output (which in turn equals income). The 45° line in Fig. 3-3 shows points at which output and aggregate demand are equal. The aggregate demand schedule in Fig. 3-3 cuts the 45° line at E, and it is accordingly at E that aggregate demand is equal to output (equals income). Only at E, and the corresponding equilibrium level of income and output,

FIGURE 3-3 DETERMINATION OF EQUILIBRIUM INCOME

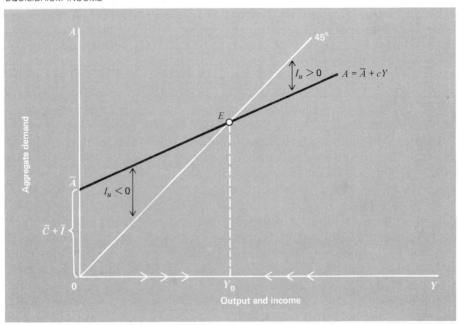

Y_0, does aggregate demand exactly equal output. At that level of output and income, planned spending exactly matches production.

We also showed in Sec. 3-1 that, at the equilibrium level of output, unintended inventory changes are zero. In Fig. 3-3, unintended changes in inventories associated with each level of output are equal to the vertical distance between the aggregate demand function and the 45° line. At levels of income below Y_0, unintended inventory changes are therefore negative because aggregate demand exceeds output. Conversely, at levels of output above Y_0, involuntary inventory changes are positive because aggregate demand falls short of output. Therefore, only at the equilibrium level of income, Y_0, are unintended inventory changes equal to zero.

The arrows in Fig. 3-3 indicate once again how we would reach equilibrium. If firms expand production whenever they face unintended decreases in their inventory holdings, then they would increase output at any level below Y_0, because below Y_0 aggregate demand exceeds output and inventories are declining. Conversely, for output levels above Y_0, firms find inventories piling up and therefore cut production. This process will lead us to the output level Y_0, where current production exactly matches planned aggregate spending. Again, the arrows in Fig. 3-3 represent the dynamic process by which the economy moves to the equilibrium level of output Y_0.[11]

Figure 3-3 sheds light, too, on the determinants of the equilibrium level of income calculated in Eq. (11). The position of the aggregate demand schedule is characterized by its slope c and intercept $\overline{A}$. The intercept $\overline{A}$ is the level of autonomous spending, that is, spending that is independent of the level of income. For our aggregate demand function, Eq. (8), autonomous spending is equal to $\overline{C} + \overline{I}$. The other determinant of the equilibrium level of income is the marginal propensity to consume, c, which is the slope of the aggregate demand schedule. Given the intercept, a steeper aggregate demand function—as would be implied by a higher marginal propensity to consume—implies a higher level of equilibrium income. Similarly, for a given marginal propensity to consume, a higher level of autonomous spending—in terms of Fig. 3-3, a larger intercept— implies a higher equilibrium level of income. These results that are suggested by Fig. 3-3 are easily verified from Eq. (11), which gives the formula for the equilibrium level of income.

Saving and Investment

A further perspective on equilibrium income can be gained from Fig. 3-4. Here we have shown separately the consumption schedule and the aggregate demand function. The vertical distance between the two schedules

---

[11]Do you see that there is once more the possibility of an inventory cycle? Refer back to footnote 7.

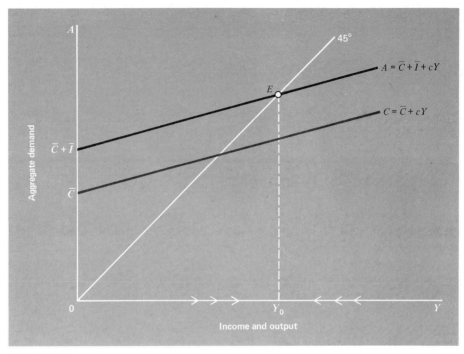

FIGURE 3-4 CONSUMPTION AND
INVESTMENT AS COMPONENTS OF
AGGREGATE DEMAND

represents the constant level of planned investment spending, $\bar{I}$. As we
saw before, the equilibrium level of income is Y_0, because only at that level
of output does aggregate planned spending—consumption plus investment
spending—equal income. The breakdown of aggregate spending into its
consumption and investment components is useful to bring out an important relationship that holds in equilibrium. Specifically, *in equilibrium
planned investment equals saving*. We recall from Fig. 3-2 that the vertical distance between the consumption schedule and the 45° line measures
saving associated with each level of income. The vertical distance between the aggregate demand schedule and the consumption schedule measures planned investment spending. At the equilibrium level of income
we note that these two distances coincide and that, accordingly, saving
equals (planned) investment.[12] By contrast, above the equilibrium level of
income Y_0, saving (the distance between the 45° line and the consumption
schedule) exceeds investment, while below Y_0 investment exceeds saving.

---

[12]Recall that we have agreed to mean "planned investment" when we use the term *investment*.

Now, is the equality between saving and investment at equilibrium an essential characteristic of the equilibrium level of income, or is it a mere curiosity? It is an essential characteristic of equilibrium. We can see that by starting with the basic equilibrium condition Eq. (9), which states that in equilibrium $Y = A$. If we subtract consumption from both Y and A, we realize that $Y - C$ is saving and $A - C$ is planned investment. In symbols,

$$Y = A$$

$$Y - C = A - C$$

$$S = \overline{I} \tag{12}$$

Thus, the initial equilibrium definition, that aggregate demand is equal to output, is equivalent to the condition that saving equals investment. The condition $S = \overline{I}$ is simply another way of stating the basic equilibrium condition.[13]

Recall also that in equilibrium, unintended inventory accumulation is zero. The saving equals investment definition of equilibrium also implies that there is no unintended inventory investment in equilibrium. Saving is income less consumption. Given the equality of income and output, saving is therefore the excess of output over consumption. That excess must exactly equal planned investment spending for there to be no unintended inventory changes. But that says that saving has to be equal to planned investment if there are to be no unintended inventory changes.

There is also a diagrammatic derivation of the equilibrium level of income that corresponds to the statement of the equilibrium condition in Eq. (12) as the balance between saving and investment. In Fig. 3-5, we show the saving function that was derived in Fig. 3-2. We have drawn, too, planned investment spending indicated by the horizontal line with intercept $\overline{I}$. Equilibrium income is shown as the level Y_0. To complete the argument, remember that from Eq. (3a) unintended inventory changes are defined as

$$I_u = Y - C - \overline{I} \tag{3a}$$

Substituting the definition of saving $S \equiv Y - C$, we have

$$I_u = S - \overline{I} \tag{13}$$

Equation (13) shows us that when saving equals investment, the unin-

---

[13]In the problem set, we ask you to derive Eq. (11) for Y_0 by starting from $S = \overline{I}$ and substituting for S from Eq. (7).

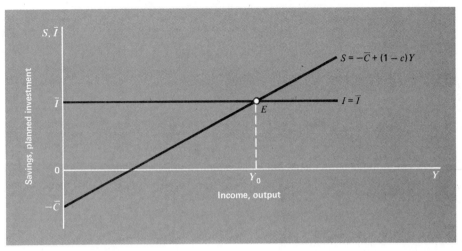

FIGURE 3-5 SAVING AND INVESTMENT

tended inventory changes are zero, and thus serves as a check on Eq. (12) as a statement of the equilibrium condition.

3-3 THE MULTIPLIER

In this section we will develop an answer to the following question: By how much does a \$1 increase in *autonomous* spending raise the equilibrium level of income?[14] There would appear to be a simple answer. Since in equilibrium income equals aggregate demand, it would seem that a \$1 increase in (autonomous) demand or spending should raise equilibrium income by \$1. That answer is incorrect. Let us now see why.

Suppose first that output increased by \$1 to match the increased level of autonomous spending. This output and income increase would in turn give rise to further *induced* spending as consumption rises because the level of income has risen. How much of the initial \$1 increase in income would be spent on consumption? The answer to that question is given by the marginal propensity to consume, c. Out of an additional dollar income, a fraction c is consumed. Assume then that production increases further to meet this induced expenditure, that is, that output and so income increase by $1 + c$. That will still leave us with an excess demand because the very

---

[14]Recall that autonomous spending $\overline{A}$ is spending that is independent of the level of income. Note also that the answer to the question posed above is contained in Eq. (11). Can you deduce the answer directly from Eq. (11)? This section provides an explanation of that answer.

fact of an expansion in production and income by $1 + c$ will give rise to further induced spending. This story could clearly take a long time to tell. We seem to have arrived at an impasse where expansion in output to meet excess demand leads to a further expansion in demand without an obvious end to that process.

It helps to lay out the various steps in this chain more carefully. We start off in the first round with an increase in autonomous spending $\Delta \overline{A}$. Next we allow an expansion in production to exactly meet that increase in demand. Production accordingly expands by $\Delta \overline{A}$. This increase in production gives rise to an equal increase in income and, therefore, via the consumption function, $C = \overline{C} + cY$, gives rise in the second round to induced expenditures of size $c\,(\Delta \overline{A})$. Assume, again, that production expands to meet the increase in spending. The production adjustment this time is $c\,(\Delta \overline{A})$ and so is the increase in income. This gives rise to a third round of induced spending equal to the marginal propensity to consume times the increase in income $c(c\,\Delta \overline{A}) = c^2\,\Delta \overline{A}$. Careful inspection of the last term shows that induced expenditures in the third round are smaller than those in the second round. Since the marginal propensity to consume, c, is less than 1, the term c^2 is less than c.

If we wrote out the successive rounds of increased spending, starting with the initial increase in autonomous demand, we would obtain

$$\Delta A = \Delta \overline{A} + c\,(\Delta \overline{A}) + c^2\,\Delta \overline{A} + c^3\,\Delta \overline{A} + \cdots$$
$$= \Delta \overline{A}(1 + c + c^2 + c^3 + \cdots) \tag{14}$$

It is obvious that for $c < 1$ the successive terms in the series become progressively smaller. In fact, we are dealing with a geometric series the sum of which is calculated as

$$\Delta A = \frac{1}{1 - c}\,\Delta \overline{A} = \Delta Y_0 \tag{15}$$

From Eq. (15) therefore the cumulative change in aggregate spending is equal to a multiple of the increase in autonomous spending. This could also have been deduced from Eq. (11).[15] The multiple $1/(1 - c)$ is called the *multiplier*, since it tells us by how much we have to multiply a given change in autonomous spending to obtain the corresponding change in equilibrium income and aggregate demand. Because the multiplier exceeds unity, we know that a \$1 change in autonomous spending increases

[15]If you are familiar with the calculus, you will realize that the multiplier is nothing other than the derivative of the equilibrium level of income, Y_0, in Eq. (11) with respect to autonomous spending. Use the calculus on Eq. (11) above and Eq. (26) below to check the statements of the text.

equilibrium income and output by more than $1.[16] The concept of the multiplier is sufficiently important to create a new notation. Defining the multiplier as α, we have

$$\alpha \equiv \frac{1}{1-c} \tag{16}$$

Inspection of the definition of the multiplier in Eq. (16) shows that the larger the marginal propensity to consume, the larger is the multiplier. For example, with a marginal propensity to consume of 0.75, the multiplier is 4; for a marginal propensity to consume of 0.8, the multiplier is 5. The reason is simply that a high marginal propensity to consume implies that a large fraction of an additional dollar income will be consumed. Accordingly, expenditures induced by an increase in autonomous spending are high and, therefore, so is the expansion in output and income that is needed to restore balance between income and demand (or spending).

Before proceeding further, we note that the relationship between the marginal propensity to consume, c, and the marginal propensity to save, s, allows us to write Eq. (16) in a somewhat different form. Remembering from the budget constraint that saving plus consumption adds up to income, we recall that the fraction of an additional dollar income consumed plus the fraction saved must add up to a dollar, or

$$1 = s + c$$

We can use the relation $s = 1 - c$ and substitute in Eq. (16) to obtain an equivalent formula for the multiplier in terms of the marginal propensity to save:

$$\alpha \equiv \frac{1}{s} \tag{16a}$$

Figure 3-6 provides a graphic interpretation of the effects of an increase in autonomous spending on the equilibrium level of income. The initial equilibrium is at point E with an income level Y_0. Consider next an increase in autonomous spending from $\overline{A}$ to $\overline{A}'$. This is represented by a parallel upward shift of the aggregate demand schedule where the shift is

---

[16]*Two warnings:* (1) The multiplier is necessarily greater than 1 in this very simplified model of the determination of income, but as we shall see in the discussion of "crowding out" in Chap. 4, there may be circumstances under which it is less than 1. (2) The term *multiplier* is used more generally in economics to mean the effect on some endogenous variable (a variable whose level is explained by the theory being studied) of a unit change in an exogenous variable (a variable whose level is not determined within the theory being examined). For instance, one can talk of the multiplier of a change in the income tax rate on the level of unemployment. However, the classic use of the term is as we are using it here—the effects of a change in autonomous spending on equilibrium output.

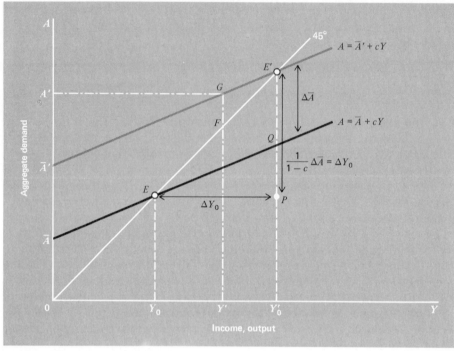

FIGURE 3-6 GRAPHICAL DERIVATION OF
THE MULTIPLIER

exactly equal to the increase in autonomous spending. The upward shift
means that now at each level of income, aggregate demand is higher by an
amount $\Delta \bar{A} \equiv \bar{A}' - \bar{A}$.

At the initial level of income Y_0, it is obvious that aggregate demand
after the increase in autonomous spending exceeds income or output and
that consequently unintended inventory decumulation is taking place at a
rate equal to the increase in autonomous spending, equal to the vertical
distance $\Delta \bar{A}$. Firms will respond to that excess demand by expanding
production, say to income level Y'. This expansion in production has two
effects. First, it gives rise to induced expenditure, increasing aggregate
demand to the level A'. Second, at the same time it reduces the gap
between aggregate demand and output, to the vertical distance FG. Additional spending is induced because the marginal propensity to consume out
of additional income is positive while the gap between aggregate demand
and output narrows because the marginal propensity to consume is less
than 1. Thus a marginal propensity to consume that is positive but less
than unity implies that a sufficient expansion in output will restore the
balance between aggregate demand and output. In Fig. 3-6 the new equi-

librium is indicated by point E' and the corresponding level of income is Y_0'. The change in income required is, therefore, $\Delta Y_0 = Y_0' - Y_0$.

The magnitude of the income change required to restore equilibrium depends on two factors. The larger the increase in autonomous spending, represented in Fig. 3-6 by the parallel shift in the aggregate demand schedule, the larger is the income change. Furthermore, the larger the marginal propensity to consume—that is, the steeper the aggregate demand schedule—the larger the income change.

As a further check on our results, we want to verify from Fig. 3-6 that the change in equilibrium income, in fact, exceeds the change in autonomous spending. For that purpose, we simply use the 45° line to compare the change in income ΔY_0 ($= EP = PE'$) with the change in autonomous spending that is equal to the vertical distance between the new and old aggregate demand schedule (QE'). It is clear from Fig. 3-6 that the change in income PE' exceeds the change in autonomous spending QE'.

Finally, there is yet another way of deriving the multiplier. The relationship between the change in equilibrium income and a change in autonomous spending can be directly derived from the concept of equilibrium. We remember that in equilibrium aggregate demand equals income or output. From one equilibrium to another it must therefore be true that the change in income ΔY_0 is equal to the change in aggregate demand ΔA:

$$\Delta Y_0 = \Delta A \tag{17}$$

Next we split up the change in aggregate demand into the change in autonomous spending, $\Delta \overline{A}$, and the change in expenditure induced by the consequent change in income—that is, $c\,\Delta Y_0$.

$$\Delta A = \Delta \overline{A} + c\,\Delta Y_0 \tag{18}$$

Combining Eqs. (17) and (18), we obtain the change in income as

$$\Delta Y_0 = \Delta \overline{A} + c\,\Delta Y_0$$

or

$$\Delta Y_0(1 - c) = \Delta \overline{A}$$

or

$$\Delta Y_0 = \frac{1}{1 - c}\,\Delta \overline{A} = \alpha\,\Delta \overline{A} \tag{19}$$

There are three important points to remember from this discussion:

1 An increase in autonomous spending raises the equilibrium level of income.

2   The increase in income is a multiple of the increase in autonomous spending.

3   The larger the marginal propensity to consume, the larger is the multiplier, arising from the relation between consumption and income.

As a check on your understanding of the material of this section, you should develop the same analysis, and the same answers, in terms of Fig. 3-5.

3-4 THE GOVERNMENT SECTOR

So far we have ignored the role of the government sector in the determination of equilibrium income. The government affects the level of equilibrium income in two separate ways. First, government spending on goods and services, G, is a component of aggregate demand. Second, taxes and transfers affect the relation between output and income, Y, and the *disposable income*—income that is available for consumption or saving—that accrues to the private sector, Y_d. In this section, we will be concerned with the way in which government spending, taxes, and transfers affect the equilibrium level of income.

We start again from the basic national income accounting identities. The introduction of the government restores government spending on the expenditure side of Eq. (1) of this chapter, and taxes less transfers on the allocation of income side. We can, accordingly, rewrite the identity in Eq. (1) as

$$C + I + G \equiv Y \equiv S + (T - R) + C \qquad (1a)$$

The definition of aggregate demand has to be augmented to include government spending on goods and services—the purchases of military equipment and the services of bureaucrats, for instance. Thus we have

$$A \equiv C + \overline{I} + G \qquad (5a)$$

Consumption will no longer depend on income but rather on *disposable* income Y_d. Disposable income Y_d is the net income available for spending by households[17] after paying taxes to and receiving transfers from the government. It thus consists of income less taxes plus transfers, $Y + R - T$. The consumption function is now

$$C = \overline{C} + cY_d = \overline{C} + c(Y + R - T) \qquad (6a)$$

A final step is a specification of *fiscal policy*. Fiscal policy is the policy of the government with regard to the level of government spending, the

---

[17] In Chap. 2 we distinguished between disposable personal income and disposable private sector (persons and corporations) income. In this section we ignore that distinction by assuming that firms pay out all their profits to households.

level of transfers, and the tax structure. We shall assume that the government spends a constant amount $\overline{G}$, that it makes a constant amount of transfers $\overline{R}$, and that it collects a fraction t of income in the form of taxes. For instance, if t equals 0.2, there is an income tax equal to 20 percent of income.

$$G = \overline{G} \qquad R = \overline{R} \qquad T = tY \qquad (20)$$

With this specification of fiscal policy we can rewrite the consumption function, after substitution from Eq. (20) for R and T in Eq. ($6a$) as

$$C = \overline{C} + c(Y + \overline{R} - tY)$$
$$C = (\overline{C} + c\overline{R}) + c(1 - t)Y \qquad (21)$$

We note from Eq. (21) that the presence of transfers raises autonomous consumption spending by the marginal propensity to consume out of disposable income c times the amount of transfers.[18] The presence of income taxes, by contrast, lowers consumption spending at each level of income. That reduction arises because households' consumption is related to disposable income rather than income itself, and income taxes reduce disposable income relative to the level of income. While the marginal propensity to consume out of disposable income remains c, the marginal propensity to consume out of income now is $c(1 - t)$, where $1 - t$ is the fraction of income left after taxes.

Equilibrium Income

We are now set to study income determination when the government's role is included. For that purpose, we return to the equilibrium condition for the goods market, $Y = A$, and after substituting from Eqs. (21) and ($5a$), we can write the equilibrium condition as

$$Y = (\overline{C} + c\overline{R}) + c(1 - t)Y + \overline{I} + \overline{G}$$
$$= (\overline{C} + c\overline{R} + \overline{I} + \overline{G}) + c(1 - t)Y$$
$$= \overline{A} + c(1 - t)Y$$

We can solve this equation for Y_0, the equilibrium level of income, by collecting terms in Y:

$$Y[1 - c(1 - t)] = \overline{C} + c\overline{R} + \overline{I} + \overline{G}$$

$$Y_0 = \frac{1}{1 - c(1 - t)}(\overline{C} + c\overline{R} + \overline{G} + \overline{I})$$

$$= \frac{1}{1 - c(1 - t)}\overline{A} \qquad (22)$$

[18]Note that we are assuming no taxes are paid on transfers from the government. As a matter of fact, taxes are paid on some transfers, such as interest payments on the government debt, and not paid on other transfers, such as welfare and unemployment benefits.

In comparing Eq. (22) with Eq. (11), we see that the government sector makes a substantial difference. It raises autonomous spending by the amount of government spending, $\overline{G}$, and by the amount of induced spending out of net transfers, $c\overline{R}$. At the same time, income taxes lower the multiplier. As can be seen from Eq. (22), if the marginal propensity to consume is 0.8 and taxes are zero, the multiplier is 5; with the same marginal propensity to consume and a tax rate of 0.25, the multiplier is cut in half to $\{1/[1 - 0.8(0.75)]\} = 2.5$. Income taxes reduce the multiplier because they reduce the induced increase of consumption out of changes in income. When there are no taxes, a dollar increase in income raises disposable income by exactly a dollar and induced consumption increases by c times the increase in disposable income. If there are taxes, however, a dollar increase in income raises disposable income by only $(1 - t)$ dollars. Induced consumption rises, therefore, only by $c(1 - t)$. In terms of Fig. 3-2 the presence of transfers shifts the intercept of the aggregate demand schedule up by $c\overline{R}$. The slope, which is the marginal propensity to consume out of income, declines because of the presence of income taxes.

Effects of a Change in Government Spending

We want now to consider the effects of changes in fiscal policy on the equilibrium level of income. We can distinguish three possible changes in fiscal variables: changes in government spending, changes in transfers, and income tax changes. The simplest case is that of a change in government spending. This case is shown in Fig. 3-7, where the initial level of income is Y_0. An increase in government spending represents a change in autonomous spending and therefore shifts the aggregate demand schedule upward in a parallel fashion by an amount equal to the increased government expenditure. At the initial level of output and income, the demand for goods exceeds output and, accordingly, firms expand production until the new equilibrium at point E' is reached. By how much does income expand? We remember that the change in equilibrium income will equal the change in aggregate demand, or

$$\Delta Y_0 = \Delta\overline{G} + c(1 - t)\,\Delta Y_0$$

where the remaining terms $(\overline{C}, \overline{R}$ and $\overline{I})$ are constant by assumption. Thus, the change in equilibrium income is

$$\Delta Y_0 = \frac{1}{1 - c(1 - t)}\,\Delta\overline{G} = \bar{\alpha}\,\Delta\overline{G} \tag{23}$$

where we have introduced the notation $\bar{\alpha}$ to denote the multiplier in the presence of income taxes:

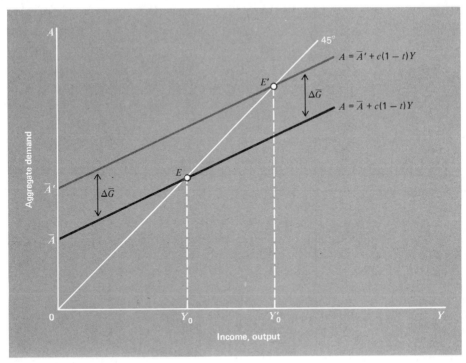

FIGURE 3-7 THE EFFECTS OF AN
INCREASE IN GOVERNMENT SPENDING

$$\bar{\alpha} \equiv \frac{1}{1 - c(1 - t)} \tag{24}$$

From Eq. (23) it is apparent that a \$1 increase in government spending will lead to an increase in income in excess of a dollar. Thus, as we have already seen, with a marginal propensity to consume of $c = 0.8$, and an income tax rate of $t = 0.25$, we would have a multiplier of 2.5: a \$1 increase in government spending raises equilibrium income by \$2.50.

Effects of Increased Transfer Payments

Consider next an increase in transfer payments. In terms of Fig. 3-7, we again have an increase in autonomous spending, so that aggregate demand increases at each level of income. The parallel shift in the aggregate demand schedule will be equal to the marginal propensity to spend out of disposable income, c, times the increase in transfers, or $c\,\Delta\bar{R}$. Again, the demand for goods will exceed production at the initial level of income and output, and an expansion in output will take place to eliminate the excess demand. To calculate the change in equilibrium income, we again use the condition that the change in aggregate demand will equal the equilibrium change in income. The change in aggregate demand in this case is the change in autonomous spending, $c\,\Delta\overline{R}$, plus induced spending $c(1-t)\,\Delta Y$, so that we can write

$$\Delta Y_0 = c\,\Delta\overline{R} + c(1-t)\,\Delta Y_0$$

or

$$\Delta Y_0 = \frac{1}{1 - c(1-t)}\,(c\,\Delta\overline{R}) = \bar{\alpha}\,c\,\Delta\overline{R} \qquad (25)$$

Equation (25) shows that an increase in transfer payments will raise the equilibrium level of income. For plausible values of c and t, it furthermore remains true that we have a multiplier effect—that a dollar increase in transfers raises equilibrium income by more than a dollar. Thus, for $c = 0.8$ and $t = 0.25$, the multiplier for transfer payments is 2.0.

The multiplier for government spending is higher than the multiplier for transfers because a $1 increase in government spending translates into a $1 increase in autonomous spending, whereas a $1 increase in transfers results in an increase of only c (less than 1) dollars in autonomous spending.

The Effects of an Income Tax Change

The final exercise in fiscal policy is a reduction in the income tax rate. This is illustrated in Fig. 3-8 by an increase in the slope of the aggregate demand function, because that slope is equal to the marginal propensity to spend out of income, $c(1-t)$. The figure shows that at the initial level of income, the aggregate demand for goods exceeds output because the increased disposable income arising from the tax reduction gives rise to increased consumption. The new higher equilibrium level of income is indicated by Y_0'.

To calculate the change in equilibrium income, we proceed as before by equating the change in income to the change in aggregate demand. The change in aggregate demand has two components. First, we have the change in spending at the initial level of income that arises from the tax cut. This part is equal to the marginal propensity to consume out of disposable income, times the change in disposable income due to the tax cut, $cY_0\,\Delta t$, where the term $Y_0\,\Delta t$ is the initial level of income times the change in the tax rate. The second component of the change in aggregate demand is the induced spending due to higher income. This is now evaluated at the new tax rate t' and has the value $c(1-t')\,\Delta Y_0$. We can therefore write[19]

---

[19]You should check Eq. (27) by using Eq. (22) to write out Y_0 corresponding to a tax rate of t, and Y_0' corresponding to t'. Then subtract Y_0 from Y_0' to obtain ΔY_0 as given in Eq. (27).

$$\Delta Y_0 = -cY_0 \,\Delta t + c(1 - t') \,\Delta Y_0 \qquad (26)$$

or

$$\Delta Y_0 = -\frac{1}{1 - c(1 - t')} cY_0 \,\Delta t \qquad (27)$$

An exercise will clarify the effects of an income tax cut. Assume initially a level of income equal to $Y_0 = 100$, a marginal propensity to consume $c = 0.8$, and a tax rate $t = 0.2$. Assume next a tax cut that reduces the income tax rate to $t' = 0.1$. At the initial level of income, disposable income therefore rises by $100(t - t') = \$10$. Out of the increase in disposable income of \$10, a fraction $c = 0.8$ is spent on consumption so that aggregate demand, at the initial level of income, increases by \$8. This corresponds to the first term on the right-hand side of Eq. (26). The increase in aggregate demand gives rise to an expansion in output and income. Per dollar increase in income, disposable income rises by a fraction $(1 - t')$ of the increase in income. Furthermore, of the increase in disposable income, only a fraction, c, is spent. Accordingly, induced consump-

FIGURE 3-8 THE EFFECTS OF A
DECREASE IN THE TAX RATE

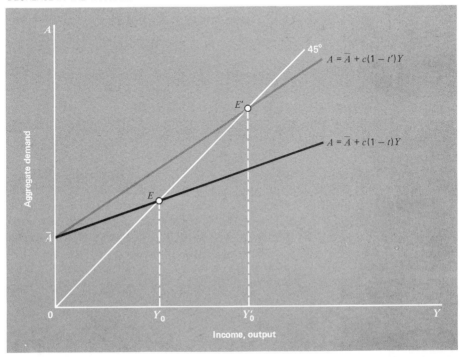

tion spending is equal to $c(1 - t') \, \Delta Y_0$, which is the second term in Eq. (26). Next we can ask how much the income tax cut achieves in terms of output expansion. Substituting our parameters in Eq. (27) we have

$$\Delta Y_0 = -\frac{1}{1 - 0.8(1 - 0.1)}(0.8)(100)(0.1 - 0.2) = (3.57)(8)$$

$$= \quad 28.56 \qquad\qquad\qquad\qquad\qquad\qquad\qquad\qquad (27a)$$

Thus, for the values we have assumed, a cut in the tax rate such that taxes fall by $10 at the initial level of income, raises equilibrium income by $28.56.

Note, however, that although taxes are initially cut by $10, the government's total taxes received fall by less than $10 between the two equilibria. Why? The reason is that the government receives 10 percent of the induced increase in income, or $2.856, as taxes. Thus the final reduction in tax receipts by the government is not the initial $10 but rather $7.144.[20]

Summary

1. Government spending and transfer payments act like increases in autonomous spending in their effects on equilibrium income.
2. Income taxes reduce disposable income relative to the level of income and thus act in the same way as a reduction in the propensity to consume in their effects on equilibrium income and output.
3. As a final comment on the material of this section, we note that all the results we have derived can be obtained in a straightforward manner by taking the change in aggregate demand *at the initial level of income* times the multiplier. (Check this proposition for each of the fiscal policy changes we have considered.) You will want to consider, too, the effect on equilibrium income of an increase in government spending combined with an *equal* reduction in transfer payments, $\Delta G = -\Delta \overline{R}$.[21]

3-5 THE BUDGET

In this section we will be concerned with the government budget. We start off by defining the well-known concept of the *budget surplus*, denoted

[20]We leave it to you to calculate the multiplier relating the change in equilibrium income to the total change in taxes received by the government. How does it compare with the multiplier for transfer payments at the new tax rate t'? Check Eqs. (27) and (25) to make sure your answer is correct.

[21]See prob. 9 at the end of the chapter.

by BuS. The surplus is simply the excess of the government's revenues, consisting of taxes, over its total spending, consisting of spending on goods and services and transfer payments:

$$\text{BuS} \equiv T - G - R \tag{28}$$

A negative budget surplus—an excess of government spending over revenues—is a *budget deficit*.

Since the budget surplus (and especially the deficit) receives much attention from politicians, economists, and the press, we want now to study the budget surplus in relation to the level of income. Substituting in Eq. (28), the assumption of a proportional income tax that yields a tax revenue $T = tY$ gives us

$$\text{BuS} = tY - G - R \tag{28a}$$

In Fig. 3-9 we plot the budget surplus as a function of the level of income for given $G = \overline{G}, R = \overline{R}$, and a given income tax rate t. We note that at low levels of income the budget is in deficit (the surplus is negative) because payments $\overline{G} + \overline{R}$ exceed income tax collection. For high levels of income, by contrast, the budget shows a surplus, since income tax collection outweighs payments in the form of government spending and transfers.

Figure 3-9 shows immediately that the budget surplus can be changed by changes in income that derive from sources other than a change in fiscal policy. Thus, for example, an increase in income that arises because of increased autonomous investment spending will give rise to an increase in

FIGURE 3-9 THE BUDGET SURPLUS

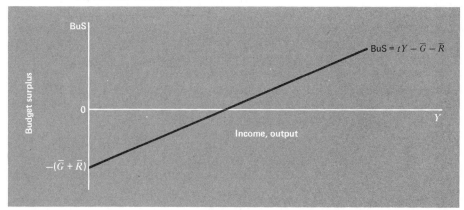

the budget surplus, or a reduction in the budget deficit. Why? Because the increase in income gives rise to an increase in income tax collection and, therefore, for a given level of government outlays, to a reduction in the deficit. To make the same point in a somewhat different manner, a reduction in economic activity, given fiscal policy as summarized by the parameters $\overline{G}$, $\overline{R}$, and t, must lead to a reduction in the budget surplus, or an increase in the deficit.

This feature of the budget, or of fiscal policy, whereby taxes are automatically reduced when income falls, is called *automatic stabilization*. Its effects were described in Sec. 3-4 as a reduction in the multiplier due to the presence of income taxes. Thus, the presence of income taxation ensures that a given reduction in autonomous spending will lead to less of a decline in income than would occur in the absence of income taxes because the multiplier $\bar{\alpha}$ is smaller than the multiplier α. In general, *automatic stabilizers* are those elements in the economy that reduce the impact of changes in autonomous spending on the equilibrium level of income. Unemployment benefits, for instance, are also an automatic stabilizer.

The Effects of Government Spending and Tax Changes on the Budget Surplus

Next we want to inquire how various changes in fiscal policy affect the budget. In particular, we will want to ask whether an increase in government spending must reduce the budget surplus. At first sight, this would appear obvious because increased government spending, from Eq. (28), is reflected in a reduced surplus, or increased deficit. At further thought it becomes apparent, however, that the increased government spending will give rise to a (multiplied) increase in income and, therefore, to increased income tax collection. This raises the intriguing possibility that tax collection might increase by more than government spending.

A brief calculation will show that the first guess is right—increased government spending reduces the budget surplus. From Eq. (23) the change in income due to increased government spending is equal to $\Delta Y_0 = \bar{\alpha}\Delta\overline{G}$. A fraction of that increase in income is collected in the form of taxes so that tax revenue increases by $t\bar{\alpha}\Delta\overline{G}$. The change in the budget surplus is therefore[22]

$$\Delta\text{BuS} = \Delta T - \Delta\overline{G}$$

$$= t\bar{\alpha}\,\Delta\overline{G} - \Delta\overline{G}$$

$$= \left[\frac{t}{1 - c(1 - t)} - 1\right]\Delta\overline{G}$$

$$= -\frac{(1 - c)(1 - t)}{1 - c(1 - t)}\Delta\overline{G} \tag{29}$$

[22]We use Eq. (24) to substitute for $\bar{\alpha}$ in Eq. (29).

which is unambiguously negative. We have, therefore, shown that an increase in government spending will reduce the budget surplus, although by considerably less than the increase in spending. For instance, for $c = 0.8$ and $t = 0.2$, a \$1 increase in government spending will create a 44-cent reduction in the surplus.[23]

In the same way, we can consider the effects of an increase in the tax rate on the budget surplus. We know that the increase in the tax rate will reduce the level of income. It might thus appear that an increase in the tax rate, keeping the level of government spending constant, could reduce the budget surplus. In fact, an increase in the tax rate increases the budget surplus despite the reduction in income that it causes.[24]

Finally, we can investigate the budgetary effects of simultaneous changes in income tax rates and government spending. We will work through these cases by using a simple example. We assume that a fiscal policy is implemented that reduces the income tax rate from $t = 0.2$ to $t = 0.1$. At an initial level of income of 100, such a tax cut results in a loss of tax revenue of \$10. In combination with the tax cut, we implement a reduction of government spending in the amount of \$10. What is the net effect on equilibrium income and the budget of the fiscal policy package, assuming a marginal propensity to consume of $c = 0.8$? With an income tax rate of $t' = 0.1$, the multiplier will be $\bar{\alpha} = 3.57$. A \$10 decrease in government spending accordingly lowers income by \$35.70. The tax cut, in turn, will raise income by $\$28.56 = (0.8)(0.1)(100)(3.57)$. The *net* effect of the package on income is therefore a reduction in income of the order of \$7.14. What is the effect on the budget? Government spending declines by \$10, tax revenue declines at the initial level of income by \$10 owing to the tax cut and suffers a further reduction, due to the decline in income, of $(0.1)(7.14) = 0.71$. The net effect of this cut in government spending combined with a decrease in taxes that *at the initial level of income* is equal to the cut in government spending, is therefore a slight increase in the budget deficit by an amount of \$0.71. The reason the budget deficit changes is that the initial cuts in both spending and taxes reduce the level of income and so reduce taxes more than they were reduced initially.

In the above example, the combined tax decrease and government spending decrease increased the budget deficit. What would happen to the level of income if government spending and taxes changed by exactly the same amount so that the budget surplus remained unchanged? The answer to this question is contained in the famous *balanced budget multiplier* result. The result is that the balanced budget multiplier is exactly 1. That is, an increase in government spending, accompanied by an equal increase in taxes, increases the level of income by exactly the amount of the

---

[23]In this case $\bar{\alpha} = 1/[1 - 0.8(0.8)] = 2.78$ (see p. 72). So $\Delta BuS = -2.78(0.2)(0.8) = -0.44$.

[24]The effects of an increase in the tax rate on the budget surplus are examined in detail in prob. 7 at the end of this chapter.

increase in government spending.[25]   The development of this interesting result is contained in the appendix to this chapter.

The major points of the preceding discussion are that a balanced budget cut in government spending lowers equilibrium income and that a $1 increase in government spending has a stronger impact on equilibrium income than a dollar cut in taxes. A dollar cut in taxes leads only to a fraction of a dollar's increase in consumption spending, the rest being saved, while government spending is reflected dollar for dollar in a change in aggregate demand.[26]

The Full-Employment Budget Surplus

A final topic to be treated here is the concept of the *full-employment budget surplus*.[27]   Recall that increases in taxes add to the surplus and that increases in government spending or transfer payments reduce the surplus. Increases in taxes have been shown to reduce the level of income, and increases in government spending and transfers to increase the level of income. It thus seems that the budget surplus is a convenient, simple measure of the overall effects of fiscal policy on the economy. When government spending increases, the level of income rises and the budget surplus falls. When taxes increase, the level of income falls and the budget surplus rises.

However, the budget surplus by itself suffers from a serious defect as a measure of the direction of fiscal policy. The defect is that the surplus can change *passively* because of changes in autonomous private spending, as we saw above. Thus, if the economy moves into a recession, tax revenue automatically declines and the budget moves into a deficit (or reduced surplus). Conversely, an increase in economic activity causes the budget to move into a surplus (or reduced deficit). These changes in the budget take place automatically for a given tax structure. This implies that we cannot simply look at the budget deficit as a measure of whether government fiscal policy is expansionary or deflationary. A given fiscal policy may imply a deficit if private spending is low and a surplus if private spending is high. Thus, it is important to note that increases in the budget deficit do not necessarily mean that the government has changed its policy

---

[25]Note that the balanced budget multiplier may well be less than 1 in the more sophisticated models of Chap. 4 in which investment spending depends on the interest rate.

[26]Rather than go through the analysis of changes in transfer payments, we will leave it to you to work through an example of the effects on the budget of a change in transfer payments in the problems at the end of the chapter.

[27]The concept of the full-employment surplus was first used by E. Cary Brown, "Fiscal Policy in the Thirties: A Reappraisal," *American Economic Review*, December 1956.

in an expansionary direction in an attempt to increase the level of income.

Since we frequently want to measure the way in which fiscal policy is being *actively* rather than *passively* used to affect the level of income, we require some measure of policy that is independent of the particular position of the business cycle—boom or recession—that we may find ourselves in. Such a measure is provided by the *full-employment budget surplus*, which we shall denote by BuS*. BuS* measures the budget, not at the actual level of income, but rather at the full-employment level of income, or at potential output. Thus, a given fiscal policy summarized by $\overline{G}$, $\overline{R}$, and t is assessed by the level of the surplus, or deficit, that is generated at full employment. Using Y_p to denote the full-employment level of income, we can write

$$\text{BuS*} = tY_p - \overline{G} - \overline{R} \tag{30}$$

In Fig. 3-10 we replicate the budget surplus schedule from Fig. 3-9 but add the full-employment level of income Y_p. The full-employment budget surplus is indicated by the corresponding point on the budget surplus schedule. To see the difference between the actual and the full-employment budget, we subtract the actual budget in Eq. (28a) from Eq. (30) to obtain

$$\text{BuS*} - \text{BuS} = t(Y_p - Y) \tag{31}$$

It is apparent that the only difference arises from income tax collec-

FIGURE 3-10 THE FULL-EMPLOYMENT
BUDGET SURPLUS

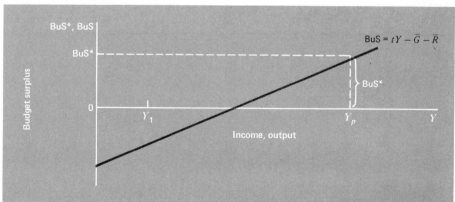

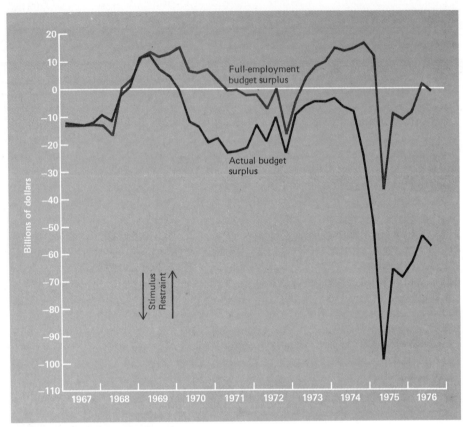

CHART 3-1   THE FULL EMPLOYMENT AND
ACTUAL BUDGET SURPLUSES, 1967–1976
(BILLIONS OF DOLLARS). (Source: *Federal
Budget Trends,* 1976)

tion.[28]   Specifically, if output is below full employment, the full-employment surplus exceeds the actual surplus.   Conversely, if actual output exceeds full-employment (or potential) output, the full-employment surplus is less than the actual surplus.

Chart 3-1 shows the actual and full-employment budget surplus for the years 1967–1976.   It is apparent that in a recession like 1974–1976 the actual deficit by far exceeds the full-employment (or high-employment)

[28]In practice, transfer payments, such as welfare and unemployment benefits, are also partly affected by the state of the economy so that R also depends on the level of income.   But the major cause of differences between the actual surplus and the full-employment surplus is the income tax.

deficit. The change in the full-employment budget from a large surplus in 1974 to a deficit in 1975 reflects the active use of fiscal policy to combat the recession—there was a substantial decrease in tax rates in early 1975. The drop in the actual budget surplus in that period is due in part to this active stimulus, and partly due to the drop in revenues resulting from the recession. By contrast, in the years 1966–1968 the actual and full-employment budgets were very close. This, by Eq. (31), is a reflection of the fact that the economy was near full employment in that period. Note that the actual budget surplus has been continuously less than the high-employment surplus since 1969. This reflects an unemployment rate that has been above the 4 percent level since 1969. Four percent is the full-employment rate used in constructing the high-employment budget.

One final word of warning should be given. The high-employment surplus is a better measure of the direction of active fiscal policy than the actual budget surplus. But it is not a perfect measure of the thrust of fiscal policy. The reason is that balanced budget increases in government spending are themselves expansionary, so that an increase in government spending matched by a tax increase that keeps the surplus constant leads to an increase in the level of income. Because fiscal policy involves the setting of a number of variables—the tax rate, transfers, and government spending—it is difficult to describe the thrust of fiscal policy perfectly in a single number.[29] But the high-employment surplus is nevertheless a useful guide to the direction of fiscal policy.

3-6 SUMMARY

1 Output is at its equilibrium level when the aggregate demand for goods is equal to the level of output.
2 Aggregate demand consists of planned spending by households on consumption, firms on investment goods, and government on its purchases of goods and services.
3 When output is at its equilibrium level, there are no unintended changes in inventories and all economic units are making precisely the purchases they had planned to. An adjustment process for the level of output based on the accumulation or decumulation of inventories leads the economy to the equilibrium output level.
4 The level of aggregate demand is itself affected by the level of output (equal to the level of income) because consumption demand depends on the level of income.
5 The consumption function relates consumption spending to income.

[29]For an attempt to do so, see Alan S. Blinder and Stephen Goldfeld, "New Measures of Fiscal and Monetary Policy," *American Economic Review*, December 1976, pp 780–796.

Income that is not consumed is saved, so that the saving function can be derived from the consumption function.

6 The multiplier is the amount by which a $1 change in autonomous spending changes the equilibrium level of output. The greater the propensity to consume, the higher the multiplier.

7 Government spending and government transfer payments act like increases in autonomous spending in their effects on the equilibrium level of income. A proportional income tax has the same effects on the equilibrium level of income as a reduction in the propensity to consume. A proportional income tax thus reduces the multiplier.

8 The budget surplus is the excess of government receipts over its spending. When the government is spending more than it receives, the budget is in deficit. The size of the budget surplus (deficit) is affected by the government's fiscal policy variables—government spending, transfer payments, and tax rates.

9 The budget surplus is also affected by changes in taxes and transfers resulting from changes in the level of income occurring as a result of changes in private autonomous spending. The *full-employment* (high-employment) budget surplus is accordingly frequently used as a measure of the active use of fiscal policy. The full-employment surplus measures the budget surplus that would exist if output were at its potential (full-employment) level.

APPENDIX

This appendix considers the *balanced budget multiplier* result mentioned in the text. The balanced budget multiplier refers to the effects of an increase in government spending accompanied by an increase in taxes such that in the new equilibrium the budget surplus is exactly the same as in the original equilibrium. The result is that the multiplier of such a policy change is unity. In other words, the *balanced budget multiplier* is 1. A multiplier of unity obviously implies that output precisely expands by the amount of the increased government spending with no induced consumption spending. It is apparent that what must be at work is the effect of higher taxes that precisely offset the effect of the income expansion, and thus maintain disposable income and hence consumption constant. With no induced consumption spending, output expands simply to match the increased government spending.

   We can derive this result formally by noting that the change in aggregate demand ΔA is equal to the change in government spending plus the change in consumption spending. The latter is equal to the marginal propensity to consume out of disposable income c times the change in disposable income ΔY_d, i.e., $\Delta Y_d = \Delta Y_0 - \Delta T$, where ΔY_0 is the change in output. Thus:

$$\Delta A = \Delta \overline{G} + c(\Delta Y_0 - \Delta T) \tag{A1}$$

Since from one equilibrium to another the change in aggregate demand has to equal the change in output, we have

$$\Delta Y_0 = \Delta \overline{G} + c(\Delta Y_0 - \Delta T)$$

or

$$\Delta Y_0 = \frac{1}{1 - c}(\Delta \overline{G} - c \, \Delta T) \tag{A2}$$

Next we note that by assumption the change in government spending between the new equilibrium and the old one is exactly matched by a change in tax collection so that $\Delta \overline{G} = \Delta T$. It follows from this last equality, after substitution in Eq. (A2), that with this particular restriction on fiscal policy we have

$$\Delta Y_0 = \frac{1}{1 - c}(\Delta \overline{G} - c \, \Delta \overline{G}) = \Delta \overline{G} = \Delta T \tag{A3}$$

so that the multiplier is precisely unity.

Another way of deriving the balanced budget multiplier result is by considering the successive rounds of spending changes caused by the government policy changes. Suppose each of government spending and taxes increases by $1. Let $c(1 - t)$, the induced increase in aggregate demand caused by a $1 increase in income in the presence of taxes, be denoted by $\overline{c}$. Now Table A3-1 shows the spending induced by the two policy changes. The first column shows the changes in spending resulting from the change in government spending and its later repercussions. The second column similarly gives the spending effects in successive rounds of the tax increase. The third column sums the two effects for each spending round, while the final column adds all the changes in spending induced so far. Since $\overline{c}$ is less than 1, $\overline{c}^n$ becomes very small as the number of spending rounds, n, increases, and the final change in aggregate spending caused by the balanced budget increase in government spending is just equal to $1.

TABLE A3-1 THE BALANCED BUDGET MULTIPLIER

| | Change in spending resulting from | | | |
Spending round	$\Delta \overline{G} = 1$	$\Delta T = 1$	Net this round	Total
1	1	$-\overline{c}$	$1 - \overline{c}$	$1 - \overline{c}$
2	$\overline{c}$	$-\overline{c}^2$	$\overline{c} - \overline{c}^2$	$1 - \overline{c}^2$
3	$\overline{c}^2$	$-\overline{c}^3$	$\overline{c}^2 - \overline{c}^3$	$1 - \overline{c}^3$
4	$\overline{c}^3$	$-\overline{c}^4$	$\overline{c}^3 - \overline{c}^4$	$1 - \overline{c}^4$
⋮				
n	$\overline{c}^{n-1}$	$-\overline{c}^n$	$\overline{c}^{n-1} - \overline{c}^n$	$1 - \overline{c}^n$

Finally, the balanced budget multiplier can also be thought of from a some-what different perspective. Consider the goods market equilibrium condition in terms of saving, taxes, investment, transfers, and government spending:

$$S + T - R = \overline{I} + G \qquad\qquad (A4)$$

Now, using the definition of the budget surplus, BuS $\equiv T - R - G$,

$$BuS = \overline{I} - S \qquad\qquad (A5)$$

If there is no change in the budget deficit, nor a change in investment, then the equilibrium change in saving is zero. For saving not to change, it is required that disposable income remain unchanged. This says that $\Delta Y_d = \Delta Y - \Delta T = 0$, and hence shows once more that the change in income equals the change in taxes. This in turn equals the change in government spending. Hence, the balanced budget multiplier, or more precisely the multiplier associated with an unchanging budget surplus or deficit, is equal to unity. This perspective on the income deter-mination process is very useful because it emphasizes the fact that a change in the surplus or deficit of one sector is matched by a corresponding change in the deficit or surplus of the remaining sectors. If the government surplus is constrained by fiscal policy to be unchanged, so too must be the private sector's surplus, $S - \overline{I}$.

PROBLEMS

1. Here we investigate a particular example of the model studied in Secs. 3-2 and 3-3 with no government. Suppose the consumption function is given by $C = 100 + 0.8Y$ while investment is given by $\overline{I} = 50$.
   a. What is the equilibrium level of income in this case?
   b. What is the level of saving in equilibrium?
   c. If for some reason output was at the level of 800, what would the level of involuntary inventory accumulation be?
   d. If $\overline{I}$ were to rise to 100 (we will discuss what determines $\overline{I}$ in later chapters), what would be the effect on equilibrium income?
   e. What is the multiplier, α, here?
   f. Draw a diagram indicating the equilibria in both 1a and 1d.
2. Suppose consumption behavior were to change in problem 1 above so that $C = 100 + 0.9Y$ while $\overline{I}$ remained at 50.
   a. Would you expect the equilibrium level of income to be higher or lower than in 1a above? Calculate the new Y_0' to verify this.
   b. Now suppose investment increases to $\overline{I} = 100$ just as in 1d above. What is the new equilibrium income?
   c. Does this change in investment spending have more or less of an effect on Y_0 than in problem 1? Why?
   d. Draw a diagram indicating the change in equilibrium in this case.
3. We showed in the text that the equilibrium condition $Y = A$ is equivalent to the $S = \overline{I}$, or saving = investment, condition. Starting from $S = \overline{I}$ and the saving function, derive the equilibrium level of income.

4 Now let us look at a model which is an example of the one presented in Secs. 3-4 and 3-5; that is, it includes government spending, taxes, and transfers. It has the same features as the one in problems 1 and 2, except that it also has a government. Thus, suppose consumption is given by $C = 100 + 0.8Y_d$ and $\overline{I} = 50$ while fiscal policy is summarized by $\overline{G} = 200$, $\overline{R} = 62.5$, $t = 0.25$.

  a What is the equilibrium level of income in this more complete model?

  b What is the new multiplier $\bar{\alpha}$? Why is this less than the multiplier in problem 1e?

5 Using the same model as in problem 4 above:

  a What is the value of the budget surplus BuS when $\overline{I} = 50$?

  b What is BuS when $\overline{I}$ increases to 100?

  c What accounts for the change in BuS from 5a to 5b?

  d Assuming that the full-employment level of income Y_p is 1,200, what is the full-employment budget surplus BuS* when $\overline{I} = 50$? 100? (Be careful)

  e What is BuS* if $\overline{I} = 50$ and $\overline{G} = 250$, with Y_p still equal to 1,200?

  f Explain why we use BuS* rather than simply BuS to measure the direction of fiscal policy.

6 Suppose we expand our model to take account of the fact that transfer payments R do depend on the level of income Y. When income is high, transfer payments like unemployment benefits will fall. Conversely, when income is low, unemployment is high and so are unemployment benefits. We can incorporate this into our model by writing transfers as $R = \overline{R} - bY$, $b > 0$. Remembering that our equilibrium income is derived as the solution to $Y_0 = C + \overline{I} + \overline{G} = \overline{C} + cY_d + \overline{I} + \overline{G}$, where $Y_d = Y + R - T$ is disposable income,

  a Derive the expression for Y_0 in this case, just as Eq. (22) was derived in the text.

  b What is the new multiplier now?

  c Why is the new multiplier less than the standard one, $\bar{\alpha}$?

7 Now we look at the role taxes play in determining equilibrium income. Suppose we have an economy of the type in Secs. 3-4 and 3-5 described by the following functions:

$$C = 50 + 0.8Y_d$$

$$\overline{I} = 70$$

$$\overline{G} = 200$$

$$\overline{R} = 100$$

$$t = 0.20$$

  a Calculate the equilibrium level of income and the multiplier in this model.

  b Calculate also the budget surplus, BuS.

  c Suppose now t is increased to 0.25. What is the new equilibrium income? The new multiplier?

  d Calculate the change in the budget surplus. Would you expect the change in the surplus to be more or less if $c = 0.9$ rather than 0.8?

  e Can you explain why the multiplier is 1 when $t = 1$?

8 Suppose the economy is operating at equilibrium with $Y_0 = 1,000$. If the government undertakes a fiscal change so that the tax rate t increases by 0.05

and government spending increases by 50, will the budget surplus go up or down? Why?

9   Suppose Congress decides to reduce transfer payments (such as welfare), but to increase government spending on goods and services by an equal amount. That is to say, it undertakes a change in fiscal policy such that $\Delta G = -\Delta R > 0$.

   a   Would you expect equilibrium income to rise or fall as a result of this change? Why? Check out your answer with the following example: Suppose initially $c = 0.8$, $t = 0.25$, and $Y_0 = 600$. Now let $\Delta \overline{G} = 10$, $\Delta \overline{R} = -10$.

   b   Find the change in equilibrium income, ΔY_0.

   c   What is the change in the budget surplus, ΔBuS? Why has BuS changed?

*10   We have seen in problem 9 that an increase in G accompanied by an equal decrease in R does not leave the budget unchanged. What would the effect on equilibrium income be if R and G change to leave the budget surplus BuS fixed?

     Notice that BuS $= T - R - G$. We want ΔBuS $= \Delta T - \Delta R - \Delta G = 0(*)$ so $\Delta R = \Delta T - \Delta G$. Since t is constant, $\Delta T = t\ \Delta Y_0(**)$. We also know that $Y_0 = \bar{\alpha}(\overline{C} + \overline{I} + \overline{G} + c\overline{R})$ and $\Delta Y_0 = \bar{\alpha}(\Delta \overline{G} + c\ \Delta \overline{R})$.

     Substituting (*) and (**) into this last equation, derive an expression for ΔY in terms of ΔG. Simplify that expression, using the fact that $\bar{\alpha} = \{1/[1 - c(1 - t)]\}$, to obtain the balanced budget result in the case of changes in transfers and government spending.

*11   In the appendix we derived the balanced budget multiplier result. It states that if $\Delta G = \Delta T$ from the initial to final equilibrium, then $\Delta Y = \Delta G$. Let us look at an example of this balanced budget multiplier in action. Consider the economy described by the following functions:

$$C = 85 + 0.75Y_d$$
$$\overline{I} = 50$$
$$\overline{G} = 150$$
$$\overline{R} = 100$$
$$t = 0.20$$

   a   Derive the multiplier $\bar{\alpha}$ and the level of autonomous spending $\overline{A}$.

   b   From 11a, calculate the equilibrium level of income and the budget surplus.

   c   Now suppose G rises to 250 while t increases to 0.28. Repeat step 11a for the new fiscal policy.

   d   Calculate Y_0' and BuS', the new income and budget surplus.

   e   What are ΔT, ΔG, ΔY, ΔBuS?

   f   In view of this result and that of problem 9, what do you think the effect on income would be if we had a balanced budget change where $\Delta R = \Delta T$?

*12   Suppose the aggregate demand function is as drawn in the figure below. Notice that at Y_0 the slope of the aggregate demand curve is *greater* than 1. (This would happen if $c > 1$.) Complete this picture as is done in Fig. 3-1 to include the arrows indicating adjustment when $Y \neq Y_0$ and show what I_u is for $Y < Y_0$ and $Y > Y_0$. What is happening in this example, and how does it differ fundamentally from Fig. 3-1?

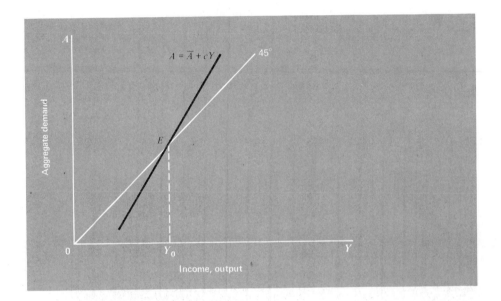

4

Money, Interest,
and Income

The stock of money, interest rates, and the Federal Reserve seemingly had no place in the model of income determination developed in Chap. 3. Clearly, though, we know that money has an important role to play in the determination of income and employment. Interest rates are frequently mentioned as an important determinant of aggregate spending, and the Federal Reserve and monetary policy receive at least as much public attention as fiscal policy. This chapter introduces money and monetary policy, and builds an explicit framework of analysis in which the interaction of goods and assets markets can be studied.

The model we will study here (called the IS-LM model) is the core of modern macroeconomics. It maintains the spirit and, indeed, many details of the previous chapter. In particular, it remains true that aggregate demand determines the equilibrium level of output. The model is broadened, though, by considering the determinants of aggregate demand. The last chapter pointed to autonomous spending and fiscal policy as the chief determinants of aggregate spending. Here we introduce the interest rate as an additional variable. We will argue that the interest rate is an additional determinant of aggregate spending and that a reduction in the rate of interest raises aggregate demand. This would seem a minor extension, and one that can readily be handled in the context of Chap. 3. This is not entirely correct, though, because we will have to ask what determines the rate of interest. That question extends our model to include the markets for (financial) assets and forces us to study the interaction of goods and assets markets. Interest rates and income are jointly determined by equilibrium in goods and assets markets.

What is the payoff for that complication? The introduction of assets markets and interest rates serves three important purposes. First, we need the extension to understand how monetary policy works. Second, the analysis qualifies the conclusions of Chap. 3. To appreciate the latter point, consider Fig. 4-1, which lays out the logical structure of the model. In Chap. 3 we looked at the submodel of autonomous spending and fiscal policy as determinants of aggregate demand and equilibrium income. Here the inclusion of assets markets—money demand and supply as we shall see—includes an additional channel. Thus, an expansionary fiscal policy, for example, would in the first place raise spending and income. That increase in income, though, would affect the assets markets by raising money demand and thereby raising interest rates. The higher interest rates in turn reduce aggregate spending and thus, as we will show, dampen the expansionary impact of fiscal policy. Indeed, under certain conditions, the increase in interest rates may be sufficiently important to *fully* offset the expansionary effects of fiscal policy. Clearly, such an extreme possibility is an important qualification to our study of fiscal policy in Chap. 3.

Third, even if the interest rate changes mentioned above only dampen (rather than fully offset) the expansionary effects of fiscal policy, they nevertheless have an important side effect. The composition of aggregate demand between investment and consumption spending will depend on the rate of interest. Higher interest rates dampen aggregate demand mainly by reducing investment. Thus, an expansionary fiscal policy would tend to raise consumption through the multiplier, but it would tend to reduce investment through the induced increase in interest rates. The side effects of fiscal expansion on interest rates and investment continues to be a sensitive and important issue in policy making. An influential view is that fiscal expansion should not be used as a tool for demand management because the increase in government spending takes place at the expense of private investment. Government spending crowds out, or displaces, private investment because it tends to raise interest rates.

These three reasons justify the more complicated model we study in this chapter. There is the further advantage that the extended model helps us to understand the functioning of financial markets.

We can use Fig. 4-1 once more to lay out the structure of this chapter. We start in Sec. 4-1 with a discussion of the link between interest rates and aggregate demand. Here we use directly the model of Chap. 3, augmented to include an interest rate as a determinant of aggregate demand. We will derive a key relationship—the IS curve—that shows combinations of interest rates and levels of income for which the goods markets clear. In Sec. 4-2 we turn to assets markets and, in particular, to the money market. We show that the demand for money depends on interest rates and income and that there is a combination of interest rates and income levels—the LM curve—for which the money market clears.[1] In Sec. 4-3 we combine the two schedules to study the joint determination of interest rates and income, as a brief glance ahead at Fig. 4-10 will show. Sec. 4-4 lays out the adjustment process toward equilibrium. Monetary and fiscal policy are discussed in Sec. 4-5 and 4-6. The political economy of monetary and fiscal policy is taken up in Sec. 4-7. We conclude the chapter with a formal statement of the model. An appendix discusses the relationship between interest rates, asset prices, and asset yields.

4-1 THE GOODS MARKET AND THE IS CURVE

In this section we will derive a "goods market equilibrium schedule"—a combination of interest rates and levels of income such that the goods market is in equilibrium. That schedule is the IS schedule, which is shown in Fig. 4-2b. To derive the IS schedule, we start with the analysis of goods market equilibrium of Chap. 3, and modify it to take account of the

---

[1] The terms IS and LM are shorthand representations of investment equals saving (goods market equilibrium) and money demand (L) equals money supply (M), or money market equilibrium. The classic article on this model and an extremely readable one is J. R. Hicks, "Mr. Keynes and the Classics: A Suggested Interpretation," *Econometrica*, 1937, pp. 147–159.

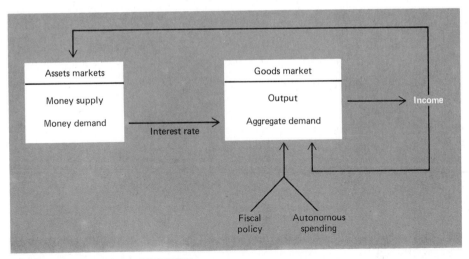

FIGURE 4-1 THE LOGICAL STRUCTURE
OF THE IS-LM MODEL

relationship between investment spending and the interest rate.

In Chap. 3 we relied on an aggregate demand function of the form:

$$A = \overline{A} + \overline{c}Y \tag{1}$$

where $\overline{A}$ denotes autonomous spending and is equal to

$$\overline{A} \equiv \overline{C} + \overline{I} + \overline{G} + c\overline{R} \tag{2}$$

and where we have introduced the shorthand notation $\overline{c} \equiv c(1 - t)$ to denote the marginal propensity to spend out of income.

Equilibrium in the goods market requires that output equals aggregate demand,

$$Y = A \tag{3}$$

and leads, by substitution from Eq. (1), to the equation

$$Y = \overline{A} + \overline{c}Y \tag{3a}$$

This can be solved for the equilibrium level of income[2]:

[2]To move from Eq. (3a) to Eq. (3b), we collect terms in Y to obtain $Y(1 - \overline{c}) = \overline{A}$. Then we divide both sides by $(1 - \overline{c})$ to yield Eq. (3b).

$$Y_0 = \frac{\overline{A}}{1 - \overline{c}} = \overline{\alpha}\overline{A} \qquad (3b)$$

In Eq. (3b) we have used the shorthand notation for the multiplier with taxes, $\overline{\alpha} \equiv 1/(1 - \overline{c})$.

The level of planned investment $\overline{I}$ in Eq. (2) was treated as constant in

FIGURE 4-2 DERIVATION OF THE IS CURVE

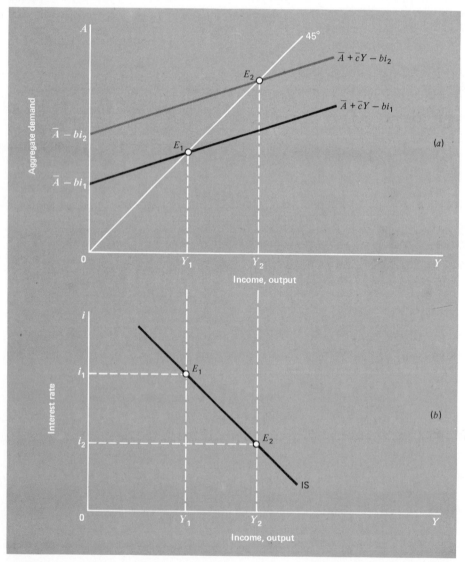

Chap. 3. However, planned investment spending is influenced by the rate of interest, being inversely related to it. We explore the determinants of investment spending in depth in Chap. 6, but a simple argument will suffice here to show why planned investment spending is negatively related to the interest rate. Investment is spending on additions to the capital stock. Such investment is undertaken with an eye to the profits that can be obtained in the future by operating machines and factories. Now, suppose firms borrow to buy the capital, in the form of machines and factories, that they use. Then the higher the interest rate, the more firms have to pay out in interest each year from the earnings they receive from their investment. Thus the higher the interest rate, the less the profits to the firm after paying interest, and the less it will want to invest. A high rate of interest lowers the profitability of additions to the capital stock and therefore implies a low rate of investment spending. Conversely, a low rate of interest makes investment spending profitable and is, therefore, reflected in a high level of planned investment.

Accordingly, we modify the assumption that investment spending is constant by specifying an investment spending function of the form:[3]

$$I = \overline{I} - bi \qquad b > 0 \qquad\qquad (4)$$

where i is the rate of interest and b measures the interest response of investment. $\overline{I}$ now denotes autonomous investment spending, that is, investment spending that is independent of both income *and* the rate of interest.[4] Equation (4) states that the lower the interest rate, the higher is planned investment, with the coefficient b measuring the responsiveness of investment spending to the interest rate.

We now modify the aggregate demand function Eq. (1) to reflect the new planned investment spending schedule Eq. (4). Aggregate demand still consists of the demand for consumption goods, investment, and government spending on goods and services. Only now investment spending depends on the interest rate. We have

---

[3]Here and in other places in the book we specify linear (straight-line) versions of behavioral functions. We use the linear specifications to simplify both the algebra and the diagrams. The linearity assumption does not lead to any great difficulties so long as we confine ourselves to talking about small changes in the economy. You should often draw nonlinear versions of our diagrams to be sure you can work with them. This would be particularly useful where, as in Fig. 4-2, the position and shape of one curve (in this case, the IS curve) depend on the position and shape of another curve (the aggregate demand schedules in the upper panel, in this case).

[4]In Chap. 3 investment spending was defined as autonomous with respect to income. Now that the interest rate appears in the model, we have to extend the definition of autonomous to mean independent of both the interest rate and income. To conserve notation, we continue to use $\overline{I}$ to denote autonomous investment, but recognize that the definition is broadened.

$$A \equiv C + I + G$$
$$= \overline{C} + c\overline{R} + c(1 - t)Y + \overline{I} - bi + \overline{G}$$
$$= \overline{A} + \overline{c}Y - bi \tag{1a}$$

where

$$\overline{A} \equiv \overline{C} + c\overline{R} + \overline{I} + \overline{G} \tag{2a}$$

From Eq. (1a) it is clear that an increase in the interest rate reduces aggregate demand at a given level of income, because an interest rate increase reduces investment spending. Note that the term $\overline{A}$, which is the part of aggregate demand unaffected by either the level of income or the interest rate, does include part of investment spending, namely, $\overline{I}$. As noted above, $\overline{I}$ is the *autonomous* component of investment spending, which is independent of the interest rate (and income).

At any given level of the interest rate, we can still proceed as in Chap. 3 to determine the equilibrium level of income and output. At each level of the interest rate, there is an equilibrium level of income. As the interest rate changes, the equilibrium level of income changes. The relationship we shall now derive between the interest rate and the equilibrium level of income in the goods market is the *IS curve*.

Figure 4-2 is used to derive the IS curve. For a given level of the interest rate, say i_1, the last term of Eq. (1a) is a constant (bi_1), and we can in Fig. 4-2a draw the aggregate demand function of Chap. 3, this time with an intercept $\overline{A} - bi_1$. The equilibrium level of income obtained in the usual manner is Y_1 at point E_1. Since that equilibrium level of income was derived for a given level of the interest rate i_1, we can plot that pair (namely, i_1, Y_1) in the bottom panel as point E_1. We now have one point, E_1, on the IS curve.

Consider next a lower interest rate, i_2. At a lower interest rate, aggregate demand would be higher at each level of income, because investment spending is higher. In terms of Fig. 4-2a, that implies an upward shift of the aggregate demand schedule. The entire aggregate demand schedule shifts upward by $-b \, \Delta i$, where Δi, the assumed change in the interest rate, is negative. The curve shifts upward because the intercept $\overline{A} - bi$ has been increased. Given the increase in aggregate demand, we note that the equilibrium level of income rises to point E_2, with an associated income level Y_2. At point E_2, in the bottom panel, we record the fact that an interest rate i_2 implies an equilibrium level of income, Y_2—equilibrium in the sense that the goods market is in equilibrium (or that the goods market *clears*). Point E_2 is another point on the IS curve.

We can apply the same procedure to all conceivable levels of the interest rate and thereby generate all the points which make up the IS curve. They have in common the property that they constitute combinations of interest rates and income (output) such that the goods market clears. We therefore refer to the IS curve as the *goods market equilibrium schedule.*

Figure 4-2 shows that the IS curve is negatively sloped, reflecting the increase in aggregate demand associated with a reduction in the interest rate. We can alternatively derive the IS curve by using the goods market equilibrium condition

$$Y = A \qquad (5)$$

Substituting from Eq. (1a) for aggregate demand in Eq. (5), we obtain

$$Y = \overline{A} + \overline{c}Y - bi \qquad (6)$$

which can be simplified to

$$Y = \overline{\alpha}(\overline{A} - bi) \qquad \overline{\alpha} \equiv \frac{1}{1 - \overline{c}} \qquad (6a)$$

From Eq. (6a) we note that a higher interest rate implies a lower level of equilibrium income for a given $\overline{A}$, as Fig. 4-2 shows. (Recall that $\overline{\alpha}$ is the multiplier of Chap. 3.)

The construction of the IS curve is quite straightforward, and may even be deceptively simple. We can gain further understanding of the economics of the IS curve by asking and answering the following questions:

• What determines the slope of the IS curve?
• What determines the position of the IS curve, given its slope, and what causes the curve to shift?
• What happens when the interest rate and income are at levels such that we are not on the IS curve?

The Slope of the IS Curve

We have already noted that the IS curve is negatively sloped, because a higher level of the interest rate reduces investment spending, therefore reduces aggregate demand, and therefore reduces the equilibrium level of income. The steepness of the curve depends on how sensitive investment spending is to changes in the interest rate, and also on the multiplier $\overline{\alpha}$ in Eq. (6a).

Suppose that investment spending is very sensitive to the interest rate, so that b in Eq. (6a) is large. Then, in terms of Fig. 4-2, a given change in the interest rate produces a large change in aggregate demand, and thus shifts the aggregate demand curve in Fig. 4-2a up by a large distance. A large shift in the aggregate demand schedule produces a correspondingly large change in the equilibrium level of income. If a given change in the interest rate produces a large change in income, the IS curve is very flat.

Thus the IS curve is flat if investment is very sensitive to the interest rate, that is, if b is large. Correspondingly, with b small and investment spending not very sensitive to the interest rate, the IS curve is relatively steep.

Consider next the effects of the multiplier $\bar{\alpha}$ on the steepness of the IS curve. Figure 4-3 shows aggregate demand curves corresponding to different multipliers. The coefficient $\bar{c}$ on the darker aggregate demand curves is smaller than the corresponding coefficient $\bar{c}'$ on the lighter aggregate demand curves. The multiplier is accordingly larger on the lighter aggregate demand curves. The initial levels of income, Y_1 and Y_1', correspond to the interest rate i_1 on the lower of each of the darker and lighter aggregate demand curves, respectively. A given reduction in the interest rate, to i_2, raises the intercept of the aggregate demand curves by the same vertical distance, as shown in the top panel. However, the implied change in income is very different. For the lighter curve, income rises to Y_2', while it rises only to Y_2 on the darker line. The change in equilibrium income corresponding to a given change in the interest rate is accordingly larger as the aggregate demand curve is steeper; that is, the larger the multiplier, the greater the rise in income. That should not be surprising since, effectively, the change in the interest rate and induced change in investment acts in the same way on the aggregate demand curves as a change in autonomous spending $\bar{A}$. As we see from Fig. 4-3b, the smaller the multiplier, the steeper the IS curve. Equivalently, the larger the multiplier, the larger the change in income produced by a given change in the interest rate.

We have thus seen that the smaller the sensitivity of investment spending to the interest rate and the smaller the multiplier, the steeper the IS curve. This conclusion can be confirmed by using Eq. (6a). We can turn Eq. (6a) around to express interest rate as a function of level of income:

$$i = \frac{\bar{A}}{b} - \frac{Y}{\bar{\alpha}b} \qquad (6b)$$

We thus see that for a given change in Y, the associated change in i will be larger in size as b is smaller and $\bar{\alpha}$ is smaller.

Given that the slope of the IS curve depends on the multiplier, fiscal policy can affect that slope. The multiplier $\bar{\alpha}$ is affected by the tax rate:

$$\bar{\alpha} = \frac{1}{1 - c(1 - t)} \qquad (7)$$

An increase in the tax rate reduces the multiplier. Accordingly, the higher the tax rate, the steeper the IS curve.

The Position of the IS Curve

We now want to answer the question of what determines the position of the IS curve, and what causes it to shift that position. Figure 4-4 shows two

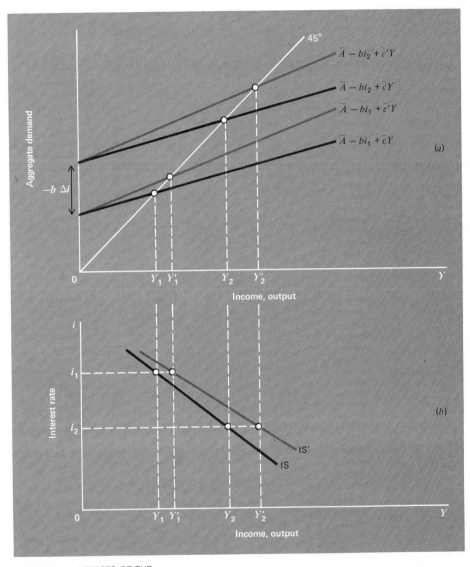

$45°$

$\overline{A} - bi_2 + \overline{c}'Y$

$\overline{A} - bi_2 + \overline{c}Y$

$\overline{A} - bi_1 + \overline{c}'Y$

$\overline{A} - bi_1 + \overline{c}Y$

(a)

$-b\,\Delta i$

(b)

FIGURE 4-3 EFFECTS OF THE MULTIPLIER ON THE STEEPNESS OF THE IS CURVE

different IS curves, the lighter one of which lies to the right and above the darker IS curve. What might cause the IS curve to be at IS' rather than at IS in Fig. 4-4? The answer is an increase in the level of autonomous spending.

In Fig. 4-4a we show an initial aggregate demand curve drawn for a level of autonomous spending $\overline{A}$ and for an arbitrary interest rate i_1. Corresponding to the initial aggregate demand curve is the point E_1 on the IS curve in Fig. 4-4b. Now, at the same interest rate, let the level of autonomous spending increase to $\bar{A}'$. The increase in autonomous spending increases the equilibrium level of income at the interest rate i_1. The point

FIGURE 4-4 A SHIFT IN THE IS CURVE
CAUSED BY A CHANGE IN AUTONOMOUS
SPENDING

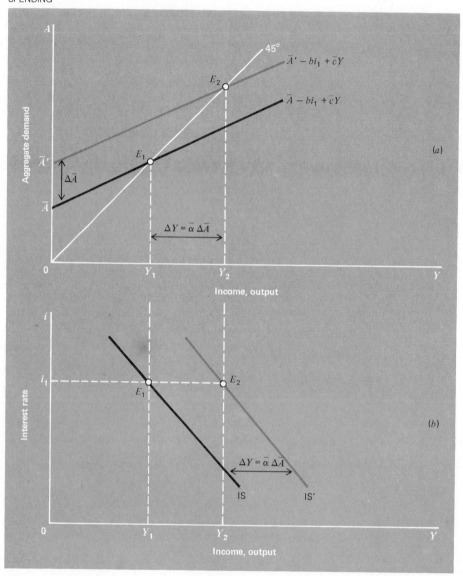

E_2, in Fig. 4-4b, is thus a point on the new goods market equilibrium schedule IS'. Since E_1 was an arbitrary point on the initial IS curve, we can perform the exercise for all levels of the interest rate and thereby generate our new curve IS'. We see that an increase in autonomous spending shifts the curve out to the right.

By how much does the curve shift? The change in income, as a result of the change in autonomous spending, can be seen from the top panel to be just the multiplier times the change in autonomous spending. That means that the IS curve is shifted horizontally by a distance equal to the multiplier times the change in autonomous spending, as can be seen from the fact that the distance between E_1 and E_2, in the lower panel, is the distance between Y_1 and Y_2 in the upper panel.

Now the level of autonomous spending is:

$$\overline{A} \equiv \overline{C} + \overline{I} + \overline{G} + c\overline{R} \qquad (2)$$

Accordingly, an increase in government spending or transfer payments will shift the IS curve out to the right, the extent of the shift depending on the size of the multiplier. An increase in taxes (reduction in transfer payments or reduction in government spending) shifts the IS curve to the left.

Positions off the IS Curve

We gain understanding of the meaning of the IS curve by considering points off the curve. Figure 4-5 reproduces Fig. 4-2, along with two additional points—the *dis*equilibrium points E_3 and E_4. Consider first the question of what is true for points off the schedule, points such as E_3 and E_4. In Fig. 4-5b, at point E_3 we have the same interest rate i_2 as at point E_2, but the level of income is lower than at E_2. Since the interest rate i_2 at E_3 is the same as at E_2 in Fig. 4-5b, we must have the same aggregate demand function corresponding to the two points. Accordingly, looking now at Fig. 4-5a, we find both points are on the same aggregate demand schedule. At E_3 on that schedule, aggregate demand exceeds the level of output. Point E_3 is therefore a point of *excess demand for goods*: the interest rate is too low, or output is too low for the goods market to be in equilibrium. Demand for goods exceeds output.

Consider next point E_4 in Fig. 4-5b. Here we have the same rate of interest i_1 as at E_1, but the level of income is higher. Given the interest rate i_1, the corresponding point in Fig. 4-5a is at E_4, where we have an *excess supply of goods*, since output is larger than aggregate demand—that is, aggregate demand given the interest rate i_1 and the income level Y_2.

The preceding discussion can be generalized by saying that points above and to the right of the IS curve—points like E_4—are points of excess supply of goods. This is indicated by ESG (excess supply of goods) in Fig. 4-5b. Points that would be noted below and to the left of the IS curve are

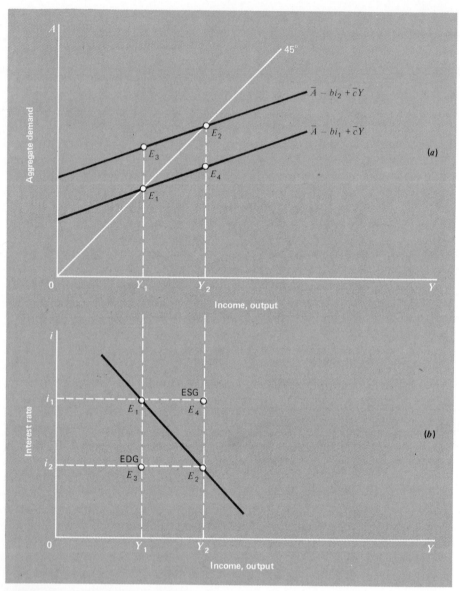

FIGURE 4-5 EXCESS SUPPLY (ESG) AND
DEMAND (EDG) IN THE GOODS MARKET TO
THE RIGHT AND LEFT, RESPECTIVELY, OF
THE IS CURVE

points of excess demand for goods. At a point like E_3, the interest rate is
too low and aggregate demand is therefore too high, relative to output.

EDG (excess demand for goods) shows the region of excess demand in Fig. 4-5.

Summary

The major points about the IS curve are:

1 The IS curve is the schedule of combinations of the interest rate and level of income such that the goods market is in equilibrium.
2 The IS curve is negatively sloped because an increase in the interest rate reduces planned investment spending, therefore reduces aggregate demand, and thus reduces the equilibrium level of income.
3 The smaller the multiplier and the less sensitive investment spending is to changes in the interest rate, the steeper the curve.
4 The IS curve is shifted by changes in autonomous spending. An increase in autonomous spending, including an increase in government spending, shifts the IS curve out to the right.
5 At points to the right of the curve, there is excess supply in the goods market, and at points to the left of the curve, there is excess demand for goods.

We turn now to examine behavior in the assets markets.

4-2 THE ASSETS MARKETS AND THE LM CURVE

In the preceding section we discussed aggregate demand and the goods market. In the present section, we turn to assets markets. The assets markets are the markets in which money, bonds, stocks, houses, and other forms of wealth are traded. Up to this point in the book we have ignored the role of those markets in affecting the level of income, and it is now time to remedy the omission.

There is a large variety of assets, and a tremendous volume of trading occurs every day in the assets markets, but we shall simplify matters enormously by grouping all available financial assets into two groups, *money* and *interest-bearing assets*.[5] By analogy with our treatment of the goods market, where we proceeded as if there was a single commodity called output, we will proceed in the assets markets as if there are only two assets,

---

[5] We shall be assuming in this section that certain assets, such as the capital that firms use in production, are not traded. That too is a simplification. A more complex treatment of the assets markets would allow for the trading of capital and would introduce a relative price for the capital operated by firms. This treatment is usually reserved for advanced graduate courses. For such a treatment of the assets markets, see James Tobin, "A General Equilibrium Approach to Monetary Theory," *Journal of Money, Credit and Banking*, February 1969, pp. 15–29, and, by the same author, "Money, Capital, and Other Stores of Value," *American Economic Review*, May 1961, pp. 26–37.

money and all others. It will be useful to think of the other assets as marketable claims to future income such as *bonds*.

A bond is a promise to pay to its holder certain agreed-upon amounts of money at specified dates in the future. For instance, a borrower sells a bond in exchange for a given amount of money today, say $100, and promises to pay a fixed amount, say $6, each year to the person who owns the bond, and to repay the full $100 (the principal) after some fixed period of time, like three years, or perhaps longer. In the above example, the interest rate is 6 percent, for that is the percentage of the amount borrowed that the borrower pays each year.

The Wealth Constraint

At any given time, an individual has to decide how to allocate his or her financial wealth between alternative assets. The more bonds she holds, the more interest she receives on her total financial wealth. The more money she holds, the less likely she is not to have money available when she wants to make a purchase. If she has $1,000 in financial wealth, she has to decide whether to hold, say $900 in bonds and $100 in money, or rather $500 in each type of asset, or else even $1,000 in money and none in bonds. We refer to decisions on the form in which to hold assets as *portfolio decisions*.

The example makes it clear that the (portfolio) decision on how much money to hold and the decision on how many bonds to hold are really the same decision. Given the level of financial wealth, once the individual has decided how many bonds to hold, she has implicitly also decided how much money to hold. There is thus a *wealth budget constraint* which implies that the sum of the individual's demands for money and bonds has to add up to her total financial wealth.

At this stage we have to reintroduce the crucial distinction between *real* and *nominal* variables. The nominal demand for money is the individuals's demand for a given number of dollars, and similarly, the nominal demand for bonds is the demand for a given number of dollars' worth of bonds. By contrast, the real demand for money is the demand for money expressed in terms of the number of units of goods that money will buy: it is equal to the nominal demand for money divided by the price level. If the nominal demand for money is $100 and the price level is $2 per good—meaning that the representative basket of goods costs $2—then the real demand for money is fifty goods. If the price level later doubles to $4 per good, and the demand for nominal money likewise doubles to $200, the real demand for money is unchanged at fifty goods. Real money balances—real balances for short—are the quantity of nominal money divided by the price level, and the real demand for money is often called *the demand for real balances*. Similarly, real bond holdings are the nominal quantity of bonds divided by the price level.

The wealth budget constraint in the assets markets states that the demand for real balances, which we shall denote L, plus the demand for real bond holdings, which we denote V, must add up to the real financial wealth of the individual. Real financial wealth is, of course, simply nominal wealth W divided by the price level P:

$$L + V = \frac{W}{P} \tag{8}$$

Note, again, that the wealth budget constraint implies, given an individual's real wealth, that a decision to hold more real balances is also a decision to hold less real wealth in the form of bonds. This implication turns out to be both important and convenient. It will allow us to discuss assets markets entirely in terms of the money market. Why? Because, given real wealth, when the money market is in equilibrium, the bond market will turn out also to be in equilibrium. We shall now show why that should be.

The total amount of real financial wealth in the economy consists of real money balances and real bonds in existence. Thus total real financial wealth is equal to

$$\frac{W}{P} \equiv \frac{M}{P} + V^s \tag{9}$$

where M is the stock of nominal money balances and V^s is the real value of the supply of bonds. Total real financial wealth consists of real balances and real bonds. The distinction between Eqs. (8) and (9) is that Eq. (8) is a constraint on the amount of assets individuals *wish* to hold, whereas Eq. (9) is merely an accounting relationship which tells us how much financial wealth there is in the economy. There is no implication in the accounting relationship in Eq. (9) that individuals are necessarily happy to hold the amounts of money and bonds that actually exist in the economy.

Now we substitute Eq. (8) into Eq. (9) and rearrange terms to obtain

$$\left(L - \frac{M}{P}\right) + (V - V^s) = 0 \tag{10}$$

Let us see what Eq. (10) implies. Suppose first that the demand for real balances L is equal to the existing stock of real balances M/P. Then, the first term in parentheses in Eq. (10) is equal to zero, and therefore the second term in parentheses must also be zero. Thus, if the demand for real balances L is equal to the supply of real balances M/P, the demand for real bonds V must be equal to the supply of real bonds V^s. Stating the same proposition in terms of "markets," we can say that the asset budget constraint implies that when the money market is in equilibrium so that $L = M/P$, so too is the bond market in equilibrium and therefore $V = V^s$. Similarly, when there is excess demand in the money market, so that $L > M/P$, Eq. (10) implies that there is an excess supply of bonds, $V < V^s$.

To repeat, we have seen that when the money market is in equilibrium, the bond market is also in equilibrium. When there is excess demand in the money market, there is *an equal* excess supply in the bond market. We can therefore fully discuss the assets markets by concentrating our attention on the money market.

The Demand for Money

We can now proceed by concentrating on the money market, and initially on the demand for real balances.[6] The demand for money is a demand for *real* balances because the public holds money for what it will buy. The higher the price level, the more nominal balances have to be held to be able to purchase a given quantity of goods. If the price level doubles, then an individual has to hold twice as many nominal balances in order to be able to buy the same amount of goods.

The demand for real balances depends on the level of real income and the interest rate. It depends on the level of real income because individuals hold money to finance their expenditures which, in turn, depend on income. This demand for money to finance regular spending on goods is known as the transactions demand for money. The demand for money depends also on the interest rate. The cost of holding money is the interest that is foregone by holding it rather than interest-bearing assets. The higher the interest rate, the more costly it is to hold money, rather than other assets, and accordingly, the less cash will be held, at each level of income. Individuals can economize on their holdings of cash when the interest rate rises by being more careful in managing their money, by making transfers from money to bonds whenever their money holdings reach any appreciable magnitude. If the interest rate is 1 percent, then there is very little benefit from holding bonds rather than money. However, when the interest rate is 10 percent, one would probably go to some efforts not to hold more money than needed to finance day-to-day transactions.

On these simple grounds, then, the demand for real balances increases with the level of real income and decreases with the interest rate.[7] The demand for real balances is, accordingly, written:[8]

$$L = kY - hi \qquad k > 0 \qquad h > 0 \tag{11}$$

[6]The demand for money is studied in depth in Chap. 7; here we only briefly present the arguments underlying the demand for money.

[7]As we shall see in Chap. 7, there are other motives than transactions motives for holding money, and they too point to a negative relationship between the demand for money and the interest rate.

[8]Once again, we write the demand for real balances as a linear function of real income and the interest rate, though that cannot be true for all levels of the interest rate. The demand for real balances cannot be negative. The linear form of the demand function applies only over a limited range of values of income and the interest rate. You should experiment with a non-linear form of the demand function in some of the diagrams below.

The parameters k and h reflect the sensitivity of the demand for real balances to the level of income and the interest rate, respectively. A \$5 increase in income raises money demand by $k \times$ \$5. An increase in the interest rate by one percentage point reduces real money demand by h times 1 percent.

The demand function for real balances, Eq. (11), implies that, for a given level of income, the demand is a decreasing function of the rate of interest. Such a demand curve is shown in Fig. 4-6 for a level of income Y_1. The higher the level of income, the larger the demand for real balances, and therefore the further to the right the demand curve. The demand curve for a higher level of real income Y_2 is also shown in Fig. 4-6.

The Supply of Money, Money Market Equilibrium, and the LM Curve

Now that we have specified a demand function for money, we next study the equilibrium in the money market. For that purpose we have to say how the supply of money is determined. The nominal quantity of money M is controlled by the Federal Reserve System, and we shall take it as given at the level $\overline{M}$. We are assuming the price level is constant at the level $\overline{P}$, so that the real money supply can be taken to be fixed at the level $\overline{M}/\overline{P}$.[9]

In Fig. 4-7 we show combinations of interest rates and income levels such that the demand for real balances exactly matches the available supply. Starting with the level of income Y_1, we have the associated demand curve for real balances L_1, in Fig. 4-7b. It is drawn, as in Fig. 4-6, as a decreasing function of the interest rate. The existing supply of real balances $\overline{M}/\overline{P}$ is shown by the vertical line, since it is given and therefore independent of the interest rate. The interest rate i_1 has the property that it clears the money market. At that interest rate, the demand for real balances equals the supply. Therefore, point E_1 is an equilibrium point in the money market. That point is recorded in Fig. 4-7a as a point on what we shall be calling the *money market equilibrium schedule*, or *LM curve*.

Consider next the effect of an increase in income to Y_2. In Fig. 4-7b the higher level of income causes the demand for real balances to be higher at each level of the interest rate, so the demand curve for real balances shifts to the right to L_2. At the initial interest rate i_1, we now have an excess demand for money. Therefore, we require an increase in the interest rate to i_2 in order to maintain equilibrium in the money market at that higher level of income. Accordingly, our new equilibrium point is E_2. In Fig. 4-7a, we record point E_2 as a point of equilibrium in the money market. Performing the same exercise for all income levels, we generate a series of points that can be linked up to generate the LM schedule, or the money

---

[9]Since for the present we are holding constant the money supply and price level, we refer to them as exogenous and denote that fact by a bar.

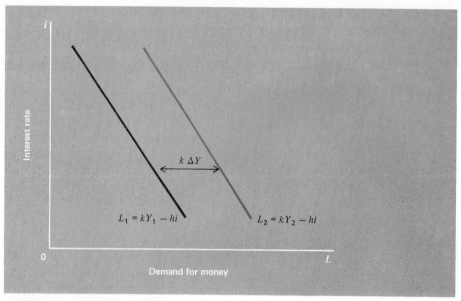

FIGURE 4-6 THE DEMAND FOR REAL
BALANCES AS A FUNCTION OF THE
INTEREST RATE AND REAL INCOME

market equilibrium schedule. Along the LM schedule the demand for real
balances is equal to the given real money supply.

Given the fixed supply of real balances, the LM curve is positively
sloped. An increase in the interest rate reduces the demand for real balances. To maintain the demand for real balances equal to the fixed supply,
the level of income has, therefore, to rise. Accordingly, money market
equilibrium implies that an increase in the interest rate is accompanied by
an increase in the level of income.

The LM curve can also be obtained from the combination of the demand curve for real balances, Eq. (11), and the fixed supply of real balances. For the money market to be in equilibrium, we require that demand equals supply, or that

$$\frac{\overline{M}}{\overline{P}} = kY - hi \tag{12}$$

Solving for the interest rate, we have

$$i = \frac{1}{h}\left(kY - \frac{\overline{M}}{\overline{P}}\right) \tag{12a}$$

The relationship (12a) is the LM curve.

Next we ask the same questions about the properties of the LM schedule that we asked about the IS curve.

The Slope of the LM Curve

The larger the responsiveness of the demand for money to income, as measured by k, and the lower the responsiveness of the demand for money to the interest rate h, the steeper will be the LM curve. This point can be established by experimenting with Fig. 4-7. It can also be confirmed by examining Eq. $(12a)$, where a given change in income ΔY has a larger effect on the interest rate i, the larger is k and the smaller is h. If the demand for money is relatively insensitive to the interest rate, so that h is close to zero, the LM curve is nearly vertical. If the demand for money is very sensitive to the interest rate, so that h is large, then the LM curve is close to horizontal. In that case, a small change in the interest rate is accompanied by a large change in the level of income to maintain money market equilibrium.

The Position of the LM Curve

The real money supply is held constant along the LM curve. It follows that a change in the real money supply will shift the LM curve. In Fig. 4-8 we show the effect of an increase in the real money supply. In Fig. 4-8b we have drawn the demand for real money balances for a level of income Y_1. With the initial real money supply $\overline{M}/P$, the equilibrium is at point E_1, with an interest rate i_1. The corresponding point on the LM schedule is E_1. Consider next the effect of an increase in the real money supply to $\overline{M}'/P$, which is represented by a rightward shift of the money supply schedule.

FIGURE 4-7 DERIVATION OF THE LM CURVE

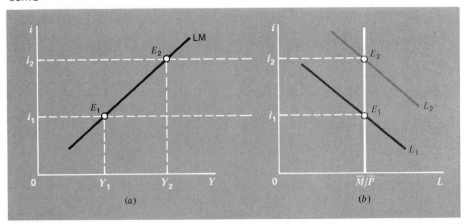

(a)   (b)

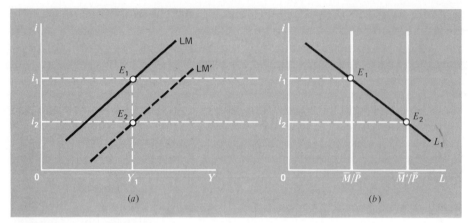

FIGURE 4-8 AN INCREASE IN THE
SUPPLY OF MONEY FROM $\bar{M}$ TO $\bar{M}'$ SHIFTS
THE LM CURVE TO THE RIGHT

At the initial level of income and, hence, on the demand schedule L_1, we now have an excess supply of real balances. To restore money market equilibrium at the income level Y_1, the interest rate has to decline to i_2. The new equilibrium is, therefore, at point E_2. This implies, that in Fig. 4-8a, the LM schedule *shifts* to the right and down to LM'. At each level of income the equilibrium interest rate has to be lower to induce people to hold the larger real quantity of money. Alternatively, at each level of the interest rate, the level of income has to be higher so as to raise the transactions demand for money and thereby absorb the higher real money supply. These points can be noted, too, from inspection of the money market equilibrium condition in Eq. (12a).

Positions off the LM Curve

Next we consider points off the LM schedule, to characterize them as points of excess demand or supply of money. For that purpose, we look at Fig. 4-9, which reproduces Fig. 4-7 but adds the disequilibrium points E_3 and E_4.

Consider first the equilibrium point E_1, where the money market is in equilibrium. Next assume an increase in the level of income to Y_2. This will raise the demand for real balances and shift the demand curve to L_2. At the initial interest rate the demand for real balances would be indicated by point E_4 in Fig. 4-9b, and we would have an excess demand for money—an excess of demand over supply—equal to the distance E_1E_4. Accordingly, point E_4, in Fig. 4-9a, is a point of excess demand for money: the interest rate is too low and/or the level of income too high for the money market to clear. Consider next point E_3, in Fig. 4-9b. Here we have the initial level of income Y_1, but an interest rate that is too high to yield money market equilibrium. Accordingly, we have an excess supply of money equal to the distance $E_3 E_2$. Point E_3 in Fig. 4-9a therefore corresponds to an excess supply of money.

More generally, any point to the right and below the LM schedule is a point of excess demand for money, and any point to the left and above the LM curve is a point of excess supply. This is shown by the EDM and ESM notations in Fig. 4-9a.

Summary

The following are the major points about the LM curve.

1   The LM curve is the schedule of combinations of the interest rate and level of income such that the money market is in equilibrium.
2   When the money market is in equilibrium, so too is the bond market. The LM curve is, therefore, also the schedule of combinations of the level of income and the interest rate such that the bond market is in equilibrium.
3   The LM curve is positively sloped. Given the fixed money supply, an increase in the level of income, which increases the demand for money, has to be accompanied by an increase in the interest rate. This reduces

FIGURE 4-9   EXCESS DEMAND (EDM) AND SUPPLY (ESM) OF MONEY TO THE RIGHT AND LEFT OF THE LM CURVE, RESPECTIVELY

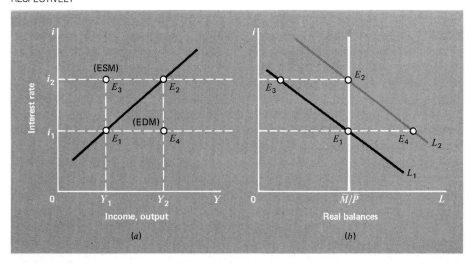

the demand for money and thereby keeps the demand for money equal to the supply.

4 The LM curve is shifted by changes in the money supply. An increase in the money supply shifts the LM curve out to the right.

5 At points to the right of the LM curve, there is an excess demand for money, and at points to its left, there is an excess supply of money.

We are now ready to discuss the joint equilibrium of the goods and assets markets.

4-3 EQUILIBRIUM IN THE GOODS AND ASSETS MARKETS

We have so far studied the conditions that have to be satisfied for the goods and money markets, respectively, to be in equilibrium. These conditions are summarized by the IS and LM schedules. The task now is to determine how these markets are brought into *simultaneous* equilibrium. For simultaneous equilibrium to be obtained, interest rates and income have to be such that *both* the goods market *and* the money market are in equilibrium. That condition is satisfied at point E in Fig. 4-10. The equilibrium interest rate is therefore i_0, and the equilibrium level of income Y_0, *given* the exogenous variables,[10] in particular, the real money supply and fiscal policy. At point E, *both* the goods market and the assets markets are in equilibrium.

Now that we have moved rather quickly from the derivation of the IS and LM curves to the equilibrium of the economy that is implied by their intersection, it is worth stepping back to review our assumptions and the meaning of the equilibrium at E. The major assumption that we are making is that the price level is constant and that firms are willing to supply whatever amount of output is demanded at that price level. Thus, we assume the level of output Y_0, in Fig. 4-10, will be willingly supplied by firms at the price level $\overline{P}$. We repeat again that this assumption is one that is needed for the development of our analysis; it will be dropped in Chap. 11 when we begin to study the determinants of the price level.

At the point E, in Fig. 4-10, the economy we are studying is in equilibrium, given the price level, because both the goods and money markets are in equilibrium. The demand for goods is equal to the level of output on the IS curve. And on the LM curve, the demand for money is equal to the supply of money. That also means the supply of bonds is equal to the demand for bonds, as our discussion of the wealth budget constraint showed. Accordingly, at point E, firms are producing the amount of output they plan to (there is no unintended inventory accumulation or decumulation), and individuals have the portfolio compositions they desire.

---

[10]Recall from Chap. 3 that exogenous variables are those whose values are not determined within the system being studied.

The equilibrium levels of income and the interest rate will change when either the IS or the LM curve shifts. Figure 4-11, for instance, shows the effects on the equilibrium levels of income and the interest rate of an increase in the rate of autonomous consumption $\overline{C}$. Such an increase raises autonomous spending $\overline{A}$, and therefore shifts the IS curve out to the right. That results in a rise in the level of income and an increase in the interest rate.

We recall from Sec. 4-2 that a change in autonomous spending, equal in this case to $\Delta\overline{C}$, shifts the IS curve to the right by the amount $\overline{\alpha}\,\Delta\overline{C}$, as we show in Fig. 4-11. In Chap. 3, where we dealt only with the goods market, we would have argued that $\overline{\alpha}\,\Delta\overline{C}$ would be the change in the level of income resulting from the change of $\Delta\overline{C}$ in autonomous spending. But it can be seen in Fig. 4-11 that the change in income here is only ΔY_0 which is clearly less than the shift in the IS curve $\overline{\alpha}\,\Delta\overline{C}$.

What explains the fact that the increase in income is smaller than the increase in autonomous spending, $\Delta\overline{C}$, times the simple multiplier, $\overline{\alpha}$? Diagramatically, it is clear that it is the slope of the LM curve. If the LM curve were horizontal, there would be no difference between the extent of the horizontal shift of the IS curve and the change in income. If the LM curve were horizontal, then the interest rate would not change when the IS curve shifts. It will be recalled that we stated in Chap. 3 that we were

FIGURE 4-10 GOODS AND ASSETS MARKET EQUILIBRIUM

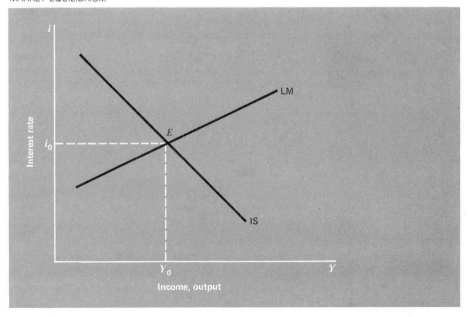

assuming a fixed interest rate, so there is no inconsistency between the results of that chapter and Fig. 4-11.

What is the economics of what is happening? The increase in autonomous spending does tend to increase the level of income. But an increase in income increases the transactions demand for money. With the supply of money fixed, the interest rate has to rise to ensure that the demand for money stays equal to the fixed supply. When the interest rate rises, investment spending is reduced because investment is negatively related to the interest rate. That means the total change in aggregate demand is less than $\bar{\alpha} \, \Delta \bar{C}$. Accordingly, the equilibrium change in income is less than the horizontal shift of the IS curve.

We have now provided an example of the uses of the IS-LM apparatus. That apparatus is most useful for studying the effects of monetary and fiscal policy on income and the interest rate, and we shall so use it in Secs. 4-5 and 4-6 below. Before we do that, however, we want to ask how the economy moves from one equilibrium, like E, to another, like E'.

4-4 ADJUSTMENT TOWARD EQUILIBRIUM

Suppose the economy were initially at a point like E in Fig. 4-11, and that one of the curves then shifted, so that the new equilibrium was at a point like E'. How would that new equilibrium actually be reached? The adjustment will involve changes in both the interest rate and the level of income. To study how they move over time, we make two assumptions:

1 Output increases whenever there is an excess demand for goods (EDG) and contracts whenever there is an excess supply of goods (ESG). This assumption reflects the adjustment of firms to involuntary decumulation and accumulation of inventories, as in Chap. 3.
2 The interest rate rises whenever there is an excess demand for money (EDM) and falls whenever there is an excess supply of money (ESM). This adjustment occurs because an excess demand for money implies an excess supply of other assets (bonds). In attempting to satisfy an excess demand for money, people sell off bonds and thereby cause their prices to fall, or their yields (interest rates) to rise.

A detailed discussion of the relationship between the price of a bond and its yield is presented in the appendix to this chapter. Here we give only a brief explanation. For simplicity, consider a bond which promises to pay the holder of the bond $5 per year forever. The $5 is known as the bond *coupon*, and a bond which promises to pay a given amount to the holder of the bond forever is known as a *perpetuity*. If the yield available on other assets is 5 percent, then the perpetuity will sell for $100 because at that price it too yields 5 percent (= $5/$100). Now suppose that the yield

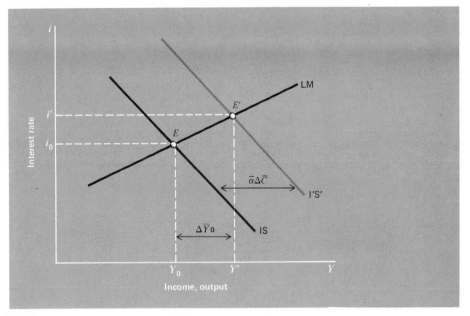

FIGURE 4-11 EFFECTS OF AN INCREASE
IN AUTONOMOUS SPENDING ON INCOME
AND THE INTEREST RATE

on other assets rises to 10 percent. Then the price of the perpetuity will
drop to $50, because only at that price does the perpetuity yield 10 percent,
that is, the $5 per year interest on a bond costing $50 gives the owner a 10
percent yield on his $50. This example makes it clear that the *price* of a
bond and its *yield* are inversely related, given the coupon.

We discussed the way in which an excess demand for money causes
asset holders to attempt to sell off their bonds, thereby causing their prices
to fall and yields to rise. Conversely, when there is an excess supply of
money, people attempt to use their money to buy up other assets, raising
their prices and lowering their yields.[11]

In Fig. 4-12 we use the analysis underlying Figs. 4-5 and 4-9 to study
the adjustment of the economy. Four regions are represented in Fig. 4-12,
and they are characterized in Table 4-1. We know from Fig. 4-9 that there
is an excess supply of money above the LM curve, and hence we show
ESM in regions I and II in Table 4-1. Similarly, we know from Fig. 4-5
that there is an excess demand for goods below the IS curve. Hence, we
show EDG for regions II and III in Table 4-1. You should be able to fill in
the remaining details of Table 4-1.

[11]We assume that the rate of adjustment in each market is proportional to the excess demand in
that market.

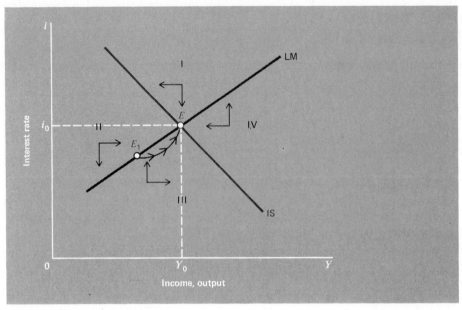

FIGURE 4-12 DISEQUILIBRIUM AND
DYNAMICS IN THE GOODS AND MONEY
MARKETS

The adjustment directions specified in assumptions 1 and 2 above are represented by arrows. Thus, for example, in region IV we have an excess demand for money that causes interest rates to rise as other assets are sold off for money and their prices decline. The rising interest rates are represented by the upward-pointing arrow. There is, too, an excess supply of goods in region IV, and, accordingly, involuntary inventory accumulation to which firms respond by reducing output. Declining output is indicated by the leftward-pointing arrow. The adjustments shown by the arrows will lead ultimately, perhaps in a cyclical manner, to the equilibrium point E. For instance, starting at E_1 we show the economy moving to E, with income

TABLE 4-1   DISEQUILIBRIUM REGIONS IN FIG. 4-12

	Goods market		Money market	
I	ESG	$(Y > A)$	ESM	$(L < M/P)$
II	EDG	$(Y < A)$	ESM	$(L < M/P)$
III	EDG	$(Y < A)$	EDM	$(L > M/P)$
IV	ESG	$(Y > A)$	EDM	$(L > M/P)$

and the interest rate increasing along the *adjustment path* indicated.

For many purposes it is useful to restrict the dynamics by the reasonable assumption that the money market adjusts very fast and the goods market adjusts relatively slowly. Since the money market can adjust merely through the buying and selling of bonds, it is reasonable to think of the interest rate as adjusting rapidly and the money market effectively being always in equilibrium. Such an assumption will imply that we are always on the LM curve: any departure from the equilibrium in the money market is almost instantaneously eliminated by an appropriate change in the interest rate. In disequilibrium, we therefore move along the LM curve as is shown in Fig. 4-13. The goods market adjusts relatively slowly because firms have to change their production schedules, which takes time. For points below the IS curve, we move up along the LM schedule with rising income and interest rates, and for points above the IS schedule, we move down along the LM schedule with falling output and interest rates until point E is reached. The adjustment process is *stable* in that the economy does move to the equilibrium position at E.

The adjustment process shown in Fig. 4-13 is very similar to that of Chap. 3. To the right of the IS curve there is an excess supply of goods, and firms are therefore accumulating inventories. They cut production in response to their inventory buildup, and the economy moves down the LM

FIGURE 4-13 ADJUSTMENT TO
EQUILIBRIUM WHEN THE MONEY MARKET
ADJUSTS QUICKLY

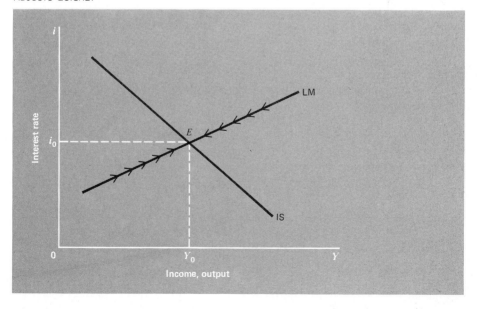

curve. The difference between the adjustment process here and in Chap. 3 is that, as the economy moves toward the equilibrium level of income here, with a falling interest rate, desired investment spending is actually rising as the interest rate falls.[12]

Now that we have established that the economy does adjust toward its equilibrium position, we turn to examine the effects of monetary and fiscal policy on the equilibrium interest rate and level of income.

4-5 MONETARY POLICY

In this section we are concerned with the effect of an increase in the real quantity of money on the interest rate and level of income. We will break up that inquiry into two separate questions. First, what is the ultimate effect of the increase in the money supply when the new equilibrium is reached? Second, how is that new equilibrium reached, or what is the *transmission mechanism*?

Through monetary policy, the Federal Reserve System manipulates the quantity of money to affect interest rates and income. We shall here take the case of an *open market purchase*. That is a government purchase of bonds and (equal) sale of money. The purchase is made by the Federal Reserve System (Fed), which pays for its purchase with money that it can create. One can usefully think of the Fed printing money with which to buy bonds, even though that is not strictly accurate, as we shall see in Chap. 8. The purpose of an open market operation is to change the available *relative* supplies of money and bonds and thereby change the interest rate or yield at which the public is willing to hold this modified composition of assets. When the Fed buys bonds, it reduces the supply of bonds available in the market and thereby tends to increase their price, or lower their yield. Only at a lower interest rate will the public be prepared to hold a larger fraction of their given wealth in the form of money, and a lower fraction in the form of bonds.

In Fig. 4-14 we show graphically how the open market purchase works. The initial equilibrium at point E is on the initial LM schedule that corresponds to a real money supply, $\overline{M}/\overline{P}$. Consider next an open market operation that increases the nominal quantity of money, and given the price level, the real quantity of money. We showed in Sec. 4-2 that as a consequence the LM schedule will shift to LM'. Therefore, our new equilibrium will be at point E' with a lower interest rate and a higher level of income. The equilibrium level of income rises because the open market purchase reduces the interest rate and thereby increases investment.

As can be seen from Fig. 4-14, the steeper the LM schedule and the

---

[12]In a more detailed analysis, one would want to allow for the possibility that desired investment would be cut back in response to excess inventories. This again raises the possibility of the *inventory cycle*, referred to in Chap. 3.

flatter the IS schedule—the lower the responsiveness of money demand to the interest rate, and the larger the responsiveness of aggregate demand to the interest rate—the larger will be the change in income. If money demand is very sensitive to the interest rate, then a given change in the money stock can be absorbed in the assets markets with only a small change in the interest rate. The effects of an open market purchase on investment spending would then be small. By contrast, if the demand for money is not very sensitive to the interest rate, a given change in the money supply will cause a large change in the interest rate and have a big effect on investment demand.[13]

Consider next the adjustment process to the monetary expansion. At the initial equilibrium point E, the increase in the money supply creates an excess supply of money to which the public adjusts by attempting to reduce its money holdings by buying other assets. In the process, asset prices increase and yields decline. By our assumption that the assets markets adjust rapidly, we move immediately to point E_1, where the money market

[13]In the problem set, we ask you to provide a similar explanation of the role of the slope of the IS curve—which is determined by the multiplier and the interest sensitivity of investment demand—in determining the effect of monetary policy on income.

FIGURE 4-14 THE ADJUSTMENT PATH OF THE ECONOMY FOLLOWING AN INCREASE IN THE MONEY STOCK

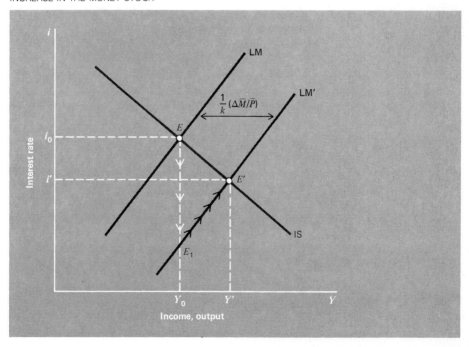

clears, and where the public is willing to hold the larger real quantity of money because the interest rate has declined sufficiently. (The lower the responsiveness of the demand for money to the interest rate, the larger the change in the interest rate that is required.) At point E_1, however, there is an excess demand for goods. The decline in the interest rate, given the initial income level Y_0, has raised aggregate demand and is causing inventories to run down. In response, output expands and we start moving up the LM schedule. Why does the interest rate rise in the adjustment process? Because the increase in output raises the demand for money and that increase has to be checked by higher interest rates.

The Transmission Mechanism

Two steps in the transmission mechanism—the process by which changes in monetary policy affect aggregate demand—are essential. The first is that an increase in real balances generates a *portfolio disequilibrium*—at the prevailing interest rate and level of income, people are holding more money than they want. This causes portfolio holders to attempt to reduce their money holdings by buying other assets, thereby changing asset yields. In other words, the change in the money supply changes interest rates. The second stage of the transmission process occurs when the change in interest rates affects aggregate demand.

These two stages of the transmission process are essential in that they appear in almost every analysis[14] of the effects of changes in the money supply on the economy. The details of the analysis will often differ—some analyses will have more than two assets and more than one interest rate, some will include an influence of interest rates on categories of demand other than investment, and so on—but these two stages will be present. For instance, here is a description of the process provided by Warren L. Smith:

> The way in which monetary policy induces portfolio adjustments which will, in due course, affect income and employment may be described briefly as follows: A purchase of, say, Treasury bills by the Federal Reserve will directly lower the yield on bills and, by a process of arbitrage involving a chain of portfolio substitutions will exert downward pressure on interest rates on financial assets generally. . . .
>
> With the expected yield on a unit of real capital initially unchanged, the decline in the yields on financial assets, and the more favorable terms on which new debt can be issued, the balance sheets of households and businesses will be thrown out of equilibrium. The adjustment toward a new equilibrium will take the form of a sale of existing financial assets and the issuance of new debt

---

[14]We say "almost every analysis" because it is sometimes argued that real balances have a direct effect on aggregate demand through the *real balance effect*. Essentially, the argument is that wealth affects consumption demand (as we shall see in Chap. 5) and that an increase in real balances increases wealth and therefore consumption demand. However, this effect is not very important empirically.

to acquire real capital and claims thereto. . . . . This stock adjustment approach is readily applicable, with some variations to suit the circumstances, to the demands for a wide variety of both business and consumer capital—including plant and equipment, inventories, residential construction, and consumer durable goods.[15]

In studying the details of the transmission process, it is important to see how much influence money has at each stage. For instance, if the demand for money is very sensitive to changes in the interest rate, or if interest rate changes have only a small effect on aggregate demand,[16] then monetary policy tends to be relatively ineffective. Conversely, to obtain a large increase in income from a monetary increase, we require a low responsiveness of money demand to the interest rate and a high responsiveness of aggregate demand to a change in the interest rate.

The Liquidity Trap

In discussing the effects of monetary policy on the economy, two extreme cases have received much attention. The first is the *liquidity trap*, a situation in which the public is prepared to hold any amount of money at a given interest rate. This implies the LM curve is horizontal and that changes in the quantity of money do not shift it. It that case, monetary policy carried out through open market operations[17] has no effect on either the interest rate or the level of income. In the liquidity trap, monetary policy is powerless to affect the interest rate.

There is a liquidity trap at a zero interest rate. At a zero interest rate, the public would not want to hold any bonds, since money, which also pays zero interest, has the advantage over bonds of being usable in transactions. Accordingly, if the interest rate ever, for some reason, got down to zero, increases in the quantity of money could not induce anyone to shift into bonds and thereby reduce the interest rate on bonds even below zero. An increase in the money supply in that case would have no effect on the interest rate and income, and the economy would be in a liquidity trap.

The belief that there was a liquidity trap at low positive (rather than zero) interest rates was quite prevalent during the forties and fifties. It was a notion associated with the keynesian followers and developers of the

[15]Warren L. Smith, "A Neo-Keynesian View of Monetary Policy," *Controlling Monetary Aggregates*, Boston, Federal Reserve Bank of Boston, 1969, pp. 105–117.

[16]We refer to the responsiveness of aggregate demand—rather than investment demand—to the interest rate because consumption demand may also respond to the interest rate. Higher interest rates may lead to more saving and less consumption at a given level of income. Empirically, it has been difficult to isolate such an interest rate effect on consumption.

[17]We say "through open market operations" because an increase in the quantity of money carried out simply by giving the money away, increases individuals' wealth and through the real balance effect has a small effect on aggregate demand. An open market purchase, however, increases the quantity of money and reduces the quantity of bonds by the same amount, leaving wealth unchanged.

theories of the great English economist, John Maynard Keynes—although Keynes himself did state that he was not aware of there ever having been such a situation.[18] The importance of the liquidity trap stems from its presenting a circumstance under which monetary policy has no effect on the interest rate and thus on the level of real income. Belief in the trap, or at least the strong sensitivity of the demand for money to the interest rate, was the basis of the keynesian belief that monetary policy has no effects on the economy. There is no strong evidence that there ever was a liquidity trap, with the 30's as a possible exception, and there certainly is not one now.

The Classical Case

The polar opposite of the horizontal LM curve—which implies that monetary policy cannot affect the level of income—is the vertical LM curve. The LM curve is vertical when the demand for money is unaffected by the interest rate. Under those circumstances, any shift in the LM curve has a maximal effect on the level of income. Check this by moving a vertical LM curve to the right and comparing the resultant change in income with the change produced by a similar horizontal shift of a nonvertical LM curve.

The vertical LM curve is called *classical* because it implies that the demand for money depends only on the level of income and not at all on the interest rate. As we shall see below, that implies not only that monetary policy has a maximal effect on the level of income, but also that fiscal policy has no effect on income. The vertical LM curve, implying the comparative effectiveness of monetary policy over fiscal policy, is sometimes associated with the view that "only money matters" for the determination of output. Since the LM curve is vertical only when the demand for money does not depend on the interest rate, the interest sensitivity of the demand for money turns out to be an important issue in determining the effectiveness of alternative policies.

4-6 FISCAL POLICY

In this section we are concerned with the effects of fiscal policy on the economy. Specifically, we are interested in the effect of an increase in government spending, given the tax structure and the real quantity of money.

The effects of an increase in government spending can be determined from Fig. 4-15. We start off at point E, where both markets clear. The increase in government spending creates an excess demand for goods at the initial point and therefore shifts the IS schedule to IS'. For goods market equilibrium we require at the initial interest rate a higher level of income,

---

[18] J. M. Keynes, *The General Theory of Employment, Interest and Money*, Macmillan, 1936, p. 207.

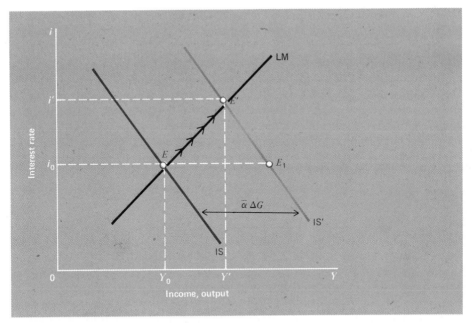

FIGURE 4-15 EFFECTS OF AN INCREASE
IN GOVERNMENT SPENDING

namely, the level indicated by point E_1, where the distance EE_1 is equal to the multiplier $\bar{\alpha}$ times the increase in government spending.

At the ultimate equilibrium position E', we have a higher interest rate and a higher level of income than at E. Therefore, an increase in government spending is expansionary with respect to income. The expansion of income is, however, less than that indicated by the simple multiplier and point E_1. This is because the interest rate rises, reduces investment, and thereby somewhat offsets the multiplier effect on private aggregate demand. The higher interest rate is required in order to maintain monetary equilibrium at the higher level of income, as we discussed in Sec. 4-3.

The flatter the LM schedule and the steeper the IS schedule, the larger is the increase in income that is generated by an increased level of government spending. Alternatively, it is larger the more responsive the demand for money with respect to the interest rate, the less responsive aggregate demand with respect to the interest rate, and the larger the multiplier $\bar{\alpha}$.

Consider next the adjustment process starting from the initial equilibrium at point E. We continue to assume that the money market clears fast and continuously, while output adjusts only slowly. This implies that as government spending increases, we stay initially at point E, since there is no disturbance in the money market. The excess demand for goods, however, causes output to be increased and that increase in output and income raises the demand for money. The resulting excess demand for money, in turn, causes interest rates to be bid up and we proceed up along the LM curve with rising output and rising interest rates, until the new equilibrium at point E' is reached.

The fact that we do not have an increase in output to the full extent of the simple multiplier $\bar{\alpha}$ times the increase in government spending, is entirely due to our now taking account of the assets markets. As income rises, the demand for money increases and people try to sell off other assets to acquire cash balances and in doing so cause asset prices to decline and interest rates to rise. This increase in interest rates, in turn, reduces investment spending and dampens the expansionary effect of increased government spending by reducing aggregate private demand relative to what it would have been at a constant interest rate.

The Liquidity Trap Again

In examining the effects of fiscal policy, there has also been a concentration on the two extreme cases we discussed in connection with monetary policy. If the economy is in the liquidity trap so that the LM curve is horizontal, then an increase in government spending has its full multiplier effect on the equilibrium level of income. There is no change in the interest rate associated with the change in government spending, and thus no investment spending is cut off. There is therefore no dampening of the effects of the increased government spending on income.

You should draw your own IS-LM diagrams to confirm that, if the LM curve is horizontal, monetary policy has no impact on the equilibrium of the economy and fiscal policy has a maximal effect on the economy. Less dramatically, if the demand for money is very sensitive to the interest rate, so that the LM curve is almost horizontal, fiscal policy changes have a relatively large effect on output, while monetary policy changes have little effect on the equilibrium level of output.

As a preview of our later discussion of monetary and fiscal policy in the 1960's, in Chap. 10, we point out one other circumstance in which fiscal policy has its full multiplier effect on the level of income. So far we have taken the money supply to be constant at the level $\overline{M}$. It is possible that the Fed might instead manipulate the money supply so as to keep the interest rate constant. In that case we could talk of a money supply *function* which is very elastic with respect to the interest rate. More simply, the Fed increases the money supply whenever there are signs of an increase in the interest rate, and reduces the money supply whenever the interest rate seems about to fall. If the money supply function is very elastic with respect to the interest rate, the LM curve again becomes very flat and fiscal policy has large impacts on the level of output.

The Classical Case Again and Crowding Out

If the LM curve is vertical, then an increase in government spending has no effect on the equilibrium level of income. It only increases the interest rate. This case is shown in Fig. 4-16, where an increase in government spending shifts the IS curve to IS' but has no effect on income. If the demand for money is not related to the interest rate, as a vertical LM curve implies, then there is a unique level of income at which the money market is in equilibrium, and fiscal policy cannot affect the level of income.

Given that an increase in government spending does not change the level of income when the LM curve is vertical, we know also that aggregate demand must be unchanged. Therefore, we have to ask what component of spending (investment or consumption) is reduced when government spending is increased but total aggregate demand remains unchanged. The answer is that investment spending is reduced by an amount exactly equal to the increase in government spending. Consumption spending does not change because the level of income is unchanged and autonomous

FIGURE 4-16 THE VERTICAL LM CURVE
AND CROWDING OUT

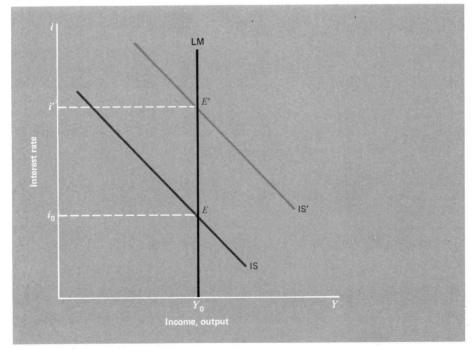

demand is unchanged.[19]   Thus we are assured that the increase in government spending is precisely offset by reduced investment spending.   This phenomenon is known as *crowding out*—the government spending crowds out some other component of spending and has no effect on total spending. The crowding out argument is one which is frequently made in the press to suggest that government spending has no effects on output and employment.

The view that government spending merely crowds out private spending is widely held by monetarist economists, such as Milton Friedman, who place primary emphasis on the role of the money stock in determining the level of income.[20]   The monetarist emphasis on the stock of money is also implied by the LM curve being vertical, so that in the IS-LM context, monetarism is consistent with the view that the LM curve is vertical, or that the demand for money does not depend on the interest rate.   However, there are other circumstances, such as a situation of full employment, in which there is crowding out.   If output is at the full-employment level, any increase in government spending has to take place at the expense of another component of aggregate demand, and crowding out will occur.[21]

In brief, in the IS-LM context in which we are now working, with the price level given and the level of output responding to aggregate demand, monetarist views on crowding out and the major importance of money are fully consistent with the LM curve being vertical.   Equivalently, they depend on the assumption that the demand for money does not depend on the interest rate.   But there are also other conditions in which there is crowding out.

The extreme cases of a vertical LM curve, or a flat LM curve, represent boundaries that are useful for reference purposes.   Beyond that their use is quite limited, since any reasonable description for policy purposes will want to assume the intermediate case of an upward-sloping LM curve, so that both monetary and fiscal policy work.   As we show in Chap. 7, the demand for real balances is definitely negatively related to the interest rate.

4-7 THE COMPOSITION OF OUTPUT

We have now seen that both monetary and fiscal policy can be used to expand aggregate demand and thus raise the equilibrium level of output.

---

[19]Note again that in principle consumption spending could be reduced by increases in the interest rate, and then both investment and consumption would be crowded out.

[20]We discuss monetarism in Chap. 16 below.

[21]Friedman has argued that his views do not depend on the demand for money not being a function of the interest rate, making essentially the second argument above for crowding out. See Milton Friedman, "Interest Rates and the Demand for Money," in his *The Optimum Quantity of Money*, Aldine, 1969.

Since the liquidity trap and the classical case represent at best extremes useful for expositional purposes, it is apparent that policy makers can use either monetary or fiscal policy to affect the level of income.

In Fig. 4-17 we address the policy problem of an economy that finds itself in equilibrium at point E with an output level Y_0, that falls short of the full-employment level Y_p. What policy choices does that economy have? From the preceding analysis, it is obvious that we could use an expansionary monetary policy. By increasing the money supply, we could shift the LM curve down and to the right, lower interest rates, and raise aggregate demand until we reach E_2. Alternatively, we could use an expansionary fiscal policy—a cut in taxes or an increase in government spending—to shift the IS curve up and to the right until we reach E_1. Finally, we can use a combination of monetary and fiscal policy. What package should we choose?

The choice of monetary and fiscal policy as tools of stabilization policy is an exceedingly important and quite controversial topic. In Chap. 9 we will address some technical issues that deal with the flexibility and speed with which these policies can be implemented and take effect. Here we do not discuss speed and flexibility, but rather look at what these policies do to the composition of aggregate demand.

FIGURE 4-17 EXPANSIONARY POLICIES
AND THE COMPOSITION OF OUTPUT

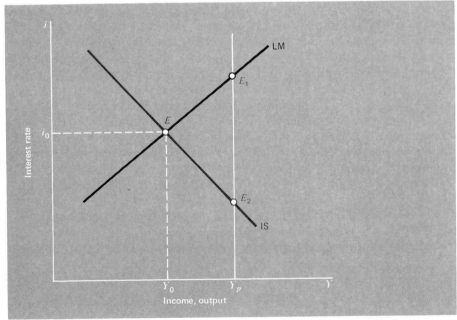

Now, in that respect, there is a sharp difference between monetary and fiscal policy. Monetary policy operates by stimulating interest-responsive components of aggregate demand (primarily investment spending and, in particular, residential construction). There is strong evidence that the immediate and strongest effect of monetary policy is on residential construction. Fiscal policy, by contrast, operates in a manner that depends on precisely what goods the government buys or what taxes and transfers it changes. Here we might be talking of government purchases of goods and services such as road paving, a reduction in the corporate profits tax, or a reduction in sales taxes or Social Security contributions. Each policy affects the level of aggregate demand and will cause an expansion in output, except that the type of output and the beneficiaries of the fiscal measures differ. A corporate tax cut, as we shall see in Chap. 10 (where we review the 1964 tax cut), affects both investment spending and, through distributed profits, personal consumption. An income tax cut has a direct effect on consumption spending. Given the quantity of money, all expansionary fiscal policies have in common that they will raise the interest rate.

Once we recognize that all the policies raise output, but that they differ significantly in their impact on different sectors of the economy, we open up a problem of political economy. Given the decision of expanding aggregate demand, who should get the primary benefit? Should the expansion take place through a decline in interest rates and increased investment spending, or should it take place through a cut in taxes and increased personal spending, or should it take the form of an increase in the size of the government?

Questions of speed and predictability of policies apart—these are taken up in Chap. 9—the issues raised above have been settled by political preferences.[22] Conservatives will argue for a tax cut anytime. They will favor stabilization policies that in a recession cut taxes and in a boom cut government spending. Over time, given enough cycles, you wind up with a government sector that becomes very small, just as a conservative would want it to be. The counterpart view belongs to those who feel that there is much scope for government spending in education, environment, job training and rehabilitation, and the like, and who, accordingly, favor expansionary policies in the form of increased government spending. Growth-minded people and the construction lobby finally argue for expansionary policies that operate through low interest rates.

What is the historical record? We study that question in more detail in Chap. 10, but we can already note that expansionary fiscal policies in the sixties, such as the 1964 tax cut, were accompanied by expansionary monetary policies so as to achieve a balanced expansion. We shall also see, though, that there were a number of episodes in which very tight monetary

[22]See Herbert Stein, "All Out for a Tax Cut," *The Wall Street Journal*, Nov. 15, 1976.

policy was used to restrain aggregate demand. In those episodes, the major impact of the restrictive policies on aggregate demand occurred through reduced investment, particularly in housing.

The recognition that monetary and fiscal policy changes have different effects on the composition of output is important. It suggests that policy makers can choose a *policy mix* that will both get the economy to full employment and also make a contribution to solving some other policy problem. We anticipate here several subsequent discussions in which we point out two other targets of policy which have been taken into account in setting monetary and fiscal policy—growth and balance of payments equilibrium.

In the sixties, policy makers were growth- and investment-oriented. The argument was that today's investment provides tomorrow's jobs. Moreover, investment in raising productivity would reduce costs and thus reduce the rate of inflation. This line of argument would suggest that expansionary policies should take the route of low interest rates so as to ensure that a significant part of the required increase in aggregate demand would take the form of investment. The counterargument came from the international side of the economy. Here it was argued that low interest rates would lead to outflows of funds and balance of payments problems. If United States interest rates declined relative to those in the rest of the world, people would get out of United States assets and into foreign assets. The United States would suffer a balance of payments deficit. With that line of argument, high interest rates were called for and an expansion in aggregate demand would preferably be achieved through fiscal expansion, rather than monetary expansion.

These side considerations—growth, price performance, and the balance of payments—were indeed important determinants of the policy mix that the Kennedy-Johnson administration opted for. In conjunction with the Fed they chose a policy of fiscal *and* monetary expansion. Side effects on the balance of payments did arise, as expected, and there were continuing attempts to deal with them through additional measures, such as restrictions on capital outflows.

*4-8 A FORMAL TREATMENT

So far we have relied on a verbal and graphical treatment of the model, and we round off the discussion now by using the equilibrium conditions in Eqs. (6a) and (12a). To determine the equilibrium level of income, we want both the goods and money markets to clear. We require, therefore, that both the equilibrium conditions in the goods and assets markets be satisfied. Repeating these equilibrium conditions here for convenience, we have

Goods market: $$Y = \bar{\alpha}(\overline{A} - bi) \tag{6a}$$

Money market:

$$i = \frac{1}{h}\left(kY - \frac{\overline{M}}{\overline{P}}\right) \tag{12a}$$

Since we wish to have equilibrium simultaneously in both markets, we may solve these two equations simultaneously for the equilibrium interest rate and income level as functions of the exogenous variables. We proceed by substitution. Substituting Eq. (12a) in Eq. (6a) yields

$$Y = \bar{\alpha}\left[\overline{A} - \frac{b}{h}\left(kY - \frac{\overline{M}}{\overline{P}}\right)\right] \tag{13}$$

or, after collecting terms in Y,

$$Y_0 = \frac{h\bar{\alpha}}{h + kb\bar{\alpha}}\overline{A} + \frac{b\bar{\alpha}}{h + kb\bar{\alpha}}\frac{\overline{M}}{\overline{P}} \tag{13a}$$

where Y_0 is now the equilibrium level of income. The terms that multiply the exogenous variables $\overline{A}$ and $\overline{M}/P$ can be thought of as more complicated multipliers that reflect the monetary repercussions that characterize this model and differentiate it from the simple keynesian model. It is useful to rewrite Eq. (13a) in a somewhat simplified form as

$$Y_0 = \beta\overline{A} + \gamma\frac{\overline{M}}{\overline{P}} \tag{14}$$

where

$$\beta \equiv \frac{h\bar{\alpha}}{h + bk\bar{\alpha}} \tag{15}$$

and

$$\gamma \equiv \frac{b\bar{\alpha}}{h + bk\bar{\alpha}} \tag{16}$$

Here β and γ will be referred to as the *fiscal* and *money multipliers*, respectively.

The fiscal multiplier β tells us by how much an increase in government spending affects the equilibrium level of income, holding the real money supply constant. Examine Eq. (13a) and consider the effect of an increase in government spending on income. The increase in government spending $\Delta \overline{G}$ is a change in autonomous spending, so that $\Delta \overline{A} = \Delta \overline{G}$. The effect of the change in $\overline{G}$ is given by

$$\frac{\Delta Y_0}{\Delta \overline{G}} = \frac{h\overline{\alpha}}{h + bk\overline{\alpha}} \equiv \beta \qquad (17)$$

We note that the expression in Eq. (17) is zero if h becomes very small and will be equal to $\overline{\alpha}$ if h approaches infinity. This corresponds, respectively, to a vertical and horizontal LM schedule. Similarly, a large value of either b or k serves to reduce the effect on income of government spending. Why? A high value of k implies a large increase in money demand as income rises and, hence, a large increase in interest rates in order to maintain money market equilibrium. In combination with a high b this implies a large reduction in private aggregate demand. Equation (17) thus presents the algebraic analysis that corresponds to the graphical analysis of Fig. 4-11.

Similarly, the money multiplier γ tells us by how much an increase in the real money supply affects the equilibrium level of income, keeping fiscal policy unchanged. Using Eq. (13a) to examine the effects of an increase in the real money supply on income, we have

$$\frac{\Delta Y_0}{\Delta (\overline{M/P})} = \frac{b\overline{\alpha}}{h + bk\overline{\alpha}} \equiv \gamma \qquad (18)$$

The smaller h and k and the larger b and $\overline{\alpha}$, the more expansionary is the effect of an increase in real balances on the equilibrium level of income. This corresponds to a constellation of a very steep LM schedule and a very flat IS schedule. Equation (18) thus corresponds to the graphical analysis presented in Fig. 4-14.

The Classical Case and Liquidity Trap Again

We return now to Eq. (13a) to consider two extreme possibilities. One is the world of constant velocity. We define the *income velocity of money* as the ratio of income to money:

$$V \equiv \frac{Y}{M/P} \equiv \frac{PY}{M} \qquad (19)$$

where PY is the level of nominal income. Income velocity V is thus the ratio of the level of nominal income to the nominal money stock. If the demand for money is unresponsive to the interest rate, then $h = 0$ and Eq. (13a) becomes

$$Y = \frac{1}{k}\frac{\overline{M}}{P} = \frac{V}{P/\overline{M}} \tag{20}$$

where

$$V \equiv \frac{1}{k}$$

or

$$PY = VM \tag{20a}$$

This is a "quantity theory world" where nominal income PY is proportional to the nominal quantity of money, and changes in the nominal quantity of money are reflected in equiproportionate changes in nominal income. This is what we previously called the classical case. From Eq. (20a) we see that, given the price level (say $\overline{P}$), and for fixed velocity, real income can change only if the nominal money supply changes. Fiscal policy is totally ineffective in this case.

The other extreme is represented by a world where h is infinite, so that money and other assets are effectively perfect substitutes. In such a world Eq. (13a) reduces to

$$Y = \overline{\alpha}\overline{A} \tag{21}$$

This is a "multiplier world" where autonomous spending entirely determines the level of real income. It occurs if the economy is in a liquidity trap.

4-9 SUMMARY

The IS-LM model presented in this chapter is a simplified, but useful, model of the economy which lays particular stress on the channels through which monetary and fiscal policy affect the economy. The analysis proceeds by first studying equilibrium in the goods and money markets, respectively. The overall equilibrium of the model is achieved when the level of income and the interest rate are such that both markets are in equilibrium. If the money market is in equilibrium, then the other assets markets, represented here by the catch-all "bond market" are also in equilibrium. We have shown how the economy adjusts to changes and that, under the reasonable dynamic assumptions made, the economy does move toward the equilibrium.

In Sec. 4-5 we saw how monetary policy affects the economy, in the first instance by disturbing the equilibrium in the assets markets and thus changing the interest rate, and then, through the effects of the interest rate on aggregate demand. Fiscal policy continues to affect the level of income as in Chap. 3, but the multiplier effects of fiscal changes on income are dampened by the effects of rising income on interest rates and thus on aggregate demand.

We also examined two extreme cases. In the liquidity trap, in which increases in the money supply affect neither the interest rate nor the level of income, only fiscal policy changes the level of income. Further, because the interest rate is unchanged by the fiscal policy action, there is no induced reduction in investment spending, and no dampening effect of output arising from falling investment. In the classical case, in which the demand for money does not depend on the interest rate, the level of income cannot change unless the demand for money changes. Fiscal policy changes affect only interest rates and the rate of investment, while leaving total spending unchanged.

The extreme cases are of interest from a historical perspective, and useful for understanding of the model, but neither is very useful for understanding the current American economy. There is much evidence that the demand for real balances is significantly related to the interest rate but not so strongly that we are in a liquidity trap.

And a final warning, that has already been mentioned: We are assuming here that any level of output that is demanded can be produced by firms at the constant price level. Price level behavior, including inflation, will be discussed in substantially more detail in Chaps. 12 and 13. Those chapters build on the analysis of the IS-LM model.

*APPENDIX: INTEREST RATES, PRESENT VALUES, AND DISCOUNTING

In this appendix we deal with the relationships among bond coupons, interest rates and yields, and the prices of bonds. In doing so, we shall introduce the very useful concept of present discounted value (PDV).

Section 1

We start with the case of a perpetual bond, or perpetuity. Such bonds have been issued in a number of countries, including the United Kingdom, where they are called Consols. The Consol is a promise by the British government to pay a fixed amount to the holder of the bond, every year and forever. Let us denote the promised payment per Consol by Q_c, the *coupon*.[23]

The *yield* on a bond is the return per dollar that the holder of the bond receives. The yield on a savings account paying 5 percent interest per year is obvi-

---

[23]The *coupon rate* is the coupon divided by the face value of the bond, which is literally the value printed on the face of the bond. Bonds do not necessarily sell for their face value, though customarily the face value is close to the value at which the bonds are sold when they first come on the market.

ously just 5 percent. Someone paying $25 for a Consol which has a coupon of $2.5 obtains a yield of 10 percent [($2.5/25) × 100].

The yield on a Consol and its price are related in a simple way. Let us denote the price of the Consol by P_c and the coupon by Q_c. Then as the above example suggests, the yield i is just

$$i = \frac{Q_c}{P_c} \qquad \text{(A1)}$$

which says that the yield on a perpetuity is the coupon divided by the price. Alternatively, we can switch Eq. (A1) around to

$$P_c = \frac{Q_c}{i} \qquad \text{(A2)}$$

which says that price is the coupon divided by the yield. So given the coupon and the yield, we can derive the price, or given the coupon and the price, we can derive the yield.

None of this is a theory of the determination of the yield or the price of a perpetuity. It merely points out the relationship between price and yield. Our theory of the determination of the yield on bonds is, of course, presented in this chapter. The interest rate in this chapter corresponds to the yield on bonds, and we tend to talk interchangeably of interest rates and yields.

We shall return to the Consol at the end of this appendix.

Section 2

Now we move to a short-term bond. Let us consider a bond which was sold by a borrower for $100, on which the borrower promises to pay back $108 after one year. This is a one-year bond. The yield on the bond to the person who bought it for $100 is 8 percent. For every $1 he lent, he obtains both the $1 principal and 8 cents extra at the end of the year.

Next we ask a slightly different question. How much would a promise to pay $1 at the end of the year be worth? If $108 at the end of the year is worth $100 today, then $1 at the end of the year must be worth $100/108, or 92.6 cents. That is the value today of $1 in one year's time. In other words, it is the *present discounted value* of $1 in one year's time. It is the present value because it is what would be paid today for the promise of money in one year's time, and it is discounted because the value today is less than the promised payment in a year's time.

Denoting the one-year yield or interest rate by i, we can write down that the present discounted value of a promised payment Q_1, one year from now, is

$$\text{PDV} = \frac{Q_1}{1+i} \qquad \text{(A3)}$$

Let us return to our one-year bond and suppose that the day after the original borrower obtained his money, the yield on one-year bonds rises. How much would anyone *now* be willing to pay for the promise to receive $108 after one year? The answer must be given by the general formula (A3). The bond is just a promise to pay $108 in one year's time, and if the yield on one year bonds is i, then the present value of the promise is given by Eq. (A3). That means that the price of the one-year bond will fall when the interest rate or yield on such bonds rises. Once again, we see that the price of the bond and the yield are inversely related, given the promised payments to be made on the bond.

As before, we can reverse the formula for the price in order to find the yield on the bond, given its price and the promised payment Q_1. Note that the price P is equal to the present discounted value (PDV) so that we can write

$$1+i = \frac{Q_1}{P} \tag{A4}$$

Thus, given the price of the bond and the promised payment, we can find the yield.

Section 3

Next we consider a two-year bond. Such a bond would typically promise to make a payment, which we shall denote Q_1, of interest at the end of the first year, and then a payment of interest and principal (usually the amount borrowed) Q_2, at the end of the second year. Given the yield i on the bond, how do we compute its PDV, which will be equal to its price?

We start by asking first what the bond will be worth one year from now. At that stage, it will be a one-year bond, promising to pay the amount Q_2 in one year's time, and yielding i. Its value one year from now will accordingly be given by Eq. (A3) except that Q_1 in Eq. (A3) is replaced by Q_2. Let us denote the value of the bond one year from now by PDV_1 and note that

$$PDV_1 = \frac{Q_2}{1+i} \tag{A5}$$

To complete computing the PDV of the two-year bond, we can now treat it as a one-year bond, which promises to pay Q_1 in interest one year from now, and also to pay PDV_1 one year from now, since it can be sold at that stage for that amount. Hence, the PDV of the bond, equal to its price, is

$$PDV = \frac{Q_1}{1+i} + \frac{PDV_1}{1+i} \tag{A6}$$

or

$$PDV = \frac{Q_1}{1+i} + \frac{Q_2}{(1+i)^2} \tag{A6a}$$

As previously, given the promised payments Q_1 and Q_2, the price of the bond will fall if the yield rises, and vice versa.

It is now less simple to reverse the equation for the price of the bond to find the yield than it was before: that is because from Eq. (A6) we obtain a quadratic equation for the yield, which has two solutions.

We have now provided the outline of the argument whereby the present discounted value of *any* promised stream of payments for any number of years can be computed. Suppose that a bond, or any other asset, promises to pay amounts Q_1, Q_2, Q_3, ..., Q_n in future years, 1, 2, 3, ..., n years away. By pursuing the type of argument given in Sec. 4-3, it is possible to show that the PDV of such a payments stream will be

$$\text{PDV} = \frac{Q_1}{1+i} + \frac{Q_2}{(1+i)^2} + \frac{Q_3}{(1+i)^3} + \cdots + \frac{Q_n}{(1+i)^n} \tag{A7}$$

As usual, the price of a bond with a specified payments stream will be inversely related to its yield.

Section 5

Finally, we return to the Consol. The Consol promises to pay the amount Q_c forever. Applying the above formula, we can compute the present value of the Consol by

$$\text{PDV} = Q_c \left[\frac{1}{(1+i)} + \frac{1}{(1+i)^2} + \frac{1}{(1+i)^3} + \cdots + \frac{1}{(1+i)^n} + \cdots \right] \tag{A8}$$

The contents of the parentheses on the right-hand side are an infinite series, the sum of which can be calculated as $1/i$. Thus

$$\text{PDV} = \frac{Q_c}{i} \tag{A9}$$

This section casts a slightly different light on the commonsense discussion of Sec. 1 of this appendix. Equations (A8) and (A9) show that the Consol's price is equal to the PDV of the future coupon payments.

PROBLEMS

1 The following equations describe an economy. (Think of C, I, G, etc., being measured in billions and i as percent; a 5 percent interest rate implies $i = 5$.)

$$C = 0.8(1 - t)Y \qquad 1$$

$$t = 0.25 \qquad 2$$

$$I = 300 - 15i \qquad 3$$

$$\bar{G} = 390 \qquad 4$$

$$L = 0.25Y - 12i \qquad 5$$

$$\frac{\bar{M}}{P} = 303 \qquad 6$$

a What is the equation that describes the IS curve?
b What is the general definition of the IS curve?
c What is the equation that describes the LM curve?
d What is the general definition of the LM curve?
e What are the equilibrium levels of income and the interest rate?
f Describe in words the conditions that are satisfied at the intersection of the IS and LM curves, and why this is an equilibrium.

2 Continuing with the same equations:
a What is the value of $\bar{\alpha}$, which corresponds to the simple multiplier (with taxes) of Chap. 3?
b By how much does an increase in government spending of $\Delta\bar{G}$ increase the level of income in this model, which includes the assets markets?
c By how much does a change in government spending of $\Delta\bar{G}$ affect the equilibrium interest rate?
d Explain the difference between your answers to 2a and 2b.
e Relate your answer to 2d to the question of *crowding out*.
f What is the money multiplier in this system? (In other words, by how much does a change in the real money stock of $\Delta\bar{M}/P$ affect the equilibrium level of income?)

3 a Explain in words how and why the multiplier $\bar{\alpha}$ and the interest sensitivity of aggregate demand affect the slope of the IS curve.
b Explain why the slope of the IS curve is a factor in determining the working of monetary policy.

4 Explain in words how and why the income and interest sensitivities of the demand for real balances affect the slope of the LM curve.

5 a Why does a horizontal LM curve imply that fiscal policy has the same effects on the economy as we derived in Chap. 3?
b What is happening in this case in terms of Fig. 4-1?
c Under what circumstances might the LM curve be horizontal?

6 We mentioned in the text the possibility that the interest rate might affect consumption spending. An increase in the interest rate could in principle lead to increases in saving and therefore a reduction in consumption, given the level of income. Suppose that consumption were in fact reduced by an increase in the interest rate; how would the IS curve be affected?

7 Suppose that the money supply, instead of being constant, increased (slightly) with the interest rate.
a How would this change affect the construction of the LM curve?
b Could you see any reason why the Fed might follow a policy of increasing the money supply along with the interest rate?

8 a How does an increase in the tax rate affect the IS curve?
b How does it affect the equilibrium level of income?
c How does it affect the equilibrium interest rate?

9 Draw a graph of how i and Y respond over time (i.e., use time as the horizontal axis) to:
a An expansion in the money supply
b An increase in taxes
You may assume that the money market adjusts much more rapidly than the goods market.

10 In Fig. 4-17 the economy can move to full employment by an expansion in either money or the full-employment deficit. Which policy leads to E_1 and which to E_2?

How would you expect the choice to be made? Who would most strongly favor moving to E_1? E_2? What policy would correspond to "balanced growth"?

11 "We can have the GNP path we want equally well with a tight fiscal policy and an easier monetary policy, or the reverse, within fairly broad limits. The real basis for choice lies in many subsidiary targets, besides real GNP and inflation, that are differentially affected by fiscal and monetary policies." What are some of the subsidiary targets referred to in the quote? How would they be affected by alternative policy combinations?

*12 a Nominal GNP in 1975 was about $1,500 billion, and the money supply was about $300 billion. What then was the income velocity of money?

b We noted that, if the demand for money is totally interest-insensitive, velocity V is just the inverse of the coefficient k of our money demand function, where k represents the income sensitivity of the demand for money. We can interpret k as the fraction of a year's income that people hold in the form of money. Using the numbers of 12a, what fraction of the year's income do people hold as money? How many weeks' income on average are people holding in the form of money?

*13 A bond promises to pay the holder $6 at the end of the first year and $106 at the end of the second year.

a If the interest rate or yield is 6 percent, what is the value of the bond?

b Without necessarily solving the arithmetic, write out an expression for how much the bond will be worth if the interest rate drops to 5 percent. Is this more or less than in 13a? Why?

PART

5

Consumption,
Income, Wealth,
and Lags

he IS-LM model developed in Chap. 4 provides a coherent macro-economic framework, which enables us to understand the interaction of some of the main macroeconomic variables. Now we retrace our steps to present a more detailed and more sophisticated treatment of the key equations in the IS-LM model. The present chapter deals with the consumption function. The following three chapters deal with invest-ment, money demand, and money supply. As a unit, these chapters flesh out the behavioral equations of the IS-LM model and thus move us toward a more realistic and reliable understanding of the working of the economy.

Our starting point in examining consumption behavior is the consump-tion function we have been using so far in the book. Thus far we have been assuming that consumption is a linear function of disposable income:

$$C = \overline{C} + cY_d \qquad \overline{C} > 0 \qquad c > 0 \tag{1}$$

CHART 5-1 THE CONSUMPTION
FUNCTION, 1946–1975 (BILLIONS OF 1972
DOLLARS)

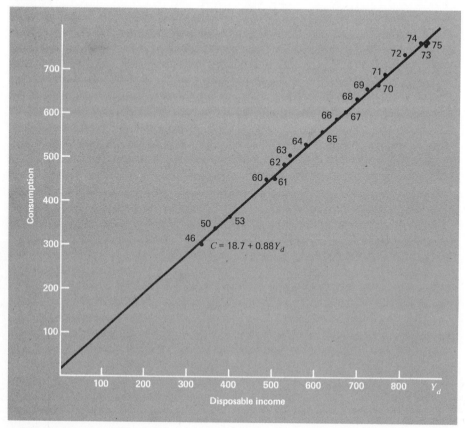

The consumption function (1) has two particular features which determine its properties. They are the intercept $\overline{C}$ and the marginal propensity to consume, c. Equation (1) implies that a \$1 increase in disposable income raises consumption spending by the marginal propensity to consume, c. It implies, too, that the average propensity to consume, C/Y_d, or the ratio of consumption to disposable income, falls with the level of disposable income. This point can be seen from Eq. (1a), where we have divided both sides of Eq. (1) by Y_d:

$$\frac{C}{Y_d} = \frac{\overline{C}}{Y_d} + c \tag{1a}$$

An increase in disposable income lowers the ratio $\overline{C}/Y_d$ and therefore reduces the average propensity to consume. As income becomes very large, the first term on the right-hand side becomes progressively smaller and the average propensity to consume approaches the marginal propensity to consume, c.

Now what is the empirical evidence in support of such a consumption function? Using annual data for real disposable income and real personal consumption expenditures for the 1946–1975 period, we can estimate a consumption function of the form given in Eq. (1). The estimated equation is

$$C = 18.7 + 0.88Y_d \tag{2}$$

In Chart 5-1 we show the regression line reported in Eq. (2), together with the consumption and disposable income data for some of the years 1946–1975. The regression line is "fitted" to the data using the method of least squares.[1] The equation clearly has the two properties we have been assuming for our standard consumption function (1): namely, a positive intercept or autonomous spending term, $\overline{C}$ = \$18.7 billion (in 1972 prices), and a positive marginal propensity to consume of c = 0.88.

For a quick check on the use of the equation, we take, say, 1974 real disposable income, which was Y_d = \$843.5 (billion). Substituting that value into the consumption function in Eq. (2), we get the predicted level of consumption of \$761 (= 18.7 + 0.88 × 843.5). Actual consumption expenditure in that year was \$760. Accordingly for that particular year the

---

[1]It is frequently useful to summarize a relationship such as that of Chart 5-1 between consumption expenditures and disposable income by writing down an equation such as Eq. (2), which has specific numerical values in it, rather than the more general form of Eq. (1), which does not specify numerical values of the coefficients $\overline{C}$ and c. The line drawn in Chart 5-1 is the line represented by Eq. (2). That line is calculated by minimizing the sum of the squares of the distances of the points in Chart 5-1 from the line, and it provides a good description of the general relationship between the two variables. For further details on the fitting of such lines, called least-squares regression lines, see Robert S. Pindyck and Daniel L. Rubinfeld, *Econometric Models and Economic Forecasts*, McGraw-Hill, 1976.

equation makes a 1- billion-dollar error—a quite small error of much less than 1 percent of consumption.

Equation (2) shows that the average propensity to consume, C/Y_d, declines with the level of income. Using that equation, the average propensity to consume is

$$\frac{C}{Y_d} = \frac{18.7}{Y_d} + 0.88 \tag{2a}$$

In 1974, for example, with a disposable income of \$843.5 billion, the equation shows that the average propensity to consume would be 0.902 (= 18.7/843.5 + 0.88). The actual number for 1974 is 0.901. In some other years, the error is greater. For instance, in 1963 the predicted value of the average propensity to consume is 0.915 and the actual value is 0.930. Table 5-1 presents actual values of the average propensity to consume for 1946–1975. Overall, the table seems to show a decline in the average propensity to consume over the course of time, but with considerable short-run fluctuations.

This introductory review of the facts suggests that our simple consumption function stands up quite well empirically. Even so, its accuracy should not be exaggerated. For instance, the error of 0.015 in the average propensity to consume in 1963 seems small, but it does mean that a prediction of consumption for that year based on the actual value of real disposable income (\$539 billion) is in error by \$8.1 billion (= 0.015 × \$539 billion). There is thus room for improvement.

However, historically, the main impetus for attempting to improve on consumption functions of the form of Eq. (2) came from a clear inconsistency between the results of two types of early study of consumption behavior. The first type of study estimated a consumption function like Eq.

TABLE 5-1 THE RATIO OF REAL CONSUMPTION SPENDING TO REAL PERSONAL DISPOSABLE INCOME, 1946–1975

1946	0.907	1956	0.913	1966	0.911
1947	0.960	1957	0.914	1967	0.901
1948	0.932	1958	0.913	1968	0.911
1949	0.952	1959	0.925	1969	0.920
1950	0.934	1960	0.930	1970	0.902
1951	0.921	1961	0.923	1971	0.900
1952	0.918	1962	0.926	1972	0.915
1953	0.916	1963	0.930	1973	0.895
1954	0.922	1964	0.916	1974	0.901
1955	0.928	1965	0.911	1975	0.895

Source: Economic Report of the President, 1976.

(2), using annual data for the short period 1929–1941, for which such data were available. Using those data, we obtain an estimate of an equation like Eq. (2) but with different values of the parameters:

$$C = 39.9 + 0.75Y_d \qquad (2b)$$

This consumption function has a much lower marginal propensity to consume—namely, 0.75—than has Eq. (2) itself. It also implies that the average propensity to consume falls quite rapidly with the level of income.[2]

The second type of study was of the long-run behavior of consumption. Simon Kuznets studied the behavior of consumption over the long period 1869–1938.[3] He found that over that long period, consumption was almost proportional to income—or that the average propensity to consume was nearly constant—in sharp contrast to the implications of the short-run equation (2b). (Proportionality of consumption to income simply means that we can write $C = cY_d$ and omit the intercept.) The long-run average propensity to consume that Kuznets found was near 0.9.

The puzzle, then, was that the short-run consumption function (2b) implies a marginal propensity to consume of 0.75, with an average propensity to consume that declines as income rises, while the long-run data showed the average propensity to consume to be roughly constant at about 0.9. Because the long-run studies show a constant average propensity to consume, they imply also that the marginal propensity to consume is equal to the average, at about 0.9.[4] This value of the marginal propensity to consume is consistent with the 0.88 implied by Eq. (2).

The difference is important because the marginal propensity to consume figures prominently in the calculation of multipliers and thus has a bearing on income determination and policy questions. At the simplest level, calculating the multiplier $\alpha = 1/(1 - c)$ implies that with $c = 0.88$, as the long-run data would suggest, we have a multiplier in excess of 8. With $c = 0.75$, as the earlier data show, the multiplier is only 4. It is therefore clearly important to find out what accounts for the difference in estimates and which one is the most appropriate empirical counterpart of our theoretical concept of a marginal propensity to consume.

To preview the substance of the following sections, modern consumption function theory has improved on equations such as Eq. (2) by sharpening our understanding of the relation between current consumption and

[2]Check this by calculating the implied value of the average propensity to consume for 1974, when real disposable income was $843.5 billion.

[3]Simon Kuznets, *National Product since 1869* and *National Income, a Summary of Findings*, New York, National Bureau of Economic Research, 1946.

[4]It is interesting to note that the inconsistency between the results of short- and long-run studies that existed on the basis of the 1929–1941 data is less obvious in the post-World War II data. For instance, dividing the period 1946–1975 in two, the estimate of the marginal propensity to consume based on data for 1946–1960 is 0.88, and the estimate based on data for 1961–1975 is 0.86.

current disposable income. The main point of these innovations is to suggest that current consumption depends on a broader measure of income than current disposable income. The broader measures we will study go under the names of *lifetime income, permanent income,* and *relative income*. These new concepts, which we shall study in Secs. 5-1, 5-2, and 5-3, have in common the recognition that consumption spending is maintained relatively constant in the face of fluctuations of current income. Consumption spending is not geared to what we earn today, but to what we earn on average. The important question obviously is what "average" means in this context.

The theories we present all imply that there is a difference between the marginal propensity to consume in the short run and the marginal propensity to consume in the long run. The short-run consumption function—the relationship between consumption spending and current disposable income—is indeed quite flat. However, this consumption function shifts upwards over time. These shifts in the relationship between consumption and current disposable income bring into the discussion the roles of *wealth* and *permanent income* in affecting consumer spending.[5] These considerations are taken up in the next two sections.

5-1 THE LIFE-CYCLE THEORY OF CONSUMPTION AND SAVING

The consumption function (1) is based on the simple notion that individuals' consumption behavior in a given period is related to their income in that period. The life-cycle hypothesis views individuals instead as planning their consumption and savings behavior over long periods, with the intention of allocating their consumption in a satisfactory way over their entire lifetimes. The life-cycle hypothesis views savings as resulting mainly from individuals' desires to provide for consumption in old age. As we shall see below, the theory points to a number of unexpected factors affecting the savings rate of the economy; for instance, the age structure of the population is in principle an important determinant of consumption and savings behavior.

To anticipate the main results of this section, we can already state here that we will derive a consumption function of the form:

[5]The theories of the consumption function developed below are also useful for explaining another empirical puzzle that we shall not go into in detail. In *cross-sectional* studies of the relationship between consumption and income—studies in which the consumption of a sample of families is related to their income—the marginal propensity to consume out of disposable income also appears to be lower than the average propensity to consume, with the average propensity to consume falling as the level of income rises. If you are interested in the reconciliation of this evidence with the long-run evidence of Kuznets, you should look at the ingenious explanation advanced by Milton Friedman, through the permanent-income hypothesis. Follow up the reference given in footnote 11 below.

$$C = a\,\frac{W}{P} + cY_d \tag{3}$$

where W/P is real wealth, a is the marginal propensity to consume out of wealth, and c is the marginal propensity to consume out of disposable income. We will show what determines the marginal propensities, why wealth should be an argument in the consumption function, and what the life-cycle consumption theory implies about the ratio of consumption to income, C/Y_d.

Consider now an individual who expects to live for L years, work and earn income for N years, and be in retirement for $(L-N)$ years. We shall in what follows ignore any uncertainty about either life expectancy or the length of working life. We shall assume, too, that no interest is earned on savings so that current saving translates dollar for dollar into future consumption possibilities. With these assumptions we can approach the saving or consumption decision with two questions. First we ask what are the individual's lifetime consumption possibilities. Second, we are interested in the way the individual will choose to distribute her consumption over her lifetime. We shall now consider the consumption possibilities.

For the moment we ignore property income (income from assets) and focus attention on labor income. We denote the annual real labor income by Z. Given N years of working, *lifetime income* (from labor) is ZN, income per working year times the number of working years. Consumption over the individual's lifetime cannot exceed this lifetime income unless she is born with wealth, which we assume is not the case. Accordingly, we have determined the first part of the consumer's problem in finding the limit of lifetime consumption.

We assume the individual will want to distribute her consumption over her lifetime so that she has a flat or even flow of consumption. Rather than consuming a lot in one period and very little in another, the preferred profile is to consume exactly equal amounts in each period.[6] Clearly, this assumption implies that consumption is not geared to *current* income (which is zero during retirement) but rather to *lifetime income*.

Lifetime consumption equals lifetime income. This means that the

---

[6]Why? The basic reason is the notion of diminishing marginal utility of consumption. Consider two alternative consumption plans. One involves an equal amount of consumption in each of two periods, the other involves consuming all in one period and none in the other. The principle of diminishing marginal utility of income implies that, in the latter case, we would be better off by transferring some consumption from the period of plenty toward that of starvation. The loss in utility in the period of plenty is *more* than compensated by the gain in utility in the period of scarcity. And there is a gain to be made by transferring consumption so long as there is any difference in consumption between the two periods. The principle of diminishing marginal utility of consumption conforms well with the observation that most people choose stable life-styles—not in general saving furiously in one period to have a big bust in the next, but rather consuming at about the same level from period to period.

planned level of consumption C, which is the same in every period, times the number of years in life L equals lifetime income:

$$CL = ZN \qquad (4)$$

Lifetime income is equal to ZN. Dividing through by L, we have planned consumption per year, C, that is proportional to labor income:

$$C = \frac{N}{L}Z \qquad (5)$$

The factor of proportionality in Eq. (5) is N/L, the fraction of lifetime spent working. Accordingly Eq. (5) states that in each year of life a fraction of labor income is consumed, where that fraction is equal to the proportion of working life in total life.

The counterpart of Eq. (5) is the saving function. Remembering that saving is equal to income less consumption, we have

$$S \equiv Z - C = \frac{Z(L - N)}{L} \qquad (6)$$

Equation (6) states that saving during the period in which the individual works is equal to a fraction of labor income, where that fraction is equal to the proportion of life spent in retirement.

Figure 5-1 shows the pattern of consumption, saving, and dissaving.[7] Over the whole lifetime, there is an even flow of consumption at the rate C, amounting to CL. That consumption spending is financed during working life out of current income. During retirement the consumption is financed by drawing down the savings that have been accumulated during working life. Therefore the shaded areas $(Z - C)N$ and $C(L - N)$ are equal, or equivalently saving during working years finances dissaving during retirement. The important idea of lifetime consumption theory is apparent from Fig. 5-1. It is that consumption plans are made so as to achieve a smooth or even level of consumption by saving during periods of high income and dissaving during periods of low income. This is, therefore, an important departure from consumption based on current income. It is an important difference because, in addition to current income, the whole future profile of income enters into the calculation of lifetime consumption. Before developing that aspect further, however, we return to Fig. 5-1 to consider the role of assets.

During the working years the individual saves to finance consumption during retirement. The savings build up assets, and we accordingly show

---

[7] Figure 5-1 was developed by Franco Modigliani in "The Life Cycle Hypothesis of Saving, the Demand for Wealth and the Supply of Capital," *Social Research*, vol. 33, no. 2, 1966.

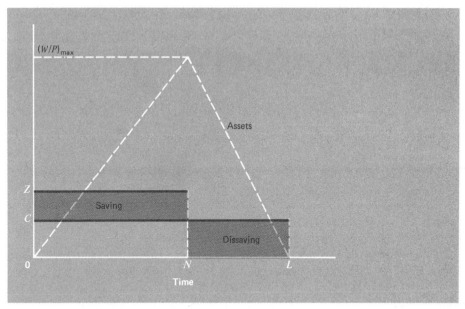

FIGURE 5-1 LIFETIME INCOME,
CONSUMPTION, SAVINGS, AND WEALTH IN
THE LIFE-CYCLE MODEL

in Fig. 5-1 how the individual's wealth or assets increase over working life
and reach a maximum at retirement age. From that time on assets decline
because we assume the individual sells assets to pay for current consumption. We can briefly ask what is the maximum level assets reach? We
remember that assets are built up to finance consumption during retirement. Consumption during retirement is equal to $C(L - N)$. Further,
since consumption is equal to $C = ZN/L$, the maximum stock of assets is
$(W/P)_{max} = ZN(L - N)/L$, which is reached exactly at the point of retirement.
From then on assets decline until they reach precisely zero at the end of
life.

Introducing Wealth

The next step is to extend this model and allow for initial assets or wealth,
that is, assuming the individual is born to wealth. We can simply draw on
the previous insight that the individual consumer will spread any resources
he has to achieve an even lifetime consumption profile. If, in addition to
labor income, he has assets, he will plan to use these assets to add to his
lifetime consumption. An individual who is at some point T in his lifetime,
with a stock of wealth W/P, and labor income accruing for another $(N - T)$

years at the rate of Z, and with a life expectancy of $(L - T)$ years to go, will behave as follows. His lifetime consumption possibilities are

$$C(L - T) = \frac{W}{P} + (N - T)Z \tag{7}$$

where we have included wealth W/P along with lifetime labor income as a source of finance for lifetime consumption. From Eq. (7) consumption in each period is equal to

$$C = a\frac{W}{P} + cZ \qquad a \equiv \frac{1}{L - T} \qquad c \equiv \frac{N - T}{L - T} \qquad N \geq T \tag{8}$$

where the coefficients a and c are respectively the marginal propensities to consume out of wealth and labor income.

It is important to recognize from Eq. (8) that the marginal propensities are related to the individual's position in the life cycle. The closer the individual is to the end of lifetime, the higher the marginal propensity to consume out of wealth. Thus, an individual with two more years of life will consume half his wealth in each of the remaining two years. The marginal propensity to consume out of labor income is related both to the number of years during which further income will be earned, $N - T$, and to the number of years over which these earnings are spread, $L - T$. It is quite clear from Eq. (8) that an increase in either wealth or labor income will raise consumption expenditures. It is apparent, too, that lengthening working life relative to retirement will raise consumption simply because it increases lifetime income. The most basic point, however, is that Eq. (8) shows *both* income and wealth as determinants of consumption spending.

To summarize where we have come so far, we note that in this form of the life-cycle model:

1 Consumption is constant over the consumer's lifetime.
2 Consumption spending is financed by lifetime income plus initial wealth.
3 During each year a fraction $1/(L - T)$ of wealth plus expected earnings will be consumed.
4 Current consumption spending depends on current wealth and income.

Before passing on to the aggregate level, leaving behind the typical consumer, we briefly note some further implications of life-cycle theory. Clearly the theory shows that during earning years consumers will save. The theory has predictions, too, about how young and old people will respond to an increase in wealth. An old person will have a much larger marginal propensity to spend out of wealth. Why? Because old people have a shorter life expectancy and therefore plan to spread the increase in wealth over a smaller number of years. Young people, by contrast, plan to consume the increase in wealth over a longer horizon and therefore will spend a smaller fraction of the increase in wealth in each year. We note, too, that if there was an increase in wealth, the ratio of consumption to income would increase. The point is that even with an unchanged income but a higher wealth, consumption spending would rise, and thus the ratio of consumption to income would rise. We will return to this point because it has a bearing on the puzzles that we set out to explain at the beginning.

Before we discuss attempts to estimate consumption functions including both wealth and income, we should discuss some extensions of the life-cycle model. First, taking account of the possibility that saving earns interest, so that a dollar not consumed today provides more than a dollar's consumption tomorrow, does not alter the essential results. Second, the analysis is little affected when it is extended to allow for the facts that individuals are uncertain of the length of their lifetimes, and also that they sometimes want to leave bequests to their heirs, so that they would not necessarily plan to consume all their resources over their own lifetimes.

Third, an individual's income is unlikely to be constant over his working life; indeed, the individual does not know exactly what his income for future years will be. It is accordingly necessary for him to make lifetime consumption plans by trying to predict future incomes. Albert Ando and Franco Modigliani, two of the three originators of the life-cycle theory,[8] argue that individuals base their predictions of future income on their current incomes, and that accordingly current income should appear in the consumption function to reflect expectations of future income.

Fourth, we want to consider the relationship between the theory as so far outlined, which is strictly a theory about consumption and saving by a single individual over the course of her lifetime, and aggregate consumption and saving. Imagine an economy in which population was constant, and GNP was constant through time. Each individual in that economy would go through the life cycle of saving and dissaving outlined in Fig. 5-1. The economy as a whole, though, would not be saving. At any one time, the saving of working people would be exactly matched by the dissaving of retired people. If population were growing, though, there would be more young people than old, thus more saving in total than dissaving, and there would be net saving in the economy. Thus, aggregate consumption depends in part on the age composition of the population. It also depends on such characteristics of the economy as the average age of retirement and the presence or absence of social security.

To move from the conceptual framework of Eq. (8) to an empirical estimate of the consumption function, we have to find a way of measuring expected labor income Z. In the original work, Ando and Modigliani assumed that expectations about labor income are made on the basis of cur-

[8]Albert Ando and Franco Modigliani, "The 'Life Cycle' Hypothesis of Saving: Aggregate Implications and Tests," *American Economic Review*, March 1963.

rent disposable income. In later work, expected labor income was assumed to be proportional to current disposable income.[9] Estimating a consumption function of the form of Eq. (3), using data for the years 1953–1975, we obtain

$$C = 0.039 \frac{W}{P} + 0.74 \, Y_d \tag{9}$$

From Eq. (9), a \$1 increase in real wealth increases consumption spending by about 4 cents. A \$1 increase in disposable income raises consumption by 74 cents. Needless to say, this marginal propensity to consume out of disposable income, $c = 0.74$, is much lower than the estimates presented previously for the post-War period.

The theoretical argument we have made assumes that individuals attempt to distribute their financial resources so as to achieve an even level of consumption over a lifetime. It also implies that both income and wealth enter the consumption function. The next question we want to discuss is what bearing Eq. (3) or Eq. (9) has on the puzzle of the difference between the approximate constancy of the average propensity to consume in the long run and the diminishing average propensity to consume implied by the short-run consumption function of Eq. (2b). For that purpose, we divide Eq. (3) on both sides by disposable income Y_d to obtain

$$\frac{C}{Y_d} = a \frac{W/P}{Y_d} + c \tag{10}$$

We argued earlier that empirically the average propensity to consume, C/Y_d, is relatively constant in the long run (i.e., on average over long periods of time) but fluctuates more in the short run. The explanation for these results suggested by Eq. (10) must lie in the behavior of the ratio of wealth to disposable income. Table 5-2 shows the ratios of consumption to disposable income and wealth to disposable income for the years 1953–1975. Low ratios of wealth to income tend to be associated with low ratios of consumption to disposable income. And Table 5-2 does provide an explanation for the constancy of the long-run average propensity to consume compared with its short-run behavior—because the ratio of wealth to income in the long run is relatively constant, while in the short run the ratio fluctuates.

We want now to bring out one very interesting feature of the behavior of consumption, which should tend to increase confidence in the life-cycle hypothesis as an explanation of consumption behavior. It used to be argued that the ratio of consumption to disposable income tends to rise dur-

---

[9]We shall see in discussing permanent income that there are alternative formulations of the way expectations are formed, which would make expected labor income depend on the disposable income of previous periods, as well as the current period.

TABLE 5-2 RATIOS OF WEALTH AND CONSUMPTION TO DISPOSABLE INCOME, 1953–1975

	$\dfrac{W/P}{Y_d}$	$\dfrac{C}{Y_d}$		$\dfrac{W/P}{Y_d}$	$\dfrac{C}{Y_d}$
1953	3.95	0.916	1965	4.40	0.911
1954	4.11	0.922	1966	4.23	0.911
1955	4.27	0.928	1967	4.33	0.901
1956	4.26	0.913	1968	4.42	0.911
1957	4.25	0.914	1969	4.34	0.920
1958	4.30	0.913	1970	3.98	0.902
1959	4.57	0.925	1971	4.11	0.900
1960	4.50	0.930	1972	4.21	0.915
1961	4.67	0.923	1973	4.12	0.895
1962	4.46	0.926	1974	3.90	0.901
1963	4.59	0.930	1975	3.95	0.895
1964	4.58	0.916	Average 1953–1975	4.28	0.914

Source: Economic Report of the President, 1976 and MPS Data Bank.

ing recessions. It is not clear from Table 5-2 that the argument was factually correct even in the fifties and early sixties, if one looks, say, at the recession years 1954, 1958, and 1961. However, for the moment, let us assume that was a fact. The life-cycle hypothesis explained that fact by the behavior of the ratio of wealth to disposable income during recessions—the ratio of wealth to disposable income was supposed to rise during recessions. Table 5-2 does show the ratio rising from 1953 to 1954 and from 1960 to 1961, so there is some plausibility in the generalization that the wealth–disposable income ratio rose during recessions in the fifties and early sixties. So the life-cycle hypothesis provided a perfectly good explanation of what were believed to be the facts. However, in the recent recession, in 1975, the average propensity to consume was very low, in contrast to what had earlier been believed to be the typical behavior of consumption during recessions. But the life-cycle hypothesis nonetheless provides a good explanation for the low ratio of consumption to disposable income in 1975—for in that year, the ratio of wealth to disposable income is also low.

We have already noted that Eq. (9) reconciles the evidence of a long-run average propensity to consume of about 0.9 with the short-run evidence of a lower marginal propensity to consume. We can see that clearly by examining the equation in conjunction with Table 5-2. Taking Eq. (9) and dividing both sides by Y_d, we obtain

$$\frac{C}{Y_d} = 0.039 \frac{W/P}{Y_d} + 0.74 \qquad (10a)$$

For the period 1953–1975, the average propensity to consume is 0.91, as seen in Table 5-2. The average ratio of wealth to disposable income is 4.28. Now, using Eq. (10a), we find that the equation predicts a ratio of consumption to disposable income equal to 0.91 (= 0.039 × 4.28 + 0.74).[10] Even though the propensity to consume out of disposable income, holding the level of wealth fixed, is only 0.74, the equation predicts an average propensity to consume of 0.91. The difference arises from the relationship between consumption and wealth.

We can also see from Eq. (9) why, as mentioned earlier, the simple consumption function of Eq. (2) should be expected to shift up over time. Over time, the level of wealth rises, and thus the constant term, the intercept $\bar{C}$ in Eq. (2), should be expected to be higher when the equation is estimated using data from a period of high wealth than when it is estimated using data from a period in which wealth is low.

In summary, then, the life-cycle model shows that consumption depends on both real wealth and disposable income. Using round numbers, the marginal propensity to consume out of disposable income is about $c = 0.7$ and the marginal propensity to consume out of wealth is about 0.04. There is obviously a range for these estimates, and the round numbers only serve as a guide that is easy to remember.

Finally, one further interesting implication of the life-cycle hypothesis is that it provides a route for the stock market to affect consumption behavior. The value of stocks held by the public is part of wealth, and should be—and is—included in W/P in Eq. (3). When the value of stocks is high—when the stock market is booming—W/P is high and tends to increase consumption, and the reverse occurs when the stock market is depressed.

5-2 PERMANENT-INCOME THEORY OF CONSUMPTION

In the long run the consumption–income ratio is very stable, but in the short run it fluctuates. The short-run marginal propensity to consume appears to be smaller than the long-run propensity to consume. The life-cycle approach explains these observations by pointing out that people want to maintain a smooth profile of consumption even if their lifetime income profile is uneven, and thus emphasizes the role of wealth in the consumption function. An alternative explanation that differs in the details, but shares entirely the spirit of the life-cycle approach, is the permanent-income theory of consumption.

---

[10]You would do as well not to be too excited about the equation predicting the mean correctly, because linear regression equations of the form of Eq. (9) all have the property that, if the mean values of the variables on the right-hand side of the equation are inserted, the resulting prediction gives the mean value of the left-hand side variable. To understand this point further, you might want to look at Pindyck and Rubinfeld, op. cit.

The theory, which is due to Milton Friedman,[11] argues that people gear their consumption behavior to their permanent or long-term consumption opportunities, not to their current level of income. A suggestive example provided by Friedman involves someone who is paid or receives her income only once a week, on Fridays. But we clearly do not expect that individual to concentrate her entire consumption on that one day on which income is received, with zero consumption on every other day. Again we are persuaded by the argument that individuals prefer a smooth consumption flow rather than plenty today and scarcity tomorrow or yesterday. On that argument consumption on any one day of the week would be unrelated to income on that particular day but would rather be geared to average daily income—that is, income per week divided by the number of days per week. It is clear that in this extreme example, income for a period longer than a day is relevant to the consumption decision. Similarly, Friedman argues, there is nothing special about a period of the length of one year that requires the individual to plan her consumption within the year solely on the basis of income within the year—rather, consumption is planned in relation to income over a longer period.

The idea of consumption spending that is geared to long-term or average or permanent income is appealing, but it leaves two further questions. The first concerns the precise relationship between current consumption and permanent income. The second question is how to make the concept of permanent income operational, that is, how to measure it.

In its simplest form, the permanent-income hypothesis of consumption behavior argues that consumption is proportional to permanent income:

$$C = cY^P \tag{11}$$

where Y^P is permanent (disposable) income. From Eq. (11) consumption varies in the same proportion as permanent income. A 5 percent increase in permanent income raises consumption by 5 percent. Since permanent income should be related to long-run average income, this feature of the consumption function is clearly in line with the observed long-run constancy of the consumption income ratio.

The next problem is how to think of and how to measure permanent income. The question is resolved in a pragmatic way by assuming that permanent income is related to the behavior of current and past incomes. To give a particular, simple example, we might estimate permanent income as a *weighted average* of current and past income:

$$Y^P = \theta Y + (1 - \theta)Y_{-1} \qquad 0 < \theta < 1 \tag{12}$$

where θ is a fraction and Y_{-1} is last year's income. To understand Eq. (12),

[11]Milton Friedman, *A Theory of the Consumption Function*, Princeton University Press, 1957.

assume we had a value of $\theta = 0.6$ and assume this year's income was $Y = \$12,000$ and last year's income was $Y_{-1} = \$11,000$. The value of permanent income would be $Y^P = \$11,600 (= 0.6 \times \$12,000 + 0.4 \times \$11,000)$. Thus, permanent income is an average of the two income levels. Whether it is closer to this year's or last year's income depends on the weight θ given to current income. Clearly, in the extreme with $\theta = 1$, permanent income is equal to current income.

An estimate of permanent income that uses only current and last year's income is an oversimplification. Friedman forms the estimate by looking at incomes in many earlier periods, as well as current income, but with weights that are larger for the more recent, as compared to the more distant incomes.[12] There is no simple theory which would tell us what the relative magnitude of the weights on different incomes should be, except for two considerations. First, income in the distant past—say more than three years ago—should have less influence on permanent income than more recent incomes. Second, current income should have a weight that is less than 1 so that we look at both current and past incomes in forming our estimate. We should also note that we cannot expect a formula like Eq. (12), based on the behavior of income in the past, to include all the factors that influence a person's beliefs about future income. The discovery of a vast amount of oil in a country, for instance, would raise the permanent incomes of the inhabitants of the country as soon as it was announced, even though a (mechanical) formula like Eq. (12) based on past levels of income would not reflect such a change.

There are some special features of Eq. (12) which deserve comment. First, if $Y = Y_{-1}$, that is, if this year's income is equal to last year's, then permanent income is equal to the income earned this year and last year. This guarantees that if an individual had always earned the same income, she would expect to earn that income in the future. Second, note that if income rises this year compared with last year, then permanent income rises by *less* than current income. The reason is that the individual does not know whether the rise in income this year is permanent. Not knowing whether the increase in income will be maintained or not, the individual does not immediately increase the expected or permanent income measure by the full amount of the actual or current increase in income.

Using Eqs. (11) and (12), we can now rewrite the consumption function:

$$C = cY^P = c\theta Y + c(1 - \theta)Y_{-1} \tag{13}$$

The marginal propensity to consume out of *current* income is then just $c\theta$, which is clearly less than the long-run average propensity to consume, c. Hence, the permanent-income hypothesis provides a simple explanation of

---

[12]Friedman also adjusts permanent income by taking into account the growth of income over time.

the difference between the short-run marginal propensity to consume and the long-run marginal (equal to the average) propensity to consume. The reason for the lower short-run marginal propensity to consume is that when current income rises, the individual is not sure that the increase in income will be maintained over the longer period on which she bases her consumption plans. Accordingly, she does not fully adjust her consumption spending to the higher level that would be appropriate if the increase in income were permanent. However, if the increase turns out to be permanent, that is, if next period's income is the same as this period's, then she will (next year) fully adjust her consumption spending to the higher level of income.

The argument is illustrated in Fig. 5-2. Here we show the long-run consumption function as a straight line through the origin with slope c, which is the constant average and marginal propensity to consume out of permanent income. The lower flat consumption function is a short-run consumption function drawn for a given history of income which is reflected in the intercept $c(1 - \theta)Y_0$. The consumption function is therefore appropriate if last year's income was Y_0. Assume in fact that we start out in long-run equilibrium with actual and permanent income equal to Y_0 and consumption therefore equal to cY_0 as is shown at the intersection of long-run and short-run consumption functions at point E. Assume next that income increases to the level Y'. In the short run, which means during the current period, we revise our estimate of permanent income upward by θ times the increase in income and consume a fraction c of that increase in

FIGURE 5-2   THE EFFECT ON
CONSUMPTION OF A SUSTAINED INCREASE
IN INCOME

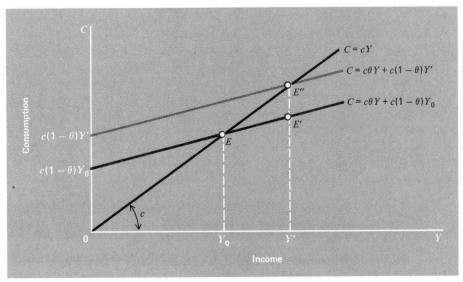

permanent income. Accordingly, consumption moves up along the short-run consumption function to point E'.

Note immediately that in the short run the ratio of consumption to income declines as we move from point E to E'. Going one period ahead and assuming that the increase in income persists so that income remains at Y', we get a shift in the consumption function. The consumption function shifts upward because, as of the given higher level of income, the estimate of permanent income is now revised upward to Y'. Accordingly, consumers want to spend a fraction c of their new estimate of permanent income Y'. The new consumption point is E'', where the ratio of consumption to income is back to the long-run level. The example makes clear the point that in the short run an increase in income causes a decline in the average propensity to consume because people do not anticipate that the increase in income will persist or be permanent. Once they do observe that the increase in income does persist, however, they fully adjust consumption to match their higher permanent income.

Like the life-cycle hypothesis, the permanent-income hypothesis has some other unexpected and interesting implications. Consider for instance the weight that should be given to current income in forming an estimate of permanent income, as a function of the extent to which current income varies for a given individual. An individual whose income has been extremely unstable in the past will not give a large amount of weight to a change in income in any one year. The weight θ in Eq. (13) for such an individual will be relatively small, and his marginal propensity to consume out of current income will accordingly be relatively small. On the other hand, an individual whose income has been very stable in the past will put a lot of weight on changes in current income, and have a relatively large θ in Eq. (13).[13] His marginal propensity to consume out of current income will therefore be relatively large. Friedman shows that this implication is borne out by the facts. Farmers, for instance, have very variable incomes and a low marginal propensity to consume out of current income.

To conclude this section, it is worth considering the relationship between the life-cycle and permanent-income hypotheses briefly. The two hypotheses are not mutually exclusive. The life-cycle hypothesis pays rather more attention to the motives for saving than the permanent-income hypothesis does, and provides convincing theoretical and empirical reasons to include wealth as well as income in the consumption function. The permanent-income hypothesis, on the other hand, pays more careful attention to the way in which individuals form their expectations about their future incomes than the original life-cycle hypothesis does. Recall that current labor income entered the life-cycle consumption function to reflect expectations of future income. The more detailed analysis of the deter-

---

[13]Recall that, although we restricted our measure of permanent income to a two-year average, there is no reason why the average should not be taken over longer periods. If current income is unstable, an appropriate measure of permanent income may well be an average over five or more years.

minants of expected future income that is provided by the permanent-income hypothesis can be and has been included in the life-cycle consumption function.

Indeed, current practice is to combine the expectations formation aspect emphasized by the permanent-income theory and the emphasis on wealth that is suggested by life-cycle consumption theory. Thus we would look for a consumption function with wealth and expected labor income as determinants of consumer spending. Using current and one-period lagged disposable income as proxies for expected labor income, we obtain for the 1953–1975 period the equation

$$C = 0.045 \frac{W}{P} + 0.55Y_d + 0.17Y_{d-1} \tag{14}$$

Equation (14) shows that both current and last period's disposable income affect current consumption, as does current real wealth. A \$1 increase in real wealth, given current and past real disposable income, raises consumption by 4.5 cents. An increase in current real disposable income raises consumption by 55 cents. Furthermore, if that real income increase persists for another period, there will be a further increase in consumption, in response to the lagged income term Y_{d-1}, of 17 cents. The short-run marginal propensity is therefore 0.55 while the long-run marginal propensity is 0.72 (= 0.55 + 0.17).[14]

Equation (14) combines the main features that are emphasized by modern consumption theory.[15] It reflects a low short-run marginal propensity to consume (0.55), and a longer-run marginal propensity to consume of 0.72 that is still small. It also shows the role of wealth which serves to reconcile the low marginal propensities to spend out of disposable income with the observed higher average propensity to consume, or the ratio of consumption to disposable income which is of the order of 0.9.

5-3 THE RELATIVE-INCOME HYPOTHESIS

Modern theories of the consumption function have in common the objective of explaining short-run fluctuations in the ratio of consumption to disposable income combined with virtual constancy of the ratio of consumption to disposable income in the long run. Life-cycle and permanent-income theory explain this behavior as an attempt to maintain a

[14]To fix ideas, the reader should draw a graph of Eq. (14) with consumption on the vertical axis and current disposable income on the horizontal axis. What is the intercept? How does the diagram differ from that in Fig. 5-2? Show now the effects of (1) transitory increases in income, (2) a sustained increase in income, and (3) an increase in wealth.

[15]Interpreting the income coefficients in Eq. (14) in terms of permanent-income theory leads us to conclude that $Y_d{}^P = 0.76Y_d + 0.24Y_{d-1}$. Problem 12 at the end of this chapter raises this question.

smooth flow of consumption that is geared to long-run consumption opportunities, as measured by lifetime income and wealth, or by permanent
income.

An earlier and influential theory along much the same lines is the
relative-income hypothesis that was advanced by James Duesenberry.[16]
The theory argues that current consumption depends not only on current
income but also on the history of income. Individuals build up consumption standards that are geared to their *peak* income levels. If income declines relative to past income, then individuals will not immediately sacrifice the consumption standard they have adopted. There is a *ratchet
effect*, and they will only adjust to a small extent to the decline in current
income. However, there is an asymmetry because an increase in income
relative to past peaks immediately raises the consumption level.

Figure 5-3 shows consumption behavior according to the relative-
income hypothesis. The dark line is the consumption function if current
income is the peak level of income. Thus, if current income is Y_d^0 *and*
exceeds previous levels of income, then consumption would be at point E
on the consumption function $C = cY_d$. If income declined from the level Y_d^0

[16]See James Duesenberry, *Income, Savings and the Theory of Consumer Behavior*, Harvard
University Press, 1952.

FIGURE 5-3 THE RELATIVE-INCOME
HYPOTHESIS

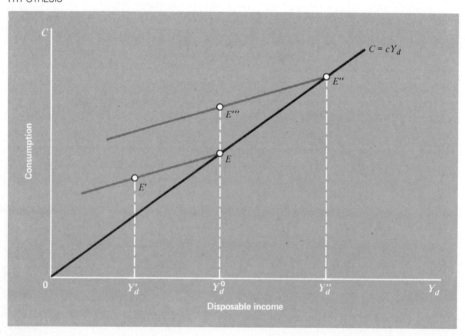

to Y_d', then consumption would adjust along the light schedule to E'. The peak level of income Y_d^0 would continue to influence consumption because it determines the consumption standard that individuals seek to maintain. In the short run, therefore, saving adjusts so as to allow consumption to be maintained close to the habitual level. Assume next that income rose to the level Y_d''. This would be a new peak level of income, and consumption accordingly would rise to E''. If income were to decline back to Y_d^0, the new peak level Y'' would continue to influence consumption so that we would find ourselves at point E'''.

The theory is very suggestive again of the attempt to smooth consumption in the face of income fluctuations. It has an intuitive appeal in its emphasis on consumption standards geared to peak income. It lacks, perhaps, the economic richness that the later theories of the life cycle and permanent income added. Its main shortcoming is the asymmetry that suggests that a current increase in income, if it exceeds a previous peak, immediately induces a new consumption standard. Here the alternative theories are more persuasive in that they suggest a partial adjustment, for both an increase and a decrease in income. But the theory does suggest that, as the level of income rises over time, consumption will rise roughly in proportion, along the line $C = cY_d$.

*5-4 LAGS AND DYNAMICS

This section uses the permanent-income consumption function of the previous section to study how the economy adjusts over time to changes in autonomous spending. In earlier chapters we argued that an increase in autonomous spending would bring about a once-and-for-all increase in income by an amount equal to the multiplier times the increase in autonomous spending. In the context of permanent-income theory, however, we have to distinguish between short-run and long-run marginal propensities. In the short run the marginal propensity to consume is $c\theta$ and thus the multiplier is $1/(1 - c\theta)$. In the long run, by contrast, the marginal propensity is c and therefore the multiplier is $1/(1 - c)$. Clearly, the long-run multiplier exceeds the short-run multiplier. This means that the economy takes time to adjust to a given change in autonomous spending.

We will now look at the adjustment process between short-run and long-run equilibrium as it occurs over time. To be specific, we focus on a simple model where investment spending $\bar{I}$ is the only autonomous spending. Equilibrium in the goods market, as will be recalled from Chap. 3, requires that output equals consumption plus investment. Using the consumption function in Eq. (13), we have[17]

---

[17]We assume for the purposes of this section that income and disposable income are equal so that $Y = Y_d$. The simplification will allow us to focus on the special issues of lags in the simplest possible model.

$$Y = \overline{I} + c\theta Y + c(1 - \theta)Y_{-1} \tag{15}$$

where Y is current income and Y_{-1} is last period's income. We remember, too, that the terms θ and c each are a fraction less than 1, and so is their product $c\theta$, the short-run marginal propensity to consume.

From Eq. (15) we can calculate the short-run equilibrium level of income as[18]

$$Y = \frac{1}{1 - c\theta}\overline{I} + \frac{c(1 - \theta)}{1 - c\theta}Y_{-1} \tag{16}$$

Given past income Y_{-1}, Eq. (16) tells us that an increase in investment spending will raise current income by the short-run multiplier $1/(1 - c\theta)$ times the increase in investment. This is simply the short-run effect, and we have to ask what happens next. Next period, looking back, income will have increased, and accordingly permanent income is revised upward. Consumption spending increases along with the upward revision of permanent income, thereby raising aggregate demand and therefore income. That process will continue over time with rising income leading to an upward revision of permanent income, increased consumption, and further increases in income.

The question naturally arises whether that process is stable and converges to a higher level of income. That is in fact the case. The reason is simply that the marginal propensity to spend is less than 1. As in the earlier analysis, the multiplier-induced expenditures become smaller and smaller until they practically vanish. We shall now proceed to examine the multiplier process in detail.

We do that by going through the sequence of income changes. For goods market equilibrium the change in demand in any period is equal to the change in investment $\Delta \overline{I}$ plus the change in consumption spending ΔC. In any period, we can therefore write

$$\Delta Y = \Delta C + \Delta \overline{I} \tag{17}$$

Now, if we use Eq. (13) we note that

$$\Delta C = c\theta \, \Delta Y + c(1 - \theta) \, \Delta Y_{-1} \tag{18}$$

Combining Eqs. (17) and (18), and after some rearrangement, we obtain

$$\Delta Y = \frac{1}{1 - c\theta}\Delta \overline{I} + \frac{c(1 - \theta)}{1 - c\theta}\Delta Y_{-1} \tag{17a}$$

[18]To go from Eq. (15) to Eq. (16), collect terms in Y to obtain $Y(1 - c\theta) = \overline{I} + c(1 - \theta)Y_{-1}$ and then divide both sides of the equation by $(1 - c\theta)$.

You should note that we could also have derived Eq. (17a) by starting from Eq. (16) and calculating ΔY directly.

Now we can use Eq. (17a) to consider the effects over time of a one-time increase in investment spending of $\overline{\Delta I}$. To bring out the details of the adjustment process, we start from a position of full equilibrium in which income is and has been constant. In year 1 we experience a once-and-for-all increase in investment $\overline{\Delta I}$. The increase in investment and the induced change in current consumption, $c\theta\,\Delta Y$, give rise to a first-period increase in income of $\Delta Y_1 = \overline{\Delta I}/(1 - c\theta)$, which is the first term on the right-hand side of Eq. (17a). This increase in income is shown as the first step in Fig. 5-4, and is also recorded in Table 5-3.

In the next period, there is no further increase in investment, so that $\overline{\Delta I}$ = 0. The only increase in aggregate demand in this period comes from the lagged adjustment in consumption. Consumers' permanent income has risen, because their income last period was higher than in the previous period. Their consumption accordingly rises by $c(1 - \theta)\,\Delta Y_1$. But this lagged adjustment in consumption raises aggregate demand, and therefore induces a further increase in income. The induced increase in income induces a further increase in current consumption equal to $c\theta\,\Delta Y$. The total increase in income in the second year is therefore given by the second term in Eq. (17a), and is shown as the second step in Fig. 5-4. It is also recorded in Table 5-3. For convenience, we define z as

---

FIGURE 5-4 CHANGES IN INCOME CAUSED BY A SUSTAINED INCREASE IN INVESTMENT SPENDING

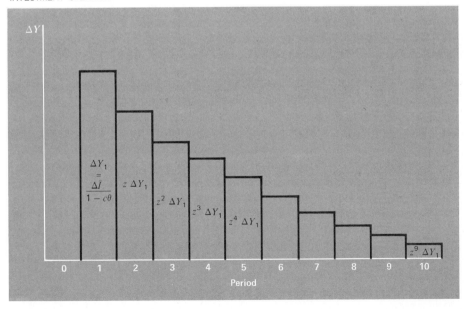

TABLE 5-3 THE DYNAMIC MULTIPLIER PROCESS

Period	ΔY_{-1}	$Y - Y_{-1}$	$Y - Y_0$
0	0	0	0
1	0	$\dfrac{1}{1-c\theta}\overline{\Delta I} = \Delta Y_1$	ΔY_1
2	ΔY_1	$\dfrac{c(1-\theta)}{1-c\theta}\Delta Y_1 = z\,\Delta Y_1$	$\Delta Y_1\,(1+z)$
3	$z\,\Delta Y_1$	$z^2\,\Delta Y_1$	$\Delta Y_1\,(1+z+z^2)$
4	$z^2\,\Delta Y_1$	$z^3\,\Delta Y_1$	$\Delta Y_1\,(1+z+z^2+z^3)$
$\vdots$			
n	$z^{n-2}\,\Delta Y_1$	$z^{n-1}\,\Delta Y_1$	$\Delta Y_1\,(1+z+z^2+\cdots+z^{n-1})$
∞	0	0	$\dfrac{\Delta Y_1}{1-z} = \dfrac{\overline{\Delta I}}{1-c}$

$$z \equiv \frac{c(1-\theta)}{1-c\theta} \tag{19}$$

Now as long as income rises, $\Delta Y > 0$, permanent income rises, and there will continue to be increases in consumption. Today's increase in income gives rise to an increase in consumption today, and also leads to an increase in consumption—and therefore in the level of income—tomorrow. What will stop the process? As in the case of the multiplier studied in Chap. 3, the process will come to an end because the induced consumption increase becomes progressively smaller over time, until it peters out entirely.

From Eq. (17a), after there are no further increases in investment, we have

$$\Delta Y = \frac{c(1-\theta)}{1-c\theta}\Delta Y_{-1} = z\,\Delta Y_{-1} \tag{20}$$

where z is defined in Eq. (19). From Eq. (20), the increase in current income is porportional to the increase in last period's income. The factor of proportionality z is less than 1,[19] so that the increases in income become progressively smaller over time. The increases in income in each period are shown in Fig. 5-4 and also in Table 5-3.

Figure 5-4 and Table 5-3 each show the dynamic process by which the change in investment in the first period sets off subsequent changes in

---

[19]Be sure you can see why z is less than 1. The coefficient z, as we use it here, has no relation to the Z used earlier in the chapter.

income. In period 1, the increase in income is $\overline{\Delta I}/(1 - c\theta)$. This increase is a result of both the investment increase itself and the induced increase in consumption. The multiplier in period 1 is the short-run multiplier $1/(1 - c\theta)$. In period 2, and subsequent periods, there is no increase in investment but there is an increase in consumption resulting from the lagged increase in income—and also from an induced increase in consumption in period 2. The increase in income in period 2 is smaller than that in period 1. Income rises in period 3 and subsequent periods for the same reasons that it rises in period 2, and the increase in income in each later period is smaller—by the factor z—than in the previous period.

Next we want to consider how the changes in income shown in Fig. 5-4 and Table 5-3 add up over time. To get the total change in income occurring as a result of the initial increase in investment spending, we have simply to add up the changes in income in each period. For that purpose, we look at the third column of Table 5-3. The difference between income in period n (Y_n) and income in period zero (Y_0) is given by

$$Y_n - Y_0 = \Delta Y_1(1 + z + z^2 + z^3 + \cdots + z^{n-1}) \tag{21}$$

where n is the period we are considering.

Figure 5-5 shows the *cumulative* change in income in any period occurring as a result of the original increase in investment spending. The total change in income proceeds over time toward the amount given by calculating the total change in income from Eq. (21) for very large values of

FIGURE 5-5 DYNAMIC MULTIPLIER OF AN AUTONOMOUS SPENDING INCREASE

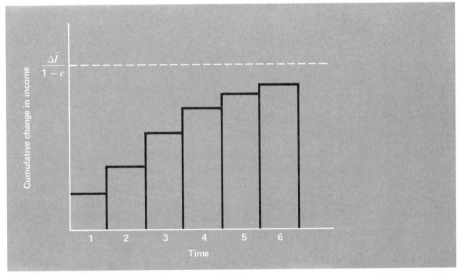

n. We know that the sum of the series $(1 + z + z^2 + \cdots)$ for z less than 1 is $1/(1 - z)$. Denoting the new steady-state level of income by Y^*, we therefore have

$$Y^* - Y_0 = \frac{\Delta Y_1}{1 - z} = \Delta Y_1 \frac{1 - c\theta}{1 - c} \tag{22}$$

Now note that

$$\Delta Y_1 = \frac{\overline{\Delta I}}{1 - c\theta}$$

and then

$$Y^* - Y_0 = \frac{\overline{\Delta I}}{1 - c} \tag{23}$$

As we should expect, the long-run change in income induced by a change in autonomous investment is given by the long-run multiplier $1/(1 - c)$.

Figure 5-5, which shows the cumulative change of income, represents the *dynamic multiplier* for autonomous spending, such as investment or government spending. It shows the *time path* of the change in income in response to a change in autonomous investment ($\overline{\Delta I}$), rather than the ultimate effect that is given by the simple multiplier $1/(1 - c)$. Dynamic multipliers are of great importance from the viewpoint of policy because they specify the effects that a given action has on a variable in the current as well as all subsequent periods. Examining a dynamic multiplier drives home the point that a given policy action does not have all its effects on income, or on any other economic variable, immediately. At any one time, the level of income will be affected by the values of policy variables at different points in the past.

Policy Implications

Consider now the policy implications of the permanent-income consumption function. Suppose there is a full-employment level of output Y_p, and suppose that policy makers wish to ensure that aggregate demand is at all times sufficient to maintain full employment. Assume next that there is for some reason a permanent decline in autonomous investment spending. The previous analysis has shown that in the short run, income would decline by $\overline{\Delta I}/(1 - c\theta)$ and would keep declining until it had fallen by $\overline{\Delta I}/(1 - c)$. Clearly, demand would fall below the full-employment level of output and an expansionary policy is called for.

One such policy would be to raise transfers and thus raise disposable income. With a short-run marginal propensity to consume out of income equal to $c\theta$, the required increase in transfers in the first period is $\Delta \overline{R} = \Delta \overline{I}/c\theta$. With that increase in transfers, consumption will expand by exactly the reduction in investment and thus make up the shortfall in demand. Thus, output remains unchanged at the full-employment level Y_p.

Suppose that the policy makers keep transfers at their new higher level. Now think of the next time period. Since disposable income has risen owing to the transfers, and since the increase persists, individuals will come to further revise upward their estimate of permanent income to the full increase in transfers. Thus, the perceived increase in permanent income in this period is $(1 - \theta) \Delta \overline{R}$, and accordingly an increase in consumption spending by $c(1 - \theta) \Delta \overline{R}$ is induced. This increase in consumption spending—if overlooked by a policy maker—will give rise to an increase in income and induced expenditures so that income rises by $c(1 - \theta)/(1 - c\theta)$ times the increase in transfers. We can go through the process over time and find that ultimately income is raised as a result of transfers by $c \Delta \overline{R}/ (1 - c)$, and is reduced because of reduction in investment by $\Delta \overline{I}/(1 - c)$. The net effect is therefore an increase in income equal to $(1 - \theta)/\theta(1 - c)$ times the initial reduction in investment.

Clearly policy went wrong. A policy designed to stabilize the level of income in the face of a reduction in investment wound up raising income. The point is that policy makers forgot about the permanent-income aspect of consumption, and thus forgot about the induced consumption effects that occur over time. What then would have been the correct policy? The correct policy would indeed require an additional increase in transfers $\Delta \overline{R} = \Delta \overline{I}/c\theta$ so as to immediately restore demand to the full-employment level. Next, however, policy recognizes that there is a difference between the short-run and long-run propensity to consume. The long-run propensity is equal to c rather than $c\theta$, and accordingly in the long run the transfer only needs to be $\Delta \overline{R} = \Delta \overline{I}/c$. The appropriate policy is therefore an immediate increase in transfers to offset exactly the reduction in investment, and then a scaling down of the transfers until they reach the lower long-run level.

There is the further question of how fast the transfers should be reduced back from their initial level toward the long-run level. The answer is that we want consumption to maintain its higher level. Therefore in the second period permanent income has to be held constant. That is, the increase in permanent income due to last period's increase in transfers has to be precisely offset by a reduction in current transfers below last period's transfers.

In Chap. 9 and 10 we shall return to the question of lags in behavior and the implications for policy. We simply note here that the question has indeed been critical in an important policy context. The policy error involved the tax increase in 1968 which the public recognized as not permanent. The tax increase was needed to reduce aggregate demand. Given that the tax increase was not considered permanent, it had very little impact on aggregate demand and certainly a smaller impact than the policy makers had predicted. By contrast a permanent tax increase, if it is perceived as such, may well have a strong immediate impact on demand as people immediately make the full adjustment in their calculation of permanent income.

The alternative theories of consumption we have presented in this chapter all include current disposable income among the factors that explain consumption behavior. Each, however, points to other factors that also affect consumption. These other factors—wealth and lagged income—have to be taken account of when consumption spending is predicted for policy purposes. Large-scale econometric models do indeed embody more sophisticated consumption theories than the simple consumption function (1) of this and earlier chapters.

5-5 SUMMARY

This chapter has studied the consumption function in great detail.

1　The chapter starts out with the simple keynesian consumption function

$$C = 18.7 + 0.88Y_d \qquad (2)$$

and finds that such a consumption function accounts well for observed consumption behavior. The equation suggests that out of an additional dollar disposable income, 88 cents are spent on consumption. The consumption function implies, too, that the ratio of consumption to income, C/Y_d, declines with the level of income.

2　Early empirical work on short-run consumption behavior showed that the marginal propensity to consume was lower than that found in longer-period studies. The evidence showed also that the average propensity to consume declined with the level of income. Long-run studies, by contrast, find a relatively constant average propensity to consume of about 0.9.

3　The evidence is reconciled by a reconsideration of consumption theory. Individuals will want to maintain relatively smooth consumption profiles over their lifetime. Their consumption behavior is geared to their long-term consumption opportunities—permanent income or lifetime income plus wealth. With such a view, current income is only one of the determinants of consumption spending. Wealth and expected income play a role, too. A consumption function that represents this idea is

$$C = 0.045\,\frac{W}{P} + 0.55Y_d + 0.17Y_{d-1} \qquad (14)$$

which allows for the role of real wealth W/P, current disposable income Y_d, and lagged disposable income Y_{d-1}. The consumption function implies that a dollar increase in wealth raises consumption by 4.5 cents. A sustained \$1 increase in income raises consumption in the first year by 55 cents and in the second year by a further 17 cents. The long-run marginal propensity to consume out of income is only 0.72, but the long-run average propensity to consume is—as a result of the presence of wealth—0.91.

4 The relative-income hypothesis argues that current consumption is related not only to current income, but also to previous peak income. The argument for this is that individuals find it difficult to reduce rates of consumption to which they have become accustomed.

5 Lagged adjustment of consumption to income results in a gradual adjustment of the level of income in the economy to changes in autonomous spending and other economic changes. An increase in autonomous spending raises income. But the adjustment process is spread out over time because the rising level of income raises consumption only gradually. This adjustment process is described by dynamic multipliers that show by how much income changes in each period following a change in autonomous spending (or other exogenous variables).

6 The dynamic adjustment of the economy to changes in policy variables, such as a change in government spending or transfers, creates a problem for policy making. The analysis of Sec. 5-4 shows that the policy maker needs detailed information about the dynamic responses of the economy, if policy is not to result in income levels that differ from the target levels. In a dynamic setting, the making of policy requires the policy maker to consider how much any particular policy action will affect income in each time period, and to calculate *time paths* for policy variables that will bring about the desired performance.

PROBLEMS

1 What is the significance of the ratio of consumption to GNP in terms of the level of economic activity? Woud you expect it to be higher or lower than normal during a recession (or depression)? Do you think the ratio would be higher in developed or underdeveloped countries? Why?

The Life-Cycle Hypothesis

2 The text states that the propensity to consume out of accumulated savings declines over time until retirement.
  a Why? What assumption about consumption behavior leads to this result?
  b What happens to this (average) propensity after retirement?

3 a Suppose you earn just as much as your neighbor, but are in much better health and expect to live longer than she does. Would you consume more or less than she does? Why? Derive this from Eq. (5).

b According to the life-cycle hypothesis, what would the effect of the Social Security system be on your average propensity to consume out of (disposable) income?

c How would Eq. (8) be modified for an individual who expects to receive $x per year of retirement benefits? Verify your result in 3b.

4 Give an intuitive interpretation of the marginal propensities to consume out of wealth and income at time T in the individual's lifetime in Eq. (8).

*5 In Eq. (5), consumption in each year of working life is given by

$$C = \left[\frac{N}{L}\right] Z \tag{5}$$

In Eq. (8), consumption is given as

$$C = a\frac{W}{P} + cZ \qquad a \equiv \frac{1}{L - T} \qquad c \equiv \frac{N - T}{L - T} \tag{8}$$

Show that Eqs. (5) and (8) are consistent for an individual who started life with zero wealth and has been saving for T years. (Hint: First, calculate the individual's wealth after T years of saving at rate $Z - C$. Then calculate the level of consumption implied by Eq. (8) when wealth is at the level you have computed.)

Permanent-Income Hypothesis

6 In terms of the permanent-income hypothesis, would you consume more of your Christmas bonus if:

a You knew there was a bonus every year.

b This was the only year such bonuses were given out.

7 Suppose that permanent income is calculated as the average of income over the past five years, i.e.,

$$Y^P = \tfrac{1}{5}\left(Y + Y_{-1} + Y_{-2} + Y_{-3} + Y_{-4}\right)$$

Suppose further that consumption is given by $C = 0.9Y^P$.

a If you have earned $10,000 per year for the past ten years, what is your permanent income?

b Suppose next year (period $t + 1$) you earn $15,000. What is your new Y^P?

c What is your consumption this year and next year?

d What is your short-run MPC? Long-run?

e Assuming you continue to earn $15,000 starting in period $t + 1$, graph the value of your permanent income in each period using the equation above.

8 Explain why good gamblers (and thieves) might be expected to live very well even in years when they don't do well at all.

*9 The graph (bottom of page) shows the lifetime earnings profile of a person who lives for four periods and earns incomes of $30, $60, and $90 in the first three periods of the life cycle. There are no earnings during retirement.

a You are asked to determine the level of consumption, compatible with the budget constraint, for someone who wants an even consumption profile throughout the life cycle. Indicate in which periods the person saves and dissaves and what amounts.

b Assume now that contrary to 9a there is no possibility for borrowing. The credit markets are closed to the individual. Under this assumption, what is the flow of consumption the individual will pick over the life cycle? In providing an answer, continue to assume that, if possible, an even flow of consumption is preferred.

c Assume next that the person described in 9b receives an increase in wealth or nonlabor income. The increase in wealth is equal to $13. How will that wealth be allocated over the life cycle with and without access to the credit market? How would your answer differ if the increase in wealth were $23.

*10 Consider the consumption function in Eq. (14). Assume autonomous investment spending is constant, as is government spending. The economy is close to full employment and the government wishes to maintain aggregate demand precisely constant. In these circumstances, assume there is an increase in real wealth of $10 billion. What change in income taxes will maintain constant the equilibrium level of income in the present period? What further changes in taxes are required next year? The year after that?

*11 Assume the income tax rate is $t = 0.2$. Using Eq. (14) and the information from Sec. 5-4, determine the size of the short-run and long-run multipliers.

12 Equation (14) shows consumption as a function of wealth, current and lagged

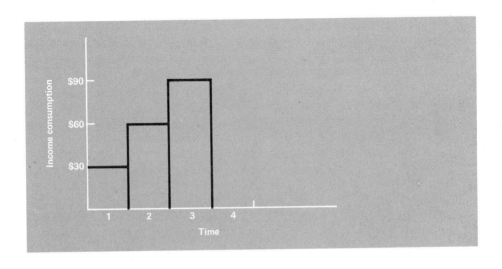

disposable income. To reconcile that consumption function with permanent income expectations formation, you are asked to use Eq. (12) and the consumption function

$$C = a\frac{W}{P} + cY_d^P$$

to determine what is the magnitude of θ and $(1 - \theta)$ that is implied by Eq. (14).

6

*Investment Spending

n this chapter we continue our in-depth analysis of the macroeconomic relationships of the IS-LM model studied in Chap. 4. Chapter 5 moved beyond the simple consumption function of Chap. 3, paying particular attention to the role of lags and the precise way in which income enters the consumption function. Similarly, this chapter moves beyond the simple investment function of Chap. 4, in which investment was treated as a function of the interest rate. This chapter will provide a theoretical foundation for understanding how interest rates affect the level of investment. In addition, we will see how lags and variables other than interest rates—including tax rates—also affect the rate of investment.

Why study investment spending? In the first place, investment is a significant component of aggregate demand. The share of investment spending in GNP is shown in Chart 6-1. In 1975, it accounted for 12 percent of aggregate demand, and it was as high as 19 percent of aggregate demand in 1950. Clearly investment spending constitutes a much smaller part of aggregate demand than consumption spending. Nonetheless, it plays an important role in the fluctuations of GNP over the course of the business cycle, because it varies proportionately much more than consumption spending. Chart 6-1 also highlights the role of investment in relation to the business cycle. Gross investment as a percentage of GNP is plotted along with the unemployment rate (note that the scale for the unemployment rate is reversed). There is quite clearly a relationship between fluc-

CHART 6-1 GROSS INVESTMENT AS A PERCENTAGE OF GNP, AND THE UNEMPLOYMENT RATE. (Source: *Economic Report of the President*, 1976)

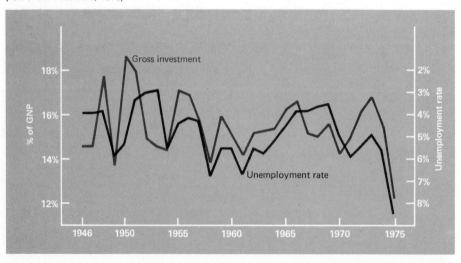

tuations in the level of economic activity, as indicated by the unemployment rate, and the share of investment spending in income. When unemployment is high, investment spending as a fraction of income is low, and vice versa. Indeed, this relationship goes back a long way. During the Great Depression, investment spending was under 4 percent of GNP in both 1932 and 1933.

Second, investment is important because it is a category of aggregate demand that is significantly affected by both monetary and fiscal policy. For instance, changes in the investment tax credit (to be described later) are a standard tool of fiscal policy, designed to affect investment spending. Monetary policy, too, has an important effect on investment, particularly on residential construction. Thus, changes in investment spending constitute one of the major channels by which monetary and fiscal policy affect aggregate demand.

One simple relationship is vital to the understanding of investment. *Investment is spending devoted to increasing or maintaining the stock of capital.* The stock of capital consists of the factories, machines, offices, and other durable manmade products used in the process of production. The capital stock also consists of residential housing as well as inventories. And investment is spending that adds to these components of capital stock. In this regard, it is necessary to recall the distinction drawn in Chap. 2 between *gross* and *net investment*. Gross investment represents total additions to the capital stock. Net investment subtracts depreciation—the reduction in the capital stock that occurs each period through wear and tear and the simple ravages of time—from gross investment. Net investment thus measures the increase in the capital stock in a given period of time.

In this chapter we disaggregate investment spending into three categories. The first is *business fixed investment*, consisting of business firms' spending on durable machinery, equipment, and structures, such as factories and machines. The second is *residential investment*, consisting largely of investment in housing. And the third is *inventory investment*, some elements of which were discussed in Chap. 3.

In 1976, investment spending in the three categories was as shown in Table 6-1. Chart 6-2 shows the components of investment spending in the post-World War II period. Inventory investment and residential investment fluctuate more, as a share of GNP, than business fixed investment does. Business fixed investment is, however, the largest component of investment spending. Note that the negative inventory investment in 1975 seen in Chart 6-2 is unusual, and that over most of the postwar period, inventory investment has been positive.[1]

---

[1] How can inventory investment be negative? Recall that investment is spending on *increases* in capital. In some years inventories are actually reduced rather than increased, and it is in those years that inventory investment is negative.

TABLE 6-1 GROSS DOMESTIC PRIVATE INVESTMENT IN 1976 *(In billions of dollars)*

1. Business fixed investment	160.0
2. Residential investment	67.7
Total fixed investment	227.7
3. Change in inventories	11.9
Gross private	
domestic investment	239.6

Source: Survey of Current Business, May 1977.

In the remainder of this chapter, we develop theories and discuss evidence about the determinants of the rate of investment in each of the three major categories shown in Chart 6-2.

6-1 BUSINESS FIXED INVESTMENT

The machinery, equipment, and structures used in the production of goods and services constitute the *stock* of business fixed capital. Our analysis of business fixed investment proceeds in two stages. First, we ask how much capital firms would like to use, given the costs and returns of using capital. That is, we ask what determines the *desired capital stock*. The desired capital stock is the capital stock which firms would like to have in the long run, abstracting from the delays they face in adjusting their use of capital. However, because it takes time to order new machines, build factories, and install the machines, firms cannot instantly adjust the stock of capital used in production. Second, therefore, we discuss the rate at which firms adjust from their existing capital stock toward the desired level of capital stock, over the course of time. The rate of adjustment determines how much firms spend on adding to the capital stock in each period; that is, it determines the rate of investment.

The Desired Capital Stock: Overview

Firms use capital, along with labor, to produce goods and services for sale. In deciding how much capital to use in production, they have to balance the contribution that more capital makes to their profits against the cost of using more capital. The contribution that an extra unit of capital makes to profits is determined by the *marginal product of capital*, the extra amount of output that can be produced by using that unit of capital. The cost of using more capital is known as the *rental cost of capital*, or the *user cost of capital*.

To derive the rental cost of capital, it is appropriate to think of the firm as financing the purchase of the capital (whether the firm produces the capital itself or buys it from some other firm) by borrowing, at an interest cost i. In order to obtain the services of an extra unit of capital, each period the firm must pay the interest cost i for each dollar of capital that it buys.[2] Thus the basic measure of the rental cost of capital is the interest rate. Later we shall go into much more detail about the rental cost of capital, but for the meantime we shall think of the interest rate as determining the rental cost.

In deciding how much capital they would like to use in production, firms compare the value of the marginal product of capital with the user or rental cost of capital. If the rental cost of capital is high, the marginal product of capital will have to be high for firms to be willing to pay the high cost of using the capital. If the rental cost of capital—the cost of using capital—is low, firms will be willing to use capital even if its marginal product is low.

To give content to this relationship, we have to specify what deter-

[2]Even if the firm finances the investment out of profits it has made in the past—retained earnings—it should still think of the interest rate as the cost of using the new capital, since it could otherwise have lent out those funds and earned interest on them, or paid them out as dividends to shareholders.

CHART 6-2 COMPONENTS OF INVEST-MENT SPENDING AS A PERCENTAGE OF GNP, 1946–1975. (Source: *Economic Report of the President,* 1976)

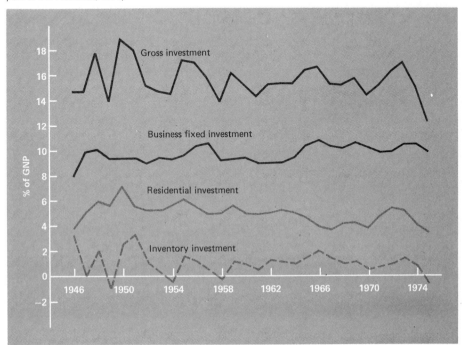

mines the productivity of capital and what determines the user (rental) cost of capital. The marginal product of capital is examined next, and then we turn to the rental cost of the capital.

The Marginal Productivity of Capital

In understanding the marginal productivity of capital, it is important to note that firms can substitute capital for labor in the production of output. Different combinations of capital and labor can be used to produce a given level of output. If labor is relatively cheap, the firm will want to use relatively more labor, and if capital is relatively cheap, the firm will want to use relatively more capital.

As the firm combines progressively more capital with relatively less labor in the production of a *given* amount of output, the marginal product of capital declines. This relation is shown in the downward-sloping schedules in Fig. 6-1. Those schedules show how the marginal product of capital falls as more capital is used in producing a given level of output. The schedule Y_1Y_1 is drawn for a level of output Y_1. The schedule Y_2Y_2 is drawn for the higher output level Y_2. The marginal product of capital, given the capital stock, say K_0, is higher on the schedule Y_2Y_2 than on Y_1Y_1. That is because more labor is being used in combination with the given amount of capital K_0 to produce the level of output Y_2 than to produce Y_1.

Figure 6-1 shows the marginal product of capital in relation to the level of output, and the amount of capital being used to produce that output. Figure 6-2 is a similar diagram which shows the desired capital stock, as related to the rental cost of capital and the level of output. Given the level of output, say Y_1, the firm will want to use more capital the lower the rental cost of capital—because at low rental costs of capital, it can afford to use capital even when its marginal productivity is quite low. If the rental cost of capital is high, the firm will be willing to use capital only if its marginal productivity is high—which means that the firm will not want to use very much capital. In producing a higher level of output, say Y_2, the firm will use both more capital and more labor, given the rental cost of capital.[3] Therefore, at higher levels of output, the desired capital stock is higher.

The general relationship among the desired capital stock (K^*), the rental cost of capital (i_c), and the level of output, is given by

$$K^* = g(i_c, Y) \tag{1}$$

Equation (1) indicates that the desired capital stock depends on the rental cost of capital and the level of output. The lower the rental cost of capital,

---

[3]Throughout this discussion, we have implicitly been assuming that the real wage paid to labor is given and does not change as the rental cost of capital changes.

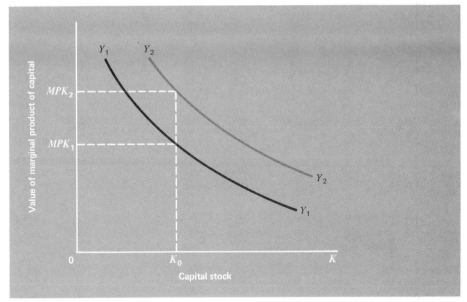

FIGURE 6-1 THE MARGINAL PRODUCT
OF CAPITAL IN RELATION TO THE LEVEL OF
OUTPUT AND THE CAPITAL STOCK

the larger the desired capital stock. And the greater the level of output, the larger the desired capital stock.

The Cobb-Douglas Production Function

While Eq. (1) provides the general relationship determining the desired capital stock, a particular form of the equation, based on the Cobb-Douglas production function,[4] is frequently used in studies of investment behavior. The particular equation that is used is

$$K^* = \frac{aY}{i_c} \qquad (2)$$

[4]The Cobb-Douglas production function is written in the form

$$Y = N^{1-a}K^a \qquad 1 > a > 0$$

where N is the amount of labor used. This production function is particularly popular because it is easy to handle, and also because it appears to fit the facts of United States economic experience quite well. The coefficient a appearing in Eq. (2) is the same as the a of the production function. The reader trained in calculus will want to show that a is the share of capital in total income.

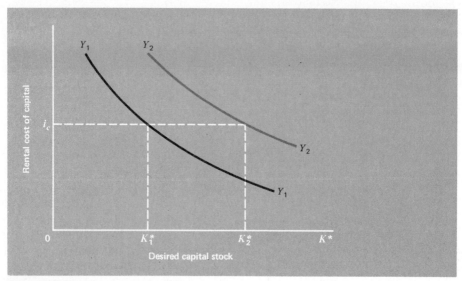

FIGURE 6-2 THE DESIRED CAPITAL
STOCK IN RELATION TO THE LEVEL OF
OUTPUT AND THE RENTAL COST OF CAPI-
TAL

where a is a constant (which is not the same as the a used in other chapters). In this case, the desired capital stock varies in proportion to output. Given output, the desired capital stock varies inversely with the rental cost of capital.

Expected Output

In determining the desired capital stock, the relevant time period for which the decision on the capital stock applies is obviously an important issue. In this section we are discussing the capital stock that the firm desires to hold at some future time. Accordingly, the level of output in Eqs. (1) and (2) should be the level of output which firms expect to be producing at that time. For some investments—such as that in machinery to produce hula hoops—the future time at which the output will be produced is a matter of months or even weeks. For other investments—such as that in airplane factories—the future time at which the output will be produced is years away.

    This suggests that the notion of permanent income (in this case permanent output) is relevant to investment as well as consumption. For longer-lived investments, the firm's capital demand is governed primarily by its views on the level of output it will be producing on average in the future.

The firm's long-run demand for business fixed capital, depending on the normal or permanent level of output, is thus relatively independent of the current level of output, and depends on *expectations* of future output levels. However, it is affected by current output to the extent that current output affects expectations of permanent output.

Summary on the Desired Capital Stock

It is worthwhile stepping back for a moment to summarize the main results so far.

1   The firm's demand for capital—the desired capital stock K^*—depends on the rental cost of capital i_c and the expected level of output.
2   Firms balance the costs and benefits of using capital. The lower the rental cost of capital, the larger the optimal level of capital relative to output. This relation reflects the lower marginal productivity of capital when it is used relatively intensively. The intensive use of capital will be profitable only if the rental cost of capital is low.
3   The higher the level of output, the larger the desired capital stock.
4   The firm plans its capital stock in relation to expected future or permanent output.
5   Current output affects capital demand to the extent that it affects expectations about future output.

The Rental Cost of Capital Again

We have already introduced the notion of the rental or user cost of capital in determining the firm's desired capital stock. As a first approximation, we identified the rental cost of capital with the interest rate, on the argument that firms would have to borrow to finance their use of capital. Now we go into more detail on the costs per period of using capital.

To use capital for a single period, say a year, the firm can be thought of as buying the capital with borrowed funds and paying the interest on the borrowing. At the end of the year, the firm will still have some of the capital left. But the capital is likely to have depreciated over the course of the year. We shall assume that the firm intends to continue using the remaining capital in production in future years, and that its depreciation simply represents the using up of the capital in the process of production—physical wear and tear. We shall now examine the rental cost, taking into account interest costs and depreciation. Although taxes affect the cost to the firm of using capital, we shall for the meantime ignore taxes and return to them later.

Leaving aside taxes, we want now to examine the two elements in the rental cost of capital in more detail. For the moment let us write the interest cost as i. Insofar as depreciation is concerned, we assume that a fixed proportion d of the capital is used up per period. At the end of the period, the firm has proportion $(1-d)$ of the original capital left, which it can continue to use in the production process. The depreciation cost, per dollar of capital, is d.[5] The rental cost, or user cost, of capital, per dollar's worth of capital, which we denote by i_c, is therefore

$$i_c \equiv i + d \qquad (3)$$

A simple numerical example should help in understanding Eq. (3). Suppose the interest rate is 10 percent per year, and the rate of depreciation is 15 percent. That means that at the end of the year, the firm will have used up 15 percent of the capital. The costs to the firm of using the capital for the year are then the interest cost, 10 cents per dollar of capital, and the depreciation cost, 15 cents per dollar of capital. The cost of using capital for a year is thus 25 cents per dollar's worth of capital.

The Real Rate of Interest

It is time now to examine the interest component of the rental cost of capital in more detail. We have not so far distinguished between the *real* and the *nominal* rates of interest. The real rate of interest is the nominal rate of interest minus the rate of inflation. In general, someone borrowing at a stated nominal rate of interest, say 10 percent, does not know what the rate of inflation over the period for which she is borrowing will be. Accordingly, the real rate of interest relevant when a loan transaction is entered into, is the *expected* real rate of interest—the stated nominal interest rate minus the rate of inflation expected over the period of the loan.

The notion of the real rate of interest is extremely important. Suppose that the nominal interest rate, the rate stated in the loan agreement, is 10 percent. Then suppose also that prices are rising at 10 percent. Someone borrowing $100 at the beginning of the year pays back $110 at the end of the year. But those dollars in which repayment is made buy less goods than the dollars lent at the beginning of the year when the loan was made. If the inflation rate is 10 percent, then the $110 paid at the end of the year buys the same amount of goods that could have been bought with the original $100 at the beginning of the year. In *real* terms, in terms of the goods which the money can buy, the lender has no more at the end than at the beginning of the year. Thus the *real* interest rate received was zero, even though the *nominal* interest rate was 10 percent. Putting things slightly differently, given the *nominal* interest rate, the higher the rate of

---

[5]Why is depreciation considered as a cost? We want to remind ourselves that the firm continues using the capital and therefore has to devote expenditures to maintaining the productive efficiency of capital and thus offset wear and tear. We are assuming that per dollar of capital d dollars per period are required to maintain productive efficiency.

inflation, the lower the *real* interest rate. In practice, nominal interest rates tend to be higher when inflation is higher.

Now it is the *expected real* rate of interest that should enter the calculation of the rental cost of capital. Why? The firm is borrowing in order to produce goods for sale. On average, across all firms, it is reasonable to believe that the prices of the goods the firms sell will be rising along with the general price level. Thus the value of what the firm will be producing in the future will be rising with the price level, but the nominal amount of interest it has to pay back on account of its borrowings does not rise with the price level. The real value of the debt it has incurred by borrowing will be falling over time, as a result of inflation, and it should take that reduction in the real value of its outstanding debts into account in deciding how much capital to employ. To put it differently, the firm will be paying off its debts with dollars of lower real value than the dollars it borrowed.

Accordingly, we can be more precise in the way we write Eq. (3) for the rental cost of capital. We write the rental cost of capital, taking account of expected inflation at the rate π^*, as

$$i_c \equiv i_r + d \equiv i - \pi^* + d \qquad (4)$$

where i_r is the real interest rate, i the nominal interest rate, and

$$i_r \equiv i - \pi^* \qquad (5)$$

Equation (5) states that the real rate of interest is the nominal interest rate minus the expected rate of inflation. Implicitly, Eq. (5) refers to the expected real rate of interest. At the end of the period, when the rate of inflation is known, we can also state what the *actual* or realized real rate of interest for the period was—namely, the nominal interest rate i minus the actual rate of inflation.

To reiterate, it is important to note that the interest rate relevant to the firm's demand for capital is the *real* rate, and not the nominal rate. This makes it clear that the nominal rate of interest is not a good guide to the rental cost of capital. If the rate of inflation is zero and is expected to be zero, and the nominal interest rate is 5 percent, then the real interest rate is 5 percent. By contrast, if the nominal interest rate is 10 percent and inflation is at the rate of 10 percent, the real interest rate is zero. Other things equal, the desired capital stock in this example would tend to be higher with the nominal interest rate of 10 percent than with the nominal rate of 5 percent—because those rates correspond to real rates of zero and 5 percent respectively. As you have no doubt deduced, and as we shall show below, investment spending tends to be higher when the rental cost of capital is lower. But because of the distinction between real and nominal interest rates, that is *not* the same as saying that investment tends to be higher when the nominal rate of interest is lower.

Taxes and the Rental Cost of Capital

We turn next to the role of taxation in affecting the rental cost of capital, and focus on two fiscal variables: the investment tax credit and the corporate income tax.[6] The investment tax credit allows firms to deduct from their taxes a certain fraction, say τ, of their investment expenditures in each year. For instance, suppose the investment tax credit is 7 percent, or 7 cents per dollar. Then a firm spending $1 million for investment purposes in a given year can deduct 7 percent of the $1 million, or $70,000, from the taxes it would otherwise have to pay the federal government. The investment tax credit should therefore reduce the rental cost of capital. We shall assume for convenience that the corporate income tax is a tax at rate t on the firm's profits.[7] That is, the firm pays t cents of taxes to the government per dollar of profit that it earns. We shall see below that the corporate income tax can be thought of as increasing the rental cost of capital.

Consider first the investment tax credit. Essentially, the investment tax credit reduces the price of a capital good to the firm by the ratio $(1-\tau)$, since the Treasury returns to the firm a fraction τ per dollar of the cost of the capital good. Accordingly, Eq. (4) is modified to

$$i_c \equiv (1 - \tau)(i + d - \pi^*) \qquad (4a)$$

The Treasury pays the firm τ percent of the cost of buying a capital good, so the rental cost, per dollar's worth of capital used in production, is reduced by the factor $(1 - \tau)$. It is thus clear that the investment tax credit does reduce the rental cost of capital to the firm.

The corporate income tax does not directly affect the rental cost of capital to the firm. But recall that the firm considers the value of the marginal product of capital in making its investment decisions. However, the relevant marginal product of capital is the marginal product *after tax*, because it is the after-tax return that the firm receives. If the value of the marginal product of 1 dollar's worth of capital is 20 cents, and the firm pays taxes at a 50 percent rate, then the contribution of that capital to the profits actually received by the firm is only 10 cents. Accordingly, the firm will calculate the after-tax marginal product of capital, that is, $(1 - t)$ times the pretax marginal product—the amount it actually receives after taxes from using one more unit of capital—in making its investment decisions. It is

[6]In addition, the tax system allows deductions from income to reflect depreciation, but we shall not discuss the depreciation adjustment here. For details see E. Cary Brown, "The New Depreciation Policy under the Income Tax: An Economic Analysis," *National Tax Journal*, March 1955, and "Tax Incentives for Investment," *American Economic Review*, May 1962, and Norman Ture, "Tax Reform: Depreciation Problems," *American Economic Review*, May 1963.

[7]The corporate income tax rate reaches its maximum 48 percent at the profit level of $50,000. From the viewpoint of large firms, the tax is practically a constant proportion of profits.

convenient, though not strictly accurate,[8] to embody this modification due to taxes by redefining the rental cost of capital so that

$$i_c \equiv \frac{(1-\tau)(i+d-\pi^*)}{1-t} \qquad (6)$$

Equation (6) shows how the investment tax credit reduces, and the corporate income tax increases, the rental cost of capital. Since π^* is the expected rate of inflation, i_c is the *expected* rental cost of capital.

Summary, and the Effects of Fiscal and Monetary Policy on the Desired Capital Stock

To summarize, we review our results in terms of the special Cobb-Douglas functional form, Eq. (2), for the desired capital stock. Substituting the formula for the user cost of capital in Eq. (6) into Eq. (2) yields Eq. (7) as the desired capital stock:

$$K^* = \frac{aY(1-t)}{(1-\tau)(i+d-\pi^*)} \qquad (7)$$

Equation (7) shows, as before, that capital demand varies in proportion to output. In addition, capital demand is larger the smaller the corporate income tax rate t, the lower the nominal interest rate i, and the smaller the rate of depreciation d. A high investment tax credit rate τ, or a high expected inflation rate, *given* the nominal interest rate i, will raise capital demand.

The major significance of Eq. (7) is that it implies that monetary and fiscal policy affect the desired capital stock. Fiscal policy exerts an effect through both the corporate tax rate t and the investment tax credit rate τ. Both these instruments were used in the 1960s to affect capital demand and thus investment spending, as will be seen in Chap. 10.

Monetary policy affects capital demand by affecting the market interest rate. The manner in which monetary policy affects capital demand is by changing the real market rate of interest relative to the marginal productivity of capital.[9] In that manner the profitability of owning and operating

---

[8]There are three reasons it is not strictly accurate. First, the corporate income tax does not directly affect the rental cost of capital itself, but rather the after-tax value of the marginal product of capital. Second, the corporate income tax does not adjust the costs of borrowing to reflect the effects of inflation. Firms are allowed to treat the nominal interest cost of their borrowing as a business expense, rather than the real cost. Equation (6) implies instead that firms are allowed to treat only *real* interest costs as a business expense. Third, the tax system has special treatment of depreciation.

[9]We should note that the Federal Reserve System is able to affect *nominal* interest rates directly by its sales and purchases of bonds. Its ability to control real interest rates is more limited.

capital is affected, and thus the demand for capital is affected. A lowering of the nominal interest rate by the Federal Reserve System (given the expected inflation rate), as reflected in a downward shift in the LM curve of Chap. 4, will induce firms to hold more capital. This expansion in capital demand in turn will affect investment spending, as we shall now see.

From Desired Capital Stock to Investment

We have now put more content into the general form of Eq. (1) for the desired capital stock, by transforming it into Eq. (7). At any given time, the actual capital stock will almost certainly differ from the capital stock firms would like to have. How then do firms change their capital stocks in order to move toward the desired capital stock? In particular, is there any reason why firms do not attempt to move to their desired capital stocks immediately?

Since it takes time to plan and complete an investment project, and because attempts to invest quickly are likely to be more expensive than gradual adjustment of the capital stock, it is unlikely that firms would attempt to adjust their capital stocks to the long-run desired level instantaneously. Very rapid adjustment of the capital stock would require crash programs by the firm which would distract management from its routine tasks and interfere with ongoing production. Thus, firms generally plan to adjust their capital stocks gradually over a period of time, rather than immediately.

The Flexible Accelerator

There are a number of hypotheses about the way in which firms plan to adjust their capital stock over time; we single out the *flexible accelerator hypothesis* here.[10] The basic notion behind the flexible accelerator hypothesis is that the larger the gap between the existing capital stock and the desired capital stock, the greater a firm's rate of investment. The hypothesis is that firms plan to close a fraction λ of the gap between the desired and actual capital stocks each period. Denote the capital stock at the end of last period by K_{-1}. The gap between the desired and actual capital stocks is $(K^* - K_{-1})$. The firm plans so that the capital stock at the end of the current period K will be such that

$$K - K_{-1} = \lambda(K^* - K_{-1}) \tag{8}$$

Equation (8) states that the firm plans to have the capital stock at the end of the period be such that a fraction λ of the gap (between the desired

---

[10]The flexible accelerator is a generalized form of the older *accelerator* model of investment, in which investment is proportional to the change in the level of GNP. The accelerator model is examined briefly in the appendix to this chapter.

capital stock K^* and the capital stock K_{-1} that existed at the end of last period) is closed. Rewriting Eq. (8),

$$K = K_{-1} + \lambda(K^* - K_{-1}) \tag{8a}$$

In order to increase the capital stock from K_{-1} to the level of K indicated by Eq. (8a), the firm has to achieve an amount of net investment, $I \equiv K - K_{-1}$ indicated by Eq. (8). We can therefore write net investment as

$$I = \lambda(K^* - K_{-1}) \tag{9}$$

which is the flexible accelerator formulation of net investment. Notice that Eq. (9) implies that investment is larger the larger the gap between actual and desired capital stocks.[11]

In Fig. 6-3 we show the adjustment process of capital in a circumstance where the initial capital stock is K_1 and the given desired capital stock is K^*. The assumed speed of adjustment is $\lambda = 0.5$. Starting from K_1, one-half of the discrepancy between target capital and current actual capital is made up in every period. First-period net investment is therefore $0.5(K^* - K_1)$. In the second period investment will be less, because the previous period's investment will have raised the actual capital stock and thus reduced the size of the gap between actual and desired capital stock. Progressively, investment reduces the gap until the actual capital stock reaches the level of target capital. The speed with which this process allows actual capital to reach target capital is determined by λ. The larger λ, the faster the gap is reduced.

In Eq. (9) we have reached our goal of deriving an investment function that shows current investment spending determined by the desired stock of capital K^* and the actual stock of capital K_{-1}. According to the flexible accelerator hypothesis, any factor that increases the desired capital stock increases the rate of investment. Thus an increase in expected output, or a reduction in the real interest rate, or an increase in the investment tax credit, will each increase the rate of investment. We thus have derived a quite complete theory of business fixed investment that includes many of the factors we should expect to affect the rate of investment. And the theory of investment embodied in Eq. (9) also contains aspects of *dynamic behavior*—that is, of behavior which depends on values of economic variables in periods other than the current period.

There are two sources of dynamic behavior in Eq. (9). The first arises from expectations. The K^* term depends on the firm's estimate of future or permanent output. To the extent that the firm forms its estimates of permanent output as a weighted average of past output levels, there will be lags in the adjustment of the level of permanent output to the actual level of

---

[11]Gross investment, as opposed to net investment described in Eq. (9), includes, in addition, depreciation. Thus, gross investment is $I + dK_{-1}$, where d is again the rate of depreciation.

output. Accordingly, the desired capital stock will adjust only slowly over time to a change in the level of output. And in turn, investment will therefore also adjust slowly to a change in the level of output. The second source of dynamic behavior arises from adjustment lags, in the specification that firms plan to close only a proportion of the gap between the actual and desired capital stocks each period, as shown in Fig. 6-3. The adjustment lags produce lagged response of investment to changes in the variables that affect the desired capital stock.

Empirical Results

At this point it is useful to ask how the investment model we have developed in Eq. (9) performs empirically. To use Eq. (9), it is necessary to substitute some specific equation for K^*, the desired capital stock. It is convenient to choose the much-used Cobb-Douglas form for the desired capital stock, as in Eq. (7). Using Eq. (7) in Eq. (9) yields a (net) investment function of the form

FIGURE 6-3 ADJUSTMENT OF THE CAPITAL STOCK

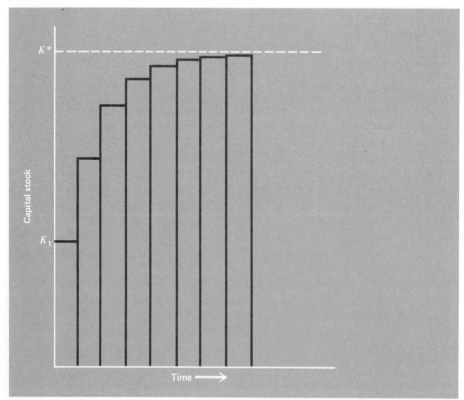

$$I = \lambda\left(\left[\frac{aY(1-t)}{(1-\tau)(i+d-\pi^*)}\right] - K_{-1}\right) \qquad (10)$$

Empirical work, in particular by Dale Jorgenson and his associates, shows that an investment function including the variables in Eq. (10) (except the expected inflation rate) provides a reasonable explanation of the behavior of business fixed investment. However, the form shown in Eq. (10) can be improved upon by allowing more scope for lagged or slow adjustment.[12] As it stands, Eq. (10), with the output variable not being explicitly permanent output, shows an immediate impact from a change in current output to investment spending. Moreover, Eq. (10) implies that if the output increase were maintained, the first-period adjustment to the increase would be larger than the second-period adjustment, and so forth, as suggested by Fig. 6-3. However, the empirical evidence suggests that the adjustment takes instead the bell-shaped form shown in Fig. 6-4. The major impact of a change in output on actual investment occurs with a two-period (year) lag. The short-run impact on investment is less than the impact two years later. Investment spending, like consumption spending, adjusts only slowly over time.

There are two, not mutually exclusive, explanations for the behavior shown in Fig. 6-4, corresponding to the two sources of dynamic behavior in Eq. (9) that we discussed above. The first possibility is that the lag pattern of Fig. 6-4 reflects the way in which expectations about future output, and thus the long-run desired capital stock, are formed. In that view, only a sustained increase in output, or for that matter, a sustained reduction in corporate taxes, will persuade firms that the capital stock should be increased in the long run. Figure 6-4 would then imply that it takes about two years for changes in the variables that determine the desired capital stock to have their major impact on expectations.

The second explanation relies less on expectations and more on the physical delays in the investment process. That interpretation would be that Fig. 6-4 reflects the long time it takes for a change in the desired capital stock to be translated into investment spending. In industries in which investment can be undertaken quickly, there may be some response within a year. But in the economy as a whole, the maximum impact on investment of a change in the desired capital stock happens only two years after the change in the desired stock.

In brief, the first explanation is that Fig. 6-4 represents the slow adjustment of the desired capital stock to changes in the variables that, in the long run, determine that desired stock. The second explanation is that Fig. 6-4 represents the long adjustment lags of investment in response to changes in the desired capital stock.

---

[12]See Dale W. Jorgenson, "Econometric Studies of Investment Behavior: A Survey," *Journal of Economic Literature*, December 1971, and Charles W. Bischoff, "Business Investment in the 1970's: A Comparison of Models," *Brookings Papers on Economic Activity*, 1:71.

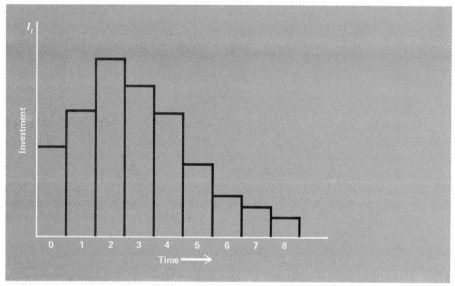

FIGURE 6-4 EFFECTS OF AN INCREASE
IN OUTPUT IN PERIOD ZERO ON NET IN-
VESTMENT IN SUBSEQUENT PERIODS

For many purposes, it does not matter which explanation of the form of Fig. 6-4 is correct, and it is difficult to tell the explanations apart empirically. It is undoubtedly true that both explanations are relevant. The important point is that lags in the determination of the level of business fixed investment are long.

Sales and Profits as Determinants of Investment

Some studies of investment find either the level of sales or total profits to be factors explaining the level of investment. It is worth noting that Eq. (10) can be interpreted as being consistent with those findings. Total output Y is the level of sales, and Eq. (10) clearly implies that Y should play a role in explaining the rate of investment. The variable $aY(1 - t)$ in Eq. (10) is the level of after-tax profits. Since a is the share of capital[13] in income, aY is therefore the total pretax income accruing to capital. The proportion $(1 - t)$ of that remains after taxation. Thus Eq. (10) implies that after-tax profits could be interpreted as playing a role in explaining investment behavior. However, Eq. (10) does not imply that both the level of output and profits should each play an independent role in explaining investment behavior.

[13]See footnote 4 on p. 179.

Summary on Business Fixed Investment

The main conclusions of the theory of business fixed investment as developed here are:

1 Over time, net investment spending is governed by the discrepancy between actual and desired capital.
2 Desired capital depends on the rental (user) cost of capital and the expected level of output. Capital demand rises with expected output and declines with an increase in either *real* interest rates or corporate taxes.
3 There is strong evidence that adjustment of actual to desired capital is a slow process. A sustained change in the profitability of capital or the level of income will not exert its maximum effect on investment for two years.
4 Although the adjustment process of actual to desired capital is a slow process, what matters for aggregate demand management is the level of investment. From this perspective, monetary and fiscal policy do exert an effect on investment, via the desired capital stock, although the short-run impact is likely to be minor. Over time, though, investment spending is more affected by monetary or fiscal policy. The lags with which these investment effects occur are important to bear in mind in shaping stabilization policy.
5 Investment theory, like consumption theory, emphasizes the role of expected or permanent income or output and other permanent variables as determinants of capital demand.

6-2 RESIDENTIAL INVESTMENT

We study residential investment separately from business fixed investment both because somewhat different theoretical considerations are relevant[14] and because institutional features of the United States economy make residential investment especially sensitive to changes in interest rates.

Chart 6-3 shows residential investment spending in constant (1972) dollars for the period 1953–1975. Residential investment declines in all recessions. Thus in 1953–1954, 1957–1958, 1960–1961, and 1970 there is a dip in residential investment. The same is true for the minirecession in 1966–1967 and certainly during the 1974–1976 recession. The 1966 minirecession is of particular interest in this context because, as we shall see in Chap. 10, the very tight monetary policy of that year fell particularly hard on residential construction. This is shown as a major dip in Chart 6-3.

---

[14]In the concluding section of this chapter we explain why different theoretical models are used in explaining business fixed investment and residential investment.

Theory

Residential investment consists of the building of single-family and mul-
tifamily dwellings which we shall call housing. Housing is distinguished
as an asset by its long life. Consequently, investment in housing in any
one year tends to be a very small proportion of the existing stock of
housing—about 3 percent. The theory of residential investment starts by
considering the demand for the existing stock of housing. Housing is
viewed as one among the many assets that a wealth holder can own.

In Fig. 6-5a we show the demand for the stock of housing in the
downward-sloping D_0D_0 curve. The lower the price of housing (P_H), the
greater is demand. The position of the demand curve itself depends on a
number of economic variables: First, the greater wealth, the greater the
demand for housing. The more wealthy individuals are, the more housing
they desire to own. Thus an increase in wealth would shift the demand
curve from D_0D_0 to D_1D_1. Second, the demand for housing as an asset
depends on the real return available on other assets. If returns on other
forms of holding wealth—such as bonds—are low, then housing looks like
a relatively attractive form in which to hold wealth. The lower the return
on other assets, the greater the demand for housing. A reduction in the
return on other assets, such as bonds or common stock, shifts the demand
curve from D_0D_0 to D_1D_1.

Third, the demand for the housing stock depends on the net real return
obtained by owning housing. The gross return—before taking costs into
account—consists of rent, if the housing is rented out, or the implicit return
that the homeowner receives by living in his own home, plus capital gains
arising from increases in the value of the housing. In turn, the costs of
owning the housing consist of interest cost, typically the mortgage interest

CHART 6-3 FIXED RESIDENTIAL IN-
VESTMENT SPENDING (BILLIONS OF 1972
DOLLARS). (Source: *Business Conditions
Digest*, May 1976)

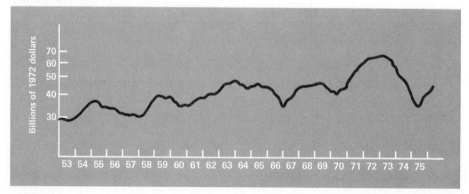

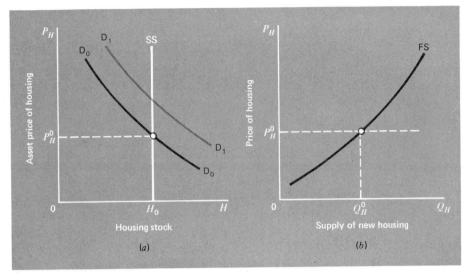

FIGURE 6-5 THE HOUSING MARKET—
DETERMINATION OF THE ASSET PRICE OF
HOUSING AND THE RATE OF HOUSING IN-
VESTMENT

rate, plus any real estate taxes, and depreciation. These costs are deducted
from the gross return to obtain the before-income tax net return. An increase in the net return on housing, caused, for example, by a reduction in
the mortgage interest rate, makes housing a more attractive form in which
to hold wealth and shifts up the demand curve for housing from D_0D_0 to
D_1D_1.

The price of housing is determined by the interaction of this demand
with the stock supply of housing. At any one time the stock supply is
fixed—there is a given stock of housing that cannot be adjusted quickly in
response to price changes. The supply curve of the stock of housing is the
SS curve of Fig. 6-5a. The equilibrium *asset price of housing*, P_H^0, is determined by the intersection of the supply and demand curves. The asset
price of housing is simply the price of a typical house or apartment. At any
one time, the market for the stock of housing determines the asset price of
housing.

We now consider the determinants of the rate of investment in housing, and for that purpose turn to Fig. 6-5b. The curve FS represents the
supply of new housing as a function of the price of housing. This curve
should be thought of in the same way as the regular supply curve of any
industry. The supply curve, it will be recalled, represents the amount of a
good that suppliers want to sell at the specified price. In this case, the
good being supplied is new housing. The position of the FS curve is

affected by the costs of factors of production used in the construction industry and by technological factors affecting the cost of building.

The curve FS is sometimes called the flow supply curve, since it represents the *flow* of new housing into the market in a given time period. In contrast, the *stock* supply curve SS represents the total amount of housing in the market at a moment of time.

Given the price of housing established in the asset market, P_H^0, building contractors supply the amount of new housing, Q_H^0, for sale at that price. The higher the asset price, the greater the supply of new housing. Now the supply of new housing is nothing other than gross investment in housing—total additions to the housing stock. Figure 6-5 thus represents our basic theory of the determinants of housing investment.

Any factor affecting the demand for the existing stock of housing will affect the asset price of housing, P_H, and thus the rate of investment in housing. Similarly, any factor shifting the flow supply curve FS will affect the rate of investment. We have already investigated the major factors shifting the DD demand curve for housing, but will briefly repeat that analysis.

Suppose the interest rate rises. Then the asset demand for housing falls and the price of housing falls; that in turn induces a decline in the rate of production of new housing, or a decline in housing investment. Or suppose that the mortgage interest rate rises: once again there is a fall in the asset price of housing and a reduction in the rate of construction. Or let there be an increase in wealth that increases the demand for housing. The asset price of housing rises and the rate of construction—the rate of housing investment—rises.

Because the existing stock of housing is so large relative to the rate of investment in housing, we can ignore the effects of the current supply of new housing on the price of housing in the short run. However, over time, the new construction shifts the SS curve of the left-hand panel to the right as it increases the housing stock. The long-run equilibrium in the housing industry would be reached, in an economy in which there was no increase in population or wealth over time, when the housing stock was constant. Constancy of the housing stock requires gross investment equal to depreciation, or net investment equal to zero. The asset price of housing would have to be at the level such that the rate of construction was just equal to the rate of depreciation of the existing stock of housing in long-run equilibrium. If population or income and wealth were growing at a constant rate, the long-run equilibrium would be one in which the rate of construction was just sufficient to cover depreciation and the steadily growing stock demand. In an economy subjected to continual nonsteady changes, that long-run equilibrium is not necessarily ever reached.

Minor qualifications to the basic theoretical structure arise chiefly because new housing cannot be constructed immediately in response to changes in P_H; rather, it takes a short time for that response to occur. Thus, the supply of new housing responds not to the actual price of housing today, but the price expected to prevail when the construction is completed. However, the lags are quite short; it takes less than a year to build a typical house. Another qualification stems from that same construction delay. Since builders have to incur expenses before they sell their output, they need financing over the construction period. They are frequently financed at the mortgage interest rate by the thrift institutions, that is, savings and loan associations and mutual savings banks. Hence the position of the flow supply curve is affected by the mortgage interest rate as well as the amount of lending undertaken by the thrift institutions.[15] We discuss below the reason that the amount of lending undertaken by the thrift institutions has an effect over and above that of the mortgage interest rate on the flow supply of housing.

Housing, Mortgages, and Regulation Q

The mortgage interest rate and the availability of mortgages play a special role in the housing market and in fluctuations in the rate of housing investment. The reason is that most mortgage lending is undertaken by thrift institutions (thrifts) on the basis of long-term debt instruments with a fixed interest rate: a mortgage is typically a debt instrument that contractually can be paid off over a twenty- to thirty-year period. Many of the liabilities of the thrift institutions, however, are relatively short-term instruments. These liabilities are essentially deposits at the savings and loan associations and mutual savings banks, most of which can be withdrawn on demand by the depositors. The savings and loans have recently been increasingly issuing longer-term liabilities of up to four-year maturity. Thus on one side of their balance sheets, the asset side, the thrift institutions have long-term assets with a fixed interest rate. On the other side of their balance sheets they have some very short-term liabilities and some of slightly longer term.

Consider now what happens to the thrifts when there is an increase in the interest rates on other short-term assets available to their depositors, perhaps the interest rate on Treasury bills, and perhaps due to inflation. If the interest rate paid by the thrifts were kept fixed, their depositors would be likely to remove their deposits and purchase other assets. On the other hand, if they raised the interest rates paid on deposits, they might well find themselves paying out more in interest payments at the new higher rate on deposits than they receive in interest payments made by individuals to whom they have lent at the old low mortgage rate. Although the interest rate on new mortgages would be raised, most of the thrifts' income would come from their outstanding mortgages. The thrifts would thus appear to be faced with the unfortunate choice between keeping the interest rates on deposits low and losing deposits, or raising interest rates on deposits and

[15]The theory of housing investment of this section is the basis of the study of the housing market undertaken by James Kearl in his 1975 MIT Ph.D. dissertation, "Inflation-Induced Distortions of the Real Economy: An Econometric and Simulation Study of Housing and Mortgage Innovation."

making losses at any time there is a large increase in the general level of interest rates.

In fact the thrifts have not had to make that choice under these circumstances, which occurred in 1966, 1969–1970, and 1974–1975. The interest rates the thrifts pay to depositors are controlled by the Federal Reserve System's regulation Q.[16] The Fed has typically kept the interest ceilings low at times of sharply rising interest rates, and the consequence has been an outflow of deposits from the thrifts at those times—the process known as *disintermediation*. Given the deposit outflow, the thrifts do not have any sources of funds with which to make loans, so that mortgages become unavailable, even at the quoted mortgage interest rates. The impact of the unavailability of mortgages on housing investment is strong, as can be observed by the fluctuations in residential investment shown in Charts 6-2 and 6-3. These impacts would be expected on the basis of the theory summarized in Fig. 6-5. The general increase in interest rates increases the attractiveness of assets other than housing. The increase in mortgage rates and the unavailability of mortgages make housing more costly or difficult to hold. Each of these factors thus shifts the DD curve downward, reducing the asset price of housing. Then the unavailability of mortgages and the increased mortgage rate shift up the FS curve. Each of these shifts reduces the rate of housing investment.

A significant part of the influence of monetary policy on aggregate demand stems from the impact of high interest rates on housing investment. Given that restrictive monetary policy is being used to affect some sector of the economy to reduce aggregate demand, it has been argued that the housing sector is a desirable target. The reason is that major changes in the rate of housing investment have very little impact in the short run on the overall availability of housing (since the housing stock is so large relative to the rate of investment) and thus cause little distress to consumers. The Fed may accordingly not be totally unhappy to use regulation Q to affect the availability of mortgages, despite the dislocation this causes for the thrift institutions and the construction industry.[17] However, the very concentrated effects of monetary policy do mean that the construction industry bears an undesirably large part of the burden of stabilization policy. This factor, among others, argues for policy measures that will ultimately lead to the disappearance of regulation Q.

---

[16]Formally, the interest ceilings for the savings and loan associations (SLAs) are set by the Federal Home Loan Bank Board, an organization whose role in relation to the SLAs is similar to that of the Fed in relation to banks. In practice, the FHLBB sets the ceiling at the regulation Q levels set by the Fed for the commercial banks.

[17]There have been suggestions that the thrifts should introduce variable rate mortgages, on which the interest payment varies with the general level of interest rates, in order to avoid the difficulties they now face when interest rates rise. Such mortgages have been introduced in California and some other states.

6-3 INVENTORY INVESTMENT

Inventories consist of goods in the process of production and completed goods held by firms in anticipation of their sale. The ratio of inventories to final sales, at an annual rate, in the United States has been in the range of 25 to 35 percent over the past eighteen years. That is, on average, firms hold inventories that constitute three to five months' worth of their final sales.

The inventories of interest to us are those held to meet future demands for goods. Firms hold such inventories because goods cannot be instantly manufactured or obtained from the manufacturer to meet demand. Some inventories are held as an unavoidable part of the production process; there is an inventory of meat and sawdust inside the sausage machine during the manufacture of sausage, for example. Inventories are also held because it is less costly for a firm to order goods less frequently in large quantities than to order small quantities frequently—just as the average household finds it useful to keep several days' supplies on hand in the house so as not to have to visit the supermarket daily.

Firms have a desired ratio of inventories to final sales that depends on economic variables. The smaller the cost of ordering new goods, and the greater the speed with which such goods arrive, the smaller the inventory-sales ratio. The more uncertainty about the demand for the firm's goods, given the expected level of sales, the higher the inventory-sales ratio. The inventory-sales ratio may also depend on the level of sales, with the ratio falling with sales because there is relatively less uncertainty about sales as sales increase. Finally there is the interest rate. Since firms carry inventories over time, they must tie up money to buy and hold them. There is an interest cost involved in such inventory holding, and the desired inventory-sales ratio should be expected to fall with increases in the interest rate. However, such a link has been difficult to establish empirically.

The most interesting aspect of inventory investment lies in the distinction between anticipated and unanticipated investment. Inventory investment could be high in two circumstances. First, if sales are unexpectedly low, firms would find unsold inventories accumulating on their shelves; that constitutes unanticipated inventory investment. This is the type of inventory investment discussed in Chap. 3. Second, inventory investment could be high because firms plan to restore depleted inventories. The two circumstances obviously have very different implications for the behavior of aggregate demand. Unanticipated inventory investment is a result of unexpectedly low aggregate demand. On the other hand, planned inventory investment can be a response to recent unexpectedly high aggregate demand. That is, rapid accumulation of inventories could be associated with either rapidly declining aggregate demand or rapidly increasing aggregate demand.

The behavior of inventory investment in the period since 1946 is shown in Chart 6-2. On the whole, inventory investment over the one-year periods of Chart 6-2 has been closely tied to the behavior of the business cycle, as represented by the unemployment rate. Inventory investment has been low when unemployment has been high, and vice versa.

However, inventory behavior over shorter time periods is more interesting and illuminating. Inventory behavior over the business cycle is well illustrated in the 1973–1975 recession. In Chart 6-4 we show real output (in 1972 dollars) as well as final sales other than for inventory. The discrepancy between GNP and final sales is equal to changes in inventories. Thus, when output exceeds final sales, inventories are increasing. Now we observe that we move into the recession with final sales declining in the fourth quarter of 1973 while output is still increasing. Throughout 1974 final sales and output decline but, throughout, output exceeds sales so that inventories keep accumulating. Firms are not yet fully adjusting production to the lower and declining level of demand. Finally, at the end of 1974 and in the first quarter of 1975 there is a dramatic reduction in output and production, and output falls below the level of final sales. Up to the third quarter of 1975 firms are decumulating inventories and meeting the excess of demand over production in that manner. Finally, in the last quarter with both sales and output back on the upswing, production roughly matches sales.

The implied behavior of the ratio of inventories to final sales is shown in Chart 6-5. It is clear that this ratio is significantly affected by the business cycle. In the early phase of a decline in aggregate demand there is relatively little production adjustment and accordingly inventories are built up. The inventory–sales ratio increases as the economy heads into a recession. Once the recession is fully under way, production is cut more severely because firms find themselves with excessive inventories and attempt to unload them. Finally, in the recovery phase demand moves ahead of production, thus allowing inventories to further decline absolutely and relative to output or sales. The inventory–sales ratio decreases as the economy moves out of the recession. The behavior of inventories thus matches rather precisely the story of the adjustment process that we told in discussing the simple keynesian model. In the initial phase of the downswing, inventories (passively) adjust to absorb the excess of production over demand. Subsequently, as involuntary inventory accumulation shows up in a high ratio of inventories to sales, firms cut production and thus actively restore the preferred ratio of inventories to sales.

As we noted in Chap. 3, the behavior of inventories not only reflects fluctuations in the economy, but also contributes to those fluctuations, through the so-called *inventory cycle*. When there is a fall in demand, inventories initially begin to increase, as can be seen at the beginning of the period shown in Chart 6-4, for instance. When firms decide to reduce their inventories, they have to cut back their orders or reduce their own production for inventory, thus reducing demand by more than the initial fall in aggregate demand. This stage worsens the decline, as can be seen

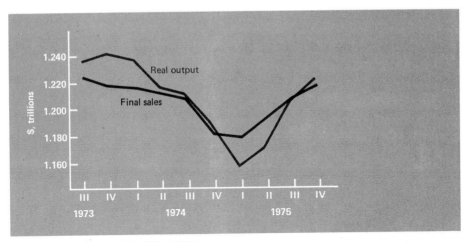

CHART 6-4 REAL GNP AND FINAL SALES
(TRILLIONS OF 1972 DOLLARS). (Source:
Economic Report of the President, 1976)

in the first quarter of 1975 in Chart 6-4. When the inventories are back to their desired level, firms will restore their inventory investment to a higher level again.

To make the point in a different way, we can consider the case of a hypothetical automobile dealer who sells, say, thirty cars per month, and holds an average of one month's sales—namely, thirty cars—in inventory. As long as sales stay steady at thirty cars per month, he will be ordering thirty cars per month from the factory. Now suppose sales drop to twenty-five cars per month, and it takes the dealer two months to respond to the change. During those two months his inventory will have climbed to forty cars. In future he will want an inventory of only 25 cars on hand. Thus, when he does respond to the fall in demand, he cuts his order from the factory from thirty to fifteen in the third month, to get his inventory back to one month's sales. After the desired inventory-sales ratio has been restored, he will then order twenty-five cars per month from the factory. We see in this extreme case how the drop in demand of five cars, instead of leading to a simple drop in car output of five cars per month, causes a drop in output of fifteen cars in one month, followed by the longer-run drop in output of five cars per month.

6-4 CONCLUSIONS

In this chapter we have seen how investment fluctuates over the business cycle. We have broken investment spending down into the three categories of business fixed investment, residential investment, and inventory investment, and we have presented theories to explain the behavior of each type of investment.

Slightly different theoretical considerations are relevant to the determination of each of the three categories of investment we have discussed. Nonetheless, there is a basic common element. That is the interaction, in each of the theories, of the demand for the stock of capital with the determinants of the rate of investment. The theory of business fixed investment started by examining the determinants of the desired capital stock, while the theory of residential investment looked at the demand for the stock of housing. The discussion of inventory investment started by examining the determinants of the desired inventory–sales ratio. Then, in each case, we went on to analyze or describe the determinants of the rate of that type of investment.

We come now to the question of why there is a difference between the theoretical models used to explain the level of business fixed investment and residential investment. The fundamental difference arises from the degree of standardization of the capital and the associated question of the existence of a good market for the used capital goods. Much of business fixed investment is in capital which is specifically designed for a given firm and is not of much use to other firms. It is, accordingly, difficult to establish a market price for the stock of that type of capital, and the theory used in discussing residential investment would be difficult to apply in that case. Although housing too varies a good deal, it is nonetheless possible to talk of a price of housing. Further, used housing is a very good substitute for new

CHART 6-5 INVENTORY–FINAL SALES RATIO, 1974–1975. (Source: *Economic Report of the President,* 1976)

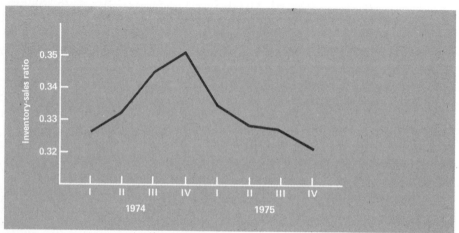

housing, whereas that is less true for many capital goods.[18] If we disaggregated business fixed investment further than we have, we might well find that the model used to study housing investment is readily applicable for certain categories of business fixed investment, for which the capital good in question is relatively standard and has a good secondhand market.

Of the factors affecting the rate of investment, the real rate of interest is important because it affects both business fixed investment and housing investment. It does not appear to have strong effects on inventory spending. Fiscal policy affects the rate of business fixed investment by affecting the rental cost of capital and can also affect residential investment by its treatment of the tax deductibility of interest payments used to finance home ownership.

Different variables affect the scale of each type of investment. The expected level of output is the major determinant of the overall scale of business fixed investment. Wealth is the major scale variable affecting the demand for housing and thus, ultimately, the rate of housing investment. The desired stock of inventory capital is related to the level of sales, but there is no simple relationship between the rate of inventory investment and changes in the level of output. A high rate of inventory investment may either be an addition to aggregate demand (if the investment is planned) or a reflection of a low level of aggregate demand (if the investment is unanticipated).

There are differences, too, in the stress placed on other factors affecting each category of investment. Lags in adjustment and lags arising from expectations that depend on past history are extremely important determinants of the rate of business fixed investment. Institutional arrangements, particularly regulation Q, play an important role in affecting the rate of residential investment. These arrangements are largely responsible for the severe fluctuations in residential construction in the United States economy.

Total investment in the economy is simply the sum of investment spending in each of the three categories that we have studied separately in this chapter. Thus, each of the factors that affects the components of investment spending also affects the level of total investment. The real interest rate is thus one of the major factors that has an unambiguous effect on investment spending. Similarly, the level of permanent output affects investment spending, as do the fiscal variables that affect the rental cost of capital. Monetary policy influences the level of investment by affecting the real rate of interest and also through the use of regulation Q.

---

[18]The two models look very different. However, you may be able to see a way of casting the analysis of the housing market in terms of the theory used in discussing business fixed investment. You can define the desired capital stock of housing as that stock which the economy will eventually reach when the price of housing reaches a constant level. Then the level of investment will be an increasing function of the difference between that stock and the existing stock.

In brief, this chapter provides the theory that explains the role of the interest rate in the investment function of Chap. 4, while pointing out that the interest rate used there should be a *real* interest rate. It also showed that other variables, such as the level of output, and the level of wealth, affect the rate of investment. Finally, it clarified the ways in which monetary and fiscal policy variables affect the rate of investment.

APPENDIX: THE ACCELERATOR MODEL OF INVESTMENT

The flexible accelerator model described in Sec. 6-1 is a substantial generalization of the original accelerator model of investment, which argued that the rate of investment is proportional to the *change* in GNP. To derive the accelerator model of investment, assume that there is complete adjustment of the capital stock to its desired level within one period (i.e., that $\lambda = 1$), so that $K = K^*$, that there is no depreciation so that $d = 0$, and that the desired capital output ratio is a constant, independent of the rental cost of capital:

$$K^* = \beta Y \tag{A1}$$

In Eq. (A1), β is a constant which should not be confused with the β in any other chapter. Substituting Eq. (A1) into Eq. (9), setting $\lambda = 1$, and noting that $K_{-1} = K^*_{-1}$, we obtain

$$I = \beta(Y - Y_{-1}) \tag{A2}$$

which is precisely the original accelerator model of investment.

While the flexible accelerator model Eq. (9) is indeed a considerable generalization of the simple accelerator model, the simpler model drives home the point that the rate of investment depends on the lagged as well as the current value of GNP. This means that any action taken this period to affect current investment and thus current GNP will also affect investment—and thus GNP—in subsequent periods. As we saw in our discussion of the permanent-income hypothesis, such a relationship presents considerable difficulties to policy makers.

PROBLEMS

1 We have seen in Chap. 5 and 6 that *permanent* income and output determine consumption and investment rather than current income and output.
   a How does this affect the IS-LM model built in Chap. 4?
   b What are the policy implications of the use of the "permanent" measures?
2 In Chap. 4 it was assumed that investment rises during periods of low interest rates. That, however, was not the case during the 1930s, when investment and interest rates were both very low. Explain how this can occur. What would have been appropriate fiscal policy in such a case?
3 According to the description of business fixed investment in this chapter, how would you expect a firm's investment decisions to be affected by a sudden increase

in demand for its product? What factors would determine the speed of its reaction?

4 Explain how the two panels of Fig. 6-5 react together over time. What would happen if the demand for housing stock (DD) shifts up and to the right over time?

5 Trace carefully the step-by-step effects on the housing market (using Fig. 6-5) of an increase in interest rates. Explain each shift and its long-run and short-run effects.

6 a Explain why the housing market usually prospers when (real) mortgage rates are low.

  b In some states, usury laws prohibit (nominal) mortgage rates in excess of a legal maximum. Explain how this could lead to an exception to the conclusion in 6a.

  c Could this happen in the absence of inflation? Explain.

7 Restrictive monetary policy can seriously hurt the housing industry in an effort to avoid excess aggregate demand.

  a What is the mechanism by which this occurs?

  b Can you suggest ways in which this heavy burden can be spread out rather than be concentrated on the housing industry?

  c Should the burden be spread?

8 a Explain how final sales and output can differ.

  b Point out from Chart 6-4 the periods of planned and unplanned inventory investment and decumulation.

  c During a period of slow but steady growth, how would you expect final sales and output to be related? Explain. Draw a hypothetical figure like Chart 6-4 for such a period.

  d Do the same as in 8c for Chart 6-5.

9 Suppose that an explicitly temporary tax credit is enacted. The tax credit is at the rate of 10 percent and lasts only one year.

  a What is the effect of this tax measure on investment in the long run (say after four or five years)?

  b What is the effect in the current year and the following year?

  c How would your answers under 9a and 9b differ if the tax credit is permanent?

7

The Demand
for Money

This chapter continues the process of filling in the details of the IS-LM model that we studied in Chap. 4. In Chaps. 5 and 6 we took a closer look at theoretical and empirical aspects of the major private sector components of demand in the goods market—consumption and investment spending. In this chapter we analyze the demand for money, and thus move over from the goods market to the assets markets. In Chap. 8 we complete our discussion of the assets markets in the IS-LM framework by examining the determinants of the supply of money and the role of the Federal Reserve System in the money markets.

We introduce the topic of money demand by returning to the concept of the demand for *real balances*, introduced in Chap. 4. One of the essentials of money demand is that individuals are interested in the purchasing power of their money holdings—the value of their cash balances in terms of the goods the cash will buy. They are not concerned with their *nominal* money holdings, that is, the number of dollar bills they hold. What this means in practice is that (1) real money demand is unchanged when the price level increases, but *all* real variables, such as the interest rate, real income, and real wealth remain unchanged; and (2) nominal money demand increases in proportion to the increase in the price level, given the constancy of the real variables specified above.[1]

We have a special name for behavior which is not affected by changes in the price level itself, all real variables remaining unchanged. We say that an individual is free from *money illusion* if a change in the level of prices, holding all real variables constant, leaves real behavior, including real money demand, unchanged. By contrast, an individual whose real behavior is affected by the price level is said to suffer from money illusion.

We shall see that empirical evidence supports the theoretical argument that the demand for money is a demand for real balances—or that the demand for nominal balances, holding other variables constant, is proportional to the price level. In Chap. 4 we also assumed that the demand for money increases with the level of real income and decreases with the interest rate. In Secs. 7-3 and 7-4 below, we examine supporting theoretical and empirical evidence on the effects of changes in the level of income, and changes in interest rates, on the demand for money. We shall see that both theory and evidence support the type of demand for money function that we used in Chap. 4.

You will also recall that the demand for money is important in determining the effectiveness of fiscal policy in changing the level of income. We showed in Chap. 4 that changes in fiscal variables, such as tax rates or government spending, affect the level of income if the demand for money changes when the interest rate changes—if the demand for money is interest-elastic. If the demand for money is totally interest-inelastic—if it does not react at all to changes in the interest rate—increases in govern-

---

[1] Be sure you understand that (1) and (2) say the same thing in slightly different ways.

ment spending totally *crowd out* private spending and leave the level of income unaffected.

The demand for money has been studied very intensively at both the theoretical and empirical levels. There is by now almost total agreement that the demand should, as a theoretical matter, and does, as an empirical matter, increase as the level of real income rises and decrease as the interest rate rises. There is accordingly no need to review major unsettled controversies in this chapter, simply because there are none with respect to money demand.

We start in Sec. 7-1 by examining the components of the stock of money in the United States. Then, in Sec. 7-2, we briefly review the traditional reasons for the use of money. Section 7-3, the longest of the chapter, presents the basic theory of the demand for money. Section 7-4 examines the evidence supporting the theoretical conclusions. Sections 7-5 and 7-6 discuss the *velocity* of money—a concept related to the demand for money—and the effects of anticipated inflation on the demand for money, respectively.

7-1 COMPONENTS OF THE MONEY STOCK

The money supply concept we shall be using in most of this chapter is M_1, which consists of currency plus demand deposits. Table 7-1 shows that M_1 in March 1977 was equal to \$316.1 billion, of which \$82.4 billion consisted of currency, and the remaining \$233.7 billion was demand deposits.

Currency is notes and coin in circulation, most of it being in the form of notes. Demand deposits are deposits at commercial banks which are checkable—against which checks can be written. At present, it is still quite accurate to say that demand deposits are deposits at commercial banks that do not earn interest. However, the distinction between demand and other deposits, as depending on whether they pay interest, is becoming difficult to maintain. Something like a check can be written against interest-earning deposits in a number of states in the northeast.[2]

We concentrate on M_1 because it is the definition of the money supply that corresponds most closely to the role of money as a *medium of exchange* or as means of making payments. Payments can be made directly with coin and notes and also, for most transactions, with a check. To make a payment using a passbook savings account, it is necessary first to transfer money out of the savings account into a checking account, and only then to write the check. Checks cannot be written directly against passbook savings accounts. That is why we do not include these accounts in our basic defini-

[2]These are the NOW, POW, and other accounts, which are merely ways around the prohibition of interest payments on demand deposits which was instituted in the 1930s, repeal of which is likely.

TABLE 7-1   COMPONENTS OF THE MONEY STOCK, MARCH 1977 (*In billions of dollars; seasonally adjusted*)

(1)	(2)	(3)	(4)	(5)	(6)	(7)
Currency	Demand deposits	M_1 $= (1) + (2)$	Time and savings deposits at commercial banks	M_2 $=$ $M_1 + (4)$	MSB deposits, SLA shares credit union shares	M_3 $=$ $M_2 + (6)$
82.4	233.7	316.1	438.0	754.2	512.0	1,266.2

Note: Details may not add to totals owing to rounding.   Monthly figures are an average of daily figures. Column 4 excludes negotiable CD's.
Source: Federal Reserve Bulletin, May 1977.

tion of the money supply.   That is also why other savings accounts, against which checks can be written, should be included in M_1.

Given the existence of certain interest-bearing deposits against which checks can be written—such as the NOW and POW accounts—and given that these deposits are formally regarded as savings accounts in the monetary statistics, it is clear that the present definition of M_1 does not correspond exactly to the role of money as a means of making payments.   Historically, there have often been changes in the type of asset which can be used as a means of payment, and simultaneous disagreements about what constituted money in those circumstances.   When checks first began to be widely used in England, at the start of the nineteenth century, there was a disagreement over whether deposits should be regarded as part of the money stock.   Now that point is not disputed.   There is no reason to believe that institutional arrangements will not change in the future so that assets we now do not regard as money—such as savings deposits—will eventually come to be thought of as money.

For instance, there is a question as to whether credit cards should not be regarded as a means of making payment.   If so—and the argument is certainly compelling—we should probably count the amount that people are allowed to charge by using their credit cards as part of the money stock.

Information on the distribution of the ownership of demand deposits is available, but there are no records of the ownership of currency.[3]   About a third of demand deposits are held by consumers, with businesses holding most of the rest.   There is no very good information on the distribution of the ownership of currency because individuals are reluctant to discuss how

[3]The data, available each quarter, are published in the *Federal Reserve Bulletin*.

much currency they hold when they are asked. The question sounds like the prelude to a robbery or a visit from the IRS.

Table 7-1 also shows two broader definitions of the money supply than M_1. Logically enough, they are M_2 and M_3.[4] M_2 adds time deposits and savings deposits at commercial banks—i.e., commercial bank deposits on which interest is paid—to M_1. There are two reasons for looking at a measure of the money stock like M_2. First, although time and savings deposits cannot be used directly to make payments, they can be used indirectly, by first making a transfer into a checking account, as described above. Second, as we shall see in Chap. 8, commercial banks have to keep reserves against time and savings deposits. Deposits at mutual savings banks (MSBs), shares at savings and loan associations (SLAs), and shares at credit unions are added to M_2 to give M_3. Each of these three assets is a savings deposit held outside the commercial banking system. From the viewpoint of their owners, they are virtually indistinguishable from savings deposits at commercial banks. They, too, can be used with relatively little trouble to make payments, and M_3, accordingly, deserves some attention as a money-stock-related measure.

In summary, there is no unique set of assets which will always constitute the money supply. At present, there are arguments for using a broader definition of the money stock than M_1, and even arguments for using a less broad definition—should $1,000 bills be included, for example? And over the course of time, the particular assets which serve as a medium of exchange, or means of payment, will certainly change.

7-2 THE FUNCTIONS OF MONEY

Money is so widely used that we rarely step back to think how remarkable a device it is. It is impossible to imagine a modern economy operating without the use of money or something very much like it. The essential role of money is to separate the acts of buying and selling goods. In a mythical barter economy, in which there is no money, every transaction has to involve an exchange of goods (and/or services) on both sides of the transaction. The examples of the difficulties of barter are endless. The economist wanting a haircut would have to find a barber wanting to listen to a lecture on economics; the peanut farmer wanting a suit would have to find a tailor wanting peanuts, and so on. Without money, modern economies could not operate. In this context, money is a *medium of exchange*, and that is its essential function.

---

[4]M_2 and M_3 both exclude negotiable certificates of deposit (CDs of over $100,000 at large commercial banks). CDs can be bought and sold in the open market like other securities, and they are thus more like commercial paper than savings deposits, even though they are liabilities of commercial banks. Corresponding to M_2 and M_3 are money supply concepts M_4 and M_5, which add the value of the outstanding stock of large CDs to M_2 and M_3, respectively. In March 1977, the stock of large CDs was $62.2 billion.

Money, as a medium of exchange, makes it unnecessary for there to be a "double coincidence of wants" in exchanges. By the double coincidence, we have in mind the above examples. The wants of two individuals would have to be identically matched for the exchange to take place. For instance, the seller of peanuts would have to find a buyer whose goods he wanted to buy (the suit) while, at the same time, the seller of suits would have to find a buyer whose goods he wanted to buy (the peanuts).

There are four traditional functions of money, of which the medium of exchange is the first.[5] The other three are store of value, unit of account, and standard of deferred payment. These stand on a different footing from the medium of exchange function.

A *store of value* is an asset that maintains value over time. Thus, an individual holding a store of value can use that asset to make purchases at a future date. If an asset were not a store of value, then it would not be used as a medium of exchange. Imagine trying to use ice cream as money, in the absence of refrigerators. There would hardly ever be a good reason for anyone to give up goods for money (ice cream) if the money were sure to melt within the next few minutes. And if the seller were unwilling to accept the ice cream in exchange for his or her goods, then the ice cream would not be a medium of exchange. But there are many stores of value other than money—such as bonds, stocks, and houses.

The *unit of account* is the unit in which prices are quoted and books kept. Prices are quoted in dollars and cents, and dollars and cents are the units in which the money stock is measured. Usually, the money unit is also the unit of account, but that is not essential. In the German hyperinflation of 1922–1923, dollars were the unit of account for some firms, whereas the mark was the medium of exchange.

Finally, as a *standard of deferred payment*, money units are used in long-term transactions, such as loans. The amount that has to be paid back in five or ten years is specified in dollars and cents. Dollars and cents are acting as the standard of deferred payment. Once again, though, it is not essential that the standard of deferred payment be the money unit. For instance, the final payment of a loan may be related to the behavior of the price level, rather than being fixed in dollars and cents. This is known as an indexed loan.

The last two of the four functions of money are, accordingly, functions which money *usually* performs, but not functions that it *necessarily* performs. And the store of value function is one that many assets perform.

There are fascinating descriptions of different types of money that have existed in the past that we do not have room to review here.[6] But there is one final point we want to emphasize about the functions of money. *Money is whatever is generally accepted in exchange.* However magnificently a piece of paper may be engraved, it will not be money if it is not

[5]See W.S. Jevons, *Money and the Mechanism of Exchange*, London, 1910.
[6]See Paul Einzig, *Primitive Money*, Pergamon Press, New York, 1966.

accepted in payment for goods and services. And, however unusual the material of which it is made, anything which is generally accepted in payment is money. The only reason money is accepted in payment is that the recipient believes that it can be spent at a later time. There is thus an inherent circularity in the acceptance of money. Money is accepted in payment because it is believed that it will also be accepted in payment by others.

7-3 THE DEMAND FOR MONEY: THEORY

In this section we review the three major theories of the demand for money. In doing so, we will concentrate on the effects of changes in income and changes in the interest rate on money demand.

The three theories we are about to review correspond to Keynes's famous three motives for holding money:[7] (1) the transactions motive, which is the demand for money arising from the use of money in making regular payments; (2) the precautionary motive, which is the demand for money to meet unforeseen contingencies; (3) the speculative motive, which arises from the uncertainties about the money value of other assets that an individual can hold. In discussing the transactions and precautionary motives, we are mainly discussing M_1, whereas the speculative motive refers more to M_2 and M_3, as we shall see below.

Although we examine the demand for money by looking at the three motives for holding it, we cannot separate out a particular person's money holdings, say $500, into three neat piles of, say, $200, $200, and $100, that are being held from each motive. Money being held to satisfy one motive is always available for another use. The person holding unusually large balances for speculative reasons also has those balances available to meet an unexpected emergency, so that they also serve as precautionary balances. All three motives influence an individual's holdings of money, and, as we shall see, each leads to the prediction that the demand for money should vary inversely[8] with the interest rate that is paid on other assets.

This final point is worth emphasizing. Money (M_1) generally earns no interest. Anyone holding money is giving up interest that she could have earned by holding some other asset, such as a savings deposit, or a bond. Money is, accordingly, costly to hold. The more of it an individual holds, the more interest is lost. Once we identify forgone interest as the cost of holding money, it becomes natural to expect the demand for money to fall when the interest rate—the cost of holding money—rises. And if money

---

[7] J. M. Keynes, *The General Theory of Employment, Interest and Money*, Macmillan, 1936, chap. 13.

[8] By "vary inversely," we mean that the demand for money increases when the interest rate paid on other assets decreases.

were to pay interest, then the cost of holding money would be the difference between the interest rate that is paid on money and the interest rate that is paid on the most comparable other asset, such as a savings deposit or, for corporations, a certificate of deposit or commercial paper.

The Transactions Demand

The transactions demand for money arises from the use of money in making regular payments for goods and services. In the course of each month, an individual makes a variety of payments for such items as rent or mortgage, for groceries, for buying the newspaper, and for other purchases. In this section we examine how much money an individual would hold for such purchases.

In analyzing the transactions demand, we are concerned with a tradeoff between the amount of interest an individual forgoes by holding money, and the costs and inconveniences of holding a small amount of money. To make the problem concrete, consider an individual paid, say, $900 each month. Assume that he spends the $900 evenly over the course of the month, at the rate of $30 per day. Now at one extreme, the individual could simply leave his $900 in cash (whether currency or demand deposits) and spend it at the rate of $30 per day. Alternatively, on the first day of the month the individual could take his $30 to spend that day and put the remaining $870 in a daily interest savings accounts. Then every morning he could go to the bank to withdraw that day's $30 from the savings account. By the end of the month he would have earned interest on the money he had each day in the savings account. This would be the *benefit* of keeping his money holdings down as low as $30 at the beginning of each day. The *cost* of keeping money holdings down is simply the cost and inconvenience of all the trips to the bank to withdraw the daily $30. To decide on how much money to hold for transactions purposes, the individual has to weigh the costs of holding small balances against the interest advantage of doing so. The smaller the amount of money held on average, the more costs the individual incurs to manage his holdings of cash and savings deposits.

We now formalize the above example in order to study the tradeoff in more detail and to derive a formula for the demand for money. Suppose the nominal monthly income[9] of the individual is Y_N. We make the simplifying assumption that Y_N is paid into his savings account, rather than his checking account, each month. The money is spent at a steady rate over the course of the month. To spend it, the individual has to get it out of the savings account and into cash, which may be currency or a checking account. If left in the savings accounts, the deposit earns interest at a rate of i per month. It earns zero interest as cash. The cost to the individual of making a transfer between cash and the savings account (which we hence-

---

[9] As a reminder, nominal income Y_N is defined as real income Y times the price level $P : Y_N \equiv PY$.

forth call bonds for convenience) is b.[10]   That cost may be the individual's time, or it may be a cost that he explicitly pays someone else to make the transfer.   For convenience we refer to it as a broker's fee.

Although we are describing an individual's transactions demand, similar considerations are relevant for firms deciding how to manage their money.   You should think of this model as applying equally well, with small changes in terminology and assumption, to firms and households.

The analysis of the demand for money we are now outlining is known as an *inventory-theoretic approach*.   Originally, the approach was developed to determine the inventories of goods a firm should have on hand. In that context, the amount Y_N would be the monthly sales of the good, b the cost of ordering the good and i the interest cost of carrying the inventory. The analogy between money as an inventory of purchasing power, standing ready to buy goods, and an inventory of goods, standing ready to be bought by customers, is quite close.   The inventory-theoretic approach to the demand for money is associated with the names of William Baumol and James Tobin, each of whom used it to study the demand for money.[11] The most famous result of Baumol and Tobin is the *square-root law* of the demand for money, which is presented in Eq. (4) below.

The individual has to decide how many transactions to make between bonds and cash each month.   If he makes just one transaction, transferring Y_N into cash at the beginning of the month, his cash balance over the course of the month will be as shown in Fig. 7-1a.   It starts at Y_N, is spent evenly over the month, and is down to zero by the end of the month, at which time a new payment is received by the individual and transferred into his checking account.   If he makes two withdrawals from the savings account, the first transfers $Y_N/2$ into cash at the beginning of the month, resulting in a cash balance that is run down to zero in the middle of the month, at which time another $Y_N/2$ is transferred into cash and spent evenly over the rest of the month.[12]   Figure 7-1b shows the individual's cash holdings in that case.

We shall denote the size of a cash withdrawal from the bond portfolio (savings account) by Z,[13] and the number of withdrawals from the bond portfolio by n.   Thus, n is the number of times the individual adds to his cash balance during the month.   If the individual makes n equal-sized withdrawals during the month, transferring funds from his savings account to his checking account, then the size of each transfer is Y_N/n, since a total of Y_N has to be transferred from the savings account into cash.   For example, if

[10]This b should not be confused with the b in earlier chapters; there are not sufficient letters of the alphabet for us to use each letter for only one concept.

[11]William Baumol, "The Transactions Demand for Cash: An Inventory Theoretic Approach," *Quarterly Journal of Economics*, November 1952; and James Tobin, "The Interest-Elasticity of Transactions Demand for Cash," *Review of Economics and Statistics*, 38, August 1956.

[12]With simple interest being paid on the savings account, it is true that the individual's transactions between bonds and cash should be evenly spaced over the month.   We leave the proof of that for the case where there are two transactions to the problem set.

[13]Please do not confuse Z in this chapter with Z in Chap. 5.

Y_N is \$900, and n, the number of transactions, is 3, then Z, the amount transferred to cash each time, is \$300. Accordingly, we can write

$$nZ = Y_N \tag{1}$$

Suppose that the amount Z is transferred from bonds to cash at each withdrawal. What then is the *average* cash balance over the course of the month? We want to find the size of the average cash balance in order to measure the interest that is lost as a result of holding cash. The interest lost will be the interest rate times the average amount of cash held during the month; if that amount were not held as cash it could be held as interest-earning bonds. In Fig. 7-1a, the average cash balance held during the month is $Y_N/2 = Z/2$, since the cash balance starts at Y_N and runs down in a straight line to zero.[14] In the case of Fig. 7-1b, the average cash balance for the first half of the month is $Y_N/4 = Z/2$, and the average cash balance for the second half of the month is also Z/2. Thus, the average cash balance for the entire month is $Y_N/4 = Z/2$. Similarly, if three withdrawals were made, the average cash balance would be $Y_N/6 = Z/2$. In general, the average cash balance is Z/2, as you might want to confirm by drawing diagrams similar to Fig. 7-1 for $n = 3$ or other values of n.

---

[14]The average cash balance is the average of the amount of cash the individual holds at each moment during the month. For instance, if he held \$300 for three days and zero for the rest of the month, the average cash balance would be \$30, or one-tenth (three days divided by thirty days) of the month times \$300.

FIGURE 7-1 THE AMOUNT OF CASH HELD DURING THE MONTH RELATED TO THE NUMBER OF WITHDRAWALS

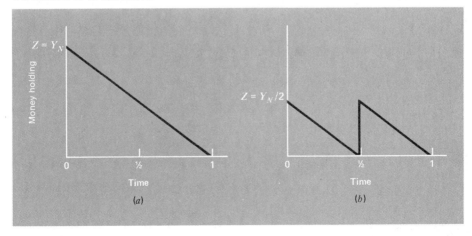

The interest cost of holding money is the interest rate times the average cash balance, or $iZ/2$. From Eq. (1), that means the total interest cost is $iY_N/2n$. The other component of the cost of managing the portfolio is the brokerage cost, or the cost in terms of the individual's time and inconvenience in managing his money. That cost is just the number of withdrawals made, n, times the cost of each withdrawal, b, and is thus equal to nb. The total cost of managing the portfolio is the interest cost plus the total brokerage cost:

$$\text{Total cost} = nb + \frac{iY_N}{2n} \tag{2}$$

Equation (2) shows formally that the brokerage cost nb increases as the number of withdrawals (transactions between bonds and money) rises, and that the interest cost decreases as the number of withdrawals increases. It thus emphasizes the tradeoff the individual faces in managing his money, and suggests that there is an optimal number of withdrawals the individual should make to minimize the total cost of holding money to meet transactions requirements for buying goods.

To derive that optimal point, we want to find the point at which the benefit of carrying out another withdrawal is less than, or just equal to, the cost of making another transaction between bonds and money. If the benefit of making another transaction were greater than the cost, then another withdrawal should be made, and the original point could not have been optimal. The cost of making another transaction is always equal to b. In Fig. 7-2, we show the costs of making a further transaction by the marginal cost curve MC, which is horizontal at the level b. The financial benefit from making another transaction is represented by the MB, marginal benefit, curve in Fig. 7-2, which represents the interest *saved* by making another withdrawal and thus having a smaller cash balance on average during the month.

The more transactions between money and bonds an individual makes, the lower the total interest cost is. But the reduction in the interest cost that is obtained by making more transactions falls off rapidly as the number of withdrawals increases. There is a substantial saving in interest costs by making two withdrawals rather than one, but very little saving in interest costs by making thirty-one transactions rather than thirty. It is impossible to reduce the interest cost below zero, however many withdrawals are made; this also suggests that the marginal benefit of making more withdrawals decreases as the number of withdrawals becomes large. The MB curve in Fig. 7-2 is, accordingly, downward-sloping.[15]

---

[15]Two points about Fig. 7-2: First, note that we have, for convenience, drawn the curves as continuous, even though you will recognize that it is only possible to make an integral number of transactions, and not, for example, 1.6 or 7.24 transactions. Second, if you can use the calculus, try to derive the equation of the marginal benefit curve from the component of costs in Eq. (2) that is due to interest lost.

In Fig. 7-2, the optimal number of transactions is given by n^*, the number at which the marginal benefit in terms of interest saved is equal to the marginal cost of making a transaction. Given the number of transactions and the individual's income, we also know his average cash balance M, using the relationship between average money holdings and the size of each transfer which we derived earlier:

$$M = \frac{Z}{2} = \frac{Y_N}{2n} \tag{3}$$

From Fig. 7-2 we can see two of the important results of the inventory theory of the transactions demand for money. First, suppose the brokerage cost rises. That shifts the MC curve up, decreases the number of withdrawals n, and therefore (from Eq. (3), where M is inversely related to n) increases the average holding of money. Second, an increase in the interest rate shifts up the MB curve, therefore increases n, and thus [again, from Eq. (3)] reduces the holding of money: when the interest rate is higher, the individual is willing to make more trips to the bank to earn the higher interest now available. Figure 7-2 thus shows one of the key results we wanted to establish—that the demand for money is inversely related to the interest rate.

In the case of an increase in income, Fig. 7-2 is unfortunately less useful. An increase in income shifts up the MB curve and thus increases

FIGURE 7-2 OPTIMAL CASH MANAGE-MENT: DETERMINING THE OPTIMAL NUMBER OF WITHDRAWALS

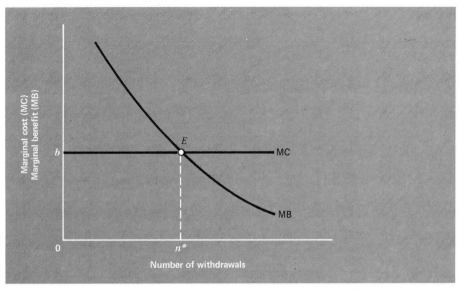

the number of transactions. But from Eq. (3), we see that an increase in the number of transactions accompanying an increase in income does not necessarily imply that the demand for money rises. If the number of transactions increases less than in proportion to the increase in income, then the income increase raises the demand for money. However, if the number of transactions increases more than in proportion to the increase in income, the increase in income could lower the demand for money. This second eventuality sounds strange and, fortunately, as a more complete algebraic analysis of the optimal behavior of the individual would show, is not possible under the assumptions we have made so far.

The famous square-root formula to which we referred above both makes the results of the graphical analysis of Fig. 7-2 more precise and resolves the ambiguity about the effects of income on the demand for money. The formula gives the demand for money that is obtained as a result of minimizing the total costs in Eq. (2) with respect to the number of withdrawals, and then using Eq. (3) to derive the cash balance.[16] The formula is

$$M^* = \sqrt{\frac{bY_N}{2i}} \tag{4}$$

Equation (4) shows that the transactions demand for money increases with the brokerage fee, or the cost of transacting, and increases with the level of income. The demand for money decreases with the interest rate.

Equation (4) also shows that an increase in income raises the demand for money proportionately less than the increase in income itself. If income rises fourfold, optimal money holdings only double. To put the same point somewhat differently, the ratio of income to money, Y_N/M, rises with the level of income. A person with a higher level of income than another holds proportionately less money than the other person. This point is sometimes put in different words by saying that there are *economies of scale* in cash management.

Yet another way of saying the same thing is to say that the income elasticity of the demand for money is less than 1 [it is equal to ½ in Eq. (4)]. The income elasticity measures the percentage change in the demand for money due to a 1 percent change in income. The income elasticity of the demand, according to Eq. (4), is ½, because a quadrupling of income only doubles the demand. Similarly, Eq. (4) implies that the elasticity of the demand for money with respect to the brokerage fee, is ½, and the elasticity with respect to the interest rate is $-$ ½.

What accounts for the fact that people can somehow manage with less cash per dollar of spending as income increases? This is the implication of

---

[16]If you can handle calculus, try to derive Eq. (4).

economies of scale, or an income elasticity of less than 1. The reason is that cash management is more effective at high levels of income, because the average cost of transactions is lower with larger-size transactions. In turn, the lower average cost of transactions results from the fixed brokerage fee per transaction; it costs as much to transfer $10 as $10 million, so that the average cost per dollar transferred is lower for large transfers.

However, in the case of households, we should recognize that the "brokerage cost" b, the cost of making withdrawals from a savings account, is, in part, the cost of time and the nuisance of having to go to the bank. Since the cost of time to an individual is likely to be higher, the higher his income, b may rise with Y_N, and in that case an increase in income would result in an increase in the demand for money by more than the income elasticity of ½ indicates—because b goes up together with Y_N.

The Demand for Real Balances

We started this chapter by emphasizing that the demand for money is a demand for real balances. It is worth confirming that the inventory theory of the demand for money implies that the demand for real balances does not change when all prices double (or increase in any other proportion). When all prices double, both Y_N and b in Eq. (4) double—that is, both nominal income and the nominal brokerage fee double. Accordingly, the demand for nominal balances doubles, so that the demand for real balances is unchanged. The square-root formula does not imply any money illusion in the demand for money. Thus we should be careful when saying the income elasticity of demand for money implied by Eq. (4) is ½. The elasticity of the demand for *real* balances with respect to *real* income is ½. But if income rises only because all prices (including b) rise, then the demand for *nominal* balances rises proportionately.

*Integer Constraints

So far we have, in the text, ignored the important constraint that it is possible to make only an integral number of transactions, such as 1, 2, 3, etc., and that it is not possible to make 1.25 or 3.57 transactions. However, when we take account of this constraint, we shall see that it implies that many people do not make more than the essential one transaction between money and bonds within the period in which they are paid.[17] Consider our previous example of the person who received $900 per month. Suppose realistically that the interest rate per month on savings deposits is ½ percent. The individual cannot avoid making one initial transaction, since income initially arrives in the savings account. The next question is whether it pays to make a second transaction. That is, does it pay to keep half the monthly

---

[17]If we had assumed that the individual were paid in cash, it would turn out that many people would not make any transactions between money and bonds in managing their transactions balances.

income for half a month in the savings account and make a second withdrawal after half a month? With an interest rate of ½ percent per month, interest for half a month would be ¼ percent. Half the income would amount to $450 and the interest earnings would, therefore, be $450 x ¼ percent = $1.125.

Now if the brokerage fee exceeds $1.125, the individual will not bother to make more than one transaction. And $1.125 is not an outrageous cost in terms of the time and nuisance of making a transfer from the savings to the checking account. Thus, for many individuals whose monthly net pay is below $1,000, we do not expect the formula (4) to hold exactly. Their cash balance would instead simply be half their income. They would make one transfer into cash at the beginning of the month; Fig. 7-1a would describe this cash balance. For such individuals, the income elasticity of the demand for money is 1, since their demand for money goes up precisely in proportion with their income. The interest elasticity is zero, so long as they make only one transaction, because they transfer all their income into cash immediately as they receive it.

The very strong restrictions on the income and interest elasticities of the demand for money of Eq. (4) are not valid when the integer constraints are taken into account. Instead, the income elasticity is an average of the elasticities of different people, some of whom make only one transaction from bonds to money, and the elasticity is therefore between ½ and 1. Similarly, the interest elasticity is also an average of the elasticities across different individuals, being between $-$ ½ and zero.[18] Because firms deal with larger amounts of money, they are likely to make a large number of transactions between money and bonds, and their income and interest elasticities of the demand for money are therefore likely to be close to the ½ and $-$ ½ predicted by Eq. (4).

*The Payment Period

Once the integer constraints are taken into account, it can also be seen that the transactions demand for money depends on the frequency with which individuals are paid (the payment period). If one examines the square-root formula (4), the demand for money does not seem to depend on how often a person is paid, since an increase in the payments period increases both Y_N and i in the same proportion. Thus the demand for money appears unaffected by the length of the period. However, consider an individual who makes only one transaction from bonds to money at the beginning of each month. His money demand is $Y_N/2$. If such a person were paid weekly, his demand for money would be only one-quarter of the demand with monthly payments. Thus we should expect the demand for money to increase with the length of the payments period.

---

[18]See Robert J. Barro, "Integer Constraints and Aggregation in an Inventory Model of Money Demand," *Journal of Finance*, March 1976.

Summary

The inventory-theoretic approach to the demand for money gives a precise formula for the transactions demand for money: The income elasticity of the demand for money is ½ and the interest elasticity is $-$ ½. When integer constraints are taken into account, the limits on the income elasticity of demand are between ½ and 1, and the limits on the interest elasticity are between $-$ ½ and zero. We have outlined the approach in terms of an individual's demand for money, but a similar approach is relevant for firms.

Some of the assumptions made in deriving the square-root formula are very restrictive. People do not spend their money evenly over the course of the month, and they do not know exactly what their payments will be. Their checks are not paid into savings accounts, and so on. It turns out, though, that the major results we have derived are not greatly affected by the use of more realistic assumptions. There is thus good reason to expect the demand for money to increase with the level of income and to decrease as the interest rate increases.

The Precautionary Motive

In discussing the transactions demand for money, we focused on transactions costs and ignored uncertainty. In this section, we concentrate on the demand for money that arises because people are uncertain about the payments they might want to, or have to, make.[19] Suppose, realistically, that an individual did not know precisely what payments he would be receiving in the next few weeks, and also that he did not know what payments he would have to make. He might decide to have a hot fudge sundae, or need to take a cab in the rain, or have to pay for a prescription. If he did not have money with which to pay, he would incur a loss. The loss could be missing a fine meal, or missing an appointment, or having to come back the next day to pay for the prescription. For concreteness, we shall denote the loss incurred as a result of being short of cash by c.[20] The loss clearly varies from situation to situation, but as usual we simplify.

The loss incurred as a result of being out of money is a cost of *illiquidity*. Since *liquidity* is a much-used term in connection with assets, it is worth a brief discussion. An asset is liquid when it can be used quickly and cheaply to make a purchase. Money is thus entirely liquid. Other assets have differing degrees of liquidity. A savings deposit is quite liquid, since it can be turned into cash quickly with little loss. An old master is highly illiquid, since it takes time to sell paintings and obtain a price close to their full value. We say that the cost of being out of money to make a purchase is a cost of illiquidity, because the individual might well have

---

[19]See Edward H. Whalen, "A Rationalization of the Precautionary Demand for Cash," *Quarterly Journal of Economics*, May 1966.

[20]This c should not be confused with the marginal propensity to consume.

other assets she could, in principle, sell in order to make whatever purchase is being considered. However, there is no quick way of selling off most assets while trying to catch a cab in the rain.

Now we return to the precautionary demand for money. The more money the individual holds, the less likely she is to incur the costs of illiquidity. But the more money she holds, the more interest she is giving up. We are back to a tradeoff situation similar to that examined in relation to the transactions demand. Somewhere between holding so little money for precautionary purposes that it is virtually certain it will be necessary to forgo some purchase (or to borrow in a hurry), and so much money that there is little chance of not being able to make any payment that might be necessary, there must be an optimal amount of precautionary balances to hold. That optimal amount will involve the balancing of interest costs against the advantages of not being caught illiquid.

Once more, we write down the total costs of holding an amount of money M.[21] This time we are dealing with expected costs, since it is not certain what the need for money will be. We denote the probability that the individual is illiquid during the month by $p(M,\sigma)$. The function $p(M,\sigma)$ indicates that the probability of the person being illiquid at some time during the month depends on the level of money balances M she holds, and the degree of uncertainty σ about the net payments she will be making during the month. The probability of illiquidity is lower the higher is M, and higher the higher is the degree of uncertainty σ. The *expected cost* of illiquidity is $p(M,\sigma)c$—the probability of illiquidity times the cost of being illiquid. The interest cost associated with holding a cash balance of M is just iM. Thus, we have

$$\text{Expected costs} = iM + p(M,\sigma)c \qquad (5)$$

To determine the optimal amount of money to hold, we compare the marginal costs of increasing money holding by \$1 with the expected marginal benefit of doing so. The marginal cost is again the interest foregone, or i. That is shown by the MC curve in Fig. 7-3. The marginal benefit of increasing money holding arises from the lower expected costs of illiquidity. Increasing precautionary balances from zero has a large marginal benefit, since that takes care of small unexpected disbursements that are quite likely. As we increase cash balances further, we continue to reduce the probability of illiquidity, but at a decreasing rate. We start to hold cash to insure against quite unlikely events. Thus, the marginal benefit of additional cash is a decreasing function of the level of cash holdings—more cash on hand is better than less, but at a diminishing rate. The marginal benefit of increasing cash holdings is shown by the MB curve in Fig. 7-3.

The optimal level of the precautionary demand for money is reached

---

[21]This paragraph contains technical material that is optional and can easily be skipped.

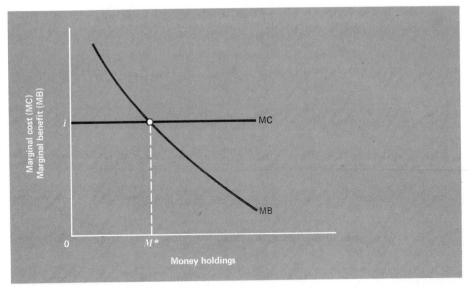

FIGURE 7-3 THE PRECAUTIONARY DE-
MAND FOR MONEY

where the two curves intersect. That level of money is shown as M^* in Fig. 7-3. Now we can use Fig. 7-3 to examine the determinants of the optimal level of the precautionary demand. It is, first, apparent that precautionary balances will be larger when the interest rate is lower. A reduction in the interest rate shifts the MC curve down and increases M^*. The lower cost of holding money makes it profitable to insure more heavily against the costs of illiquidity. An increase in uncertainty leads to increased money holdings because it shifts up the MB curve. With more uncertainty about the flow of spending, there is more scope for unforeseen payments and thus a greater danger of illiquidity. It therefore pays to insure more heavily by holding larger cash balances. Finally, the lower the costs of illiquidity c, the lower is money demand. A reduction in c moves the MB curve down. Indeed, if there were no cost to illiquidity, no one would bother to hold money. There would be no penalty for not having it, while at the same time, holding it would mean a loss of interest.

Before we conclude this section, we note that the model of precautionary demand can be applied to goods other than money. It is a broad theory that applies to any commodity inventory that is held as insurance against contingencies. For instance, cars carry spare tires. The reader can work out circumstances under which one would want to have more than one spare tire in a car, and even circumstances in which zero would be the optimal number. The idea of the precautionary demand for money or for goods is quite general. So, too, are the determinants of the precautionary demand: the alternative cost in terms of interest forgone, the cost of il-liquidity, and the degree of uncertainty that determines the probability of illiquidity.

The Speculative Demand for Money

The transactions demand and the precautionary demand for money em-phasize the medium of exchange function of money, for each refers to the need to have money on hand to make payments. Each theory is more relevant to the M_1 definition of money than any other, though the pre-cautionary demand could certainly explain part of the holding of savings accounts and other relatively liquid assets which are part of M_3. Now we move over to the store of value function of money and concentrate on the role of money in the investment portfolio of an individual.

An individual who has wealth has to hold that wealth in specific assets. Those assets make up a *portfolio*. In general, one would think an investor would want to hold the asset which provides the highest returns. How-ever, given that the return on most assets is uncertain, it is unwise to hold the entire portfolio in a single *risky asset*. You may have the hottest tip that a certain stock will surely double within the next two years, but you would be wise to recognize that hot tips are far from infallible, and that you could lose a lot of money in that stock as well as make money. The pru-dent, risk-averse investor does not put all her eggs in one basket. Uncer-tainty about the returns on risky assets leads to a diversified portfolio strategy.

As part of that diversified portfolio, the typical investor will want to hold some amount of a safe asset, as insurance against capital losses on assets whose prices change in an uncertain manner. The safe asset would be held precisely because it is safe, even though it pays a lower expected return than risky assets. Money is a safe asset in that its nominal value is known with certainty.[22] In a famous article,[23] James Tobin argued that money would be held as the safe asset in the portfolios of investors. The title of the article, "Liquidity Preference as Behavior towards Risk," ex-plains the essential notion. In this framework, the demand for money—the safe asset—depends on the expected yields on other assets, as well as the riskiness of the yields on the other assets. The riskiness of the return on other assets is measured by the variability of the return. Using reason-able assumptions, Tobin shows that an increase in the expected return on other assets—an increase in the opportunity cost of holding money (that is, the return lost by holding money)—lowers money demand. By contrast,

[22]Of course, when the rate of inflation is uncertain, the real value of money is also uncertain, and money is no longer a safe asset. Even so, the uncertainties about the values of equity are so much larger than the uncertainties about the rate of inflation, that money can be treated as a relatively safe asset.

[23]James Tobin, "Liquidity Preference as Behavior towards Risk," *Review of Economic Studies*, February 1958.

an increase in the riskiness of the returns on other assets increases money demand.

An investor's aversion to risk certainly generates a demand for a safe asset. The question we want to consider is whether that safe asset is money. That is, we want to ask whether considerations of portfolio behavior do generate a demand for money. The relevant considerations in the portfolio are the returns and the risks on assets. From the viewpoint of the yield and risks of holding money, it is clear that time or savings deposits have the same risks as currency or demand deposits. However, they pay a higher yield. The risks in both cases are the risks arising from uncertainty about inflation. Given that the risks are the same, and with the yields on time and savings deposits higher than on currency and demand deposits, portfolio diversification can explain the demand for assets such as time and savings deposits, but not the demand for M_1. The speculative demand is not a valid reason for holding M_1, but it is a reason for holding M_2 or M_3.

Nonetheless, the implications of the speculative, or risk-diversifying, demand for money, are similar to those of the transactions and precautionary demands. An increase in the interest rate on nonmoney assets, such as long-term bond yields or equity yields, will reduce the demand for M_2. An increase in the rate paid on time deposits will increase the demand for time deposits, perhaps even at the cost of the demand for M_1, as people take advantage of the higher yields they can earn on their investment portfolios to increase the size of those portfolios. One important difference between the speculative and the other two categories of demand is that here the level of wealth is clearly relevant to the demand for M_2. The level of wealth determines the size of the total portfolio, and we expect that increases in wealth lead to increases in the demand for the safe asset, and thus in M_2 demand.

One final point on the speculative demand. Many individuals with relatively small amounts of wealth will indeed hold part of that wealth in savings accounts, in order to diversify their portfolios. But bigger investors are sometimes able to purchase other securities which pay higher interest and also have fixed (i.e., risk-free) nominal values. Large CDs (in excess of $100,000) are sometimes an example of such assets, as are Treasury bills on occasion. For such individuals or groups, the demand for a safe asset is not a demand for money.

7-4 EMPIRICAL EVIDENCE

This section examines the empirical evidence—the studies made using actual data—on the demand for money. We noted in Chap. 4, and again at the beginning of Sec. 7-3, that the *interest elasticity* of the demand for money plays an important role in determining the effectiveness of monetary and fiscal policies. We then showed in Sec. 7-3 that there are good theoretical reasons for believing the demand for real balances should depend on the interest rate. The empirical evidence supports that view very strongly. Empirical studies have established that the demand for money is responsive to the interest rate. An increase in the interest rate reduces the demand for money.

The theory of money demand also predicts that the demand for money should depend on the level of income. The response of the demand for money to the level of income, as measured by the *income elasticity* of money demand, is also important from a policy viewpoint. The income elasticity of money demand provides a guide to the Fed as to how fast to increase the money supply to support a given rate of growth of GNP without changing the interest rate.

Suppose that the aim is for GNP growth of 10 percent, 6 percent real growth and 4 percent inflation. If the Fed wants to provide a sufficient growth rate of money to prevent interest rates from rising, it has to know the income elasticity of the demand for real balances. Suppose the real income elasticity is ½. Then the Fed would have to produce monetary growth of 7 percent to prevent an increase in interest rates. Why? First, the demand for nominal money increases in proportion to the price level, since money demand is a demand for real balances. Thus 4 percent growth in money is needed to meet the increased demand from the 4 percent increase in the price level. The 6 percent growth in real income would increase the demand for real balances by 3 percent (= 6 percent × ½), given the real income elasticity of ½. Hence, the needed 7 percent (= 4 + 3) growth in the nominal money supply to meet the increased demand arising from the increase in income.

The empirical work on the demand for money has introduced one complication that we did not study in the theoretical section. That is that the demand for money adjusts to changes in income and interest rates *with a lag*. When the level of income or the interest rate changes, there is first only a small change in the demand for money. Then, over the course of time, the change in the demand for money increases, slowly building up to its full long-run change. Reasons for this lag are not yet certain. The two usual possibilities exist in this case too. The lags may arise because there are costs of adjusting money holdings, or they may arise because money holders' expectations are slow to adjust. If a person believes that a given change in the interest rate is temporary, she may be unwilling to make a major change in her money holdings. As time passes and it becomes clearer that the change is not transitory, she is more willing to make a larger adjustment.

The empirical evidence on the demand for money in the United States has been reworked and reviewed in a very comprehensive study by

[24]Stephen M. Goldfeld, "The Demand for Money Revisited," *Brookings Papers on Economic Activity*, 1973, 3. A review of other work on the demand for money is contained in the very readable book by David Laidler, *The Demand for Money: Theories and Evidence*, Dun-Donnelley, 1977.

Stephen Goldfeld of Princeton University.[24] Goldfeld studies the demand for M_1, using quarterly post-World War II data. Table 7-2 summarizes the conclusions that are of major importance for us. The table shows the elasticities of the demand for real balances with respect to real income Y (real GNP), and interest rates. The rate on time deposits, i_{TD}, and the rate on commercial paper, i_{CP}, are the interest rates used by Goldfeld. Commercial paper represents short-term borrowing by corporations. That interest rate is relevant to the demand for money because commercial paper is an asset which is very liquid for (other) corporations that can hold it instead of money for short periods of time.

In the short run (one quarter), the elasticity of demand with respect to real income, is 0.19. This means that a 1 percent increase in real income raises money demand by 0.19 percent, which is considerably less than proportionately. The table shows that the interest elasticity of money demand with respect to interest rates is negative: an increase in interest rates reduces money demand. The short-run interest elasticities are quite small. An increase in the rate on time deposits from 4 percent to 5 percent, that is, a 25 percent increase ($\frac{5}{4} = 1.25$), reduces the demand for money by only 1.12 percent ($=0.045 \times 25$ percent). An increase in the rate on commercial paper from 4 to 5 percent would reduce money demand by only 0.47 percent.

The long-run elasticities exceed the short-run elasticities by a factor of more than 3, as Table 7-2 shows. The long-run real income elasticity is 0.68, meaning that in the long run the increase in real money demand occurring as a result of a given increase in real income is only 68 percent as large as the proportional increase in income. Real money demand thus rises less than proportionately to the rise in real income. The long-run interest elasticities sum to a little over 0.2, meaning that an increase in *both* i_{TD} and i_{CP} from 4 percent to 5 percent would reduce the demand for money by a little over 5 percent.

How long is the long run? That is, how long does it take the demand for money to adjust from the short-run elasticities of Table 7-2 to the long-run elasticities shown in the table? Actually, it takes forever for the full

TABLE 7-2 ELASTICITIES OF REAL MONEY DEMAND

	Y	i_{TD}	i_{CP}
Short run	0.19	−0.045	−0.019
Long run	0.68	−0.16	−0.067

Source: S. Goldfeld, "The Demand for Money Revisited," *Brookings Papers on Economic Activity*, 1973, 3, p. 602, Regression A.

long-run position to be reached. Table 7-3, however, shows the elasticities of the demand for real balances in response to changes in the level of income and interest rates after one, two, three, four, and eight quarters. Three-fourths of the adjustment is complete within the first year, and over 90 percent of the adjustment is complete within the first two years.

In summary, we have so far described three essential properties of money demand:

1 The demand for real money balances responds negatively to the rate of interest. An increase in interest rates reduces the demand for money.
2 The demand for money increases with the level of real income. However, the income elasticity of money demand is less than 1 so that money demand increases less than proportionately with income.
3 The short-run responsiveness of money demand to changes in interest rates and income is considerably less than the long-run response. The long-run elasticities are estimated to be over three times the size of the short-run elasticities.

There is one more important point with which we conclude this section. The question is how money responds to an increase in the level of prices. Here Goldfeld, like other researchers before him, finds strong evidence that an increase in prices raises nominal money demand in the same proportion. We can add, therefore, a fourth conclusion:

4 The demand for nominal money balances is proportional to the price level. There is no money illusion; in other words, the demand for money is a demand for *real* balances.

*7-5 THE INCOME VELOCITY OF MONEY

The *income velocity of money* is the number of times the stock of money is turned over per year in financing the annual flow of income. Thus in 1976, GNP was about $1,700 billion, the money stock (M_1) was $304 billion, and velocity was therefore about 5.5. The average dollar of money balances financed $5.5 of spending on final goods and services, or the public held on average just under 20 cents of M_1 per dollar of income.[25] While we usually calculate velocity for the economy as a whole, we can also calculate it for an individual. For instance, for someone earning $12,000 per year, who has average money balances during the year of $1,000, the income velocity of money holdings is 12.

[25]Why do we say income velocity and not plain velocity? There is another concept, transactions velocity, that is the ratio of total transactions to money balances. Total transactions far exceed GNP for two reasons. First, there are many transactions involving the sale and purchase of assets that do not contribute to GNP. Second, a particular item in final output typically generates total spending on it that exceeds the contribution of that item to GNP. For instance, 1 dollar's worth of wheat generates transactions as it leaves the farm, as it is sold by the miller, as it leaves the baker for the supermarket, and then as it is sold to the household. One dollar's worth of wheat may involve several dollars of transactions before it is sold for the last time. Transactions velocity is thus higher than income velocity.

TABLE 7-3 DYNAMIC PATTERNS OF ELASTICITIES OF MONEY DEMAND WITH RESPECT TO REAL INCOME AND INTEREST RATES

Quarters elapsed	Y	i_{TD}	i_{CP}
1	0.19	−0.045	−0.019
2	0.33	−0.077	−0.033
3	0.43	−0.100	−0.042
4	0.50	−0.117	−0.049
8	0.63	−0.148	−0.062
Long run	0.68	−0.160	−0.067

Source: S. Goldfeld, "The Demand for Money Revisited," *Brookings Papers on Economic Activity,* 1973, 3.

Income velocity (from now on we shall refer to velocity rather than income velocity) is defined, as in Section 4-8, as

$$V = \frac{Y_N}{M} \tag{6}$$

the ratio of nominal income to nominal money stock. If we rewrite (6) as

$$Y_N = VM \tag{6a}$$

we see one of the major reasons economists have examined the behavior of velocity. Given the nominal money stock and the velocity, we know the level of nominal income. Thus, if we can predict the level of velocity, we can predict the level of nominal income, given the money stock.

Further, *if* velocity were constant, changing the money supply would result in proportionate changes in nominal income. Any policies, including fiscal policies, that did not affect the money stock would not affect the level of income. You will probably now recognize that we have previously discussed a case of constant velocity, without so naming it. In Chap. 4, we discussed the effectiveness of fiscal policy when the demand for money is not a function of the interest rate. We concluded there that if the demand for money is not a function of the interest rate, the LM curve is vertical and the quantity of money uniquely determines the level of nominal income. That vertical LM curve is the same as the assumption of constant velocity.

The discussion of constant velocity suggests that the behavior of velocity is closely related to the behavior of the demand for money. We shall examine that relationship in more detail in the next paragraph. Indeed, the notion of velocity is important because it is a convenient way of talking about money demand. For that reason, the term is frequently used in policy discussions. Discussions about monetary policy would be difficult to follow (or even more difficult to follow than they now are) without knowledge of the meaning of velocity.

We now examine the relationship between velocity and the demand

for money. Let the demand for real balances be written $L(i,Y)$ consistent
with Chap. 4. Recall that Y is real income. Then, when the supply of
money is equal to the demand for money, we have

$$\frac{M}{P} = L(i,Y) \qquad (7)$$

or

$$M = P \cdot L(i,Y) \qquad (7a)$$

Now we can substitute Eq. (7a) into Eq. (6) to obtain

$$V = \frac{Y_N}{PL(i,Y)} \qquad (6b)$$

$$= \frac{Y_N/P}{L(i,Y)}$$

$$= \frac{Y}{L(i,Y)}$$

where we have recognized that Y_N/P is the level of real income. Income
velocity is the ratio of the level of real income to the demand for real
balances.

From Eq. (6b) we note that velocity is a function of real income and the
interest rate. Consider first the effects of a change in the interest rate on
velocity. An increase in the interest rate reduces the demand for real
balances and therefore increases velocity: when the cost of holding money
increases, money holders make their money do more work, and thus turn it
over more often.

The way in which changes in real income affect velocity depends on
the income elasticity of the demand for money. If the income elasticity of
the demand for real balances were 1, then the demand for real balances
would change in the same proportion as income. In that case, changes in
real income would not affect velocity. For suppose that real income Y
increased by 10 percent. The numerator Y in Eq. (6b) would increase by
10 percent as would the denominator, and velocity would be unchanged.
However, we have seen that the income elasticity of the demand for money
is less than 1. That means that velocity *increases* with increases in real
income. For example, suppose that real income rose 10 percent, and the
demand for real balances increased only by 6.8 percent ($= 0.68 \times 10$ percent) as Goldfeld's results suggest. Then the numerator of Eq. (6b) would
increase by more than the denominator, and velocity would rise.

The empirical work reviewed in Sec. 7-4 makes it clear that the demand for money and, therefore, also velocity does react systematically to
changes in interest rates and the level of real income. The empirical evidence therefore decisively refutes the view that velocity is unaffected by

changes in interest rates and that fiscal policy is, accordingly, incapable of affecting the level of nominal income. In terms of Eq. (6*b*), and using the analysis of Chap. 4, expansionary fiscal policy can be thought of as working by increasing interest rates, thereby increasing velocity, and thus making it possible for a given stock of money to support a higher level of nominal GNP.

The empirical evidence we reviewed in Sec. 7-4 is useful in interpreting the long-run or *trend* behavior of velocity, shown in Chart 7-1. The chart shows a striking and steady increase in velocity since the mid-fifties. Velocity has risen from about 3 then, to more than 5 in the mid-seventies, that is, an increase of 70 percent. The public now holds a smaller ratio of money to income than it did twenty years ago. The average dollar thus finances a significantly larger flow of income now than it did then.

This 70 percent increase in velocity since the mid-fifties is broadly consistent with what we should expect, given the characteristics of the demand for money outlined in Sec. 7-4. Table 7-4 summarizes the calculation of the changes in velocity that can be attributed to the behavior of real income and interest rates on the basis of the estimates of Sec. 7-4. Examining Eq. (6*b*), we note that an increase in real income directly increases velocity by increasing the numerator of the expression for velocity. Real income has increased about 80 percent since the mid-fifties, and that direct effect tends to increase velocity by 80 percent, as Table 7-4 shows.

Velocity is decreased by any factor (other than income) tending to increase the demand for money and increased by any factor tending to decrease the demand for money. Now the increase in income of 80 percent increases the demand for real balances by 54 percent (= 0.68 × 80 percent). But interest rates have increased since the mid-fifties. Commercial paper rates have about doubled, or increased by 100 percent. That would reduce the demand for real balances by about 7 percent (−0.067 × 100 percent) and increase velocity by about 7 percent. Time deposit rates have increased by about 120 percent since the mid-fifties, and that would decrease the demand for real balances by 19 percent (= 0.16 × 120 percent).

Summing these influences on velocity, we see that velocity should have increased by 52 percent (= 80 − 54 + 7 + 19 percent) since the mid-fifties, on the basis of the estimated demand for money functions and behavior of real income and interest rates. The predicted 52 percent increase in velocity is in the neighborhood of the actual 70 percent, but less. The empirical results explain most of the increase in trend velocity, but not all of it. The unexplained part could be the result of increasing sophistication in the management of their cash balances by firms over the past twenty years.

In the last few years there have been quite a number of changes in bank regulations that have had the effect of reducing "brokerage fees." What has happened is effectively a reduction in the cost of transferring money balances from saving to checking accounts. Thus, in 1975, it be-

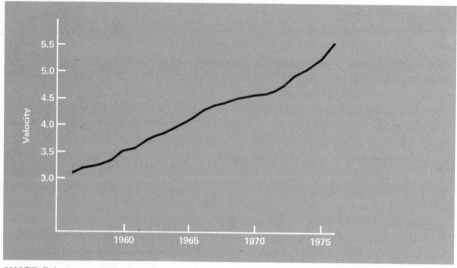

CHART 7-1 THE INCOME VELOCITY OF
MONEY (M_1): THE TREND

came possible to make transfers by telephone instruction rather than actually going to the bank. Along with the reduction in brokerage costs there has been an increasing tendency to make it possible for corporations to manage cash more effectively. Corporations now can hold savings accounts and thus collect interest. There are, too, "bank-managed checking accounts" where the bank undertakes to monitor the account and invest automatically any excess balances in short-term financial assets. The net effect of all these changes is to bring about a reduction in M_1 per dollar income or an increase in velocity.

By contrast to the longer-term trends we have been discussing, the importance of the behavior of velocity (or money demand) in the short run and the way in which the behavior of velocity is discussed in policy making is brought out by events at the end of 1975. Chart 7-2 shows a rapid rise in velocity from the second quarter of 1975. This rise in velocity played an important role in the recovery from the recession. Monetary growth was quite slow in those quarters, and the Fed set itself a goal of increasing the M_1 money stock at a rate of only 5 to 7 percent. Since the inflation rate that was expected for the period was in the 7 to 8 percent range, the Fed was implicitly setting a target for the growth rate of real balances of zero or less.[26] Many outside economists feared that low growth of real balances would result in an increase in interest rates that would choke off the recov-

[26]Be sure you understand why planned monetary growth of say 6½ percent and expected inflation of 7½ percent implies that real balances are expected to fall.

ery. However, the Fed stuck to its guns, arguing that velocity typically increases during business cycle recoveries.

Commenting later, Arthur Burns, the chairperson of the Fed, testified to Congress:[27]

> We knew from a careful reading of history that the turnover of money balances tends to rise rapidly in the early stages of an economic upswing. Consequently, we resisted the advice of those who wanted to open the tap and let money flow out in greater abundance. Subsequent events have borne out our judgments ... increases in the turnover of money balances have been larger than we at the Federal Reserve had anticipated.

We shall make two brief comments on Burns' statement. First, "turnover" of money balances is nothing other than velocity. Second, note that the very small short-run income elasticity of demand for real balances shown in Sec. 7-4 implies that velocity should rise rapidly when income increases. In the short run, increases in income during a recovery do not increase the demand for money by very much, and velocity thus tends to increase much more rapidly than it would given the same increase in income maintained for a longer period. Nonetheless, it remains true that velocity in the last part of 1975 increased even more rapidly than the results of Sec. 7-4 predicted, and, as Burns notes, also more rapidly than the Fed had predicted. There is not yet a satisfactory explanation of the behavior of

[27]Statement by Arthur F. Burns before the Committee on Banking, Currency, and Housing, U.S. House of Representatives, Feb. 3, 1976. Reprinted in the *Federal Reserve Bulletin*, February 1976, pp. 119–125.

TABLE 7-4   INCREASE IN VELOCITY, MID-FIFTIES TO MID-SEVENTIES

Source of velocity change	Calculation	Contribution to change in velocity
1. Increase in real income	80%	80%
2. Increased demand for real balances arising from increase in income	0.68 × 80% = 54% (elasticity times percent change in income)	−54%
3. Decreased demand for real balances arising from 120% increase in time deposit rate	−0.16 × 120% = −19% (elasticity times percent change in interest rates)	+19%
4. Decreased demand for real balances arising from doubling (100% increase) of commercial paper rate	−0.067 × 100% = −7% (elasticity times percent change in interest rates)	+7%
Total		52%

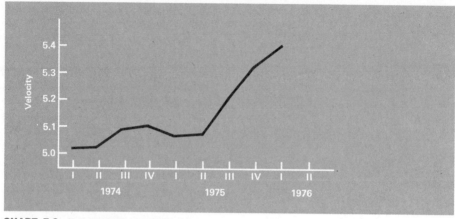

CHART 7-2 THE INCOME VELOCITY OF MONEY IN THE SHORT RUN. (Source: *Economic Report of the President*, 1977)

the demand for money or velocity during that period. Without that increase in velocity, and given the slow growth of money (2.7 percent in the second half of 1975) at the time, the recovery could not have taken place as quickly as it did. Of course, if velocity had not increased as it did, the Fed could have increased the growth rate of money.

7-6 VELOCITY AND INFLATION

We begin to discuss inflation systematically only in Chap. 13, but we can take up here an important and fascinating aspect of inflation. The question is: How does inflation affect the demand for money? It is especially important to distinguish here between the demand for *nominal* and *real* money balances. Earlier in the chapter we have seen that (1) an increase in the price level, all real variables remaining unchanged, leaves the demand for real balances unchanged and increases the demand for nominal balances in proportion to the increase in the price level, and (2) an increase in the rate of interest reduces the demand for real balances. In discussing the role of the interest rate in affecting the demand for money, we pointed out that the interest rate is the return that can be obtained by holding an asset alternative to money, and that it therefore represents the cost of holding money.

These two points are relevant in discussing the effects of expected inflation—expected continuing increases in prices—on the demand for real balances. We have seen that a one-time increase in the price level, all real variables remaining unchanged after the increase in the price level, leaves the demand for real balances unaffected. But now assume that prices increase and that the public interprets the price increases as merely the prelude to further continuing price increases. That is, the public believes there will be inflation.

By raising the price level, inflation reduces the purchasing power of money. Thus inflation at the rate of 5 percent reduces the real value of a nominal dollar that is held for a period of one year by 5 percent. Inflation acts as a tax on real balances.[28] Someone holding $100 for a year during which inflation is 5 percent, in effect pays $5 for holding that money during the year. If she held less money, she would pay a smaller tax; if she reduced her cash holdings to $50, the tax would be only $2.50. There is thus an incentive, when increased inflation is expected, to try to reduce holdings of real balances and instead hold assets whose value is not as adversely affected by inflation. It is precisely this consideration that causes the public to reduce the demand for real balances when inflation is expected.

The effects of expected inflation on the demand for real balances have a strong influence on the behavior of the price level when money supply growth increases. Suppose the money supply had been growing at 5 percent, that real income was constant, and that the inflation rate had been a steady 5 percent. Then let the money supply start growing more rapidly, say at 10 percent. Ultimately, prices will increase at a 10 percent rate as well. But with 10 percent inflation expected, the demand for real balances is lower than when the expected inflation rate is only 5 percent. That means that at some stage during the process by which the economy adapts from an inflation rate of 5 percent to a rate of 10 percent, real balances have to be reduced. The only way real balances can fall is if prices increase more rapidly than the money supply. Accordingly, at some point during the adjustment process, prices have to increase more rapidly than at 10 percent, which is the rate at which the nominal money supply is growing. That means that an increase in the growth rate of money to a new higher level produces, at some point, a rate of inflation higher than the rate of growth of money. The adjustment of real balances during an inflationary period will imply that prices increase more rapidly than the nominal money stock.

How does this observation link up with evidence on money demand during inflationary periods? Phillip Cagan of Columbia University studied the demand for real balances during *hyperinflations*—extremely rapid inflations—in an interesting and famous article.[29] His evidence shows that the demand for real balances declines dramatically as inflation reaches very high levels. As we noted above, expected inflation reduces the demand for money because it is a cost of holding money. For instance, during the

---

[28]We explore the notion of inflation as a tax on real balances in more detail in Chap. 14, which deals with the budget.

[29]Phillip Cagan, "The Monetary Dynamics of Hyperinflation," in Milton Friedman (ed.), *Studies in the Quantity Theory of Money,* University of Chicago Press, 1956.

Austrian hyperinflation in 1922–1923, the *monthly* rate of inflation rose from roughly zero to more than 80 percent. This extraordinary increase in inflation brought about a decline in real money demand to one-fifth the level that had been held at zero inflation. Velocity increased by a factor of 5. The evidence for other countries is, if anything, even more striking.

Cagan's evidence raises the question of how real money demand, or velocity, can be so flexible. How do people manage to reduce their money holdings per dollar, or crown, of income by so much? As inflation increases, the public takes more care in how it manages its cash balances. Money is spent more rapidly after it is received. Firms begin to pay their workers more frequently. Money becomes like a hot potato with people anxious to pass it on rapidly. One can almost see the velocity of circulation increasing as people scurry to get rid of cash. These changes in payments patterns and shopping habits do impose costs on money holders that are the major cost of expected inflation, as we shall see in Chap. 15.

The adjustment of the demand for money to expected inflation is, in principle, no different from the adjustment to changes in the interest rate, which also increase the cost of holding money. Indeed, in countries with sufficiently well-developed capital markets, expected inflation is reflected in nominal interest rates. When inflation is expected, a borrower knows that he will repay his debts in money that has lower purchasing power than the money he originally borrowed, and the lender knows that too. Lenders, accordingly, become more reluctant to lend at any given level of the nominal interest rate, and borrowers become more anxious to borrow at a given nominal interest rate. The result is that the *nominal* interest rate rises when inflation is expected, thus compensating lenders for the loss of purchasing power of money.

The rise in the nominal interest rate that we are talking about reminds us of the distinction between *real* and *nominal* interest rates made in Chap. 6. When the expected rate of inflation rises, nominal interest rates—interest rates which specify how many dollars have to be repaid—increase. The real interest rate—the nominal interest rate minus the expected rate of inflation—need not rise and may even fall. Undoubtedly, one of the major reasons for the increase in nominal interest rates in the United States since the fifties is the increase in the expected rate of inflation. In high-inflation countries, nominal interest rates become very high. In Britain, with its inflation rate in 1975 of 15 percent, interest rates were also around 15 percent. Similarly, in some Latin American countries where inflation rates have reached 50 to 100 percent per year, no one is surprised by bank loan rates of, say, 80 percent.[30]

---

[30]To give a concrete example, think of a chair that costs $100 this year and, say, the inflation rate is 100 percent per year. Next year, therefore, the chair would cost $200. Now if you could get a bank loan at 80 percent interest, you could borrow $100, buy the chair, and sit on it for a year. At the end of the year you resell it for nearly $200, pay the $80 in interest charges on your bank loan and come out ahead. Since everybody recognizes the simple arithmetic of interest and inflation, we would expect loan rates to reflect expected inflation rates.

In talking about both the expected rate of inflation itself and also nominal interest rates as influences on the demand for money, we raise the question of whether each is a separate influence on the demand for money. In well-developed capital markets, in which interest rates are free to move to reflect expected inflation, the nominal interest rate is the relevant opportunity cost of holding money. That is because individuals could make investments at that interest rate. In markets where interest rates are controlled, and rates do not rise to reflect expected inflation, individuals begin to think of the alternative of buying goods rather than holding money when the expected rate of inflation rises. The expected inflation rate itself then becomes a separate influence on the demand for money. Franco Modigliani has offered the following useful rule of thumb to decide whether the nominal interest rate or the expected rate of inflation should be included as determining the demand for money: If the nominal interest rate exceeds the expected rate of inflation, the nominal interest rate should be thought of as the cost of holding money. If the expected inflation rate exceeds the nominal interest rate, think of the expected inflation rate as the cost of holding money.

7-7 SUMMARY

1 The demand for money is a demand for real balances. It is the purchasing power, not the number, of their dollar bills that matters to holders of money.
2 The money supply M_1 is made up of currency and demand deposits at commercial banks. A broader measure, M_2, includes time and savings deposits at commercial banks.
3 The chief characteristic of money is that it serves as a means of payment.
4 There are two broad reasons why people hold money and thus forgo interest that they could earn by holding alternative assets. These reasons are transactions costs and uncertainty.
5 Transactions costs are an essential aspect of money demand. If it was costless to move (instantaneously) in and out of interest-bearing assets, nobody would hold money. Optimal cash management would involve transfers from other assets (bonds or saving deposits) just prior to outlays, and it would involve immediate conversion into interest-bearing form of any cash receipts. The existence of transactions costs— brokerage costs, fees, and time costs—makes it optimal to hold some money.
6 The inventory-theoretic approach shows that an individual will hold a stock of real balances that varies inversely with the interest rate but increases with the level of real income and the cost of transactions. The income elasticity of money demand is less than unity so that there are economies of scale.

7 Transactions costs, in combination with uncertainty about payments and receipts, give rise to a precautionary demand for money. Money holdings provide insurance against illiquidity. Optimal money holdings are higher, the higher the variability of net disbursements and the higher the cost of illiquidity. Since money holdings involve forgoing interest, the optimal money holding will vary inversely with the rate of interest.

8 Portfolio diversification involves the tradeoff between risk and return. Saving deposits form part of an optimal portfolio because they are not risky—their capital value is constant. Saving deposits dominate currency or demand deposits, which are also safe assets, because they bear interest. Thus the speculative portfolio demand for money is a demand for saving deposits or CDs.

9 The empirical evidence provides strong support for a negative interest elasticity of money demand and a positive income elasticity. Because of lags, short-run elasticities are much smaller than long-run elasticities. The long-run income elasticity is about 0.7, and the long-run interest elasticity is about -0.2.

10 The income velocity of money is defined as the ratio of income to money or the rate of turnover of money. Since the fifties, velocity has risen to a level in excess of 5.5.

11 The empirical evidence implies that an increase in real income raises velocity, as does an increase in the rate of interest. At higher levels of income or at higher interest rates, there is a lower demand for money in relation to income. Higher interest rates lead people to economize on cash balances.

12 Inflation implies that money loses purchasing power and inflation thus creates a cost of holding money. The higher the rate of inflation, the lower the amount of real balances that will be held. Hyperinflations provide striking support for this prediction. Under conditions of very high expected inflation, money demand falls dramatically relative to income. Velocity rises as people use less money in relation to income.

PROBLEMS

1. To what extent would it be possible to design a society in which there was no money? What would the problems be? Could currency at least be eliminated? How? (Lest all this seems too unworldly, you should know that some people are beginning to talk of a "cashless economy" in the next century.)

2. Evaluate the effects of the following changes on the demand for M_1, M_2, and M_3. Which of the functions of money do they relate to?

   a "Instant cash" machines which allow twenty-four-hour withdrawals from savings accounts at banks.

   b The same at savings and loan associations.

   c An increase in inflationary expectations.

d   Widespread acceptance of credit cards.

e   Fear of an imminent collapse of the government.

f   The interest rate on time deposits at commercial banks rises while interest on deposits at other financial institutions remains unchanged.

*3.   The assumption was made in the text that in the transactions demand for cash model it is optimal to space transactions evenly throughout the month. Prove this as follows in the case where $n = 2$: Since one transaction must be made immediately, the only question is when to make the second one. For simplicity, call the beginning of the month $t = 0$, and the end of the month $t = 1$. Then a transaction strategy which performs the second transaction at time t_0 will look like the picture that follows. If income is Y_N, then this will require moving $t_0 Y_N$ into cash now, and $(1 - t_0)Y_N$ at time t_0. Calculate the total cost incurred under this strategy, and try various values of t_0 to see which is optimal. (If you are familiar with calculus, prove that $t_0 = \frac{1}{2}$ minimizes total cost.)

*4.   For those students with calculus, derive Eq. (4) from Eq. (2) by minimizing total cost with respect to n.

5.   a   Determine the optimal strategy for cash management for the person who earns $1,600 per month, can earn 0.5 percent interest per month in the savings account, and has a transaction cost of $1.

b   What is the individual's average cash balance?

*c   Suppose her income rises to $1,800. By what percentage does her demand for money rise? (Pay attention to the integer constraints.)

6.   Discuss the various factors which go into an individual's decision regarding how many travelers' checks to take on a vacation.

7.   In the text, we said that the transactions demand for money model can also be applied to firms. Suppose a firm sells steadily during the month, and has to pay its workers at the end of the month. Explain then how it would determine its money holdings.

8.   a   Why has the increase in velocity since the mid-fifties exceeded that explained by Table 7-4?

b   Is V high or low relative to trend during recessions? Why?

c   Can the Fed influence velocity? How?

9.   This chapter emphasizes that the demand for money is a demand for real balances. At the same time, inflation causes the real demand to fall. Explain how these two assertions can both be correct.

10.   "Muggers favor deflation." Comment.

8

The Money
Supply Process

W e have so far taken the money supply to be given and determined by the Federal Reserve System. By and large, the Fed is indeed able to determine the money supply quite accurately, but it does not set the money supply directly. In this chapter we study the way in which the actions of the Fed, the commercial banks, and the public interact in determining the stock of money.

In conducting monetary policy, the Fed pays attention to the behavior of both interest rates and the money supply. We will show that the Fed cannot simultaneously set both the money supply and the interest rate at whatever levels it wants, though it can set either the money supply or the interest rate. In addition, we shall talk about a money supply function—the supply of money as a function of the interest rate.

8-1 DEFINITIONS

We noted in Chap. 7 that the money supply measure M_1 is the sum of demand deposits DD plus currency held outside the banks CU.

$$M_1 \equiv DD + CU \tag{1}$$

A broader measure of the money supply is M_2, which includes, in addition to M_1, time deposits TD at commercial banks:

$$M_2 \equiv M_1 + TD \tag{2}$$

Chart 8-1 shows the history of these aggregates and their components. (Currency is not shown but is the difference between M_1 and demand deposits.) Time deposits have been growing more rapidly than the other components of the money supply. M_2 has accordingly been growing more rapidly than M_1. Over the 1970–1976 period, net time deposits[1] grew at an annual rate of 15 percent, while currency increased at an annual rate of 9.7 percent and demand deposits at 6.2 percent. M_1 grew at 7 percent per annum and M_2 at 11 percent. The 7 percent growth rate of M_1 from 1970 to 1976 is nearly double the average rate of growth of M_1 from 1947 to 1976 of 3.6 percent.

Table 8-1 reproduces part of Table 7-1 and shows the March 1977 components of the money stock. M_1 is about $300 billion, approximately one-quarter of that consisting of currency, and the rest of demand deposits. Time deposits are over $400 billion.

For simplicity, we shall now ignore the distinction between demand and time deposits and consider the money supply process as if there were

---

[1]Recall from Chap. 7 that net time deposits excludes large CDs.

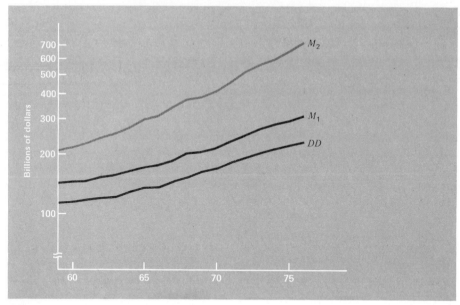

CHART 8-1 MONETARY AGGREGATES
(BILLIONS OF DOLLARS). (Source: *Economic Report of the President*, 1977)

only a uniform class of deposits D. Using that simplification, we define money as deposits plus currency:

$$M \equiv CU + D \qquad (3)$$

Starting from Eq. (3), we now begin to develop the details of the process of money stock determination. It is apparent from Eq. (3) that both the public and the commercial banks have an influence on the determination of the money supply. The public has a role because its demand for currency affects the currency component CU. The commercial banks have a role because the other component of the money stock, deposits D, is a liability of the banks—that is, a debt the banks owe their customers. We know too that the Fed has a part (the most important) in determining the money supply. The interactions among the actions of the public, the banks, and the Fed determine the money supply. We shall summarize the behavior of each of the public, the banks, and the Fed in the money supply process by a single variable.

From the viewpoint of money supply determination, the variable on which we concentrate as representing the behavior of the public is the *currency-deposit ratio*, that is, the ratio of the public's holdings of currency to their holdings of deposits. In early 1977 that ratio was 0.35 (= \$82 billion of currency ÷ \$234 billion of demand deposits), using the M_1 definition of money stock. We denote the currency-deposit ratio, CU/D, by cu.

The behavior of the banks is summarized by the *reserve-deposit ratio*. *Reserves* are assets held by the banks to meet (1) the demands of their customers for cash and (2) payments their customers make by checks which are deposited in other banks. Reserves consist of notes and coin held by the banks—*vault cash*—and also of deposits held by the banks at the Fed. This latter reserve category deserves some attention. Commercial banks which are members of the Federal Reserve System[2] have bank accounts at the Fed. They can use those accounts to make payments among themselves. Thus, when my bank has to make a payment to your bank because I paid you with a check drawn on my bank account, it makes the payment by transferring money from its account at the Fed to your bank's account at the Fed. Bank reserves thus consist of vault cash to meet customers' demands for cash and member bank deposits at the Fed to make payments to other banks. We examine the determinants of the banks' demand for reserves, RE, in more detail in Sec. 8-3 below, but in the meantime we summarize that behavior by the reserve-deposit ratio, $RE/D \equiv r$. The reserve ratio is less than 1, since banks hold assets other than reserves, such as loans they make to the public, and securities, in their portfolios. Banks in 1977 held about \$40 billion of reserves. With (demand) deposits of \$234 the reserve-deposit ratio was $r = 0.16$.

[2]Not all banks are members of the Federal Reserve System. We will not go into the details of membership of the Fed here; instead we refer the interested reader to a money and banking text, such as Lawrence Ritter and William Silber, *Principles of Money, Banking, and Financial Markets*, Basic Books, 1977. Deposits at banks which are members of the Fed make up about 75 percent of total demand deposits, so that the nonmember banks are not very important in the full picture. Fed relations with nonmember banks are under continuing review.

TABLE 8-1 COMPONENTS OF THE MONEY STOCK, MARCH 1977 (*In billions of dollars*)

(1) Currency	(2) Demand deposits	(3) M_1 ≡ (1) + (2)	(4) Time and savings deposits at commercial banks	(5) $M_2 \equiv$ $M_1 +$ (4)
82.4	233.7	316.1	438.0	754.2

Note: Details may not add to totals owing to rounding.
Source: Federal Reserve Bulletin, May 1977.

The Fed's behavior is summarized by the stock of *high-powered money,* or the *monetary base, H.* High-powered money consists of currency (notes and coin) and banks' deposits at the Fed. Part of the currency is held by the public—that is, the $82 billion referred to above. The remaining currency, about $13 billion, is held by banks as vault cash. The notes that constitute most of the outstanding stock of currency are issued by the Fed,[3] and the reserves held by member banks as Fed deposits are a liability of the Fed—that is, a debt of the Fed to the member banks.

8-2 THE MONEY MULTIPLIER

In this section we develop a simple diagrammatic approach to money stock determination. We will show how the supply of high-powered money, which is determined by the Fed, interacts with the demand for high-powered money arising from currency demand by the public and bank reserve demand, in determining the equilibrium stock of money.

At any point in time we have a given stock of high-powered money or a given monetary base (we use these terms interchangeably) which is determined by the Fed. We denote that stock of high-powered money $\overline{H}$, where the bar shows that it is exogenous. As we noted above, high-powered money is used for two purposes. First, the public's holdings of currency are one use of high-powered money. And second, banks hold their reserves in the form of high-powered money (as vault cash and deposits at the Fed). The demand for high-powered money H^d, accordingly, arises from currency demand CU by the public, and reserve demand by commercial banks RE:

$$H^d = CU + RE \qquad (4)$$

The balance between supply and demand for high-powered money requires that

$$\overline{H} = H^d = CU + RE \qquad (5)$$

The next step is to develop the right-hand side of Eq. (4), the demand for high-powered money, in terms of the ratios cu and r, as well as the money stock M. We start with the currency holdings of the public, which can be expressed in terms of the money stock M and the currency deposit ratio cu:

---

[3]Coins are actually minted by the Treasury and sold to the Fed by the Treasury. This detail complicates the bookkeeping but is of no real importance to the process of money supply determination.

$$CU = \frac{CU}{M} M = \left(\frac{CU}{D+CU}\right) M \tag{6}$$

or

$$CU = \left(\frac{cu}{1+cu}\right) M \tag{6a}$$

In Eq. (6) we have simply multiplied and divided by the money supply M and then substituted the definition of the money stock, $M \equiv D + CU$. In moving from Eq. (6) to Eq. (6a), we have divided numerator and denominator of the term in parentheses by deposits D, and then substituted the definition of the currency-deposit ratio, $cu \equiv CU/D$. Equation (6a) gives us an expression for currency demand in terms of the currency-deposit ratio and the money stock. The equation says that the public wants to hold a fraction $cu/(1+cu)$ of their money balances in the form of currency. The higher cu, the higher the fraction of money balances the public wants to hold in the form of money, and the lower the fraction to be held in the form of deposits. (That latter fraction is $1/(1+cu)$)

We can proceed in a manner parallel to Eq. (6) in deriving an expression for reserves in terms of the money stock and the reserve ratio r. Here we write reserves as

$$RE = \left(\frac{RE}{M}\right) M = \left(\frac{RE}{D+CU}\right) M \tag{7}$$

Dividing both numerator and denominator of the term in parentheses by D and using the definitions $cu \equiv CU/D$ and $r \equiv RE/D$,

$$RE = \left(\frac{r}{1+cu}\right) M \tag{7a}$$

Equation (7a) states that reserve demand is equal to a fraction $r/(1+cu)$ of the money stock. The fraction is larger the higher the reserve ratio r. It is lower the higher the currency-deposit ratio cu.[4]

We now have developed expressions for both reserves and currency in terms of money and the cu and r ratios. Substituting Eqs. (6a and (7a) as the total demand for high-powered money in Eq. (4), we obtain

$$H^d = \frac{cu}{1+cu} M + \frac{r}{1+cu} M$$

$$H^d = \left(\frac{cu+r}{1+cu}\right) M \tag{4a}$$

[4]We could have derived Eq. (7a) directly by remembering that $RE = rD$ and that deposits are a fraction $1/(1+cu)$ of the money supply $D = M/(1+cu)$. Substituting that expression for deposits, we have $RE = rD = [r/(1+cu)]M$.

Equation (4a) shows the relation between the demand for high-powered money H^d, the reserve and currency ratios, and the money supply.

Next, substitute Eq. (4a) into Eq. (5), thus equating the demand for high-powered money H^d to the supply of high-powered money $\overline{H}$:

$$\overline{H} = \left(\frac{cu + r}{1 + cu}\right) M \tag{5a}$$

The last step is to turn Eq. (5a) around to read:

$$M = \left(\frac{1 + cu}{cu + r}\right) \overline{H} \tag{8}$$

Equation (8) is the final form that expresses the money stock in terms of the three determinants, $\overline{H}$, cu, and r. The equation states that the money stock is higher the higher the supply of high-powered money. Furthermore, the money stock is higher the lower the reserve ratio and the lower the currency ratio. Low reserve and currency ratios imply that banks and the public demand relatively little high-powered money *per dollar of money stock*, and therefore that a given supply of high-powered money can support a larger stock of money.

The relationship between the money stock and high-powered money is illustrated in Fig. 8-1. The horizontal line shows the given supply of high-powered money $\overline{H}$. The demand for high-powered money is shown as the upward-sloping schedule. That schedule shows the demand for high-powered money H^d associated with each level of the money stock, and thus represents Eq. (4a). The slope of that schedule is equal to the term in parentheses in Eq. (4a), $(cu + r)/(1 + cu)$. Two points deserve notice here. First, that slope is less than 1 if the reserve-deposit ratio r is less than 1, as indeed it is. Second, we observe that the slope is larger and closer to unity, the larger the reserve-deposit ratio and the larger the currency-deposit ratio.

Point E in Fig. 8-1 shows the equilibrium between the supply and demand for high-powered money. Given cu and r and a stock of high-powered money $\overline{H}$, the equilibrium money stock is M_0. If the money stock were larger, say M', there would be an excess demand for high-powered money, and conversely if the money stock were below M_0.

Equation (8) and Fig. 8-1 give us the mechanics of the determination of the money supply. Now we want to develop a more intuitive economic interpretation of money stock determination. In the process we will show why we talk about the monetary base as "high-powered money" and we will introduce the concept of the *money multiplier*. The principal idea is that the public and banks have preferences about the composition of their balance sheets. More specifically, the public wants to hold a particular fraction $cu/(1 + cu)$ of their total money holdings in the form of currency. Banks want to hold a fraction r of their deposit liabilities in the form of

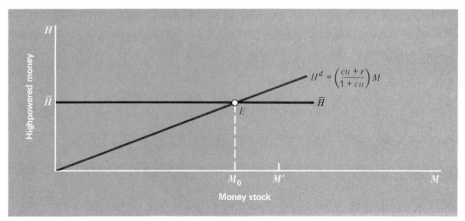

FIGURE 8-1 MONEY STOCK DETERMI-
NATION

reserves. Both the demand for currency and the demand for reserves are a demand for high-powered money. Given the supply of high-powered money, there is a unique level of the money stock such that, first, the public and banks have their preferred *composition* (r and cu) of balance sheets, and, second, the demand for high-powered money is equal to the supply. In this sense we speak of $\bar{H}$, cu, and r as the principal determinants of the money supply.

FIGURE 8-2 AN INCREASE IN THE DE-
MAND FOR HIGH-POWERED MONEY

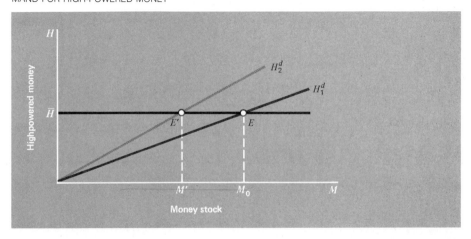

The interpretation of the equilibrium money stock brings out the fact that an increase in r or cu would raise the demand for high-powered money at each level of the stock of money. In Fig. 8-2 we show this as an upward rotation of the demand for high-powered money from H_1^d to H_2^d. The figure shows that the increased demand for high-powered money gives rise to a decline in the equilibrium money stock to M'.

The effect of an increase in the supply of high-powered money is shown in Fig. 8-3. An increase in the supply of monetary base shifts the $\overline{HH}$ schedule upward by $\Delta \overline{H}$. At the initial money stock the supply of high-powered money exceeds the demand. The money supply expands until we reach point E', where we have a new equilibrium with a higher stock of money. We will not discuss yet what causes the money supply to expand when there is an excess of high-powered money, but will instead concentrate on the relation between the expansion in high-powered money, $\Delta \overline{H}$, and the increase in the equilibrium stock of money. We note, from Fig. 8-3, that the increase in the equilibrium money stock exceeds the increase in high-powered money. A dollar increase in high-powered money increases the money stock by a multiple of $1. This is the reason why we refer to the monetary base as "high-powered" money.

The precise relationship between the increase in the monetary base and the increase in the equilibrium money stock depends obviously on the slope of the H^d schedule in Fig. 8-1. A steep slope means that a given stock of high-powered money supports only a small stock of money. Conversely, when the slope is very flat, a given supply of monetary base leads to a large stock of money. The term $(1 + cu)/(cu + r)$ in Eq. (8) is the reciprocal of the slope of the H^d schedule and is called the *money multiplier*. The ratio tells us by how much an increase in high-powered money, $\Delta \overline{H}$, increases the money stock:

$$\Delta M = \left(\frac{1 + cu}{cu + r} \right) \Delta \overline{H} \qquad (8a)$$

It is apparent from Eq. (8a) that, the lower the cu and r ratios, the larger the multiplier. The lower the increase in demand for high-powered money per dollar increase in the money stock, the larger the increase in the money stock we require for the increased monetary base to be absorbed. Assume that, as in the United States, $cu = 0.35$ and $r = 0.16$ so that the multiplier is 2.64 ($= 1.35/0.51$). In this case a $1 increase in high-powered money leads to an expansion of the money stock of $2.64. Why?

An increase in the money stock of $1 raises the demand for high-powered money only by a fraction. In our example, using Eq. (4a), it raises the demand for monetary base by 38 cents. This immediately suggests than an expansion of the money stock equal to $1/0.38 = $2.64 is required to create a $1 increase in demand for high-powered money. This is the multiplier relation between the monetary base and the equilibrium money stock. The lower the demand for high-powered money per dollar money

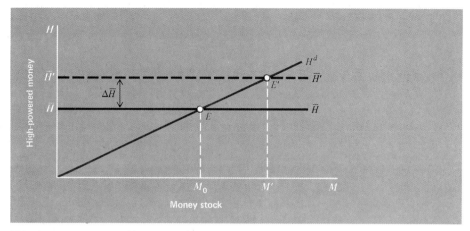

FIGURE 8-3 AN INCREASE IN THE MON-
ETARY BASE

stock, the larger the increase in money required to absorb a given increase in the monetary base.

The money multiplier is sufficiently important and central to warrant some new notation. Let m denote the money multiplier:

$$m \equiv \frac{1 + cu}{r + cu} \tag{9}$$

and with that notation we can rewrite the equation for the money supply in Eq. (8) as

$$M = m\overline{H} \tag{8b}$$

This shows that the money supply is determined by two factors: (1) high-powered money, which is controlled by the Fed, and (2) the money multiplier, which reflects the currency and reserve behavior of the public and commercial banks.

Inspection of Eq. (9) immediately shows that because the reserve deposit ratio is less than 1, the money multiplier is larger than 1. In our example, it was equal to 2.64. The actual figures for the money multiplier are shown in Chart 8-2.[5] A glance at Chart 8-2 suggests that the money multiplier is far from constant. Since the Fed controls $\overline{H}$, it would be able

---

[5]The monetary base used in the calculations shown in Chart 8-2 includes some uses of the base we have omitted, such as Treasury deposits at the Fed. The base used in the calculations underlying Chart 8-2 is, accordingly, larger and the calculated multiplier $M_1/\overline{H}$ is lower than the number we use. For a revision of the monetary base series, see Federal Reserve of St. Louis, *Review*, July 1977.

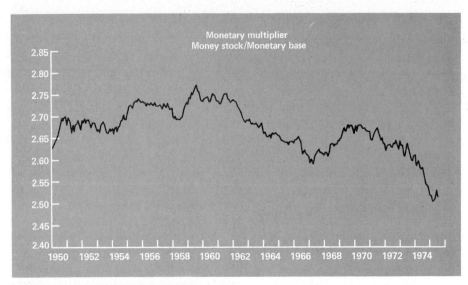

CHART 8-2 THE M_1 MONEY MULTIPLIER, 1950–1975. (Source: Federal Reserve Bank of St. Louis, *Review*, September 1975)

to control M exactly if the multiplier were constant. However, the money multiplier varies, not entirely predictably, and it is not always possible for the Fed to set the money supply at precisely the level it wants. We now take a closer look at the reasons why the money multiplier varies.

8-3 THE STOCK OF HIGH-POWERED MONEY

Table 8-2 shows a highly simplified form of the Fed's balance sheet,[6] listing its assets and liabilities. On the left-hand side are the Fed's main assets, and its liabilities appear on the right. The major assets the Fed owns are gold and government securities. The two main classes of liabilities are currency and member bank deposits. High-powered money, or monetary base, is created when the Fed acquires assets (on the *sources* side) and pays for these assets by creating liabilities.

   The operation by which the Fed most often changes the stock of high-powered money is an *open market operation*. We will examine the mechanics of an open market *purchase*, an operation in which the Fed buys,

[6]We have simplified the balance sheet by lumping together a number of assets and liabilities in the entries "Net other credit" and "Net other liabilities." More detail on the Fed's balance sheet and the monetary base can be obtained by examining the *Federal Reserve Bulletin*'s tables. See also Albert E. Burger, *The Money Supply Process*, Wadsworth, 1971, or a money and banking text.

say, $1 million of government bonds from a private individual. The accounting for the Fed's purchase is shown in Table 8-3. The Fed's ownership of government securities rises by $1 million, which is reflected in the government securities entry on the assets side of the balance sheet. How does the Fed pay for the bond? It writes a check on itself. In return for his bond, the seller receives a check instructing the Fed to pay him (the seller) $1 million. He takes the check to his bank, which credits him with the $1 million, and then deposits the check at the Fed. That bank has an account at the Fed, which is credited for $1 million, and the member bank deposits entry on the liabilities side of the balance sheet rises by $1 million. The commercial bank has just increased its reserves by $1 million, held in the first instance as a deposit at the Fed. The Fed owns more government securities, and the stock of high-powered money has been increased by the amount of the open market purchase. That increase in high-powered money shows up as an increase in member bank deposits. You should now trace out the way in which an open market sale reduces the stock of high-powered money.

The only strange part of the story of the open market purchase is that the Fed can write checks on itself. The check instructs the Fed to pay $1 million to the order of the seller of the bond. The payment is made by giving the eventual owner of the check a deposit at the Fed. That deposit can be used to make payments to other banks, or it can be exchanged for currency. Just as the ordinary deposit holder at a commercial bank can obtain currency in exchange for deposits, the commercial bank deposit holder at the Fed can acquire currency in exchange for its deposits. When the Fed pays for the bond with a deposit at the Fed, it creates high-powered money with a stroke of the pen. Further, since it is the issuer of currency, it also creates high-powered money with the printing press. In either

TABLE 8-2 SIMPLIFIED FORM OF FED BALANCE SHEET, SHOWING SOURCES AND USES OF HIGH-POWERED MONEY

Assets (billions of dollars)			Liabilities (billions of dollars)	
Gold and foreign exchange		12.9	Currency	102.9
Federal reserve credit		116.4	Held by the public	87.1
Loans, discounts, and			Vault cash	15.3
advances	.9		Member bank deposits	
Government securities	107.9		at Fed	27.1
Net other credit	7.5			
Less: Net other liabilities		−1.5		
Monetary base (sources)		130	Monetary base (uses)	130

Note: Numbers may not total owing to rounding.
Source: *Federal Reserve Bulletin*, February 1978.

TABLE 8-3 EFFECTS OF AN OPEN MARKET PURCHASE ON FED BALANCE SHEET

Assets (millions of dollars)		Liabilities (millions of dollars)	
Government securities	+1	Currency	0
All other assets	0	Member bank deposits	+1
Monetary base (sources)	+1	Monetary base (uses)	+1

event, the Fed can create high-powered money at will, merely by buying assets such as government bonds and paying for them with its liabilities.

We return now to the balance sheet, starting by examining the assets. The purchase of assets generates high-powered money. The gold and foreign exchange that the Fed owns was acquired in the past, when the Fed paid for it by writing checks on itself. There is, accordingly, almost no difference between the way in which an open market purchase of gold affects the balance sheet and the way in which an open market purchase of bonds affects the balance sheet. The Fed's 1976 holdings of gold were about $12.0 billion, valued at $42 an ounce. The market value of the gold is much higher, since the market price of gold is far above $42 per ounce.[7]

Table 8-2 points to the effects of Fed purchases of foreign exchange on the monetary base. As we shall see in Chap. 18, the Fed sometimes buys and sells foreign currencies in an attempt to affect exchange rates. These purchases and sales of foreign exchange—*foreign exchange market intervention*—have effects on the base. Note from the balance sheet that if the central bank buys gold or foreign exchange, there is a corresponding increase in high-powered money, as the Fed pays with its own liabilities for the gold or foreign exchange that is purchased. The first point to note, then, is the direct impact of foreign exchange market operations on the base.

The second point concerns *sterilization*. By that term we denote attempts by the Fed to neutralize the effects on the base of exchange market intervention. What is done here is an offsetting open market operation. On one side the Fed creates monetary base by buying foreign exchange, but at the same time an offsetting open market sale of debt reduces the base. The net effect, therefore, is to leave the base unchanged but to change the portfolio composition of the Fed's balance sheet. There will be an increase in the gold and foreign exchange entry and an offsetting reduction in Federal Reserve credit. Thus, by sterilization, the Fed breaks the

---

[7]In the problem set, you are asked to show how the balance sheet would be affected if the Fed decided to value its gold at the free market price. For that purpose you will have to adjust the item "Net other liabilities" appropriately.

link between foreign exchange operations and the money supply.

The Fed's role as a lender is reflected by the "Loans, discounts, and advances" item. The Fed will provide high-powered money to banks that need it by lending to them (crediting their account at the Fed) against the collateral of government securities. The rate at which the Fed typically lends is called the *discount rate*, and it is a rate set by the Fed. If a bank is short of reserves, it can try to borrow from the Fed. The Fed does not automatically lend to banks that want to borrow, even if they are willing and able to pay the discount rate for the borrowing, in part because it does not want banks to use the Fed habitually as a source of reserves. The willingness of banks to borrow from the Fed is partly affected by the rate the Fed charges, and the discount rate accordingly influences the volume of borrowing. Since borrowed reserves are also part of high-powered money, the Fed's discount rate has some effect on the monetary base.

At one time, the discount rate had considerable importance as a signal of the Fed's intentions with regard to the behavior of interest rates. In one famous episode in December 1965, President Johnson reacted strongly and publicly to a discount rate increase which was seen as being the start of a more restrictive monetary policy.[8] More recently, the Fed has tended to use discount policy passively, letting the discount rate adjust occasionally as the general level of interest rates changes.

The balance sheet of Table 8-2 conceals one important item in the "Net other liabilities" entry. Among those liabilities are deposits that the Treasury holds at the Fed. The Treasury makes almost all its payments for the purchases of goods and services and to repay maturing government debt out of its accounts at the Fed. That has the interesting implication that Treasury purchases affect the stock of high-powered money. For suppose the Treasury makes a payment of $1 billion to buy weapons out of its Fed account, by writing a check on that account. Such a check would look much like any other check, except that it would instruct the Fed, rather than a commercial bank, to pay $1 billion to the bearer of the check. The seller of the weapons deposits the check in his bank, which in turn presents it to the Fed. The Fed then credits the commercial bank account at the Fed for $1 billion. Member bank deposits have risen.[9] We show these changes in the balance sheet in Table 8-4.

Because payments by the Treasury from its Fed accounts affect the stock of high-powered money, the Treasury attempts to prevent those accounts from fluctuating excessively. For that purpose, it also keeps accounts at commercial banks, the so-called *tax and loan accounts*. When the Treasury receives tax payments, it typically deposits them in commercial banks, rather than the Fed, so that it does not affect the stock of high-

[8]See Arthur M. Okun, *The Political Economy of Prosperity*, Norton, 1970, p. 69.

[9]Recall that a bank deposit is a *debt* or liability of the bank in which the deposit is held—it is an amount the bank owes the depositor.

powered money. Then, before it has to make a payment, it moves the money from the commercial bank to the Fed. If the payment is made fairly soon after the money is moved into the Fed then the stock of high-powered money is only temporarily affected by the Treasury purchase. The Treasury's attention to the effects of its operations on the stock of high-powered money has varied over the years.

The relationship between the Fed and the Treasury is important also in understanding the financing of government budget deficits. Such deficits can be financed by the Treasury's borrowing from the public. In that case, the Treasury sells bonds to the public. The public pays for the bonds with checks, which are deposited in a tax and loan account. This, accordingly, does not affect the stock of high-powered money. When the Treasury makes payment, it moves the money in and out of its Fed account, leaving the monetary base the same after it has made its payment as it was before the money was transferred into the Fed from the tax and loan account. Thus Treasury deficit financing through borrowing from the public has only a temporary effect on the monetary base, and no effect on the base after the Treasury has used the borrowed funds to make the payments for which the funds were raised.

Alternatively, the Treasury can finance its deficit by borrowing from the Fed. It is simplest to think of the Treasury selling a bond to the Fed instead of to the public. When the bond is sold, the Fed's holdings of government securities increase, and simultaneously the liability "Net other liabilities" increases because Treasury deposits at the Fed have risen. But then when the Treasury uses the borrowed money to make a payment, the stock of high-powered money rises, just as in Table 8-4. Accordingly, when a budget deficit is financed by Treasury borrowing from the Fed, the stock of high-powered money is increased. We sometimes talk of central bank financing of government deficits as financing through the printing of money. It is not necessarily true that the deficit is literally financed by the central bank through the printing of money, but it is true that central bank financing increases the stock of high-powered money, which comes to much the same thing.

TABLE 8-4 FED BALANCE SHEET: EFFECT OF TREASURY PAYMENT

Assets (billions of dollars)		Liabilities (billions of dollars)	
Less:			
Net other liabilities*	+1	Currency	0
Other assets	0	Member bank accounts	+1
Monetary base (sources)	+1	Monetary base (uses)	+1

*The Treasury's payment *reduces* net other liabilities by $1 billion, therefore *increasing* assets by $1 billion.

The main point of this section is that the Fed controls the stock of high-powered money primarily through open market operations, which it can undertake whenever it feels the necessity. It also has some influence over the stock of high-powered money through the indirect route of changing the discount rate and thereby affecting the volume of member bank borrowing. Finally, Treasury financing of its deficits through borrowing from the public leaves the stock of high-powered money unaffected, whereas Treasury financing by borrowing from the Fed increases the monetary base. The Fed does not have to finance Treasury borrowing. Thus it still retains its ability to control the stock of high-powered money, even when the Treasury is running a budget deficit.

8-4 THE CURRENCY-DEPOSIT RATIO

The next element in the money supply formula (8) is the currency-deposit ratio, which reflects the behavior of the public. The currency-deposit ratio is determined primarily by payment patterns, and has a strong seasonal pattern; it is highest around Christmas. The ratio increases when the ratio of consumption to GNP increases, since currency demand is more closely linked to consumption than GNP, while deposit demand is more closely linked to GNP.

The currency-deposit ratio has been increasing, as can be deduced from the behavior of currency and demand deposits since 1970 shown in Chart 8-1. Currency has increased at a 9.7 percent rate since 1970, whereas demand deposits have increased at a 6.2 percent rate. The increase in the currency-deposit ratio accounts for some of the decline in the money multiplier shown in Chart 8-2. For the remainder of the chapter we shall treat the ratio as independent of interest rates and constant.

8-5 THE RESERVE-DEPOSIT RATIO

The commercial banking system affects the supply of money through the reserve-deposit ratio r. The reserve-deposit ratio is determined by two sets of considerations. First, the banking system is subject to Fed regulation in the form of *minimum reserve requirements*. The reserve requirements vary by type of deposit and also by bank size and location. The reserve requirements against time deposits are lower than those against demand deposits; reserve requirements are lower for smaller banks than for large banks, and so on.[10] The variety of the reserve requirements creates some difficulties for control of the money stock because shifts of deposits between different categories of deposits change the level of required re-

---

[10]Reserve requirements are published in the *Federal Reserve Bulletin.*

serves even if the level of deposits is unaffected. There is no compelling logic to the way in which the reserve requirements have evolved, and we shall not discuss them further.

Second, banks may want to hold *excess reserves* beyond the level of required reserves. In deciding how much excess reserves to hold, a bank's economic problem is very similar to the problem of the individual in deciding on a precautionary demand for money. Banks hold reserves to meet demands on them for cash or payments to other banks. If they cannot meet those demands, they have to borrow, either from the Fed or from other banks that happen to have spare reserves. The explicit cost of borrowing from the Fed is the discount rate, while the implicit cost is Fed disapproval of the bank's imprudent behavior (if it is short of reserves frequently) and possible future refusal of the borrowing privilege. The cost of borrowing from other banks is the *federal funds rate*, where federal funds are simply reserves that some banks have in excess and others need. The federal funds rate varies with the overall availability of reserves to the banking system, and can be affected by the Fed through open market operations. When the Fed buys assets in the open market, it increases the availability of reserves and reduces the federal funds rate. In brief, there is a cost to a bank of being short of reserves, and that cost is affected by the Fed's actions.

There is also a cost to a bank of holding reserves. Reserves do not earn interest. By holding smaller reserves, a bank is able to invest in interest-earning assets and increase its profits. A simplified commercial bank balance sheet is shown in Table 8-5. By reducing its reserves, the bank is able to increase its loans or investments on which it earns interest. There is thus a tradeoff of the sort examined in Chap. 7 in discussing the precautionary demand for money. The more reserves a bank holds, the less likely it is to have to incur the costs of borrowing. But the more reserves it holds, the more interest it forgoes.

The bank's choice of reserve ratio therefore depends on three factors, in addition to the required reserve ratio, which we denote r_R. The first is the uncertainty of its net deposit flow. The more variable the inflows and

---

TABLE 8-5 COMMERCIAL BANK BALANCE SHEET

Assets	Liabilities
Reserves	Deposits
Commercial bank credit	
Loans	
Investments	
Less:	
Borrowing from Fed	
Borrowing in the Fed funds	
market (net)	

outflows of cash a bank experiences, the more reserves it will want to hold. The second is the cost of borrowing when the bank runs short of reserves. We shall take the discount rate i_D to be the cost of borrowing. The third factor is the interest forgone by holding reserves, which we shall take as the market interest rate i. We can therefore write the bank's reserve-deposit ratio r as a function of the market interest rate, the discount rate, the required reserve ratio r_R, and σ:

$$r = r(i, i_D, r_R, \sigma) \tag{10}$$

where σ indicates the uncertainty characteristics of the bank's deposit inflows and outflows.

How does each of the factors in Eq. (10) affect the reserve ratio? An increase in the interest rate on earning assets decreases the reserve ratio, since it makes reserves more costly to hold. An increase in the discount rate increases the ratio, since it makes it more costly to run short of reserves. And an increase in the required reserve ratio increases the actual reserve ratio. We thus see that the reserve ratio is a function of market interest rates, which suggests that the supply of money itself may also be a function of market interest rates.

Excess reserves in the last ten years have been less than 1 percent of total reserves. Indeed, in the entire postwar period, they have been small compared with the levels reached in the thirties. The thirties were a period of great economic uncertainty, during which there were many bank failures; that is, banks were unable to meet the demands of their depositors for cash. If you have a deposit in a failed bank, you cannot "get your money (currency) out."

In the thirties, it became necessary for banks to hold large reserves. The reason is that a bank that holds relatively few reserves, with most of its assets in loans or securities, cannot quickly meet its depositors' demands for currency. Banks that hold low reserves are exposed to the risk that a run by depositors—an attempt to convert their deposits into currency— drives the bank into default. But it is precisely when depositors are afraid that a bank is in danger of defaulting that they are likely to attempt to withdraw their money from that bank before it is too late. That is to say that a run may occur on a bank precisely because its depositors believe that a run on the bank is likely to occur. In a general atmosphere of suspicion—such as prevailed in the thirties—it therefore became important for banks to demonstrate their ability to meet cash withdrawals by holding large reserves, that is, by holding excess reserves. Only by actually being in a position to meet large cash demands could the banks avoid their depositors' actually making those demands. The massive bank failures of the thirties, as a consequence of runs on banks, gave rise to an important institutional reform, the creation of the Federal Deposit Insurance Corporation (FDIC). That institution insures bank deposits, so that depositors get paid, even if a bank fails.

There are three main reasons why excess reserves are now so small. First, bank deposits are now insured, mainly through the FDIC. An individual depositor now knows that her deposit will ultimately be paid back. The threat of runs on banks is accordingly much reduced, and banks do not have to hold large reserves to guard against runs.[11] Second, the development of financial markets and communications has reduced the cost to banks of managing their balance sheets in such a way as to keep excess reserves small. Third, the relatively high level of interest rates makes it costly for banks to hold idle reserves rather than earning assets.

8-6 COMMERCIAL BANK CREDIT AND THE ADJUSTMENT PROCESS

This section extends the discussion of commercial banks to explore the relationship between *bank credit* and the money stock, and to show how the money stock adjusts toward its equilibrium value when the monetary base $\overline{H}$ is changed.

Commercial Bank Credit

Commercial bank credit consists of the loans and investments made by banks. We can use the bank's balance sheet, Table 8-5, together with the diagrams of Sec. 8-2 to examine the relationship between bank credit and the money stock. Note from the balance sheet, Table 8-5, that commercial bank credit CC plus reserves RE equals deposits D:

$$CC + RE \equiv D \tag{11}$$

or, equivalently, that commercial bank credit is equal to deposits less reserves:

$$CC \equiv D - RE \tag{11a}$$

Adding and subtracting currency on the right-hand side yields

$$CC \equiv (D + CU) - (RE + CU) \tag{12}$$

or

$$CC \equiv M - \overline{H} \tag{12a}$$

where we have substituted the definition of the money supply and high-powered money into Eq. (12) to obtain Eq. (12a).

[11]See Milton Friedman and Anna Schwartz, *A Monetary History of the United States*, Princeton University Press, 1963, and Thomas Mayer, *Monetary Policy in the United States*, Random House, 1968.

Equation (12a) states that commercial bank credit is equal to the money supply less high-powered money. In Fig. 8-4 this is shown by introducing a 45° line into the diagram so that we can measure the money supply M_0 by the vertical distance to that line. Accordingly, with a money supply M_0 and a stock of high-powered money $\overline{H}$, the equilibrium supply of commercial bank credit is given by the distance AE, the difference between M and $\overline{H}$, as in Eq. (12a).

The relationship (12a) between the money stock and bank credit can be understood by thinking of how a bank creates credit. When banks expand credit by making loans or purchasing securities, they pay for the assets they acquire by creating deposits. A bank that makes a loan to a customer does not give the customer cash but rather gives the loan in the form of a deposit at the bank, and allows the customer to draw on the deposit. The customer is obviously free to draw down the account by taking out currency or else may write a check on the account and make payments in that manner.

The important aspect of credit creation is that it leads automatically to money creation. A bank creates a deposit in making a loan. Deposits are part of our definition of the money supply and, therefore, bank credit creation implies money creation. Even if the loan customer collected the loan entirely in the form of currency, it is still true that the money supply would have increased by the increase in the public's holding of currency.[12]

It is apparent, too, that an increase in high-powered money, as in Fig. 8-4, would increase commercial bank credit as would a reduction in either cu or r. The diagram is useful in another respect. It emphasizes the makeup of the money supply in terms of the credit and high-powered money components. The higher the reserve ratio—the more nearly the H^d schedule coincides with the 45° line—the larger the high-powered money component of the money supply and the smaller the fraction that has as its counterpart commercial bank credit.

The Adjustment Process

Here we briefly describe the adjustment process toward the equilibrium money stock shown in Fig. 8-4. We assume that the public is always in balance sheet equilibrium, by which we mean that the public always holds currency and deposits in the preferred proportion, cu. Consequently, whenever there is an excess of monetary base $\overline{H}$ over the demand for high-powered money H^d, banks have more reserves than they desire, and therefore fewer earning assets than they desire.

Recall now that banks create money when they expand credit. They purchase earning assets by making loans or purchasing securities. In doing so, they create deposits and, therefore, expand the money supply.

[12] You are asked to explain this in the problem set.

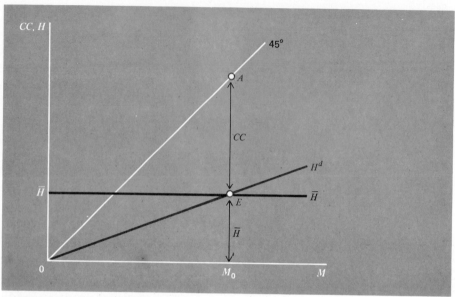

FIGURE 8-4 THE EQUILIBRIUM MONEY
STOCK AND COMMERCIAL BANK CREDIT

The expansion in the money supply, in turn, reduces excessive reserve holdings. This is true for two reasons. First, the expansion of deposits raises the demand for reserves and therefore leaves banks with fewer excess reserves. Second, part of the deposits banks create as they expand credit will be taken out by customers in the form of currency, thereby causing banks to lose excess reserves. It is clear, therefore, that the expansion of credit will cause a reduction in excess reserves, both because of increased reserve demand and a loss of reserves as customers withdraw currency.

An adjustment process based on credit expansion when banks have excess reserves, and on credit contraction when they have deficient reserves, therefore ensures that the financial system will reach a point like E in Fig. 8-4. At point E, banks and the public wish to hold the existing stock of monetary base and are precisely satisfied with the composition of their balance sheets. Banks have the preferred ratio of reserves to deposits (and therefore the preferred ratio of credit to deposits). The public has the preferred composition of its money holdings between currency and deposits.

Figure 8-5 explains the adjustment process in more detail. Here we have separated out the demand for currency CU from the demand for high-powered money. The vertical distance between the H^d and CU schedules is the commercial bank demand for reserves RE. Since, by assumption, the public always is on the CU schedule, the vertical distance between CU and the existing stock of high-powered money, $\overline{H} - CU$, is equal to *actual* bank reserves. At any point to the left of M_0 there is an excess of actual over desired bank reserves. Thus at a money stock level such as M', actual bank reserves exceed the demand for reserves. Whenever there is an excess of actual over desired reserves, banks expand credit. They increase deposits by making loans and thus cause the money supply to expand. The expansion continues until they achieve precisely their reserve target. This is true at point E, where actual and desired reserves coincide.

8-7 THE MONEY SUPPLY FUNCTION

We have in Secs. 8-3 to 8-5 gone behind the formula (8) for the determinants of the money supply and studied the behavior of the three variables in that formula. We now return to Eq. (8) to summarize the implications of Secs. 8-3 to 8-5 by writing a *money supply function* that takes account of the behavior of the banking system and the public:

$$M = \frac{1 + cu}{cu + r(i, i_D, r_R, \sigma)} \overline{H}$$

$$= m(i, i_D, r_R, cu, \sigma)\overline{H} \tag{13}$$

In Eq. (13) we have written the money multiplier m as a function of interest rates, the discount rate, required reserves, the currency-deposit ratio, and the variability of deposit flows.

FIGURE 8-5   THE ADJUSTMENT PROCESS

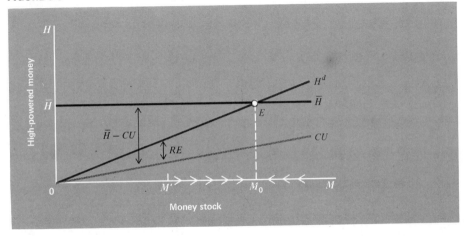

Given the stock of high-powered money, the supply of money in-creases with the money multiplier m. The multiplier, in turn, increases with the level of market interest rates, and decreases with the discount rate, the required reserve ratio, and the currency-deposit ratio. We refer to Eq. (13) as a supply function because it describes the behavior that determines the money supply, given $\overline{H}$. Note that the Fed affects the money supply through three routes: $\overline{H}$, controlled primarily through open market opera-tions, the discount rate i_D, and the required reserve ratio r_R. Of these three channels of control, the stock of high-powered money is the one most fre-quently used.

8-8 EQUILIBRIUM IN THE MONEY MARKET

We can now combine the money supply function in Eq. (13) with the money demand function, developed in Chap. 7 to study money market equilibrium. For that purpose we will continue to assume, as we generally have so far, that the price level is given at the level $\overline{P}$. Furthermore, for the purposes of this section, we will take the level of real income as given, $Y = Y_0$. With both the price level and level of income fixed, money demand will depend only on the interest rate, while the money supply depends on the arguments in Eq. (13). The money market equilibrium will determine the equilibrium interest rate and quantity of money, for given $\overline{P}$ and Y_0.

The equilibrium condition in the money market is that the real money supply M/P equals the demand for real balances, or

$$\frac{M}{P} = L(i,Y) \tag{14}$$

Substituting the expression (13) for M in the money market equilibrium condition (14), and noting $P = \overline{P}$ and $Y = Y_0$ by assumption, we obtain

$$m(i,i_D,r_R,cu,\sigma)\frac{\overline{H}}{\overline{P}} = L(i,Y_0) \tag{14a}$$

We now have the money market equilibrium condition in terms of interest rates and the other variables affecting the supply of, and demand for, money.

In Fig. 8-6 we show the real money demand function as a downward-sloping schedule, drawn for a given level of real income. The real money supply (given $\overline{P}$, σ, cu, i_D, and r_R) is an upward-sloping function of the market interest rate and is drawn for a given stock of high-powered money $\overline{H}$. The positive slope of the money supply function reflects the fact that at higher interest rates, banks prefer to hold fewer reserves, so that the money

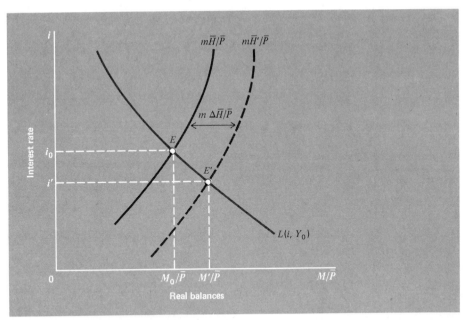

FIGURE 8-6 EQUILIBRIUM IN THE MONEY
MARKET

multiplier is higher.[13] The equilibrium money supply and interest rate are
jointly determined at point E.

Figure 8-6 can be used to study the effects of monetary policy on
interest rates, given the price level and the level of income. In terms of the
LM curve of the IS-LM analysis of Chap. 4, we will be asking how the LM
curve shifts, given the level of income, when monetary policy changes.
Figure 8-7 shows the LM curve, with the initial curve, LM_0, corresponding
to the initial stock of high-powered money $\bar{H}$. We consider first the effects
of an open market purchase. As we saw in Sec. 8-2, an open market purchase increases the stock of high-powered money, and therefore shifts the
supply curve of money in Fig. 8-6 to the right by the money multiplier
times the increase in the base $m \, \Delta \bar{H}/\bar{P}$. The supply curve of money shifts to
the position shown by the broken line, corresponding to the larger stock of
high-powered money $\bar{H}'$. Given the level of income, the increase in the
base via an open market purchase raises the real money supply from $M_0/\bar{P}$ to
$M'/\bar{P}$ and reduces the interest rate from i_0 to i'. Corresponding to the
increase in the base, the LM curve in Fig. 8-7 shifts down and to the right to
$L'M'$.

[13]At sufficiently high interest rates the money supply schedule becomes vertical. Why?

The decline in interest rates shown in Fig. 8-6 does, to some extent, offset the effects of the increase in the monetary base on the money stock. If the money multiplier remained constant, the money stock would increase in proportion to the increase in the base. However, given the fall in interest rates, banks will find it less expensive to hold excess reserves and so choose a higher reserve-deposit ratio. Accordingly, the money multiplier falls, and the money supply increases less than in proportion to the increase in the base. There is, nonetheless, a definite increase in the money stock, as the diagram shows.

The interest responsiveness of the money supply is called the "new view" to contrast it with an earlier and mechanical approach that viewed the money multiplier m as constant. Professor Robert Rasche,[14] in reviewing the empirical literature on the interest-responsiveness of money supply concludes:

> The available evidence suggests quite conclusively that the short-run feedbacks through interest rate changes which would be generated by policy changes in reserve aggregates, are very weak and should cause little, if any, difficulty for the implementation of policy actions aimed at controlling the money stock through the control of reserve aggregates.

[14]Robert Rasche, "A Review of Empirical Studies of the Money Supply Mechanism," Federal Reserve Bank of St. Louis, *Review*, July 1972, p. 19.

FIGURE 8-7 EFFECTS OF MONETARY POLICY ON THE LM CURVE

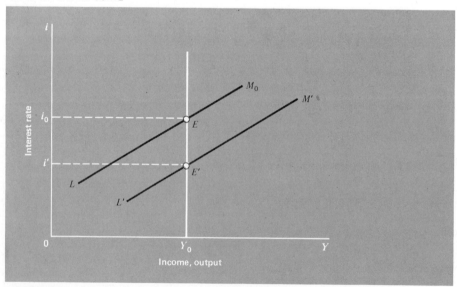

The conclusion, then, is that induced interest rate movements will dampen the money supply expansion brought about by an increase in high-powered money, but that this dampening effect is not very important.

We can similarly analyze the effects of an increase in the discount rate on the money stock and the LM curve. An increase in the discount rate causes banks to want to hold more reserves, since the costs of running short of reserves are raised when the discount rate rises. Accordingly, the supply schedule shifts to the left and equilibrium interest rates increase, while the money supply declines. Similarly, an increase in reserve requirements causes an increase in the reserve-deposit ratio, a decline in the money multiplier, and a leftward shift of the money supply schedule. The resulting effect is again an increase in equilibrium interest rates and a reduction in the money supply.

8-9 CONTROL OF THE MONEY STOCK AND CONTROL OF THE INTEREST RATE

We make a simple but important point in this section: the Fed cannot simultaneously set both the interest rate and the stock of money at any given target levels that it may choose. If the Fed wants to achieve a given interest rate target, like 5 percent, it has to supply the amount of money that is demanded at that interest rate. If it wants to set the money supply at a given level, say \$400 billion in the month of June 1979, it has to allow the interest rate to adjust to equate the demand for money to that supply of money.

Figure 8-8 illustrates the point. Suppose that the Fed, for some reason, decides that it wants to set the interest rate at a level i^*, and the money stock at the level M^*, but that the demand for money function is as shown in $L(i, Y_0)$. The Fed is able to move the money supply function around as in Fig. 8-8, but it is not able to move the money demand function around. It thus has to accept that it can only set combinations of the interest rate and the money supply that lie along the money demand function. At the interest rate i^*, it can have the money supply $M_0/\overline{P}$. At the target money supply $M^*/\overline{P}$, it can have the interest rate i_0. But it cannot have both $M^*/\overline{P}$ and i^*.

The point is sometimes put more dramatically as follows. When the Fed decides to set the interest rate at some given level and keep it fixed—a policy known as *pegging* of the interest rate—it loses control over the money supply. It has to supply whatever amount of money is demanded at that interest rate. If the money demand curve were to shift, because of income growth, say, the Fed would have to increase the stock of high-powered money to increase the money supply.

As an operational matter, it is easier for the Fed in its day-to-day operations to control interest rates exactly than to control the money stock exactly. The Fed buys and sells government securities—primarily Treasury bills—from its *open market desk* in the New York Fed every day. If

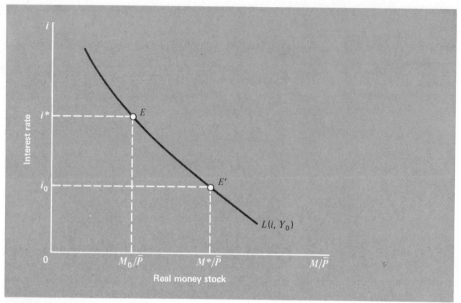

FIGURE 8-8 CONTROLLING THE MONEY
STOCK AND INTEREST RATES

the Fed wanted to raise the price of government securities (lower the interest rate), it would have to buy the securities at the price it wanted. If it wanted to reduce prices of government securities (raise the interest rate), it would have to sell a sufficient amount of securities from its large portfolio. Thus on a day-to-day basis, the Fed can determine interest rates quite accurately.[15]

However, the Fed cannot determine the money supply precisely on a day-to-day basis. For one thing, there is a lag in obtaining data on the money stock. It is some weeks until reasonably good money supply data for a given date become available. That would not affect the Fed's ability to control the money stock if the money multiplier were constant, for then it would be able to deduce from the behavior of the monetary base what the money stock was. But the multiplier is not constant. It varies as a result of changes in the currency-deposit and reserve-deposit ratios. Thus, in the short run, the Fed cannot control the money stock exactly. Over a longer period of time, the Fed is able to determine the money stock fairly accurately. As data on the behavior of the money stock and the money multiplier become available, the Fed can make mid-course corrections in its

[15]For a discussion of techniques of monetary control see the papers by William Poole, "The Making of Monetary Policy: Description and Analysis," and Paul Meek, "Nonborrowed Reserves or the Federal Funds Rate as Desk Targets—Is There a Difference," in *New England Economic Review*, March/April 1975.

setting of the monetary base. Suppose the Fed was aiming for monetary growth of 5 percent over a given period, and initially started the base growing at 5 percent. If it found halfway into the period that the money multiplier had been falling and that the money supply was therefore growing at less than 5 percent, it could step up the growth rate of the base to compensate for the fall in the multiplier.

8-10 MONEY STOCK TARGETS

In March 1975 the Fed, at the direction of the Congress, began to announce target rates of growth of the money stock for the coming twelve months. For instance, Table 8-6 shows the *target* growth rates for money stock measures M_1 through M_3 announced by the Fed for various periods.[16] Table 8-6 also shows the *actual* growth rates of money achieved over these periods. Although the Fed approximately achieved the target growth rates for M_2 and M_3, the M_1 money supply sometimes grew more slowly than the target rate.

Why? The main reason the Fed does not achieve all its targets is that it has too many of them. The Fed cannot control the rates of growth of the different monetary aggregates sufficiently finely that it can achieve growth rates for each of them. If the public decides to move out of demand deposits and into time deposits (perhaps because NOW accounts, which are like checking accounts, but pay interest, are invented), the growth rate of M_1 will tend to be low at the expense of a high rate of growth of M_2. There

---

[16]Recall from Chap. 7 that M_3 is defined as M_2 plus savings accounts at nonbank thrift institutions. The latter include savings and loan associations, mutual savings banks, and credit unions

TABLE 8-6   TARGET AND ACTUAL GROWTH RATES OF MONEY

Period (percent change from a year earlier)	M_1	M_2	M_3
March 1976:			
Projected range	5–7½	8½–10½	10–12
Actual	4.9	9.6	12.2
1976/II			
Projected range	5–7½	8½–10½	10–12
Actual	5.2	9.6	12.0
1976/III			
Projected range	5–7½	7½–10½	9–12
Actual	4.4	9.3	11.5
1976/IV			
Projected range	4½–7½	7½–10½	9–12
Actual	5.4	10.9	12.8

Source: Economic Report of the President, 1977.

is not much the Fed can do about that, though it can change the interest rates banks are allowed to pay on time deposits (through the use of the famous regulation Q which regulates bank interest rates), but it cannot control the growth rates of the different aggregates precisely.

The Fed also has interest rate targets, which are not stated in Table 8-6. The Fed did not want interest rates to go much below 5 percent during the period covered by Table 8-6 at the same time as it wanted M_1 to grow at 5 to 7.5 percent.

However, in the last quarter of 1975, the demand for money was unexpectedly low. In terms of Fig. 8-9, money demand had been expected to be at a position like that shown by the upper demand curve. That would have produced interest rates of about 5 percent along with monetary growth of about 6 percent. Instead, the money demand curve was at a position like that shown by the lower line. The Fed at that stage could either have stuck to its money growth target and pushed interest rates down, or stuck with its interest rate target and allowed the money supply to grow slowly. In the event, it did a little of each. M_1 money growth was below the target rate, and the interest rate fell below 5 percent. The Fed moved to a position like E' on the lower money demand curve in Fig. 8-9, where i_0 and $M_0/\overline{P}$ indicate the compromise levels of the interest rate and the money stock.

8-11 SUMMARY

There are four major points in this chapter.
1 The nominal money supply is determined by the actions of the public through the currency-deposit ratio, the commercial banks' reserve-deposit ratio, and by the Fed.
2 The Fed affects the money supply primarily through open market operations which control the monetary base, or high-powered money. The Fed can also affect the money supply indirectly through the effects of the discount rate and required reserve ratios on the banks' reserve-deposit ratio.
3 Given the stock of high-powered money, the supply of money is a function of the interest rate.
4 The Fed cannot set both the interest rate and the stock of money at whatever target levels it chooses. If it controls the interest rate, it gives up control over the money supply, and vice versa.

PROBLEMS

1 Use Figs. 8-4 and 8-5 to show the equilibrium amounts of currency and deposits.
2 In the 1930s the stock of money fell despite a substantial increase in high-powered money. How do you explain that fact?

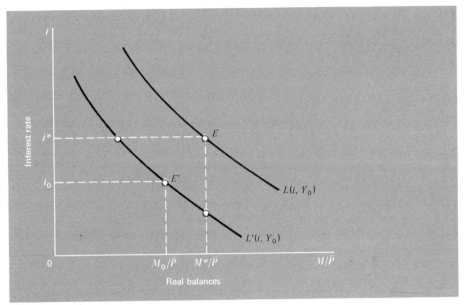

FIGURE 8-9 TARGETS AND COM-
PROMISES IN MONETARY POLICY

3   When the Fed buys or sells gold or foreign exchange, it automatically offsets or sterilizes the impact of these operations on the monetary base by compensating open market operations. Show the effects on the Fed balance sheet of a purchase of gold and a corresponding sterilization through an open market operation.

4   Explain how the Fed's balance sheet would be affected if it valued gold at the market price.

5   "All money is credit." Discuss.

6   "All credit is money." Discuss.

7   A proposal for "100 percent banking" involves a reserve-deposit ratio of unity. Such a scheme has been proposed for the United States in order to enhance the Fed's control over the money supply. Indicate (a) why such a scheme would help monetary control and (b) what bank balance sheets would look like under this scheme.

8   Suppose a bank has excess reserves and makes a loan to someone who immediately withdraws the deposit the bank gives him, and holds it as currency. Why does the bank's granting of the loan increase the money supply?

9   Discuss the impact of credit cards on the money multiplier.

*10   This problem extends the analysis of the chapter by distinguishing between M_1 and M_2. Assume a currency–demand deposit ratio cu and a desired ratio of demand to time deposits of the public, $d = DD/TD$. Assume, too, that banks have reserve preferences described by r_D and r_T with respect to demand and time deposits, where the reserve ratio for time deposits r_T is lower than that for demand deposits r_D.

a Use the definition of M_1 and the ratios d, r_T, and r_D to derive an expression for the equilibrium stock of M_1.

b Use the definition of M_2 and the ratios to derive an expression for the equilibrium stock of M_2.

c Show the effects of an increase in the demand-time deposit ratio on credit.

11 By using Figs. 8-1, 8-6, and 8-7, show the effect of an increase in required reserves on:

a The equilibrium money supply

b Interest rates

c The equilibrium level of income

12 The Federal Deposit Insurance Corporation (FDIC) insures commercial bank deposits against bank default. Discuss the implications of that deposit scheme for the money multiplier.

13 Until 1933 the Fed bought and sold gold in transactions with private residents at $20 an ounce. Discuss the implications of a hypothetical gold discovery in Illinois for the money supply, interest rates, and income, under the assumption that the Fed would buy or sell any amount of gold at $20 an ounce.

14 Assume required reserves were zero. Would banks hold any reserves?

15 The growth targets for various monetary aggregates for 1977 and early 1978 are shown below. Use the *Federal Reserve Bulletin* to find the actual growth rates of these monetary aggregates.

Period (range of percent change from a year earlier)	M_1	M_2	M_3
1977/I	4.5–7	7.5–10	9–12
1977/II	4.5–7	7.5–9.5	9–11
1977/III	4.5–6.5	7.5–10	9–11.5
1977/IV	4.5–6.5	7–10	8.5–11.5
1978/I	4.5–6.5	7–9.5	8.5–11

Source: *Economic Report of the President*, 1977, and *Federal Reserve Bulletin*, March and June 1977.

Problems of Stabilization Policy

T his is the first of two chapters that discuss the problems of macroeconomic policy making. An understanding of the general difficulties
of carrying out successful stabilization policies—policies to reduce the
fluctuations of the economy—helps in explaining why economic performance over the past thirty years has been less satisfactory than might be
expected. Chart 9-1, which shows the unemployment rate over the last
fifty years, gives the clear impression that stabilization policy has left something to be desired. Even before the recession of 1974–1975, unemployment has frequently been high in the post-World War II period.

The reason for discussing the problems of stabilization policy here is
that the preceding chapters have laid out a clear body of theory that seems
to show exactly the policy measures that can be used to maintain full employment. We saw that high unemployment, or a large GNP gap, can be
reduced by an expansion in aggregate demand. An increase in aggregate
demand in turn can be achieved by expansionary monetary or fiscal
policies: an increase in the money supply, a reduction in taxes, an increase
in government spending, or an increase in transfers. Similarly, a boom can
be contained by restrictive monetary or fiscal policies.

The policies needed to prevent the fluctuations in unemployment
shown in Chart 9-1 accordingly appear to be simple and obvious. How,
then, did the fluctuations occur? The answer obviously is that policy making is far from simple. Part of the difficulty of policy making arises from the
possible *conflict between the maintenance of full employment and the
target of low inflation.* That important issue is discussed in the second of
the two general chapters on the problems of policy making, Chap. 15.
Chapters 10 and 16 apply some of the lessons of the two policy chapters to
examine policy making in the United States economy in the sixties and
seventies, respectively.

In this chapter we discuss in detail three problems in the carrying out
of policy that suggest why policy should not be expected to achieve its
targets, such as full employment, at all times. The three *handicaps of
policy making* are:

1 *Lags* in the effects of policy
2 The role of *expectations* in determining private sector responses to policy
3 *Uncertainty* about the effects of policy

In a nutshell, we are going to argue that a policy maker who (1) ob-
serves a disturbance, (2) does not know whether it is permanent or not, (3)
takes time to develop a policy which (4) takes still more time to affect
behavior and (5) has uncertain effects on aggregate demand, is very poorly
equipped to do a perfect job of stabilizing the economy.

Before identifying in more detail the various obstacles in the way of

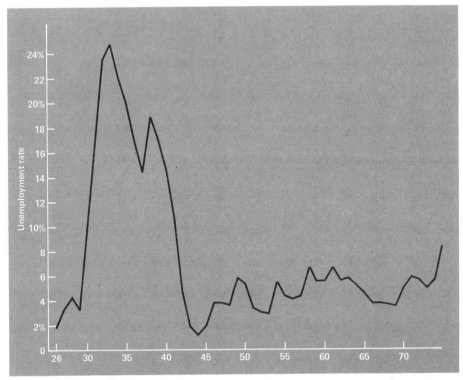

CHART 9-1 UNEMPLOYMENT RATE IN THE
UNITED STATES, 1926–75. (Source: *Economic Report of the President,* 1953 and 1977)

successful policy making, we discuss *economic disturbances* in terms of
their sources, persistence, and importance for policy making. We define
disturbances loosely as shifts in aggregate demand or supply, or shifts in
money demand or supply, that cause output, interest rates, or prices to
diverge from the target path. A few examples of such disturbances can be
given here: In 1976 there was a shortfall of federal government spending.
The government spent less than had been planned, in part because contracts were not awarded in time, and as a consequence aggregate demand
was less than planned. A supply disturbance, to give a different example,
arose in 1973–1974 when the oil price shock raised materials prices and
thereby reduced output supply and created inflationary pressure. A
money demand disturbance occurred in 1975–1976 when money demand
was unexpectedly low as a consequence of financial innovations, as we saw
in Chap. 7. Finally, as another demand disturbance, in 1976 investment
spending was unexpectedly low and as a consequence the recovery in the
second part of the year proceeded at a slower pace than had been planned.

9-1 ECONOMIC DISTURBANCES

For the discussion of economic disturbances in this chapter we can return to the simple keynesian aggregate demand framework of Chap. 3. Figure 9-1 shows the standard aggregate demand diagram with the full-employment level of output represented by Y_p, that is, potential output. Our initial equilibrium is at point E with aggregate demand, including government spending, precisely sufficient to sustain full-employment output.

Suppose next, starting from the initial equilibrium, that there are variations in aggregate demand caused by economic disturbances. What disturbances might cause the economy to move from the full-employment level of output and therefore suggest the use of stabilization policy to restore aggregate demand to the full-employment level? It is clear from Fig. 9-1 that any one of the components of aggregate demand might change.

In terms of overall economic impact, the major disturbances to the economy have been wars. The effects of the increases in government spending associated with World War II, the Korean war, and the Vietnam war can be seen in Chart 9-1. Of these, World War II had the largest impact on the economy. At the height of the war, in 1944, federal government spending exceeded 45 percent of GNP.

As shown in Fig. 9-1, an increase in government spending would cause an upward shift in aggregate demand and therefore an excess demand for

FIGURE 9-1 THE EFFECTS OF AN
ECONOMIC DISTURBANCE

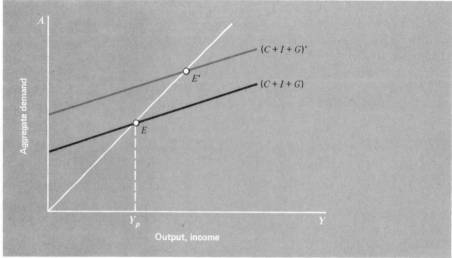

goods. To contain aggregate spending to the full-employment level of output, increased government spending would have to be offset by a reduction in private demand, that is, a reduction in investment and/or consumption spending. Investment spending can be reduced by allowing the interest rate to rise, and consumption spending can be reduced by increasing income taxes. These conventional economic policies may not be sufficient in wartime, however. In World War II more direct methods of reducing investment and consumption were used. A system was set up in which investment projects had to be licensed. That system served to reduce the overall rate of private investment and also to direct investment toward areas helpful for the war effort. There was also some rationing of consumption goods, which reduced consumption expenditure as some of the rationed demand spilled over into increased saving rather than being diverted toward other goods. Thus, the aggregate level of consumption spending was reduced by using rationing to reduce the consumption of various goods essential for the war effort (gasoline, tires, meat, shoes, etc.).[1]

Changes in government spending or tax policies not connected with wars may also constitute economic disturbances. Government spending or taxes may be increased or reduced for reasons which have to do with the government's view of desirable social policies. Those changes too may affect the level of aggregate demand if not accompanied by appropriate monetary and fiscal policies.

Other economic disturbances that lead to changes in aggregate demand originate in the private sector. They are reflected in Fig. 9-1 as shifts in the consumption or investment function. If consumers decide to consume more out of their disposable income at any given level of income, the consumption function of Fig. 9-1 shifts upward, tending to increase the level of income. If there is no economic explanation for the shift in the consumption function, then it is attributed to a change in the tastes of consumers between consumption and saving. In such a case, we describe the shift as a disturbance.

Similarly, if investment spending increases for no apparent economic reason, then we attribute the increase to an unexplained change in the optimism of investors about the returns from investment. Again, we regard that change in investment behavior as a disturbance to the system. Changes in the optimism of investors are sometimes described as changes in their *animal spirits*—a term that suggests that there may be little rational basis for those spirits.[2] Some shifts in the investment function are caused

[1] In passing, it is worth considering for a moment why partial rationing might work as a macroeconomic policy, that is, as a policy reducing aggregate demand. The reason must be that part of the expenditure that is precluded by rationing does not fall on other goods but instead falls on saving, that is, future consumption.

[2] Keynes, in particular, argued that shifts in the investment function were a major cause of fluctuations in the economy. See John Maynard Keynes, *The General Theory of Employment, Interest and Money*, Macmillan, 1936, chap. 22.

by new inventions that require large amounts of investment for their successful marketing, such as the development of the railroads in the nineteenth century and the spread of the automobile in the 1920s.

Shifts in the demand for money may affect the interest rate, and thus indirectly affect the rate of investment; they, too, constitute a possible source of private sector economic disturbances.

Disturbances that we have not yet incorporated in our basic theoretical framework also affect the level of income. These include increases in exports, caused by changes in foreigners' demand for our goods, which tend to increase the level of income. Changes in supply conditions, such as the oil embargo of 1973–1974, will affect the level of income. In Chap. 13 we also discuss the possibility that the behavior of wages may constitute a source of economic disturbances.

Finally, there is the interesting possibility that disturbances may be caused by the policy makers themselves. There are two different arguments concerning this possibility. First, since policy making is difficult, it is entirely possible that the attempts of policy makers to stabilize the economy could be counterproductive. Indeed, a forcefully stated and influential view of the causes of the Great Depression[3] argues that an inept monetary policy by the Federal Reserve System was chiefly responsible for the severity of the depression. The argument of Friedman and Schwartz is basically that the officials in charge of the Federal Reserve System in the early 1930s did not understand the workings of monetary policy and therefore carried out a policy that made the depression worse rather than better.

The second argument that policy makers themselves may be responsible for economic disturbances arises from the relationship between election results and economic conditions in the period before the election.[4] It appears that incumbents tend to be reelected when economic conditions, primarily the unemployment rate, are improving in the year before the election. Accordingly, it is tempting for incumbents to attempt to *improve* economic conditions in the period before the election; that may involve tax reductions or increases in government spending. It is now quite common to talk of the *political business cycle*, meaning that business fluctuations are significantly affected by government economic policies undertaken for political reasons.

It has been argued that election results are significantly affected by the growth rate, rather than the level, of income, in the year leading up to an election. If that is so, then it is tempting indeed for governments to start an expansion in an election year. Despite the difficulties of policy making, it is always easy to start an economic expansion in the short run—though not

---

[3]See Milton Friedman and Anna J. Schwartz, *The Great Contraction*, Princeton University Press, 1965. See also Peter Temin, *Did Monetary Forces Cause the Great Depression?* Norton, 1975, for a skeptical view of the Friedman-Schwartz argument.

[4]See Ray Fair, "Growth Rates Predict November Winners," in *New York Times*, Business & Finance section, p. 12, Jan. 25, 1976, particularly the concluding paragraph.

to control it later when its inflationary consequences appear. While there is some evidence to support the notion of a political business cycle, the argument should be regarded as tentative because the link between economic conditions and election results is not yet firmly established.

We proceed next to discuss the three factors that make the task of policy makers far more difficult than an over-literal interpretation of the simple income-expenditure model in Fig. 9-1 might suggest.

9-2 LAGS IN THE EFFECTS OF POLICY

Suppose that the economy was at full employment and has been affected by an aggregate demand disturbance that reduces the equilibrium level of income below full employment in Fig. 9-2 toward point E'. Suppose further that there was no advance warning of this disturbance and that accordingly no policy actions were taken in anticipation of its occurrence. Policy makers now have to decide *whether at all* and *how* to respond to the disturbance.

The first concern—and the first difficulty—should be over the permanence of the disturbance and its subsequent effects. Suppose the disturbance is only transitory, such as a one-period reduction in consumption

FIGURE 9-2 AN AGGREGATE DEMAND DISTURBANCE

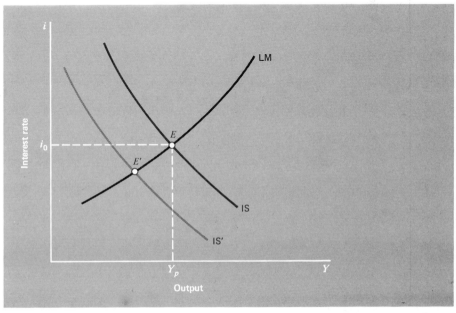

spending. If the disturbance is transitory so that consumption rapidly reverts back to its initial level, then the best policy may be to do nothing at
all. Provided suppliers or producers do not mistakenly interpret the reduction in demand as permanent but rather perceive it as transitory, they will
absorb it by production and inventory changes rather than capacity adjustments. The disturbance will affect income this period but will have very
little permanent effect. Policy actions generally do not affect the economy
immediately. Any policy actions taken to offset the disturbance this
period, for example a tax reduction, will have their impact on spending and
income only over time. In later periods, however, the effects of the initial
reduction in demand on the level of income will be very small, and without
the policy action the economy would tend to be very close to full employment. The effects of a tax reduction therefore would be to raise income in
later periods and move it away from the full-employment level. Thus, if
the disturbance is temporary and it has no long-lived effects and policy
operates with a lag, then the best policy is to do nothing.

Fig. 9-3 illustrates the main issue. Assume an aggregate demand
disturbance reduces output below potential, starting at time t_0. Without
active policy intervention output declines for a while but then recovers and
reaches the full-employment level again at time t_2. Consider next the path
of GNP under an active stabilization policy, but one that works with the
disadvantage of lags. Thus, expansionary policy might be initiated at time
t_1 and start taking effect some time after. Output now tends to recover
faster as a consequence of the expansion and, because of poor dosage and/or
timing, actually overshoots the full-employment level. By time t_3 restrictive policy is initiated, and some time after, output starts turning down
toward full employment and may well continue cycling for a while. If this
were an accurate description of the potency or scope of stabilization policy,
then the question must seriously arise whether it is worth trying to stabilize
output or whether the effect of stabilization policy is actually to make things
worse. Stabilization policy may actually *destabilize* the economy.

One of the main difficulties of policy making is in establishing whether
or not a disturbance is temporary. It was clear enough in the case of World
War II that a high level of defense expenditures would be required for
some years. However, in the case of the Arab oil embargo of 1973–1974, it
was not clear at all how long the embargo would last or whether the high
prices for oil that were established in late 1973 would persist. At the time
there were many who argued that the oil cartel would not survive and that
oil prices would soon fall—that is, that the disturbance was temporary.
That did not turn out to be the case. Let us suppose, however, that it is
known the disturbance will have effects that will last for several quarters,
and that the level of income will, without policy, be below the full-
employment level for some time. Now, what lags do policy makers encounter?

We now consider the steps required before a policy action can be taken
after a disturbance has occurred, and then the process by which that policy

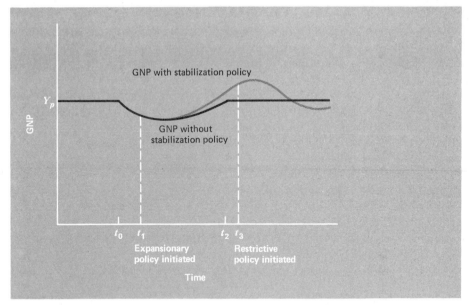

FIGURE 9-3 LAGS AND DESTABILIZING POLICY

action affects the economy. There are delays, or lags, at every stage. It is customary and useful to divide the lags into an *inside* lag, which is the time period it takes to undertake a policy action—such as a tax cut, or an increase in the money supply—and the *outside* lag, which describes the timing of the effects of the policy action on the economy. The inside lag in turn is divided into *recognition*, *decision*, and *action* lags.

The Recognition Lag

The recognition lag is the period that elapses between the time a disturbance occurs and the time it is recognized by the policy makers that action is required. This lag could in principle be *negative* if the disturbance could be predicted and appropriate policy actions considered *before* it even occurs. For example, we know that seasonal factors affect behavior. Thus it is known that at Christmas the demand for currency is high. Rather than allow this to exert a restrictive effect on the money supply, the Fed will accommodate this seasonal demand by an expansion in high-powered money.

In other cases the recognition lag has been positive so that some time elapsed between the disturbance and the recognition that active policy was required. This was true, for example, of the 1974–1975 recession. As can be seen from Chart 1-2 the unemployment rate started increasing very rapidly in the third and particularly the fourth quarter of 1974. It is now clear that expansionary action was required no later than September 1974. Yet in October 1974 the administration was still calling for a tax *increase* to reduce aggregate demand and inflation. By December a sharp increase in the unemployment rate led forcefully to the recognition by most economists that there was need for expansionary action. Only in January, in his State of the Union address, did the President call for a tax reduction, which was implemented in the Tax Reduction Act of 1975. Solow and Kareken have studied the history of policy making. In their study they find that on average the recognition lag is about five months.[5] That lag was found to be somewhat shorter when the required policy was expansionary and somewhat longer when restrictive policy was required.

The major reason that there is any recognition lag at all, apart from the delay in collecting statistical data, is that it is never certain what the consequences of a disturbance will be. That uncertainty in turn is a result of economists' lack of knowledge of the workings of the economy (which is discussed in Sec. 9-4 below) as well as political uncertainties.

The Decision and Action Lags

In the case of the recognition lag, there is no great difference between the lags for fiscal policy and monetary policy. The Federal Reserve Board, the Treasury, and the Council of Economic Advisers are in constant contact with each other and share their predictions about the future course of the economy. For the decision lag—the delay between the recognition of the need for action and a policy decision—by contrast there is a difference between monetary and fiscal policy. The Federal Reserve System's Open Market Committee meets at least monthly to discuss and decide on policy. Thus once the need for a policy action has been recognized, the decision lag for monetary policy is short. Further, the action lag—the lag between the policy decision and its implementation—for monetary policy is also short. The major monetary policy actions, we have seen, are open market operations, changes in the discount rate, and changes in interest rate ceilings through regulation Q. Each of these policy actions can be undertaken almost as soon as it has been decided. Thus, under the existing arrangements for the Federal Reserve System, the decision lag for monetary policy is short, and the action lag practically zero.

However, fiscal policy actions are less rapid. Once the need for a fiscal policy action has been recognized, the administration has to prepare legislation for that action. Next, the legislation has then to be considered and

[5]See John Kareken and Robert Solow, "Lags in Monetary Policy," in *Stabilization Policies*, prepared for the Commission on Money and Credit, Englewood Cliffs, NJ., Prentice-Hall, 1963. See, too, the review of the evidence in Thomas Mayer, *Monetary Policy in the United States*, Random House, 1968, chap. 6, and Michael J. Hamburger, "The Lag in the Effect of Monetary Policy: A Survey of the Recent Literature," Federal Reserve Bank of New York, *Monthly Review*, December 1971.

approved by both houses of Congress before the policy change can be made. Depending on the degree of agreement between the administration and the Congress, that may be a lengthy process. Even after the legislation has been approved, the policy change has still to be put into effect. If the fiscal policy takes the form of a change in tax rates, it may be some time before the changes in tax rates begin to be reflected in pay checks—that is, there may be an action lag. On occasion, though, as in early 1975 when taxes were reduced, the fiscal decision lag may be short; in 1975 it was about two months.

It is primarily because of the different institutional arrangements with regard to monetary and fiscal policy that fiscal policy changes tend to be used less frequently than monetary policy changes in the United States economy. But there are different arrangements in other countries. In Britain, for instance, the government can have tax changes approved very rapidly because the government usually controls a majority in the House of Commons, and that majority is subject to stronger party discipline than in the United States Congress.

The lengthy legislative process for fiscal policy in the United States has led to repeated suggestions that the President be granted the authority to undertake certain fiscal actions without legislation. One proposal is that the President should be allowed to vary tax rates by limited amounts in either direction without first obtaining specific authorization from Congress, but subject to congressional veto.[6] This proposal would reduce the decision lag. Whether such a change is desirable from the economic viewpoint depends obviously on whether the President would on average make changes in tax rates that tend to offset disturbances to the economy. Do remember, though, the political business cycle.

The existence of the inside lag of policy making focuses attention on the *built-in* or *automatic stabilizers* that we discussed in Chap. 3. One of the major benefits of automatic stabilizers is that their inside lag is zero. Recall from Chap. 3 that the most important automatic stabilizer is the income tax. It stabilizes the economy by reducing the multiplier effects of any disturbance to aggregate demand. Recall also from Chap. 3 that the multiplier for the effects of changes in autonomous spending on GNP is inversely related to the income tax rate. The higher the tax rate, the smaller the effects of any given change in autonomous demand on GNP. Similarly, unemployment compensation is another automatic stabilizer. When a worker becomes unemployed and reduces his consumption, that reduction in consumption demand tends to have multiplier effects on output. Those multiplier effects are reduced when the worker receives unemployment compensation because his disposable income is reduced by less than his loss in earnings.

[6]Report of the Commission on Money and Credit, *Money and Credit—Their Influence on Jobs, Prices and Growth*, Prentice-Hall, 1961, pp. 133–137.

Chart 9-2 shows the practical importance of automatic stabilizers (and active fiscal policy) in the United States economy. The chart shows personal disposable income as a fraction of national income. Personal disposable income, as you will remember from Chap. 2, is the income that actually accrues to households after all taxes but inclusive of all transfers. The chart brings out the fact that during periods of a high GNP gap—the early sixties, the 1969–1971 period, and most particularly 1974–1975—personal disposable income rises relative to national income. In these periods transfer payments rise and the growth in income tax collection slows down. For the whole period 1960–1976 the ratio of personal disposable income to national income is on average 84.7 percent. In a recession such as 1974–1975, however, the ratio increases sharply whereas during a period of high aggregate demand and expansion, such as in 1965–1969, the ratio declines below average.[7] In passing, we leave you with this question: What is the counterpart of the increase in the ratio of personal disposable income to national income in a recession? What ratio would you expect to decline sharply?

Although built-in stabilizers have desirable effects, they cannot be carried too far without also affecting the overall performance of the economy.

CHART 9-2 AUTOMATIC STABILIZERS:
THE RATIO OF PERSONAL DISPOSABLE
INCOME TO NATIONAL INCOME. (Source:
Economic Report of the President, 1977)

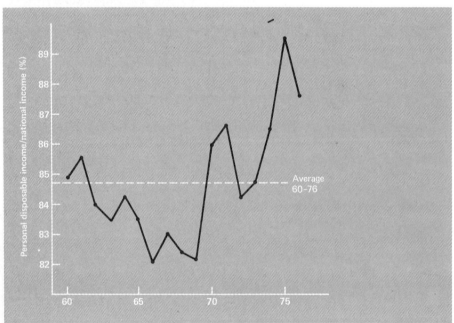

The multiplier could be reduced to 1 by increasing the tax rate to 100 percent, and that would appear to be a stabilizing influence on the economy. But with 100 percent marginal tax rates, the desire to work and consequently the level of GNP would be reduced. Thus there are limits on the extent to which automatic stabilizers are desirable.[8] Nonetheless, automatic stabilizers play an important role in the economy; it has been argued that the absence of significant unemployment compensation in the 1930s was one of the major factors making the Great Depression so severe, and that the existence of the stabilizers alone makes the recurrence of such a deep depression unlikely.

The Outside Lag

The inside lag of policy is a *discrete* lag in which policy can have no effects on the economy until it is implemented. The outside lag is generally a *distributed* lag: once the policy action has been taken, its effects on the economy are spread over time. There is usually a small immediate effect of a policy action, but other effects occur later.

The idea that policy operates on aggregate demand and income with a distributed lag is shown in Fig. 9-4 a and b. Suppose that we are considering a once-and-for-all increase in high-powered money in period 1, as shown in Fig. 9-4 a. This increase in high-powered money, by affecting interest rates and therefore aggregate spending, changes the level of income in subsequent quarters by the amounts indicated in Fig. 9-4 b. The height of the bars shows the amount by which GNP exceeds the level that it would have had in the absence of the policy change. Figure 9-4 b is thus a *dynamic multiplier* of the type examined in Chap. 5. The main point to be made is that monetary or fiscal policies taken now affect the economy over time, with most of the effects typically not occurring in the first quarter. Thus in Fig. 9-4 a given increase in high-powered money in the short run raises GNP by only a small amount although over the full adjustment period the increase in GNP is substantial.

Figure 9-4 makes it clear that the impact of an increase in high-powered money (corresponding to an open market purchase by the Federal Reserve) is initially very small, and that it continues to increase over a long period of time. Thus if it were necessary to increase the level of employment rapidly to offset a demand disturbance, a large open market purchase would be necessary. But in later quarters, the larger initial open market purchase would build up large effects on GNP, and those effects would

---

[7]To be precise the chart reflects both automatic stabilizers and discretionary changes in taxes and transfers. Thus the increase in the ratio in 1975 reflects not only automatic transfers but also the tax rebate of early 1975. The data that would separate out the automatic stabilizers are not conveniently available.

[8]For a discussion of the history of automatic stabilizers see Herbert Stein, *The Fiscal Revolution in America*, University of Chicago Press, 1969.

probably overcorrect the unemployment, leading to inflationary pressures. It would then be necessary to reverse the open market purchase and conduct open market sales to avoid the inflationary consequences of the initial open market purchase.[9]

It should thus be clear that when policy acts slowly, with the impacts of policy building up over time, considerable skill is required of policy makers if their own attempts to correct an initially undesirable situation are not to lead to problems that themselves need correcting. Recall also that we have been talking here about the *outside* lag, and that the policy action we are considering would only be taken six months after the initial disturbance if the inside lag is six months long.

Why are there such long outside lags? We have already discussed some of the reasons for these lags in Chap. 5 on the consumption function,

---

[9]In Chap. 5 we explicitly worked out what would be required for fiscal policy if it were used to stabilize income in the face of a temporary reduction in consumption demand. The principles of that example apply also to the monetary policy problem discussed here.

FIGURE 9-4a TIME PATH OF
HIGH-POWERED MONEY

FIGURE 9-4b DYNAMIC MULTIPLIERS
FOR THE EFFECTS OF THE CHANGE IN
HIGH-POWERED MONEY ON GNP

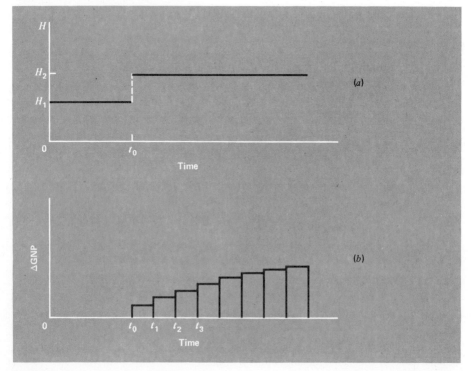

where current consumption depends on lagged income, and also in Chap. 6 on investment, where the accelerator models imply that investment depends on lagged and current income. Similar lags are also present in the financial sector of the economy, where the demand for money depends on lagged income. Each of these sources of lags creates an outside lag, and their interaction generally produces longer lags than each of the underlying lags.

Because the point is so important, let us describe in more detail how the lags of monetary policy arise. Suppose the Fed conducts an open market purchase. Because aggregate demand depends heavily on lagged values of income, interest rates, and other economic variables, the open market purchase initially has effects mainly on short-term interest rates and not on income. Short-term interest rates, such as the Treasury bill rate, affect long-term interest rates with a lag. The long-term interest rates in turn affect investment with a lag, and also affect consumption by affecting the value of wealth.[10] Then when aggregate demand is affected by the initial open market purchase, the increase in aggregate demand itself produces lagged effects on subsequent aggregate demand through the fact that both consumption and investment depend on past values of income. So the effects of an initial open market purchase will be spread through time, as in Fig. 9-4.

Monetary and Fiscal Policy Lags

The discussion of the previous paragraph suggests that fiscal policy and certainly changes in government spending, which act directly on aggregate demand, may affect income more rapidly than monetary policy. This is indeed the case. However, the fact that fiscal policy acts faster on aggregate demand than monetary policy must not lead us to overlook the fact that fiscal policy has a considerably longer inside lag. Moreover, the inside lag for government spending is longer than that for taxes because, when the government purchases goods and services, it has to decide what goods to buy, have bids for the sale of those goods submitted by the private sector, and then decide on the award of the contracts. In summary, therefore, fiscal policy is attractive because of the short outside lag, but that advantage is more than offset by a potentially long inside lag.

Our analysis of lags indicates clearly one difficulty in undertaking stabilizing short-term policy actions: it takes time to set the policies in action, and then the policies themselves take time to affect the economy. But that is not the only difficulty. Further difficulties considered in Secs. 9-3 and 9-4 arise from uncertainty about the exact timing and magnitude of the effects of policy. The dynamic multiplier of Fig. 9-4 itself is not un-

[10]Recall that in Chap. 5 we discussed the life-cycle model of consumption demand in which consumption is affected by the level of wealth. Part of wealth is the value of stock market assets; the value of stock market assets rises when the long-term interest rate falls. Thus, interest rates affect consumption through a wealth effect.

changing, and we do not know for sure how a particular policy will affect income in subsequent periods.

9-3 THE ROLE OF EXPECTATIONS

We have discussed the two basic sources of lags in economic behavior in earlier chapters. The first source is the costs of rapid adjustment. For example, in Chap. 6 we showed how the costs of adjusting the actual capital stock to the desired capital stock led to lags in the investment function. The second source of lags is expectations. In this section we focus on expectations, their formation, and the effects they have on policy and its effectiveness.

While it is undoubtedly true that the past behavior of a variable influences expectations about its future behavior, it is also true that consumers and investors will sometimes use more information than is contained in the past behavior of a variable when trying to predict its future behavior. Consider in particular forecasts of permanent income—long-run average income. In Chap. 5, as in Friedman's original work on the consumption function, permanent income is estimated as an average of income in the recent past. Suppose, however, that you were a resident of a small country that had just discovered vast gold deposits. You would then take the information about the gold discovery into account in forming an estimate of your permanent income. You would *immediately* estimate a permanent income substantially higher than your historical average income. Or suppose that you have been estimating the expected rate of inflation as an average of past rates of inflation, at a time when the inflation rate is high, and a new government is elected on a strictly anti-inflationary platform. Then you would lower your estimate of the inflation rate; that is, you would use more information in predicting it than is contained solely in its past behavior. It should be clear that it is in general very difficult to incorporate *all* relevant information that is used by economic agents within a simple economic model. That means there will inevitably be errors in what the models predict for the consequences of various policy actions, meaning in turn that it is difficult to control the economy precisely.

Reliance on formulas in which expectations are based on past behavior can lead to policy mistakes. To make that point clear, let us consider the most famous recent example in which use of a model with expectations formed only on the basis of past behavior, turned out to be a poor policy guide. The year 1968 was a period of rising inflation. At the time, the rate of inflation of 4 percent was viewed with more alarm than a similar rate would be viewed today, since the rate of inflation had been low throughout the sixties. In addition, the rate of unemployment was low. Contractionary policy was called for, and the administration decided to ask for a tax increase. The decision was to ask for a 10 percent surcharge on personal and corporate income taxes; that is, every taxpayer and corporation would have to pay 10 percent more taxes on the same income than in the past year.

To predict the effects of the policy, it was obviously necessary to consider the effects of the tax surcharge on consumer spending and thus on the level of income. Typically this was done using a consumption function that related the level of consumption to current and past levels of disposable income, as in our formulation of the permanent income consumption function. To calculate the effects of the tax increase, it was thought necessary only to combine this consumption function with a model of the rest of the economy, which was duly done. Predictions were that the tax increase would have a substantial effect on the level of aggregate demand and income—so much so that the Federal Reserve System decided to undertake an expansionary monetary policy to offset part of the contactionary effects of the tax increase. However, the combined contractionary fiscal policy and expansionary monetary policy did not reduce the rate of inflation.

What went wrong? The major clue is that the tax increase was explicitly stated to be a *temporary* tax surcharge that was supposed to last only one year. But that meant that the tax increase would have a much smaller effect on consumers' estimates of their permanent income than would a similar permanent tax increase. A 10 percent increase in taxes in one year has a much smaller effect on lifetime income than a permanent 10 percent tax increase. Thus if a tax increase is temporary, and is expected to be temporary, as the 1968 tax increase was known to be, its effects on consumption will be smaller than if the increase is permanent.

It is now clear that calculation of the effects of the tax surcharge should have taken account of the temporary nature of the surcharge. Does the lesson that economists learned from the 1968 experience guarantee that similar mistakes will not be made in the future? Unfortunately, there is no such guarantee. Expectations enter economic models in many places, and in order to estimate the models using actual data, it is necessary to include some method of calculating the expectations, such as permanent income, or the expected rate of inflation. A careful user of an economic model will no doubt try to check for the reasonableness of the expectations that it includes, but because there are so many places in which expectations matter, it is unlikely that expectations will always be treated appropriately.

It is particularly important to consider the effects of a given policy action itself on expectations, since it is possible that a new type of policy will affect the way in which expectations are formed.[11] Suppose that the Federal Reserve System announced a new monetary policy designed to stabilize the average level of income and avoid booms and recessions. The new policy would be to reduce the money supply whenever the income level rose and to increase the money supply whenever the income level

[11]The role of expectations in economics and the interaction between policy and expectations in particular have been the subject of much recent research. See, for example, Thomas J Sargent and Neil Wallace, "Rational Expectations and the Theory of Economic Policy," *Journal of Monetary Economics*, April 1976.

fell. Such a *countercyclical rule* has implications for expectations. Clearly it would be entirely inappropriate in the presence of such monetary policy to use an expectations mechanism that implies that an increase in income will persist. The monetary policy rule implies that the money supply would be reduced following an increase in income, and one expects the reduction in money to exert at least a dampening effect on income. While correct expectations mechanisms must therefore use information about policy responses to disturbances, such care is difficult to apply in practice. Most expectations mechanisms embodied in econometric models of the United States economy and used for the assessment of policies assume that expectations affecting consumption and investment spending are based entirely on past values.

This section has made two important points about the role of expectations in explaining the difficulties of policy making. The first general point is that the difficulties of modeling the way in which expectations are formed will inevitably lead to errors in economists' forecasts of the effects of particular policy actions on the economy. The second particular point is that expectations themselves are likely to be affected by policy measures, and that failure to take account of the effects of policy on expectations will lead to mistaken predictions of the effects of those policies.

9-4 UNCERTAINTY

In Secs. 9-1 and 9-3 we discussed two major sources of uncertainty that make it difficult to control the economy. In Sec. 9-1 we discussed disturbances that affect the economy, and the problem of predicting how long a given disturbance and its effects will last. In Sec. 9-3 we emphasized that it is never certain exactly what expectations are at any given time and how they are formed. Thus the effects of any given policy action can never be predicted exactly. In this section we point to other uncertainties complicating the task of policy making.

First, though, we want to extend the discussion of economic disturbances of Sec.9-1. In that section we considered major disturbances to the economy. However, there are countless minor disturbances, of the same general nature as the major disturbances outlined in Sec. 9-1, that continually affect the economy and make it impossible to predict the effects of any policy action exactly. The weather and other natural phenomena affect the level of output and employment. Consumption and investment are subject to changes resulting from changes in tastes and animal spirits. Strikes—which have important economic causes, but probably also some noneconomic causes—take place, and affect the level of output temporarily. Political events affect the economy. New inventions lead to economic changes. Disturbances of these sorts occur all the time, and need not be major, but they do mean that there will always be uncertainty about the future behavior of the economy.

In addition, major uncertainties arise from economists' uncertainty about the structure of the economy. It is convenient to distinguish between uncertainty about the correct model of the economy and uncertainty about the precise values of the parameters or coefficients within a given model of the economy, even though the distinction is not watertight. First, there is considerable uncertainty about the correct model of the economy. There is disagreement among economists on some of the behavioral functions of the economy. Thus we discussed a number of models of consumption. As yet, there has not been decisive evidence that has clearly demonstrated that one and only one of those models is correct. Accordingly, different economists use different models of consumption. Of course, the models have much in common, but they are not identical. There are also minor disagreements on the demand for money function, and those disagreements in turn lead to different predictions about the effects of policy.

Reasonable economists can and do differ about what theory and empirical evidence suggest are the correct behavioral functions of the economy. Generally, each economist will have reasons for favoring one particular form, and will use that form. But, being reasonable, the economist will recognize that the particular formulation being used may not be the correct one, and will thus regard the predictions made by using it as subject to a margin of error. Policy makers in turn will know that there are different predictions about the effects of a given policy, and will want to consider the range of predictions that is being made in deciding on policy.

Second, even within the context of a given model, there is uncertainty about the numerical values of the parameters of the model. Suppose for a moment that all economists agree that the life-cycle model of consumption, precisely as specified in Chap. 5, was the only correct model of consumption behavior. On the basis of the historical evidence that we have, it is still not possible to measure the values of the marginal propensities to consume out of labor income and wealth in that consumption function without error. We stated in Chap. 5 that the propensity to consume out of wealth is 0.045. However, we cannot be certain that the number is 0.045 and not 0.06, say, because the statistical evidence we have is not strong enough to enable us to specify the number exactly. The statistical evidence does enable us to say something about the likely range of the parameter[12], so that we could be relatively certain that the true coefficient is between, say, 0.03 and 0.06, but at present, and for the foreseeable future, we would not know it exactly. That uncertainty about the exact values of parameters in our models again means that the effects of policy cannot be predicted with accuracy.

This type of uncertainty has been called *multiplier uncertainty* to emphasize the fact that policy makers will not know what is the correct magnitude of policy actions such as tax cuts, because they do not know what the

---

[12]We are discussing here *confidence intervals* about estimates of parameters; see Pindyck and Rubinfeld, *Econometric Models and Economic Forecasts*, McGraw-Hill, 1976, p. 28, for further discussion.

multiplier is. Thus, with a marginal propensity to consume of 0.7, the multiplier would be 3.3 (=1/1 − 0.7) while a marginal propensity to consume of 0.6 would imply a multiplier of 2.5. If the GNP gap were estimated at, say, $30 billion, a multiplier of 3.3 would call for a $9 billion increase in spending while a multiplier of 2.5 would require $12 billion. If 3.3 was the true multiplier but policy makers erroneously picked 2.5, they would find themselves overshooting their target by $6 billion.

What is optimal behavior in the face of such multiplier uncertainty? The more precisely policy makers are informed about the relevant parameters, the more activist the policy can afford to be. Conversely, if there is a considerable range of error in the estimate of the relevant parameters—in our example the multiplier—then policy should be more modest. With poor information, very active policy runs a large danger of introducing unnecessary fluctuations in the economy.

9-5 ACTIVIST POLICY

We started this chapter asking why there are any fluctuations in the American economy when the policy measures needed to iron out those fluctuations seem to be so simple. The list of difficulties in the way of successful policy making that we have outlined may have raised a different question: Why should one believe that policy can do anything to reduce fluctuations in the economy?

Indeed, considerations of the sort spelled out in the previous three sections have led Milton Friedman and others to argue that there should be no use of active countercyclical monetary policy,[13] and that monetary policy should be confined to making the money supply grow at a constant rate. The precise value of the constant rate of growth of money, Friedman suggests, is less important than the fact that monetary growth be constant and that policy should *not* respond to disturbances. At various times he has suggested growth rates for money of 2 percent or 4 percent or 5 percent. As Friedman has expressed it, "By setting itself a steady course and keeping to it, the monetary authority could make a major contribution to promoting economic stability. By making that course one of steady but moderate growth in the quantity of money, it would make a major contribution to avoidance of either inflation or deflation of prices."[14]

In discussing the desirability of active monetary and fiscal policy, we want to distinguish between policy actions taken in response to major disturbances to the economy, and fine tuning in which policy variables are continually adjusted in response to small disturbances to the economy. We see no case for arguing that monetary and fiscal policy should not be

---

[13]See Milton Friedman, *A Program for Monetary Stability*, New York, Fordham University Press, 1959.

[14]Milton Friedman, "The Role of Monetary Policy," *American Economic Review*, March 1968.

used actively in the face of major disturbances to the economy. Most of the considerations of the previous three sections of this chapter indicate some uncertainty about the effects of policy, but there are still clearly definable circumstances in which there can be no doubt that the appropriate policy is expansionary or contractionary. An administration coming to power in 1933 should not have worried about the uncertainties associated with expansionary policy that we have outlined above. The economy does not move from 25 percent unemployment to full employment in a short time (precisely because of those same lags that make policy difficult). Thus expansionary measures such as a rapid growth of the money supply or increased government expenditures or tax reductions or all three would have been appropriate policy since there was no chance they would have an impact only after the economy was at full employment. Similarly, contractionary policies for private demand are called for in wartime. Early in 1975 with unemployment at 8.2 percent and rising rapidly and forecasts of unemployment for the next two years being very high, policies designed to reduce unemployment were appropriate.[15] In the event of large disturbances in the future, active monetary and/or fiscal policy should once again be used.[16]

Fine tuning presents more complicated issues. The basic question is whether policy variables should be adjusted at frequent intervals to attempt to smooth out minor disturbances to the economy. For instance, should an increase of 0.5 percent in the unemployment rate lead to a small tax reduction, or a small increase in the rate of growth of the money supply, or should policy simply not respond to such disturbances? One possibility is that the initial increase in the unemployment rate is transitory and thus that policy action is inappropriate; the other is that the initial disturbance is permanent, and perhaps even the first sign of a major disturbance, in which case a policy reaction is appropriate. If the disturbance is permanent, the appropriate policy response to a small disturbance is a small change in the course of policy. Thus even if it turned out that the policy action was inappropriate because the disturbance was transitory, the (undesirable) consequences of the policy action would be limited because only a small adjustment had been made. Accordingly, we believe that fine tuning is appropriate provided that policy responses are always kept small in response to small disturbances.

However, we should emphasize that the argument for fine tuning is a controversial one. The major argument against fine tuning is that in practice policy makers cannot behave as suggested—making only small adjustments to small disturbances. Rather, it is argued, they tend to try to do too

---

[15]Because the inflation rate was high in early 1975, policy making then required some judgment about the costs of inflation compared with those of unemployment, a topic discussed in Chap. 15 below. Policy in early 1975 was thus more difficult than policy in 1933.

[16]Interestingly, Friedman argues for the use of active policy in the face of major disturbances in the article cited in footnote 14.

much, if allowed to do anything. Instead of merely trying to offset disturbances, they try to keep the economy always at full employment and therefore undertake inappropriately large policy actions in response to small
disturbances.

The major lesson of the previous three sections of this chapter is not
that policy is impossible, but that policy that is too ambitious in trying to
keep the economy always at full employment (with zero inflation) is impossible. The lesson is to proceed with extreme caution, always bearing in
mind the possibility that policy itself may be destabilizing. We see no
reason why the Federal Reserve System should try to keep the money
supply always growing at the same rate, and believe on the contrary that the
stability of the economy would be improved by its following a careful
countercyclical policy. Similarly, if fiscal policy were not subject to a long
inside lag, we would believe it possible for cautiously used fiscal policy to
be stabilizing.

Rules versus Discretion

Finally in this chapter, we want to discuss an issue that has perhaps had
more attention in the economic literature than it deserves. This is the
issue of "rules versus discretion." The issue is whether the monetary
authority and also the fiscal authority should conduct policy in accordance
with a preannounced rule that describes precisely how their policy variables will be determined in all future situations, or whether they should be
allowed to use their discretion in determining the values of the policy
variables at different times. One example of a rule is the constant growth
rate rule—say at 4 percent—for monetary policy. The rule is that no matter what happens, the money supply will be kept growing at 4 percent.[17]
An example of another rule would be that the money supply growth rate
will be increased by 2 percent per year for every 1 percent unemployment
in excess of, say, 5 percent. Algebraically such a rule would be expressed
as

$$\frac{\Delta M}{M} = 4.0 + 2(u - 5.0) \tag{1}$$

where the growth rate of money $\Delta M/M$ is at an annual percentage rate, and
u is the percentage unemployment rate.

The activist monetary rule is shown in Fig. 9-5. On the horizontal axis
we show the unemployment rate and on the vertical axis the growth rate of
the money stock. At 5 percent unemployment monetary growth is 4 percent. If unemployment rises above 5 percent, monetary growth is *au-*

---

[17]Recall from Chap. 8 that although the monetary authority cannot control the money supply
and its growth rate exactly, it is able to control the money stock with considerable accuracy.

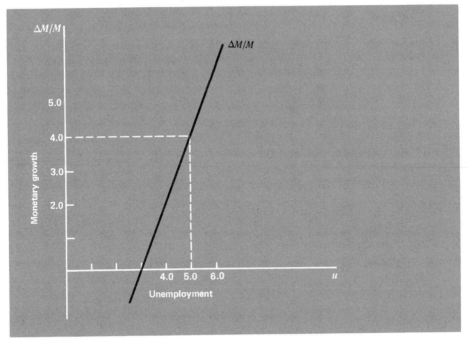

FIGURE 9-5 AN ACTIVIST MONETARY
RULE

tomatically increased. Thus with 7 percent unemployment monetary growth would be 8 percent. Conversely, if unemployment dropped below 5 percent, monetary growth would be lowered below 4 percent. The rule, therefore, gears the amount of monetary stimulus to an indicator of the business cycle. By linking monetary growth to the unemployment rate an activist, anticyclical monetary policy is achieved, but this is done without any discretion.

The issue of rules versus discretion has been clouded by the fact that most proponents of rules have been nonactivists, whose preferred monetary rule is a constant growth rate rule.[18] Thus the argument has tended to center on whether activist policy is desirable or not. The fundamental point to recognize is that we can design *activist rules*. We can design rules that have countercyclical features without at the same time leaving any discretion in their actions to policy makers. The point is made by Eq. (1), which is an activist rule because it expands money when unemployment is high and reduces it when unemployment is low. It leaves no room for policy discretion and in this respect is a rule.

[18]An assessment of the issues is provided in Arthur Okun, "Monetary-Fiscal Activism: Some Analytical Issues," *Brookings Papers on Economic Activity*, 1:1972.

Given that the economy and our knowledge of it are both changing over time, there is no case for stating permanent policy rules that would tie the hands of the monetary and fiscal authorities permanently. The practical issue in rules versus discretion then becomes whether the policy makers should announce in advance what policies they will be following for the foreseeable future. This would seem to be a desirable development, in that it aids private individuals in forecasting the future course of the economy. In fact, since 1975 the chairperson of the Federal Reserve Board has been required to announce to Congress the Fed's forecasts of its policies over the next year.[19]

9-6 SUMMARY

1 Despite the apparent simplicity of policies needed to maintain continuous full employment, the historical record of the behavior of unemployment, shown in Chart 9-1, implies that successful stabilization policy is difficult to carry out.

2 Many of the complications in the execution of stabilization policy are a result of the tradeoff between inflation and unemployment in the short run. This important topic is deferred to Chap. 15. The present chapter concentrates on other sources of difficulty for stabilization policy.

3 The potential need for stabilizing policy actions arises from economic disturbances. Some of these disturbances, such as changes in money demand, consumption spending, or investment demand, arise from within the private sector. Others, such as wars, may arise for noneconomic reasons.

4 Inappropriate economic policy may also tend to move the economy away from full employment. Policy may be inappropriate because policy makers make mistakes or because policy is manipulated for political reasons, leading to the political business cycle.

5 The first difficulty of carrying out successful stabilization policy is that policy works with lags. The *inside* lag—divided into recognition, decision, and action lags—is the period between which an action becomes necessary and when it is taken. The *outside* lag is the period between which a policy action is taken and when it affects the economy. The outside lag is generally a distributed lag: the effects of a policy action build up over the course of time.

6 The behavior of expectations is a further source of difficulty for policy making. First, it is difficult to know exactly what determines expectations and to capture those factors in a simple formula. Second, policy actions themselves are likely to affect expectations.

7 More generally, there is always uncertainty about the effects of a given

[19]See Table 8-6 for the targets announced in 1975 and 1976.

policy action on the economy. Economists are not agreed on the "correct" model of the economy, and evidence is not likely to be at hand soon to settle decisively disagreements over some behavioral functions—such as the consumption function. And even if we did know the form of the behavioral functions, the statistical evidence would be insufficient to pinpoint the values of the relevant parameters.

8 There are clearly occasions on which active monetary and fiscal policy actions should be taken to stabilize the economy. These are situations in which the economy has been affected by major disturbances.

9 Fine tuning—continuous attempts to stabilize the economy in the face of small disturbances—is more controversial. If fine tuning is undertaken, it calls for small policy responses in an attempt to moderate the economy's fluctuations, rather than to remove them entirely. A very active policy in response to small disturbances is likely to destabilize the economy.

10 The real issue in rules versus discretion is whether policy actions should be announced as far in advance as possible. Such announcements are desirable in that they aid private individuals in forecasting the future behavior of the economy.

10

The Kennedy and Johnson Years: The New Economics and the Emergence of Inflation

The early sixties were the heyday of the New Economics, which applied the keynesian analysis we have studied so far to reduce the unemployment rate and increase the growth rate of the United States economy. By the mid-sixties, the unemployment rate, which was 6.7 percent in 1961, had fallen to 4.5 percent, close to full employment, and it continued to fall thereafter through 1969. The second half of the sixties was a period of full employment and high aggregate demand of the kind progressive democracies are committed to achieve. Essentially full employment was attained even before the Vietnam war increase in government spending.

This chapter uses the analytical tools we have developed so far to interpret and understand developments in the United States economy during the Kennedy and Johnson years. The sixties are worth studying both because economic policy applied keynesian economics and because knowledge of the economic events of the period is important for understanding current problems, policies, and controversies.

Perspectives on economic policy in the sixties appear to differ widely. In one view, the period was one of high employment and prosperity, thanks to the activist stance of policy. An alternative view is that over-expansionist policies in that period were responsible for the inflation that was to prove the economic policy problem of the seventies. Actually, both views are correct. Policy in the early sixties was indeed successful. And economic policy in the second half of the period was over-expansionary or equivalently, not sufficiently contractionary, in the face of increases in government spending related to the Vietnam war.

Both the major achievement and the major cost of economic policy in the sixties can be seen in Chart 10-1 and Table 10-1. The main achievement is the decline in the unemployment rate from 6.7 percent in 1961 to 3.5 percent in 1969. The main cost is the increase in the inflation rate over the period, from 1.0 percent in 1961 to 5.4 percent in 1969. The lowering of unemployment was accompanied by a growth rate of real GNP at an average annual rate from 1961 to 1969 of 4.8 percent per year, substantially greater than the average growth rate of real GNP of 2.2 percent over the five years from 1956 to 1961.

This chapter reviews macroeconomic policy in the sixties in six sections. First we study and outline the main tenets of the New Economics which the economic advisers of the Kennedy and Johnson years brought to bear on policy. Then we briefly discuss economic policy in the early years of the Kennedy administration, during which the administration failed to follow very expansionary policies. In Sec. 10-3 we look at the 1964 tax cut, which stands out as the textbook example of successful expansionary fiscal policy. The *credit crunch* of 1966 is examined in Sec. 10-4. In Sec. 10-5 we look at the 1968 tax surcharge and use it to discuss the role of transitory taxes and the importance of the coordination of monetary and fiscal policies. Finally, Sec. 10-6 briefly considers the end of the sixties and the onset of restrictive policies in 1969 to fight the inflationary pressure in the economy.

We are not at this stage equipped to analyze inflation, and so continue the discussion of economic policy in the late sixties and the seventies in Chap. 16.

The appendix to this chapter contains a chronological review of the fiscal policy actions undertaken during the 1961–1969 period. It can be used as a reference for details of the various policies and episodes discussed in the text.

The chapter is intended to serve two purposes. One is to use the theoretical tools of the previous chapters to show how they are useful, and

CHART 10-1 INFLATION AND UNEMPLOYMENT. (Source: *Economic Report of the President, 1977*)

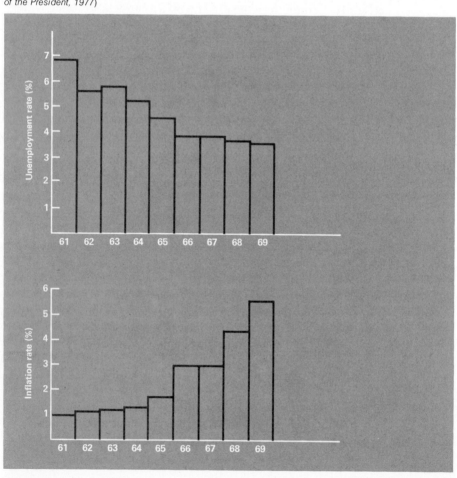

TABLE 10-1 INFLATION AND UNEMPLOYMENT IN THE SIXTIES

	Year								
	61	62	63	64	65	66	67	68	69
Inflation (percentage change in consumer price index)	1.0	1.1	1.2	1.3	1.7	2.9	2.9	4.2	5.4
Unemployment (percentage of labor force)	6.7	5.5	5.7	5.2	4.5	3.8	3.8	3.6	3.5

Source: Economic Report of the President, 1977

indeed essential, to an understanding of macroeconomic policy problems. In so doing, we also illustrate some of the problems of policy making that were discussed in Chap. 9. The second purpose of the chapter is to show how the experience of the sixties shaped much of the thinking that goes into current economic policy making and led to many of the economic problems faced in the seventies.

10-1 THE NEW ECONOMICS

The "New Economics" is a term that has come to be used to describe the analytical and philosophical approach to economic policy making used by the Kennedy and Johnson administrations in the 1960s. The analytical approach consists basically of the tools we have outlined in Chaps. 3 through 7. The philosophy characterizing that approach to economics is a mix of activism and optimism. It is well characterized by a paragraph from a chapter on the "Promise of Modern Economic Policy" by Walter Heller, written in 1966 when the New Economics was at the pinnacle of esteem:

> The significance of the great expansion in the 60's lies not only in its striking statistics of employment, income, and growth but in its glowing promise of things to come. If we can surmount the economic pressures of Vietnam without later being trapped into a continuing war on inflation when we should be fighting economic slack, the "new economics" can move us steadily toward the qualitative goals that lie beyond the facts and figures of affluence.[1]

Walter Heller, now a professor at the University of Minnesota, was one of the chief architects of economic policy in the early sixties. He was chairperson of the Council of Economic Advisers (CEA) under both Presidents Kennedy and Johnson. The CEA is a body of professional economists that advises the President on economic policy. The council became more influential in the Kennedy and Johnson administrations than it had been before, and attracted as members and staff a succession of distinguished economists. Among these were James Tobin of Yale, Gard-

[1]W. W. Heller, New Dimensions of Political Economy, Norton, 1967, p. 58.

ner Ackley of the University of Michigan, Robert Solow of MIT, Otto Eckstein and Kenneth Arrow of Harvard, and Arthur Okun, then of Yale and now at the Brookings Institution, to name only a few.

The New Economics emphasized the goal of reattaining full employment after the high unemployment levels of the late 1950s. The first goal of policy was to move to a full utilization of resources. The analysis of how that was to be done led to the introduction of a number of concepts, some of which, such as the full employment budget surplus, we have already met. We shall briefly review the basic analytical concepts of the New Economics, before concluding this section by discussing what was new in the New Economics.

Potential Output and the GNP Gap

To focus attention on the target of full employment, and for use as an operating guide to policy, the Council (CEA), and particularly Arthur Okun, developed and stressed the concept of *potential output*.[2] Potential output, or full-employment output, measures the level of real GNP the economy can produce with full employment. The full-employment rate of unemployment used in defining potential output in the sixties was 4 percent. The 4 percent rate was taken as an unemployment rate that was consistent with price stability. Unemployment could be pushed even lower with expansionary policies, but it was feared this could only be done at the cost of incurring high rates of inflation.[3]

Along with the concept and measurement of potential output went the notion of the *GNP gap*. The gap is simply the difference between actual and potential real output. An excess of potential over actual output means that the economy is operating at less than full employment, that resources are therefore being wasted, and that expansionary policy is called for. Chart 10-2 shows potential and actual output. Potential output grows at a constant 3.75 percent rate, taken to be consistent with labor force growth and the growth of productivity of labor. For the years 1961–1965, actual GNP is below its potential level and the GNP gap is therefore positive. Chart 10-2 shows that at the beginning of 1961, the GNP gap was an extraordinary $60 billion, measured in 1972 dollars, or nearly 8 percent of GNP. A gap of that magnitude seemed clearly to call for expansionary policy. Either monetary or fiscal policy could be used to raise aggregate demand and increase actual output to a level closer to the economy's potential.

The notions of potential output and the GNP gap seem very simple, but they are important. They dramatize the costs of unemployment in easily

[2]We introduced potential output in Chap. 1.

[3]Remember that in Chap. 1 we pointed out that a new measure of potential output takes an unemployment rate of 4.9 percent to represent full employment in the 70's.

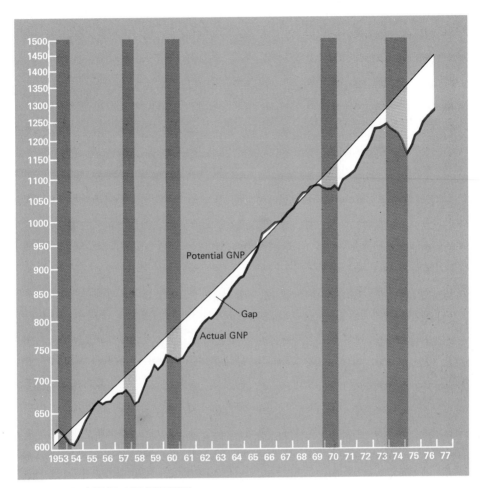

CHART 10-2 ACTUAL AND POTENTIAL
GNP (BILLIONS OF 1972 DOLLARS). (*Source:*
Current Business Conditions, September
1976)

understood terms—in terms of output loss due to unemployment—and
make it easy to understand what alternative target levels of GNP, at which
policy makers might aim, would mean for the level of unemployment.

The Full-Employment Budget Surplus

The full-employment budget surplus was discussed at some length in
Chap. 3, and we will therefore be brief here. The concept had been introduced to the economics literature before the 1960s. As a reminder, the
full-employment budget surplus is the budget surplus measured as it
would be if unemployment were at the full-employment level, or, equiva-

lently, if output were at its potential level. The concept is important and useful because it directs attention away from the actual budget, which is a misleading indicator of fiscal policy, toward the full-employment surplus—a more relevant, although still imperfect, indicator of policy.

The actual budget is a misleading indicator of the direction of fiscal policy, because the actual budget can change for reasons having nothing to do with fiscal policy. In particular, a decline in aggregate demand will reduce income and tax collections, and therefore increase the actual budget deficit. But this certainly does not mean that fiscal policy has become more expansionary. In this example, although the actual budget deficit increases, the full-employment deficit (or surplus) remains constant.

The New Economists planned to use fiscal policy as the instrument with which to close the GNP gap. It was important to get across to Congress and the public the idea of the full-employment surplus because the unemployment rate was high in 1961, and the federal budget was in an actual deficit. Any proposals to increase spending or cut taxes would certainly imply a larger deficit if GNP were to remain unchanged. Members of Congress could be relied upon to look with great suspicion on any policy that might increase the budget deficit. By focusing attention on the full-employment budget, the New Economists appropriately succeeded in shifting attention away from the state of the actual budget to concern with how the budget would look at full employment—which had the side benefit of focusing attention on the full-employment issue itself.

Fiscal Drag and the Fiscal Dividend

Growth of potential output over time implies that aggregate demand must increase to maintain full employment. Suppose that income taxes increase with the level of income, but that government spending does not automatically increase along with income. In that case, the full-employment budget surplus increases over time as the economy grows. That increase in the full-employment surplus tends to exert a restraining effect on aggregate demand. The restraining influence on aggregate demand implied by a fixed level of government spending and a given tax structure[4] in a growing economy, and the resultant increase in the full-employment surplus, is called *fiscal drag*. In order to offset the deflationary effect of increased tax revenues that come with increased income, either government spending has to rise or taxes have to be cut to allow private spending to rise, and thus support the increased level of potential output.

The policy implication of fiscal drag is that *fiscal dividends* should be paid. To offset the net deflationary effects of fiscal drag, government spending can be increased or tax rates can be reduced. These increases in spending or reductions in taxes are known as the fiscal dividend. How is the fiscal dividend possible? Suppose that potential output is rising, and

---

[4]By "a given tax structure" we mean the set of rules, including tax rates, exemption levels, etc., used to calculate taxes.

that taxes would rise along with potential output. To maintain a constant full-employment surplus, tax rates can be reduced. The same amount of taxes in total can be realized at lower tax rates if output rises. Alternatively, government spending can increase to match the increase in taxes, so that the full-employment surplus remains constant despite the increase in output.

Walter Heller assesses the distribution of fiscal dividends between 1961 and 1965 as in Table 10-2. The table shows that $48 billion was distributed as fiscal dividends in the form of tax cuts or increased expenditures between 1961 and 1965. The table makes the basic point about fiscal drag: with a given tax structure, expansions in income raise taxes that can be used to finance increased government spending without changing the full-employment surplus;[5] alternatively, tax rates can be reduced to keep the full-employment surplus constant as potential output rises.

Growth

The New Economics emphasized economic growth, in two ways. First, there was the need for aggregate demand to grow in order to achieve full employment. In that respect, growth was a matter of achieving full employment and maintaining it. Second, there was an emphasis on achieving a high rate of growth of potential output itself. The emphasis was on investment spending to encourage growth in productive potential. We delay consideration of that aspect until Chap. 17.

The Behavior of Money Wages

We have to be brief in discussing the emphasis placed by the New Economists on the behavior of money wages relative to productivity, in affecting the rate of inflation, because we have not yet integrated the theory

[5]In the 1970s, there has been concern that fiscal dividends are committed in advance. Certain government spending programs, such as Social Security, imply increasing government payments in the future, which will probably use up the fiscal dividend.

TABLE 10-2 FISCAL DIVIDENDS, 1961–1965 (*Billions of dollars*)

Tax reductions		Expenditure increases	
Personal income tax	$11	Defense and space purchases	$11
Corporate income tax	6	Personal transfer payments	9
Excise tax	2	Grants-in-aid	5
Payroll tax increase	−2	Interest and subsidies	4
		Domestic nondefense purchases	3
Net tax reduction	$16	Expenditure increases	$32

Source: Walter Heller, *New Dimensions of Political Economy*, Norton, 1967, p. 71. Figures may not add up because of rounding.

of inflation with our analysis of aggregate demand.   At this stage we merely note that there was great concern over the behavior of money wages throughout the Kennedy and Johnson years, and that early in the period in 1962, the Council of Economic Advisers set up *guideposts* for the behavior of money wages.[6]   The basic guidepost was that money wages should not grow faster than the average rate of productivity increase in the economy. In 1965 and 1966, the guideposts were made more explicit and the rate of wage increase of 3.2 percent became the general criterion for noninflationary wage increases.

In setting up the criterion for noninflationary wage increases—that wages should not increase faster than labor productivity—the CEA also suggested that rapid investment could contribute to price stability.   The notion was that rapid investment would increase the amount of capital employed in the production of output, and would thus increase the productivity of labor.   For a given rate of wage increase, this greater productivity would mean less inflation.   High investment spending was thus thought helpful in containing inflationary pressures.

As we have already noted, we shall not discuss wage behavior further in this chapter.   By the end of Chap. 13, the apparatus for analyzing the proposals of the CEA for wage behavior and the role of investment and productivity increase in determining inflation will have been presented. At that stage we will invite the reader to return to this section to review the proposals of the CEA.

What Was New?

What was new about the New Economics?   Was the approach to stabilization policy along the lines of fiscal activism, potential output objectives, and the emphasis on the full-employment budget surplus in fact new?   The answer here is not simple.   It is true that the activism the CEA displayed was unprecedented.   But it is true, too, that the tools and concepts the Council used were main-line professional macroeconomics.   The idea of active fiscal policy as a countercyclical measure and the notion that there was nothing particularly desirable about a balanced budget were certainly not new.

Even so, the active use of fiscal policy met much resistance in the political process at the time.   Herbert Stein, himself chairperson of the CEA under President Nixon, reviews the progress toward the major policy measure of the early sixties, the 1964 tax cut, in his book *The Fiscal Revolution in America*.[7]   He shows how the Kennedy administration first had to get accustomed to the idea that, during recession, a move toward an in-

---

[6]For an interesting, and sometimes amusing, discussion of the guideposts, see George P. Shultz and Robert Z. Aliber (eds.), *Guidelines*, University of Chicago Press, 1966. See, too, the evaluation in Otto Eckstein, "The Economics of the 1960's: A Backward Look," *Public Interest*, Spring 1970.

[7]Herbert Stein, *The Fiscal Revolution in America*, University of Chicago Press, 1969.

creased budget deficit was not a step toward fiscal irresponsibility. By the same token, Congress had to find its way toward expansionary fiscal policies, away from balanced budgets or tax cuts accompanied by offsetting reductions in public spending. Eventually, many recognized that a measure to expand aggregate demand was necessary in order to cope with high unemployment. But there was considerable disagreement on whether to use tax cuts or expenditure changes and if tax cuts were used, who should get them.

Stein's account is borne out by the inside view presented by Walter Heller:[8]

> As I reflect on the early months of the Kennedy Administration, I must agree with those who feel that, judged only in terms of policies actually proposed and adopted, modern economics established a firm beachhead on the New Frontier, but not much more, in 1961. And one should probably heed the judgement of authorities like Seymour Harris that Kennedy "at first seemed allergic to modern economics." One should not infer, however, that his allergy was inbred. Much of it was simply a political sensitivity to the sting of Republican charges of fiscal irresponsibility and a consciousness that tax cuts did not fit his call for sacrifice. . . .

Then Heller goes on to explain that it was not until 1962 that President Kennedy himself seemed convinced by the arguments of his advisers. And it was not until 1964, when the tax cut was carried out, that the Congress seemed convinced by those arguments.

Thus, what was new about the New Economics was not the analysis, but the active and successful use of that analysis in the operation of fiscal policy.

10-2 ECONOMIC POLICY: 1961–1963

The initial moves in fiscal policy were modest indeed. Although the Kennedy administration took over an economy in 1961 with unemployment near 6.7 percent, no major expansionist fiscal policies were undertaken.[9]

---

[8]Heller, *New Dimensions of Political Economy*, op. cit., p. 30.

[9]Part of the explanation for the modesty of these initial efforts is that the administration was concerned about the effects of any expansion of aggregate demand on the balance of payments. Effects of increases in aggregate demand on the balance of payments are studied in Chap. 18.

Concern over the balance of payments also lay behind Operation Twist, which was supposedly the basis for monetary policy in the early sixties. Twist was an attempt to reduce long-term interest rates, in order to increase investment spending, while not reducing short-term interest rates, which were thought to determine capital flows from abroad to the United States. As we see in Chap. 18, capital inflows improve the balance of payments, and it was desired to keep short-term interest rates (such as the Treasury bill rate) high, in order to attract foreign capital and to prevent outflows of American capital. Interest rates were to be affected by the Fed's buying long-term debt (thus reducing the interest rate on it) and selling short-term debt (thus increasing the interest rate on it). Interest rates did move in the desired directions in that period though it is not clear that was due to the Fed's actions. Phillip Cagan briefly reviews the policy in Cagan *et al.*, *Economic Policy and Inflation in the Sixties*, American Enterprise Institute, 1972, p. 94. He suggests that the Fed merely paid lip service to Operation Twist.

The only indication of an expansionist philosophy in fiscal policy was that the increase in defense spending associated with the Berlin military build-up in 1961 was *not* accompanied by increased taxes. The resultant increase in the high-employment budget deficit accordingly exerted some expansionary effects toward a recovery.

By January 1962, though, with unemployment still at 6 percent, the administration reverted to orthodoxy by presenting a balanced budget proposal for fiscal year 1963. Only after June 1962, with the recovery not taking off but faltering instead, did the administration develop a strong commitment toward fiscal activism. A first step was the investment tax credit measure of October 1962 together with more liberalized depreciation guidelines. The purpose of these measures was to raise the profitability of investment spending and thereby raise aggregate demand. In January 1963 the administration finally asked for a major change in the tax structure. In proposing a permanent cut in the income tax rates for individuals and corporations, it set the basis for the Revenue Act of 1964.

10-3 THE 1964 TAX CUT

In this section we will study the effects of the Revenue Act of 1964. That measure, enacted in February 1964, more than a year after the initial recommendation, provided for a permanent cut in income tax rates for individuals and corporations. The one-year lag provides an illustration of the decision lag of fiscal policy. Marginal tax rates for individuals that had ranged from 20 to 91 percent were reduced to a range of 14 to 70 percent. The tax rate for most corporations was reduced from 52 to 48 percent. It was estimated that the tax cut package amounted to a reduction in personal taxes of $10 billion and in corporate taxes of $3 billion. These tax cuts were very substantial. The personal tax cut of $10 billion was equivalent to a 20 percent reduction in personal tax payments and the corporate tax reduction amounted to 8 percent of corporate taxes.

The effects of the tax cut are studied in this section in two ways, First, we provide some calculations for what we would expect the impact of the tax cut to be, using the theory developed in Chaps. 3 through 8 and estimates of the empirical magnitudes. Second, we look at the actual path of GNP and its components and attempt to infer the contribution of the tax cut and make a comparison with the predicted effects. Throughout this section we rely strongly on an important paper by Arthur Okun which develops an analysis of the tax cut and its expected macroeconomic impact.[10]

An important aspect of the analysis to follow is that it emphasizes fiscal policy and generally ignores monetary policy. It will be seen that we use the multiplier apparatus of Chap. 3, rather than the full IS-LM apparatus of

---

[10]See Arthur Okun, "Measuring the Impact of the 1964 Tax Reduction," in W. W. Heller (ed.), *Perspectives on Economic Growth*, Random House, 1968.

Chap. 4. In Chap. 3, the interest rate was implicitly held constant. Accordingly, income expansion due to fiscal policy was not dampened in that chapter by increases in the interest rate. The assumption that the interest rate remained constant following the tax cut, which is required if we are to use the analysis of Chap. 3 rather than the full IS-LM analysis of Chap. 4, turns out to be justified. Monetary policy following the tax cut was *accommodating*. The Fed did allow the money supply to increase following the tax cut to keep the interest rate constant. If the money supply had not been increased, then the interest rate would have risen, and some investment spending would have been choked off. The actual monetary policy that followed the tax cut avoided cutting off investment by expanding the money supply enough to prevent interest rates from rising. As Okun puts it, "The monetary authorities supplied a good sound set of tires for the economy to roll on, but they did not contribute the engine."[11] The expansion was due to fiscal policy but it was supported, or accommodated, by an expansionary monetary policy. We will not discuss monetary policy further in this section.

*Long-Run Effects

We noted that the tax package consisted of a cut of about $10 billion in personal income taxes, and a cut in corporate profit taxes worth $3 billion. The cut in personal income taxes would increase disposable personal income and thereby increase consumption spending directly. The corporate tax cut, by raising corporate after-tax profits, would increase both investment spending and the payments of dividends out of the now higher profits. These increases in dividends would increase personal disposable income and thus consumption spending. Finally, both consumption and investment spending would increase in response to any changes in GNP—these are induced expenditures.

Tables 10-3 and 10-4 summarize these impacts on GNP. First, there are three components of the *direct* impact of the tax package on demand. Estimates of the direct effects of the tax cut on GNP depend on a number of *parameters*—that is, numerical values of coefficients like the long-run marginal propensity to consume and the propensity of corporations to pay dividends out of profits. In each case we use Okun's estimates of these parameters. In turn, they are based on a variety of studies to which Okun refers in the article cited above.

The first direct effect of the tax cut on aggregate demand arises from the $10 billion cut in personal income taxes. The long-run marginal propensity to consume is estimated at 0.949, which means that consumption spending increases by $9.49 billion as a result of the cut in personal income taxes. Second, the cut of $3 billion in corporate profit taxes is assumed to lead to an increase in corporate investment of $2.25 billion, on the assump-

[11]Okun, op. cit., p. 44.

TABLE 10-3 DIRECT LONG-RUN EFFECTS OF 1964 TAX CUT

	Action	Effect	Explanation
1.	$10 billion cut in income taxes: $10 billion × 0.949 =	$9.49 billion increase in consumption	Long-run marginal propensity to consume (MPC) = 0.949
2.	$3 billion cut in corporate profit taxes: $3 billion × 0.75 =	$2.25 billion increase in investment	Corporations invest 75% of after-tax profits
3.	$3 billion cut in corporate profit taxes $3 billion × 0.625 = $1.875 billion increase in distributed profits $1.875 billion × 0.879 = $1.648 billion increase in personal disposable income $1.648 billion × 0.949 =	$1.56 billion increase in consumption	Firms distribute 62.5% of additional after-tax profits Only 87.9% of these dividends is available for spending after income taxes Long-run MPC is 0.949
4.	Total direct effect	$13.3 billion increase in aggregate demand	

tion that firms invest 75 percent of their after-tax profits. Third, the increased dividends paid out by corporations increase consumption. The table shows three steps in the computation of that increase in consumption. Since corporations distribute 62.5 percent of their additional after tax profits, there is an increase of $1.875 billion in dividends.[12] But those dividends are taxed, at the average rate of 12.1 percent, so that only 0.879 (= 1 − 0.121) of the increase in dividends remains as an increase in disposable income. And then 0.949 of that increase in disposable income is consumed. The three direct effects of the tax cut on aggregate demand add up to an increase in aggregate demand of $13.3 billion.

Table 10-4 shows the *induced* effects of the increase in income created by the tax cuts. There are two induced components of spending. First, it

[12]Note that the $3 billion cut in corporate taxes leads to an increase of $2.25 billion in corporate investment and a $1.875 billion increase in dividends. The total exceeds $3 billion, implying that corporations finance part of the increase in investment by borrowing.

is estimated that only about half—0.505 is the estimate—of an increase in GNP represents an increase in disposable personal income. Then the long-run marginal propensity to consume is applied to the 0.505 to calculate the induced consumption resulting from a \$1 increase in GNP. Second, there is induced investment as a result of an increase in GNP. A \$1 increase in GNP leads to a 20.6-cent increase in after-tax corporate profits, of which 75 percent is invested. Thus there is a 15.4-cent increase in investment spending as a result of a \$1 increase in GNP.

Applying the long-run propensity to consume, 0.949, to the change in disposable income, we have

$$\Delta C = 0.949\,\Delta Y_d = (0.949)\,(0.505\,\Delta Y) = 0.479\,\Delta Y \qquad (1)$$

The induced change in investment is

$$\Delta I = (0.75)(0.206)\,\Delta Y = 0.154\,\Delta Y \qquad (2)$$

These assumptions imply a long-run multiplier of 2.72, calculated using the equations of Chap. 3 together with Eqs. (1) and (2) as follows:

$$\Delta Y = \Delta A = \Delta \overline{A} + \Delta C + \Delta I$$
$$= \Delta \overline{A} + 0.479\,\Delta Y + 0.154\,\Delta Y \qquad (3)$$

or

$$\Delta Y(1 - 0.479 - 0.154) = \Delta \overline{A} \qquad (4)$$

$$\Delta Y = 2.72\,\Delta \overline{A} \qquad (4a)$$

TABLE 10-4   INDUCED LONG-RUN EFFECTS OF THE 1964 TAX CUT *(Per dollar increase in income)*

		Effect	Explanation
1. Consumption	\$1 × 0.505 = \$0.505		Only about half of the increase in GNP turns into increases in disposable income
	\$0.505 × 0.949 =	\$0.479 increase in consumption	Long-run MPC = 0.949
2. Investment	\$1 × 0.206 = \$0.206 increase in after-tax corporate profits		A dollar increase in income raises corporate after-tax profits by \$0.206
	\$0.206 × 0.75 =	\$0.154 increase in investment	Corporations invest 75% of after-tax profits

Now $\Delta \overline{A}$ is the change in spending of $13.3 billion so that

$$\Delta Y = 2.72 \times \$13.3 \text{ billion} = \$36.2 \text{ billion} \qquad (5)$$

which is the total effect on spending of the tax cut.

Table 10-5 suggests two ways of breaking down the total increase in GNP of about $36 billion. We can attribute part of the increase in GNP to the cut in personal income taxes and part to the corporate income taxes, by reading across the table. The $10 billion cut in personal taxes increases consumption by $9.49 billion and, allowing for the multiplier, has a total effect of $25.81 billion on demand (equal to $9.49 billion $\times$ 2.72). The corporate tax cut of $3 billion directly increases aggregate demand by $3.81 billion, through its effects on investment and consumption. The total effects of the corporate tax cut on GNP are that $3.81 billion times the long-run multiplier of 2.72, or $10.3 billion. The corporate tax cut thus has a higher multiplier (10.36/3=3.45) than the multiplier associated with the personal tax cuts (25.8/10 = 2.58). The corporate tax cut thus seems more effective in increasing aggregate demand per dollar of tax revenue lost. We return later to the question of the relative effectiveness of the two types of tax cut.

The second way of breaking down the effects of the tax cuts can be seen by reading down the columns of Table 10-5, which focus on the way in which the various components of aggregate demand are affected. Investment increases by $7.8 billion. This is composed of the initial increase in investment of $2.25 billion plus further induced investment of $(0.154)(\$36.2) = \$5.57$ billion. Consumption demand increases by the initial increase of $11.05 (= \$9.49 + \$1.56) plus induced consumption spending of $17.34 billion (= 0.949 \times 0.505 \times \$36.2$ billion).

The above calculation of the long-run impacts of the tax cuts follows a multiplier approach similar to that outlined in Chap. 3 and illustrates the uses of that type of analysis. It is also appropriate to bear in mind the warnings of Chap. 9. Some of the numbers in Table 10-5 are estimated with a wide margin of uncertainty. In particular, the details of the way in which increases in corporate profits affect investment spending and dividends are quite uncertain. Thus, Table 10-5 represents Okun's best esti-

TABLE 10-5   TOTAL LONG-RUN EFFECTS OF THE 1964 TAX CUT

	Consumption	Investment	GNP
Corporate tax cut	$ 6.52	$3.83	$10.36
Personal tax cut	21.85	3.97	25.81
Total effect	$28.39	$7.80	$36.17

Note: Billions of dollars. Numbers may not add up because of rounding.

mates, but, as he notes, "these estimates should be viewed as the center of a sizable range."[13] Indeed, many would consider multipliers in excess of 2 as unusually large.

*Lags and the Short-Run Effects of the Tax Cut

The long-run effects of the tax cut estimated in Table 10-5 were expected to take place over a period of years. From the viewpoint of policy, it is also important to calculate how rapidly the tax cuts would affect GNP. Chart 10-3 shows the predicted response of GNP to the tax cut in the first six quarters, that is, from the start of the tax cut at the end of the first quarter of 1964 to the second quarter of 1965. The lower shaded part of each bar shows the increase in GNP arising from an increase in consumption, and the upper part shows the contribution of increased investment spending to the increase in GNP. Chart 10-3 is nothing other than the dynamic multiplier of the tax cut.[14] It is important to note how the GNP effects of the tax cut occur over time. They start with a minor impact on consumption but soon build up as both consumption and investment spending increase. By 1965/II the increase in GNP has reached $25 billion, over 70 percent of the final $36 billion, with a third of it in increased investment and two-thirds in increased consumption. Further, as the chart suggests, the increase in GNP has not yet petered out. GNP is still growing in response to the fiscal expansion.

We now ask what *lags* are responsible for the shape of the dynamic multiplier of Chart 10-3. Note that it takes four quarters before the increase in GNP caused by the tax cut exceeds the size of the tax cut itself. By the end of the sixth quarter,[15] GNP has increased by more than twice the cut in taxes. The way in which GNP responds to the tax cuts over time depends crucially on the lags in consumption and investment behavior that we reviewed in Chaps. 5 and 6. The main lags that arise are:

1   The lag with which consumption adjusts to a change in personal disposable income. As emphasized in Chap. 5, the short-run marginal propensity to spend is significantly smaller than the long-run marginal propensity. A sustained dollar increase in personal disposable income raises consumption by only 60 cents in the first two quarters, while in the long run consumption spending increases by as much as 95 cents. Clearly the difference between short-run and long-run spending pro-

[13]Okun, op. cit.

[14]Dynamic multipliers were introduced in Chaps. 5 and 9.

[15]There is some ambiguity about how many quarters' lag any particular quarter in Chart 10-3 represents. The tax cut was instituted in March 1964 and the total cut in 1964/I was only $3 billion, versus the full amount in later quarters. We refer to 1964/I as the first quarter, but the first quarter in which there was a full tax cut was 1964/II.

pensities stretches out the effects of the tax cut on GNP until consumption fully adjusts to the higher level of personal disposable income.

2 The second lag is that between changes in corporate after-tax profits and changes in dividends, which in turn lead to changes in consumption. We found out above that in the long run a sustained dollar increase in after-tax corporate profits gives rise to an increase in dividends of 62.5 cents. That increase in dividends, however, occurs only after an adjustment period. Corporations are reluctant to vary (reduce) their dividends and therefore do not rapidly adjust dividend payments to an increase in profits for fear the increased profits are transitory. Again drawing on Okun's estimates, in the short run of two quarters only 10 cents of a dollar increase in profits is distributed. This lag in the distribution of dividends is important because it implies that the effect of the corporate tax cut on consumption spending takes some time to filter through. First there is an increase in dividends due to the increase in corporate profits from the tax cut and then, once increased dividends start raising personal disposable income, there is still the consumption lag to reckon with. A corporate tax cut, therefore, operates with the double handicap of the dividend lag and the consumption lag.

3 The third important lag is that between changes in corporate after-tax profits and changes in business fixed investment. In the long run we found that a sustained dollar increase in after-tax profits leads to 75 cents increase in business fixed investment spending. Within the first two quarters, however, only about 30 cents of an additional dollar of profits is spent on fixed investment.

The lags in the consumption and investment process account for the important difference between short-run and long-run responses of GNP to the tax cut. For each quarter shown in Chart 10-3, there is a multiplier calculation similar to the calculations that underlie the long-run analysis above. We can illustrate those calculations by examining the second-quarter multipliers of the tax cut. For that purpose, we use the short-run two-quarter propensities specified in items (1) through (3).

First for the multiplier we have

$$\frac{1}{1 - 0.6(0.505) - 0.3(0.206)} = 1.57$$

where we have used the short-run propensities to consume (0.6) and invest (0.3) and the fraction of a dollar increase in GNP that accrues, respectively, as personal disposable income (0.505) and corporate after-tax profits (0.206) within two quarters. Clearly the short-run (two-period) multiplier is much smaller that the long-run multiplier of 2.72 calculated above.

Next we calculate the initial change in demand. This is a change in consumption due to the personal tax cut of 0.6 ($10 billion) or $6 billion, an increase in investment spending of 0.3 ($3 billion) or $0.9 billion and increased consumption due to the corporate tax cut.   The latter is a bit harder to compute   It is equal to $0.10(0.879)(0.6)(3 billion) = $0.158 billion, where we recognize that, per dollar increase in corporate profits, only 10 cents is distributed in the short run as dividends, of which only 87.9 percent is left after personal taxes.   The increase in disposable income leads to increased consumption spending with a short-run propensity of 0.6.   The corporate tax cut therefore raises consumption initially by $0.16 billion. The total impact on demand is therefore $7.06 billion, and with a multiplier of 1.57, we get an increase in income of $11 billion as a short-run response of income to the tax cut.   This is in fact close to what Chart 10-3 shows to be happening by the third quarter of 1964.[16]

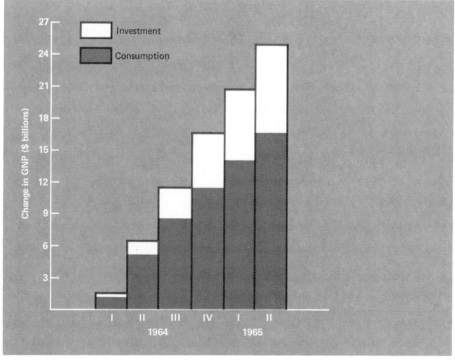

CHART 10-3   THE CHANGE IN GNP DUE TO THE 1964 TAX CUT (Source: Arthur Okun, "Measuring the Impact of the 1964 Tax Reduction," in W.W. Heller (ed.), *Perspectives on Economic Growth,* Random House, 1968)

[16]Why the third quarter and not the second quarter of 1964?   The reason is that the tax cut went into effect only in March 1964 and it thus had very little impact in the first quarter of 1964. Accordingly, 1964/III is basically the second quarter after the tax cut rather than the third.

TABLE 10-6 SHORT-RUN (TWO-QUARTER) EFFECTS OF THE 1964 TAX CUT

	Consumption	Investment	GNP
Corporate tax cut	$0.66	$1.00	$ 1.67
Personal tax cut	8.86	0.58	9.45
Total	$9.52	$1.58	$11.11

Note: Billion dollars. Numbers may not add up because of rounding.

The short-run (two-quarter) impacts of the tax cut are summarized in Table 10-6, constructed in the same way as Table 10-5. In Table 10-6 the bulk of the effects of the tax cuts come from the impact of increased consumption spending as a result of the cut in personal income taxes.

So far the discussion has disregarded one important component of aggregate demand, namely, inventory investment spending. The tax measures we have considered have no significant effect on inventory investment in the long run, and we could therefore disregard such investment in calculating the long-run impact of the tax cut package. In the very short run, firms meet increased demand out of inventories, and for that reason the increase in aggregate demand falls short of the tax-induced effects on consumption and investment demand, as inventory investment is negative. This reduction in inventories, together with the increase in GNP, leads firms to restore their inventory-sales ratios and therefore undertake inventory investment. Thus, a sustained dollar increase in income would cause firms to spend on additions to their inventories for some time until the level of stocks had increased sufficiently to match the higher level of income and sales. This effect is therefore strictly transitory, but it is very important in the short run. In fact, in Chart 10-3, the impact of the tax cut on investment shown as the upper portion of each bar includes this inventory investment spending. Over time this component of investment diminishes and is replaced by the permanent increase in fixed investment spending. We should increase the estimates of the effects of both the corporate and personal income tax cuts in Table 10-6 somewhat to account for induced inventory investment spending. Inventory investment, however, makes no difference to the relative size of the effects of the two types of tax cut, nor does it affect the long-run multipliers since the spending on inventories is strictly transitory.

Short- and Long-Run Effects of the Tax Cuts

The discussion of lags and the short-run impact of the tax cut brings out strongly the difference between the effectiveness of corporate and personal income tax cuts. The corporate tax cut contributes only $1.67 billion to income (in the short run). The multiplier for a corporate tax cut in the short run is less than 1. (The multiplier here is defined as the total change in

TABLE 10-7 SHORT-RUN AND LONG-RUN MULTIPLIERS OF DIFFERENT TAX CUT MEASURES

	Corporate tax cut	Personal tax cut
Short run	0.55	0.95
Long run	3.45	2.58

income due to the corporate tax cut from Table 10-6, divided by the size of the tax cut or 1.67/3 billion = 0.56.) By contrast the personal tax cut has a quite high short-run multiplier of 0.95 (= 9.45 billion/10 billion), although it is still less than 1.

The difference is obviously that for the corporate tax cut the lags, particularly with respect to dividends and consumption, are much more important. It is important to recognize this because it shows that corporate tax cuts are a poor instrument if fast effects on GNP are required. To judge the short-run effectiveness of policy instruments clearly, the short-run multipliers that we just calculated and not the long-run multipliers are relevant.

A comparison of these multipliers between instruments and short run and long run is revealing, as seen in Table 10-7. What the table brings out is that in the long run a corporate tax cut is very effective, working both through increased disposable income on consumption and through increased investment spending. In the short run the lags in investment, dividends, and consumption make a corporate tax cut relatively ineffective since a dollar cut in corporate taxes yields only a 51-cent increase in income. By contrast a dollar cut in personal taxes has a relatively significant short-run impact in that it raises GNP by 94 cents. In the long run, however, the additional gain is somewhat less than for the corporate tax.

A Look at the Data

In this part we look briefly at the actual data to see whether and how the tax cut worked. In doing so, we also illustrate the difficulties of evaluating the effects of past policy measures. These difficulties arise from the problem of deducing what would have happened if the policy measure had not been undertaken.

The analysis so far suggests plausible values for (1) the order of magnitude of the long-run effects, (2) the components of aggregate demand we expect to be affected, and (3) the likely time path of the reaction of GNP and its components to the tax cut. The problem in isolating the effects of the tax cut, however, is that there were a lot of other things affecting aggregate demand at the same time; particularly, adjustments to past changes in income were still affecting aggregate demand. There is no entirely certain and correct procedure that will identify the exact contribution of the tax cut to GNP. Ideally, we would like a procedure that allows us to find out what GNP would have been in the absence of the tax cut had everything else been the same. If we had that path of GNP, we would compare it to the path GNP actually took as a consequence of the tax cut and attribute the difference, in a diagram like Chart 10-3, to the tax cut. The fact is that we cannot construct very exactly the *counterfactual* history of GNP and therefore have to rely on procedures such as outlined above to try to discern the predicted results from the actual data.

With this preface we can turn to the actual data. In particular, we will look at changes in real GNP and its components for the period 1963–1966, shown in Table 10-8. In the table we show for GNP and each major component both the change in constant dollars and the percentage change. Consider first real GNP (in 1972 dollars). From a low growth rate in 1963 over 1962, growth increases very significantly in the year of the tax cut and the subsequent year. This bears out our previous analysis that suggests that the effect of the tax cut will start within the year in which the cut takes place but with the major part of the effects occurring say between the third and eighth quarters, which would be from fall 1964 to early 1966. The growth rate for 1965 is even higher than that for 1964, thus bearing out our predictions about the time path of GNP adjustment.

The order of magnitude of the change in GNP will be studied next. Here we have to deal with the fact that GNP would have grown somewhat even in the absence of the tax cut. The problem is, by how much? In 1963 GNP grew relative to 1962 by almost 4 percent. If we assume, perhaps heroically, that GNP would have grown at 4 percent in the absence of the tax cut, then we can attribute the difference between 4 percent and actual growth in 1964 and 1965 to the tax cut. The resulting numbers in turn can be compared to our predictions in the previous parts.

With 4 percent growth in 1964 and 1965 the increase in income would have been $33 billion for 1964 over 1963 and $35 billion for 1965 over 1964. The differences between these hypothetical increases in income in the absence of a tax cut and the actual number in Table 10-8 are respectively $10.7 billion for 1964 and $16.5 billion for 1965, or $27.2 billion for the combined effect. The 1964 number of $10.7 falls slightly short of the $11 billion we calculated as the impact by the third quarter of 1964 in the previous part, but it is a number very clearly in the ballpark. Allowing for full adjustment, we found the long-run effect on GNP of the tax cut to be $36.2 billion. Our two-year effect of $27.2 billion falls short of that, as it should because it is just two years and not the long run. Again, however, it is a number very close to that predicted by Okun, as seen in Chart 10-3. We conclude, therefore, that if in the absence of the tax cut GNP had grown at the rate of 4 percent, then the actual behavior of GNP reflects the impact of the tax cut in roughly the timing and order of magnitude that the empirical analysis of the preceding estimates would have suggested.

Next we look at the components of GNP. Here we would expect a

TABLE 10-8   CHANGES IN GNP AND ITS COMPONENTS, 1963–1966 (*In billions of 1972 dollars*)

	GNP		Consumption		Fixed investment		Inventory investment	
1963/1962	$31.6	3.9%	$18.5	3.8%	$ 7.5	6.8%	$−0.3	−3.7%
1964/1963	$43.7	5.2%	$27.3	5.4%	$ 8.0	6.8%	$−0.5	−6.4%
1965/1964	$51.5	5.8%	$30.0	5.6%	$14.0	11.2%	$ 4.0	54.0%
1966/1965	$55.1	5.9%	$28.0	5.0%	$ 5.8	4.2%	$ 5.4	47.0%

Note: These comparisons are midyear to midyear.
Source: Economic Report of the President, 1975.

relatively faster adjustment for consumption than for fixed investment because of the difference in lags. From the table it is apparent that consumption did increase significantly in 1964 and 1965. The rate of increase in those years was certainly much higher than in 1963. Thus in 1964 an actual increase of $27 billion was $7 billion in excess of what consumption growth would have been if it had followed a 4 percent growth path. That difference of $7 billion can therefore be taken as a rough measure of the short-run consumption effects of the tax cut. It is somewhat on the low side of the impact effect on consumption that our previous analysis suggested, but it is again a ballpark figure.

We observe rather clearly from Table 10-8 the lag with which fixed investment spending reacts to policy. There is no change in investment spending in 1964 relative to 1963, but in 1965 there is a very dramatic increase in investment that reflects the tax cut and induced investment spending in adjustment to the increased growth in income. The initial increase in income is thus essentially led by consumption spending, with increased fixed investment following with a lag. Finally consider inventory investment. As we would expect from an expansion in aggregate demand led by a consumption increase, the first effect is to lead to a reduction in inventories. However, in 1965 inventory investment is extremely strong and thus reflects the adjustment of planned inventory stocks to the higher level of income.

The data in Table 10-8 confirm in more than a rough way the predictions we formed earlier about the effects of a tax cut. The data show the sharp increase in income over time in response to the fiscal expansion. The time path of the expansion of GNP and its components reflects the lags in consumption and investment spending. The total impact, relative to a hypothetical 4 percent growth path, reflects roughly the order of magnitude that we would expect. During the first six quarters, the economy proceeded about three-quarters of the way to full adjustment.

We have studied the 1964 tax cut in considerable detail because it is the textbook case of a tax cut. From an initial position of slow growth the tax cut strongly raised aggregate demand and real growth in income from about 4 percent to the higher level of 6 percent. The strong increase in aggregate demand in turn was reflected in a continuously falling unemployment rate. From an unemployment rate of 5.7 percent in 1963, the expansion led to a reduction in unemployment to only 3.8 percent in 1966. Clearly the 1964 tax cut had an important macroeconomic impact, turning the economy from low growth and a large GNP gap back to high growth and full-employment.

10-4 THE 1966 CREDIT CRUNCH

The credit crunch of the second half of 1966 was the first occasion in the post-World War II period that the Fed sharply cut back on monetary growth and caused rapid and, for the time, large increases in interest rates. For reasons to be explained in this section, banks and other financial institutions were not able to make their usual volume of loans. As Phillip Cagan describes the episode:[17]

> Increasingly, normally acceptable borrowers had to be disappointed, even though banks stretched their resources. During these months interest rates soared, and many corporations that borrow short-term funds on a regular basis began to doubt whether they would be able to meet upcoming financial commitments. The financial and business community developed a severe case of the jitters. Few had ever experienced a general financial stringency.

The crunch was the period of high interest rates, reduced availability of loans from financial institutions, and simple fear of financial disaster that prevailed from about August to October 1966.

In this section we analyze the causes and the consequences of the credit crunch.

The Onset of Inflation

The vigorous expansion in economic activity set off by the 1964 tax cut and supported by the accompanying monetary expansion led to a significant increase in inflation by 1965–1966. Chart 10-1 shows a clear break in the economy's inflation performance in 1965, with inflation increasing from the 1.0 to 1.5 percent range of 1961–1964 to the 2.9 to 5.4 percent range of 1966–1969. Unemployment fell to 4 percent by early 1966, and the economy not only reached the level of potential output, but was soon operating at a level of GNP in excess of potential output. The increase in inflation led to the Federal Reserve policies that produced the credit crunch.

[17]Phillip Cagan, "Monetary Policy," pp. 99–101 in Phillip Cagan et al., *Economic Policy and Inflation in the Sixties*, American Enterprise Institute, 1972.

Monetary Policy and Disintermediation

The Fed was alarmed by the emergence of inflation and, as early as February 1966, determined that monetary conditions should become tighter. The tighter monetary conditions, however, did not come about until the second quarter of 1966. From then on, for the rest of 1966, the money supply actually remained constant. The reduction in monetary growth, from an average of 4.5 percent in the preceding year to exactly zero, proved to be a very deflationary move. The demand for nominal balances was still growing because nominal income was increasing. By keeping the nominal money supply constant in the face of growing demand, the Fed forced up interest rates and thereby depressed spending. Table 10-9 shows interest rates for 1965–1967, with the Treasury bill and commercial paper rates peaking in the fourth quarter of 1966.

The financial markets were affected not only by a relatively slow growth in the monetary base, but also by increased reserve requirements that were imposed on time deposits and, most importantly, by regulation Q.[18] Regulation Q imposes ceilings on interest rates which banks are allowed to pay on their time deposits. As interest rates in the market rose, they soon hit the ceiling set by the Fed, and commercial banks found that they became uncompetitive in raising funds. The public preferred Treasury bills and commercial paper rather than time deposits, whose regulated low yield now made them unattractive. As a consequence commercial banks could not raise the funds with which to expand their lending.

What happened to the commercial banks and other thrift institutions, such as the mutual savings banks and savings and loan associations in 1966, was that the interest rates they were allowed to pay on deposits held with them were less that the interest rates that could be earned by buying Treasury bills and commercial paper. Commercial paper is a short-term bond (called a note) issued by firms, for the purpose of borrowing for short periods (up to six months). When the commercial paper rate exceeds the regulation Q rate banks can pay, depositors withdraw their funds from the

---

[18]Regulation Q and disintermediation were discussed in Chap. 6.

TABLE 10-9   INTEREST RATES, 1965–1967

	1965	1966				1967
		I	II	III	IV	
Treasury bill rate	4.0	4.6	4.6	5.1	5.3	4.3
Government long-term bond yield	4.2	4.6	4.6	4.8	4.7	4.9
Prime commercial paper	4.4	4.9	5.4	5.9	6.0	5.1

Source: Economic Report of the President, 1968.

banks to invest in the higher-yielding assets. Chart 10-4 compares the Fed discount rate, the yield on four- to six-month prime commercial paper, and the regulation Q maximum rate. The period of the credit crunch coincides with the period in Chart 10-4 in which the commercial paper rate was above the regulation Q rate.

The process in which depositors withdraw funds from banks and other financial institutions as a result of interest rate ceilings is known as *disintermediation*.[19] As a result of the loss of funds, the banks can no longer make loans. Borrowers have to turn away from banks and rather raise funds by borrowing directly in the money market. Lenders and borrowers get together directly, avoiding the financial intermediaries, and thus avoiding the regulation interest rate ceilings. That is, firms no longer try to raise money for investment from bank loans but by selling debt (commercial paper) to investors in the money market.

One might think that this process of bypassing the financial intermediaries is quite unobjectionable since it gets the credit to those who need it most while giving lenders rates higher than those regulation Q will permit banks to pay. There are, however, two major problems. The first is that disintermediation inevitably hurts small business and consumers. Small business and consumers cannot place their credit demands directly in the market. They cannot issue commercial paper or other credit instru-

---

[19] A second and perhaps more important instance of disintermediation occurred in 1969. See Cagan, op. cit., pp. 117-125.

CHART 10-4 INTEREST RATES AND REGULATION Q CEILING. (Source: *Survey of Current Business,* 1969 Supplement, and *Federal Reserve Bulletin*)

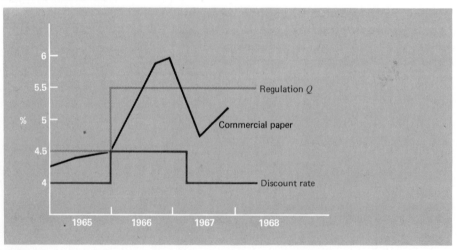

ments in the way large corporations can. Indeed, it is precisely the role of banks and similar institutions to channel credit efficiently to these sectors and "intermediate" between borrowers and lenders. Regulation Q, when it becomes effective, therefore discriminates against consumer loans and small business credit. The other major problem arises for mortgages. Savings and loan associations specialize in mortgage credit which finances construction. Whenever ceiling interest rates on time deposits become effective, these institutions, exactly like banks, lose their competitiveness in attracting funds and consequently have a reduced volume of credit to loan out. This in turn means that less credit is available for construction, and as a consequence there is a strong impact on construction, as we see in Chart 10-5.[20]

The Fed's decision to allow interest rates to increase and stop monetary growth had been long delayed. In the two preceding years, the money stock had been allowed to grow to accommodate the fiscal expansion. Only in the face of sharply increased inflation did the Fed consider a move toward restraint and high interest rates, which have a strong impact on particular sectors of the economy, most importantly on housing construction. Tight money meant, too, a more general slowdown in the growth of aggregate demand and therefore no further cuts in the unemployment rate. The choice between restraining aggregate demand to reduce inflationary pressure and accomodating high demand to reduce unemployment further was not then, nor is it usually, an easy one. It was already apparent to administration economists that rising defense expenditures were putting excessive demand pressure on the economy, and that fiscal policy could offset that pressure. However, a tax increase did not come until 1968. In the meantime, at least in 1966, the full burden of restraining aggregate demand was taken up by the Fed in a "go-it-alone" tight monetary policy.

Effects of the Credit Crunch on Economic Activity

The tightness of monetary policy started to affect aggregate demand by late 1966. Private investment spending as shown in Chart 10-5 responded dramatically to the high interest rates and credit tightness. This was particularly true for residential construction, which declined sharply under the impact of tight credit. We note, too, the relative timing of reduced residential construction and the reduction in business fixed investment spending. Residential construction reacted very quickly to tightness in money and credit markets. The adjustment in business investment was considerably slower.

The credit crunch is reflected in a sharp reduction in real income growth in 1966 and early 1967. From a high rate of growth of 8 percent in

[20]For further aspects of regulation Q see Albert Burger, "A Historical Analysis of the Credit Crunch of 1966," *Federal Reserve Bank of St. Louis, Review*, September 1969. pp. 13–30.

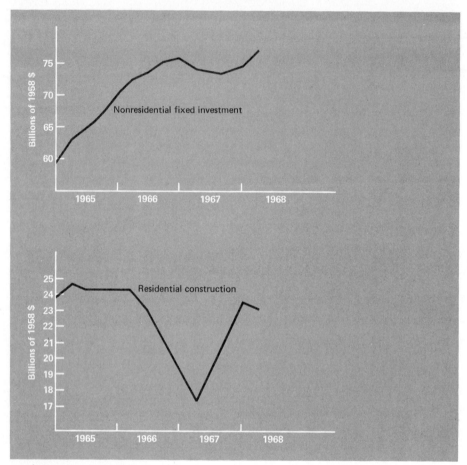

CHART 10-5 COMPONENTS OF
INVESTMENT SPENDING, 1965–1967
(BILLIONS OF 1958 DOLLARS). (Source:
Survey of Current Business, 1969
Supplement)

1965 the rate of increase of real output falls as shown in Table 10-10. Much of the slowdown of growth preceded the crunch itself, but was probably a result of the fall in residential construction that began in the second quarter of 1966 as interest rates rose.

What accounts for the reduced real growth? The 5-billion-dollar reduction in housing construction and the flattening out of business fixed investment spending were each partially responsible. While residential construction accounts for less than 4 percent of GNP and the reduction in construction spending accounts for less than 1 percent of GNP, it is

TABLE 10-10 REAL OUTPUT GROWTH

1965	1966				1967				1968
	I	II	III	IV	I	II	III	IV	
8.1	7.6	3.6	3.1	4.8	−0.1	2.4	4.4	3.2	5.1

Source: *Survey of Current Business*, 1969 Supplement.

nevertheless sufficiently important a reduction to start off a dampening in real growth that is reflected in Table 10-10. Subsequently as high interest rates slowed down business fixed investment, the economy entered a *minirecession* in early 1967. The minirecession was the short period of negative growth which, however, did not last long enough even to reduce output below its potential level. Real growth in the first quarter was close to zero. With a growing labor force, failure of real output and employment to grow means rising unemployment. We only record this fact here but will return to it in Chap. 13 below.

The effects of the 1966 credit crunch were soon overcome, and the economy returned once more to high growth rates of real spending and output. Charts of actual and potential output, such as Chart 10-2, show that the following period, 1968–1969, was one in which the GNP gap was negative and output was at or even above the full-employment level. The 1966 credit crunch made only a very transitory dent in growth performance for two reasons. One was the very sizeable buildup of military spending, and the other was a monetary policy that resumed a highly expansionary path.

10-5 THE 1968 TAX SURCHARGE

Monetary policy in 1966 slowed down the growth rate of real output and produced the minirecession of early 1967. By late 1967, however, the economy had resumed a high growth rate of output and spending, despite declines in residential construction and business fixed investment. The explanation for the resumption of growth can be seen in Chart 10-6, which shows a rapid increase in federal government outlays between 1965 and 1967. The spending was in good measure for defense purposes, but there were, too, the Great Society programs of President Johnson. Along with the increased government spending went a more expansionary monetary policy, which we shall discuss below.

The high level of employment combined with the increasing rate of inflation led administration economists to discuss the desirability of a tax increase to offset the expansionary impact of the high aggregate demand. Although the economy was still in a minirecession in the first quarter of

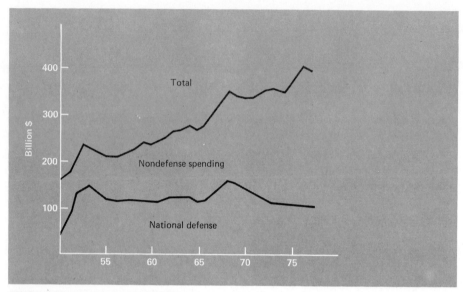

CHART 10-6 FEDERAL GOVERNMENT
OUTLAYS (BILLIONS OF 1977 DOLLARS).
(Source: *The Budget of the United States
Government,* 1977)

1967, it was clear that some restrictive policies were necessary, in the face
of high levels of government spending.

There were three options for restrictive policy. The first was to run a
tight monetary policy by reducing the growth rate of the money supply—
the policy of 1966 and the credit crunch. Both the memory of the credit
crunch and the impact of tight money on investment and particularly housing construction argued against the use of tight monetary policy.[21]
Second, it might have been possible to cut government spending.
Government spending on goods and services had grown in the last few
years by more that $20 billion, and federal spending on goods and services
had increased from 9 percent to 11 percent of GNP. However, military
spending could not be cut because of the war, and the administration was
not anxious to cut spending on its Great Society programs. This left the tax
increase as the option actually chosen.

In January 1967 the administration asked Congress for a temporary tax
surcharge, to start July 1. A tax surcharge is a proportional increase above
existing taxes. Essentially, taxes are calculated using existing tax rates,

[21]Of course, the administration could not itself choose the course of monetary policy, but it
could make its views known to the Fed.

exemptions, etc., and then when the bill has been added up, a given percentage is added to it. Congress was reluctant to pass the legislation then, primarily because the minirecession was still on. As Okun puts it:[22]

> Politically, a tax increase seemed considerably more feasible in 1967, because of the experience of 1966, which had underlined the costs of inflation and the distortions involved in using monetary brakes to offset a fiscal accelerator. Yet restrictive tax action could not be taken until the immediate economic slowdown had been surmounted and a rebound was visible to the congressional eye. This strategy of shifting the fiscal-monetary mix depended upon accurate forecasting and appropriate timing of policy measures. The existing slowdown permitted the monetary brakes to be released without an imminent threat of inflation. Then it was necessary for the economy to get back on its feet and show vigor. Finally, it was essential that fiscal stimulus be curbed by the timely enactment of a substantial tax increase.
>
> As matters developed, the strategy earned a top grade in economics and a failing grade in politics.

In referring to a shifting of the fiscal monetary mix, Okun means a shift from tight monetary policy and expansionary fiscal policy in 1966 to easier monetary policy and tighter fiscal policy later.

The tax surcharge was finally enacted only in June 1968, after a period of strong monetary expansion and an increase in the budget deficit. Chart 10-7 shows that the full-employment budget (HE) moved from a small surplus in 1966 to a deficit of $16 billion by the middle of 1968. The shift to a full-employment deficit was largely the result of the increase in government spending.

The Tax Package

The Revenue and Expenditure Control Act of 1968 featured a 10 percent surcharge on income taxes paid by individuals, retroactive to April 1, 1968, and by corporations, retroactive to January 1, 1968. The act further provided for a reduction in some proposed federal expenditures and a ceiling on government spending for the fiscal year 1969. The surcharge was explicitly recognized as temporary and was due to expire in June 1969.

The tax surcharge was the main feature of the act. It was estimated that the surcharge would create an additional $10 billion in actual fiscal revenue per full year when estimated at the 1968 income level. The revenue effect shows up in Chart 10-7 as an increase in the full-employment budget surplus (HE) that moved from a deficit of $16 billion in the second quarter of 1968 to the much smaller deficit of $1 billion at the end of 1968.

[22]Arthur Okun, *The Political Economy of Prosperity*, Norton, 1969, pp. 83–84.

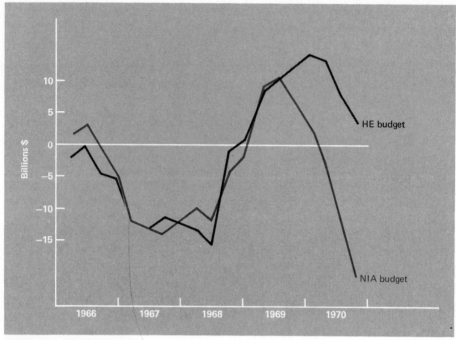

CHART 10-7 ACTUAL AND FULL
EMPLOYMENT BUDGET. (Source: *Federal
Budget Trends,* various issues)

Results of the Tax Surcharge

The question we have to address now is what amount of restraint in terms
of reduced aggregate spending we would expect to arise from this restrictive fiscal action. The first guess is that we should simply reverse the
analysis of the 1964 tax cut. Now we have a tax increase rather than a cut in
taxes, but of roughly the same order of magnitude. There is, though, the
potentially important difference that the 1968 surcharge was quite
explicitly recognized as *temporary.* This means, in line with our analysis
of the consumption function in Chap. 5, that individuals would plan to
spread the current increase in tax liabilities over a much longer consumption and saving horizon. They would plan to finance the one-time extra tax
liability by reducing saving a lot and reducing consumption rather little.
By contrast, if the tax surcharge were viewed as permanent, rather more of
it would come out of reduced consumption and quite a bit less out of
reduced saving.

Was the 1968 tax surcharge effective in restraining aggregate demand?

As usual, the question is hard to answer because we cannot be certain as to what might have happened in the absence of the surcharge. Moreover, the point is still controversial among researchers.[23] The facts do suggest some answers, though. The most important fact that stands out is the sharp reduction in the saving rate in 1968–1969. Table 10-11 shows that the saving rate in 1968–1969 declined quite significantly and that the timing of the decline roughly accorded with the imposition of the surcharge.

What do we expect the savings rate to do in a permanent-income view of consumption behavior? We know that the tax surcharge will reduce personal disposable income and therefore should to some extent affect both consumption and saving. What happens, though, to the *fraction* of personal income saved? Figure 10-1 returns to the short-run and long-run consumption functions of Chap. 5. Starting from an initial equilibrium at point E with a disposable income of Y_d^0, we experience a transitory decline in disposable income to Y_d'. In the short run the adjustment is to point E', with a relatively small adjustment in consumption and a relatively large decline in saving. If the decline in disposable income were maintained, we would ultimately move to point E'' on the long-run consumption function. In the short run the ratio of consumption to income rises as we move from E to E'. It follows that the ratio of saving to income, the saving rate, declines. This is precisely the result observed in Table 10-11. Again, if the tax surcharge persisted, we would expect a downward shift of the consumption function over time until point E'' was reached, with consumption and saving ratios back to the initial levels that they showed at point E. By contrast, if the tax increase were permanent, the adjustment would be directly from E to E'' with the savings rate remaining constant.

To illustrate the effect we are talking about, we look in Table 10-12, at some numbers for the transition from the second to the third quarter of 1968 at the time the surcharge became effective. From the table it is quite apparent that a major part of the increased tax payments were financed by a

[23]See A. Okun, "The Personal Tax Surcharge and Consumer Demand, 1968–1970," *Brookings Papers on Economic Activity*, 1971, 1, and W. L. Springer, "Did the 1968 Surcharge Really Work?" *American Economic Review*, September 1975, and the follow-up in the *American Economic Review*, March 1977.

TABLE 10-11   THE SAVING RATE IN RESPONSE TO THE 1968 TAX SURCHARGE

1967	1968				1969				1970
	I	II	III	IV	I	II	III	IV	
7.3	7.2	7.6	6.0	6.2	5.3	5.3	6.6	6.8	7.9

Source: W. L. Springer, "Did the 1968 Surcharge Really Work?" *American Economic Review*, September 1975.

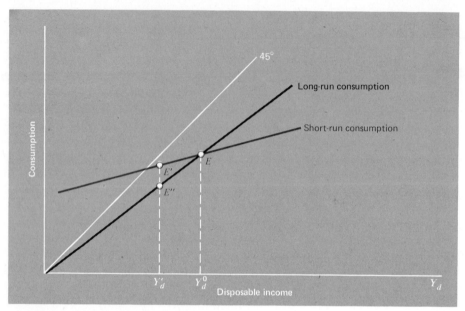

FIGURE 10-1 THE SHORT-RUN EFFECT OF A TRANSITORY TAX SURCHARGE

reduction in saving. Taxes rose by $11 billion, of which $9 billion was financed by reducing saving. Consumption spending in fact increased along with personal income.

The evidence we are considering here would seem to argue quite strongly that the 1968 surcharge had only a minor effect on consumption spending. With most of the increase in taxes financed by a reduction in saving, the marginal propensity to consume out of disposable income appropriate for a transitory surcharge appears to be small. Indeed marginal propensities to consume out of transitory income that have been suggested in the discussion of this tax increase range between 0.1 and 0.3.[24]

While there is no complete answer yet to the question of the effects of transitory changes in fiscal policy on aggregate demand, the basic outlines of the answer are clear. Both the theory of consumption of Chap. 5 and the experience of the tax surcharge of 1968 suggest that the impacts of temporary tax increases on consumption spending are relatively small. A transitory tax change of the 1968 type, scheduled to last a year, seems to have less than half the effect on consumption that a permanent change does.

[24]See R. Eisner, "What Went Wrong?" *Journal of Political Economy*, May/June 1971, and A. Blinder and R. Solow, "Analytical Foundations of Fiscal Policy" in A. Blinder, et al., *The Economics of Public Finance*, Brookings, 1974. pp. 105–109.

Monetary Policy

Returning to the course of the economy in 1968, we note that real income continued to expand strongly despite the restrictive fiscal policy. The growth rate did decline a little. From a growth rate of real income of 4 percent at the beginning of the year, real growth fell to 3 percent at the end of the year. What sustained the increase in aggregate demand? We have seen that the reduction in the savings rate absorbed much of the restrictive fiscal policy. Beyond that, however, one has to look to monetary policy as a significant contributor to strength in aggregate demand. Table 10-13 shows the annual growth rates of money, first quarter to first quarter for M_1, that is, currency plus demand deposits.

It is striking that after the credit crunch of 1966, reflected in the very low growth rate of money for 1966 of 2.2 percent, money growth increases very sharply and is sustained at a high level around 7 percent for two years. From early 1967 until early 1969 money grew at a rate higher than it had for any two-year period since the 1940s. This provides an explanation for the continued high level of aggregate demand and rapidly increasing inflation in this monetary expansion. Not only was monetary growth sufficiently vigorous to overcome the deflationary impact of restrictive fiscal policy, but it also contributed to expansion in aggregate demand and inflationary pressure. Indeed, in the period 1967 to 1968, inflation increased from the 3 percent that had prevailed in 1967 to 4.7 percent by late 1968.

Chart 10-8 helps interpret monetary policy. Here we show the interest rate on medium-term (three- to five-year) Treasury bonds, the growth rate of money (M_1), and the rate of inflation (CPI). The growth rate of the nominal quantity of money, after a decline in 1966–1967, increased sharply in 1968 and continued to be high in 1969. From this point of view, monetary policy was very expansionary in 1968 and thus explains why the fiscal tightness, reflected in the sharp increase of the high-employment budget in

TABLE 10-12   THE EFFECTS OF THE 1968 TAX SURCHARGE ON CONSUMPTION AND SAVING (*Billions of dollars at annual rates*)

	1968/II	1968/III	Change
Personal income	681	699	18
Less: Taxes, etc.	93	104	11
Equals: Personal disposable income	588	595	7
Less: Consumption	543	559	16
Equals: Personal saving	45	36	−9

Source: *Survey of Current Business,* 1973 Supplement.

TABLE 10-13 GROWTH RATE OF MONEY (M_1)

1966/65	1967/66	1968/67	1969/68	1970/69
5.4	2.2	6.7	7.9	3.1

Source: Federal Reserve Bank of St. Louis.

Chart 10-7, was not more deflationary in its impact on economic activity.

A look at interest rates might, on the contrary, suggest that monetary policy was tight. Interest rates increased from 1967 on, and reached their highest level for the sixties in 1969. However, here it is important to return to the distinction between nominal and real interest rates. The expected real interest rate is the nominal interest rate minus the expected rate of inflation, and it is the expected real interest rate that is relevant for investment. In Chart 10-8 we show the actual rate of inflation. We do not have any exact measure of the expected rate of inflation, so that we cannot calculate the expected real rate of interest. But since the actual rate of inflation increased throughout the sixties, with a particularly sharp acceleration in 1967, it is reasonable to suppose that the expected rate of inflation too rose through the sixties, and perhaps a little more rapidly in 1967 than earlier. In that case the expected real rate of interest would not have been rising as fast as the nominal interest rate, shown in Chart 10-8, and might even have been falling after 1967. If so, we could regard monetary policy as expansionary from the viewpoint of both the behavior of the growth rate of money and the behavior of expected real interest rates.

The interpretation of the economic events of 1968 is an important question in macroeconomics. One view is that the continued expansion was entirely due to the high growth of money, *and* that fiscal policy does not matter. The other is that while both monetary and fiscal policy are potentially important, the effects of the fiscal policy in the form of the temporary surcharge were small compared to the effects of a strong monetary expansion. The view we have taken throughout this book is that both monetary and fiscal policy matter. The net effect will depend on the relative dosage and any special consideration that may be appropriate. For 1968 the net effect was undoubtedly caused by a monetary expansion that was more than sufficient to overcome the deflationary effects of the move toward a temporary budget surplus.

Why Did the Fed Do It?

In concluding this section we must raise the question of why monetary policy was so very expansionary in the 1967–1968 period. There were two main factors. The first was a desire to avoid a repetition of the credit crunch, with its effects on housing and small business, and near financial panic. Second, the effects of the proposed tax surcharge in reducing aggregate demand were undoubtedly overestimated. The crucial distinction between the effects of permanent and transitory tax changes was not made. It was therefore anticipated that the tax increase would lead to a significant reduction in aggregate demand, and that monetary policy should cushion the anticipated shock. In a sense, the success of the tax cut of 1964 was partly responsible for the failure of the tax surcharge of 1968, because it led to an overestimate of the effectiveness of fiscal policy.

10-6 RESTRICTIVE MONETARY AND FISCAL POLICY IN 1969

The previous sections have shown how the New Economics was strikingly successful in moving the economy to full employment. When at full employment, however, the policies ran into trouble. As Walter Heller recognized:

> The margin for error diminishes as the economy reaches the treasured but treacherous area of full employment. Big doses of expansionary medicine

CHART 10-8 INTEREST RATE, INFLATION, AND MONETARY GROWTH. (Source: *Survey of Current Business.* 1969 Supplement, and *Federal Reserve Bulletin*)

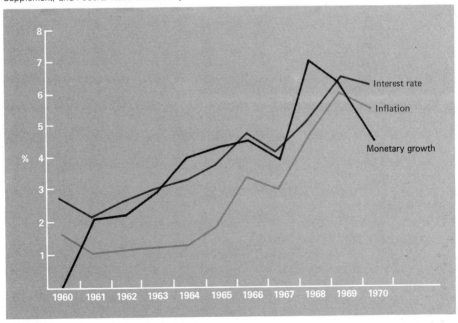

were easy—and safe—to recommend in the face of a $50 billion gap and a hesitant Congress. But at full employment, targets have to be defined more sharply, tolerances are smaller, the line between expansion and inflation becomes thinner . . . . [25]

We do not yet have the analytical tools to discuss the economic policies and problems of the late sixties and early seventies. In this section we briefly set the scene for the discussion of recent policy to be carried out in Chap. 16. The failure to coordinate monetary and fiscal policy, the failure to raise taxes to offset the increased defense spending in 1965–1967, and the failure to control monetary growth in 1967–1968 led inevitably to a buildup of inflation that left the incoming Nixon administration with inflation at the then "intolerably" high level of 5.4 percent. Unemployment in early 1969 was only 3.5 percent.

The low rate of unemployment allowed policy to shift to a fight against inflation. The incoming administration immediately reconsidered the budget for fiscal year 1970. Cuts in spending were proposed along with an extension of the surcharge at a 5 percent level and the repeal of the investment tax credit. Monetary policy, too, became more restrictive in 1969, with the growth rate of the money stock in the second half of the year being less than 2 percent, as compared with the nearly 8 percent growth rate in 1968. We will study the effects of these policies on the economy in Chap. 16.

REFERENCES

Bach, G. L., *Making Monetary and Fiscal Policy*, Brookings, 1971, chap. 6.

Diamond, J. J. (ed.), *Issues in Fiscal and Monetary Policy*, DePaul, 1971.

Cagan, Phillip, et al., *Economic Policy and Inflation in the Sixties*, American Enterprise Institute, 1972.

Friedman, M., *An Economist's Protest*, Horton, 1972.

———, *Dollars and Deficits*, Prentice-Hall, 1968.

——— and W. Heller, *Monetary vs. Fiscal Policy: A Dialogue*, Norton, 1969.

Gordon, R. A., *Economic Instability and Growth: The American Record*, Harper and Row, 1974.

Heller, W., *New Dimensions of Political Economy*, Norton, 1967.

Okun, A., *The Political Economy of Prosperity*, Norton, 1970.

Poole, W., "Monetary Policy in the United States," *Proceedings of the American Academy of Political Science*, vol. 31, no. 4, 1975.

Stein, H., *The Fiscal Revolution in America*, The University of Chicago Press, 1969.

Tobin, J., *The New Economics One Decade Older*, Princeton University Press, 1974.

[25] W.W. Heller, *New Dimensions of Political Economy*, op. cit., p. 69.

APPENDIX: MAJOR CHANGES IN TAX LAWS IN THE 1960s*

Measure	Date recommended	Date enacted	Remarks
Investment tax credit	April 1961	October 1962	Provided a sizeable incentive for new investment in depreciable equipment for domestic use. A 7 percent credit against income tax liabilities is allowed on most such investment.
Revenue Act of 1964	January 1963	February 1964	A permanent cut in income tax rates for all individual and corporate taxpayers. Personal taxes were cut by more than 20 percent and corporate taxes by about 8 percent. Before the cut the marginal personal tax rates ranged from 20 to 91 percent; afterwards the range was 14 to 70 percent. For most corporations the rate fell from 52 to 48 percent.
Excise Tax Reduction Act of 1965	January 1965	June 1965	Repealed federal excise taxes on appliances, radios, television sets, jewelry, furs, and certain other items.
Tax Adjustment Act of 1966	January 1966	March 1966	Restored excise tax rates on transportation equipment and telephone services.
Temporary suspension of the investment tax credit	September 1966	November 1966	As of October 10, 1966, temporarily suspended the 7 percent investment tax credit.
Restoration of the investment tax credit	March 1967	June 1967	As of March 10, 1967, restored the 7 percent investment tax credit.
Revenue and Expenditure Control Act of 1968	January 1967	June 1968	Levied 10 percent surtax on personal income taxes effective April 1, 1968, and on corporate income effective January 1, 1968. The surtax was scheduled to expire on June 30, 1969. Postponed reduction in the respective 7 and 10 percent excise tax rates on automobiles and telephone services.

Extension of surtax	April 1969	August 1969	Extended the 10 percent surtax on personal incomes, previously scheduled to expire on June 30, 1969, to December 31, 1969.
Tax Reform Act of 1969	January 1969	December 1969	Increased personal exemptions and standard deductions. Introduced a maximum marginal rate of 50 percent on earned income. The maximum rate on unearned income remained at 70 percent. Extended the surtax from January 1, 1970, to June 30, 1970, at a 5 percent rate. Generally repealed the investment tax credit for corporations for property constructed, reconstructed, or acquired after April 18, 1969.

*During this period Social Security tax rates were increased. This is not shown here.

Source: Adapted from Federal Reserve Bulletin, various issues.

PROBLEMS

1 The New Economics, while not theoretically novel in the early 1960s, was politically dangerous. President Kennedy ran instead on a balanced-budget platform. How does such a fiscally conservative approach fit in with the New Economics? What would be the implications for stabilization policy of a commitment to a balanced budget every year?

2 The New Economics is based on a keynesian approach to macroeconomics, just as Chaps. 3 and 4 are.
   a Indicate the problem of a GNP gap on the keynesian cross diagram of Chap. 3. (Note: Indicate by a vertical line the level of potential output at one point in time.)
   b Draw on such a diagram the effect of a tax cut like the Revenue Act of 1964.
   c Show how a *negative* GNP gap can come about. What would be appropriate fiscal policy in such a case?

3 a Show in an IS-LM figure what the effect of the 1964 tax cut was. What would have happened if the Fed had kept the money supply constant?
   b Indicate the actual events of 1964–1965 on the IS-LM diagram, illustrating the meaning and effects of "accommodating" monetary policy.

4 Evaluate the general effectiveness and influence of monetary policy using Chart 10-1 and the table below. What are the policy implications of long-delayed and unpredictable responses to changes in the money supply? What is the proper role of monetary policy in view of the experience of the 1960s?

GROWTH RATES OF M_1 *(Percent change, January to January)*

1960	1961	1962	1963	1964	1965	1966	1967	1968	1969
−0.3	3.0	1.7	3.7	4.0	4.8	1.5	7.1	7.9	3.8

Source: Federal Reserve Bulletin, various issues.

5 Explain why many people believe that the inflationary problems of the 1970s have their roots in the 1960s. How can this be so? What would be the cause? What could have been done to avoid such "heating up" of the economy, in this view?

6 The following quote is from a column by Milton Friedman in the December 9, 1968, issue of *Newsweek*. He goes on to point out that inflation rose dramatically during the Kennedy and Johnson years, as did government spending. Is this a fair appraisal of the New Economics? Would you agree or disagree with him? Explain.

> The Nixon Administration will confront major economic problems in three areas: inflation, balance of payments, and the government budget.... In each area, the New Economics has managed in eight years to turn a comfortable, easy situation into a near-crisis, to squander assets and multiply liabilities.

7 Discuss the notion of the "monetary-fiscal policy mix." What determines the "mix" that is chosen? How did the effects of the mixes of 1966 and 1968 differ? Illustrate using an IS-LM diagram. (Assume the level of income was the same.)

8 Explain the role of Regulation Q in the credit crunch of 1966.

PART

11

Aggregate Supply

U p to this point we have assumed that firms produce and supply all the output that is demanded at the current price level, and have concentrated our attention on aggregate demand. We left in abeyance the questions of the determination of the price level and the rate of inflation, and of the interaction between changes in output and changes in prices. Even though our theoretical chapters did not discuss changes in the price level, you no doubt noticed that in Chaps. 9 and 10 we mentioned several times the likelihood that rapidly rising output would be accompanied by increases in the price level. It is now time to begin our study of the determinants of the aggregate price level and its changes over time—that is, the rate of inflation.

The first element we develop in this chapter is the theory of aggregate supply. Then in Chap. 12 we combine aggregate supply and aggregate demand to see how the price level is determined, and how shifts in aggregate supply and demand affect the price level. Chapter 1 has already provided us with the outlines of the interaction of aggregate supply and demand in the determination of the price level—but as we warned there, there is much that lies behind the aggregate supply and demand curves.

The aggregate supply curve is the relationship between the amount of output firms supply and the aggregate price level. The aggregate supply curve and the aggregate demand curve between them explain how changes in aggregate nominal GNP are divided between changes in the price level and changes in real GNP. A given change in nominal GNP can always be broken down into a change in real GNP and a change in the value of output due to price changes, as can be seen in Eq. (1).[1]

$$\Delta Y_n = P \, \Delta Y + Y \, \Delta P \tag{1}$$

where $Y_n = PY$ is the level of nominal GNP, P the aggregate price level, and Y the level of real GNP.

We should not expect a given percentage change in nominal GNP always to translate into changes in real output and prices in the same proportions. Rather, the way in which a change in nominal GNP is divided depends on a number of factors, including how close the economy is to full employment. If the economy were always at full employment, the first term in Eq. (1) would be zero because output is limited by factor supplies.

[1] The relation between changes in nominal income, price changes, and changes in real income is brought out in the following example, using data for 1974 and 1975:

	P	Y	Y_n
1974	1.16	1,214	1,413
1975	1.27	1,192	1,516
	$\Delta P = 0.11$	$\Delta Y = -22$	$\Delta Y_n = 103$

Using Eq. (1) we have: $1.27(-22) + 1,214(0.11) = 105.6 = \Delta Y_n$, where the difference is due to rounding error and where GNP is measured in billions of dollars.

At the other extreme, one can imagine a world where there is considerable unemployment and prices are entirely unresponsive to aggregate demand. In that case the second term would be zero. Generally, the response would be in between those extremes, with any given change in nominal income changing both prices and output. However, to a surprising extent, current aggregate demand appears to have relatively little impact on prices. As William Nordhaus of Yale has put it: "After three decades, the major intellectual problem continues to be the fact that so little response to demand shifts comes through prices and wages."[2]

This chapter develops the notion of a short-run aggregate supply schedule which is quite flat, and a long-run supply schedule which is vertical. In the short run, an expansion in output has relatively little effect on costs and prices so that the IS-LM analysis remains relevant for the determination of output. Over time, however, rates of unemployment below normal give rise to wage and cost increases and thus shift upward the aggregate supply schedule. In the longest run, the level of output supplied is independent of the level of prices.

The theory of aggregate supply is among the most difficult and least settled aspects of modern macroeconomics. Accordingly, the theory we present in this chapter is not well established. Important as aggregate supply is to issues of public policy, there are no definitive theories of aggregate supply. The area is one in which there is much current research, which absorbs interest and effort under the heading "the new microeconomics of inflation and unemployment."[3]

We shall build the theory in this chapter using three main elements: (1) the determination of firms' level of employment, (2) wage behavior, and (3) the pricing decision by firms. The story we will tell is that firms hire a labor force that corresponds to their expected or *normal* level of output. Firms price their output at the level of *normal costs* (the cost of production corresponding to the normal level of output) rather than charging at each moment what the market will bear. Normal costs are made up primarily of wage costs which in turn are determined by the level of unemployment. The elements, correctly assembled, will give us an aggregate supply schedule or a relation between output and prices.

The aggregate supply theory we present is essentially *dynamic*; that is, the supply relationship between output and prices is different in the short run and the long run. In the short run (of about a year) the aggregate supply curve is quite flat. Changes in the value of output which occur as a result of aggregate demand changes are, in the short run, primarily quantity changes and not price changes. Over time, the state of the labor market affects costs and therefore shifts the supply schedule. The long-run re-

[2]William Nordhaus, "Inflation Theory and Policy," *American Economic Review*, May 1976, p. 62.
[3]See Edmund S. Phelps (ed.), *Microeconomic Foundations of Employment and Inflation Theory*, Norton, 1969, for a difficult but interesting set of papers describing some original research in this area.

sponse of prices to shifts in aggregate demand is therefore greater than the short-run response.

The chapter starts by examining an idealized economy in which prices and wages adjust instantly to changes in demand. It will be seen that in this *neoclassical* economy, the aggregate supply curve is vertical—changes in aggregate demand change the price level but have no effect on real output. Such a frictionless economy is continuously at full employment, and so aggregate demand changes do not have any effect on employment and therefore on the level of real output.

The neoclassical model provides a background against which it is easier to understand the development of the theory of aggregate supply in the rest of the chapter. The determination of the firm's level of employment is studied in Sec. 11-2. Section 11-3 examines the way in which wages and prices are determined. Then in Sec. 11-4 we combine the three elements (1) employment determination, (2) wage behavior, and (3) firms' pricing decisions, to produce the aggregate supply curve.

11-1 THE FRICTIONLESS NEOCLASSICAL MODEL

We will introduce our problem—the relationships between output and employment, and output and prices—by studying an idealized frictionless case. That is the case where wages and prices are flexible, where there are no costs to workers in finding a job and no costs to firms in increasing or reducing their labor force, and where firms behave competitively and expect to sell all they produce at prevailing prices. That case will serve as a benchmark for the discussion of more realistic cases, but it also allows us to introduce some useful concepts such as the production function and the demand for labor. Throughout, we will assume that labor is the only variable factor of production in the short run.

The Production Function

A production function provides a relation between the quantity of factor inputs, such as the amount of labor used, and the maximum quantity of output that can be produced using those inputs. The relation reflects only technical efficiency. In Eq. (2) we write the production function

$$Y = F(N, \ldots) \tag{2}$$

where Y denotes real output, N is labor input, and the dots denote other cooperating factors that are in short-run fixed supply. The production function is shown in Fig. 11-1. It exhibits "diminishing returns," which means that output increases proportionately less than labor input.

Diminishing returns are shown in the production function by the fact that it is not a straight line through the origin (constant returns) or an

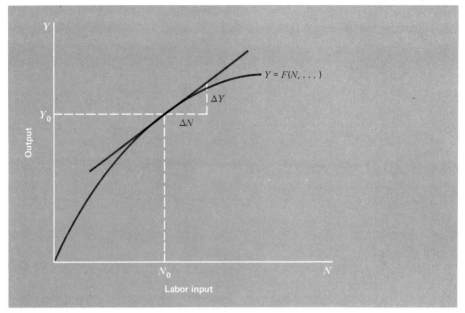

FIGURE 11-1 THE PRODUCTION
FUNCTION AND THE MARGINAL PRODUCT
OF LABOR

upward-curling line (increasing returns). Diminishing returns are explained by the fact that as employment increases, and other inputs remain
constant, each laborer on the job has fewer machines with which to work
and therefore becomes less productive. Thus, increases in the amount of
labor progressively reduce the addition to output that further employment
can bring. An increase in the labor force will always raise output, but
progressively less so as employment expands. The marginal contribution
of increased employment is indicated by the slope of the production function, $\Delta Y/\Delta N$. It is readily seen that the slope flattens out as we increase
employment, thus showing that increasing employment makes a positive
but diminishing contribution to output.

Labor Demand

From the production function we can proceed to the demand for labor. We
are asking how much labor a firm would want to hire. The rule of thumb is
to continue hiring additional labor and expand production as long as the
increase in the value of output exceeds the increase in the wage bill. A
firm will hire an additional hand as long as she will bring in more in
revenue than she costs in wages. The contribution to output of additional
labor is called the marginal product of labor and has already been identified

in Fig. 11-1 with the slope of the production function. That marginal product, as we saw above, is both positive—additional labor is productive—and diminishing, which means that additional employment becomes progressively less productive. We noted above that a firm will employ additional labor as long as the marginal product of labor, MPN for short, exceeds the cost of additional labor. The cost of additional labor is given by the real wage, that is, the nominal wage divided by the price level. The real wage measures the amount of real output the firm has to pay each worker. Since hiring one more worker results in an output increase of MPN, and a cost to the firm of the real wage, firms will hire additional labor if the MPN exceeds the real wage. This point is formalized in Fig. 11-2, which looks at the labor market.

The downward-sloping schedule in Fig. 11-2 is the demand for labor schedule which, as we shall now see, is the MPN schedule: firms hire labor up to the point at which the MPN is equal to the real wage. The MPN schedule shows the contribution to output of additional employment. In line with our reasoning above, the MPN is positive, but additional employment reduces it so that the MPN schedule is negatively sloped.

Now assume a firm currently employs a labor force N_1 and the real wage is $(w/P)_0$, where w is the money wage and P the price of output. At an employment level N_1 in Fig. 11-2, the firm is clearly engaging too much labor—the real wage exceeds the MPN of that level of employment. What would happen if the firm reduced employment? The reduction in employment would reduce output by the MPN times the change in employment, MPN $\cdot \Delta N$, and therefore reduce revenue to the firm. On the other side of the calculation we have the reduction in the wage bill. Per unit reduction in employment, the wage bill falls at the rate of the real wage, $(w/P) \Delta N$. The net benefit of a reduction in the level of employment is thus equal to the vertical excess of the real wage over the MPN in Fig. 11-2. It is apparent that at the level of employment N_1 that excess is quite sizable, and it pays the firm to reduce the employment level. Indeed it pays to reduce employment until the firm gets to point N_0. Only at that point does the cost of additional labor—the real wage—exactly balance the benefit in the form of increased output. The same argument applies to the unemployment level N_2. Here employment is insufficient because the contribution to output of additional employment, MPN_2, exceeds the cost of additional employment and it therefore pays to expand the level of employment. It is readily seen that the only level of employment that precisely balances the costs and benefits is the level N_0. Therefore, given *any* real wage, the firm's demand for labor is shown by the MPN curve.

Equilibrium in the Labor Market

We have now developed the relation between output and employment (the production function) and the optimal employment choice for a given real wage that is implied by the demand for labor. It remains to consider the determination of the real wage, as part of labor market equilibrium. What we have not yet dealt with is the supply of labor. Adding labor supply will permit us to determine equilibrium in the labor market, employment, real wages, and the supply of output, all together.

We will make a quite simple assumption concerning labor supply. We will assume that the supply of labor is fixed at $\overline{N}$ and that it is independent of the real wage.[4] This is shown in Fig. 11-3 as the vertical schedule, $\overline{NN}$. The equilibrium real wage is clearly $(w/P)_0$.

How does the labor market get to that equilibrium? We argue that the real wage will fall whenever there is an excess supply of labor and that it will rise whenever there is an excess demand. In terms of Fig. 11-3 this means that the real wage will decline whenever it is above $(w/P)_0$. At $(w/P)_1$, for example, labor demand is only N_1 and thus falls short of labor supply. This puts downward pressure on the real wage, causes the real wage to fall, and thus makes it profitable to expand employment. Exactly the reverse argument holds for real wages lower than $(w/P)_0$, where we have an excess demand for labor.

From Fig. 11-3 we see that adjustment of the real wage will bring the

[4]The exposition of this chapter would be little affected if we assumed that labor supply increased as the real wage increased. The major change then would be that the full-employment level of employment would depend on the level of the real wage. You might want to experiment with an upward-sloping labor supply curve as you continue reading.

FIGURE 11-2 THE OPTIMAL EMPLOYMENT CHOICE FOR A GIVEN REAL WAGE

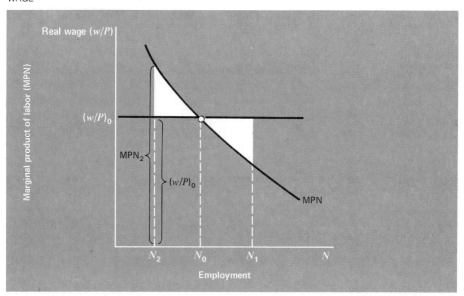

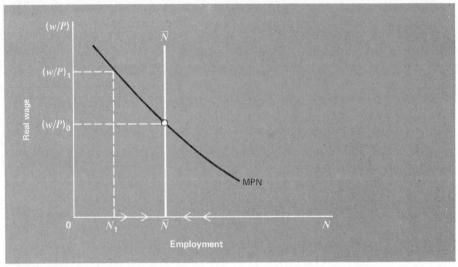

FIGURE 11-3 EQUILIBRIUM IN THE
LABOR MARKET

labor market into full-employment equilibrium at a real wage $(w/P)_0$ and with an employment level equal to the given labor supply $\overline{N}$. Figure 11-4 summarizes the complete equilibrium in the labor market and the corresponding level of *full-employment output* Y_p which is the level of output associated with employment equal to the given labor supply.

Neoclassical Goods and Labor Market Equilibrium

We have now derived the full-employment supply of output and have to complete the neoclassical model by asking how *money* wages and prices are determined. How can we be sure that goods produced can actually be sold? Here we make two important assumptions: (1) goods prices will rise or fall instantaneously to clear the goods market and (2) money wages will instantaneously rise or fall to clear the labor market. How will that adjustment work?

In the labor market the flexibility of money wages ensures that at each price level the money wage rises or falls to achieve the necessary level of the real wage. We are therefore continuously in labor market equilibrium and, whatever the level of prices, firms will employ the full-employment labor force $\overline{N}$ and supply the corresponding level of output Y_p. This is shown in Fig. 11-5 in the aggregate supply curve Y_pY_p. The aggregate supply schedule is vertical to show that the equilibrium level of output supplied—when the labor market is in equilibrium—is independent of the price level. If prices rose relative to wages, firms would be making profits.

In an attempt to secure even larger profits, they would attempt individually to expand their employment level at the going money wage. In the aggregate, though, all they would do would be to compete for the given labor force and drive up the money wage until it had risen in proportion to the increase in prices, thus leaving real output unchanged.

Next we proceed to Fig. 11-6, where we draw both an aggregate supply and an aggregate demand curve. We have to determine why changes in

FIGURE 11-4 EQUILIBRIUM IN THE LABOR MARKET AND FULL-EMPLOYMENT OUTPUT

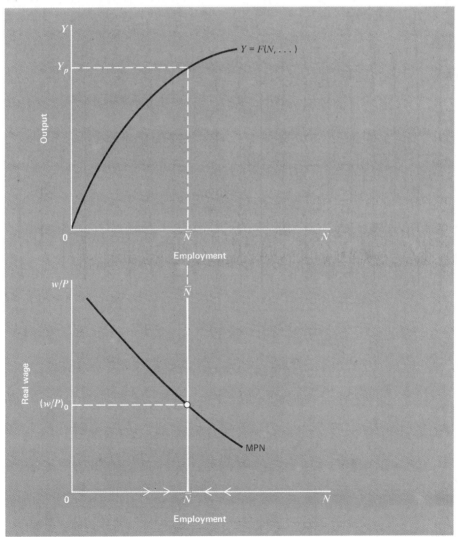

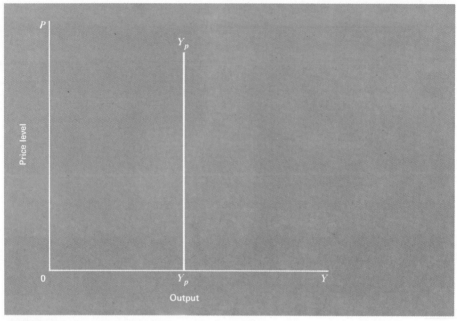

FIGURE 11-5 THE AGGREGATE SUPPLY
CURVE WITH WAGE FLEXIBILITY

the level of prices should affect aggregate demand at all, and thus have the potential of affecting the goods market. The argument, anticipating the details of the next chapter, is that given the nominal quantity of money, a reduction in the price level raises the real quantity of money, $\overline{M}/P$. At each level of real output the higher real money supply causes interest rates to fall and, therefore, aggregate demand to rise. Thus, the price level affects aggregate demand via the real balances–interest rate channel.

Given the downward-sloping aggregate demand curve Y^d, and our aggregate supply schedule $Y_p Y_p$, the equilibrium price level is P_0. We need not be concerned yet with a full understanding of the details of the adjustment process of the price level. It suffices to recognize that it is plausible that the economy will converge to a full-employment equilibrium with all markets in equilibrium. Given the equilibrium price level P_0, the nominal wage will adjust so that the real wage is $(w/P_0)_0$. Furthermore, *if* wages and prices adjust rapidly, and *if* firms respond rapidly in their production decisions to changing conditions, and *if* labor moves rapidly between jobs as some firms expand and others contract, we would expect to be in equilibrium continuously. Any disturbance, such as an increase in the nominal money supply or an improvement in technology, would immediately be reflected in changes in wages and prices that restore the full-employment equilibrium.

The neoclassical full equilibrium is a useful reference point for the study of more realistic descriptions of macroeconomics. We should expect to converge to the neoclassical equilibrium in the long run. But in the short run, problems of transactions costs and information problems associated with finding and taking jobs, together with simple stickiness of wages and prices due to contractual arrangements, will affect the adjustment process. If, for example, prices do not fall fast enough in response to a decline in the nominal quantity of money, then we would expect to get transitory disequilibrium and unemployment. Such unemployment would not occur in the neoclassical model. It is exactly this range of issues such as short-run adjustment and unemployment with which the macroeconomics of the short run is concerned. We therefore retain the neoclassical analysis as a reference point and turn next to a discussion of the adjustment process under less ideal conditions.

There are, as we noted before, three factors underlying slow adjustment in the goods and labor markets. (1) The money wage adjusts only slowly. It takes unemployment to bring the money wage rate down. (2) It is costly to hire and fire workers, and firms therefore do not stay precisely on their neoclassical demand function for labor as in Fig. 11-3. (3) Connected with the preceding point, the costs of changing employment imply that firms look ahead in making employment decisions and base these both

FIGURE 11-6 THE INTERACTION OF AGGREGATE SUPPLY AND DEMAND IN THE DETERMINATION OF THE EQUILIBRIUM PRICE LEVEL

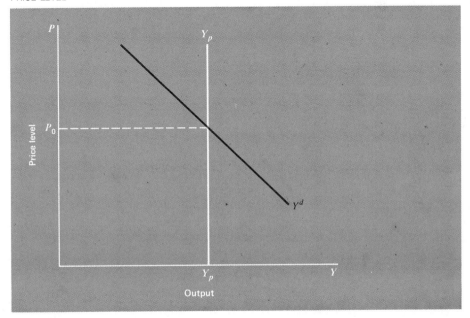

on the real wage, as above, and on their expected sales. The remainder of this chapter explores the implications of these modifications.

11-2 OUTPUT AND EMPLOYMENT

The neoclassical analysis of the previous section will now be modified to recognize that in the short run firms will not be on their marginal product of labor schedule, MPN. Two important departures from the neoclassical assumptions arise. One is that a firm can achieve a *transitory* or temporary increase in output by working a given labor force somewhat harder, perhaps including overtime. The counterpart is that during a transitory decline in demand a firm may want to hold on to its employees rather than laying them off. The firm will incur the wage costs but will save the costs of rehiring the labor force once demand recovers. The fact that variations in demand and sales may be seen as transitory suggests that it may be profitable to separate the production decision from the employment decision. To go a step ahead we would think, if there are significant costs in hiring and firing, that firms will have a relatively stable level of employment but may vary output as demand for their goods varies.[5]

Chart 11-1 shows the average workweek of production workers in manufacturing. It shows, too, the number of layoffs per hundred employees. As the preceding argument suggests, layoffs and reductions in overtime move together. Firms adjust to a decline in demand in part by reducing their employment level and in part by reducing the workweek. This is particularly evident for the 1974–1975 recession, but is similarly true, for example, in the 1958 recession. By contrast, during a period of high aggregate demand, such as 1964–1966, overtime is high and layoffs fall below 1 percent. There is a further point in Chart 11-1 that is quite important. We see for 1974 a decline in overtime that starts quite perceptibly in the middle of the year. However, the steep decline in layoffs starts a quarter later, once sales expectations had definitely turned down and firms knew that the economy was in a recession.

Productivity

We have made the point that firms can vary their labor input (hours of work) without necessarily changing employment. Firms can practice *labor hoarding* when demand declines, and they can increase overtime when demand temporarily expands. This practice has an implication for labor productivity. Figure 11-1, the production function, suggests that as output

---

[5]Even output itself need not vary, since firms can sell from inventory whenever demand transitorily rises and produce to replenish their inventory whenever demand declines.

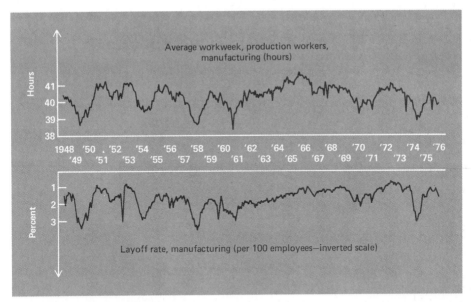

CHART 11-1 AVERAGE WORKWEEK AND
LAYOFF RATE. (Source: *Business Conditions,*
November 1976)

expands, the marginal and average contribution of labor to output declines.[6]
However, productivity actually moves *procyclically*. This means that as
output expands in the recovery phase of the business cycle, the productivity of labor—the ratio of output to employment—rises. The reason is simply that when output expands, firms have more work for their labor force to
do, and labor works harder each hour that it is on the job.[7] Conversely,
when output declines but firms hoard labor, the ratio of output to employment declines. Thus measured productivity—the ratio of output to
employment—moves with the level of output or procyclically. This point
is forcefully brought out by Chart 11-2, which shows output per hour in the
private nonfarm economy. The chart shows that an index of productivity
moves with economic activity. Productivity declines as the economy
moves into the deep recession at the end of 1974 and recovers along with
output, starting the second quarter of 1975.

[6]Be sure you can see why Fig. 11-1 implies that the average productivity of labor, namely Y/N,
declines as N increases.

[7]Another reason that labor productivity rises in the short run when output increases is that the
firm has certain *overhead* labor—such as management—which is needed to keep the firm
operating at all, but which is not expanded with output.

Employment

The next question we have to address is the employment level a firm will select. How closely will employment move with output? We have already seen that firms can vary output as of a given employment level by using the labor force more or less intensively. That is an efficient short-run adjustment but is clearly not a reasonable long-run strategy. A firm that expects a doubling in its sales volume can achieve these sales at much lower cost with an increase in regular employment than by getting the same increase in hours out of overtime of its given employees. The question then is, what determines the employment level?

Unlike the neoclassical firms of the first section, an actual firm will experience significant costs in changing employment in the short run. These costs arise from advertising, screening, and interview costs for new employees, but more importantly, from the costs of having to train those employees.

Given these costs of changing employment, firms, in making their employment decisions, will look ahead to the levels of output they expect to be producing in the future. The demand for labor depends therefore not only on the current level of output but also on the expected level of output. In addition to future output levels, firms are concerned about the cost of labor (the real wage) they expect to prevail over the period for which they make employment decisions. The essential departure from the neoclassical model lies in the idea of a *sales constraint*.[8] Firms do not believe that

CHART 11-2 OUTPUT PER HOUR IN THE
PRIVATE NONFARM BUSINESS SECTOR
(INDEX 1967 = 100). (Source: *Economic
Report of the President.* 1977)

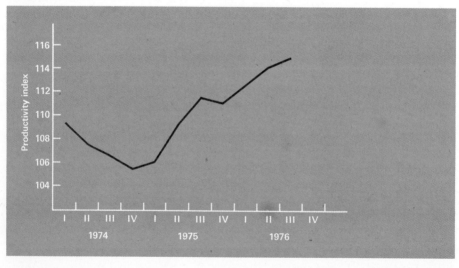

they can sell any amount of output at the going price but rather believe, realistically, that their market is limited and that there is a given level of output that they can sell at the prevailing level of prices. This sales constraint is reflected in their demand for labor.

Figure 11-7 shows the role of sales expectations in the employment decision. Assume the real wage is $(w/P)_0$. The competitive (unconstrained) firm would move to point E, where the marginal product of labor equals the real wage, $MPN = (w/P)_0$. Next assume that the firm can in fact only sell an amount of output which it takes N' units of labor to produce. Clearly the firm would not hire more than N' units of labor because it has no use for more labor. The firm does not expect to be able to sell more output, and therefore any labor beyond N' has implicitly a zero marginal product. Therefore with a sales constraint, the demand for labor is less than in the neoclassical world. Corresponding to the employment level N' we observe profits which arise from the excess of the marginal product of labor over the real wage.

Figure 11-7 overemphasizes the difference between the competitive

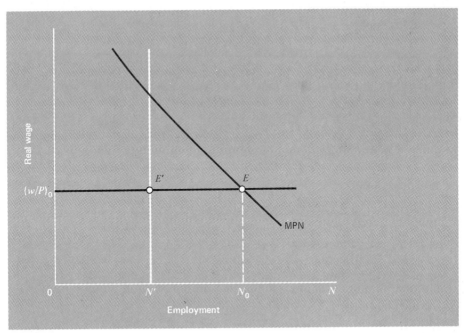

FIGURE 11-7   THE DEMAND FOR LABOR
IN THE PRESENCE OF SALES CONSTRAINTS

[8]Emphasis on sales constraints is central to the new *disequilibrium approach* to macroeconomics. For an exposition, see R.J. Barro and H.I. Grossman, "A General Equilibrium Model of Income and Employment," *American Economic Review*, March 1971.

firm and firms that face a sales constraint. Figure 11-7 suggests that an increase in the real wage above $(w/P)_0$ has no impact on employment because firms with an employment level of only N' are still in a position where MPN $> (w/P)$. Conversely, a decline in real wages simply raises profits but does not change employment. In fact, however, we would expect the employment level to depend on *both* sales expectations and the real wage. The argument relies on a *speculative* demand for labor. The speculative demand for labor arises because firms are not certain about their future sales, and therefore their precise future labor requirement. They know that their expectations may prove incorrect.

Now, if the real wage is very low, firms will find it profitable to hire more cheap labor and to speculate on making extra profits if demand turns out to be unexpectedly high. Conversely, if real wages are very high, firms will hold less labor because they face the risk that if they have overestimated labor use, they will wind up with a large wage bill and small sales. We are back, therefore, with a demand for labor that depends on the real wage rate, but also on sales expectations.

This labor demand is shown in Fig. 11-8 as the downward-sloping schedule. At a real wage $(w/P)_0$ the firm (or firms in the aggregate) will hire an amount of labor N_0, given that they hold sales expectations Y_0. A reduction in expected sales shifts the demand curve for labor to the left. With expected sales $Y_1 < Y_0$, the demand for labor at the real wage $(w/P)_0$ declines to N'.

A reduction in the real wage below $(w/P)_0$ would raise labor demand because firms at each level of sales expectations would find it profitable to take an increased speculative position in the labor market. With labor cheaper, firms would take the risk of having more labor on the payroll to face unexpectedly high demand. However, while the speculative demand provides for an impact of real wages on labor demand, and thus gives rise to a negatively sloped demand schedule for labor, the effect may be quite small.

Now that we have reformulated the theory of labor demand, we can return to the neoclassical theory and recognize that the downward-sloping demand for labor in Fig. 11-8 need not only depend on a speculative effect. Indeed, not all firms are sales-constrained and therefore, for the competitive sector, we would expect the ordinary adjustment of labor demand to the real wage as described in Sec. 11-1. Accordingly, we can interpret the downward-sloping demand for labor as arising both from a speculative effect for sales-constrained firms, and from an adjustment to real wages of the unconstrained sectors.

In summary we have shown that (1) the aggregate demand for labor and employment depends on sales expectations and the real wage; (2) increased sales expectations increase the level of employment; and (3) a reduction in the real wage increases labor demand and employment.

Our theory of employment relies on costs in changing the level of employment. Because of these costs, the firm looks beyond current real wages and sales and considers also future real wages and future labor demand. These considerations raise two questions: First, how do firms form their expectations about future sales and real wages? Second, how do firms respond to a change in sales that they consider transitory?

We can start with the second question, which turns out to have a relatively obvious answer. If a firm faces a transitory increase in the demand for its output, but if at the same time it is costly to hire and fire additional labor, then the firm will not expand employment substantially but rather meet the increased demand out of inventories and through overtime. Obviously, though, the longer the increase in demand is expected to persist (or the less transitory it is) and the larger the increase in demand, the more likely that the firm will want to expand employment somewhat.

Next we turn to the very difficult question of expectations. We will for the purposes of this chapter assume that firms expect the current level of real wages to persist. Expected future real wages are equal to the real wages that currently prevail. For sales we adopt a different convention. Here we recognize that if current sales are very low, firms do not believe that sales will be low indefinitely. On the contrary, they would expect

FIGURE 11-8 REDUCED SALES EXPECTATIONS DECREASE THE DEMAND FOR LABOR AT EACH REAL WAGE

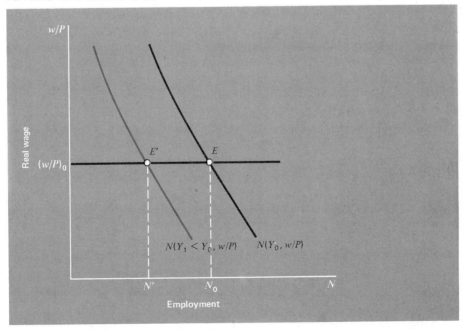

sales to improve. Conversely, if sales currently are very high, firms anticipate some decline. Whether current sales are very high or low must obviously be judged relative to some benchmark. We take full-employment
output Y_p to be the benchmark. The expectations formation we have just
described can be formalized as in Eq. (3):

$$Y^e = aY + (1 - a)Y_p \qquad 0 \le a \le 1 \tag{3}$$

where Y^e is *expected sales* or expected output.[9]

Equation (3) shows expected output Y^e as an average of full-
employment output Y_p and current output Y. We treat the weight a in Eq.
(3) as given. If all disturbances, causing the level of output to diverge from
the full-employment level, are believed to be entirely temporary, then a
should be close to zero and changes in current output have almost no effect
on expected output and therefore on employment. Conversely, if disturbances are expected to persist, and it is believed that the economy takes a
long time to move toward the full-employment level, then the weight a
should be close to unity. Current output should receive a larger weight in
the formation of expected output, and current employment would be more
closely linked to current output.

In summary, the aggregate employment decision, taking all types of
firms together, depends on expected sales and the real wage. We can write
a labor demand curve that is appropriate for the short run:

$$N = N\left(Y^e, \frac{w}{P}\right) = N\left(Y_p, Y, \frac{w}{P}\right) \tag{4}$$

The labor demand function shows that the total level of employment depends on expected output and the real wage. Expected output, in turn,
depends on both potential output and the current level of output. At a
given real wage, the higher the output, the higher the demand for labor.
And, given the level of output, the lower the real wage, the higher the
demand for labor.

11-3 WAGE AND PRICE SETTING

This section continues the derivation of the aggregate supply schedule by
discussing wage and price setting. Since the chapter is already quite long,
it is worthwhile stepping back for a moment to explain where we are going,
and how we got to where we are now. What we are out to find is a relation-

---

[9]As we have noted frequently, modelling expectations with simple formulas is always difficult.
You might want to consider the implications of an alternative formulation such as:
$$Y^e = aY + (1 - a)Y_p + \lambda(Y_{-1} - Y_p) \qquad 0 \le \lambda \le 1$$
as you continue reading.

ship between the supply of output and the level of prices—that is, the aggregate supply schedule. We started in Sec. 11-2 by examining the relationship between the level of output and the level of employment. Now in this section we will examine the relationship between the level of employment and wages, and then between wages and prices. Then, linking output to employment, employment to wages, and wages to prices, in Sec. 11-4 we will finally derive the aggregate supply schedule.

It is also worth recalling that we expect the aggregate supply schedule to be flat in the short run—unlike the neoclassical schedule in Fig. 11-4—but we expect the long-run aggregate supply schedule to resemble the neoclassical supply function.

We will start in this section by examining the link between wage behavior and the level of employment. As for most of the elements of the theory of aggregate supply, empirical evidence on wage behavior is not yet conclusive. Most existing empirical evidence is related to the famous Phillips curve, introduced in Chap. 1, and which will be reviewed in greater depth in Chaps. 13 and 15. In the late fifties, the Phillips curve was treated as a relationship between the rate of unemployment and the rate of increase of *nominal* wages.[10] Wages would increase when (measured) unemployment was very low, and would stay constant and perhaps even fall if unemployment was very high. Later the argument was modified to take account of the effects of expected changes in the price level on nominal wages,[11] but we will not deal with that important modification in this chapter, deferring it for the later chapters on the Phillips curve.

For purposes of this chapter, it is sufficient to take the view that the state of the labor market determines the rate of change of money wages. Whenever employment is abnormally high, wages will be rising. Conversely, whenever employment is low, wages will be falling. The idea here is that wages move only slowly in response to labor market disequilibrium and that, in the short run, overemployment and underemployment are quite possible—even though the economy tends to move toward full employment in the absence of disturbances to aggregate demand and supply.

Once wage behavior has been studied, we move over to price behavior. The prices firms charge for their output are based mainly on the costs of producing output, and in particular, on the most important of those costs, the money wage, or the cost of labor. Accordingly, there will be a link between the unemployment rate and the behavior of the price level.

---

[10]We should also note that the Phillips curve designation is now often used to describe a relationship between the rate of change of *prices* and the unemployment rate, rather than the wage-unemployment relation.

[11]Without going into detail, expected changes in the price level should affect nominal wages because labor and firms are both concerned with real wages. If the nominal wage for which labor contracts to sell its services remains fixed for, say, a year, then labor would be concerned with how the price level would change over the contract year since the price level changes affect the real wage to be received. Hence, expected changes in the price level should affect the nominal wage.

Wage Setting

The notion that the state of the labor market determines the behavior of money wages is formalized in Fig. 11-9, where we show a demand for labor curve (NN), drawn for the expected full-employment level of output, Y_p. We show, too, the supply of labor $\overline{N}$. If the real wage were initially at a level such as $(w/P)_0$, there would be unemployment of labor equal to the distance $N_0\overline{N}$. That unemployment would in turn cause wages to start declining—this is precisely the insight of the Phillips curve. Given the price level—the behavior of which we shall examine later—real wages would decline, adding to employment. However, the effect might be very slow because money wages might fall only slowly.

Now we will develop the simple notion illustrated in Fig. 11-9 more formally. First, we have to explain that in this chapter we are abstracting from *frictional* unemployment—the unemployment that results from the rate at which people normally change jobs, and from the fact that it takes new workers some time to find their first job. This frictional unemployment is studied in detail in Chap. 15, under the name of the *natural rate of unemployment,* which can also be called the "full-employment rate of unemployment." Once we recognize that some unemployment is normal, because of frictions in the labor market, we realize that overemployment is possible as well as underemployment. From now on we shall take $\overline{N}$ to be the level of employment that would exist at normal full employment. If the employment level is $\overline{N}$, we shall say that there is zero unemployment, even though the unemployment statistics, measuring also frictional unemployment, would report the actual unemployment rate at around 5 percent. Employment can exceed $\overline{N}$, in which case we say in this chapter that there is negative unemployment.

Wages respond to unemployment. If employment is below $\overline{N}$, nominal wages will decline. Conversely, if employment is above $\overline{N}$—or unemployment is negative—wages will increase. This idea is formalized in Eq. (5):

$$w = w_{-1}(1 - \epsilon u) \qquad 0 < \epsilon < 1 \qquad (5)$$

where u is the unemployment rate and ϵ measures the responsiveness of wages to unemployment. Now consider first the case where unemployment is zero, $u = 0$. In that case current wages w are equal to last period's wages so wages neither rise nor fall. Next we look at the case where there is some unemployment, $u > 0$. Now the term in parentheses is less than 1, and accordingly current wages are less than last period's wages. Therefore, Eq. (5) reflects the fact that unemployment causes wages to decline.

To emphasize the percentage rate of change of wages—or wage inflation—we can rewrite Eq. (5):[12]

---

[12]To get from Eq. (5) to Eq. (5a), we divide both sides by w_{-1} and subtract 1 from both sides of the equation to obtain $w/w_{-1} - 1 = -\epsilon u$, which can be rewritten as Eq. (5a).

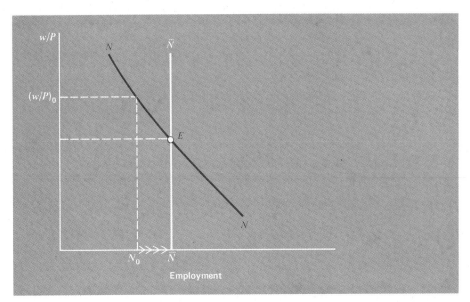

FIGURE 11-9 ADJUSTMENT IN THE
LABOR MARKET

$$\frac{w - w_{-1}}{w_{-1}} = -\epsilon u \tag{5a}$$

To fix ideas, we look at Table 11-1. We assume last period's wage was $4 per hour. We also assume that $\epsilon = 0.5$. In the table we show the current wage as implied by the unemployment rate and past wages through Eq. (5). We show the change in wages absolutely and in percentage terms.

The table brings out several points. First, if there is overemployment, u is less than zero and wages are rising, and if there is unemployment, wages are falling. Second, the larger the unemployment rate, the larger the decline in wages. Third, the percentage change in wages, in the last column, is proportional to the unemployment rate. Because we have chosen a value of $\epsilon = 0.5$, the percentage change in wages is half of the unemployment rate.

The unemployment rate u in Eq. (5) or Eq. (5a) is defined as the fraction of the full-employment labor force $\bar{N}$ that is not employed:

$$u \equiv \frac{\bar{N} - N}{\bar{N}} \tag{6}$$

Thus, if the full-employment labor force is equal to 100 people of whom 94 are employed, then the unemployment rate is $u = (100 - 94)/100 = 6$

TABLE 11-1 WAGE ADJUSTMENT TO UNEMPLOYMENT ($\epsilon = 0.5$).

w_{-1}	u	w	Δw	$(w - w_{-1})/w_{-1}$
$4	−0.02	$4.04	$0.04	0.01
$4	0	$4.00	0	0
$4	0.02	$3.96	−$0.04	−0.01
$4	0.05	$3.90	−$0.10	−0.025
$4	0.08	$3.84	−$0.16	−0.04

percent. Using the definition of the unemployment rate in Eq. (6), we can rewrite the *wage equation* as

$$w = w_{-1}\left[1 - \epsilon\left(1 - \frac{N}{\overline{N}}\right)\right] \tag{5b}$$

From Eq. (5b) it is apparent that the current wage depends on two elements. One is last period's wage. Other things equal, the current wage is last period's wage. The other determinant of wages is employment, or more particularly, employment relative to the full-employment labor force $N/\overline{N}$. When employment exceeds the supply of labor, wages are rising, and when employment falls short, wages are falling.

In Fig. 11-10 we show the current wage as a function of the level of employment, given the past wage. In studying Fig. 11-10, we first observe that when employment is equal to the full-employment labor supply $\overline{N}$, the current wage is equal to the past wage or $w = w_{-1}$. Next we note that deviations from full employment affect the wage rate. An increase in employment, relative to $\overline{N}$, raises the wage and a reduction in employment lowers the wage.

In Fig. 11-11 we make the point that if employment were, somehow, kept below the full-employment level, then the money wage would keep on falling. To see that, we start at point E with full employment. Then we have a decline in employment because firms' sales expectations decline. The decline in employment takes us to the employment level N_0, and the corresponding decline in money wages lowers the wage rate relative to last period. The money wage rate is now at w', having fallen from w_{-1}^0. The next step is to recognize that as we move ahead one period, unemployment is still the same, so there continues to be downward pressure on wages.

The new wage equation is based on the most recent money wage w'. It is shown as the dashed schedule, crossing the $\overline{N}$ schedule at a wage rate $w_{-1} = w'$. The low employment level this period also exerts downward pressure on wages and we therefore move to point A'' with a further decline in wages. The process will continue in this manner until the falling money wages lower costs and prices sufficiently to expand aggregate demand and thereby raise output and employment.

In summary, we have said that wages are set on the basis of last period's money wage with an adjustment for the state of the labor market. When labor markets are tight, $N > \bar{N}$, wages are increasing. Conversely, when there is unemployment, $N < \bar{N}$, wages are falling. The slope of the wage equation in Fig. 11-10 indicates the impact of a change in employment on the money wage rate. A steep schedule means that a change in current employment has a large impact on current money wages.

Price Setting

In the neoclassical framework of Sec. 11-1, it was assumed that prices are somehow adjusted by the "market." Now we shall instead assume that firms set prices, and that they set their prices on the basis of the costs of production. If a firm experiences an increase in costs, then it will pass on that cost increase in the form of higher prices.[13] This is true for cost increases arising both from increases in wages and from increases in materials costs (for example, the cost of oil). We write costs per unit of output z as a function of wages w and materials costs P_m:

---

[13]For some evidence on wage-price behavior see Otto Eckstein (ed.), *Parameters and Policies in the U.S. Economy*, North-Holland, 1976, chap. 3; and Otto Eckstein (ed.), *The Econometrics of Price Determination*, Board of Governors of the Federal Reserve, 1972.

FIGURE 11-10 THE WAGE EQUATION

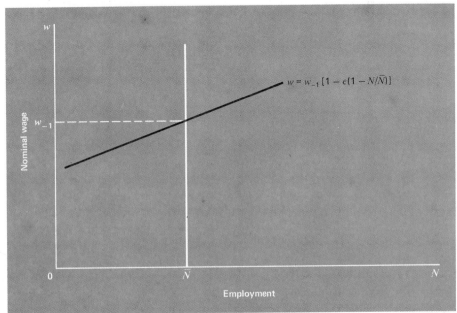

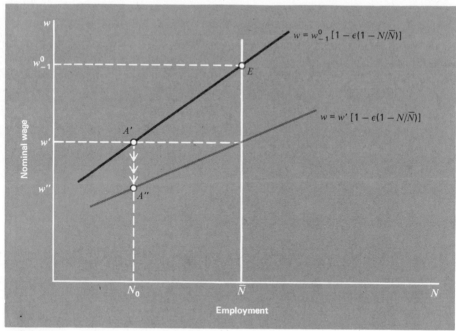

FIGURE 11-11 WAGE ADJUSTMENT IN
RESPONSE TO LABOR MARKET
CONDITIONS

$$z = z(w, P_m, \ldots) \tag{7}$$

The dots indicate that factors other than wages and the price of materials can affect the cost of production. For instance, changes in taxes that business firms have to pay, or changes in technology, will affect the cost of producing output.

The firm's pricing follows costs, though we shall assume that firms do not base their current price exactly on their current costs of production. A firm may view some cost changes as temporary, say as a result of temporary shortages, and not adjust their list prices in response to such temporary changes. It is costly to change prices, both because firms have to inform purchasers of the price changes and because price changes (increases) annoy customers and lose goodwill for firms. Accordingly, firms will want to maintain some stability in their prices and will base prices on their normal costs—the costs they anticipate they will have on average over some future period.

If a current cost change is maintained, a firm can stay in business only if it passes on the cost increase. To reflect the fact that the firm prices goods in line with normal cost, we make the supply price of output a function of both current and past cost. Again, this is a reflection of a particularly simple way in which firms might form expectations about normal costs.

We use the price equation:

$$P = bz + (1 - b)z_{-1} \qquad 0 \le b \le 1 \qquad (8)$$

In Eq. (8) we have the *price equation*, an equation that tells us the current *supply price* as a function of current and past costs. Unit costs, in turn, depend on wages as well as material costs. The unit costs are assumed to include normal profits. The weights b and $1 - b$ in Eq. (8) reflect the fact that a firm will not fully pass on an increase in current costs but will do so only if it is a sustained increase. Thus, if unit costs rose by 10 percent, and b, the coefficient of current cost, was $b = .8$, then the firm would raise price currently by 8 percent. If the cost increase persisted, we would find in the next period a further adjustment of 2 percent to complete the *passthrough* of higher costs. If, on the contrary, costs declined to their initial level, we would have a net effect on prices equal to $-(.8)$ (10 percent) + (.2) (10 percent) = -6 percent. The fact that price does not fully decline is due to the persisting effect of past cost increases that only now affect the pricing decision. In subsequent periods that effect wears out.

There is one further property of Eqs. (7) and (8) to which we want to draw attention. What happens if we double material costs P_m and money wages? We assume that Eq. (7) has the property that if all input prices increase in some proportion, then unit costs increase in the same proportion. Further, from the price equation in Eq. (8), as we noted, a sustained increase or decrease in costs changes prices in the same proportion. Thus, we have built into our pricing system the assumption that there is no long-run money illusion. In the long run, an equiproportionate factor price increase is fully passed on into a price increase of the same proportion.

In summary, our price equation states that supply prices are based on costs—labor and material costs. Sustained increases in costs are fully passed on. Current changes in costs are only partially passed through into higher prices and are partially absorbed by a change in profit margins. A sustained equiproportionate increase in input prices will be fully passed on in an equiproportionate change in output prices.

11-4 AGGREGATE SUPPLY

We have completed now the discussion of employment, wages, and prices, and can summarize it by looking at the aggregate supply schedule. The aggregate supply schedule tells us the level of prices associated with each level of output. The relationship between current output and prices that is the short-run aggregate supply function relies on three partial adjustments:

(1) the partial adjustment of sales expectations to a change in output studied in Sec. 11-2, (2) the slow adjustment of wages to a change in employment, and (3) the partial passthrough of increases in labor cost into higher prices. The latter two adjustments were examined in Sec. 11-3.

In Fig. 11-12 we show the short-run aggregate supply schedule Y^s. That schedule is drawn for a given level of past costs. The slope of the schedule reflects the fact that current changes in output are accompanied by current changes in prices. The channels for that effect were developed in Secs. 11-2 and 11-3 and are illustrated schematically as follows:

$$\Delta Y \longrightarrow \Delta Y^e \longrightarrow \Delta N \longrightarrow \Delta w \longrightarrow \Delta z \longrightarrow \Delta P$$
$$\text{(1)} \qquad \text{(2)} \qquad \text{(3)} \qquad \text{(4)} \qquad \text{(5)} \qquad \text{(6)}$$

The links in the relation between changes in current output and prices were formed in Eqs. (3) through (8). Moving along the aggregate supply schedule, we have the following chain of events: (1) An increase in output, say, because of an expansion in aggregate demand. (2) The increase in current output affects expected output. An increase in current output is, in part, thought of as indicating a permanent increase in output. To that extent, expected output is revised upward by some fraction a of the increase in output, as shown in Eq. (3). (3) The increase in expected output raises labor demand at each real wage as shown in Eq. (4). (4) From the analysis of wage setting we know that an increase in employment will cause money wages to rise. The speed with which money wages react to

FIGURE 11-12 THE SHORT-RUN AND LONG-RUN AGGREGATE SUPPLY SCHEDULES

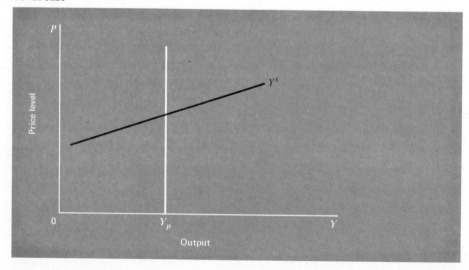

changes in employment is shown in the wage-setting equation ($5b$). (5) The increase in wages raises labor costs. (6) The increase in labor costs, through the price-setting equation (8), is partly passed on into an increase in output prices. It will be apparent that not only are there a lot of links in the chain from output to prices, but also there is a lot of partial adjustment in the transmission mechanism. This is the reason why the aggregate supply schedule is relatively flat in the short run.

There is a further important point about the aggregate supply schedule that we have to recognize, and that concerns the way the supply curve shifts over time. A given aggregate supply schedule such as the schedule Y^s is drawn for a given level of past costs z_{-1}, as is apparent from the price-setting equation (8). The *slope* of the aggregate supply schedule is determined by the effects of current output on current costs. The *location* of the aggregate supply schedule is determined by past costs.

This point is important because it implies that an expansion in output has effects on price not only in the current period—the movement along the aggregate supply schedule—but also in subsequent periods. The reason is that wages will keep changing as long as employment is at a level different from $\overline{N}$, the full-employment level. The change in wages, even with given sales expectations, will affect costs and therefore will be passed on into higher prices. This means that the continuing cost adjustments will *shift* the aggregate supply schedule.

Figure 11-13 makes this point in more detail. Here we start at point E with a situation of full employment. Costs have been constant in the past by assumption. Next we have an increase in demand that raises output to Y_0 and maintains it at that higher level. Our question is: What happens to the supply schedule over time as wages adjust to the change in employment that is induced by the changed sales expectations?

Starting at point E, the first-period impact is to raise prices from P_0 to P_1 as the economy adjusts to the increased output along the initial supply schedule Y_0^s, drawn for a given level of past costs. In the next period we still have the higher level of employment induced by the increased sales expectation, and wages therefore continue to increase. The increase in wages, in turn, raises costs, and these costs now are passed on in the form of higher prices. The aggregate supply curve shifts up because costs are increasing. But it also shifts up because past wage changes are incorporated only slowly in current prices.

Given the higher wages, supply prices are higher at each level of output, or, in other words, the supply schedule shifts up and to the left to Y_1^s. The new price at a level of output Y_0 is now P_2. Obviously, the wages will keep on rising as long as employment is above normal and, therefore, the supply curve shifts upward and prices keep rising as long as output is above normal. The very important point, then, is that a level of output above full employment will be accompanied by ever-increasing prices. Conversely, if output were sustained below normal levels, wages and prices would keep falling. As we shall see in the next chapter, this is an impor-

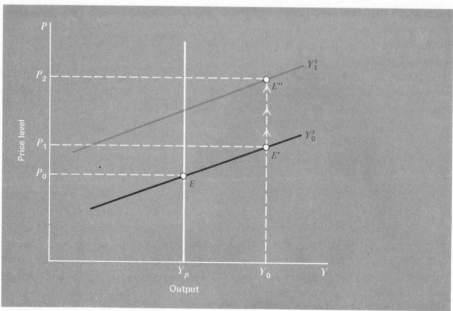

FIGURE 11-13 WAGE AND PRICE
ADJUSTMENT WHEN OUTPUT IS ABOVE
NORMAL

tant adjustment process. In fact, it is precisely the neoclassical adjustment process described earlier with the one exception that we think of it as spread out over time.

The relationship we have discussed in the last paragraph will be used extensively in Chap. 13, and we therefore want to flag it at this stage. We have just shown that there is a relationship between the rate of change of prices and the level of output, in relation to the level of potential output. When output is above the potential output level, prices tend to rise, and when output is below the full-employment level, prices tend to fall. Going back a step to the level of unemployment, we have just seen that when there is unemployment (recall that we are here abstracting from frictional unemployment), prices tend to fall, and when there is excess employment, prices tend to rise. We thus have a relationship like that shown in Fig. 11-14 between the unemployment rate and the inflation rate. That relationship is called, like Eq. (5), the Phillips curve. The inflation-unemployment Phillips curve of Fig. 11-14 will play a major role in the dynamic theory of aggregate supply we present in Chap. 13. However, recall that we have here abstracted from the effects of the expected price level on the current wage rate. In Chap. 13 we will augment the Phillips curve of Fig. 11-14 to take account of expected changes in the price level.

11-5 SUMMARY

This chapter has covered a lot of very hard ground. The major point to be established was that output variations along the short-run aggregate supply schedule are accompanied by only moderate price increases. In the short run, the price level varies little with the level of output. Over time, however, wages, costs, and prices will keep rising if output is above normal and keep falling if output is below normal.

We summarize now the contents of the chapter.

1 The neoclassical theory of the demand for labor relates labor demand only to the real wage, given the quantity of other factors the firm is using. Competitive firms that are free to change the quantity of labor they use, costlessly and immediately, will hire labor up to the point where the real wage is equal to the marginal product of labor (MPN).

2 With wages and prices freely flexible, the equilibrium full-employment level is determined in the labor market. The labor market is continuously in equilibrium at the full-employment level, and aggregate supply will therefore be the amount of output which that amount of labor produces. Given that the labor market is in equilibrium, the aggregate supply curve is vertical at the level of potential output—the aggregate supply is independent of the price level.

3 The aggregate supply theory we present starts from the recognition

FIGURE 11-14 THE INFLATION-UNEMPLOYMENT PHILLIPS CURVE

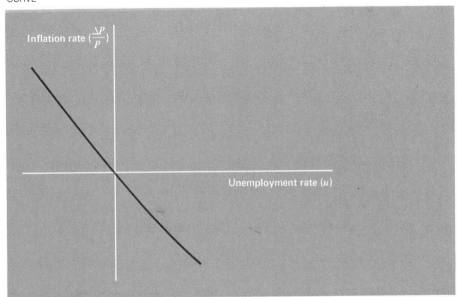

that it is costly for the firm to change the level of employment. In deciding how much labor to employ today, firms look ahead to the output level they expect to be producing in the future.

4   Firms accommodate temporary changes in output largely by changing the amount of overtime their existing labor force works.

5   The employment decision depends on both the real wage and the expected level of output. The expected level of output in turn depends on the full employment level of output and the current level of output. Increases in expected output lead to increases in employment, and increases in the real wage reduce employment.

6   Current output affects current employment by affecting the expected level of output.

7   Nominal wages change in accordance with the state of excess demand in the labor market. When there is unemployment, wages fall, and when there is negative unemployment, wages rise. In this connection, it should be recalled that we abstract in this chapter from the existence of frictional unemployment.

8   Firms base the prices they charge on their costs of production. Thus, when wages rise, because the level of employment is above the full-employment level, prices are increased too. However, firms base their pricing decision on normal costs, and so do not immediately pass on increases in wages completely.

9   Assembling these elements, an increase in output is accompanied by an increase in prices. An increase in output, resulting, say, from an increase in aggregate demand, affects expected output, leading to an increase in employment. The increase in employment increases the nominal wage, which leads to some increase in the prices firms charge.

10   The full impact of changes in aggregate demand on prices occurs only over the course of time. A permanent increase in aggregate demand feeds slowly into an increased demand for labor, which in turn means wages rise slowly, which in turn means that prices are adjusted only over the course of time. If employment is somehow held above the full-employment level, wages and prices will continue to rise without end.

PROBLEMS

1   In 1972, nominal GNP was $1,171 billion as was real GNP (i.e., 1972 is the base year for which the GNP deflator is equal to 100). In 1974, the price level (GNP deflator) was 116.2 and real GNP was $1,121 billion. How much did nominal GNP increase from 1972 to 1974? (Hint: Be sure to measure ΔP correctly as 0.162.)

2   Suppose a new method of production is invented which increases the marginal product of labor at each level of employment.

   a   What effect does this have on the (neoclassical) demand for labor?

   b   What effect does it have on the equilibrium real wage if the supply of labor is fixed and independent of the real wage?

   c How would your answer to (2b) be affected if the supply of labor increased with the real wage?

*3 Suppose now that the new method of production increases the average product of labor at each level of employment as well as the marginal product, and revert to the assumption that labor supply is independent of the real wage.

   a What effect does the invention have on the equilibrium level of real output?

   b What effect does the invention have on the equilibrium price level? (You will have to use the aggregate demand diagram here.)

   c What effect does the invention have on the *nominal* wage?

   d How are your answers to 3a to 3c affected if the supply of labor increases with the real wage?

4 What effect does a rightward shift in the supply curve of labor have on the aggregate supply curve, the equilibrium real wage, and the price level?

We move over now to the nonneoclassical aggregate supply curve developed in Secs. 11-2 through 11-4.

5 a How do you account for the short-run behavior of labor productivity?

   b What does the neoclassical model imply about the short-run behavior of labor productivity, if one assumes that short-run fluctuations in output are accompanied by movements along a stable demand for labor curve of the sort presented in Fig. 11-3?

6 a Given expected output, why does the real wage affect employment?

   b In the theory of aggregate supply presented in this chapter, how does the real wage behave (does it go up or down?) when there is an increase in output?

7 Suppose that all firms believed that the current level of output Y, whatever its level, was the long-run level of output Y^e, so that the weight a in Eq. (3) was one.

   a How would that affect the slope of the aggregate supply curve? Be careful.

   b Explain for what particular aspects of the behavior of the economy in the short run the value of a in Eq. (3) matters. Choose from (i) the slope of the aggregate supply curve, (ii) the behavior of the real wage, (iii) the behavior of labor productivity in the short run, and (iv) the behavior of the money wage in the short run. Explain your answer.

* 8 How does (a) the variable ϵ affect the slope of the aggregate supply curve? (b) the weight b affect the slope of the supply curve? Explain.

9 How does an increase in materials prices P_m affect the aggregate supply curve? Be sure to distinguish between the short- and long-run effects.

*10 Assume that wages are the only element of cost so that $z = w$ and $z_{-1} = w_{-1}$. With this assumption we can write the price equation (8) as

$$P = bw + (1 - b)w_{-1} \tag{8a}$$

Use Eq. (8a) together with Eq. (5) to derive a relationship between:

   a prices, current wages, and unemployment

   b the current real wage and the current rate of unemployment

12

Income, Prices,
and Unemployment

n this chapter we combine aggregate supply, studied in Chap. 11, with aggregate demand, as studied in Chap. 4. The resulting analysis leads to the simultaneous determination of most of the important macroeconomic variables—the level of output, the price level, interest rates, and (un)employment.[1] This chapter, therefore, extends the analysis of Chap. 4 by explicitly introducing the price level as one of the variables to be determined. Recall that throughout Chap. 4 we took the price level P to be fixed. The price level is, of course, far from constant. The extension of the IS-LM analysis to examine the determination of the price level is therefore an extremely important step.

The analysis in this chapter further differs from the IS-LM framework in that it is essentially dynamic. The discussion of the supply side in the previous chapter introduced the distinction between the short-run and the long-run aggregate supply curves. That distinction is important in this chapter because it is the basis on which we distinguish between the short-run, intermediate-run, and long-run effects of monetary and fiscal policies on output and prices.

12-1 AGGREGATE DEMAND

In this section we will derive an *aggregate demand function*. The aggregate demand function is a relationship between the planned level of real spending or demand for goods, and the level of prices, *given* the quantity of money and fiscal policy. Since it is a relationship between the quantity of goods demanded and the price level, and since it will be seen to be downward-sloping, it looks similar to the regular demand curve of microeconomics. In this case, however, we consider the *aggregate* demand for all goods and services as a function of the *aggregate* price level rather than the demand for a single good as a function of its (relative) price. Further, as we noted in Chap. 1, there is a lot behind the aggregate demand curve. As we shall see, it summarizes the equilibrium of both goods and assets markets.

The aggregate demand function we shall use was introduced in Chap. 4 as Eq. (14) and is repeated here for convenience:

$$Y = \beta \overline{A} + \gamma \frac{\overline{M}}{P} \tag{1}$$

$$\beta \equiv \frac{h\bar{\alpha}}{h + bk\bar{\alpha}} \qquad \gamma \equiv \frac{b\bar{\alpha}}{h + bk\bar{\alpha}}$$

where the terms β and γ are respectively the "multipliers" associated with fiscal and monetary policy and incorporate the interaction between goods

[1] The only important macroeconomic variable that is not studied explicitly in this chapter is the inflation rate; its behavior is analyzed in detail in Chap. 13.

and money markets. The term $\overline{A}$ denotes autonomous spending, including fiscal variables, $\overline{M}/P$ is the quantity of real balances, and Y is measured in *real* terms. Although we derived the present equation (1) in Chap. 4, we did not use it there to draw an aggregate demand relationship that express-es the demand for goods as a function of the price level. In Chap. 4, we took the price level as given, and obtained Eq. (1) as describing the inter-section of the IS and LM curves for given levels of autonomous spending and the real money supply.

Equation (1) expresses the *joint* equilibrium of the goods and assets markets. It summarizes the basic results of Chap. 4: first, that the higher the level of autonomous spending (the further out to the right the IS curve), the higher the equilibrium level of income; and, second, that the higher the real money supply (the further to the right the LM curve), the higher the equilibrium level of income.

In deriving Eq. (1), we explicitly assumed that any level of real output that was demanded could be produced, at the given price level. We thus ignored any constraints that might exist on aggregate supply. In this chap-ter, we shall explicitly consider the interaction of supply and demand. Accordingly, we do not treat Eq. (1) as determining the level of output, but only as determining the level of demand *at a given price level*. If demand does not equal supply at that price level, then the price level is not an equilibrium price level and output is not at the equilibrium level either. The interaction of supply and demand will determine the equilibrium levels of prices and real output.

We shall now use Eq. (1), together with the IS-LM analysis on which it is based, to study the relationship between the level of spending—the demand for goods—and the price level, given the nominal quantity of money and autonomous spending. It is obvious from inspection of Eq. (1) that a higher price level implies lower real balances and therefore a lower equilibrium level of income and spending. This relationship is shown as the $Y^d(F, M/P)$ curve in Fig. 12-1, where F represents the term $\beta\overline{A}$ in Eq. (1).[2] To understand the relationship between aggregate demand and the price level that is shown in Fig. 12-1, we turn to the IS and LM curves that underlie that relationship.

In the upper panel of Fig. 12-2 we show the familiar IS and LM schedules. In the lower panel we show the aggregate demand schedule. Consider first a price level P_0. Given fiscal policy we have an IS curve. A given nominal quantity of money together with the price level P_0 will imply a quantity of real balances M/P_0 and an associated LM_0 curve. The equilib-rium level of income is Y_0^d. Accordingly, we show point E_0 in the lower panel as one point on the aggregate demand schedule, or one combination of price and output levels such that both the goods market and money market are in equilibrium.

Consider next a lower price level P_1. Given the nominal quantity of

[2]We use the symbol F to emphasize that fiscal variables affect the position of the aggregate demand curve, by affecting the term $\beta\overline{A}$.

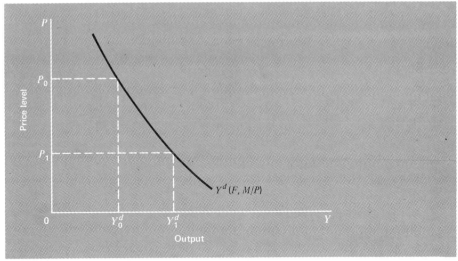

FIGURE 12-1 THE AGGREGATE DEMAND
CURVE

money, the decline in the price level raises *real* balances to M/P_1, and therefore shifts the LM schedule to the right to LM'. The LM schedule shifts down and to the right because in order to induce the public to hold a larger quantity of real balances, income would have to be higher or interest rates would have to be lower. The new equilibrium level of income and spending is Y_1^d and we record E_1 as another point on the aggregate demand schedule in the lower panel. The schedule of points on the aggregate demand curve in the lower panel is obtained by considering all possible price levels. It is the schedule generated by the intersection of the IS and LM curves as the price level changes, namely, $Y^d(F,M/P)$ in Fig. 12-1, that we refer to as the aggregate demand schedule. It is clear from the way we have derived the schedule that we can think of it as a *market equilibrium* schedule—the locus of points along which *both* the money market and the goods market are in equilibrium, given the value of autonomous spending and the nominal money supply.

Before we conclude this section, we want to give an economic interpretation of the aggregate demand relationship. Suppose that the goods and money markets are initially in equilibrium, so that we are at a point on the aggregate demand curve. Then let the price level increase. The higher price level reduces real balances and thereby creates an excess demand for real money balances at the given level of income. The excess demand for real balances in turn raises interest rates. The increase in interest rates in turn reduces real spending by discouraging investment, and therefore leads to a decline in the equilibrium level of income. Thus the initial price increase leads to a decline in income, so that the aggregate demand curve is negatively sloped.

There are two critical points to remember about the aggregate demand curve. The first is that autonomous spending and the nominal money supply are held constant as we move along the schedule. The second point can be seen by noting that the interest rate at E_1 in Fig. 12-2 is lower

FIGURE 12-2 THE AGGREGATE DEMAND CURVE AS DERIVED FROM THE IS AND LM CURVES

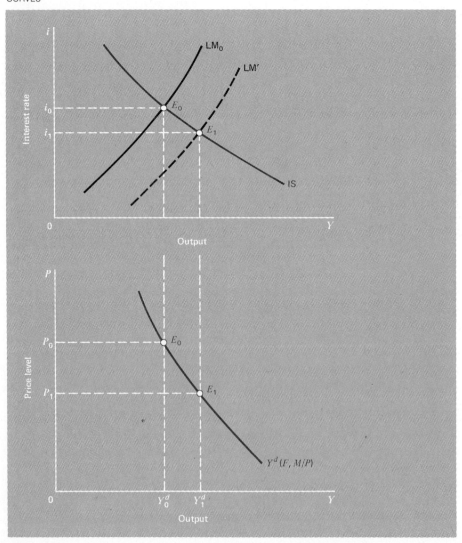

than the interest rate at E_0—the point is that the interest rate declines as the level of income rises along the aggregate demand curve. The declining interest rate derives from the fact that with a given *nominal* quantity of money, a decline in the price level implies an increase in *real* balances. This increase in real balances lowers interest rates. The lower interest rate in turn raises investment spending and has an expansionary effect on aggregate demand and income. Thus as we move down the aggregate demand curve, a falling rate of interest accompanies a rising level of real demand and a falling price level.

12-2 PROPERTIES OF THE AGGREGATE DEMAND SCHEDULE

There are two sets of questions we look at here: First, what determines the slope of the aggregate demand schedule? Second, how does the aggregate demand schedule shift in response to changes in fiscal policy and the nominal money supply?

The Slope of the Aggregate Demand Curve

The answer to the first question is fortunately very easy. We can draw on considerations developed in the discussion of monetary policy in Chap. 4. We asked there what determines the effectiveness of monetary policy—the increase in income associated with an increase in the money supply. We studied that question by increasing the money supply at a given price level, that is, by increasing the real money supply. The slope of the aggregate demand schedule in Fig. 12-2 reflects the answer to exactly the same question. The reason that the question is the same is that Fig. 12-2 relates a change in the real money supply to the resulting change in the equilibrium level of income and spending. However, this time the real money supply changes because the price level changes. The amount by which a given change in prices, and therefore in the real money supply, changes the equilibrium level of income and spending depends primarily on the response of money demand to the interest rate and the response of aggregate spending to the interest rate.

A low interest response of money demand and a high interest response of aggregate spending ensure a large effect of real money changes on output. The reason, as will be remembered from Chap. 4, is that a low interest response of money demand implies that a given change in real balances brings about a large change in interest rates. Given a change in interest rates, a large interest response of aggregate spending serves to translate the interest reduction into a large increase in spending. It follows, therefore, that the aggregate demand schedule is relatively flat—large changes in income and spending are associated with small changes in the price level—if monetary policy is very effective, that is, if the interest response of money demand is low and the interest response of spending is high.

The slope of the aggregate demand curve depends also on the multiplier $\bar{\alpha}$. Other things equal, a given reduction in the price level and increase in real balances gives rise to a larger increase in income and spending, the larger the multiplier or the larger the marginal propensity to spend. Accordingly, a large multiplier serves to flatten the aggregate demand function.[3]

The Effects of Monetary and Fiscal Policy Changes on the Aggregate Demand Curve

We turn now to the second question, which asks about the effects of changes in fiscal policy and the nominal money supply on the location of the aggregate demand curve. We are now examining the effects of variables that cause the entire aggregate demand curve to *shift*. In Sec. 12-1 of this chapter, by contrast, we were considering only movements along a *given* aggregate demand curve, on which fiscal variables and the nominal money supply are kept constant. Before we proceed to a detailed graphical examination of the effects of an increase in the nominal money stock or expansionary fiscal policy on the aggregate demand curve, it is worth stepping back for a moment to ask what we expect to find.

We already know from Chap. 4 and Eq. (1) that an increase in the nominal money supply increases aggregate demand as of a fixed price level. Thus we should expect an increase in the nominal money supply to shift the aggregate demand curve of Fig. 12-1 outwards, reflecting the increase in the demand for goods at a given price level that is caused by the change in the money stock. Similarly, we know that expansionary fiscal policy, such as an increase in government spending or a reduction in taxes, increases aggregate demand at a given price level. Accordingly expansionary fiscal policy should also be expected to shift the aggregate demand curve outwards.

We will now examine the effect of the policy changes in more detail. In Fig. 12-3 we show the effects on the aggregate demand curve of an increase in the nominal quantity of money. Similarly, in Fig. 12-4 we consider the effects of an increase in government spending.

Consider first an increase in the nominal quantity of money. We are asking the following question: What is the effect of an increase in the nominal quantity of money on the equilibrium level of income and spending *at a given price level P_0*? The answer to that question will be the shift in the aggregate demand schedule. We know that for a given price level, an increase in the nominal quantity of money implies an increase in the real quantity of money. There is, therefore, a rightward shift in the LM curve to LM', as in the upper panel of Fig. 12-3. As a consequence, the equilibrium level of income rises to Y_1^d. What happens is that at the given level of

---

[3]It will be useful for you to show the above propositions on the slope of the aggregate demand curve using Fig. 12-2. See prob. 2 at the end of the chapter.

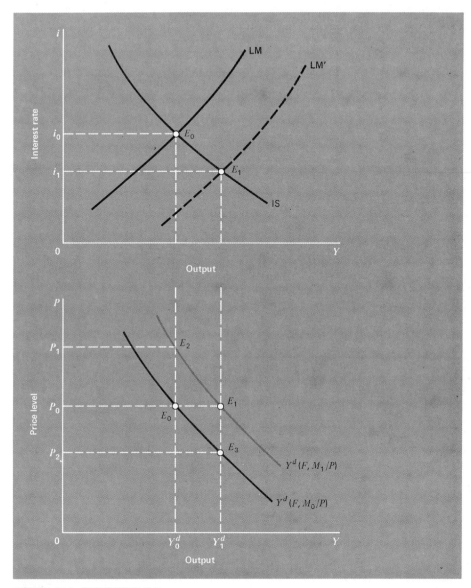

FIGURE 12-3 THE SHIFT IN THE
AGGREGATE DEMAND CURVE DUE TO AN
INCREASE IN THE NOMINAL MONEY
SUPPLY ($M_1 > M_0$)

prices P_0, the higher nominal quantity of money implies a higher real quantity of money and therefore lower interest rates and higher equilibrium income and spending. We record this fact in the lower panel of Fig. 12-3 by noting that point E_1 is a point on the new aggregate demand schedule.

The initial equilibrium price level was chosen arbitrarily. We could have started with any price level and thereby shown that the aggregate demand schedule shifts to the right.

FIGURE 12-4 A SHIFT IN THE
AGGREGATE DEMAND SCHEDULE DUE TO
INCREASED GOVERNMENT SPENDING
$(F_1 > F_0)$

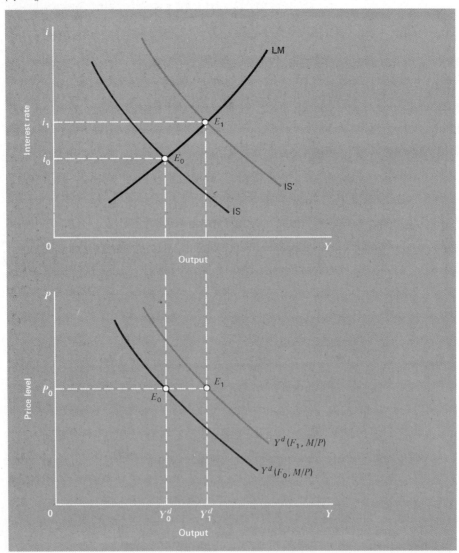

There is an alternative and important way of recognizing the same point. When the nominal money supply increases, we could ask by how much the equilibrium price level would have to rise, at each level of income and spending, in order for aggregate demand to remain unchanged. It is clear from Eq. (1) that aggregate demand would remain unchanged if the real money supply remained unchanged. Given an increase in the nominal money supply, we would therefore require prices to increase in such a way that M/P remains constant. In terms of Fig. 12-3, this implies that an increase in the nominal money supply shifts the aggregate demand schedule up in exactly the same proportion as the increase in the nominal money stock. Thus the ratio P_1/P_0 in Fig. 12-3 is the same as the ratio P_0/P_2, and each ratio is equal to M_1/M_0. This upward shift reflects an essential characteristic of aggregate demand, namely, that an equiproportionate increase in money and prices leaves the real money supply and therefore interest rates and real spending unchanged.[4]

Consider next the effect of an expansionary fiscal policy on the aggregate demand schedule. In Fig. 12-4 we show that an expansionary fiscal policy in the form of increased government spending, or reduced taxes, leads to an upward shift of the IS curve and a resulting increase in real income. At a given price level P_0, the fiscal expansion raises the equilibrium level of income and spending. In the lower graph this fact is recorded by point E_1 as a point on the new aggregate demand schedule. Since we could have started with any price level and corresponding LM curve in the upper panel, it is immediately apparent that corresponding to the easier fiscal policy we have a new aggregate demand schedule that lies everywhere to the right of the initial schedule. In fact, the rightward shift of the aggregate demand schedule at each price level, $\beta\Delta\bar{A}$, is related to the multiplier β in the equation for equilibrium aggregate demand, Eq. (1). From the definition of β, it is apparent that the shift in the aggregate demand curve is larger the larger the interest response of money demand, the lower the interest response of aggregate spending, and the smaller the income response of money demand.

Before proceeding, we summarize here the main points about aggregate demand: (1) The concept of aggregate demand provides a relation between the equilibrium level of income and spending, and the level of prices. (2) The aggregate demand schedule is negatively sloped because a reduction in the price level raises real balances, reduces interest rates, and thereby raises the equilibrium level of income and spending. (3) An increase in the nominal quantity of money, or an expansionary fiscal policy, shifts the aggregate demand schedule up and to the right; equivalently, an expansionary monetary or fiscal policy raises the equilibrium level of income and spending at each level of prices.

---

[4]As a technical point, we refer to this property of the aggregate demand function as *homogeneity* of degree zero in money and prices. This means that an equiproportionate increase in money and prices leaves *real* demand unchanged.

12-3 THE INTERACTION OF AGGREGATE DEMAND AND AGGREGATE SUPPLY

We now combine aggregate demand and supply in order to derive the full equilibrium of the system, including supply constraints. In Fig. 12-5 we draw the aggregate demand schedule corresponding to a given fiscal policy and nominal quantity of money. The short-run aggregate supply curve was derived in Chap. 11. Its positive slope reflects the sluggish adjustment of wages to output changes.[5] The long-run supply curve is vertical and corresponds to the vertical $Y_p Y_p$ line, at the level of potential output.

As we have drawn it, the initial equilibrium at E is one of under-employment. Output is below the level of potential output and, accordingly, the level of unemployment is above normal. How does the economy adjust over time from the equilibrium at point E? The high level of un-employment at E will imply declining wages. Declining wages, in turn, reduce costs and shift the supply schedule down and to the right over time. The downward shift in the supply schedule, in turn, causes equilibrium prices to decline, real balances to rise, interest rates to fall, and aggregate spending to increase. The adjustment process is therefore one of falling prices and increasing aggregate spending. The process of adjustment is represented by the arrows along the aggregate demand curve in Fig. 12-5. This *automatic* process will continue until prices have declined sufficiently (and wages have declined sufficiently) for aggregate demand to support the full-employment level of output Y_p at point E_1.

There is a critical lesson here. The point is that the levels of output and employment depend on aggregate demand which in turn depends on the real money supply, as we have seen in Eq. (1). If wages are sluggish in the short run, then the real money supply (given the nominal supply of money) cannot rise fast enough to support full employment. Only over time and with protracted unemployment will wages decline to lower prices and raise real balances sufficiently to support full employment. In a world of perfect wage and price flexibility, we would always be at full employ-ment. With sluggish wages and prices, by contrast, there is no assurance that we are always at full employment. Accordingly, monetary and fiscal stabilization policy may be called upon to improve the macroeconomic performance implied by this *automatic* adjustment process.

Specifically, if aggregate demand, *at the current level of prices,* is insufficient to support the full-employment level of output, as at point E in Fig. 12-5, an expansion in aggregate demand is called for. As we saw above, an expansion in the nominal quantity of money, or expansionary fiscal policy, would by shifting the aggregate demand schedule raise equilibrium income and spending at each level of prices. Expansionary aggregate demand policies can therefore be used to support full employ-ment at the prevailing level of wages. In terms of Fig. 12-5, expansionary

[5]Recall that the aggregate supply curve developed in Chap. 11 explicitly does *not* take account of the role of expected inflation in affecting wages. We examine the very important role of expected inflation in Chap. 13.

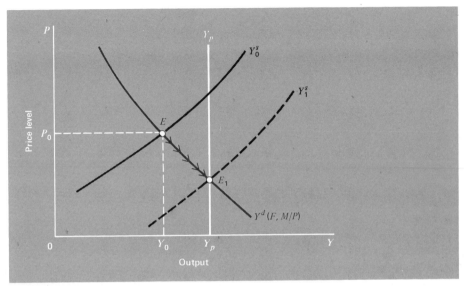

FIGURE 12-5 THE INTERACTION OF
AGGREGATE DEMAND AND SUPPLY

policies shift the $Y^d(F,M/P)$ curve up and to the right. We have seen how
the economy can undergo deflation to adjust the level of wages and prices
to the prevailing quantity of money to reach the equilibrium at E_1.
Alternatively, we may use monetary and fiscal policy to shift the aggregate
demand curve to the right and thus move output to its full-employment
level at the given wage rate.

There is a compelling logic to the argument that we should adapt the
level of the nominal quantity of money to the prevailing level of wages and
prices, rather than use unemployment or inflation to adapt wages and prices
to whatever is the quantity of money. In the next two sections we shall
study in considerably more detail how monetary policy and fiscal policy
work in this more complete model. In particular, we are interested in the
distinction between short-run and long-run effects of policies. The crucial
point we shall make is that in the short run both monetary and fiscal policy
can be expansionary. In the long run neither is expansionary, although
fiscal policy retains some important real effects.

12-4 MONETARY POLICY

In this section we examine the effects of an increase in the money stock. In
Fig. 12-6 we show the effect of an increase in the *nominal* quantity of
money from M_0 to M_1 as a rightward shift in the aggregate demand

schedule. As was shown in Fig. 12-3, the aggregate demand schedule shifts upward in the same proportion as the increase in the nominal quantity of money. In Fig. 12-6 we start with equilibrium at E, where output is at its potential level. In the short run, the increase in the money supply creates excess demand for goods at the initial price level. The excess demand in turn gives rise to an expansion in output and an increase in prices. The position of short-run equilibrium is at point E_1, where aggregate demand equals short-run supply. E_1 is also a point at which output exceeds potential output.

It is important to go behind the schedules for a moment to examine again the factors that account for the change in *real* output as a consequence of a change in the *nominal* quantity of money. On the supply side, the basic factor is the slow adjustment of nominal wages. The more sluggish the wages, the flatter the aggregate supply schedule and, accordingly, the larger the short-run expansion in output. Thus we retain the result from the supply side that sluggish wages imply that an increase in prices allows an expansion in real output.

On the aggregate demand side, we note that an increase in the nominal money stock also increases the real money stock *provided* prices do not rise to fully offset the increase in the nominal money supply. We recall from

FIGURE 12-6 THE EFFECTS OF MONETARY EXPANSION IN THE AGGREGATE DEMAND AND SUPPLY MODEL

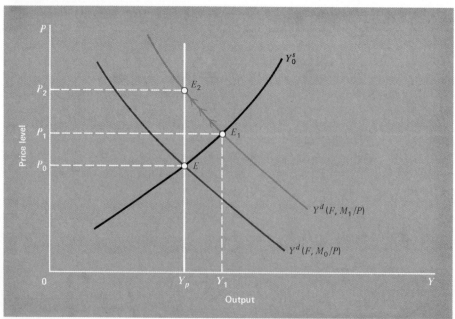

Sec. 12-2 that the increase in the nominal money supply shifts the aggregate demand schedule up in the same proportion as the increase in the money stock. Thus $(P_2 - P_0)/P_0$ in Fig. 12-7 is the proportionate increase in the money stock. Since in the short run prices increase by only $(P_1 - P_0)/P_0$, we clearly have an increase in real balances. The increase in real balances causes a reduction in interest rates and, therefore, an increase in real aggregate demand. The fact that prices increase proportionately less than nominal money·accounts for the expansion in real demand that sustains the higher level of output. At point E_1, therefore, we have a lower interest rate than at E, and that decline in the interest rate accounts for the higher level of real aggregate demand.

However, the short-run equilibrium at point E_1 is only transitory. Unemployment at E_1 is below its normal level, and that implies that wage pressure will set in and start raising costs. The effect of wage pressure as we saw in Chap. 11 is to shift the aggregate supply schedule upwards. The upward shift in aggregate supply, in turn, will cause an increase in equilibrium prices and a reduction in equilibrium supply. Over time the economy moves up the aggregate demand schedule with rising prices (inflation) and falling output until point E_2 is reached. We emphasize again that the driving force in the adjustment process is wage pressure. As long as output is above normal, unemployment is below normal and wages are rising. The rising wages raise costs and shift the supply schedule upwards. The resulting excess demand for goods raises prices, reduces real balances, raises interest rates, and reduces aggregate real demand.

How long will the process continue? Wages will continue rising as long as output is above potential. Accordingly, the supply schedule will keep shifting until point E_2 is reached. At that point, output has returned to normal: wages, prices, and the nominal quantity of money *all* have increased in the same proportion. All real variables, including output and interest rates, have returned to their initial equilibrium.

The property of the economy whereby changes in the nominal quantity of money affect only nominal variables (the price level and wages), leaving all real variables unchanged, is referred to as the *neutrality of money*. We have just seen that money is neutral in the long run for an economy starting at full employment. We saw in Sec. 12-3 that when the economy is not initially at full employment, it adjusts over time until full employment is reached. Thus even if the economy does not start at full employment, an increase in the money stock is neutral in the long run since it has no long-run effects on real variables. While it should be well understood that money is neutral in the long run, it should also be understood that monetary expansion causes an increase in output in the short run. Thus money is not neutral in the short run. Accordingly, monetary policy can be used as a tool of stabilization policy to affect the behavior of real variables such as the levels of output and unemployment.

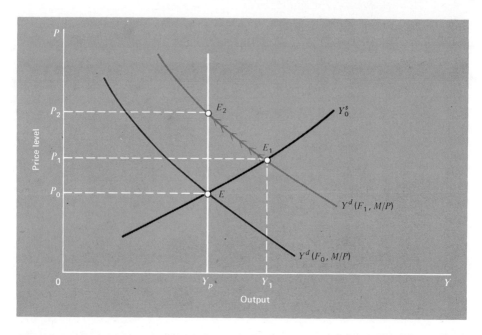

FIGURE 12-7 THE EFFECTS OF
EXPANSIONARY FISCAL POLICY

12-5 FISCAL POLICY

Consider next the effects of an expansionary fiscal policy. Referring to Fig. 12-7, we again start with a full-employment equilibrium at point E with output at its potential level Y_p. An expansion in government demand, or a cut in taxes, will shift the aggregate demand schedule to the right and accordingly create an excess demand for goods at the initial level of prices. The resulting increase in output and prices serves to clear markets and establish a short-run equilibrium at point E_1. On the supply side, as in the discussion of monetary policy, we note that the sluggishness of wages allows an expansion in output and employment when prices rise. On the aggregate demand side at point E_1, a higher level of real spending is sustained by a higher level of government spending, or higher private spending due to tax cuts.

An important question concerns the interest rate at point E_1. Unlike the case of a monetary expansion, the interest rate at point E_1 is actually higher than at point E. It has increased to maintain balance between the demand for and supply of real balances. To establish that point, we observe that the increase in prices between E and E_1 implies that we have a lower quantity of real balances. Further, the expansion in output causes an increase in real money demand. To reduce the demand for real money to the new lower level of real supply, we clearly require a higher interest rate.

In the short run, a fiscal expansion raises output and employment. As in the case of monetary expansion, it will be more expansionary the flatter the aggregate supply curve—equivalently, the lower the responsiveness of costs to an expansion in output. Now consider again the adjustments that arise from the reduction in unemployment below normal. The resulting wage pressure will raise costs and thereby shift up the supply schedule. Again, the resulting price increase will reduce the real money supply, raise interest rates, and reduce real spending. Accordingly, we will move up and along the aggregate demand schedule from E_1 to E_2 until output has returned to the potential output level.

The next question to ask is what will have happened once we return to the potential output level at E_2. It is apparent from Fig. 12-7 that prices will have risen. The higher level of prices, given money, will have raised interest rates just sufficiently to reduce private real spending by exactly the increase in government spending. It is therefore true that, with long-run output given, increased purchases (absorption) of goods by the government leave fewer resources available for private purchases. The process by which the private sector is *crowded out*[6] in the long run is through higher prices and therefore higher interest rates.

The fact that in the long run private sector spending is displaced by increased government spending is entirely a consequence of the assumption that long-run output is fixed so that if the government absorbs more, less is left to the private sector. This long-run crowding-out feature does not imply, however, that in the short run government spending is ineffective in expanding output and aggregate demand. Again, it is critical to bear in mind that the long-run equilibrium is primarily an indication of a position to which the economy will adjust, given enough time. It should not be thought of as the point toward which the economy moves as the immediate short-run consequence of expansionary fiscal policy. It is true that the long-run interpretation of this model confirms the view that increased government spending always occurs at the expense of private real spending. While this view may be correct in the long run,[7] it does not establish the case against active fiscal policy as a tool of short-run stabilization.

The relationship between fiscal policy and interest rates can be inferred too from Fig. 12-8, which includes the familiar IS curve. We have drawn in the initial IS schedule and the IS′ schedule corresponding to the increase in government spending. We also include a vertical line indicating potential output. Starting from the initial equilibrium at point E, the fiscal expansion first raises output and interest rates to some point like E_1. Subsequently, the rising prices cause the LM schedule (not drawn) to shift

---

[6]Crowding out was defined in Chap. 4. As an exercise, show the effect of a tax cut on the long-run level and composition of private spending.

[7]We say "may be" because we have here disregarded the effects of fiscal policy on the rate of investment and thus on the capital stock. See the problem set in Chap. 17 for further discussion.

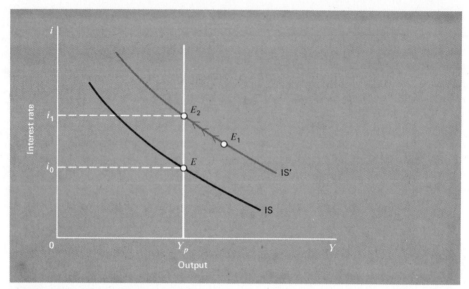

FIGURE 12-8 THE LONG-RUN EFFECT OF
FISCAL EXPANSION ON INTEREST RATES

up and to the left so that the equilibrium moves along the IS′ schedule until
potential output is reestablished. At that point, the interest rate will have
risen just enough to restore goods market equilibrium at the initial level of
output.

12-6 DISTURBANCES, POLICY RESPONSE, AND SUPPLY MANAGEMENT

The preceding discussion prepares us for an analysis of macroeconomic
disturbances and appropriate policy responses. Now that we have extended the IS-LM framework to include aggregate supply as well as aggregate demand, we can consider disturbances that arise either on the supply
or the demand side of the economy. On the demand side we can consider
disturbances such as autonomous changes in money demand or shifts in the
consumption or investment functions. Each such change would shift the
aggregate demand function and therefore disturb the macroeconomic equilibrium. On the supply side, we can look at disturbances such as exogenous increases in materials costs, or changes in taxes on goods or labor, that
shift the supply schedule.

The extension of our basic IS-LM framework to include supply considerations allows us to discuss the new interest in fiscal policy as a tool of
supply management. This view holds that fiscal policy in the form of
variations in indirect taxes or payroll taxes can be used to offset supply
disturbances while both monetary and fiscal policy can be used to maintain

aggregate demand at the full-employment level of output.

We will now go through the effects of an increase in payroll taxes on aggregate supply. The analysis will show that the macroeconomic effects of such a policy are to *increase* prices and *reduce* output. Obviously, then, a *cut* in payroll taxes can be used as a stimulative, noninflationary stabilization policy.

To explore this view of fiscal policy effects on aggregate supply, we consider the case of an increase in payroll taxes, that is taxes on wages. When there is a tax on wages, the wage paid to workers is less than the wage paid by employers. We assume that the wage paid to workers adjusts only with changes in the unemployment rate. More technically, we assume that in the short run the *incidence* of the payroll tax is on employers. Accordingly, an increase in labor costs due to payroll taxes will lead firms to pass on that cost increase in the form of higher prices. It follows that the supply schedule shifts up and to the left at each level of output. In Fig. 12-9 we show that an increase in payroll taxes causes the economy to move from its initial equilibrium at point E to a new equilibrium at point E_1 with higher prices and lower output. An increase in payroll taxes raises prices because it raises costs, given the wage rate. Output declines because the cost and price increases reduce the real money supply, raise interest rates, and therefore reduce real spending.

FIGURE 12-9 THE SUPPLY EFFECT OF A PAYROLL TAX INCREASE

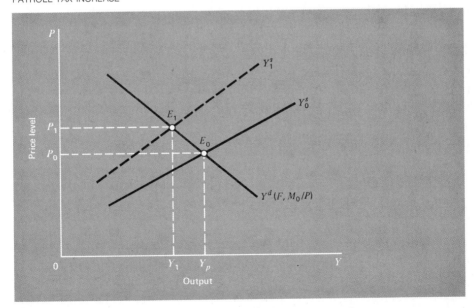

In Fig. 12-9 we have *not* considered a second aspect of the payroll tax increase that operates on the aggregate demand side. A payroll tax increase obviously reduces disposable income at each level of output since the government now collects more taxes. Accordingly, aggregate demand declines at each level of output unless this deflationary effect is offset by increased transfers or increased government spending. In the absence of such compensating policies, the aggregate demand schedule would therefore shift to the left in Fig. 12-9 and further add to the output reduction, but at the same time make the effect on the price level ambiguous.

The preceding discussion suggests two questions about the choice of fiscal policies. First, there is the question of comparing payroll taxes, which have both supply and demand effects, to other fiscal policy instruments such as changes in government spending or transfers. Second, there is the question of determining what type of disturbances would be best countered by policies that have supply effects and what type of disturbances should be countered mainly by aggregate demand policies.

The answer to these questions must rely on the general principle that policies should be geared, as closely as possible, to the disturbances they are supposed to offset. Thus for aggregate demand disturbances, say an autonomous reduction in investment, the appropriate response is an aggregate demand policy. These policies, if timely, and precisely set up, will maintain aggregate demand close to full employment and keep the price level constant. They therefore prevent the need to adjust output and prices to a transitory change in aggregate demand. We note also that in the case of aggregate demand variations, policies that mainly affect aggregate supply are inappropriate. They are inappropriate because they may stimulate output in the right direction but they do so at the costs of changing prices.

Consider next a disturbance that arises entirely on the supply side. Assume a temporary increase in raw material prices that raises costs and thus shifts the aggregate supply schedule upward. In the absence of policy changes, we would experience both an increase in prices and a reduction in equilibrium output, as shown in Fig. 12-9. An appropriate policy response would be, for example, a cut in payroll taxes. The payroll tax cut would exert an offsetting effect by reducing costs, thus leaving the supply schedule unaffected. Again we remember, however, that the payroll tax cut reduces tax revenue and therefore exerts an expansionary effect on aggregate demand. To neutralize this side effect of the tax cut, we would require an offsetting cut in government spending or a cut in transfers.

It is clear from the preceding discussion that certain fiscal policy measures may have a perhaps surprising ability to cope with disturbances. This potential role in offsetting supply disturbances has led to the suggestion that supply management be used as a systematic part of macroeconomic stabilization policy. Fiscal policy changes in the form of payroll tax changes, and indirect tax changes could, according to this new policy view, be used to offset inflationary supply shocks while aggregate demand policies would continue to be used to maintain full employment.[8]

It is fair to say that there has been relatively little experience with fiscal policy as a tool of price and supply management. Nevertheless, the concept is intriguing.[9] Because there are at least three macroeconomic policy targets—full-employment, price stability, and growth—successful stabilization policy may well require the use of fiscal policies that operate on aggregate supply as well as monetary and fiscal policies that affect both the level and composition of aggregate demand.

12-7 SUMMARY

1 The aggregate demand function describes the equilibrium relationship between aggregate spending and the price level. The equilibrium in question is the simultaneous equilibrium of the goods and assets markets.

2 The aggregate demand curve slopes downwards because an *increase* in the price level reduces real balances, increases the interest rate, and thereby *reduces* aggregate spending.

3 The aggregate demand curve is shifted up and to the right by an increase in the money stock or expansionary fiscal policy. At a given level of output, the aggregate demand curve shifts up in exactly the same proportion as the nominal money supply increases.

4 The short-run equilibrium of the economy is determined by the intersection of the short-run aggregate supply curve and the aggregate demand curve.

5 An increase in the money stock increases both output and the price level in the short run. In the long run, the aggregate supply curve shifts in response to positive or negative unemployment so that output moves back to its potential level.

6 In the long run, money is *neutral*, meaning that an increase in the money stock results only in an equiproportionate increase in prices.

7 Expansionary fiscal policy increases the levels of output and prices in the short run, but in the long run only increases prices. In the long run, expansionary fiscal policy merely *crowds out* other expenditures and has no effect on output.

8 *Supply management policies* are attempts to move the aggregate supply curve, for example, by changes in payroll taxes. There is as yet little experience with such policies. Conventional monetary and fiscal policies which move the aggregate demand curve are called *demand management policies*.

---

[8]George L. Perry, "Stabilization Policy and Inflation," in Henry Owen and Charles L. Schultze (eds.), *Setting National Priorities*, Brookings Institution, 1976.

[9]See, too, our further discussion in Chap. 13.

9 In deciding what policies to use in response to disturbances, the general rule is to use policies which most directly offset the effects of the disturbance. A shift in demand should be countered by a demand management policy and a supply shift should be offset by supply management policy.

PROBLEMS

1 a Explain why the aggregate demand curve slopes down.
  b What happens to interest rates as we move down along this schedule and why?
  c What happens to the nominal stock of money as we move down along the aggregate demand curve? The real money stock?
2 The text states that a higher multiplier $\bar{\alpha}$ would flatten out the aggregate demand curve.
  a Give an economic interpretation of this fact.
  b Use Eq. (1) to prove this, noting that

$$\gamma \equiv \frac{b\bar{\alpha}}{h + bk\bar{\alpha}}$$

  (If $\bar{\alpha}$ increases, what happens to γ?) How is γ related to the slope of the aggregate demand curve?
3 a What would be the effect on the aggregate demand curve of a cut in transfer payments?
  b Would this effect be greater or smaller if the multiplier $\bar{\alpha}$ were higher?
  c Verify this answer using Eq. (1) and the fact that

$$\beta \equiv \frac{h\bar{\alpha}}{h + bk\bar{\alpha}}$$

  *d Can you calculate $\Delta Y^d/\Delta R$ at a *fixed* level of price in terms of the variables we have already introduced? (Recall that R is transfer payments).
4 Is it true that in the short run expansionary fiscal or monetary policy can only increase output by also raising prices? Explain.
5 Suppose the aggregate supply curve were vertical. (Do you remember from Chap. 11 what would cause this?)
  a What would be the effects of expansionary fiscal and monetary policy in the short run on output, prices, and interest rates?
  b The long run?
6 In the text it is noted that monetary policy is neutral in the long run even if the economy is not initially at full employment as in Fig. 12-6. Draw a diagram which demonstrates this fact and comment on the economic implications of this result. Does it seem to be a plausible one to you?
7 a Draw a diagram like Fig. 12-7 indicating the effects of a tax increase in both the short and long runs.
  b Is such a change in fiscal policy neutral in the long run? If not, what is the real effect?

8 Suppose investors suddenly become more optimistic than in the past and decide to invest more at given levels of income and interest rates. Trace the effects of such a shift through the IS and LM curves to see its effect on equilibrium income as derived with the aggregate supply and demand curves. Explain the effects of the change in optimism on interest rates, prices, and income.

*9 A sales tax at the rate of 1 percent is imposed on all final goods. At the same time income taxes are cut so as to maintain the budget in balance at the initial equilibrium. GNP initially is $1,500 billion.

a   What is the size of the income tax cut?

b   What is the short-run effect of the policy package on output and prices?

c   What is the long-run effect on output and prices?

13

Inflation, Output, and Unemployment

This chapter studies the behavior of output, unemployment, and inflation. Our focus moves here from Chap. 12's analysis of *price level* determination, to the behavior of the *inflation rate*. Since the inflation rate is the rate of change of the price level, a theory which explains how the price level is determined—as did the theory of Chap. 12—must also explain how the inflation rate is determined. Accordingly, this chapter does not introduce a different theory from that of Chap. 12, but rather looks at the theory of Chap. 12 in a slightly different light.

The type of question we are addressing is brought out by Chart 13-1, which shows combinations of inflation rates and unemployment rates over the past few years. Evidently, no extremely simple explanation—such as the view that unemployment declines when inflation increases—can account for that behavior. From 1969 to 1970, and from 1973 to 1974, both the rate of inflation and the rate of unemployment increased. From 1970 to 1971, and from 1974 to 1975, the rate of unemployment increased, while the rate of inflation decreased. From 1971 to 1972, and from 1975 to 1976, both the rate of inflation and the rate of unemployment decreased.

Our major aim is to try to understand the behavior of the economy illustrated in Chart 13-1. We want to develop an understanding of the factors that explain inflation and unemployment and to find answers to such questions as: Why do inflation and unemployment sometimes increase together? Is inflation explained by lax monetary and fiscal policies? Can monetary or fiscal policy be used to raise the level of output permanently? Is it true that "inflation is always and everywhere a monetary phenomenon"?[1]

These questions are very much at the center of public discussion and controversy.[2] It turns out that a simple extension and reformulation of the aggregate supply-demand model of Chap. 12 goes far in providing answers. The major new element of theory in this chapter is the introduction of expectations of inflation, which affect aggregate supply. We shall see that the way in which expectations are formed plays a crucial role in determining the dynamic responses of the economy to changes in monetary and fiscal policy.

In Sec. 13-1 we begin the analysis of inflation by discussing the long-run relationship between monetary growth and inflation. We show that in the long run inflation is indeed a monetary phenomenon: in the long run the rate of inflation is determined by the growth rate of the money stock. From that long-run equilibrium, we turn to the much more controversial issues surrounding the behavior of inflation in the short run. We shall see that in the short run the inflation rate is determined by monetary and fiscal policy, by autonomous spending, by expectations of inflation, and by supply shocks. Section 13-2 presents an informal outline of the

[1]See Milton Friedman, *Dollars and Deficits*, Prentice-Hall, 1968, p. 39.

[2]See, for example, Lindley H. Clark, *The Secret Tax*, Dow Jones, 1976, and John Flemming, *Inflation*, Oxford University Press, 1976.

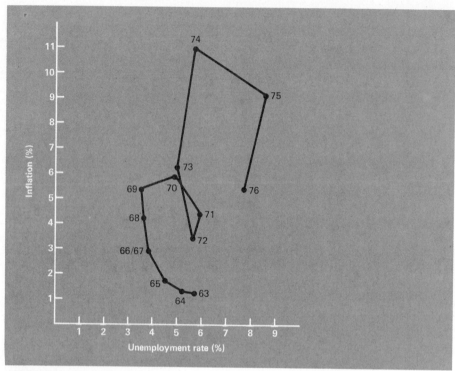

CHART 13-1 INFLATION AND
UNEMPLOYMENT. (Source: *Economic Report
of the President,* 1977)

theory of inflation and output in the short run, explaining also how short-run behavior is linked with that of the long run.

The theory of aggregate supply and the Phillips curve is developed in Sec. 13-3. The theory implies that the rate of inflation is higher, the higher the expected rate of inflation and the lower the GNP gap. The introduction of expectations into aggregate supply is a new dynamic element of the theory. Section 13-4 establishes the aggregate demand relationship between the inflation rate and aggregate spending. Aggregate demand is related to monetary and fiscal policy variables. Increases in the budget deficit or monetary growth in excess of the inflation rate give rise to increases in aggregate demand. Aggregate supply and demand are combined in Sec. 13-5 to determine the short-run rate of inflation and level of output.

Section 13-6 takes up the adjustment process that links the short-run to the long-run equilibrium. An increase in the growth rate of money is shown to raise output and inflation in the short run. Over time, the increase in output subsides and inflation increases until it fully matches the higher growth rate of the nominal money stock. The effects of fiscal policy changes on the inflation rate and output in the short and long run are examined in Sec. 13-7. Section 13-8 considers supply shocks and supply management policies. In a brief appendix to the chapter we discuss the important Okun's law relationship between the unemployment rate and the GNP gap.

13-1 MONEY AND INFLATION IN THE LONG RUN

In this section we look at the long-run relationship between money and the inflation rate. We consider a situation in which the money stock is growing at a constant rate, and in which inflation has settled down to a constant rate. Everybody is aware of the inflation, has adjusted to it, and expects it to continue. To begin with, we discuss an economy in which the growth rate of potential output is zero, and in which output has adjusted to its potential level. The long-run equilibrium we describe, with a constant rate of inflation and a constant output level, is also called a *steady state*. Later we shall modify our analysis to account for the possibility that potential output is growing over time.

In an economy with a constant growth rate of money, a constant level of output, and with everyone fully adjusted to the presence of inflation, there is a very simple relationship between the growth rate of money and the inflation rate. In such an economy, prices will rise exactly at the rate at which the nominal money stock is increasing.

We can formalize this relationship be denoting the *growth rate* of money by $m \equiv \Delta M/M$ and the rate of inflation by $\pi \equiv \Delta P/P$:

$$\pi = m \tag{1}$$

Equation (1), which we will derive and discuss in detail below, is a central statement in macroeconomics. It points out that, in the long run, or on average, there is a link between monetary growth and inflation. More precisely, in a *stationary* economy—an economy where real income is constant—the rate of inflation is equal to the growth rate of the nominal quantity of money.

Before explaining Eq. (1) in more detail, we look briefly at some evidence. Chart 13-2 shows the rate of inflation and the growth rate of money for the United States in the post-World War II period. The rates shown for each year are average rates over the past four years. Thus Chart 13-2 presents rough measures of long-run growth rates of money and the inflation rate. The chart suggests that the growth rate of money and the inflation rate do move together over long periods. However, the relationship is not exact. In part, this lack of an exact relationship reflects the role of other factors—such as fiscal policy changes and aggregate de-

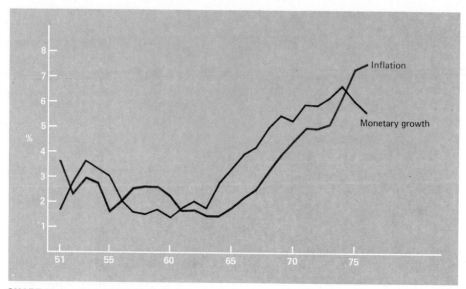

CHART 13-2 LONGTERM INFLATION AND
MONETARY GROWTH (*Note:* Inflation and
monetary growth are four-year moving
averages of annual growth rates of the GNP
deflator and of M_1. Data from the Federal
Reserve Bank of St. Louis.)

mand and supply disturbances. A second factor making the relationship
inexact is trend growth in output. We shall see later that the relationship
(1) between the growth rate of the money stock and the inflation rate has
to be modified to take account of long-run growth in output.

Now we return to Eq. (1) to establish the long-run relation between
inflation and monetary growth. For that purpose we turn to the equilibrium condition in the money market, familiar from the LM curve:

$$\frac{M}{P} = L(i,Y) \tag{2}$$

or

$$M = PL(i,Y)$$

$$\tag{2a}$$

Equations (2) and (2*a*) state that monetary equilibrium requires that
money demand equals money supply. Equation (2) states this equilibrium condition in terms of real money demand and supply; Eq. (2*a*) states
the condition in terms of nominal money demand and supply.

Now consider long-run equilibrium where, by definition, all adjustments have taken place and, therefore, output and interest rates are constant. With output and interest rates constant, the demand for real money balances is constant. Therefore, to maintain the equality between the supply and demand for money, changes in the nominal money supply must be matched by corresponding changes in prices. For instance, if the stock of money were increasing by 5 percent per year, then prices would have to be rising at the rate of 5 percent per year so as to maintain constant the real money supply M/P, and thus maintain equilibrium in the money market. Here we have, therefore, the first way of establishing that in long-run equilibrium, money and prices must grow at the same rate.

An alternative way of making the same point starts from Eq. (2a). Again we recognize that with constant real output and constant interest rates there will be a given, constant *real* demand for money L. Looking at Eq. (2a), we see that if the left-hand side—the nominal quantity of money—is increasing at some rate, the right-hand side—the demand for nominal balances—must be increasing at the same rate. But in the steady state, the only factor changing on the right-hand side is the price level, since $L(\ )$ is constant. Therefore the price level must be increasing at the same rate as the nominal money stock. And that is precisely the message of Eq. (1): in long-run equilibrium, the rate of inflation is equal to the growth rate of money.

The argument that "inflation is always and everywhere a monetary phenomenon" is thus entirely correct as a description of long-run equilibrium. It is simply an implication of monetary equilibrium. The real money supply that yields monetary equilibrium is equal to real money demand. To maintain a constant real money supply, an increasing nominal money stock has to be matched by rising prices. Thus, if the growth rate of the nominal money stock is 5 percent, the rate of inflation will be 5 percent. If the nominal money stock grows at the rate of 1,000 percent, as it has in some hyperinflations, then the rate of inflation will be 1,000 percent, in long-run equilibrium.

Now we have to step back for a moment to ask how reasonable it is to look at the long run. After all, the economy is really never in long-run equilibrium. There is always some disturbance that upsets equilibrium and causes inflation and output to be different from their long-run values. That point is well taken, and, indeed, reduces the interest we would otherwise have in long-run equilibrium. But there is a different way of looking at long-run equilibrium which makes it a less precise but much more powerful concept. This alternative is to think of the long-run equilibrium as the *average* behavior of the economy over long time periods. To give an example, if on average over a five-year period the money stock had grown at 10 percent per year, with some variation, say, between 8 and 12 percent, then we would expect the inflation rate to be about 10 percent. It might be a bit smaller or higher depending on economic disturbances during the period, but it will be roughly 10 percent. The reason this average interpretation of the long run is powerful is that we are not trying to be more precise than is reasonable. We wind up with only a rule of thumb, but it is a very sturdy one.

Output Growth and Long-Run Inflation

The relationship (1) between monetary growth and inflation requires a minor correction to account for output growth. It is clear that growth in real income raises real money demand, and that, therefore, the assumption of a constant demand for real balances is not appropriate when output is growing. How should we account for the effects of output growth on the relationship between monetary growth and inflation? For instance, how does the average growth rate of real income of 3.5 percent in the United States in the post-World War II period affect Eq. (1)?

In studying money demand in Chap. 7, we introduced the income elasticity of money demand. We noted there that a 1 percent increase in real income raises real money demand by about 0.7 percent. The income elasticity of money demand is 0.7. Thus, if real income grows at the average rate of 3.5 percent, as it has in the United States, and if the income elasticity of money demand is 0.7, as it is in the United States, then real money demand grows at the average rate of 2.45 percent (= 3.5 percent × 0.7) per year.

If real money demand is rising—say, at the rate of 2.45 percent per year—as a result of income growth, then monetary equilibrium requires that the real money supply increases at that same rate. Now the growth rate of the real money supply is just the difference between the growth rate of the nominal money stock and the rate of inflation. For instance, if the nominal money stock is increasing at 10 percent, and the rate of inflation is 6 percent, the real money supply is growing at 4 percent. If the real money supply has to be growing at 2.45 percent to maintain monetary equilibrium, then the rate of inflation has to be 2.45 percent less than the rate of monetary growth, or, in symbols,

$$\pi = m - 2.45 \tag{1a}$$

Equation (1a) states that the rate of inflation is equal to the growth rate of money *less* an adjustment arising from real income growth. Thus, if nominal money grows precisely at the rate of 2.45 percent, then prices will be constant and real money balances will grow just fast enough to meet the growing money demand. If the nominal quantity of money grows faster, then the rate of inflation has to be higher for the supply of real balances to be growing at 2.45 percent.

Equation (1a) partly explains why in Chart 13-2 there is some discrepancy between the average rate of monetary growth and the rate of inflation. We observe from the chart that monetary growth usually exceeds the inflation rate, and Eq. (1a) explains that fact by the growth in real money demand that results from real income growth.

Equation (1a) generalizes to the statement that the rate of inflation in the long run (or on average) is equal to the growth rate of the nominal money supply less the growth rate of real money demand. To give another example, if real income grew at the rate of 6 percent and the income elasticity of money demand were as high as 1.2, we would have growth in real money demand of 7.2 percent (= 6 percent × 1.2). This means that with a growth rate of nominal money of, say, 10 percent, the rate of inflation would be only 2.8 percent (= 10 percent − 7.2 percent). Clearly, then, for a given growth rate of nominal money, the inflation rate is higher the lower the growth rate of real income, or the lower the income elasticity of money demand.

Summary

Here we briefly summarize the long-run or average relation between inflation and monetary growth.

1 Inflation in the long run is a monetary phenomenon. By this we mean that inflation arises from growth in the nominal money supply in excess of growth in real money demand.
2 The higher the growth rate of the nominal money supply, the higher the rate of inflation.
3 The rate of inflation is lower the higher the growth rate of real money demand. This means that inflation is lower the faster the growth rate of output, and the more real money demand rises with increased real income or output.

The simple long-run relationship between monetary growth and inflation contains one extremely important lesson. If a country wants to reduce its average inflation rate, it has somehow to reduce the average growth rate of the money stock.

13-2 INFLATION AND OUTPUT IN THE SHORT RUN: AN OVERVIEW

Chart 13-3 shows the short-run rates of inflation and growth rate of money over the post-World War II period. The growth rates in Chart 13-3 are annual data. The picture emerging from Chart 13-3 is very different from that of Chart 13-2. It is clear from Chart 13-3 that there is no close link in the short run between the growth rate of money and the inflation rate.

The absence of a close link between the growth rate of money and the inflation rate in the short run suggests that there are other factors accounting for inflation in the short run. We now turn our attention to those factors. At the same time, we are interested in short-run fluctuations in

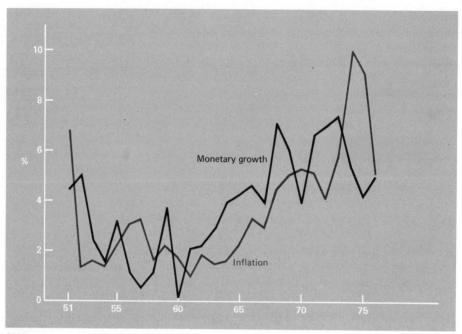

CHART 13-3 INFLATION AND MONETARY
GROWTH IN THE SHORT RUN. (Source:
Federal Reserve Bank of St. Louis. *Note:*
Inflation is the annual rate of change of the
GNP deflator. Monetary growth is the annual
growth rate of M_1.)

output and unemployment in the economy, and the relationship between
output fluctuations and inflation. Chapter 12 has already suggested that
the behavior of the price level and the behavior of output are closely related in the short run, and we will again find that to be true.

The determination of the level of output and rate of inflation in the
short run depends on aggregate supply and demand, as in Chap. 12. We
will reformulate the theory of Chap. 12 to emphasize: (1) Aggregate demand is equal to last period's aggregate demand plus (or minus) any
changes induced by changes in real balances or changes in fiscal policy.
(2) The aggregate supply relationship is affected by the expected rate of
inflation. Nominal wages adjust in response to both unemployment, and
expected inflation because both firms and workers are concerned with the
real wages they will by paying or receiving over the course of their labor
contracts. If prices are expected to increase at, say, 10 percent, during the
course of a labor contract, then nominal wages will tend, for that reason, to
increase at a rate of 10 percent over the course of the contract. Wage rises
are passed on into price rises, and the inflation rate thus reflects expected
inflation.

In this section we use the diagrammatic analysis of Chap. 12, slightly modified, to examine the long- and short-run equilibria of the economy. We make two modifications to the aggregate supply and demand analysis of Chap. 12. It is convenient to start from a situation of long-run equilibrium. Suppose that the money stock has been growing at a constant rate, say 10 percent, that the inflation rate has been 10 percent, and that the inflation that has been taking place is fully built into expectations and wage increases, so that wages too are rising at the rate of 10 percent.

Figure 13-1 shows how the aggregate supply and demand curves move over time in this inflationary economy. The first modification we make to the analysis of Chap. 12 is to note that the aggregate demand curve will be moving up over time at the same rate as the money supply is growing. Since aggregate demand depends on the level of real balances, any given level of aggregate demand will be maintained with a growing money stock only if the price level increases in the same proportion as the money stock. Thus, the aggregate demand curve moves up at the same rate as the stock of

FIGURE 13-1 STEADY-STATE INFLATION

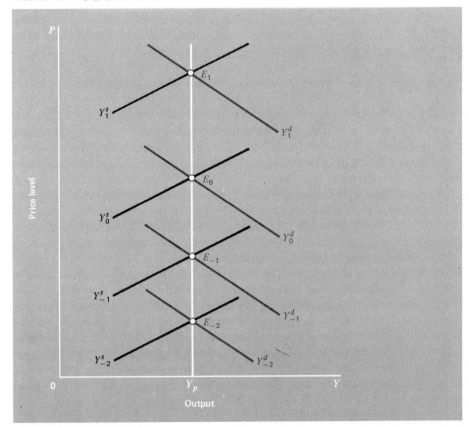

money grows, assuming that there are no other disturbances to demand, such as fiscal policy changes.

The second modification is that the aggregate supply curve moves up at the same rate as the price level is expected to increase. Since both firms and labor are concerned with *real* wages, they will adjust nominal wages in proportion to the changes they expect to take place in the price level. Those wage increases, in turn, are passed on into prices. If the price level is expected to be increasing at 10 percent per period, then the aggregate supply curve will, for that reason, be moving up at the rate of 10 percent per period.

In Fig. 13-1 the aggregate demand curve moves from Y_{-2}^d to Y_{-1}^d to Y_0^d in successive periods, shifting up 10 percent each period as a result of the 10 percent growth of the money stock. The aggregate supply curve similarly moves up from Y_{-2}^s to Y_{-1}^s to Y_0^s in successive periods, as a result of the expected inflation at the rate of 10 percent.

As a result of these shifts in the aggregate demand and supply curves, the price level increases by 10 percent from period to period. Output is at its potential level, and not changing. If the growth rate of the money stock and the expected rate of inflation both continue to be 10 percent, the next period's aggregate demand and supply curves will be Y_1^d and Y_1^s, respectively, each 10 percent above their current position, and next period's price level will be 10 percent higher than this period's. Output will remain at its potential level.

An Increase in Monetary Growth

Consider now a current disturbance, which breaks the pattern of regular or *steady-state* inflation. For concreteness, suppose that inflation had been proceeding at 10 percent for some time, as in Fig. 13-1. The corresponding equilibrium points are shown as E_{-2} and E_{-1} in Fig. 13-2. Now suppose that during this period the rate of monetary growth increases to 20 percent, and that the expected rate of inflation continues to be 10 percent. The expected rate of inflation remains at 10 percent because individuals have become used to that steady rate of inflation, which has persisted for some time.

What happens now? The aggregate demand curve moves up by 20 percent, in proportion to the increase in the money stock, to Y_0^d. The aggregate supply curve moves up only 10 percent to the position Y_0^s. We see immediately in Fig. 13-2 that the increase in monetary growth and the expansionary effect it exerts on aggregate demand—combined with the slower shift in the aggregate supply curve—drives us to the equilibrium point E_0. The impact of the increased rate of growth of money is to raise both real output and the inflation rate. The inflation rate is now $(P_0 - P_{-1})/P_{-1}$, which is greater than the expected rate of 10 percent, and less than the growth rate of money of 20 percent. The increase in inflation is accompanied by an increase in output to Y_0.

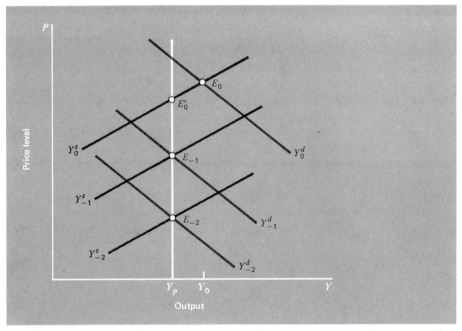

FIGURE 13-2 AN INCREASE IN
MONETARY GROWTH

We have already established two very important results. The first is that an increase in monetary growth can raise the level of output in the short run. This is exactly the same result as we obtained in Chap. 12, where we were not, however, studying a process of ongoing inflation. In Chap. 12, the increase in the stock of money exerted an expansionary influence because wages were slow to adjust. A very similar mechanism is at work here. Wages adjust slowly on the basis of built-in expectations of inflation, and therefore changes in monetary growth result in output increases. If the aggregate supply curve moved up by the same amount as the aggregate demand curve, it is clear that there would be no effect on output.

The second result, which we have already mentioned, is that the inflation rate changes by less in the short run than the growth rate of money. It is precisely that fact which is responsible for the increase in output to Y_0 that we observe in the equilibrium of the economy at E_0. Aggregate demand expands because real balances rise—and real balances rise because the nominal money stock increases more rapidly than the price level. Thus, even before we turn to other factors which affect the inflation rate in the short run, we have a possible explanation for the behavior shown in Chart 13-2—in which the link between inflation and monetary growth in the short run is weak.

The Adjustment Process

We have seen that in the short run an increase in monetary growth will (1) raise inflation but raise it by less than the increase in monetary growth and (2) raise the level of output. Now we want to link up the short run with the long run. We know that in the long run monetary growth is exactly matched by inflation, and our question therefore is: What is the adjustment process that drives the rate of inflation up to that higher level?

We turn to inflationary expectations to find the answer. Assume that monetary growth is maintained at the higher level of 20 percent indefinitely. In terms of Fig. 13-2 this means that the aggregate demand schedule will keep shifting up by 20 percent per year, year after year. The upward shift of the aggregate supply will depend on inflationary expectations. The supply schedule will shift up each year by the amount of inflation that is expected and, therefore, reflected in wages and costs.

We clearly have to ask how these expectations are formed. A simple answer is to assume that inflationary expectations are based on past experience. If inflation has been 10 percent for a long time, then people expect inflation at a rate of 10 percent. If inflation today rises to 13 percent—say in the move from E_{-1} to E_0 in Fig. 13-2—then the increased actual inflation will be reflected in somewhat higher inflationary expectations of perhaps 12 percent. The increase in actual inflation thus drives up expected inflation and causes the aggregate supply schedule to shift up faster and faster until it eventually catches up with the aggregate demand schedule. At that point (1) the economy is back to potential output and (2) the actual inflation rate is 20 percent and thus equals the monetary growth rate. We have therefore reached the new steady state.[3]

Preview

We present here a brief preview of the rest of the chapter. The aim is to provide an idea of what is to come, though not a complete understanding. In the remaining sections, we develop the ideas presented so far in more detail. There are two main changes. First, we introduce a more convenient diagrammatic treatment, which focuses on the *inflation rate* rather than the *price level*. We need a diagram which focuses on the inflation rate because we could not use Fig. 13-2 to pursue the inflation process for more than a few periods before running off the page. Secondly, we look more carefully at aggregate supply and demand.

The supply side establishes the link between actual inflation, expected inflation, and output. We develop the aggregate supply curve

---

[3]Below we ask whether there may be a period of overshooting in which the inflation rate actually rises above 20 percent before settling down at the new long-run level.

$$\pi = \pi^* + \alpha\epsilon(Y - Y_p) \tag{3}$$

Equation (3) states that the actual inflation rate π is equal to the expected inflation rate π^*, plus a term that depends on the difference between actual and potential output. The second term is already familiar from the development of aggregate supply in Chap. 11. When output is high relative to potential output, unemployment is low and wages are therefore rising, and being passed on into price increases. The first element, the expected rate of inflation, means that there is a potential for inflation even at full employment. Wages, and therefore prices, will rise when output is at the full-employment level if inflation is expected and nominal wages adjust accordingly. Thus, on the supply side, the level of output (relative to potential) and the expected rate of inflation, are the determinants of the inflation rate.

On the aggregate demand side we develop Eq. (4):

$$Y^d = Y_{-1}^d + \gamma f + \phi(m - \pi) \tag{4}$$

Equation (4) states that current real aggregate demand is equal to last period's aggregate demand, *plus* the increase that results from an expansionary fiscal policy f, *plus* the increase that results from growth in real balances, $m - \pi$.

Each of Eqs. (3) and (4) is a relationship between the inflation rate and the level of output, and we can, therefore, draw Eq. (3) as the aggregate supply curve and Eq. (4) as the aggregate demand curve. Their intersection will determine the short-run inflation rate and level of output.

The rate of inflation and the level of output in the short run will obviously depend on the positions of the supply and demand curves. It is clear, therefore, that the inflation rate and level of output are in the short run determined by the variables that appear in Eqs. (3) and (4). These variables are the expected inflation rate π^*, last period's output Y_{-1}^d, fiscal policy f, and the growth rate of the money stock m.

There are two important points which follow from the list of variables that determine the inflation rate and level of output in the short run. (1) In the short run the growth rate of money is not the only influence on the inflation rate. Fiscal policy, the expected inflation rate, and lagged output also affect the inflation rate and output in the short run. (2) *Persistence effects* are vital to an understanding of the inflationary process. The inflation rate today depends on last period's level of output, and, therefore, on last period's unemployment. And the inflation rate also depends on the expected rate of inflation, which is likely to change only slowly over time. It is these persistence effects which make it difficult to reduce inflation without affecting the unemployment rate.

We now move on to a fuller development of the analysis summarized in this section.

*13-3 AGGREGATE SUPPLY AND THE PHILLIPS CURVE

This section develops the relationship among the rate of inflation, aggregate supply, and inflationary expectations that is summarized by Eq. (3) above.

Our starting point is the theory of aggregate supply developed in Chap. 11. Our theory there builds on the assumption that overemployment leads to increases in nominal wages, which increase production costs, and are passed on into prices. Unemployment leads to falling nominal wages, which reduce the cost of production, and are passed on into falling prices. The dynamic adjustment of wages and prices comes to an end once the economy is at the level of potential output, with full employment.

In this chapter we want to include the fact that there is some frictional unemployment, even when the economy is at full employment. The frictional unemployment consists of people who are between jobs, and those who are unemployed because they have just entered the labor force and are looking for their first jobs. The rate of unemployment corresponding to full employment is called the *natural rate of unemployment*, and we shall denote it by $\bar{u}$.[4] Once we include the natural rate of unemployment in our theory, we recognize that it is unemployment in excess of the natural rate $(u - \bar{u})$, rather than the rate of unemployment itself, which tends to cause wages to fall. Unemployment below the natural rate causes nominal wages to rise.

However, the major change in the theory of aggregate supply introduced in this chapter is not the inclusion of the natural rate of unemployment $\bar{u}$. Rather, the major change is the incorporation of expectations of inflation as another influence affecting the behavior of wages, therefore costs, and therefore prices. In the face of expected inflation, labor wants to protect its real wages by having nominal wages rise, and firms can afford to pay the higher wages because they expect to be able to pass on the rising costs in the form of higher prices. The effect of expected inflation on wages and prices was not included in Chaps. 11 and 12 because the equilibrium there assumed a constant long-run level of prices.

These ideas can be combined in a relationship among actual inflation, expected inflation, and the difference between the unemployment rate and the natural rate of unemployment:

$$\pi = \pi^* - \epsilon(u - \bar{u}) \tag{5}$$

where π is the actual rate of inflation, $\pi*$ is the expected rate of inflation, and u is again the unemployment rate.

Equation (5) is shown in Fig. 13-3. Suppose, first, that unemployment is at the natural rate $\bar{u}$. If labor and firms expect the inflation rate to be π_0^*, then money wages will be rising at that rate. Labor is seeking to protect its

---

[4] We study the determinants of the natural rate of unemployment in detail in Chap. 15.

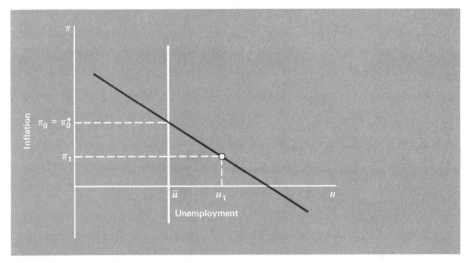

FIGURE 13-3 THE EXPECTATIONS-
AUGMENTED PHILLIPS CURVE

real wage, and firms are willing to pay the rising wages because they expect
to be able to pass on those wage increases into prices. With u equal to $\bar{u}$,
the actual rate of inflation will be equal to the expected rate π_0^*. In addition, there is an adjustment for labor market conditions. If unemployment
exceeds the natural rate, $(u - \bar{u}) > 0$, wages will rise at a lower rate than π_0^*.
Accordingly, there is a dampening effect from unemployment to actual
inflation. Conversely, if unemployment is below the natural rate, wages
will rise more rapidly than at the expected rate of inflation, and actual
inflation will therefore exceed the expected rate of inflation. The relationship between inflation and unemployment in Fig. 13-3 is, therefore, negatively sloped. Equation (5), the schedule shown in Fig. 13-3, is called an
expectations-augmented Phillips curve.

Before we come to the details of expectations formation, we complete
the relationship between output and inflation by adding Eq. (6). Equation
(6) is a relationship between unemployment and the GNP gap, of the sort
derived in Chap. 11. The higher the unemployment rate, the higher the
gap between actual and potential output:

$$u - \bar{u} = -\alpha(Y - Y_p) \qquad \alpha > 0 \qquad (6)$$

Equation (6) is a form of Okun's law, which is briefly described in the
appendix to this chapter. Okun's law is an empirical law which relates
short-run changes in output to changes in unemployment, and examines
the sources of output changes which go along with changes in unemployment. It turns out that, empirically, changes in unemployment are accom-

panied by changes in the productivity of labor and overtime (as argued in Chap. 11), and also by changes in the number of people in the labor force, or labor force *participation*. When unemployment falls, more people tend to come into the labor force to find work. For all those reasons, reductions in unemployment and increases in output occur together. The empirical law that Okun discovered is that in the short run a 1 percent change in the unemployment rate tends to accompany a three-percentage point reduction in the GNP gap.

Now we can combine Eqs. (5) and (6) to obtain the relationship between output and inflation that we are looking for:

$$\pi = \pi^* + \alpha\epsilon(Y - Y_p) \qquad \alpha\epsilon > 0 \tag{7}$$

Equation (7) presents, in an exceedingly simple form, a key macroeconomic relation sometimes referred to as the *price equation*. We want to think of it as an aggregate supply schedule to emphasize the connection with Chaps. 11 and 12.

The aggregate supply function (7) has two important properties. First, current inflation is related to inflationary expectations. The higher the expected rate of inflation, the higher the actual rate of inflation. Second, the state of the labor market is reflected in current inflation. A high GNP gap, $Y - Y_p < 0$, reduces the inflation rate below the expected inflation rate. By contrast, a level of output beyond full employment, $Y - Y_p > 0$, means overemployment and, therefore, inflation at a rate greater than π^*.

To emphasize the connection with Chap. 11, consider briefly the case where inflationary expectations are zero as we explicitly assumed in that chapter. Then the aggregate supply schedule is as shown in Fig. 13-4. At full employment, $Y = Y_p$, inflation is zero because wages are constant.

FIGURE 13-4 THE AGGREGATE SUPPLY SCHEDULE

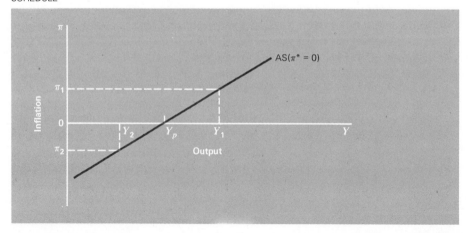

There are neither inflationary expectations nor unemployment or over-employment acting through wage changes on cost and prices. For an output level above potential, such as Y_1, the implied overemployment causes money wages to rise and is thus reflected in inflation. Conversely, for an output level Y_2, which implies unemployment, we have falling wages and, therefore, falling prices or deflation.

The extent to which the GNP gap operates on inflation is reflected in the slope of the aggregate supply schedule or the term $\alpha\epsilon$ in Eq. (7). This term reflects the relation between unemployment and the GNP gap α, and the sensitivity of money wages to unemployment ϵ. The higher either of these parameters, the higher the rate of inflation that is associated with a given level of the gap, or, in other words, the steeper the aggregate supply schedule. There is still another way of putting the same issue. The steeper the aggregate supply schedule, the more adverse the *inflation-output trade off*; that is, the more inflation we get from a given expansion in output and employment.

Expectations

The role of inflationary expectations in influencing wage formation and therefore costs and prices is central to an understanding of the inflation process. Because labor contracts fix nominal wages for a given period ahead, labor will be concerned about its real wage over the period of the contract. A given money wage rate negotiated today will have less purchasing power two years from now if the inflation rate is 10 percent, than if it is zero. It is obvious therefore that labor and firms will look ahead when they set current wages to the inflation they expect over the period of the contract.

Typically, the environment is not one where the inflation rate has been constant for a long period and can be accurately predicted. More likely the inflation rate in the recent past has varied somewhat and future inflation cannot be predicted with great accuracy. Given that uncertainty, we would expect the expectation of inflation to be based in part on inflation rates actually experienced in the recent past. Labor would seek wage increases equal to the "habitual" rate of inflation that has actually been experienced in the recent past, and thus find some insurance against the expected price increases.

Before proceeding to discuss how expectations are formed, we briefly reemphasize the critical role of inflationary expectations in the inflation process. Expectations are so critical because the simple fact that people expect inflation causes inflation. When wages increase because inflation is expected, costs increase and produce inflationary pressure as firms seek to pass on cost increases into higher prices.

When inflationary expectations are slow to adjust, monetary and fiscal policies will have quite large effects on the level of output, and relatively small effects on the inflation rate. Two instances from recent economic history are relevant here. First, in the sixties, aggregate demand kept rising, partly as a result of the 1964 tax cut, and then as a result of increases in government spending and monetary growth that were associated with the Vietnam war. However, inflation was very slow to develop, largely because the long period of moderate inflation of the late fifties and early sixties kept down expected inflation. Second, repeated attempts in the seventies to reduce actual inflation by restrictive monetary policy proved largely ineffective, resulting in unemployment rather than lower inflation. Expectations of inflation did not come down fast, and therefore actual inflation could not be reduced without substantially increasing unemployment.

Now we return once more to expectations formation. There is no generally accepted way in which to model inflationary expectations.[5] Traditionally, inflationary expectations have been thought of as some average of past inflation rates. One example would be a weighted average of inflation rates in the last four years, with relatively heavy weight on the more recent past. We show such a weighted average for the postwar period in Chart 13-4, in which we observe the gradual upturn of this measure of inflationary expectations in the late sixties, and the slow downturn after the 1973–1974 inflationary explosion. There is no particular advantage that attaches to a four-year average, nor any evidence that makes us select that number. Nor need expectations be based only on the past behavior of the inflation rate. Any information that is available about the future course of monetary and fiscal policies would also be relevant to inflationary expectations.

For the purpose of the next few sections we will make the simplifying assumption that the expected rate of inflation is equal to last period's rate of inflation:

$$\pi^* = \pi_{-1} \tag{8}$$

We adopt this oversimplified formulation only because it is easy to manipulate. Taking a long-run average over three to five years is more appropriate and important as a practical matter but really does not change the theory. All it does is to draw out the adjustment process over time and make for longer lags.

Later we will substitute for Eq. (8) an alternative assumption which bases expectations of inflation on the growth rate of the money stock:

$$\pi^* = m \tag{8a}$$

The argument here is that, since people know that monetary growth affects the inflation rate, they take account of that growth in forming their expectations. Like Eq. (8), Eq. (8a) is a very simplified formulation, but it will

[5]See Robert M. Solow, "Down the Phillips Curve with Gun and Camera," in David A. Belsley, et al. (eds.), *Inflation, Trade and Taxes*, Ohio State University Press, 1976.

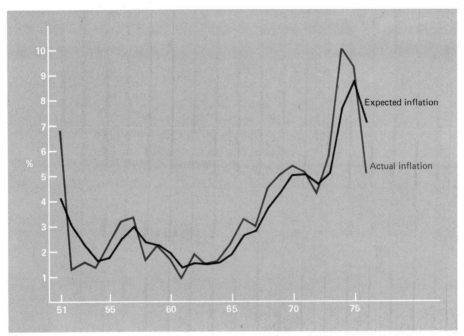

CHART 13-4 ACTUAL AND EXPECTED INFLATION. (*Note:* The expected rate of inflation is a four-year weighted average formed as follows: $\pi^* = 0.5\pi_{-1} + 0.3\pi_{-2} + 0.15\pi_{-3} + 0.05\pi_{-4}$, where the π_{-i} are the annual rates of inflation of the GNP deflator. Data from the Federal Reserve Bank of St. Louis.)

help us see how important expectations are to the dynamic behavior of the economy.

In Fig. 13-5 we return to the aggregate supply schedule to show the role of expectations. We have reproduced the aggregate supply schedule AS_0, drawn for a zero expected inflation rate from Fig. 13-3. An increase in the expected rate of inflation from zero to, say, $\pi^* = 5$ percent, will shift up the aggregate supply schedule so that now at full employment we would have a 5 percent rate of inflation. This is shown by the aggregate supply schedule AS_1. Conversely, a reduction in expected inflation below zero— the expectation of deflation—will shift the aggregate supply schedule downward to AS_2. The schedule AS_2, drawn in Fig. 13-5, reflects the expectation of prices falling at the rate of 2 percent. For higher rates of expected deflation, the aggregate supply schedule would shift down further.

Embodying inflationary expectations in the aggregate supply schedule completes the picture of inflation and output on the supply side. Inflation

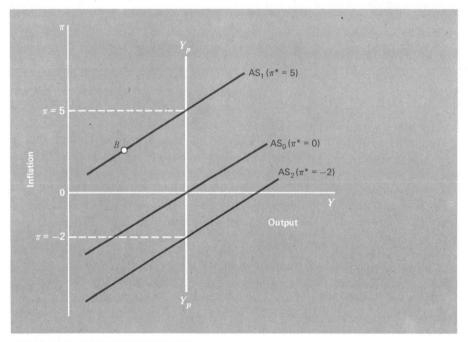

FIGURE 13-5 AGGREGATE SUPPLY AND
EXPECTED INFLATION

depends on the state of the labor market, here measured by the GNP gap, and on inflationary expectations. Inflation is higher the higher is actual output relative to potential output and the higher is expected inflation.

It is quite possible that we can have both inflation and unemployment (point *B*). That possibility arises because the expectation of inflation causes wages and prices to rise, and unemployment may not exert sufficient dampening pressure on wage settlements to restore full employment. Clearly this is the combination of facts observed in the seventies where persistent unemployment appeared together with inflation.

In concluding this section, we comment on a critical aspect of the aggregate supply schedule: in the long run the aggregate supply schedule is vertical at the full-employment level. The long-run aggregate supply schedule is the schedule Y_pY_p: the level of output is independent of the rate of inflation, as is the rate of unemployment. The reason for these strong results—sometimes referred to as the *long-run vertical Phillips curve*—is that expectations will ultimately adjust to the actual rate of inflation. Thus, by Eq. (7), equality of actual and expected inflation implies that output is at the full-employment level whatever the rate of inflation. Deviations of output from the full-employment level require expectational errors or deviations of the inflation rate from its habitual level. In the long run, by definition, there are no errors in expectations and therefore output is at the full-employment level.

*13-4 AGGREGATE DEMAND

The preceding section showed that aggregate supply theory can be extended in a simple way to link output and the rate of inflation. Inflationary pressure on the supply side arises from expectations and/or overemployment. In this section we establish a relationship between aggregate demand and inflation.

Current aggregate demand depends on autonomous spending, including fiscal influences, and the real quantity of money. In Chaps. 4 and 12 we saw that we can write aggregate demand as a function of fiscal and monetary variables:

$$Y^d = Y^d\left(F, \frac{M}{P}\right) \qquad (9)$$

Here F is a measure of fiscal policy, which we take to be represented by the full-employment budget deficit. The aggregate demand function in Eq. (9) states that an increase in the full-employment deficit increases real aggregate spending, as does an increase in the real money supply. An increase in the real money supply exerts an expansionary effect on spending because it reduces interest rates and thereby leads to an increase in real spending.

We will now restate aggregate demand as depending on the growth rate of real balances and fiscal policy. From Eq. (9), aggregate demand increases when the full-employment budget deficit expands and when real balances increase.

$$\Delta Y^d = \gamma f + \phi(m - \pi) \qquad (10)$$

In Eq. (10) the change in aggregate demand ΔY^d depends on the *change* in fiscal policy f and on the growth rate of real money balances $m-\pi$. The growth rate of real money balances is equal to the growth rate of nominal balances less the rate of inflation. (Assume prices increase by 6 percent but the nominal quantity of money increases by 10 percent. In that case the real quantity of money increases by 4 percent.) The terms γ and ϕ translate changes in the full-employment deficit and in real balances into changes in income, and therefore correspond to the fiscal and monetary multipliers studied before.

Now what is the interpretation of Eq. (10)? If fiscal policy is expansionary, aggregate demand will rise. Thus an increase in the full-employment deficit, by increased spending or reduced taxes, clearly raises aggregate demand. Similarly, if the real money supply grows, because nominal money grows faster than prices, the increased real money balances will raise aggregate spending and make it larger than it was last period. We can underline that fact by writing aggregate demand this period, Y_d, as output (aggregate demand) last period, Y_{-1}, plus the change in demand that arises from current changes in monetary and fiscal variables:[6]

$$Y^d = Y_{-1} + \alpha f + \phi(m - \pi) \tag{10a}$$

where we have substituted $\Delta Y^d = Y^d - Y_{-1}$.

We immediately recognize from Eq. (10a) that we now have a relationship between aggregate demand and the rate of inflation. Given last period's income, the change in fiscal policy, and the growth rate of money $(Y_{-1}, f,$ and $m)$, we are left with a relationship between current demand and the current rate of inflation. Equation (10a) shows that the higher the rate of inflation, the lower is the level of aggregate demand (again, *given* $Y_{-1}, f,$ m). There is a very simple explanation for this relationship. Given the growth rate of money m, the higher the rate of inflation, the lower is the growth rate of real money balances, and therefore the smaller the increase in aggregate demand. Indeed, with inflation in excess of the growth rate of money, $m - \pi < 0$, real balances are declining and therefore interest rates are increasing. In this case current demand falls short of last period's demand because inflation has cut down the real money supply and thereby raised interest rates.

In Fig. 13-6 we plot the aggregate demand schedule on the assumption that current changes in fiscal policy are zero, $f=0$. The aggregate demand schedule is downward-sloping. Given the growth rate of money, a lower rate of inflation implies that real balances are higher and that therefore the interest rate is lower and spending is higher. The negative slope results from this connection between lower inflation and higher spending.

Given the negative slope of the curve, what determines its location? We observe from Eq. (10a) (remember that we assume $f = 0$) that when $m = \pi$, current aggregate demand equals last period's output, $Y^d = Y_{-1}$. Thus the aggregate demand schedule passes through point B in Fig. 13-6 where, at an inflation rate equal to the monetary growth rate, we have no change in real balances and therefore no change in spending. For a lower rate of inflation, current spending exceeds last period's. Conversely, for a higher rate of inflation, current spending falls short of last period's.

The aggregate demand schedule in Fig. 13-6 is drawn on the assumption of a given growth rate of money m and zero change in fiscal policy. We now briefly ask how changes in these policy variables would affect aggregate demand. In Fig. 13-7 we show that an increase in monetary growth to m' will shift upward the aggregate demand schedule to pass through point

---

[6]In going from Eq. (10) to Eq. (10a), we substitute Y_{-1} in place of Y_{-1}^q. This is justified because, as we shall see below, last period's output was equal to last period's aggregate demand.

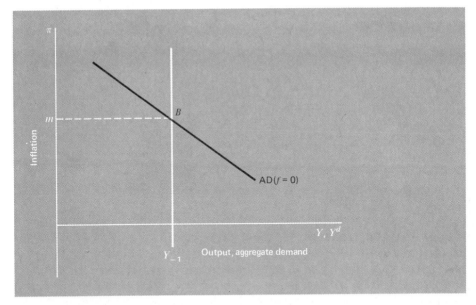

FIGURE 13-6 THE AGGREGATE
DEMAND SCHEDULE

FIGURE 13-7 THE EFFECT OF
INCREASED MONETARY GROWTH ON
AGGREGATE DEMAND

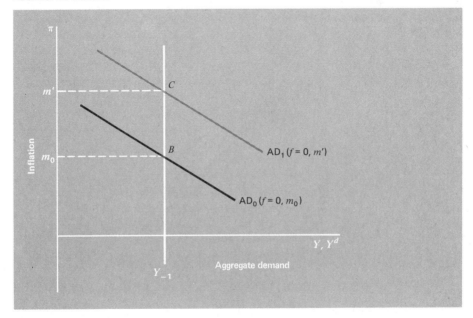

C. With higher monetary growth we need higher inflation if real balances and, therefore, aggregate demand are to remain constant over time. From Eq. (10*a*) it is apparent that an expansionary fiscal policy will likewise shift the aggregate demand schedule up and to the right. For each growth rate of nominal money and rate of inflation, a fiscal expansion provides extra expansionary force (over and above that from changing real balances) and therefore raises aggregate demand. Conversely, a move toward fiscal tightness shifts the aggregate demand schedule down and to the left.

In summary:

1 Current aggregate demand depends on past aggregate demand and the current stimulus that comes from fiscal expansion or growth in real balances.
2 The aggregate demand curve is a downward-sloping relationship between the inflation rate and the level of output.
3 The position of the aggregate demand curve depends on last period's output (Y_{-1}), the growth rate of money (m), and changes in the full employment deficit (f). Increases in any of Y_{-1}, m, or f increase aggregate demand and shift the aggregate demand curve upwards.

*13-5 DETERMINING THE INFLATION RATE AND OUTPUT LEVEL IN THE SHORT RUN

To determine the inflation rate and the level of output in the short run, we have only to put together our aggregate demand and supply curves. This is done in Fig. 13-8. The intersection of the aggregate supply and demand curves at point E determines the inflation rate and the level of output this period, π_0 and Y_0, respectively.

Now, on what do the current rate of inflation and the level of output depend? They clearly depend on the positions of the aggregate supply and demand curves. Thus changes in any of the variables which shift the aggregate supply and demand curves will affect the current inflation and output levels.

In Fig. 13-9 we show the consequences of a shift in the aggregate supply curve. Assume the AS curve shifts upwards as a result of an increase in the expected rate of inflation. The upward shift produces a higher inflation rate and lower level of output. Instead of the economy being at point E, it is at E_1. Thus we see that an increase in the expected inflation rate produces a (smaller) increase in the actual inflation rate and that it also causes a decline in output. The increase in the expected inflation rate causes wages to increase, and therefore makes the inflation rate associated with any level of output higher. Given the higher inflation rate, the demand for goods is reduced so that the level of output falls.

In Fig. 13-10 we show the consequences of an upward shift in the aggregate demand curve. The equilibrium of the economy shifts from E to

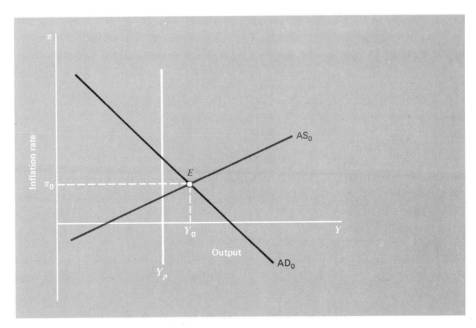

FIGURE 13-8   THE DETERMINATION OF
THE INFLATION RATE AND OUTPUT IN THE
SHORT RUN

FIGURE 13-9   THE SHORT-RUN EFFECTS
OF A SHIFT IN THE AGGREGATE SUPPLY
CURVE

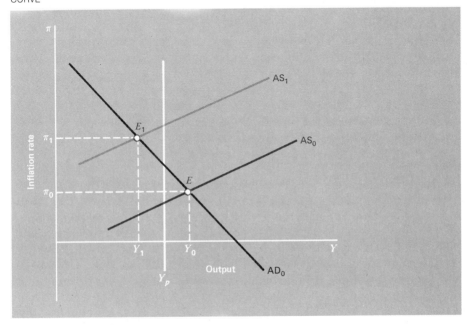

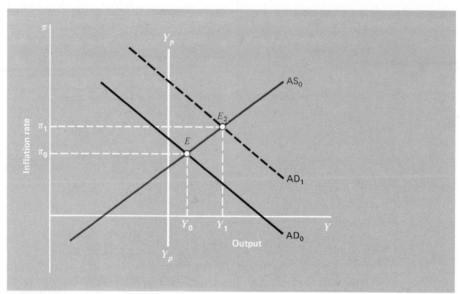

FIGURE 13-10 THE SHORT-RUN
EFFECTS OF A SHIFT IN THE AGGREGATE
DEMAND CURVE

E_2, at which point both the inflation rate and the level of output are higher than they were at E. Upward shifts in the aggregate demand curve therefore result in increases in both the level of output and the inflation rate in the short run. We have already seen what determines the position of the AD curve and therefore what causes it to shift. The higher the lagged level of income Y_{-1}, the higher the aggregate demand curve; the greater the change in the full-employment budget deficit f, the higher the AD curve; and the higher the growth rate of money, the higher the AD curve. Therefore the inflation rate is higher and the level of output is higher in the short run, the higher last period's income, the greater the change in the full-employment budget deficit, and the greater the growth rate of money.

We thus have four factors affecting the inflation rate and the level of output in the short run: the expected rate of inflation and the three variables that determine the location of the aggregate demand curve. If policy makers want to change the behavior of the inflation rate in the short run, they have to try to affect the expected inflation rate, or the change in the full-employment budget surplus, or the growth rate of the money supply. The level of income last period is not something that can be changed by policy makers today.

This analysis, like that of Chap. 12, points to the potential role of *supply management*. If policy makers want to reduce the inflation rate in the short run, then they can use *demand management* policies which shift the AD curve downwards. But such policies will tend to reduce output along with the inflation rate. If policies could be found which would shift the AS curve, those would make it possible to reduce the inflation rate without reducing the level of income.

We shall now turn to the analysis of the effects of monetary and fiscal policy on the rate of inflation and the level of output in the short and long runs in Secs. 13-6 and 13-7.

*13-6 THE ADJUSTMENT TO AN INCREASE IN MONETARY GROWTH

We have now looked at the short-run impact of shifts in the aggregate demand and supply schedules and can proceed to study the adjustment process that links short-run and long-run equilibria. We deal in this section with the adjustment to an increase in the growth rate of money.

We start by using the expectations equation (8) in which the expected rate of inflation is the rate of inflation that occurred last period. Substituting that assumption about expectations into the aggregate supply curve, Eq. (7), we have

$$\pi = \pi_{-1} + \alpha\epsilon(Y - Y_p) \tag{7a}$$

as the aggregate supply curve. In this section we shall assume that the full-employment deficit is kept constant $(f = 0)$, so that the aggregate demand curve is described by Eq. (10b):

$$Y^d = Y_{-1} + \phi(m - \pi) \tag{10b}$$

The point of departure of our analysis is the long-run equilibrium at point E in Fig. 13-11. What does long-run equilibrium imply in the model

FIGURE 13-11 LONG-RUN EQUILIBRIUM

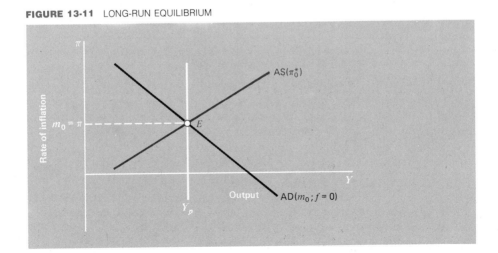

shown by Eqs. $(7a)$ and $(10b)$? Long-run equilibrium implies: (1) the economy is at full employment, $Y = Y_p$; (2) actual and expected inflation are equal, $\pi = \pi^*$; (3) the rate of inflation is equal to the growth rate of money, $\pi = m_0$; (4) aggregate demand equals aggregate supply, $Y^d = Y$; and (5) aggregate demand remains constant over time, $Y^d = Y_{-1}$.

These conditions are an exhaustive description of the equilibrium, but they are not all independent. Start with Eq. $(7a)$ and note that equality of the actual and expected inflation rates implies that output is at the full-employment level.

Next consider Eq. $(10b)$ and note that equality of the growth rate of money and the rate of inflation, $\pi = m$, implies that current output equals past output. In other words, over time, aggregate demand remains constant. Finally, the condition that demand equals supply ensures that aggregate demand is equal to full-employment output.

Diagrammatically, in long-run equilibrium, the supply and demand curves intersect at point E in Fig. 13-11. At E, the inflation rate is equal to the growth rate of money (by condition 3), and output is at its potential level (by condition 1).

Now, starting from a position of full equilibrium at point E in Fig. 13-12, the growth rate of money rises from m_0 to m' and stays at that higher level indefinitely. In Fig. 13-12 the increased monetary growth is shown by an upward shift of the aggregate demand schedule to AD_1. The impact effect, with as yet unchanged expectations, and therefore an unchanged supply schedule, is to raise both the rate of inflation and real output. Inflationary expectations, because they are sticky, keep down the actual rate of inflation and prevent it from responding fully to the increased monetary growth. Consequently, the real money supply expands and real output rises to meet the increased demand for goods. This takes us to point E_1; however, the economy will not remain at point E_1. The increased rate of inflation will be reflected in higher inflationary expectations and therefore in an upward shift of the aggregate supply schedule. Similarly, the expansion in real output is reflected in an upward shift of the aggregate demand schedule.

Accordingly, in period 2, the period after the rise in the growth rate of money, both the aggregate supply and demand curves shift. The aggregate supply curve shifts because the expected rate of inflation has increased— and π^* has increased because the inflation rate at E_1 is higher than the inflation rate at E. We can tell precisely how the supply curve shifts by looking at Eq. $(7a)$. The new aggregate supply curve AS_2 crosses the Y_p line at precisely the inflation rate that occurred in period 1. The aggregate demand curve shifts because of the increase in lagged output, as can be seen from Eq. $(10b)$. The extent to which it shifts can also be calculated precisely. By looking at Eq. $(10b)$ it will be seen that $\pi = m$, when Y is equal to Y_{-1}. Therefore, at the inflation rate m', the output level on AD_2 is exactly equal to Y_{-1}, which is the output level at E_1. (Be sure you see this in Fig. 13-12.)

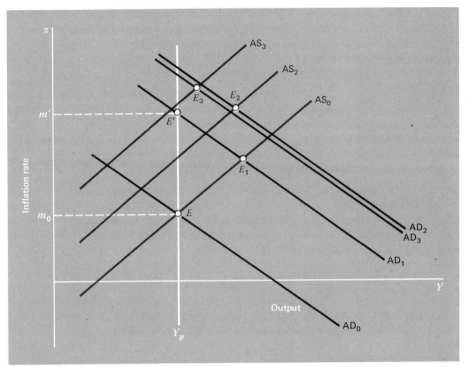

FIGURE 13-12 SHORT-RUN
ADJUSTMENT TO A CHANGE IN THE
GROWTH RATE OF MONEY

In period 2 the inflation rate and level of output are determined at E_2. The inflation rate is undoubtedly higher than it was at E_1, while we have shown the output level at E_2 to be less than output in the previous period. However, it is possible that output in period 2 could exceed output in period 1, depending on the slopes of the aggregate supply and demand curves.[7]

In subsequent periods the two curves continue to shift. As long as the inflation rate keeps rising, the aggregate supply curve will keep rising, since the actual inflation rate last period determines today's expected rate of inflation. And as long as the level of output keeps rising, the aggregate demand curve will keep shifting up, because of the presence of the lagged output term in the aggregate demand curve. When the level of output begins to drop, the aggregate demand curve starts to shift down. For instance, because the level of output at E_2 is less than that at E_1, the aggregate demand curve shifts down from AD_2 to AD_3 in period 3. Period 3's

---

[7]In the problem set, we ask you to draw a diagram similar to Fig. 13-12 in which output at E_2 will exceed output at E_1.

equilibrium is at E_3, with an inflation rate higher than in period 2 and an output level below that of period 2. In fact, in both periods 2 and 3, the rate of inflation is even higher than it will eventually be in the long-run equilibrium at E'.

It is not worth following the shifts of the aggregate supply and demand curves during the adjustment process in much further detail. Figure 13-13 shows the pattern of adjustment as the economy moves from E_1, its first-period equilibrium, to the eventual long-run equilibrium at E'. We do not include the shifting supply and demand curves that underlie the pattern of adjustment shown so as to keep the diagram clear. And we have, for con-venience, smoothed the time path of adjustment. The first few points E_1, E_2, and E_3 that we traced in Fig. 13-12 are also shown in Fig. 13-13.

There are two special features of the adjustment process that deserve comment, and that can be seen in Fig. 13-13. First, given the expectations assumption (8), the economy does not proceed directly to the point of long-run equilibrium E'. Rather, the level of output will fall below Y_p at some stages in the adjustment process as a result of shifts in the aggregate supply and demand curves, and will, at other times, be above Y_p, as it is at E_1, E_2, and E_3. Similarly, the rate of inflation will sometimes be above its long-run

FIGURE 13-13 THE ADJUSTMENT PATH
TO AN INCREASE IN MONETARY GROWTH

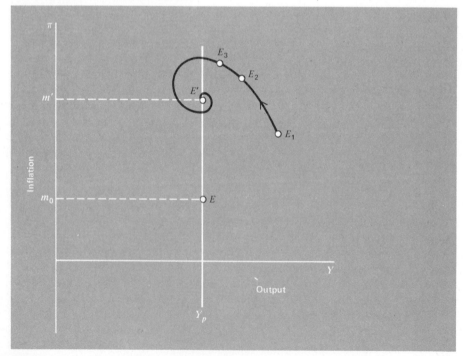

equilibrium level m', as it is at E_2, and sometimes below it, as at E_1. Eventually, the economy settles down to its long-run rate of inflation m' and output level Y_p.

The second feature of the adjustment process that is important is that in the course of the adjustment, there are times at which output decreases, while the inflation rate increases. For instance, between E_2 and E_3, in Figs. 13-12 and 13-13, the inflation rate increases while output decreases. This inverse relationship between output and inflation is a result of the shifts of the supply curve caused by changes in the expected rate of inflation.

The inverse relationship between the rate of inflation and the level of output at some stages of the adjustment process predicted by our theory is significant, for it often occurs in practice. However, it is widely believed that the Phillips curve implies that there cannot be such an inverse relationship. If one ignores the role of expected inflation in the Phillips curve, it is easy to conclude that periods in which the inflation rate and output move in opposite direction—and particularly periods in which output is falling while the inflation rate is rising—cannot be explained by economics. In fact, in 1969–1970 and 1973–1974, when both inflation and unemployment were increasing, there were complaints in the press that the laws of economics no longer seemed to be working.[8] There is no law of economics that says the inflation rate and the level of output move in the same direction at all times. We should not be surprised if the level of output and the inflation rate move in opposite directions at some stages of the adjustment process. That is one of the major lessons of this section; it is the phenomenon of *stagflation*—stagnation with inflation.

The other major lesson, which we have mentioned several times, is that the details of the adjustment process depend on the formation of expectations. In a general way, it is easy to see that the details of the economy's adjustment must depend on the formation of expectations, since changing expectations are responsible for the way in which the aggregate supply curve shifts. We shall make the point more specifically now, however, by using the expectation assumption (8a), namely, that the expected rate of inflation is equal to the growth rate of the money stock.

Perfect Foresight Expectations

The analysis so far has assumed that expected inflation is equal to last period's actual rate of inflation. This was taken up as a simple representation of expectations based on an average of past inflation rates. Now we change the expectations assumption quite radically. We assume here that people use their information about monetary growth to form inflationary expectations. Specifically, we assume in Eq. (8a) that people look at the

[8]See, for example, the Sunday *New York Times* for Jan. 25, 1970, sec. 4, pp. 1–2, "Impossible! Recession *and* Rising Prices?"

long-run relation between monetary growth and inflation explored in Sec. 13-1, and thus have an expected rate of inflation equal to the growth rate of money:

$$\pi^* = m \tag{8a}$$

If expectations are based on the growth rate of the money stock, then the growth rate of the money stock has to be known. We therefore assume that the central bank announces the growth rate of the money stock it will be producing in each period, as it now does in the United States.

If the expected rate of inflation is equal to the growth rate of the money stock in each period, we can write the aggregate supply curve, Eq. (7), as

$$\pi = m + \alpha\epsilon(Y - Y_p) \tag{7b}$$

The aggregate demand curve continues to be Eq. (10b).

Once again we start in a situation of long-run equilibrium, with inflation rate m_0 and output level Y_p, in Fig. 13-14. Now the growth rate of the money stock is to be increased from m_0 to m' in period 1, and that change is announced. The aggregate demand curve moves up to AD_1, precisely as it

FIGURE 13-14 SHORT-RUN ADJUSTMENT TO A CHANGE IN THE GROWTH RATE OF MONEY WITH PERFECT FORESIGHT EXPECTATIONS

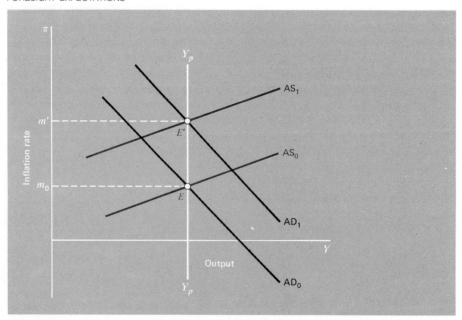

did in Fig. 13-12. At the point where Y is equal to Y_p, on AD_1, the inflation rate is equal to m', as can be seen from Eq. $(10b)$. The aggregate demand curve shifts upwards by precisely the increase in the growth rate of money. So far nothing has changed from the situation in Fig. 13-12.

But how does the aggregate supply curve behave? In Fig. 13-12 the AS curve did not shift in period 1, since the expected rate of inflation there was last period's rate of inflation. Now, however, the change in the growth rate of money causes a change in expectations, and the AS curve therefore shifts in period 1, to AS_1. It shifts upwards by precisely the increase in the growth rate of money, as can be seen from Eq. $(7b)$. When Y is equal to Y_p, the rate of inflation on AS_1 is equal to m'. The AS and AD curves therefore move up by exactly the same distance.

That means that the rate of inflation in period 1 is exactly equal to m', and that the level of output is equal to Y_p. The first-period equilibrium in Fig. 13-14 is at E'. What happens to output and inflation in subsequent periods? They do not change at all. There is no force tending to shift either curve.

We have just shown that the economy's adjustment to a change in the growth rate of money is immediate when expectations are formed according to Eq. $(8a)$. The economy moves in one period to its long-run equilibrium and stays there.

In this case, the expectations formula $(8a)$, in which expectations are based solely on the growth rate of money, turned out to be right. That is, expectations of inflation were that the rate of inflation would be equal to the growth rate of money. And the actual rate of inflation in each period was indeed equal to the growth rate of money. Expectations which turn out to be correct are called *perfect foresight expectations*, and sometimes *rational expectations*.[9]

The analysis we have just undertaken shows that changes in the growth rate of money have no *real* effects—effects on the level of output—in this economy if expectations adjust instantly to the actual behavior of inflation. In particular, if expectations show perfect foresight, changes in the growth rate of money are immediately reflected in the rate of inflation, and do not affect the growth rate of output and the unemployment rate. Here errors in expectations are responsible for the short-run real effects of money.

In a context such as that of Chap. 11 in which prices do not adjust instantly to demand changes, monetary changes can have real effects through channels other than errors in expectation. If wage rises are passed on only slowly into price changes as they were in Chap. 11, then a change in the growth rate of money would be reflected instantly in the growth rate of wages—if expectations are based on the growth rate of money—but

---

[9]We shall not pursue perfect foresight expectations in detail (including a subtlety about a once-and-for-all jump in the price level) here, but note again (as in Chap. 9) that such and similar expectations and their policy implications are being intensively studied by economists. See Thomas J. Sargent and Neil Wallace, "Rational Expectations and the Theory of Economic Policy," *Journal of Monetary Economics*, April 1976.

would only slowly be passed through into prices. In that case, prices would not adjust instantly to the change in the growth rate of money, and the aggregate supply curve would not shift up by the increase in the growth rate of money, as it does in Fig. 13-14. Output would then increase as a consequence of the increase in the growth rate of money.

Realistically, stickiness of wage and price adjustment remains an essential feature of the adjustment process.

Summary

The main points made in this section were:
1 If inflationary expectations are based in a simple way on the past behavior of the inflation rate, then an increase in the rate of growth of the money stock increases both the inflation rate and the level of output in the short run. Both the rate of inflation and the level of output continue to fluctuate thereafter, tending eventually to move to the long-run equilibrium of the economy.
2 There are stages in the adjustment process of the economy to a change in the growth rate of money at which the level of output and the rate of inflation move in opposite directions. This occurs as a result of shifts in the aggregate supply curve caused by changes in expectations.
3 If expectations show perfect foresight, the response of the simple economy studied in this section to a change in the growth rate of money is immediate. The economy moves in one period to its long-run equilibrium position and stays there when the growth rate of money changes. In that case, output remains at its potential level throughout and the change in the growth rate of money affects only the inflation rate and not real income.
4 Even if expectations do show perfect foresight, changes in the growth rate of money can have effects on the level of real output if prices adjust only slowly to changes in demand. Such a mechanism was included in Chap. 11 and omitted here only to keep the analysis relatively simple.

*13-7 FISCAL POLICY CHANGES

In the long run, the full-employment budget deficit is constant, and therefore f, the change in the full-employment deficit, is zero. Hence the inflation rate is in the long run independent of fiscal policy, and is determined solely by the growth rate of money, as we saw in Sec. 13-1.

Fiscal policy may affect the level of potential output but not through channels we have been considering in this chapter. The route through which fiscal policy can affect the level of potential output is by affecting the mix of investment and consumption. If fiscal policy encourages investment, then the capital stock and level of potential output are likely to be higher in the long run, and so fiscal policy affects potential output. In this

chapter, though, we have not included sufficient detail to study that alloca-
tive (between consumption and investment) role of fiscal policy. Instead
we treated fiscal policy as simply a method of affecting aggregate
demand—and that is the way we shall continue to treat it in examining its
short-run effects.

We will now consider what happens when there is an increase in the
full-employment budget deficit, so that f, our measure of the *change* in the
full-employment deficit, becomes positive in period 1. Thereafter it reverts to zero. We assume the growth rate of money is constant at m_0. In
the long run, we know, there are no effects of the fiscal policy change on
either the inflation rate or the level of output.

Figure 13-15 is used for the analysis of the short-run effects of the
increase in the full-employment deficit. The initial increase in the deficit
moves the aggregate demand curve up from AD_0 to AD_1. We shall assume
here that the expected rate of inflation is equal to last period's rate of
inflation.[10] That ensures that the aggregate supply curve does not shift in

[10]In the problem set, we ask you to carry out this analysis under the alternative expectations
assumption (8a), that the expected inflation rate is equal to the growth rate of money.

FIGURE 13-15 SHORT-RUN EFFECTS OF
FISCAL POLICY

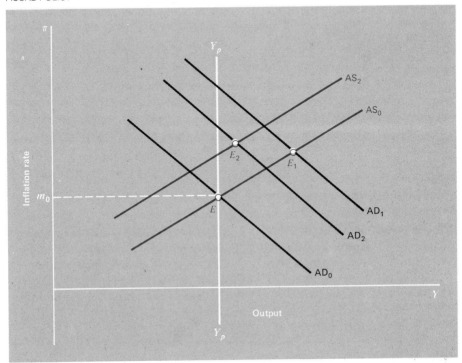

the first period. The first-period equilibrium is, accordingly, at E_1, with both output and the inflation rate above their long-run levels.

Next period both the supply and demand curves shift. The aggregate supply curve shifts up from AS_0 to AS_2 as a result of the change in the expected rate of inflation, which is now equal to last period's inflation rate. The aggregate demand curve moves down to AD_2 because f is no longer positive but rather is at zero—the full-employment deficit is no longer changing. Although lagged output at E_1 is higher than at E—and thus examination of Eq. (10) might suggest that the AD curve could move up—the net effect of the return to zero of f and the increase in Y_{-1} is to move the AD curve down. As a result of these two shifts, the level of output at the second-period equilibrium, E_2, is undoubtedly lower than at E_1, and may even be below the level of potential output. The inflation rate at E_2 may be either higher or lower than at E_1.

In subsequent periods, the rate of inflation and the level of output both continue to change, moving eventually to their long-run equilibrium levels. During the process of adjustment, the inflation rate and the output rate move both above and below their long-run equilibrium levels.

The analysis of both this section and the last makes it very clear that quite complicated patterns of adjustment of the economy can result from very simple assumptions about the way in which expectations adjust, and in which aggregate demand is determined. We have simplified greatly here; for instance, we have assumed that aggregate demand is determined solely by the current fiscal policy and current real balances, rather than also by lagged fiscal policy and real balances. We simplified the dynamics of the Phillips curve, by omitting the influence of lagged unemployment rates. We used a very simple model of expectation formation. And even so, we do not get to tell a very simple story about how the economy adjusts to policy changes—or for that matter to other disturbances. This reinforces the message of Chap. 9 about the difficulties of stabilization policy, for it is precisely the dynamics of the response of the economy to changes in policy that policy makers have to be able to predict if they are to carry out successful policy.

*13-8 AGGREGATE SUPPLY DISTURBANCES AND POLICY CHOICES

This section considers the impact of supply disturbances on inflation and output in the short run. We also discuss the optimal policy response to a supply disturbance which tends to increase the inflation rate and reduce the level of output. There is a question of whether the optimal policy response is to *accommodate* the disturbance, so as to prevent output falling (but at the cost of increased inflation) or perhaps to *offset* the disturbance by preventing the inflation (at the cost of further reducing output).

The particular example we consider is an exogenous, transitory increase in the rate of wage inflation, perhaps because of an unwarranted

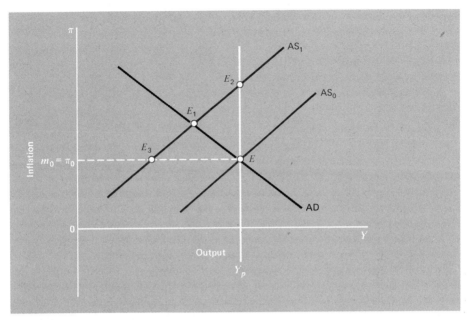

FIGURE 13-16 SUPPLY SHOCKS AND
POLICY RESPONSES

increase in inflationary expectations. In Fig. 13-16 this is shown by an
upward shift of the aggregate supply schedule from AS_0 to AS_1. The increased wage inflation is translated into higher price inflation. Given the
rate of monetary growth m_0, the impact effect of the disturbance is to reduce
output and increase inflation, as can be seen at point E_1.

The reduction in real output occurs because monetary growth falls
short of the higher rate of inflation. Accordingly, aggregate demand declines in response to lower real balances and higher interest rates.
Since, by assumption, the wage disturbance is only transitory, the subsequent adjustment of the economy would return us over time to point E.
Clearly, though, that adjustment process would be time-consuming, and
the question arises whether an active stabilization policy should be attempted.

We can consider two extreme policies. The first is to fully accommodate the supply shock to maintain the level of output constant.
Such a policy requires an increase in aggregate demand through expansionary monetary or fiscal policy. Accommodating policy will move the
economy to point E_2. Inflation increases sharply but output and employment are maintained constant. The alternative policy is oriented toward
keeping the rate of inflation from rising. Such a policy would require
moving to point E_3 in the short run and thus implies a reduction in monetary growth or a tightening of fiscal policy. Thus policy that seeks to main-

tain constant the rate of inflation in the face of supply shocks will actually add to the deflationary impact on output. The response to the 1973–1974 oil price increase in many ways resembled the latter strategy. In that case an adverse shift of the aggregate supply schedule sharply raised inflation and reduced output. The reduction in output was further magnified and the inflationary effect was dampened by a tightening of fiscal policy and continued tightness of monetary policy.

There is no simple answer as to which policy reaction is preferable—accommodation or offsetting. Nor, for that matter, are those the only two policies. Indeed, any combination of the two policies, including doing nothing, constitutes a possible policy reaction. We return to this important issue in Chap. 15, where we discuss the targets of macropolicy—inflation and unemployment—and the relative costs of high unemployment and high inflation.

Offsetting or accommodating policies such as monetary or fiscal policy are aggregate demand policies. An alternative line of policy would seek to cope with the adverse effects of the supply disturbance by supply management. Rather than allowing the supply schedule to shift and thus affect macroeconomic equilibrium, a supply management policy would offset the supply disturbance on the supply side. These policies include wage and price controls, but they include, too, the use of excise taxes and taxes on wages to shift the aggregate supply schedule.

In the case of the wage disturbance being discussed here, we can think of an offsetting reduction in, say, Social Security contributions paid by employers. We remember from Chap. 11 that firms pass on taxes on output or wages into higher prices. To prevent the increased wage inflation from being passed on into increased price inflation, we could lower the employer contribution to Social Security and thus maintain constant the rate of increase in labor cost as seen by employers. In this scenario, take-home pay increases, profits remain unchanged, and the increased take-home pay is financed effectively by a reduction in Social Security tax collection.

This policy response seems very attractive because it promises fully to offset the macroeconomic impact of the wage disturbance. However, there are several difficulties in the use of such policies. First, the reduction in Social Security taxes reduces tax collection and thus brings about an increase in the budget deficit that will somehow have to be financed. An obvious method of financing is to compensate for the reduced payroll tax collection by increasing income taxes, so as to restore budgetary balance and keep the aggregate demand curve from shifting. It would, though, be very difficult to calculate the exact dosages of the two types of tax changes needed to keep both the aggregate supply and demand curves from shifting.

The second objection is that a given structure of taxes, in principle, is set up with the aim of collecting taxes efficiently to finance the budget with a minimum of distorting side effects on the allocation of resources. Adjusting the tax structure to meet the purpose of macroeconomic stabilization may affect resource allocation adversely. There may thus be a tradeoff between efficient resource allocation and improved macroeconomic performance. The dimensions of this tradeoff are not clear at present.

The third objection is that very little is currently known about the way such policies would affect the economy. As we have noted previously, particularly in Chap. 9, there is always the danger that policy actions which seem to be stabilizing may end up being destabilizing.

These objections notwithstanding, supply management has received considerable interest in recent years. The main reason for this interest is that the policies present the possibility of avoiding the choice between more inflation and more unemployment.

13-9 SUMMARY

1   Using fundamentally the aggregate supply-demand framework of Chap. 12, we can draw aggregate supply and demand curves relating the level of output to the inflation rate rather than the price level.

2   The short-run aggregate supply curve is upward-sloping—higher inflation rates are associated with higher levels of output, in the short run. The slope of the aggregate supply curve is greater the more unemployment reacts to changes in output (the larger is α) and the more rapidly wages respond to changes in unemployment (the larger is ϵ). The position of the aggregate supply curve depends on the expected rate of inflation.

3   The long-run aggregate supply curve is vertical.

4   The short-run aggregate demand curve is downward-sloping. It is steeper the less sensitive is aggregate demand to changes in real balances (the smaller is ϕ). The position of the aggregate demand curve depends on lagged output, the rate of change of the full-employment deficit, and the growth rate of the money stock.

5   In the short run, the rate of inflation and the level of output are determined by the expected rate of inflation, the lagged level of output, the change in the full-employment surplus, and the growth rate of the money stock. An increase in the expected rate of inflation increases the actual rate of inflation and reduces output. Increases in the remaining three variables increase both the rate of inflation and output.

6   In the long run, the level of output is equal to potential output. The rate of inflation is equal to the growth rate of the money stock.

7   In the short run, an increase in the growth rate of money produces increases in output and inflation, if expectations are based on the past behavior of inflation. At stages during the adjustment process of the economy to the increased money growth, output and inflation will be moving in the opposite directions.

8   If expectations show perfect foresight, and if prices adjust immediately to wage changes, then the response of the economy to a change in the

growth rate of money is immediate—the economy moves instantly to its new long-run equilibrium, and the changed monetary growth affects only inflation, not output.

9 In the short run, an increase in the full-employment deficit increases both output and the inflation rate. A one-time increase in the full-employment deficit has no permanent effects on the rate of inflation and the level of output.

10 Supply disturbances—increases in materials prices, wage disturbances, excise taxes, and payroll taxes—shift the aggregate supply schedule. A transitory increase in wage inflation reduces output and raises inflation. Policy responses might be accommodating or offsetting on the aggregate demand side. An alternative response involves supply management, that is, a cut in excise taxes or payroll taxes that leaves the macroeconomic equilibrium unaffected.

APPENDIX: OKUN'S LAW

One of the key rules of thumb in macroeconomics is the relationship between the unemployment rate and the GNP gap. This empirical relationship, developed by Arthur Okun, and extensively used by the Kennedy-Johnson Council of Economic Advisers, is stated in Eq. (A1):

$$\text{GNP gap} = a(u - \bar{u}) \tag{A1}$$

where $\bar{u}$ is the natural rate of unemployment, taken in the 1960s to be 4 percent, and the parameter a is about 3. Okun's law as stated in Eq. (A1) says that for every 1 percent unemployment above 4 percent, there is a 3 percent GNP gap. The GNP gap here is defined as the percentage shortfall of actual from full-employment output.

$$\text{GNP gap} \equiv \frac{Y_p - Y}{Y_p} \tag{A2}$$

Equations (A1) and (A2) allow us to calculate the loss in output due to unemployment. For instance, if the unemployment rate is 7 percent, we have a 9 percent (= 3 × 3 percent) GNP gap. With a level of potential output of $1,500 billion, this means a loss in output equal to $135 billion.

Okun's law describes the short-run relationship between the GNP gap and unemployment. The underpinnings of the law can be developed in terms of the determinants of short-run output. We write output as follows:

$$Y = qh(1 - u)\overline{N} \tag{A3}$$

In Eq. (A3), q is the productivity of labor, h is the average number of hours worked, u is the unemployment rate, and $\overline{N}$ is the labor force. Equation (A3) states that short-run output is equal to employment, $h(1 - u)\overline{N}$, times productivity, q. The total number of hours worked in the economy is equal to the fraction of the labor force employed, $1 - u$, times the labor force, $\overline{N}$, times the average number of hours worked, h. Employment times productivity or output per hour gives total output, Y.

Now from Eq. (A3) it is apparent that there are four sources of increased output. Increased output can arise from an increased labor force, increased average hours worked, a reduction in the unemployment rate, or finally an improvement in productivity. Okun's observation was that, in the short-run, these sources of output growth move together, in a relatively stable manner. This fact allows a simple relationship between output and employment, recognizing that unemployment itself is a proxy for all four of the sources of increased output. The detailed breakdown of the contribution to increased output of the various sources when the unemployment rate falls by 1 percent (e.g., from 5 percent to 4 percent) is shown in Table A13-1.

Consider a simple numerical example which illustrates the lesson of Table A13-1. Suppose the unemployment rate drops by two percentage points from 7 percent to 5 percent. Output then rises by 6 percent. Of that 6 percent increase, 2.1 percent arises from the output produced by those who were previously unemployed. Those who were previously employed now work longer each week on average, and that source of growth accounts for 0.8 percent of the increase in output. People who were not previously looking for work enter the labor force and obtain jobs (we discuss this point in more detail immediately below), and their production contributes 1.3 percent to output. Finally, output per hour worked increases, increasing output by the final 1.8 percent.

It is worth noting explicitly that the relationship between changes in output and changes in unemployment that we presented in Chap. 11 in the theory of aggregate supply is entirely consistent with Okun's law. Our theory relating output and unemployment included both changes in hours worked and in productivity, as does Okun's law. The only element of Table A13-1 we did not include is the change in labor force participation.

One important point about Table A13-1 is that increased labor input derives from two sources. The first source is the obvious one of the reduced unemployment rate—putting people who were looking for work back into productive activity. The second source is less obvious. The labor force itself typically increases when the unemployment rate drops. The point is that not all persons out of work are actually measured as "unemployed." To be counted as unemployed, an individual must engage in "specific job-seeking activity within the past four weeks." In a poor labor market, some people stop looking for work and are not counted in the

TABLE A13-1 THE OUTPUT EFFECT OF A 1 PERCENT DROP IN UNEMPLOYMENT

Source of output change		Percent change in output
u	Jobs for the unemployed	1.05
h	Lengthened workweek	0.40
$\overline{N}$	Increased labor force	0.65
q	Improved productivity	0.90
Increase in output		3.00

Source: Arthur Okun, "Upward Mobility in a High-Pressure Economy," *Brookings Papers on Economic Activity*, 2, 1973.

official measures of the labor force. Once the labor market improves as the unemployment rate drops and employment prospects look brighter, such people reenter the labor market and the labor force $\bar{N}$ increases.

A second important point about the table is that a reduction in unemployment, or an increase in labor input, is usually accompanied by an improvement in productivity. Equivalently, productivity and output move in the same direction: output per worker increases when total output increases, and output per worker decreases when total output declines. The basic reason for this stems from the costs to firms of hiring and laying off workers, as discussed in Chapter 11.

Okun's law is only a rule of thumb, not a relationship that holds very precisely at each point in time. Even so, it has proved remarkably sturdy as a simple device to assess the required expansion in output to achieve a given unemployment target. Since the middle sixties, when the analysis was first developed, the unemployment rate taken to represent full employment has increased. Many argue that the full-employment unemployment rate now is more nearly 5 percent than 4 percent. This obviously means that potential output is less than that corresponding to a 4 percent unemployment rate. It does not, however, impair the usefulness of either the concept of potential output and the GNP gap, or the relation between changes in output and changes in unemployment. The recognition of a higher natural rate of unemployment changes GNP targets and unemployment targets, but it does not change the 3:1 rule of thumb.

Finally, we shift to a somewhat longer-run perspective. It is often said that the economy has to grow at 4 percent just to keep the unemployment rate from rising. We want to use Eq. (A3) to show why that should be. Suppose that the labor force were growing at some constant rate, say, 2.1 percent, and the productivity of labor were growing at a constant rate, say, 1.8 percent. These numbers are broadly descriptive of United States experience.

Now, *given* those longer-run growth rates of productivity and the labor force, output will have to grow at 3.9 percent if unemployment is to remain constant. We return to Eq. (A3) and turn it into a relationship among the growth rates of the variables in it:

$$g_Y = g_q + g_h + g_{1-u} + g_N \tag{A4}$$

In Eq. (A4) g with a subscript denotes the growth rate of the particular variable. We shall assume that the number of hours worked per worker is constant, so that g_h is zero, and, accordingly:

$$g_Y = g_q + g_{1-u} + g_N \tag{A4a}$$

Now, what does Eq. (A4a) tell us about the rate of output growth that is required to keep unemployment constant? Given $g_q = 1.8$ percent, and $g_N = 2.1$ percent, we have

$$g_Y = 1.8 + g_{1-u} + 2.1 = 3.9 + g_{1-u} \tag{A4b}$$

If the unemployment rate is to remain constant, we must have $g_{1-u} = 0$ and, accordingly;

$$g_Y = 3.9 \tag{A4c}$$

Equation (A4c) tells us that output has to grow at the sum of the growth rates of the labor force and productivity if unemployment is to remain constant. If output grows more slowly, then unemployment will be increasing.

How do Eq. (A4c) and the statement that the economy has to grow at 4 percent (which is close enough to 3.9 percent) to keep unemployment from rising, relate to the Okun's law relationship between the unemployment rate and deviation of output from the potential output level? All that Eq. (A4c) does is to tell us how fast potential output will be growing, given the assumed behavior of the labor force and productivity. Okun's law applies to short-run deviations of output around the path of potential output.

PROBLEMS

*1   a   Explain how the size of α and the size of ϵ affect the slope of the aggregate supply curve. Be sure to provide an intuitive explanation along with any other explanation.

      b   Why is it the *product* $\alpha\epsilon$ (rather than, for example, the sum $\alpha + \epsilon$) that determines the slope of the AS curve?

2   Explain in words why the expected rate of inflation affects the position of the aggregate supply curve.

3   Suppose we have an economy where real output grows at the rate of 6 percent per year. The nominal quantity of money grows at the rate of 5 percent. The income elasticity of money demand is 0.5.

      a   What is the rate of inflation in long-run equilibrium?

      b   What is the growth rate of nominal income? (Remember that nominal income can grow because prices increase or because real output rises, or both.)

      c   How would your answers to 3a and 3b change if the income elasticity of money demand was unity?

4   Suppose that the rate of inflation is 3 percent, that real wages are rising by 2 percent, and real balances are rising by 4 percent. What is:

      a   The rate of increase of nominal wages?

      b   The rate of growth of the nominal money stock?

*5   How far *upwards* does the aggregate demand curve, Eq. (10a), shift at a given level of income for:

      a   A 1 percent increase in the growth rate of the money stock?

      b   An increase of one unit in f?

      c   A one-unit increase in Y_{-1}?

      Explain why increases in each of those variables shift the AD curve up, and also try to explain the extent to which the curve is shifted in each case—5a, 5b, and 5c.

*6   a   How does the *slope* of the aggregate demand curve determine the short-run effects on the rate of inflation and output of an increase in the growth rate of money—assuming that the expected rate of inflation is unaffected by the change in monetary growth?

      b   How does the slope of the AS curve affect the way in which a change in the growth rate of money changes the rate of inflation and output in the short run?

Provide a verbal explanation along with any diagrams you draw in both cases.

7 a   Suppose that there is a one-time increase in Y_p, which thereafter remains constant. How does that affect the *long-run* inflation rate?

   b   Suppose that Y_p began to grow steadily at a rate $\bar{x}$. How would that affect the long-run rate of inflation?

*8 Draw an aggregate supply-demand diagram like Fig. 13-12, but with a very flat aggregate supply curve. Then, assuming that $\pi^* = \pi_{-1}$, allow the growth rate of money to increase and show how the supply and demand curves shift in the first two periods. Show what happens to the rate of inflation and the level of output in the first two periods, starting from the period in which the growth rate of money increases. Compare your results with those of Fig. 13-12, and explain the reasons for any differences.

*9 In analyzing the effects of a change in f in one period, we assumed that the expected rate of inflation was given by Eq. (8). Now use the alternative assumption of Eq. (8a) that $\pi^* = m$.

   a   Analyze the dynamic consequences of a one-time increase in f, as studied in Fig. 13-15.

   b   Does the expectations assumption, Eq. (8a) show perfect foresight this time? Explain.

10 At the beginning of the chapter, in discussing Chart 13-1, we said that we wanted to be able to explain behavior such as that shown in the chart. How does the analysis of this chapter explain the type of behavior seen in the chart, particularly the periods when the unemployment rate and the inflation rate were increasing together?

14

The Budget,
Government
Financing,
and the
Public Debt

The federal government's spending for 1977 was over $400 billion, or about 22 percent of GNP. The budget deficit for 1976 was nearly $59 billion, which means that the federal government spent about $59 billion more in that year than it received as taxes. The national debt at the end of 1976 was over $400 billion, or over $2,000 for every person in the United States. State and local governments spent about $250 billion in 1976, or 15 percent of GNP, compared with 5.5 percent in 1946. Facts like these are frequently cited in discussions about the size and growth of the government's role in the economy. They naturally cause concern about the way the government affects the economy. But what does a large deficit mean for the behavior of the economy? Is it bound to lead to inflation? Is an ever-growing national debt certain to lead to economic disaster? This chapter will examine these and similar questions.

The chapter discusses a number of questions connected with the budget, government spending, and taxes. In Sec. 14-1 we describe the financing of the federal government budget deficit—that is, how the government pays for the excess of its spending over its income from taxes. In Sec. 14-2 we examine the facts about the federal budget, federal government spending, the financing of that spending, and about the national debt. In Sec. 14-3 we study the effects on the economy of different methods of financing the budget, and the economic significance of the national debt. Section 14-4 discusses state and local government spending and financing. Section 14-5 briefly discusses the issue of the size of the government.

14-1 THE MECHANICS OF FEDERAL GOVERNMENT SPENDING AND FINANCING

In this section we examine how the federal government finances its spending. We are particularly interested in the relationship between the federal government's deficit and changes in the stocks of money and government debt.

How does the government pay for its spending? Directly it pays for most of its spending with checks, drawn on a Federal Reserve bank. Aside from the fact that the check is drawn on a bank in which private individuals do not have accounts, a payment made by the government looks much like a check payment made by anyone else. Like an individual, the federal government must have funds in the accounts on which it writes checks. So the question of how the federal government finances its spending is the same as the question of how the federal government makes sure that it has funds in the bank accounts (at the Federal Reserve System) on which it writes its checks.

The Treasury is the agency of the federal government that collects government receipts and makes payments for the government. The government's accounts at the Federal Reserve System are held and operated by the Treasury. The Treasury receives the bulk of its receipts from taxes.

Tax payments by the private sector are usually made to the Internal Revenue Service, which is a branch of the Treasury. When the Treasury receives the checks by which individuals and firms pay taxes, they are deposited in bank accounts held by the Treasury in private banks—so-called tax and loan accounts—and moved from there to the Treasury's account with the Fed.

In some years, taxes are less than federal government expenditures. Those are the years in which the federal government runs a budget deficit, as in 1975 and 1976. Total government spending consists of spending on goods and services G and on transfers R. Denoting taxes by T and the deficit by DF, with all variables measured in real terms, we know that

$$DF \equiv (G + R) - T \equiv -\text{BuS} \tag{1}$$

Equation (1) reminds us that the budget deficit DF is just the negative of the budget surplus BuS. Thus in 1976, the deficit was $59 billion, or the surplus was minus $59 billion.

Now, how does the Treasury make payments when its tax receipts are insufficient to cover its expenditures? The answer is that it has to borrow. In describing how the Treasury borrows to finance its deficit, we shall step back a moment from the particular institutional arrangements of the United States economy, and talk in general terms of a treasury financing its budget deficit either by borrowing from the public or by borrowing from its central bank. We shall talk as if the treasury can borrow directly from the central bank by selling it securities. Alternatively, it can sell securities (debt) to the public.[1] We shall see later that the process by which the U.S. Federal Reserve finances a deficit by lending to the Treasury is a little more complicated than the process of direct lending we describe, but that nothing essential is lost by our simplifying description of the process.

When the treasury borrows from the private sector, it sells treasury securities or debt to the private sector. In return, it receives checks from individuals and firms (including banks) in exchange for the securities it sells them. These checks are deposited either in treasury accounts at private banks or at the central bank, and can then be spent by the treasury in the same way as tax receipts.

Alternatively, the treasury can borrow from the central bank. This is done by the central bank purchasing some of the debt of the treasury. However, there is a major difference between the treasury's borrowing from the public and from the central bank. When the central bank lends to the treasury by buying treasury debt, it pays for debt by giving the treasury a check on the central bank—that is, by creating high-powered money. When the treasury spends the deposit it has received at the central bank in exchange for its debt, it leaves the private sector with larger holdings of

[1]Foreign central banks and financial institutions buy some U.S. Treasury securities and thus help finance the deficit. We shall treat sales of securities to foreign institutions as sales to the public.

high-powered money. By contrast, when the treasury borrows from the public, it receives and then spends high-powered money, thus leaving the amount of high-powered money in the hands of the public unchanged— except for a brief transition moment between sale of securities and expenditures by the treasury. Since the stock of high-powered money is an important macroeconomic variable, the distinction between selling debt to the public and selling it to the central bank is in fact a critical distinction.

The distinction can be further clarified by noting that treasury sales of securities to the central bank are referred to as *monetizing the debt*, meaning that the central bank creates (high-powered) money to finance the debt purchase. Yet another way of looking at the distinction between sales to (borrowing from) the central bank and the public is the following. We ask ourselves: What is the net change in the private sector's portfolio after the treasury has made *and* financed its expenditures? Consider first the case of borrowing from the public or selling debt to the public. In this case the public holds more debt, having bought the treasury offering, and holds an unchanged quantity of high-powered money since the treasury spends the money it obtains from the debt sale to cover its deficit. Consider next the case where the deficit is financed by sale of debt to the central bank. In this event the private sector's debt holding is unchanged while the holding of high-powered money is increased. The reason is that treasury expenditures were financed by creation of high-powered money on the part of the central bank.

We thus see that the government deficit can be financed in two ways, by sales of securities, or debt, to the private sector, and by borrowing from the central bank. The borrowing from the central bank in turn creates high-powered money. Let ΔB_p be the change in the number of government bonds (securities) held by the private sector, ΔB_f be the change in the number of bonds held by the central bank, and P_b be the price in dollars paid for one bond. Let H be the stock of high-powered money. We have just seen that[2]

$$P \cdot DF = P_b \cdot \Delta B_f + P_b \cdot \Delta B_p \simeq \Delta H + P_b \cdot \Delta B_p \qquad (2)$$

Equation (2) is called the government's *budget constraint*. It states that the nominal budget deficit is financed either by borrowing from the central bank $(P_b \, \Delta B_f)$ or by borrowing from the private sector $(P_b \, \Delta B_p)$. The change in the central bank's holdings of treasury debt causes a corresponding change in high-powered money (ΔH), so that we can say that the budget deficit is financed either by selling debt to the public or by increasing the stock of high-powered money. It is in this sense that the central bank "monetizes" the debt. Note that the government budget constraint (2) also

---

[2]As we saw in Chap. 8, the stock of high-powered money may change for reasons other than open market operations. For that reason we use the symbol for "approximately equal to" ($\simeq$) in Eq. (2). The change in the central bank's holdings of government bonds is only approximately equal to the change in high-powered money.

shows that, for a given value of the deficit, changes in the stock of high-powered money are matched by offsetting changes in the public's holdings of government debt. A positive ΔH matched by a negative $P_b \Delta B_p$ is nothing other than an open market purchase.

The view that the deficit is financed either by selling debt to the public or by increasing the stock of high-powered money is essentially a view that looks at the government sector as a whole, including or "consolidating" the central bank along with the treasury in the government sector. When one thinks of the government sector as a whole, relative to the private sector, the transactions in which the central bank buys debt from the treasury, or lends to the treasury, are seen as mere bookkeeping entries within the government sector.

Now, in many countries it is useful to think of the government sector as a whole, without bothering to distinguish between the actions of the treasury and the central bank. However, in the United States it should always be remembered that the Fed retains considerable power and independence as to how it will act. Indeed, in the United States the Fed does not generally buy debt directly from the Treasury, and so does not directly finance the deficit in the way described above. The great bulk of Fed purchases of debt are made directly from the public. However, that should be thought of as only an institutional detail. For, although the Fed by and large does not buy debt directly from the Treasury, it does so indirectly by buying securities from the public. Suppose that the Fed is conducting open market purchases at the same time as the Treasury is selling debt to the public. The net effect of the combined Treasury sale of debt and Fed open market purchase is that the Fed ends up holding more Treasury debt, which is precisely what would happen if it bought directly from the Treasury.

In the United States the important institutional arrangement is that the Fed is largely responsible for the division of the total deficit DF, in Eq. (2), between the change in high-powered money and the change in government debt held by the private sector. There is no *necessary* association between the size of the government deficit in the United States and increases in the stock of high-powered money. If the Fed does not conduct open market purchases when the Treasury is borrowing, the stock of high-powered money is not affected by the Treasury's deficit.

Nonetheless, there have been occasions in the past when there was a more or less automatic association between Fed open market purchases and Treasury borrowing. This link was most direct when the Fed was essentially committed to maintaining constant the nominal interest rates on government bonds, in the period from 1941 to 1951. As we saw in Chap. 4, an increase in the government deficit tends to increase the nominal interest rate. If the Fed were committed to maintaining constant the nominal interest rate, an increase in the deficit would force it to conduct an open market purchase to keep the nominal interest rate from rising. Thus there was a link between Treasury borrowing and Fed open market purchases.

Any time the Treasury undertook borrowing that would have increased the nominal interest rate in the absence of an increase in the money stock, the Fed was compelled to undertake an open market purchase. The Fed's commitment to maintaining the nominal interest rates on bonds constant ended formally in 1951 in the "Accord" between the Fed and the Treasury.

Even though, after 1951, the Fed had no formal commitment to maintaining constant nominal interest rates, its long-time policy of having target nominal interest rates—which could change from time to time—also led to an association between deficits and Fed open market purchases. For, given the Fed's target interest rates, Treasury borrowing which would have led to interest rate increases, triggered Fed open market purchases to keep the interest rate from rising above its target level. Thus for much of the fifties and sixties there was a link between increased Treasury borrowing and Fed open market purchases.

Recently, the Fed has moved over to policies which concentrate on the behavior of the nominal money stock. As we saw in Chap. 8, the Fed now specifies target growth rates of the money stock. A Fed commitment to producing a given money stock breaks the link between government deficits and the creation of high-powered money. As Sherman J. Maisel, a former governor of the Federal Reserve, notes;

> The Federal Reserve in recent years has given no special consideration to the Treasury's demand for funds when selecting monetary targets. . . . In general, the Federal Reserve policy is that the government must pay the going market rate of interest.[3]

Now the Fed creates high-powered money at a rate that should result in money growing at the target rate, and the change in the stock of high-powered money is therefore not directly associated with the size of the government deficit.

We return now to Eq. (2). We shall treat any indirect purchases of Treasury securities by the Fed—through open market purchases when the Treasury is running a deficit—as direct lending by the Fed to the Treasury. It follows from Eq. (2) that when the budget is not balanced, the Treasury changes the net amount of *claims* on it held by the private sector and the Fed. Those claims are the securities the Treasury sells to the private sector and (indirectly) the Fed, and they represent claims for future interest payments. The total stock of such claims constitutes the *national debt*.[4] When the budget is in deficit, the national debt increases—the stock of claims against the Treasury increases. When the budget is in surplus, the national debt decreases. The Treasury takes in more in taxes than it pays

---

[3]Sherman J. Maisel, *Managing the Dollar*, Norton, 1973, p. 149.

[4]Note that we are not counting in the national debt those claims on the Treasury that are held by government agencies other than the Fed. We regard those claims as canceling out within the government sector.

out, and can use the excess to retire (or buy back) previously issued debt.[5]

The national debt is, as we have seen, a direct consequence of past deficits in the federal budget. The national debt increases when there is a budget deficit and decreases when the budget is in surplus. The way the national debt is divided between private sector claims on the Treasury and high-powered money depends on past monetary policy. If the Fed has financed a large proportion of each deficit in the past, then the proportion of high-powered money to the national debt is large. If the Fed has financed only a small part of each deficit in the past, then the proportion of high-powered money to national debt is small.

The Treasury sells securities more or less continuously. There is, for instance, a weekly Treasury bill auction, at which prospective buyers of Treasury bills (lenders to the federal government) submit sealed bids specifying how much they are prepared to lend at different interest rates. The Treasury sells the amount of Treasury bills it has offered at the auction to the bidders who offer the highest prices, or the lowest interest rates.[6] Longer-term debt issues are less frequent. Issues of Treasury debt are not all made for the purpose of financing the budget deficit. Most debt issues are made to refinance parts of the national debt which are maturing. For example, the Treasury has to pay the amount it borrowed to a Treasury bill holder when the Treasury bill matures. Six months after a 180-day Treasury bill is issued, the Treasury has to pay the face amount of the Treasury bill to the holder. Typically, the Treasury obtains the funds to make those payments by further borrowing. The process by which the Treasury (with the help and advice of the Fed) finances and refinances the national debt is known as *debt management*. Only part of debt management is concerned with financing the current budget deficit. Most of it is concerned with the consequences of past budget deficits.

Summary

Five main points have been made in this section.
1 Federal government spending is financed through taxes and through borrowing, which is necessary when the budget is in deficit.
2 Borrowing may be from the private sector or indirectly from the Federal Reserve System.

[5]Periodically, the Congress votes to raise the maximum amount of the debt the federal government can issue. The amount of debt subject to the ceiling imposed by Congress includes some of the debt owned by federal agencies along with what we are calling the national debt.

[6]Technically, there is no interest paid on Treasury bills. Instead a Treasury bill is a promise by the Treasury to pay a given amount on a given date, say $100 on June 30. Before June 30 the Treasury bill sells for a *discount* at less than $100, with the discount implying a rate of interest. For instance, if the Treasury bill described above sold for $97.50 on January 1, the holder of the bill for six months would earn a little more than 5 percent per annum, or 2.5 percent for six months.

3 Lending to the Treasury by the Fed changes the stock of high-powered money, whereas lending by the private sector to the Treasury, to finance the deficit, does not affect the stock of high-powered money.

4 The stock of claims held by the Fed and the private sector against the Treasury—the national debt—changes with the budget deficit. The national debt increases when there is a budget deficit and decreases when there is a budget surplus.

5 Because the deficit can be financed in two ways, there is no *necessary* connection between the budget deficit and changes in the stock of high-powered money. Equation (2), the government budget constraint, says only that the *sum* of changes in the stock of debt and changes in high-powered money is approximately equal to the budget deficit.

14-2 BUDGETARY FACTS

In this section we briefly review some facts about the federal budget. Chart 14-1 shows the *real* actual and high-employment budgets for the 1952–1976 period.[7] The actual budget was in deficit most of the time since 1965, except during 1969. Before 1965 the actual budget was in surplus more frequently. The high-employment budget behaved rather differently from the actual budget. It was in continuous surplus from 1955 through 1965. The full-employment budget was in deficit from 1965 to 1969 but tended to be in surplus after 1969.

Note that the full-employment budget surplus exceeded the actual budget surplus throughout the period shown except for the years 1965–1968. Remember from the definition of the full-employment budget that it is calculated at "potential output" or 4 percent unemployment. Accordingly, the actual budget surplus exceeds the full-employment surplus whenever the unemployment rate is below 4 percent. This was the case in 1965–1968. Note, too, that the full-employment budget was in surplus even at the end of 1974 as the recession of 1974–1975 began to accelerate. The effects of the tax cut of early 1975 can be seen in the drop of the full-employment surplus in 1975.

Examine next Chart 14-2, which shows the size and Federal Reserve holdings of federal government debt. Changes in the stock of debt correspond to the state of the actual budget surplus. The debt declined during 1956 and 1957, when the budget was in surplus. It declined again in 1960, when the budget was in surplus. The reader should be able to match up other periods of decline in the debt with actual budget surpluses. Similarly, the debt was increasing very rapidly with the budget deficits of 1967–1968 and again from 1970 to 1973. Finally, the largest post-World War II budget deficit, that of 1975, shows up in Chart 14-2, in the very sharp rise in the national debt during 1975.

[7]The high-employment or full-employment budget was introduced in Chap. 3.

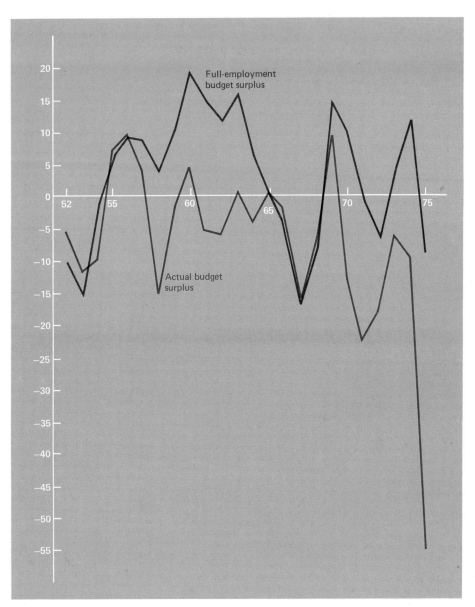

CHART 14-1 ACTUAL AND
FULL-EMPLOYMENT BUDGET SURPLUS
(BILLIONS, 1972 DOLLARS). (*Source:* Federal
Reserve Bank of St. Louis.)

As can be seen from the chart, part of the national debt is held by foreigners. Those foreigners may be either private individuals or official foreign institutions, such as foreign central banks. Foreign central banks hold reserves in the currencies of other countries, as we shall see in Chap.

18.   Part of their reserves are held in dollars, in interest-bearing form, and that is what can be seen in Chart 14-2. Some of the national debt is held by international institutions, such as the World Bank (International Bank for Reconstruction and Development).

Chart 14-2 also shows the Federal Reserve System's holdings of federal debt. There is some similarity between the time patterns of the total debt and the Fed's holdings of the debt, but it is not strong. For instance, in late 1972, when the debt was rising rapidly, the Fed's holdings of debt actually fell. This reinforces the point made at the end of Sec. 14-1, that there is no necessary connection between the size of the deficit and the Fed's holdings of government debt.

CHART 14-2 THE PUBLIC DEBT (BILLIONS OF DOLLARS). (Source: *Federal Reserve Bulletin*, various issues.)

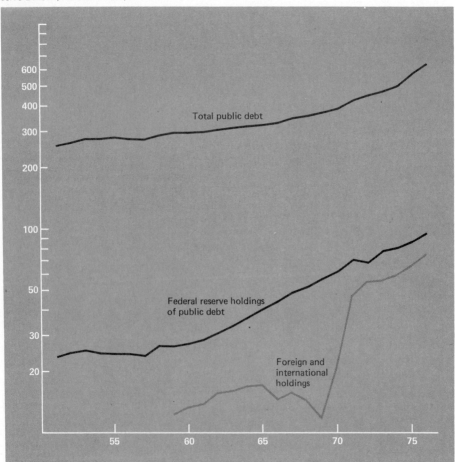

Although the national debt has been rising over the post-World War II period, it has not risen as fast as GNP, This can be seen in Chart 14-3, which plots the national debt as a percentage of GNP. In 1946, after the heavy borrowing by the federal government during the war, the debt was larger than GNP. By 1975 the debt was down to 30 percent of GNP. This is very much the historical pattern for the United States; the national debt usually rises substantially during wartime and then declines relative to GNP after wars. It is interesting to note that the debt has actually fallen in *real* terms since 1946. Over the 1946–1976 period the nominal debt slightly more than doubled, but the price level (CPI) almost tripled. So, alarming as the growth of the national debt might appear, the debt has been declining rapidly in size (in the post-World War II period) relative to the size of the economy as measured by GNP.

So far we have presented some facts about the size of the budget deficit, its relation to the national debt, the financing of the deficit, and the size of the debt. We turn now to examine the budget itself in more detail. Table 14-1 presents the sources of receipts by the federal government, as a percentage of GNP. The major sources of receipts for the federal government are the individual income tax, the corporate income tax, and contribu-

CHART 14-3 FEDERAL GOVERNMENT DEBT AS A PERCENTAGE OF GNP, 1946–1976. (Source: *Economic Report of the President,* 1977)

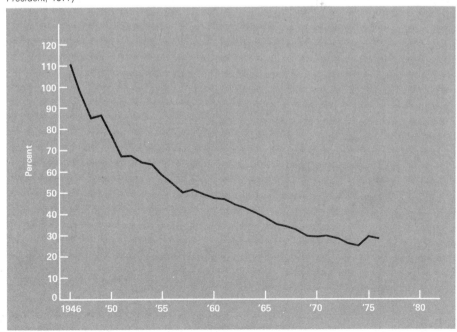

TABLE 14-1   FEDERAL RECEIPTS BY SOURCE (*As a percentage of GNP*)

Source	1955	1960	1965	1970	1975	1976
Individual income taxes	8	8	8	9	9	8
Corporate profits taxes	5	4	4	3	3	3
Social insurance taxes and contributions	2	3	3	5	6	6
Other taxes and receipts	3	3	3	3	2	2
Total receipts	17	19	18	20	20	19

Source: Congressional Budget Office. Totals may not add because of rounding.

tions to social insurance (Social Security.)   The ratios of individual and corporate income taxes to GNP have remained fairly steady since 1955, though corporate profits taxes have declined as a percentage of GNP.[8]   Social insurance taxes and contributions have increased rapidly as a share of GNP over the last twenty years, and particularly in the last ten years. Other taxes and receipts are largely indirect taxes, such as current excise taxes on tires, tobacco, and gasoline, as well as tariffs on imported goods. Reliance on indirect taxes has been declining over the last twenty years.

Table 14-2 shows how federal outlays are allocated among several broad categories of expenditure.   In 1955 more than half the budget was devoted to national defense, and only one-sixth to transfer (benefit) payments to individuals.   The share of national defense in the budget, and national defense spending as a share of GNP, have fallen in the last twenty years, with a temporary increase during the period of the Vietnam war. Transfer payments have increased rapidly since 1955, with the most rapid increase coming between 1970 and 1975.   Now transfer payments exceed defense spending and account for nearly half of federal government spending.

Table 14-3 shows the breakdown of transfer payments from 1965 to 1976.   In large part, the increase in transfer payments is due to rapid in-

[8]The share of profits in GNP has also declined over the period.

TABLE 14-2   FEDERAL OUTLAYS BY MAJOR COMPONENT (*As a percentage of GNP*)

Major component	1955	1960	1965	1970	1975	1976
National defense	11	9	7	8	6	6
Benefit payments for individuals	3	5	5	6	9	10
Grants to state and local governments	1	1	1	2	2	3
Net interest	1	1	1	2	2	2
Other federal operations	2	3	4	3	3	3
Total budget outlays	18	19	18	21	22	24

Source: Congressional Budget Office.

TABLE 14-3 DOMESTIC TRANSFER PAYMENTS *(In billions of dollars)*

Fiscal year	Total	Retire-ment and disa-bility*	Hospital and supple-mentary medical insurance	Food stamps	Veteran benefits and insurance	Unem-ployment benefits	Other
1965	28.3	20.2	†	†	4.7	2.5	0.9
1970	54.8	35.6	6.7	0.6	6.9	3.0	2.0
1975 (est.)	128.2	82.6	13.2	3.3	11.9	13.7	3.5
1976 (est.)	143.0	91.3	14.1	3.1	11.6	17.2	5.7

*Includes black-lung benefits, supplemental security income benefits, and military retired pay.

†Less than $50 million.

Source: Special Analyses: Budget of the United States Government Fiscal Year 1976.

creases in payments for retirement (Social Security) and disability. Medicare payments too have increased rapidly. In part, the high level of transfer payments in 1975 and 1976 was a result of the recession. This caused unemployment benefits to rise from $5 billion in 1974 to $17 billion in 1976. Nonetheless, even in 1976, unemployment benefits were only 12 percent of total transfer payments.

Grants to state and local governments have increased as a share of GNP in the last twenty years, as has net interest.[9] The reason net interest has increased as a share of GNP is not that the national debt has risen as a percentage of GNP (Chart 14-3 shows that the national debt fell as a per-centage of GNP over the period) but that the interest rate paid by the federal government on the debt has risen rapidly.

So much for the facts about the federal budget. Next we consider what the facts mean.

*14-3 THE BUDGET AND MACROECONOMIC EQUILIBRIUM

In earlier chapters we discussed the effects of monetary and fiscal policy on the equilibrium of the economy. In those chapters we measured fiscal policy by the full-employment deficit. We have now seen that the actual budget deficit affects the stock of government debt held by the private sector and/or the Fed. We did not take account of the interactions between the state of the budget and changes in the national debt in our earlier

[9]Because of rounding, Table 14-2 exaggerates the rise in net interest payments. The rise from 1 percent to 2 percent shown in the table is in fact a rise from 1.37 percent in 1955 to 1.73 percent in 1975.

analysis. We now want to consider the effects of the creation or retirement of the debt associated with an actual budget deficit or surplus on the macroeconomic adjustment process. We first discuss the effects of a budget deficit that is financed by the Fed. Then we discuss the so-called *inflation tax*. Following that, we examine the effects of a deficit that is financed by borrowing from the private sector. Finally in this section, we briefly discuss the issue of the burden of the national debt.

Federal Reserve Financing of the Deficit

We distinguish between the effects of a temporary, say one-year, deficit that is financed by borrowing from the Fed and the effects of a continuing deficit. Suppose first that the budget is in deficit for a single year, and that the deficit is financed entirely by the Fed. Such a budget deficit might be caused by a one-year increase in government spending, which thereafter falls back to its original level.

Figure 14-1 reproduces the aggregate demand–aggregate supply framework of Chap. 12. We will use this framework to show that a transitory budget deficit financed by money creation permanently raises the price level, even though the increase in government spending does not persist. Government spending by assumption reverts to its initial level after one period. However, that transitory government spending is financed by creation of money and that increase in the money stock is

FIGURE 14-1 THE EFFECT OF A MONEY-FINANCED, TRANSITORY INCREASE IN GOVERNMENT SPENDING

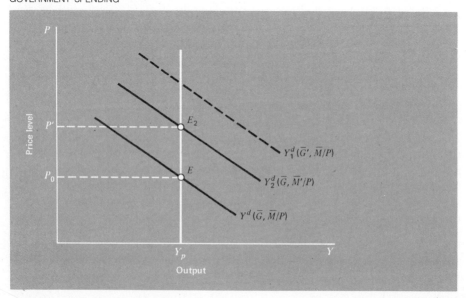

permanent. As we saw in Chap. 12, an increase in the stock of money permanently raises the long-run price level.

Now consider the argument in more detail using Fig. 14-1 starting from full equilibrium at point E. The initial increase in government spending will shift the aggregate demand schedule out and to the right to Y_1^d because the demand for goods and services is raised. The effect of increased spending in the short run is to raise output and prices.[10] If we ignored the financing of the deficit, we would conclude that the economy returns to point E once government spending declines back to its initial level. In fact, however, the government spending, when financed by the Fed, gives rise to an increase in the stock of money that will remain even after the government spending falls back to the initial level. The effect of that increase in the money stock, with government spending back at the initial level $\overline{G}$, is shown by the aggregate demand schedule Y_2^d. We are not concerned here with the adjustment process but rather with the long-run effects. These can be directly inferred from Fig. 14-1 by recognizing that output in the long run will be unaffected by the money-financed transitory government spending. Accordingly with output at the level Y_p the long-run effect of the financing is to raise prices to the level P'. A transitory, money-financed deficit thus leads to a once-and-for-all permanent increase in the level of prices. Note that the analysis implies that fiscal and monetary policy are interrelated, through the financing of deficits.

Consider next the effects of a small *permanent* budget deficit, financed by the Fed. Assume initially that the government keeps the deficit fixed in real terms. We assume a "small" real deficit because we shall argue presently that there is a maximum deficit that can be financed by money creation. Attempts to go beyond that maximum deficit lead to uncontrolled inflation. We have now to use the analysis of Chap. 13, since we shall be dealing with a process of continuing or ongoing inflation. Assume that the government increases its spending. That results in an increase in the full-employment deficit which shifts the aggregate demand curve AD in Fig. 14-2 out to the right. In addition, because the Fed is financing the deficit, the growth rate of the nominal money stock increases, and shifts the aggregate demand curve further out for that reason. These two factors shift the aggregate demand curve from AD_0 to AD_1 and move the economy from an equilibrium at E to E_1. Both the inflation rate and growth rate of output rise. In subsequent periods the aggregate demand curve shifts back to the left somewhat, as a result of the fact that the full-employment deficit is no longer increasing. However, because the money stock has to grow (at a higher rate) to finance the deficit, the aggregate demand curve remains permanently higher than it was initially, and the inflation rate at the new long-run equilibrium E_2 is permanently higher than it was initially at E.

[10]The levels of output and prices in the short-run would be given by the intersection of the Y_1^d curve and a short-run aggregate supply curve (not shown).

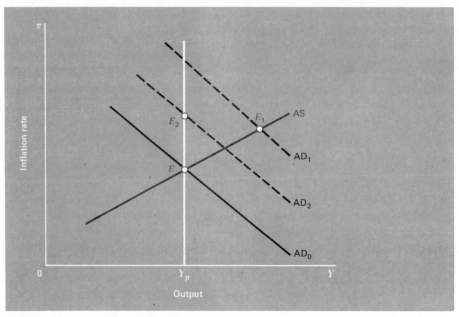

FIGURE 14-2 EFFECTS OF A PERMANENT
INCREASE IN THE DEFICIT FINANCED BY
BORROWING FROM THE FEDERAL RESERVE

Inflation and the Deficit

In the analysis of the permanent deficit above, we assumed that the deficit
was fixed in real terms, that is, independently of the price level. In the
United States economy, there are important elements of the tax system that
depend on the price level. An increase in the price level tends to reduce
the deficit unless definite action is taken to change tax rates. There are two
main reasons for that. The first is that tax rates are fixed in relation to
nominal income and are progressive. That is, taxes rise as a proportion of
income as income increases. The second is that some government outlays
are fixed in nominal terms, and hence decline in real value when the price
level rises.

To make the first point, consider the example of a tax payer shown in
Table 14-4. We are comparing an initial situation with a price level of 100
and pretax nominal income of $20,000 with a later situation in which both
the price level and pretax nominal income have doubled. Initially taxes of
$7,000 are paid on nominal income of $20,000. After the price level doubles, a higher proportion of nominal income, namely $20,000, is paid in
taxes. That is because the income tax is progressive. That means that the
real value of after-tax income falls with the price level and that the real
value of taxes paid to the government rises with the price level—taxes

TABLE 14-4   EFFECTS OF INFLATION ON AFTER-TAX INCOME

Price level	Pretax income, nominal	Taxes, nominal	After-tax income, nominal	After-tax income, real
100	$20,000	$ 7,000	$13,000	$13,000
200	40,000	20,000	20,000	10,000

increase from $7,000 to $20,000 in Table 14-4. In terms of the initial price level, taxes increase in real value by $3,000. Thus, with tax rates unchanged, and a progressive tax system, inflation tends to raise real taxes and reduce the real deficit.

How important is the effect described in the above paragraph in the United States economy? Over the post-World War II period there have been sufficient reductions of tax rates that the percentage of GNP paid in income taxes has remained fairly stable, as seen in Table 14-2. In the short run, with tax rates fixed, it has been estimated that the 12 percent inflation of 1974 increased the taxes received by the federal government by at least $20 billion in real terms.[11]

There have been a number of suggestions that the tax system be altered so that real taxes do not change with changes in the price level. These are proposals for *indexing* the tax system[12] In an indexed tax system, tax brackets would increase in proportion to the price level. The result would be that changes in the price level would not affect *real* taxes. For instance, in an indexed tax system, the nominal taxes in Table 14-4 would only double from $7,000 to $14,000 with doubling of the price level. Canada, for example, has indexed its income tax system.

The major economic argument against indexation of the tax system is that a progressive tax system in nominal terms provides an automatic stabilizer for the economy in response to changes in the price level. We recall the role of automatic stabilizers from Chap. 3. The argument there was that a proportional income tax would reduce the marginal propensity to spend out of income and therefore would reduce the size of the multiplier. The argument here is that with progressive taxation of nominal income— that is, taxes that increase as a proportion of income as nominal income rises—we would have further stabilizing effects. With progressive taxation of nominal income an increase in the price level such as would arise from an aggregate demand disturbance would be dampened because tax rates rise with the increase in nominal income and thus reduce multipliers.

[11]See William Fellner, Kenneth W. Clarkson, and John H. Moore, *Correcting Taxes for Inflation*, American Enterprise Institute, 1975, and Milton Friedman, "Monetary Correction," in Herbert Giersch et al. (eds.), *Essays on Inflation and Indexation*, American Enterprise Institute, 1974.

[12]See, for instance, the article by Milton Friedman referred to in footnote 11.

While a simple proportional tax system provides for a built-in stabilizer, the further benefits of progressive taxation for built-in stabilizer purposes are small. Thus the economic argument against indexation of the tax system is weak.

Aside from the progressive nature of the tax system in *nominal* terms, there is a second factor that leads increases in the price level to reduce the real deficit. That is that some of the payments the federal government makes are fixed in nominal terms. Of these, interest payments on the national debt are the major example. An increase in the price level reduces the real value of these payments and thus reduces the real deficit.

There are three major points in this part.

1 A temporary increase in government spending financed by borrowing from the central bank has a permanent effect on the price level because it increases the money stock.
2 A permanent increase in the real deficit, financed through borrowing from the Fed, permanently increases the inflation rate.
3 In the United States economy, a rising price level tends to reduce the real deficit, given real government spending on goods and services. That is mainly because tax rates are fixed in nominal terms and are progressive. Further, some budget outlays are fixed in nominal terms.

The Inflation Tax

In discussing the effects of a permanent real deficit, we said that it was possible that a deficit of given size could not be financed by borrowing from the central bank. To establish that fact, it is useful to think of inflation as a tax on the holdings of real money balances. To simplify the exposition, we shall talk only of equilibrium long-run inflation, in which the expected rate of inflation is equal to the actual rate of inflation.[13]

Inflation is a tax on the holdings of real balances because anyone who holds money when there is inflation, loses part of the value of that money owing to the inflation. Inflation reduces the purchasing power of money, as shown in Chap. 7. An individual starting the year with $100 will have to add $5 to his money holdings during the year merely to maintain their real value or purchasing power constant if there is 5 percent inflation. Alternatively, if he keeps his nominal money holdings constant at $100 over the year, he loses 5 percent of the value of the money owing to inflation. The effect of the inflation is thus the same as the effect of a tax on the holding of the money.

---

[13]Inflation is often rhetorically described as "the cruelest tax of all." This statement does not refer to the analysis we are about to carry out of inflation as a tax on real balances in the long run with actual inflation equal to expected inflation. Instead, it refers to the effects of unexpected inflation on those who have saved in nominal assets—such as time deposits—for their retirement. Such individuals are obviously adversely affected by inflation. If the inflation is unexpected, they will find themselves with assets of lower real value than they had expected to have, and with a lower standard of living than they had planned.

In long-run equilibrium assuming, for simplicity, no real growth in the economy, real balances will be constant. That means that in long-run equilibrium each individual adds to her nominal balances at a rate equal to the rate of inflation. With 5 percent inflation, everyone adds 5 percent to nominal balances each year. The inflation tax per year can then be thought of as 5 percent of the total value of real balances in the economy.

Let us spell out the argument more carefully. The value of the inflation tax is the amount that individuals have to add to their cash balances every year to maintain the real value of their cash balances constant. Let ΔM be the amount of nominal balances added to cash balances and P be the price level. Denote the real value of the inflation tax by T_I. Then

$$T_I = \frac{\Delta M}{P} \tag{3}$$

Now we can multiply and divide in Eq. (3) by M to obtain

$$T_I = \frac{\Delta M}{M} \cdot \frac{M}{P} = \pi \cdot \frac{M}{P} \tag{3a}$$

In the absence of growth, and in the long run, $\Delta M/M$, the growth rate of the money stock, is equal to the rate of inflation π. Hence the inflation tax can be thought of as the inflation rate times holdings of real balances. In the long run real balances are constant in the absence of growth, so that M/P is constant in the long run.

Now, how does the inflation tax behave as the inflation rate changes? At first glance, it might seem from Eq. (3a) that the total inflation tax rises with the rate of inflation π. However, we know that holdings of real balances depend on the costs of holding real balances, and thus should be expected to fall with the expected rate of inflation, which is the cost of holding real balances. Figure 14-3 draws a demand curve for real balances (LL) as a function of the expected inflation rate, holding other variables affecting the demand for money, such as real income, constant. That demand curve is downward-sloping because individuals reduce their holdings of *real* balances when the expected inflation rate increases.

In long-run equilibrium, in which the expected rate of inflation is equal to the actual rate, $\pi = \pi^*$, the inflation tax is given by the area of the rectangle shown in Fig. 14-3. The tax from Eq. (3a) is the product of the inflation rate and the level of real balances or the "tax base," and that is precisely given by the area of rectangles such as that shown, with sides of length π_0^* and $(M/P)_0$.

For the demand curve shown in Fig. 14-3, the inflation tax as a function of the inflation rate is shown in Fig. 14-4. As the inflation rate rises from zero, the total tax rises. Eventually, though, increases in the inflation rate drive down the demand for money so much that the total tax revenue falls. T_I^* is the maximum inflation tax revenue. In general we would expect the

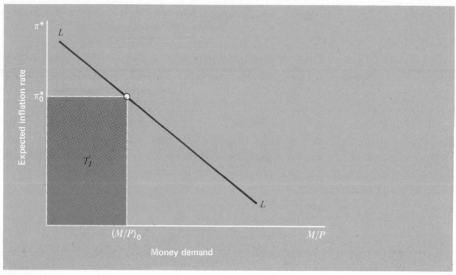

FIGURE 14-3 THE DEMAND FOR REAL
BALANCES AS A FUNCTION OF THE EX-
PECTED RATE OF INFLATION

total revenue from the inflation tax to behave in a way similar to that shown
in Fig. 14-4. At a zero inflation rate, there is no tax and so no tax revenue.
Thus increases in the inflation rate from zero will increase total revenue
from the inflation tax. Eventually, though, the tax rate becomes high
enough to drive demand down to the point where total revenue begins to

FIGURE 14-4 THE INFLATION TAX AS A
FUNCTION OF THE RATE OF INFLATION

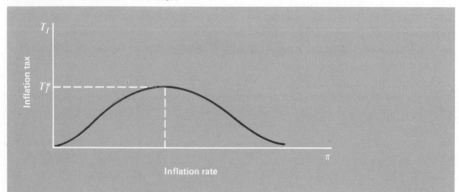

decline.[14]   There is nothing special about a tax on real balances as opposed to a tax on any other commodity in this regard.

Inflation is not referred to as a tax merely because individuals find that the real value of their money balances is reduced by inflation.   The counterpart of the public's payment of the inflation tax—additions to nominal money balances so as to keep their purchasing power constant and thus offset the effect of inflation—is the government's receipt of the inflation tax. How does the government "receive" the tax?   The government, in the form of the combined Treasury and central bank, creates the money that the public adds to its nominal money holdings to maintain constant its real balances.   How does the public "buy" the money from the government? The private sector does that by using part of its income to add nominal money to its money balances.   The private sector gives up some goods or services to the government, which pays with the money it uses to finance the deficit.   Thus the government collects the tax by buying goods and services from the private sector with the money the private sector adds to its nominal balances.   This budgetary aspect of the inflation tax completes the reason why inflation can be thought of as a tax collected from money holders and accruing to the government.   Furthermore it is this tax aspect of money-financed deficits that has led some to argue that there are only two ways the deficit can be financed, taxation or borrowing from the public. The third way, borrowing from the Fed and corresponding money creation, it is argued, is in fact a form of taxation.[15]

Now, what does all this have to do with the budget and macroeconomic adjustment?   The major point of this part is that, in long-run equilibrium, there is a maximum amount of revenue that can be raised through the inflation tax.   Treasury borrowing from the Fed results in increases in the stock of high-powered money.   That means that Treasury borrowing from the Fed is equivalent to the government's raising revenue through issues of high-powered money.   But we have seen that there is a maximum amount of revenue that can be obtained in that way.

If the government attempts to raise more revenue than the maximum it can obtain through issues of high-powered money, and if it prints more high-powered money whenever it finds itself unable to cover its expenses, the rate of inflation will continue increasing.   The public and the government will be competing for goods with the government printing money and the public trying to get rid of it.   Eventually the economy will experience an extremely rapid inflation or a *hyperinflation*.   For instance, in the Ger-

[14]Can you show that the elasticity of demand for real balances with respect to the expected rate of inflation is one at the point of maximum revenue?

[15]It should be noted that in the United States and most other countries only part of the money supply—high-powered money—is issued by the government.   The inflation tax collected by the government is based on its "sales" of high-powered money, and not on the change in the total money supply.   The commercial banks too "collect" some of the inflation tax as the interest rates they charge on loans rise with inflation while they pay zero interest on deposits.

man hyperinflation of 1922–1923, the average rate of inflation was 322 percent *per month*.

Keynes, in a masterful description of the hyperinflation process in Austria after World War I, tells of how people would order two beers at a time because they grew stale at a rate slower than their price was rising.[16] Other stories include those of a person who carried her (worthless) currency in a basket and found that, having set down the basket for a moment, it was stolen, but the money had been left.

To return now to the budget deficit, we see why the government could not finance a deficit in excess of the maximum revenue from the inflation tax by borrowing from the central bank. In other words, there are real deficits that simply could not, in the long run, be financed by borrowing from the central bank, that is, by the issue of high-powered money. Attempts to finance in that way would lead to hyperinflation. The fear that hyperinflation will result from large budget deficits may be one of the arguments in the minds of those most concerned over the budget deficit. But it is foolish to assume that any budget deficit, however small, will lead to a hyperinflation, even if it is financed by borrowing from the Fed.

The analysis of the inflation tax is not of great importance for the U.S., with its well-functioning tax system and independent central bank. In other countries, with less well-developed tax systems, the printing of money may be one of the few ways the government has of obtaining resources. To put it differently, in some countries, large parts of government spending are financed by borrowing from the central bank and thus by inflation.

Private Sector Financing of the Deficit

Once again we want to distinguish between the effects of a temporary budget deficit, financed by borrowing from the private sector, and the effects of a permanent budget deficit financed in that way. We particularly want to compare the effects of financing by borrowing from the private sector with financing by the central bank, which was discussed above. We shall refer to financing of the deficit by borrowing from the private sector as *debt financing,* and to financing by borrowing from the Fed as *money financing*.

Figure 14-5 presents the familiar aggregate demand and supply diagram of Chap. 12. The initial effect of an increase in government spending is to move the aggregate demand curve out to Y_1^d from its initial position at Y^d. The extra government spending is financed by selling debt to the private sector. Thus the private sector accumulates government debt over the period during which government spending is at its higher level. Now, what effect does that higher stock of government debt held by the private

---

[16]See John Maynard Keynes, *A Tract on Monetary Reform*, Macmillan, which remains one of the most readable accounts of inflation. See also Phillip Cagan, "The Monetary Dynamics of Hyperinflation," in Milton Friedman (ed.), *Studies in the Quantity Theory of Money*, University of Chicago Press, 1956.

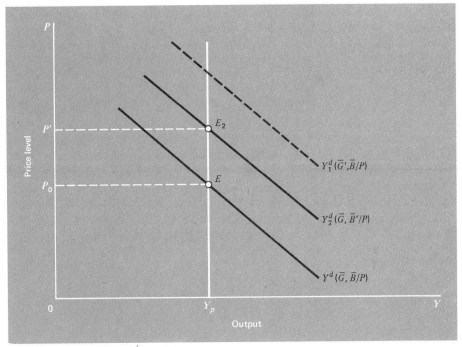

FIGURE 14-5 EFFECT OF A TEMPORARY INCREASE IN GOVERNMENT SPENDING FINANCED BY BORROWING FROM THE PUBLIC

sector have on aggregate demand?

Any individual holding government bonds regards those bonds as part of her wealth. Thus it would seem that, given the level of income, aggregate demand should rise when the stock of government bonds rises, because individuals holding those bonds have higher wealth. The higher wealth increases consumption demand.[17] Accordingly, the aggregate demand curve would shift out to the right as a result of the increase in privately held wealth. Hence, we show the final aggregate demand curve at Y_2^d, above the initial curve Y^d. The difference between the two aggregate demand schedules Y^d and Y_2^d arises from the higher stock of government bonds $\bar{B}'$, compared to $\bar{B}$ on the initial aggregate demand curve. Since the effects of the higher wealth on consumption demand are likely to be small, we show the final aggregate demand curve Y_2^d below the aggregate demand curve Y_1^d.

There are two complications to this analysis. The first is that the existence of the higher stock of debt raises the amount of interest payments in the federal budget. If the budget was originally balanced at point E, it

[17]Recall the discussion of wealth as a factor in consumption spending in Chap. 5.

may not be balanced at E_2. Of course, since the price level at E_2 is higher than at E, tax receipts may have risen at E_2 compared with E, and perhaps the budget would be balanced. But it need not be. If it were not, then further financing of the deficit would have to be undertaken, and that would have subsequent effects on the equilibrium. We discuss the effects of a permanent deficit below.

The second complication is related to the first. It is possible that individuals in the economy calculate their wealth taking into account the tax payments they will have to make in the future. Suppose that everyone believed that the national debt would eventually be paid off. Then everyone would know that at some point in the future, the federal government would have to run a surplus. Individuals might think the federal government would at some future date have to raise taxes in order to pay off the debt. To that extent, an increase in the debt would increase their wealth and at the same time suggest to them that their taxes would be higher in future. The net effect on aggregate demand might then be zero.[18] The issue raised by this argument is sometimes posed by the question "Are government bonds wealth?"

There is another way of looking at the above argument. Now, instead of concentrating on wealth we concentrate on disposable income. An increase in the debt raises disposable income for the private sector because it raises the interest payments the private sector receives. The federal government has to finance those interest payments in some way. Suppose that it financed them by raising taxes or reducing other transfer payments. Then disposable income would be unaffected, despite the higher debt. Consumption demand in this case would be little affected by the increase in the national debt. With such a combined change in the debt and taxes that leaves the budget balanced in the long run, the aggregate demand curve would return to its initial position at Y^d. There would be no (or little) long-run effect from the higher debt if the higher debt did not result in an unbalanced budget.

The theoretical and empirical issue of whether an increase in the national debt increases aggregate demand is not yet settled. It is difficult to isolate the effects of changes in the debt on consumption demand in empirical studies of consumption. The theoretical arguments we have are not conclusive. We are not certain whether individuals do take account of their future tax liabilities when they calculate their wealth. Thus we have to leave this question in an unresolved state.

There is one important difference between debt financing and money financing of a given short-run budget deficit. Money financing of the deficit, as we saw in Chap. 12, tends to reduce the interest rate in the short run compared with debt financing. That is because money financing increases the nominal money stock whereas debt financing does not. In the

---

[18]For an eclectic view of this argument, see Robert J. Barro, "Are Government Bonds Net Wealth?" *Journal of Political Economy,* December 1974.

short run, then, debt financing reduces the level of investment compared with money financing. That is one of the issues connected with the crowding-out question that we studied in Chap. 4.

We want also to compare the effects on the price level of money and debt financing of a temporary increase in government spending. There is no question that the price level is higher with money financing than with debt financing, There are two reasons. First, money financing increases the money stock and debt financing does not. The higher the money stock, the greater the aggregate demand at any given price level. Second, we attributed a price level rise in the case of debt financing to the wealth effect of a greater stock of debt on consumption. While there is some argument about whether bonds are wealth, there is no question that money is wealth. So the wealth effect on consumption is larger in the case of money financing than debt financing. That, too, means that aggregate demand at any given price level will be higher with money than with debt financing.

We now summarize the effects of a temporary budget deficit financed by debt creation. Such financing probably increases aggregate demand but, because of the possible effects of anticipated future tax liabilities on consumption, that is not certain. Debt financing, starting from a balanced budget and if not compensated for by higher taxes or reductions in other transfer payments, leads to a permanent deficit in the budget. Debt financing raises the interest rate and reduces investment in the short run as compared with the effects of money financing.

We turn now to a permanent real deficit. An attempt to run a permanent real deficit financed by debt must imply reductions in other transfer payments or increases in taxes. For, as the debt accumulates over time, interest payments on the debt increase. Without changes in other variables affecting the deficit, the deficit would continue to increase through the increasing interest payments. Such a policy cannot be maintained forever because eventually government spending and other transfers would be reduced to zero and taxes would have to continue to increase forever. That cannot be done forever without having adverse effects on the level of output. Thus we conclude that attempts to finance a given real deficit purely through debt financing cannot be viable in the long run in an economy that is not growing.[19]

We have now discussed the two extreme cases of financing of the deficit purely through the creation of high-powered money and purely through borrowing. In practice, neither of these extremes is followed.

Chart 14-4 shows Federal Reserve holdings of public debt as a fraction of the total public debt outstanding. The chart shows the large increase in the fraction of the debt held by the Fed throughout the sixties. This reflects the fact that the Fed is purchasing part of the growing public debt

---

[19]The long-run effects of debt-financed changes in government spending are described in a widely discussed paper by Alan Blinder and Robert Solow, "Analytical Foundations of Fiscal Policy," in A. S. Blinder et al., *The Economics of Public Finance*, Brookings, 1974.

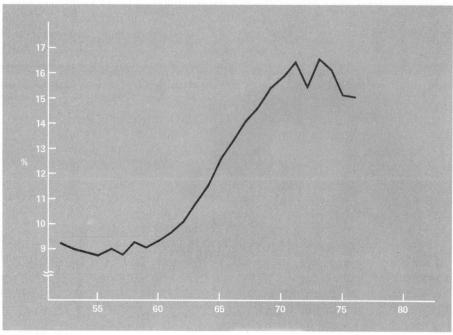

CHART 14-4 FEDERAL RESERVE
HOLDING OF PUBLIC DEBT AS
PERCENTAGE OF TOTAL DEBT. (*Source:*
Economic Report of the President, 1977)

and is thus monetizing budget deficits. The chart shows also that the Fed need not monetize the deficits. Thus in 1972, for example, the public debt increased by $25 billion, reflecting that year's deficit. The Fed did not add in that year to holdings of public debt, and as a consequence their share declined as shown in Chart 14-4. In practice, part of the deficit has been financed by the Fed, but the link between deficits and Fed holdings of government debt is not automatic.

We should also note that the discussion of the financing of permanent deficits fixed in real terms represents the analysis of an abstract case in the sense that few governments make decisions to run permanent deficits fixed in real terms. The results of the analysis are nonetheless useful. We saw that an increase in the real deficit financed through money creation increases the steady-state rate of inflation, provided that the inflation tax could generate that amount of revenue. That result is indicative of the inflationary effects of the financing of deficits through the printing of high-powered money. We also saw that a permanent increase in the real deficit could not in the long run be financed purely through borrowing from the private sector, since the interest on the debt would also have to be financed.

The Burden of the Debt

We stated at the beginning of the chapter that the national debt now exceeds $2,000 per person in the United States. That seems to be a heavy debt for each individual to bear. It is the notion that every person in the country has a large debt that makes the existence of the debt seem so serious.

However, we should realize that corresponding to the debt that every person has as his share of the national debt, are the Treasury bonds and bills that every person (on average) has. By and large we owe the national debt to ourselves. Each individual shares in the public debt, but many individuals own claims on the government that are the other side of the national debt. If there is a debt for individuals taken together, it arises from prospective taxes to pay off the debt. The taxes that different individuals would pay to retire the debt would also vary among the population. To a first approximation, one could think of the liability that the debt represents as canceling out the asset that the debt represents to the individuals who hold claims on the government.

You will recognize that we are now discussing the question of whether the debt is counted as part of wealth for the population as a whole. Earlier we started from the view that the government bonds and Treasury bills that individuals hold are part of their wealth. We then asked whether the possibility that all individuals consider the future tax liabilities connected with the hypothetical paying off of the debt at some future date, meant that on balance the debt was not part of the wealth. In this section we started from the other side: we first talked of the national debt as a debt, and then pointed out that there were assets held by individuals corresponding to that debt. We pointed out earlier that it was not yet certain whether individuals taken together in fact count the national debt as a part of wealth. There certainly does not seem to be any argument that the liability represented by some possible paying off of the debt at some unknown future time outweighs the value of the assets that individuals hold at present. At this level, then, there is no persuasive argument that the debt is a burden in the sense that the economy as a whole regards the national debt as a reduction in its wealth.

The only factor ignored in the previous paragraph is that part of the debt is owned by foreigners. In that case, for the United States economy as a whole, part of the asset represented by the debt is held by foreigners, while the future tax liability accrues entirely to residents. Then that part of the debt held by foreigners might represent a net reduction in the wealth of United States residents.

Although the debt is not a burden in the fairly crude sense in which one asks whether individuals regard themselves as being poorer because of the existence of the debt (leaving aside the part of the debt owned by foreigners), there are more sophisticated senses in which it might be a burden. The most important sense in which there is a possible burden arises from the potential long-run effects of the debt on the capital stock. We saw earlier that debt financing increases the interest rate and reduces investment. That would mean that the capital stock would be lower with debt financing than otherwise. If individuals regard the debt as part of their wealth, then they tend to increase their consumption at a given level of income, which results in a smaller proportion of GNP being invested.[20] In the long run, that would result in a lower capital stock and thus a lower level of real output. In that sense, then, the debt could be a burden. Secondly, the debt might be a burden because debt servicing in the long run could require higher tax rates. If those tax rates have adverse effects on the amount of work that individuals do, then real output would be reduced. But it is far from certain that higher tax rates in fact reduce the amount of work that individuals do.

Thus, if the debt is a burden, it is a burden for reasons very different from those suggested by the statement that every person in the United States has a debt of $2,000 as a share of the national debt. The major possible source of burden arises from the possible effects of the national debt on the capital stock.

14-4 STATE AND LOCAL GOVERNMENT SPENDING AND FINANCING

Chart 14-5 shows state and local government expenditures annually in the period since 1946. As a percentage of GNP the share of state and local government spending has increased steadily. By 1976 the share was almost 15 percent and thus had become a very important component of aggregate demand.

Most of state and local government spending is on purchases of goods and services. In fact, state and local governments spend more on goods and services than the federal government does. The relative expenditures on goods and services can be seen in Chart 14-6. In 1975 state and local governments spent $208 billion on goods and services as compared to $123 billion for the federal government. The rapid increase in state and local government spending relative to federal spending on goods and services began in the late sixties. The goods and services that state and local governments buy are typically education, highways, hospitals, fire protection, garbage removal, and police protection. State and local governments spend relatively small amounts on transfer payments. With regard to interest payments, state and local governments actually on balance receive more interest than they pay out. This is a result of the budget surpluses they have been running which have enabled them, taken together, to purchase federal securities. Although many state and local governments run deficits (e.g., New York City) and have to borrow, thus accounting for

[20]For articles dealing with the burden of the debt, see J. M. Ferguson (ed.), *Public Debt and Future Generations*, Chapel Hill, University of North Carolina Press, 1964.

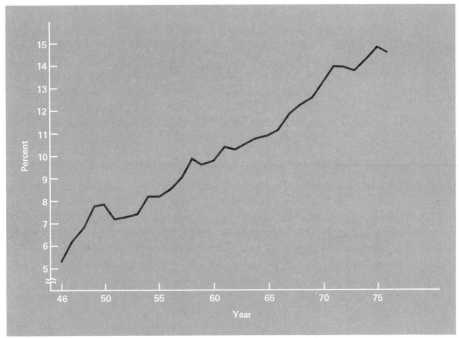

CHART 14-5 STATE AND LOCAL GOV-
ERNMENT SPENDING AS A PERCENTAGE
OF GNP, 1946–1976. (Source: *Economic Re-
port of the President*, 1953 and 1977)

the existence of state and local government securities, others run surpluses and purchase the securities issued by the federal government.

The major sources of state and local government revenues are indirect taxes, largely the sales tax. Other large sources of funds are state income taxes, property taxes, and grants-in-aid from the federal government.

State and local government financing differs from federal financing mainly in that the state and local governments cannot borrow from the Fed. Thus when a state or local government runs a deficit, it has to borrow by selling securities to the private sector.

Two major questions arise in connection with state and local governments' role in the economy. The first concerns the determinants of state and local government spending. In large part, this is determined through the political process. Although state and local spending as a proportion of GNP has been rising, it would not be wise to assume that this trend will continue. Indeed, the recent recession reduced tax revenues for some state and local governments and put pressure on them to reduce spending. There have also been political indications that it is popular to run against big state government.

The second question concerns the effects of state and local government

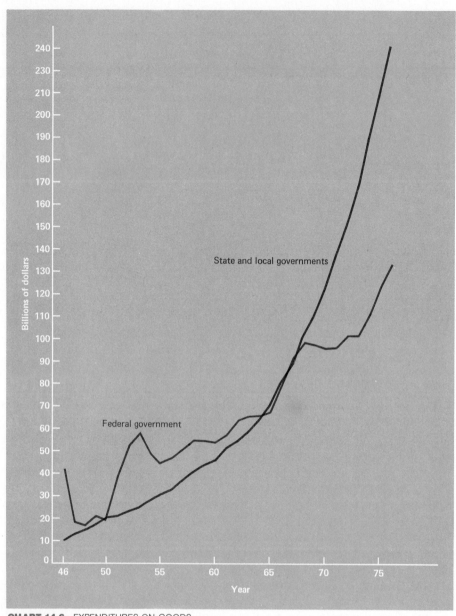

CHART 14-6 EXPENDITURES ON GOODS
AND SERVICES: FEDERAL VS STATE AND
LOCAL GOVERNMENTS. (*Source: Economic
Report of the President,* 1977)

spending on the economy. Here the analysis of federal government spending and taxing of earlier chapters is relevant. There are multiplier effects associated with changes in state and local spending just as there are for changes in federal spending.

14-5 THE SIZE OF THE GOVERNMENT

A recurring theme in political discussion concerns the size of the government. A vocal part of those influential in public policy argue that the size of the government has been increasing almost continuously in the last twenty-five years and that the government "spends our money" in ways we could do better ourselves. Such a view has been put forth by a great many conservative economists. The question whether we get our money's worth from the government is too complex to permit a simple test or answer. Certainly that answer has not been provided in any definite form so far.

A different, and in some ways intriguing, perspective on the size of the government is provided by Table 14-5. That table shows federal government spending as a fraction of GNP. One view is that government spending as a fraction of GNP has continuously risen since the early fifties. Such a view was advocated, for example, by William F. Buckley, the distinguished columnist and author (*Saving the Queen*). Senator Edward Kennedy, however, has argued that quite to the contrary, government spending as a fraction of GNP in the early 1950s jumped to 20 percent and has hovered around that level all the time since with variations influenced by wars and business cycle.[21] If that interpretation is correct, then indeed the

[21]*Boston Globe*, June 18, 1976.

TABLE 14-5 GOVERNMENT SPENDING AS A FRACTION OF GNP (*Calendar years*)

Year	Percent	Year	Percent
1949	16.0	1963	19.2
1950	14.3	1964	18.6
1951	17.5	1965	18.0
1952	20.5	1966	19.1
1953	21.6	1967	20.6
1954	19.1	1968	20.8
1955	17.1	1969	20.1
1956	17.1	1970	20.8
1957	18.0	1971	20.7
1958	19.8	1972	20.9
1959	18.7	1973	20.3
1960	18.4	1974	21.3
1961	19.5	1975	23.8
1962	19.6	1976	22.9

Source: Economic Report of the President, 1977.

current outcry against big government is primarily a reflection of the fact that the composition of government outlays has changed away from defense and toward transfers (including veterans).

There is nothing inevitable about growth in the federal budget as a share of GNP. Indeed, Charles Schultze, first chairperson of the Council of Economic Advisers in the Carter administration, has calculated that if present spending programs are maintained, federal government spending will be about 18 percent of GNP by 1986. With the current tax laws, taxes will be about 23 percent of GNP in 1986.[22] The 5 percent difference provides room for a fiscal dividend, which will almost certainly be taken partly in the form of tax cuts and partly through increased government spending. Political decisions will determine the proportions finally chosen.

14-6 SUMMARY

1   Federal government spending is financed through taxes and borrowing. The borrowing takes place directly from the public, and may indirectly be from the Fed.
2   Under present institutional arrangements, there is no necessary link between Treasury borrowing and changes in the stock of high-powered money. Federal Reserve financing of the deficit increases the stock of high-powered money.
3   When the Fed tries to control the level of interest rates, it creates an automatic link between Treasury borrowing and the creation of high-powered money.
4   Federal government receipts come chiefly from the individual income tax, the corporate income tax, and social insurance taxes and contributions. The share of the last category has increased rapidly in the postwar period, especially since 1965.
5   Federal government spending is chiefly on defense and transfer payments to individuals. The share of defense in federal spending has fallen over the past twenty years, while transfers have risen.
6   A temporary increase in government spending financed by an increase in the stock of high-powered money increases the price level permanently.
7   A permanent increase in government spending financed by money creation results in a permanent increase in the inflation rate.
8   Inflation can be regarded as a tax on real balances. The federal government collects the tax through the quantity of high-powered money that it provides during inflation to meet the increased demand for high-powered money. There is a maximum revenue that can be raised through the inflation tax.

[22]C. L. Schultze, "Federal Spending: Past, Present, and Future," in H. Owen and C. L. Schultze *Setting National Priorities*, Brookings, 1976.

9 A temporary increase in government spending financed by debt creation increases the price level permanently.

10 Debt financing of a permanent increase in government spending is not
viable if potential output remains fixed. The interest payments on the
debt would continually increase, making for a rising deficit that has to
be funded by borrowing.

11 The major sense in which the national debt may be a burden is that it
may lead to a decline in the capital stock in the long run.

12 In the late sixties and early seventies, the share of state and local
governments in GNP has increased steadily and now amounts to about
15 percent of GNP.

PROBLEMS

1 What effect does a federal government surplus have on the stock of money
and the stock of debt? Explain in detail the mechanics of how the stocks of
money and bonds are affected.

2 Suppose the Treasury issues $1 billion in Treasury bills which are bought by
the public. Then the Fed conducts open market purchases of $300 million.
Effectively, how has the debt been financed?

3 Under what circumstances are fiscal and monetary policy related rather than
two completely independent instruments in the hands of the government?

4 In some countries there is virtually no capital market in which the government
can borrow, and only a rudimentary tax system, so that taxes produce only
very small revenues.
  a What is the relationship between monetary and fiscal policy in such countries?
  b What does the inflation tax analysis imply about the ability of the government in such a country to spend a large share of GNP permanently?

5 Analyze the difference in the impact on the interest rate, investment, and the
price level of a temporary change in government spending, financed by
money creation and borrowing, respectively.

6 What would be the effect of inflation on real income taxes if income taxation
was:
  a Regressive?
  b Proportional?
  c Indexed?

*7 Recall that the elasticity of demand for real balances with respect to the
expected inflation rate (see Figs. 14-3 and 14-4) is defined as

$$\frac{\Delta(M/P)}{\Delta\pi^*} \cdot \frac{\pi^*}{(M/P)}$$

Prove that if $(\pi_0^*, (M/P)_0)$ is the point in Fig. 14-3 where T_I is maximized, then
at π_0^* this elasticity is 1.

*8   Analyze the effects on the economy of a permanent increase in the level of government spending, financed by money creation.

*9   Trace out the path the economy follows when there is a permanent increase in government spending that is financed by borrowing from the public. Take account of the size of the deficit in each period. (Do not follow this sequence of events for more than three periods. Use the diagrams of Chap. 13.)

10   Examine Chart 14-6 and then calculate how the share of total government spending (by federal and state and local governments) on goods and services in GNP changed from 1965 to 1975. (You will have to use one of the charts in Chap. 1 that shows the level of GNP.) How has total government spending changed relative to the size of the federal budget? Why is there so much more concern about the size of the federal budget than about total government spending on goods and services?

11   Some people say that a huge government debt is a burden in that each individual on average owes over $2,000 as her share of the debt. Others point out that a large debt means individuals own large amounts of government securities and thus are wealthier. Who is right?

15

Stabilization Policy: The Phillips Curve and the Tradeoffs between Inflation and Unemployment

With 5 percent inflation and 3.5 percent unemployment in 1969, the Nixon administration decided that restraint in aggregate spending was called for. A cooling off in aggregate spending would reduce inflationary pressure. There would, inevitably, be higher unemployment in the short run, but that cost would be worth the price of reduced inflation in the long run. Similarly, in the recovery from the recession in 1975, monetary and fiscal policy were only moderately stimulative. The policy decision was to move the economy along a path of relatively slow but safe recovery, to make inroads on inflation in preference to a rapid reduction in unemployment.

These policy choices reflect an assessment of the relative costs of inflation and unemployment. They certainly reflect the judgment that there is a cost to inflation, and that this cost is sufficiently important to warrant a period of unemployment in order to reduce inflation. The policies imply, too, the belief that inflation can be reduced in the long run without the cost of a permanently higher rate of unemployment. Finally the policies reflect the judgment that a gradual approach to lower inflation is preferable to a rapid approach. This chapter investigates the premises of such policy choices. We address the question of the costs of inflation and of unemployment, the meaning of unemployment, and the *tradeoff* between inflation and unemployment.

You will find that the problems in this chapter do not have definite answers. The problems discussed are among the most lively and controversial in current economic research. Furthermore, the inflation-unemployment problem is the key issue in political economy. It is a campaign platform issue, and it is frequently an issue of legislation. The Humphrey-Hawkins bill, before the Congress in the high-unemployment year 1976, attempted to reduce unemployment in four years to 3 percent. The bill raised the issues of whether such a reduction in unemployment is feasible, whether it could be sustained in the long run, or whether it would give rise to uncontrolled inflation as some opponents claimed. Although the answers in this area are few, it is well worth laying out the relevant considerations and analyzing the areas of agreement and controversy.

This chapter starts by revisiting the Phillips curve of Chap. 13 and investigating the tradeoff between inflation and unemployment. In Chap. 13 we argued that, in the short run in which the expected inflation rate is constant, the Phillips curve is relatively flat. That implies there is a short-run tradeoff between inflation and unemployment: in the short run the unemployment rate can be reduced at the cost of higher inflation. By contrast, we argued that in the long run the unemployment rate is equal to the natural rate. This implies that there is no long-run tradeoff between inflation and unemployment, or alternatively, that the long-run Phillips curve is vertical. That view is not universally held. It has been, and is, argued that lower unemployment can be bought *in the long run* at the cost of higher inflation. We examine the arguments and evidence about the slope of the long-run Phillips curve in Sec. 15-1.

In Sec. 15-2 we proceed to examine the factors underlying any given unemployment rate, say 6 percent. We find that a given unemployment rate implies durations and frequencies of unemployment that differ considerably across different groups in the labor force. The discussion of Sec. 15-2 also treats the question of how the natural or long-run rate of unemployment can be lowered, by policies that intervene in the labor market. The costs of inflation and unemployment are considered in the next sections, and the chapter concludes with a discussion of alternative adjustment strategies—cold turkey versus gradualism.

15-1 IS THE PHILLIPS CURVE VERTICAL?

The vertical Phillips curve is controversial. The issue is basically whether in the long run the unemployment rate is independent of the rate of inflation. If so, then one cannot use stable macropolicies to maintain low unemployment indefinitely. If, by contrast, the Phillips curve is not vertical in the long run, then there is a long-run choice to be made, involving a cost-benefit decision between higher inflation and lower unemployment.

The problem of this section then is to establish (1) whether or not there is reason to believe that the long-run Phillips curve is vertical and (2) what implications follow from a long-run vertical Phillips curve.

It is best to start the discussion with a concrete example. Thus Professor Saul Hymans of the University of Michigan has estimated the long-run Phillips curve shown in Chart 15-1.[1] This *long-run* Phillips curve is negatively sloped and thus implies a long-run tradeoff between inflation and unemployment. The schedule implies that the unemployment rate can be *permanently* reduced if we are prepared to accept an increase in inflation. Hymans notes: "According to this empirical trade-off relation, maintaining an unemployment rate of 4 percent eventually leads to an inflation rate of 4 percent as well. A 6 percent unemployment rate, if maintained, would be accompanied by an inflation rate of only 1.7 percent." This view of the long-run tradeoff between inflation and unemployment is the hypothesis that A. W. Phillips initially derived from the data. It is also the view that was held quite firmly by policy makers and advisers in the early sixties. Clearly, if the world is as represented by Chart 15-1, then the policy maker can choose the long-run mix of inflation and unemployment that is socially preferred, and set out to use aggregate demand management to set output and hence unemployment at the chosen level.

Current thinking on the inflation-unemployment problem has moved away from this long-run tradeoff concept. Although there is no agreement yet, the following issues are clearly recognized: (1) The short-run Phillips

---

[1]Saul Hymans, "The Inflation-Unemployment Trade-Off: Theory and Experience," in Warren Smith and Ronald Teigen (eds.), *Readings in Money, National Income, and Stabilization Policy*, Irwin, 1974.

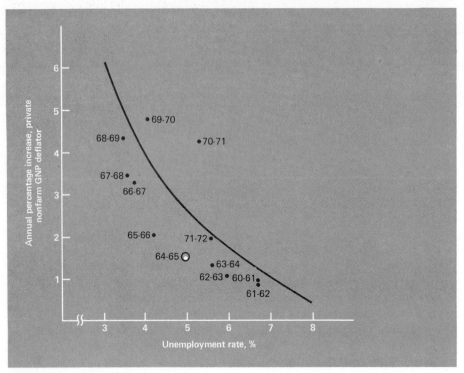

CHART 15-1 THE MICHIGAN PHILLIPS
CURVE

curve is likely to shift over time in response to changes in the expected rate of inflation. (2) The center of controversy has been the question of whether the long-run Phillips curve is actually vertical. As we see below, this is the question whether a low level of unemployment can be sustained by a high but constant rate of inflation.

The basis for these two issues arises from the role of expectations in determining the relation between inflation and unemployment. We recall that in Chap. 13 we used the expectations-augmented Phillips curve:

$$\pi = \pi^* - \epsilon(u - \bar{u}) \tag{1}$$

In that chapter we argued that the inflation rate depends on both the expected inflation rate π^* and the unemployment rate (or the deviation of the unemployment rate from the natural rate, $u - \bar{u}$). In terms of Fig. 15-1, we would have one Phillips curve for *each* expected rate of inflation. Thus in Fig. 15-1 we show the Phillips curve $P^0 P^0$ that is drawn for an expected rate of inflation of $\pi^* = 2.5$ percent. The schedule $P'P'$ is drawn for a higher expected rate of inflation of 5 percent and therefore associates with each

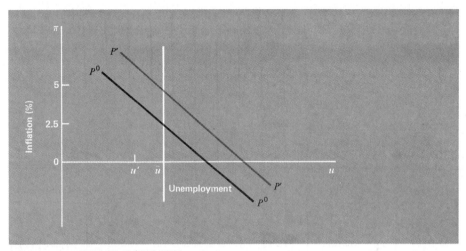

FIGURE 15-1 PHILLIPS CURVES WITH
DIFFERENT EXPECTED RATES OF
INFLATION AND DIFFERENT
EXPECTATIONS COEFFICIENTS

unemployment rate a higher rate of actual inflation. In fact, we could draw a whole family of Phillips curves, only two of which we have drawn in Fig. 15-1. We ask what is the inflation rate associated with the unemployment rate $u = \bar{u}$. The answer is simply that the inflation rate is equal to the expected rate. With actual equal to expected inflation, the unemployment rate is $u = \bar{u}$, and there is no tradeoff. The long-run unemployment rate—the unemployment rate when actual equals expected inflation—is equal to the natural rate $\bar{u}$.

This latter aspect is exceedingly important because it has implications for long-run policy options. This view was suggested by Edmund Phelps of Columbia University and Milton Friedman,[2] who argued that the only scope for macropolicy in influencing unemployment lies in the short run. In the short run the actual inflation rate can rise relative to the expected rate and thereby reduce unemployment. However, macropolicy cannot influence the long-run rate of unemployment. The argument is made more specific in Eq. (2), where we have an expectations-augmented Phillips curve with a twist. Instead of including π^* on the right-hand side, we write $\beta\pi^*$, where β is no longer necessarily unity as in Eq. (1).

$$\pi = \beta\pi^* - \epsilon(u - \bar{u}) \tag{2}$$

How does the value of β affect the position of the short-run Phillips

[2]See Milton Friedman, "The Role of Monetary Policy," *American Economic Review*, March 1968, and Edmund Phelps, *Inflation Policy and Unemployment Theory*, Norton, 1973.

curve? The value of β tells us by how much an increase in the expected inflation rate causes the actual inflation rate to rise, holding the unemployment rate constant. In drawing Fig. 15-1, we implicitly assumed a value of $\beta = 1$ as indicated by Eq. (1). Now we use Fig. 15-1 to compare Phillips curves with $\beta = 1$ and $\beta = 0.5$, respectively. Assume the expected rate of inflation is 5 percent. The schedule $P'P'$ shows the Phillips curve for $\beta = 1$ as before. The schedule P^0P^0 shows the Phillips curve for $\beta = 0.5$ but an expected rate of inflation of 5 percent. Clearly then a value of β less than unity associates a lower rate of inflation with each level of the unemployment rate.

However, there is a further and even more important implication. Consider the long-run Phillips curve implied by Eq. (2). Again, the long run means that actual equals expected inflation. Thus subtracting π^* from both sides of Eq. (2) and setting $\pi = \pi^*$, we obtain the long-run tradeoff as:

$$u = \bar{u} - \frac{1 - \beta}{\epsilon}\pi \tag{3}$$

Equation (3) implies that there is a long-run tradeoff between inflation and unemployment unless $\beta = 1$. In particular, if β is less than 1, then there is a negatively sloped long-run Phillips curve. Higher inflation is associated with lower unemployment, even in the long run.

Figure 15-2 shows the relation between short-run and long-run Phillips curves for $\beta = 0.5$. The schedules P^0P^0 and $P'P'$ are drawn for expected inflation rates of 5 percent and 10 percent, respectively. Now assume that the actual inflation rate were indeed 5 percent. Then point A would be a point on the long-run Phillips curve because at that point the actual and expected inflation rates are equal. Similarly, point B would be a point on the long-run curve if the actual inflation rate were 10 percent. We can connect all such points as A and B and thus derive the long-run Phillips curve $P_L P_L$ that is implied by Eq. (3).

What are the important points to note about the long-run curve $P_L P_L$? First, the long-run tradeoff is steeper than the short-run tradeoff represented by Phillips curves such as P^0P^0 and $P'P'$, on which the expected rate of inflation is constant. The reason is that expectations adjust over time and are *partly* reflected in increased inflation. Thus a reduction of unemployment from 4 percent to 3 percent in the short run, given expected inflation, can be achieved at the cost of relatively little increase in inflation. In the long run we can only do so at a cost in terms of inflation implied by the long-run tradeoff. But we can still do it. If we raise inflation enough, we can sustain rates of unemployment much below $\bar{u}$.

This is precisely the line of argument challenged by Friedman and Phelps. Friedman and Phelps note that in the long run inflation will be fully anticipated. Nobody will allow her real wage to be affected simply because the inflation rate is high. The argument implies the following:

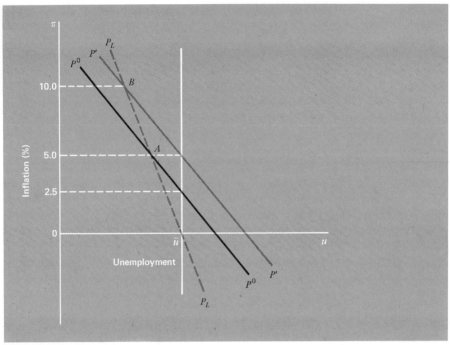

FIGURE 15-2 SHORT-RUN AND
LONG-RUN PHILLIPS CURVES

Expected inflation will be *fully* reflected in actual wage settlements, and actual wage settlements or the rate of increase in money wages will be *fully* reflected in price inflation. Therefore, with fully anticipated inflation—as is appropriate for the long run—the coefficient β must be equal to 1. This in turn implies that the long-run Phillips curve is not only steeper than the short-run Phillips curve but is actually vertical.

If this argument is accepted—and it is worth noting that it is increasingly accepted—then long-run unemployment is independent of the rate of inflation. In the long run, in which the expected rate of inflation is equal to the actual rate of inflation, unemployment will be at the natural rate $\bar{u}$. This *natural-rate hypothesis* appears to reduce severely the scope for long-run macropolicies. Equation (1) shows that the way the unemployment rate can be kept at a level other than $\bar{u}$ is by having the expected rate of inflation differ from the actual rate. Rewriting (1), we have

$$\pi - \pi^* = -\epsilon(u - \bar{u}) \tag{1a}$$

For u to be less than $\bar{u}$, π has to be greater than π^*. Thus, if unemployment is to be kept below the natural rate, individuals must *permanently* expect less inflation than actually occurs. But it can hardly be expected that, in the long run, the government can control the inflation rate in such a way that the public never comes to expect the inflation rate that actually occurs.

The logic of this argument can be understood better by describing the *accelerationist* viewpoint. When Friedman originally made his argument about the natural rate, he suggested that the government might be able to keep the unemployment rate below the natural rate by having accelerating inflation. The idea here was that the public takes time to catch on to the rate of inflation, and that by the time it had caught on to, say, an inflation rate of 5 percent, the government could already have moved the rate of inflation up to 6 percent. Then by the time the public had begun to expect 6 percent inflation, the actual rate of inflation could be moved to 7 percent—and so on. However, it is hard to believe that the public would not eventually come to understand that the inflation rate was accelerating. One can then argue that the acceleration of the inflation rate could be ever-increasing, but again, the public should eventually catch on. Thus the final argument is that there is no way the government can, in the long run, affect the unemployment rate by manipulating the inflation rate.

Clearly, then, the long-run implications of a vertical Phillips curve for the scope of macroeconomic policy have made it a controversial proposition. A broader reason why the vertical Phillips curve or natural rate hypothesis can be thought of as controversial is that it appears to suggest that *nothing* can be done about long-run unemployment. This is not correct. Whether the long-run Phillips curve is vertical or downward-sloping, it may be possible to reduce the natural rate $\bar{u}$ through labor market policies. These are policies designed to make the labor market more efficient. In terms of Fig. 15-2, labor market policies would imply a leftward shift of the vertical or long-run Phillips curve by reducing $\bar{u}$. Indeed, the idea of shifting the Phillips curve was discussed long before the issue of long-run vertical versus downward-sloping curves arose.

We have already noted that the suggestion of a long-run vertical Phillips curve is increasingly accepted as a reasonable description of long-run policy alternatives. The question remains, though, of why that view is still controversial. The reason is primarily that the Phillips curve started off as an empirical regularity just as we presented it in Chaps. 12 and 13. It was introduced by Phillips as a mainly nontheoretical observation about the relation between labor market conditions and wage inflation. Since the curve was based on data of almost a century, it certainly did appear as a long-run relation. Further, during the early sixties empirical work seemed to confirm that it provided a good description of the facts. The early sixties was a period of low inflation in the United States and the United Kingdom, and there was no pressing reason to think that the expected rate of inflation had an important impact on wage and price inflation. Since the expected rate of inflation was low, its omission from empirical studies did no harm to the predictions made using the Phillips curve.

The important change in ideas came in the late sixties, when the Phillips curve seemed to be shifting. In the late sixties and early seventies it became apparent that at a given rate of unemployment, the inflation rate was increasing over time. A Phillips curve without expectations was unstable.[3] At that time, concentration shifted to the role of expectations of inflation in the process of wage bargaining. The suggestion was that with high expected inflation labor would hold out for a more rapidly rising money wage and that in this way inflation expectations would enter the Phillips curve. The next step was to argue that not only should inflation expectations enter the Phillips curve, as in Eq. (2), but that they should enter with a coefficient of unity. Initial work in the late sixties found β in Eq. (2) to be less than unity. But as more evidence for the United States became available, estimates of β in equations like Eq. (2) moved increasingly toward unity.[4] Accordingly, we have now reached a stage at which theory and evidence are both consistent with the view that the long-run Phillips curve is vertical. That is the view we have adopted in this book.

While there may be considerable agreement on a long-run vertical Phillips curve, that agreement is not unanimous.[5] Nor, for that matter, do we feel completely confident that the Phillips curve is vertical at *all* rates of inflation. Thus we would not be surprised to see that the Phillips curve has a shape such as that shown in Fig. 15-3. At positive rates of inflation (to which our actual experience since 1945 is limited) the curve is for all practical purposes vertical. At negative rates of inflation it may well be practically horizontal. Even high unemployment will not cause prices to fall rapidly. The basis for the Phillips curve of Fig. 15-3 is the suggestion that money wage behavior is asymmetrical. Wages rise in the face of excess demand for labor or expected inflation, but do not fall in the face of even heavy unemployment or expected deflation.[6] There seems to be some evidence for that view, and, if it is correct, the long-run Phillips curve might well be kinked, as in Fig. 15-3. You will recognize that this Phillips curve is merely an extreme version of that shown in Chart 15-1.

What practical conclusions can we draw from our discussion of the Phillips curve? The first important point is that the short-run Phillips

---

[3]See Robert J. Gordon, "Wage Price Controls and the Shifting Phillips Curve," *Brookings Papers on Economic Activity*, 1972.

[4]Robert E. Lucas, "Some International Evidence on Output Inflation Tradeoffs," *American Economic Review*, June 1973, presents a statistical and economic argument that the failure of β in equations like Eq. (2) to equal unity does not prove that there is a tradeoff between inflation and unemployment that can be used by policy makers.

[5]See, for example, Robert Solow, "Down the Phillips Curve with Gun and Camera," in David A. Belsley, et al. (eds.), *Inflation, Trade and Taxes*, Ohio State University Press, 1976, and James Tobin, "Inflation and Unemployment," *American Economic Review*, March 1972.

[6]In fact, money wages might not fall at all but simply remain constant. In that event, the rate of decline in prices would at most be equal to the rate of productivity growth. This is so because the rate of change of prices is approximately equal to the rate of change of wages less the growth rate of productivity. Accordingly, with money wages constant, productivity growth puts a floor on the rate of deflation.

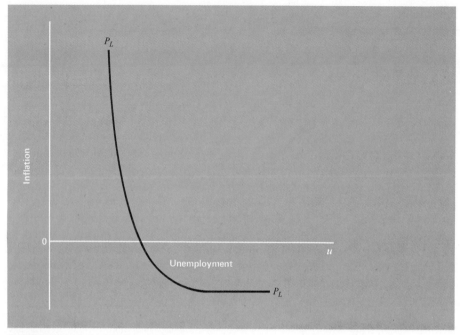

FIGURE 15-3 THE LONG-RUN PHILLIPS
CURVES WITH MONEY WAGES THAT ARE
STICKY DOWNWARD

curve may well be quite flat—large reductions in unemployment can be
achieved with little increase in inflation. The next proposition is that
expectations adjust and shift the Phillips curve up after an expansion of
aggregate demand and reduction of unemployment. The expectations adjustment certainly raises the inflation cost of sustaining a lower unemployment level. The last proposition is that there is no *usable* long-run
inflation-unemployment tradeoff in the United States economy. This
means that for all practical purposes the long-run Phillips curve is vertical
and that expansionary aggregate demand policies cannot be used to reduce
long-run unemployment. In the short run, though, increases in aggregate
demand can be used as a means of reducing unemployment.

15-2 THE ANATOMY OF UNEMPLOYMENT

It is time to take a closer look at unemployment now that we have reviewed
the unemployment-inflation tradeoff. The traditional notion of unemployment is that there is a pool of workers who remain unemployed for
long periods of time, with little chance of finding work. That picture is

incorrect. There is a pool of unemployed people, but there is considerable movement in and out of the pool with a relatively short spell of unemployment on average.

It is useful to organize discussion of unemployment around the relationship between the aggregate *unemployment rate u*, the average *duration* of a spell of unemployment D_u, and the *frequency* of unemployment F_u:

$$u = \text{duration} \times \text{frequency} = D_u \times F_u \tag{4}$$

From Eq. (4), the unemployment rate is the product of the average duration of unemployment and the average frequency of unemployment. Thus, for example, suppose the average duration or length of a spell of unemployment is five weeks and suppose that on average each person—or rather each member of the civilian labor force—is unemployed once every two years. What will the unemployment rate be? The unemployment rate is the fraction of a year the average person in unemployed (D_u = 5 weeks/52 weeks = 0.096) times the number of times per year (F_u = 0.5) that the average person becomes unemployed. For our example it works out that the average member of the civilian labor force experiences spells of unemployment of almost 0.1 year, or more than a month, in duration with a frequency of once every two years or on average half a time per year. The unemployment rate therefore works out to u = 4.8 percent (= 0.5 × 0.096). To give another example assume that the average duration of unemployment is much larger, say one year, but that the frequency of unemployment is considerably smaller, say once every twenty years. In this case, we have an unemployment rate of u = 5 percent (= 1 × 0.05) just as before. An aggregate unemployment rate, of say 5 percent, is consistent with considerably different durations and frequencies of unemployment. We will see that United States unemployment is more like the first example above than the second. Unemployment in the United States results from frequent short spells of unemployment rather than infrequent long spells.

Equation (4) is a description of unemployment that characterizes the unemployment of the average member of the civilian labor force. For many purposes we are interested not in the average person but rather in different groups. From this point of view the unemployment rate in Eq. (4) can be thought of as the weighted average of the unemployment rates of various subgroups or categories of members of the labor force. Thus we can write

$$u = w_1 u_1 + w_2 u_2 + \ldots + w_n u_n \tag{5}$$

In Eq. (5) the weights w_i are the fraction of the civilian labor force that fall within a specific group, say, black teenagers. The u_i are the unemployment rates for those subgroups. An equation like Eq. (5) emphasizes the possibility that the average unemployment rate conceals unemployment rates that vary dramatically across groups that differ by race, age, and sex. In fact, we could think of the same aggregate unemployment rate as made up of equal unemployment rates across, say two groups or as coming from quite different unemployment rates for different groups. Specifically for 1975, the aggregate unemployment rate was 8.5 percent, white unemployment was 7.8 percent, and nonwhite unemployment was 13.9 percent. In terms of Eq. (5) we have

$$8.5 \text{ percent} = (0.885)7.8 \text{ percent} + (0.115)13.9 \text{ percent} \tag{5a}$$

where the shares of the two groups in the labor force are 88.5 percent and 11.5 percent, respectively. Clearly Eq. (5a) shows dramatically that a given aggregate unemployment rate can conceal a large discrepancy in unemployment rates across groups. More importantly, it is possible for the unemployment rate of a subgroup to be very high indeed without this being significantly reflected in the aggregate numbers simply because the group is small as a fraction of the labor force.

After this preview we now turn to the characteristics of aggregate unemployment in terms of Eq. (4) and (5). First we study the finding that the average unemployment experience is one of frequent short spells of unemployment. Next we look at the composition of unemployment, which is concentrated quite heavily in the groups of young people and minorities. In concluding this section, we look at the characteristics of United States unemployment to ask what policies can be used to reduce the unemployment rate. For that purpose it is important to know the anatomy of unemployment.

Flows In and Out of Unemployment

An unemployed person is defined as one who is out of work *and* who (1) has either actively looked for work during the previous four weeks, or (2) is waiting to be recalled to a job from which she has been laid off, or (3) is waiting to report to a new job within four weeks. For most people unemployment is a temporary state.

Figure 15-4 shows how people enter and leave the *unemployment pool*. A person may become unemployed for one of four reasons: (1) The person may be a new entrant into the labor force looking for work for the first time or else after not having looked for work for more than four weeks. (2) A person may quit a job in order to look for other employment and register as unemployed while searching. (3) The person may be laid off. The definition of *layoff* is a suspension without pay lasting or expected to last more than seven consecutive days, initiated by the employer "without prejudice to the worker." The latter qualification means that the worker was not fired but rather is expected to return to the old job. A firm will typically adjust to a transitory decline in product demand by laying off some

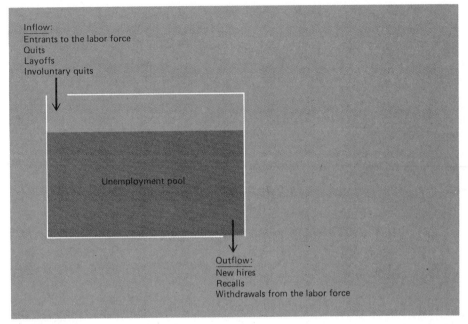

FIGURE 15-4 FLOWS IN AND OUT OF
THE UNEMPLOYMENT POOL

labor. A firm may also rotate layoffs among its labor force so that the individual laid-off worker may expect a recall even before product demand has fully recovered. In manufacturing it appears that over 75 percent of laid-off workers actually return to jobs with their original employers.[7] (4) A worker may be fired "with prejudice," so that there is no hope of returning to the initial job. This last way of becoming unemployed is more politely referred to as "involuntary quits."

These sources of inflow into the pool of unemployment have a counterpart in the outflow from the unemployment pool. There are essentially three ways of moving out of the pool of unemployment. (1) A person may be hired into a new job. (2) Someone laid off can be recalled. (3) An unemployed person can stop looking for a job and thus, by definition, leave the labor force.

Recent research has concentrated on the flows into and out of unemployment.[8] The research starts from the recognition that the flows are

[7] See Martin Feldstein, "Temporary Layoffs in the Theory of Unemployment," *Journal of Political Economy*, October 1976.

[8] See Charles C. Holt, "Job Search, Phillips' Wage Relation and Union Influence: Theory and Evidence," in E. S. Phelps (ed.), *Microeconomic Foundations of Employment and Inflation Theory*, Norton, 1970; Robert E. Hall, "Why Is the Unemployment Rate So High at Full Employment?" *Brookings Papers on Economic Activity*, 1970, 3; Martin S. Feldstein, "The Economics of the New Unemployment," *Public Interest*, Fall 1973.

TABLE 15-1 UNEMPLOYED PERSONS BY DURATION OF UNEMPLOYMENT

	May 1973	May 1975
Overall unemployment rate (percent)	4.9	8.9
Percentage of total, *unemployed for:*		
Less than 5 weeks	49.3	34.7
5-14 weeks	27.0	26.9
15 weeks and over	23.8	38.3
Average duration of *unemployment* (weeks)	11.2	14.8
Frequency of unemployment (times per year)	0.23	0.32

Source: Employment and Earnings, June 1973 and June 1975.

large relative to the average level of unemployment. A first way of looking at the flows emphasizes the low average duration of unemployment. This point is brought out in Table 15-1 and Chart 15-2, where we look at the distribution of unemployment according to duration. For comparison we choose the rates for May 1975, when the unemployment rate in the aggregate was at a postwar high, and May 1973, when it was close to what is regarded as the natural rate.

In May 1973, about half the unemployed had been unemployed for less than five weeks. Less than 10 percent of the unemployed had been unemployed for over six months. The average duration of unemployment was just over eleven weeks. By May 1975, the average duration of unemployment had lengthened to almost fifteen weeks, but even so, over half the unemployed had been in that state for less than ten weeks. The frequency of unemployment rose over the two years, from 0.23 in May 1973 to 0.32 in May 1975.

At both dates shown in Table 15-1, most of the unemployed had been in that state for less than ten weeks. We draw from this observation the important conclusion that average unemployment is not the result of a few people being unemployed for a long period of time. Rather unemployment is the result of people entering and leaving the pool of unemployment fairly often. This implies that flows in and out of the unemployment pool are large relative to the level of unemployment. It is not correct, though, to conclude that unemployment is no problem because it is spread widely and for short periods. It is not correct to argue that a 5 percent unemployment rate means that every person is unemployed for 2.6 weeks (= 52 weeks × 5 percent per year) per year. On the contrary, unemployment is a phenomenon which affects some people for longer periods and some—and perhaps the same—people more often than it does others. This is why we discuss the distribution of unemployment below.

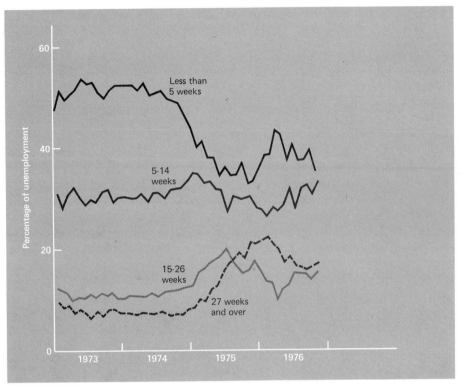

CHART 15-2 DURATION OF UNEMPLOYMENT. (Source: *Economic Indicators*, December 1976)

A second way of examining flows in and out of unemployment is by direct estimates of the rate at which the labor force turns over in manufacturing establishments. Those data, for the months of May 1973 and May 1975, respectively, are presented in Table 15-2. They support our conclusions above about large flows in and out of the pool of unemployment. "Accessions" are names added to the payroll of a company in a given month. Thus in May 1973 manufacturing companies on average added 4.7 names to their payrolls per hundred employees. "Separations" are names removed from the payroll during the month. In May 1975, manufacturing companies on average removed 4.1 names from their payrolls per hundred employees. Note first that the levels of accessions and separations (per hundred employees) are consistently high, each in the vicinity of 4 percent per month. Second, note that even when the unemployment rate was at the high level of 8.9 percent, accessions were equal to 3.5 percent of the manufacturing work force. Even in the depths of the recession, firms were hiring new people and calling back workers who had earlier been laid off. Perhaps even more surprisingly, in May 1975, 1.3 percent of the workers in

TABLE 15-2   LABOR TURNOVER RATES IN MANUFACTURING *(Per 100 employees)*

	May 1973		May 1975	
1. Total accessions	4.7		3.5	
New hires		3.9		1.8
Recalls		0.8		1.7
2. Total separations	4.7		4.1	
Quits		2.7		1.3
Layoffs		0.9		2.6
Other, including involuntary quits		1.1		0.2

Source: Employment and Earnings, June 1973 and June 1975.

manufacturing quit their jobs voluntarily.   Table 15-2 presents a remarkable picture of movement in the labor force.   People are taking and leaving jobs, even during times of very high unemployment.

Now that we have a picture of the labor market as being in a constant state of movement, we can ask about the factors changing the rate of unemployment, and those determining the overall level of unemployment. Figure 15-4 makes it clear that unemployment increases when the flow into unemployment exceeds that out of the pool.   Thus increases in quits and layoffs increase unemployment, as does an increase in the flow of new entrants into the labor market, since new entrants typically take time to find a job once they decide to become employed.   Unemployment is reduced by increases in hiring rates, and by unemployed workers leaving the labor force.

Table 15-3 and Chart 15-3 provide some information about the breakdown of the reasons for unemployment.   The categories in this table do not precisely match those in Fig. 15-4.   Nevertheless, they indicate that when the average unemployment rate is low, as in May 1973, less than 40 percent of unemployment is due to job loss.   By contrast, when unemployment is high, as in May 1975, job loss becomes by far the most important reason for unemployment.   In fact, the "true" unemployment due to job loss is even

TABLE 15-3   UNEMPLOYED PERSONS BY REASON FOR UNEMPLOYMENT

	May 1973 (percent)	May 1975 (percent)
Job losers	38.7	57.6
Job leavers	13.7	9.2
Reentrants	32.5	23.5
New entrants	15.0	9.6
Total	100	100

Source: Employment and Earnings, June 1973 and June 1975.

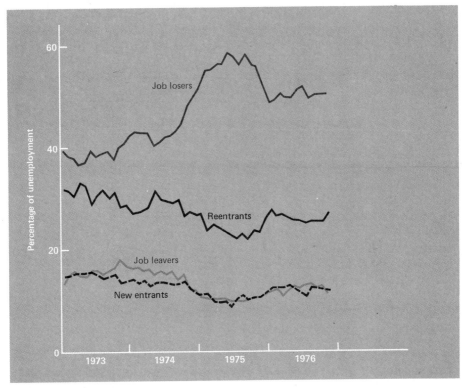

CHART 15-3 REASONS FOR UNEMPLOYMENT (Source: *Economic Indicators*, December 1976)

larger than suggested by this table because of those called "discouraged workers," that is, people who cease to look for jobs, and thus are no longer counted as unemployed.

Figure 15-4 explains changes in the level of unemployment at a mechanical level. Each of the factors contained in Fig. 15-4 is in part determined by economic variables, such as the level of aggregate demand, and the actual and expected real wage rate. When aggregate demand rises (at a given real wage), firms increase their hiring. When aggregate demand falls, firms lay off workers. Thus there is an immediate link between the factors emphasized in Fig. 15-4 and aggregate demand. However, it should be noted that the relationship between aggregate demand and the variables affecting the rate of unemployment is not unambiguous. For instance, an increase in the demand for labor increases quits at the same time as it reduces layoffs. A person thinking of leaving his job to search for another would be more likely to quit when the job market is good and demand is high, than when there is heavy unemployment and the prospects of finding a good job quickly are low. In fact, it can be seen from Table

15-2 that quits and layoffs moved in the opposite direction between May 1973 and May 1975: quits fell from 2.7 percent to 1.3 percent per month, while layoffs rose from 0.9 percent to 2.6 percent per month.

We now know what causes the unemployment rate to change. When the unemployment rate is constant, flows in and out of unemployment just balance each other. Flows in and out of unemployment can match at any level of unemployment. The *natural rate of unemployment,* however, is that rate of unemployment at which flows in and out of unemployment just balance,[9] *and* at which expectations of firms and workers as to the behavior of prices and wages are correct.

The determinants of the natural rate of unemployment can be thought of in terms of the duration and frequency of unemployment. The *duration* of unemployment is the average length of time it takes to find and accept a job, after entry into the pool of unemployed. That depends on(1) the organization of the labor market, in regard to the presence or absence of employment agencies, youth employment services, etc., (2) the demographic makeup of the labor force, as discussed below, (3) the ability and desire of the unemployed to keep looking for a better job, and (4) the availability and type of jobs. If all jobs are the same, then an unemployed person will take the first one offered. If some jobs are better than others, then it is worthwhile searching and waiting for a good one. If it is very expensive to remain unemployed, say, because there are no unemployment benefits, then an unemployed person is more likely to accept a job offer than to continue looking for a better one. If unemployment benefits are high, then it may be worthwhile for the unemployed person to continue looking for a better job rather than accepting a poor job when one is offered.

The behavior of workers who have been laid off is particularly important when considering the duration of unemployment. Typically, a worker who has been laid off returns to her original job and does not search for another job. The reason is quite simple: once a worker has been with a firm for a long time, she has special expertise in the way that firm works which makes her valuable to that firm but is not of great benefit to another firm. That means that such an individual could not expect to receive as good a job if she searched for a new one. Her best course of action may be to wait to be recalled.

There are two basic determinants of the *frequency* of unemployment. The first is the variability of the demand for labor across different firms in the economy. The second is the rate at which new workers enter the labor force. Even when aggregate demand is constant, some firms are growing and some are contracting. The contracting firms lose labor and the growing firms hire more labor. The greater this variability of the demand for

---

[9]We should recognize that when the labor force is growing, and the unemployment rate is constant, the pool of unemployed grows over time. For example, with a labor force of 80 million and 5 percent unemployment, total unemployment is 4.0 million people. With a labor force of 90 million and 5 percent unemployment, there are 4.5 million unemployed, and the unemployment pool has grown by ½ million people.

labor across different firms, the higher the unemployment rate. Further, the variability of aggregate demand itself will affect the variability of the demand for labor. Second, the more rapidly new workers enter the labor force—the faster the growth rate of the labor force—the higher the natural rate of unemployment.

The four factors affecting duration and the two factors affecting frequency of unemployment are the basic determinants of the natural rate of unemployment.

You should note that the factors determining the level of the natural rate of unemployment are not immutable. The structure of the labor market and the labor force can change. The willingness of workers to remain unemployed while looking for, or waiting for, a new job can change. The variability of the demand for labor by different firms can change. As Edmund Phelps has noted, the natural rate is not "an intertemporal constant, something like the speed of light, independent of everything under the sun."[10] Indeed, the natural rate is difficult to measure, and estimates of it have changed over the last few years from about 4 percent in the 1960's to near 5 or 5.5 percent in the late seventies.

The Distribution of Unemployment

Unemployment is distributed very unevenly across the population. Chart 15-4 shows unemployment rates by age, sex, and race categories. The message of Chart 15-4 is simple. First, sex differences are associated with some differences in unemployment rates, given age and race. However, these differences are relatively small. Differentials between male and female unemployment rates were reduced between May 1973 and May 1975. Second, nonwhite unemployment is substantially greater than white unemployment, with the unemployment rate for black teenagers being twice the corresponding rate for white teenagers. In all age and sex groups, black unemployment rates are at least 1½ times as large as white unemployment rates. And third, unemployment rates fall with age, up to the age of 65.

The data on the durations of unemployment presented in Table 15-4 tell another interesting story. The average duration of unemployment rises with age, and the frequency of unemployment for the young is eight or more times the frequency for mature workers. The frequency of unemployment for blacks is greater than that for whites, but the differences between blacks and whites are smaller than those between the young and the more mature.

The evidence tells an unambiguous story. Unemployment is much higher among the young than among the older. But the nature of the unemployment is very different. The young tend to be unemployed more often and for short spells, whereas older workers are unemployed much less often but for longer periods. To the extent that long periods of unem-

[10]See E. Phelps, "Economic Policy and Unemployment in the Sixties," *Public Interest,* Winter 1974.

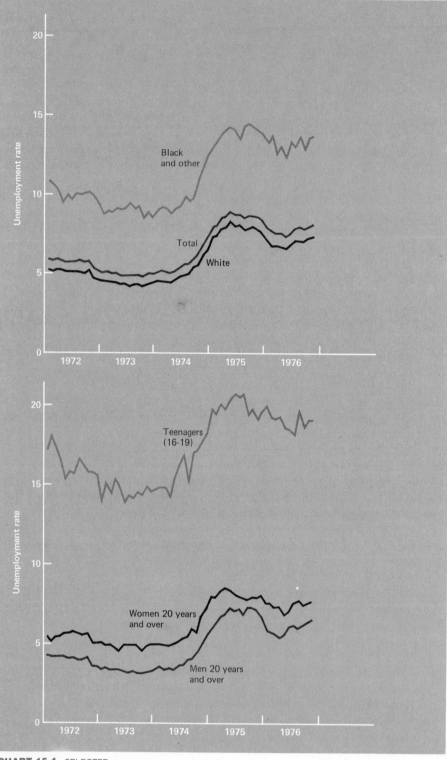

CHART 15-4 SELECTED
UNEMPLOYMENT RATES. (Source: *Economic Indicators*, December 1976)

TABLE 15-4   RATES, DURATION, AND FREQUENCY OF UNEMPLOYMENT, BY AGE, SEX, AND RACE

	Unemployment rate (percentage of labor force)		Average duration (weeks)		Average frequency (times per year unemployed)	
	May 1973	May 1975	May 1973	May 1975	May 1973	May 1975
Males						
16–19	12.1	18.1	8.8	11.0	0.72	0.86
20–24	7.1	14.9	9.8	14.9	0.38	0.52
25–64	2.4	5.8	16.1	18.0	0.08	0.17
Females						
16–19	13.3	19.3	7.1	9.3	0.98	1.08
20–24	7.9	13.3	8.0	10.4	0.50	0.67
25–64	3.5	7.3	11.1	16.2	0.16	0.23
White						
Males	3.4	7.2	12.9	15.5	0.14	0.24
Females	4.6	8.5	8.9	13.5	0.27	0.35
Nonwhite						
Males	7.4	13.1	12.5	17.8	0.31	0.38
Females	8.9	13.5	10.7	13.4	0.43	0.53
All workers	4.9	9.0	10.1	13.5	0.25	0.35

Source: *Employment and Earnings*, June 1973 and June 1975.

ployment are a more serious concern than short periods, a given rate of unemployment (say 5 percent) among older workers is a more serious concern than the same rate of unemployment (5 percent) among youths. But the level of unemployment among the young is so high that youth unemployment is indeed a serious problem.

Reducing the Natural Rate of Unemployment

Discussions of methods for reducing the natural rate of unemployment tend to focus on the distribution of unemployment across different groups in the labor force.[11]   Unemployment rates are lowest among mature white males. If unemployment rates for other groups of workers could be reduced toward those levels, the overall unemployment rate would obviously drop.

   The place to start is with teenage unemployment.   We have pointed out above that teen-agers are unemployed more frequently than others. Reasons for their unemployment can be examined with the help of Table 15-5.   It can be seen that many of the unemployed teenagers are new entrants to the labor force, and also that more teenagers than adult males are reentrants to the labor force.   The unemployment rate among teen-

[11]See Martin S. Feldstein, "The Economics of the New Unemployment," *Public Interest*, 33, Fall 1973, and Robert E. Hall, "Prospects for Shifting the Phillips Curve through Manpower Policy," *Brookings Papers on Economic Activity*, 1971, 3.

TABLE 15-5   UNEMPLOYED PERSONS BY REASON FOR UNEMPLOYMENT BY SEX, AGE, AND RACE

	Males, 20+		Females, 20+		Both sexes, 16 to 19		White		Nonwhite	
	May 1973	May 1975	May 1973	May 1975	May 1973	May 1975	May 1973	May 1975	May 1973	May 1975
Total unemployed (percent distribution)	100	100	100	100	100	100	100	100	100	100
Job losers	57.3	74.2	34.7	54.1	15.2	26.2	39.5	58.2	36.0	54.0
Job leavers	13.7	7.9	16.4	12.7	10.3	6.6	14.1	9.5	12.0	8.1
Reentrants	25.5	15.6	42.9	28.9	30.0	32.2	31.4	23.3	36.9	24.6
New entrants	3.5	2.3	6.1	4.3	44.5	35.0	15.0	8.9	15.0	12.7

Source: Employment and Earnings, June 1973 and June 1975.

agers could be reduced if the length of time it takes a teenager to find a first job is reduced, and also if their entry and exit from the labor force were made less frequent. In order to reduce delays in the finding of jobs, it has been suggested that a *Youth Employment Service* should be set up to help school leavers locate jobs.

One of the main reasons teenagers enter and leave the labor force often is that the jobs they hold when they are working are not particularly attractive. It is a matter of some controversy as to how to improve existing jobs. Martin Feldstein has suggested that part of the reason jobs are unattractive is that the minimum wage is too high to make it worthwhile for employers to spend more money training the labor they hire in order to make their employees more skilled in their line of work.[12] He points to the apprentice system in other countries, in which young workers either receive very low pay or else actually pay to get jobs, while they are learning skills. He argues that a reduction in the minimum wage would help make such on-the-job training more attractive to employers in the United States. He also suggests that there should be a system of scholarships for this type of training, since he doubts that a lower minimum wage by itself would be sufficient to encourage the right amount of on-the-job training.

By contrast, Peter Doeringer and Michael Piore[13] doubt that measures such as reducing the minimum wage will do much to improve the nature of jobs in what they call the *secondary labor market*. They suggest that there are a host of noneconomic factors affecting the nature of the jobs that are typically available in the economy. The major economic variables they point to as determining the nature of jobs are the stability and level of aggregate demand. They argue that the instability of aggregate demand is

[12]Martin Feldstein, "The Economics of the New Unemployment," op. cit.

[13]Peter B. Doeringer and Michael J. Piore, "Unemployment and the 'Dual Labor Market'," *Public Interest*, 38, Winter 1975.

the major reason firms rely on temporary labor and subcontracting to meet high levels of demand. If demand were maintained at a high *and* stable level, firms would have more incentive to create good stable jobs for their entire work force.

When we move away from teen-age unemployment to other categories of unemployment, it is clear from Table 15-5 that reentry rates into the labor force are much higher for all categories other than mature males. This suggests that these other groups, too, move in and out of the labor force. Thus the same policies that might increase the stability of teen-age employment should be expected to work for these groups. These would include policies to provide such workers with more training, perhaps in government manpower training schemes. There have been a number of such programs, the success of which is difficult to evaluate.[14] They would also include attempts to create "job banks" which would make it possible to match the characteristics of available jobs with those of workers looking for jobs in a computerized system. Better day-care facilities would also contribute to more stable labor market participation.

Finally, we return to the system of unemployment benefits. Unemployment benefits are not taxed, but wages are. It appears that unemployment benefits typically are at least 50 percent as high as after-tax wage incomes. A rough comparison is provided by the average weekly unemployment check in the third quarter of 1975, which was about $71. Weekly earnings (after income and Social Security tax) in private nonagricultural employment were about $149 in the same time period.[15] The assumption that unemployment compensation amounts to roughly 50 percent of after-tax earnings is thus a good working hypothesis. A high level of unemployment benefits makes it less urgent for an unemployed person to obtain a job. Further, the fact that a laid-off worker will not suffer a large loss from being laid off makes it more attractive for an employer to lay off a worker temporarily than to attempt to keep her on the job.

There seems to be little doubt that unemployment compensation does add to the natural rate of unemployment. This does not imply, though, that unemployment compensation should be abolished. What is appropriate is a scheme that will create less incentive for firms to lay off labor while at the same time ensuring that the unemployed are not exposed to economic distress.[16]

It has become fashionable to argue that unemployment does not present a serious social problem because the unemployed essentially choose to be unemployed and live off unemployment compensation. This argument is wrong in assuming that all unemployment is covered by unem-

[14]See the articles by Hall, cited in footnotes 8 and 11, and by Feldstein, cited in footnotes 7 and 8. See also the annual *Employment and Training Report of the President.*

[15]See *Economic Report of the President,* 1975, Tables B26 and B29.

[16]See Feldstein, "The Economics of the New Unemployment," op. cit., for discussion of the ways in which the current system could be improved.

ployment benefits. In fact, insured unemployment is less than two-thirds of total unemployment.

15-3 THE COSTS OF UNEMPLOYMENT

The costs of unemployment are so obvious that this section might seem superfluous. Society on the whole loses from unemployment because total output is below its potential level. The unemployed as individuals suffer both from their income loss while unemployed and from the low level of self-esteem that long periods of unemployment cause.[17]

This section provides some estimates of the costs of forgone output resulting from unemployment, and clarifies some of the issues connected with the costs of unemployment and the potential benefits from reducing unemployment. We distinguish between cyclical unemployment, associated with short-run deviations of the unemployment rate from the natural rate, and "permanent" unemployment that exists at the natural rate.

Cyclical Unemployment

We have already studied Okun's law, which estimates the short-run loss of output associated with a one-percentage-point increase in the unemployment rate. The cost of a one-percentage-point increase in the unemployment rate in the short run is a three-percentage-point fall in the level of real output. This is the fundamental cost of cyclical unemployment.

Are there any other costs of unemployment or, for that matter, offsetting benefits? It is possible to imagine offsetting benefits. We do not discuss here the benefit arising from a temporary reduction in the inflation rate accompanying a temporary increase in unemployment, but rather we focus on the costs of unemployment taken by itself. A possible offsetting benefit occurs because the unemployed are not working and have more leisure. However, the value that can be placed on that leisure is small. In the first place, much of it is unwanted leisure.

Second, there is a fairly subtle issue that we shall have to explore. If a person were free to set her hours of work, she would work up to the point at which the marginal value of leisure to her was equal to the marginal return from working an extra hour. We would then be able to conclude that, if her workday were slightly reduced, the overall loss to her would be extremely small. The reason is that she acquires extra leisure from working less, at the cost of having less income. But she was previously at the point where the marginal value of leisure was equal to the after-tax marginal wage, so that the benefit of the increased leisure almost exactly offsets the private loss of

---

[17]See Robert J. Gordon, "The Welfare Cost of Higher Unemployment," *Brookings Papers on Economic Activity*, 1973, 1; and Edmund S. Phelps, *Inflation Policy and Unemployment Theory*, Norton, 1972.

income. However, the net marginal wage is much less than the value of the marginal product of an employed person to the economy. The major reason is that society taxes the income of the employed person, so that society as a whole takes a share of the marginal product of the employed person. When the employed person stops working, she loses for herself only the *net* of tax wage she had been receiving. But society also loses the taxes she had been paying. The unemployed person values her leisure at the net of tax wage, and that value is smaller than the value of her marginal product for society as a whole. Therefore, the value of increased leisure provides only a partial offset to the Okun's law estimate of the cost of cyclical unemployment.

Note that we do not count both the loss of the individual's income to herself and the Okun's law estimate of forgone output as part of the cost of unemployment. The reason is that the Okun's law estimate implicitly includes the individual's own loss of income—it estimates the total loss of output to the economy as a whole as a result of the reduction of employment. That loss could in principle be distributed across different people in the economy in many different ways. For instance, one could imagine that the unemployed person continues to receive benefit payments totaling close to her previous income while employed, with the benefit payments financed through taxes on working individuals. In that case, the unemployed person would not suffer an income loss from being unemployed, but society would still lose from the reduction in total output available.

However, the effects of an increase in unemployment are, in fact, borne heavily by the unemployed themselves. There is thus an extra cost to society of unemployment that is very difficult to quantify. The cost arises from the uneven distribution of the burden of unemployment across the population. Unemployment tends to be concentrated among the poor, and that makes the distributional aspect of unemployment a serious matter. It is not one we can easily quantify, but it should not be overlooked. Further, there are many reports of the adverse psychic effects of unemployment that, again, are not easy to quantify but should not be ignored.[18]

"Permanent" Unemployment

The benefits of reducing the natural rate of unemployment are more difficult to estimate than the costs of cyclical unemployment. It is clear that the Okun's law estimate of a 3 percent change in output resulting from a one-percentage-point change in the unemployment rate is not appropriate here. The reason is that the increase in output associated with cyclical changes in unemployment results in part from the fact that the labor put back to work in the short run is able to use capital that had not been fully utilized when unemployment was high. However, in the long run, which

[18]See E. W. Bakke, *The Unemployed Worker: A Study of the Task of Making a Living without a Job*, Archon, 1969.

is relevant when considering a reduction in the natural rate of unemployment, it would be necessary to invest to provide for the capital with which the newly employed would work. The Okun 3:1 ratio is therefore too high for the long-run benefits of reducing the natural rate of unemployment. One estimate of benefit is that a one-percentage-point reduction in the natural unemployment rate from 5 percent would increase long-run output by only 0.76 percent.[19]

The available estimates of the social benefits of a reduction in long-run unemployment cannot be narrowed down to very solid numbers. Even more difficult is the estimate of an "optimal" long-run unemployment rate. Here we ask the question whether any—and, if so, how much— unemployment is desirable in the long run. A first guess at the answer to that question is that all unemployment is wasteful, since the unemployed labor could usefully be employed. However, that answer is not totally persuasive. Those people who are unemployed in order to look for a better job are performing a valuable service not only for themselves. They are also performing a service for society by attempting to put themselves into a position in which they earn the most and are the most valuable. Because the composition of demand shifts over time, we can expect always to have some firms expanding and some contracting. This is true even with a stable level of aggregate demand. Those who lose their jobs will be unemployed, and they benefit both society and themselves by not taking the very first job that comes along but rather searching for the optimal employment. Accordingly, we can conclude that some unemployment is a good thing in an economy in which the composition of demand changes over time. It is one thing to recognize this and quite another to pin down the optimal rate of unemployment numerically. Gordon's estimate in the article referred to in footnote 17 is 2.0 percent. Feldstein[20] has argued that the unemployment rate could be lowered to less than 3 percent and perhaps even close to 2 percent, though he has cautiously avoided specifying the precise number.

15-4 THE COSTS OF INFLATION

The costs of inflation are much less obvious than those of unemployment. There is no direct loss of output from inflation, as there is from unemployment. In studying the costs of inflation, we again want to distinguish the short run from the long run. In the case of inflation, though, the relevant distinction is between inflation that is *perfectly anticipated* and taken into account in economic transactions, and *imperfectly anticipated*, or unexpected inflation. We start with perfectly anticipated inflation because that

[19]See Robert J. Gordon, op. cit., p. 175.

[20]In "The Economics of the New Unemployment," op. cit.

case provides a useful bench mark against which to judge unanticipated inflation.

Perfectly Anticipated Inflation

Suppose that an economy has been experiencing a given rate of inflation, say 5 percent, for a long time, and that it is correctly anticipated that the rate of inflation will continue to be 5 percent. In such an economy, all contracts would build in the expected 5 percent inflation. Borrowers and lenders will both know and agree that the dollars in which a loan will be repaid will be worth less than the dollars which are given up by the lender when he makes the loan. Nominal interest rates[21] would be 5 percent higher than they would be in the absence of inflation. Long-term wage contracts will increase wages at 5 percent per year to take account of the inflation, and then build in whatever changes in real wages are agreed to. Long-term leases will take account of the inflation. In brief, any contracts in which the passage of time is involved will take the inflation into account. In that category we include the tax laws, which we are assuming would be indexed. That is, as discussed in Chap. 14, the tax brackets themselves would be increased at the rate of 5 percent per year.[22] Inflation has no real costs in such an economy, except for a minor qualification to be noted below.

That qualification arises because the interest rate that is paid on money might not adjust to the inflation rate. No interest is paid on currency—notes and coin—throughout the world, and no interest is paid on demand deposits in many countries. It is very difficult to pay interest on currency, so that it is likely that the interest rate on currency will continue to be zero, independent of the perfectly anticipated inflation rate. Interest can be paid on demand deposits, and is paid in some states on what are essentially demand deposits.[23] Thus it is reasonable to expect that in a fully anticipated inflation, interest would be paid on demand deposits, and the interest rate paid on demand deposits would adjust to the inflation rate. If so, the only cost of perfectly anticipated inflation is that the inflation makes it more costly to hold currency.

The cost of holding currency is the interest forgone by not holding an interest-bearing asset. When the inflation rate rises, the nominal interest rate rises, the interest lost by holding currency increases, and the cost of

---

[21]Nominal interest rates were defined in Chap. 6. The nominal interest rate is the stated interest rate in money terms, such as 5¼ percent on a savings deposit, distinguished from the expected real interest rate, which is the nominal rate minus the expected rate of inflation.

[22]The taxation of interest would have to be on the *real* (after-inflation) return on assets for the tax system to be properly indexed.

[23]These are the NOW accounts. A NOW account is a negotiable order of withdrawal account. It is difficult to distinguish it with the naked eye from a checking account. Interest is paid on NOW accounts.

holding currency therefore increases. Accordingly, the demand for currency falls. In practice, this means that individuals economize on the use of currency by carrying less currency in their wallets and making more trips to the bank to cash smaller checks than they did before. The costs of these trips to the banks are often described as the "shoe-leather" costs of inflation. The costs are related to the amount by which the demand for currency is reduced by an increase in the anticipated inflation rate, and they are trivial.

We should add that we are assuming throughout inflation rates that are not too high to effectively disrupt the payments system. This disruption was a real problem in some instances of hyperinflations, but it need not concern us here. We are abstracting, too, from the cost of "menu change." This cost arises simply from the fact that with inflation—as opposed to price stability—people have to devote real resources to marking up prices, changing pay telephones and vending machines as well as cash registers. These costs are there, but one cannot get too excited about them.

On balance, the costs of fully anticipated inflation are trivial.

The notion that the costs of fully anticipated inflation are trivial does not square well with the strong aversion to inflation reflected in policy making and politics. The most important reason for that aversion is probably that inflations in the United States have not been steady, and that the inflationary experience of the United States is one of imperfectly anticipated inflation, the costs of which are substantially different from those discussed in this part.

There is a further line of argument that explains the public aversion to inflation, even of the fully anticipated, steady kind we are discussing here. The argument is that such a state is not likely to exist, that it is a mirage to believe that policy makers could and would maintain a steady inflation rate at any level other than zero. The argument is that policy makers are reluctant to use restrictive policy to compensate for transitory increases in the inflation rate. Rather than maintain a constant rate of inflation in the face of inflation shocks, the authorities would accommodate these shocks and therefore validate them. Any inflationary shock would add to the inflation rate rather than being compensated by restrictive policy. In this manner, inflation, far from being constant, would, in fact, be rising as policy makers validate any and every disturbance rather than using policy to rigidly enforce the inflation target. Zero inflation, it is argued, is the only target that can be defended without this risk.[24]

Although there are many examples of countries with long inflationary histories, there does not appear to be any tendency for the inflation rate of those countries to increase over time. The argument thus seems weak. However, it is true that the inflation rate has been more stable in countries

[24]See William J. Fellner, "Criteria for Demand Management Policy in View of Past Failures," in Fellner (ed.), *Contemporary Economic Problems*, American Enterprise Institute, 1976.

with low rates of inflation than in countries with inflation rates that are on average higher,[25] perhaps providing a germ of validity to the notion.

Imperfectly Anticipated Inflation

The idyllic scene of full adjustment to inflation painted above does not describe economies that we actually know. Modern economies include a variety of institutional features representing different degrees of adjustment to inflation. Economies with long inflationary histories, such as those of Brazil, or Israel, have made substantial adjustments to inflation through the use of indexing. Others in which inflation has been episodic, such as the United States economy, have made only small adjustments for inflation.

One of the important effects of inflation is to change the real value of assets fixed in nominal terms. A doubling of the price level, such as the United States has experienced in the period from 1955 to 1975, cuts the purchasing power of all claims or assets fixed in money terms in half. Thus, someone who bought a twenty-year government bond in 1955 and expected to receive a principal of, say, $100 in constant purchasing power at the 1975 maturity date, actually winds up with a $100 principal that has purchasing power of only $50 in 1955 dollars. The doubling of the price level has effectively reduced the real value of the asset by one-half. It has transferred wealth from creditors—holders of bonds—to debtors. This effect operates with respect to all assets fixed in nominal terms, in particular, money, bonds, savings accounts, insurance contracts, and some pensions. Obviously it is an extremely important effect since it can certainly wipe out the purchasing power of a lifetime's saving that is supposed to finance retirement consumption. In 1975 the total value of assets fixed in nominal terms was about $5 trillion, or almost $24,000 per head. A one-percentage-point increase in the price level would reduce the real value of these assets by $51 billion, or an amount equal to 3.5 percent of GNP.

Those figures by themselves seem to explain the public concern over inflation. There appears to be a lot riding on each percentage-point change in the price level. That impression is slightly misleading. Many individuals are both debtors and creditors in nominal assets. Almost everyone has some money, and is thus a creditor in nominal terms. Much of the middle class owns housing, financed through mortgages whose value is fixed in nominal terms. Such individuals benefit from inflation because it reduced the real value of their mortgages. Other individuals have borrowed in nominal terms to buy consumer durables such as cars, and to that extent have their real indebtedness reduced by inflation.

Table 15-6 shows the net position of different sectors in the economy in terms of the amounts of nominal assets they own or owe. In other words, the table shows the net debtor or creditor status in terms of nominal or

[25]Arthur M. Okun, "The Mirage of Steady Inflation," *Brookings Papers on Economic Activity*, 2, 1971.

TABLE 15-6 NET DEBTOR OR CREDITOR STATUS IN NOMINAL ASSETS OF MAJOR ECONOMIC SECTORS
(Billions of dollars)

	1960	1970	1975
Households	+337	+706	+1,130
Unincorporated businesses	− 21	− 93	− 142
Nonfinancial corporations	− 67	−190	− 324
Financial corporations	+ 32	− 76	− 89
Governments	−251	−340	− 518

Note: A plus sign indicates a net monetary creditor.
Source: Federal Reserve Flow-of-Funds Accounts.

"monetary" assets and liabilities.[26]   The household sector shows up as a net monetary creditor with the government the offsetting major monetary debtor.   Nonfinancial corporations are to a large extent monetary debtors reflecting their debt-financed capital structure.   Similarly, financial corporations are net monetary debtors.   For example, the banks' net debtor position is reflected by their liabilities in the form of debt and deposits while their assets include some real assets like land and structures.

The important point about Table 15-6 is the recognition that a change in the price level brings about a major redistribution of wealth between sectors.   Thus an inflation rate of 10 percent in 1975 would have resulted in a transfer of $51.8 billion from the household sector to the government. Obviously we must be careful in assessing the implications of that statement.   A redistribution of wealth from corporations to the household sector for example, means that as a household the average person has gained, but as owner of a corporate stock the average household has lost. Rather than looking at the total amount of nominal assets outstanding to judge the potential impact of inflation, we should look at the net effect of a change in the price level on the real wealth of different individuals.   This singles out transfers between the government and the private sector as particularly important because here the offset is much less immediate.

We are talking here about inflation because that is the current issue.   It should be apparent though that much the same problems arise with deflation or falling prices.   Thus from 1929 to 1933 the consumer price index fell by almost 25 percent, and that decline meant an extremely large increase in the real value of liabilities, in particular, the real debt of farmers.   Inflation redistributes wealth within society from creditors to debtors, and deflation redistributes wealth from debtors to creditors.

---

[26]Table 15-6 is an updated version of a similar table in G. L. Bach and James B. Stephenson, "Inflation and the Distribution of Wealth," *Review of Economics and Statistics*, vol. 56, no. 1 (February 1974).

However, we must go beyond Table 15-6 in two respects. First, Table 15-6 really indicates the vulnerability of different sectors to inflation. It does not tell us to what extent inflation was anticipated when the contracts behind the figures in Table 15-6 were entered into. The 10 percent inflation referred to above might have been correctly anticipated, so that the wealth transfer occurring as a result of the inflation would not cause any surprises. However, that does not mean that the creditors would not benefit from higher rates of inflation, and the debtors from lower rates. Second, the gains and losses from the wealth transfers occurring as a result of inflation basically cancel out over the economy as a whole. When the government gains from inflation, the private sector might have to pay lower taxes later. When the corporate sector gains from inflation, owners of corporations benefit at the expense of others. If we really did not care about the distribution of wealth among individuals, the costs of unanticipated inflation would be negligible. Included in the individuals of the previous sentence are those belonging to different generations, since the current owners of the national debt might be harmed by inflation to the benefit of future taxpayers.

The costs of unanticipated inflation are thus largely distributional costs. There is some evidence[27] that the old are more vulnerable to inflation than the young in that they own more nominal assets. Offsetting this, however, is the fact that Social Security benefits are indexed, so that a substantial part of the wealth of those about to retire is protected from unanticipated inflation. There appears to be little evidence supporting the view that the poor suffer unduly from unanticipated inflation.

Inflation redistributes wealth between debtors and creditors, as shown in Table 15-6, because changes in the price level change the purchasing power of assets fixed in money terms. There is room, too, for inflation to affect income positions by changing the distribution of income. A popular line of argument has always been that inflation benefits capitalists or recipients of profit income at the expense of wage earners. Unanticipated inflation, it is argued, means that prices rise faster than wages and therefore allow profits to expand.[28] For the United States in the postwar period there is no persuasive evidence to this effect. There is evidence that the real return on common stocks—that is, the real value of dividends and capital gains on equity—is reduced by unanticipated inflation. Thus, equity holders appear to be adversely affected by unanticipated inflation.[29]

The last important distributional effect of inflation concerns the real

[27]See Bach and Stephenson, op. cit.

[28]Louis De Alessi, "Do Business Firms Gain from Inflation? Reprise," *Journal of Business*, April 1975. See also Nancy Jianakoplos, "Are You Protected from Inflation?" Federal Reserve Bank of St. Louis, *Review*, January 1977.

[29]See Charles R. Nelson, "Inflation and Rates of Return on Common Stocks," *Journal of Finance*, May 1976.

value of tax liabilities. We recall from Chap. 14 that a failure to index the tax structure implies that inflation moves the public into higher tax brackets and thus raises the real value of their tax payments or reduces real disposable income. Inflation acts as if Congress had voted an increase in tax schedules. An estimate of this overtaxation due to the approximately 10 percent inflation from 1973 to 1974 is $7 billion (in 1974 dollars) on account of increased personal income taxes alone.[30]

The fact that unanticipated inflation acts mainly to redistribute wealth, the net effects of which redistribution should be close to zero, has led to some questioning of the reasons for public concern over inflation. The gainers, it seems, do not shout as loudly as the losers. Since some of the gainers (future taxpayers) have yet to be born, this is hardly surprising. There is also a notion that the average wage earner is subject to an illusion when both his nominal wage and the price level increase. The wage earner is thought to attribute increases in nominal wages to his own merit rather than to inflation, while the general inflation of prices is seen as causing an unwarranted reduction in the real wage he would otherwise have received. It is hard to know how to test the validity of this argument.

It does appear that the redistributive effects of unanticipated inflation are large, and that, accordingly, some parts of the population could be seriously affected by unanticipated inflation. It is difficult to be more precise in discussing this complicated question, which, like others in this chapter, remains the subject of ongoing research.

*15-5 SHORT-RUN AND LONG-RUN TRADEOFFS ONCE AGAIN

Chapter 13 studied the determination of the rates of inflation and unemployment, and the response of the economy to various shocks. In this section we ask what the scope for stabilization policy might be in response to shocks. We have already considered issues of uncertainty about the dynamic response of the economy and the size of multipliers. We have also reviewed some evidence on the costs of inflation and unemployment. The remaining question is this: How fast should policy makers try to reach their target? Given the long-run unemployment rate, there is a unique long-run growth rate of money that will satisfy the inflation target. The problem is to know whether, from some initial situation, one should try to proceed to that inflation target at maximum speed—and suffer a large unemployment cost in the transition—or whether on the contrary a more gradual approach is called for.

Assume the economy to be in full equilibrium with an inflation rate of 10 percent and that a move to a lower long-run rate of inflation is planned. Further, assume that only monetary policy will be used to achieve that

[30]See William Fellner et al., *Correcting Taxes for Inflation*, American Enterprise Institute, Washington, D.C., June 1975, p. 8.

reduction in inflation. Now a first possibility arises if the government commands total credibility with the public and all prices and wages adjust freely. In that case it is sufficient to announce and implement a reduction in monetary growth to the new long-run target level. The inflation rate will immediately respond because the credibility that the government commands will instantaneously be reflected in a revision of expectations to the new lower rate of inflation. The free adjustability of prices and wages will ensure that the expectations are immediately reflected in actual price behavior.

It is more likely that the government does not command such credibility so that expectations continue to be formed—entirely or predominantly—on the basis of past observations of inflation. That case is analyzed in Fig. 15-5. The initial equilibrium is at point E, and the long-run target is at point E'. Now we shall examine two strategies which we refer to as *gradualist* and *cold turkey*. A gradualist policy involves an immediate reduction in monetary growth toward the new long-run level, while a cold-turkey policy goes for an immediate reduction in the inflation rate to the long-run level.

The gradualist approach is a compromise. It recognizes that in the transition to the new long-run equilibrium unemployment will occur, and that inflation can be reduced faster with a more restrictive policy. The

FIGURE 15-5 ALTERNATIVE
ADJUSTMENT POLICIES

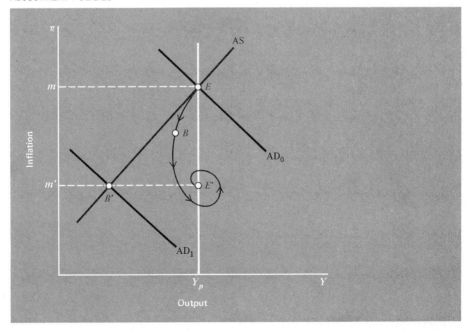

gradualist approach recognizes, too, that more rapid adjustment of inflation will imply higher unemployment. The compromise is to achieve the target of reduced inflation gradually, over a period of time.

Figure 15-5 illustrates the two policy options. The gradualist approach is shown by the cyclical adjustment path. Starting at point E, monetary growth with this strategy is reduced somewhat so that there is an immediate reduction in inflation but also some increase in unemployment because output declines (say at point B). Over time the reduction in inflationary expectations shifts the aggregate supply schedule downward and the decline in output shifts the aggregate demand schedule down. With this improvement in the inflation-unemployment tradeoff, further reductions in monetary growth become possible until the new long-run equilibrium at point E' is reached. The approach to that equilibrium may well be cyclical,[31] but the outstanding aspect of the policy is not to seek an immediate full achievement of the inflation target.

The cold-turkey strategy immediately implements the new inflation target by sharply reducing monetary growth *below* the new long-run level m'. The strategy is to reduce inflation immediately to the new long-run level. This requires a reduction in the growth rate of money over and above what is appropriate in the long run. This is shown by the shift of the aggregate demand schedule to AD_1 in Fig. 15-5. The cold-turkey policy immediately moves to point B'. The reduction in output and the sharp increase in unemployment exert a sufficiently deflationary effect to cut down the rate of inflation. From then on the policy faces the problem of building up aggregate demand without raising inflation as the economy moves from B' to the long-run equilibrium at point E'.

How should we evaluate the two policies? It is apparent that the cold-turkey strategy involves much higher unemployment in the short run. It has the compensating advantage that it achieves the target inflation immediately and that, perhaps, it is a more credible demonstration of policy intent. If the latter were true, then it might be argued that expectations adjust faster and that, accordingly, the adjustment process might be faster. By comparison the gradualist approach chooses adjustment to reduced inflation along a path that involves a lower unemployment rate with the offsetting cost of an inflation rate that declines less rapidly. Also, because the policy reduces inflation only gradually, it may act more slowly in causing people to revise downward their expectations and therefore may lengthen the adjustment process.

We have painted a picture of two extreme policies, of which one goes soft on unemployment and the other achieves a reduction in inflation immediately at any cost in terms of unemployment. Even though these may be extremes, they nevertheless make the point that there is a policy prob-

---

[31]In principle, a careful economic policy could move the economy from E to E' without a cyclical approach. In practice, a direct approach requires more knowledge of the economy than the policy maker is likely to have.

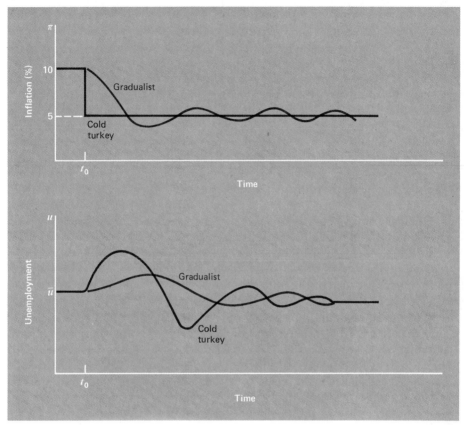

FIGURE 15-6 ALTERNATIVE PATHS OF INFLATION AND UNEMPLOYMENT

lem in evaluating the path along which stabilization policy moves the economy to long-run targets. Figure 15-6 shows the implications for unemployment and inflation of the two adjustment paths. It is apparent that the cold-turkey strategy produces a higher initial unemployment rate. In choosing, the policy maker has to trade off more unemployment now for less inflation. In addition, though, the policy maker has to recognize the lagged effects of monetary policy, and must be aware of the possible inaccuracies of her predictions or information about the economy.

How is the policy maker to choose among paths of the type shown? This depends to a large extent on her evaluation of the costs of inflation and unemployment. Someone who is persuaded that the costs of inflation are low would not be willing to incur much unemployment to reduce the inflation rate. Even if such a policy maker agreed that ultimately a lower rate of inflation was desirable, she would not do anything as extreme as is implied by the cold-turkey policy. Rather, she might chip away over time at the inflation rate, slowly trying to move the economy toward a lower rate, but always remaining acutely conscious of the effects of her policies on unemployment. Someone concerned that inflation undermines the political fabric of democracy, and that some unemployment does not, would be willing to incur the costs of high unemployment in the short run to rid the country of the curse of inflation.

The discussion of the costs of inflation and unemployment in Sec. 15-4 suggested that the aggregate costs of cyclical unemployment are relatively easy to measure. Okun's law is useful in this regard. However, there are distributional costs of unemployment that are more difficult to quantify, and the costs of unanticipated inflation are largely distributional and equally difficult to quantify. Thus, although economic analysis can help in identifying the costs of inflation and unemployment, it cannot pin them down accurately. Further, it should be recognized that the weights given to the losses suffered by different groups of people are likely to differ between policy makers. If it were demonstrated that unanticipated inflation hurt group X and benefited group Y, that would not guarantee that all policy makers would agree on the costs of unanticipated inflation. Some policy makers would regard damage done to group X as not very costly, if not beneficial, and benefits for group Y as a good thing. Other policy makers would doubtless have an opposite view.

This section has raised the question of how fast policy makers should attempt to reach their targets. There is the final question, though, of choosing long-run targets and recognizing that the cost of adjustment may be excessive compared to the benefits. Those who hold this view argue that inflation should be stabilized at the current level, rather than reduced. They argue that a stable rate of inflation removes some and perhaps most of the cost of inflation so that the residual benefits of reducing inflation may look small compared to the adjustment costs. Thus Herbert Stein, a chairperson of the Council of Economic Advisers in the Nixon administration and now a professor at the University of Virginia, has argued:

> ... it will probably not be possible for us to establish the expectation of something like zero inflation without our going through a period in which that actually is the rate. Nothing the government says will be believed without such a demonstration, and the demonstration is likely to be extremely painful. ... The rate has been around 6 percent for over seven years, and interest rates, wage contracts, annuities, and many other arrangements have been adjusted to it. On balance what seems crucial is to try to assure that the rate does not rise above 6 percent, or gets back promptly if it does. Beyond that, if opportunities arise to get the rate lower, they should be taken, but no great sacrifice should be made in order to achieve that.[32]

[32]Herbert Stein, "Fiscal Policy: Reflections on the Past Decade," in William Fellner (ed.), *Contemporary Economic Problems*, American Enterprise Institute, 1976, p. 83.

15-6 Summary

1 The long-run Phillips curve is essentially vertical. In the long run there is no inflation-unemployment trade-off.

2 The short-run Phillips curve is flatter than the long-run schedule because expectations are sticky and wages and prices are slow to adjust. But the Phillips curve shifts over time as expectations adjust to the actually realized rate of inflation.

3 If expectations do not fully adjust, or if the expectation of inflation is not fully passed through into higher inflation, then even in the long run there is a negatively sloped Phillips curve or inflation-unemployment tradeoff. The long-run Phillips curve is steeper than the short-run tradeoff.

4 If the long-run Phillips curve is vertical, then labor market policies rather than inflation must be used to reduce the long-run rate of unemployment.

5 The unemployment rate can be attributed to the frequency of unemployment (F_u) and the duration of unemployment (D_u), $u = F_u \times D_u$. The anatomy of unemployment for the United States reveals frequent and short spells of unemployment. Near full employment, in 1973, half the unemployed experienced unemployment for less than five weeks and the frequency of unemployment averaged once every 4½ years.

6 A significant part of the unemployment arises from the time involved in locating jobs for new entrants or the time spent between jobs for those who change employers.

7 The concept of the natural rate of unemployment singles out that part of unemployment which would exist even at a high level of aggregate demand. The unemployment arises in part because of a high frequency of job changes, in particular for teenagers. The high frequency is explained partly by the poor quality of jobs available to people without training. The natural rate of unemployment is hard to conceptualize and even harder to measure. The consensus is to estimate it around 5 percent, up from the 4 percent of the mid-sixties.

8 There is a significant difference in unemployment rates across age groups, sex, and race. Unemployment among black teenagers is highest and that of white adults is lowest. The young, women, and minorities have significantly higher unemployment rates than middle-aged, male whites.

9 Policies to reduce the natural rate of unemployment involve labor market policies and aggregate demand policies. The economy needs a stable, high level of aggregate demand. Disincentives to employment and training, such as minimum wages, and incentives to extended job search, such as untaxed unemployment benefits, also tend to raise the natural rate.

10 The cost of unemployment is the psychic and financial distress of the unemployed as well as the loss of output. The loss of output is not compensated by the unemployed enjoying leisure. For one thing, a large part of unemployment is involuntary. For another, the social product of labor exceeds the wage rate because of income taxes.

11 The economy can adjust to perfectly anticipated inflation by moving to a system of indexed taxes and to nominal interest rates that reflect the expected rate of inflation. In the absence of regulations that prevent these adjustments (such as usury laws or interest rate ceilings, etc.), there are no important costs to perfectly anticipated inflation. The only costs are those of changing price tags periodically and the cost of suboptimal holdings of currency. Perfectly anticipated inflation has negligible costs.

12 Imperfectly anticipated inflation has important redistributive effects between sectors. Unanticipated inflation benefits monetary debtors and hurts monetary creditors. The government gains real tax revenue, and the real value of government debt declines.

13 Optimal adjustment in reducing the rate of inflation involves the policy choice between a strategy that lowers inflation fast with high initial unemployment, and an alternative slow and gradual policy. The assessment of these policy options involves the costs and benefits of inflation and unemployment. The lower the cost of unemployment and the higher the cost of inflation, the more likely that a rapid adjustment is appropriate. The faster expectations adjust and the more credible the policy, the faster it can be implemented without generating high unemployment.

PROBLEMS

1 During the 1960s, an effort was made to improve the Phillips curve relationship through the use of "wage-price guideposts" and presidential jawboning. The idea was to give firms guidelines publicly for determining nominal wage increases. How would such a policy reduce inflation? Would you expect it to work in the short run? In the long run? What factors determine its effectiveness?

2 One frequently hears of the "wage-price spiral." The underlying idea is that wage increases cause price increases, and then these in turn cause more wage increases. These feed on each other in a never-ending spiral. Can the economy get caught in such a spiral? How would it get in? Out? Explain this notion in terms of the Phillips curve.

3 Discuss strategies whereby the government (federal, state, or local) could reduce unemployment in or among:
   a Depressed industries
   b Unskilled workers
   c Depressed geographical regions
   d Teenagers

Include comments on the *type* of unemployment you would expect in these various groups (i.e, relative durations and frequencies).

4 Discuss how the following changes would affect the natural rate of unemployment. Comment also on the side effects of these changes.
   a Elimination of unions
   b Increased participation of women in the labor market
   c Larger fluctuations in the *level* of aggregate demand
   d An increase in unemployment benefits
   e Elimination of minimum wages
   f Larger fluctuations in the *composition* of aggregate demand

5 Discuss the differences in unemployment between men and women in view of Table 15-5. What does this imply about the types of jobs (on average) the different sexes are getting?

6 Some people say that inflation can be reduced in the long run without an increase in unemployment, and so we should reduce inflation to zero. Others say a steady rate of inflation at, say, 6 percent is not so bad, and that should be our goal. Evaluate these two arguments and describe what, in your opinion, are good long-run goals for inflation and unemployment. How would these be achieved?

7 In the past ten years, Americans' awareness of inflation has increased markedly.
   a Suppose people now adjust their expectations more rapidly than earlier because of this experience. What are the implications in terms of the effects of policy?
   b Suppose instead people now take the view that inflation is going to be 6 percent no matter what the government does. What would this do to government efforts to reduce inflation below that figure? Explain.

*8 How would the model in Chap. 13 be affected if a long-run Phillips curve like the one in Chart 15-1 were used, rather than a vertical long-run Phillips curve? Trace the short- and long-run effects of a decrease in the full-employment surplus in such a model.

9 The following information is to be used for calculations of the unemployment rate. There are two major groups, adults and teenagers. Teenagers account for 10 percent of the labor force and adults for 90 percent. Adults are divided into men and women. Women account for 25 percent of the adult labor force. The following table shows the frequency and duration of unemployment statistics for the various groups and subgroups, expressed on a per year basis.

Group	Frequency (F_u)	Duration (D_u)
Teenagers	0.70	0.20
Adults:		
Men	0.15	0.30
Women	0.30	0.20

   a How do the numbers in this table compare (roughly) with the numbers for the United States economy?
   b Calculate the aggregate unemployment rate, using Eqs. (1) and (2) and the information provided above.
   c Assume the frequency of unemployment for women rises from 0.3 to 0.5, but that all the other numbers in the table stay constant. What is the effect

on female unemployment? What is the effect on the aggregate unemployment rate?

d Assume the share of women in the adult labor force increases to 40 percent. What is the effect on the adult unemployment rate? What is the effect on the aggregate unemployment rate?

e Consider the impact of a policy that improves the opportunities for young people to find jobs. Through what channel would the unemployment rate be affected?

10 Use the *Economic Report of the President* to find the unemployment data and the duration of unemployment (all workers) for the years 1968, 1973, and 1976.

a Use graph paper and plot the combinations of $F_u = u/D_u$ and D_u. Plot the duration of unemployment on the vertical axis and the frequency on the horizontal axis.

b Use your chart to make comparisons of the structure of unemployment between 1968 and 1973 and between 1973 and 1975. What general observations can you make?

11 Use the data from *Employment and Earnings* to make comparisons among various subgroups of the labor force in their unemployment characteristics.

a Find the duration and frequency of unemployment data for the following groups: teenage—adults; female—male; nonwhite—white. Calculate F_u and D_u as percentage numbers. Find also the 1976 averages for all workers.

b Plot the data in a chart with D_u on the vertical axis and F_u on the horizontal axis. How do the groups compare with each other and with the national average?

16

Economic Policy 1969-1976: The Problems of Inflation and Unemployment

This chapter follows up on our Chap. 10 discussion of economic policy in the sixties. The Kennedy administration came into office in 1961 with an inheritance of low inflation and high unemployment, as we saw in Chap. 10. The sixties was a period of expansionary economic policy, with the consequence that the Nixon administration took over in 1969 with an altogether different scene. Unemployment was down to 3.5 percent, but inflation was above 5 percent.

The policy problems of the 1969–1976 period initially revolved around attempts to reduce inflation. These attempts led to a recession in 1970–1971 during which the inflation rate fell very little. The economy boomed during 1972–1973, but was then faced with unprecedentedly large supply shocks in the form of increases in agricultural and oil prices in 1973–1974. Attempts to deal with the supply shocks through restrictive demand policies were unsuccessful, and the economy in 1975 was in its deepest recession of the postwar period. Recovery began at the end of 1975 and continued, fitfully, through 1976. The Carter administration came to office with an inflation rate that, at 6 percent, was lower than in the preceding years. Similarly, the high unemployment rate in excess of 7 percent was lower than the 1975 peak of 8.9 percent.

The understanding of macroeconomics increased significantly over this period. The period started with demand management policies based largely on control of the money supply. It ended with the use of both monetary and fiscal policy as instruments of stabilization policy. There was, too, increasing attention being paid to the potential role of supply management policies. Policy makers emerged from the 1969–1976 experience with the recognition that "there is a lesson to be drawn from past policy mistakes. The history of monetary and fiscal policies demonstrates that we have a great deal to learn about implementing discretionary policies."[1]

The present chapter focuses on these lessons. We start by discussing *monetarism*—an economic doctrine that seemed simple, useful, and persuasive in the late 1960s and early 1970s. From there we proceed to a detailed discussion of gradualism, the economic policy approach of the 1969–1970 period. The New Economic Policy (NEP) of the 1971–1973 period follows next. The recession that started in 1973–1974 and an analysis of the recovery, which started in mid-1975, conclude the chapter. Since many details and issues crop up in the experience of these years, it is useful to start with a brief preview of the facts, policies, and problems.

16-1 A PREVIEW

In this section we sketch the main phases of the economy and economic policies in the 1969–1976 period. Table 16-1 provides a summary outline

---

[1] *Annual Report of the Council of Economic Advisers*, 1976, p. 20.

TABLE 16-1   ECONOMIC PROBLEMS AND POLICIES IN 1969–1976

Year	Inflation (percent)	Unemployment (percent)	Economic activity	Policy
1969	5.4	3.5	Decline	Gradualism: tightening of
1970	5.9	4.9	Recession	monetary and fiscal policy
1971	4.3	5.9	Recession—recovery	NEP: wage and price controls in
1972	3.3	5.6	Recovery—boom	phases I–IV; expansionary monetary and
1973	6.2	4.9	Boom—decline	fiscal policy until mid-1973
1974	11.0	5.6	Decline—recession	Tight monetary and fiscal
1975	9.1	8.5	Recession—recovery	policy Tax cut, relatively
1976	5.3	7.7	Recovery—pause	tight money

Source: Economic Report of the President, 1977.   The inflation data are year-to-year changes in the consumer price index.

of the topics of this chapter which are introduced here. Chart 16-1 presents the details of key macroeconomic variables. The time period falls broadly into three parts. At the outset there is the attempt to reduce inflation by a tightening of monetary and fiscal policy. The policy was described as *gradualism* to suggest that there would be no attempt to impose an outright recession of sufficient depth to choke off inflation very quickly.

Nevertheless the policies did give rise to a recession, and with that opened up another subperiod, that of the New Economic Policy, or *NEP*. The policies pursued in this period were a combination of wage and price controls together with a vigorous expansion in aggregate demand. By 1972–1973 NEP reduced unemployment back down below 5 percent and achieved a transitory reduction in inflation. However, the expansion in aggregate demand was so vigorous, aided by expansionary monetary and fiscal policy, that inflation was soon to worsen again. In fact from the end of 1971 to mid-1973 monetary growth proceeded at an average annual rate of 7.5 to 8 percent. As measured a critic as Phillip Cagan has commented that "the failure of policy in 1972 and early 1973 to restrain monetary growth was a monumental blunder."[2]

By mid-1973 the progressive softening of price and wage controls to-

[2]Phillip Cagan, "Controls and Monetary Policy," in Cagan et al., *A New Look at Inflation*, American Enterprise Institute, 1973, p. 27.

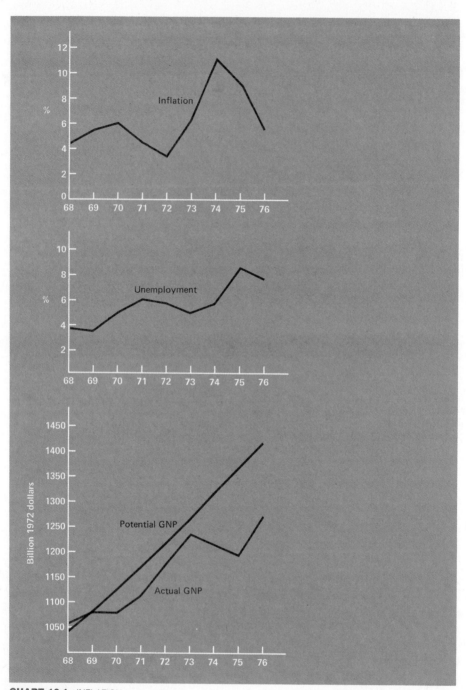

CHART 16-1 INFLATION, UNEMPLOYMENT, AND REAL GNP. (Source: *Economic Report of the President*, 1977)

gether with expansionary policies had brought inflation up to 6 percent. Once again, inflation became a chief concern of policy. At the same time the oil shock and reductions in food supplies exerted strong inflationary pressure along with a reduction in real aggregate demand. Throughout 1974 the economy moved into a decline as judged by the behavior of GNP, although unemployment increased only slowly. There was a quite determined effort to choke off inflationary pressures by tight monetary and fiscal policies. By late 1974 and early 1975 the economy had moved steeply into a recession. Soon that recession proved to be the deepest in the postwar period. Unemployment reached almost 9 percent, and at the depth of the recession in the second quarter of 1975 the GNP gap was 12–15 percent.

The recession called for strong expansionary policies. The administration was concerned, however, that too rapid a recovery would be reflected in continuing high inflation. The choice, therefore, was for a moderate recovery path. A tax cut was passed in early 1975. Monetary policy remained relatively tight, but an unpredicted increase in velocity or decline in money demand offset the monetary tightness and furthered the expansion. By the end of 1976 unemployment was below 8 percent and inflation had come down to around 5 percent.

In the 1960s unemployment was the chief target of policy; in the seventies it was inflation. Along with the change in targets, there was a change in policy makers and persuasions. Keynes—and fiscal policy—had made the cover of *Time* magazine in 1965. In 1969 Milton Friedman—and monetarism—made the cover of *Time*. Friedman's monetarist theories laid heavy stress on money stock behavior affecting GNP. Monetarism was strong in the early 1970s. But as much as the failure of the 1968 tax surcharge marked the end and failure of the magic of the New Economics, so the failure of gradualist policies in 1969–1971 was to mark the end of the magic of monetarism. Economics would emerge from the 1960s and 1970s more balanced, less activist, less monetarist, and less self-confident.

We have noted the advent of monetarism in economic policy. Along with an emphasis on monetarism and restrictive aggregate demand policies came a new cast of macroeconomic actors. At the head of the CEA we find in those years successively Paul McCracken of the University of Michigan; Herbert Stein, now at the University of Virginia; and Alan Greenspan from the consulting firm of Townsend-Greenspan. The CEA continued to attract other distinguished academics, among them William Fellner of Yale and Hendrik Houthakker of Harvard. While the CEA in the 1960s had been decidedly expansionist, there was no doubt that an important shift toward conservative policies had taken place. That shift was matched elsewhere at the macroeconomic controls. Arthur Burns became chairperson of the Fed and after 1973 set a quite single-minded course of tight money. George Shultz and subsequently William Simon headed the Treasury and left little doubt about their conservative outlook.

16-2 MONETARISM

Milton Friedman and monetarism are almost synonomous. Monetarism appears, however, in many shades and covers quite a spectrum from a harder monetarism than the Friedman variety to eclectic keynesians. In that spectrum one would include distinguished economists such as Karl Brunner of the University of Rochester and his student Allan Meltzer of Carnegie-Mellon, Thomas Mayer of the University of California at Davis, Phillip Cagan of Columbia University, and David Laidler and Michael Parkin of the University of Western Ontario, to name only some of the most prominent. Monetarism is not confined to academic economists. Indeed, the Federal Reserve Bank of St. Louis has long been a haven of a monetarist perspective on macroeconomics. If monetarism admits of some diversity, it nevertheless comes down to the proposition that money is extremely important for macroeconomics, that money is more important than other things such as fiscal policy, and, in some variants, that money is virtually *all* that matters.

Friedman's views on macroeconomics have been laid out in a series of scholarly articles, books, and popular writing.[3] Outstanding among his writings is *A Monetary History of the United States, 1867–1960*, a book written jointly with Anna J. Schwartz of the National Bureau of Economic Research. Despite its length the *Monetary History* is an absorbing book that skillfully relates the behavior of the economy to the behavior of the stock of money. The book generally attributes changes in the level of prices and in economic activity—including the Great Depression—to movements in the stock of money.

Emphasis on the Stock of Money

Monetarism emphasizes the importance of the behavior of the money stock in determining (1) the rate of inflation in the long run and (2) the behavior of real GNP in the short run. Friedman has said:[4]

> I regard the description of our position as "money is all that matters for changes in *nominal* income and for *short-run* changes in real income" as an exaggeration but one that gives the right flavor of our conclusions.

The view that the behavior of the money stock is crucial for determining the rate of inflation in the long run is consistent with the analysis of Chap. 13, as we noted there. The view that the behavior of the money stock—by which Friedman usually means the *growth rate* of the money

[3] Some of his major articles are reprinted in *The Optimum Quantity of Money*, Aldine, 1969. See also Friedman's book *A Program for Monetary Stability*, Fordham University Press, 1959, and Milton Friedman and Anna J. Schwartz, *A Monetary History of the United States, 1867–1960*, Princeton University Press, 1963.

[4] "A Theoretical Framework for Monetary Analysis," *Journal of Political Economy*, March/April 1970, p. 217.

stock—is of primary importance in determining the behavior of nominal and real GNP in the short run is not one we have accepted. Our treatment so far has given emphasis to *both* monetary and fiscal variables in determining the short-run behavior of nominal and real GNP. We have also studied the role of shocks other than changes in monetary and fiscal policy, such as the oil price increase, in affecting GNP. But there is no doubt that monetary variables play an important role in determining nominal and real GNP in the short run.

An important part of monetarism is the insistence that changes in the growth rate of money—accelerations and decelerations—account for changes in real activity. Instability in monetary growth is mirrored in variability in economic activity. Thus Friedman argues:[5]

> Why should we be concerned about these gyrations in monetary growth? Because they exert an important influence on the future course of the economy. Erratic monetary growth almost always produces erratic economic growth.

Monetarists point to a number of economic expansions and recessions as being caused by monetary accelerations and decelerations. These would certainly include the 1966 slowdown of economic activity in response to the credit crunch, the failure of the 1968 tax surcharge because it was swamped by expansionary monetary policy, and the 1970 recession.

Friedman's view of the primary importance of money is based in part on his careful historical studies, in which he was able to relate the booms and recessions of United States economic history to the behavior of the money stock. In general, it appeared that increases in the growth rate of money produced booms and inflations, and decreases in the money stock produced recessions and sometimes deflations. In part, his view of the primary importance of money is based on a theoretical analysis of the effects of fiscal policy, as discussed in Chap. 14's analysis of the different methods of financing the government budget deficit. We showed there that a money-financed deficit has a permanent effect on the price level whereas a debt-financed deficit has a smaller permanent effect on the price level. These permanent effects are long-run effects. It is less clear why Friedman places primary emphasis on monetary policy—as opposed to fiscal policy—in affecting the behavior of real and nominal GNP in the short run.

Long and Variable Lags

Monetarism has emphasized that, although the growth rate of money is of prime importance in determining the behavior of GNP, the effects of

---

[5]Milton Friedman, "Irresponsible Monetary Policy," *Newsweek,* Jan. 10, 1972. Reproduced in his collection of public policy essays, *There's No Such Thing as a Free Lunch,* Open Court Publishing Co., 1975, p. 73.

changes in the growth rate of money on the subsequent behavior of GNP occur with long and variable lags. On average, it takes a long time for a change in the growth rate of money to affect GNP, so the lag is long. In addition, the time it takes for the change in the growth rate of money to affect GNP varies from one historical episode to another—the lags are variable. These arguments are based on empirical and not theoretical evidence. Friedman estimates the lags may be as short as six months and as long as two years.

The Monetary Rule

Combining the preceding arguments, Friedman argues against the use of active monetary policy. He suggests that, because the behavior of the money stock is of critical importance for the behavior of real and nominal GNP, and because money operates with a long and variable lag, monetary policy should not attempt to "fine-tune" the economy. The active use of monetary policy might actually destabilize the economy, because an action taken in 1978, say, might affect the economy at any of various future dates, in 1979 and 1980, say. By 1980, the action taken in 1978 might be inappropriate for the stabilization of GNP. Besides, there is no certainty that the policy will take effect in 1980 rather than 1979. For example, suppose that the economy is currently in a recession, and that the money supply is increased rapidly today to increase the growth rate of real GNP. Today's increase in the growth rate of money might affect GNP within six months, and achieve its purpose. However, it might work only in two years, by which time GNP might well already have increased without the aid of the monetary policy action. And if the expansionary monetary policy affects an economy by then close to full employment, inflation will result.

Thus Friedman reaches the conclusion that although monetary policy has powerful effects on GNP, it should not be actively used, lest it destabilize the economy. Accordingly, he argues that the money supply be kept growing at a constant rate, to minimize the potential damage that inappropriate policy can cause.[6]

The Unimportance of Interest Rates

In the IS-LM model of Chap. 4, changes in the money stock affect the economy primarily by affecting interest rates which, in turn, affect aggregate demand and thus GNP. Accordingly, the level of interest rates seems to provide a guide to the effects of monetary policy on the economy. When interest rates are low, monetary policy seems to be expansionary, encouraging investment, and thus producing a high level of aggregate demand. Similarly, high interest rates seem to indicate contractionary policy.

[6]For a concise statement see Milton Friedman, "The Case for a Monetary Rule," *Newsweek*, Feb. 7, 1972. Reprinted in *There's No Such Thing as a Free Lunch*, pp. 77–79. Arguments about active policy making were discussed in Chap. 9.

Further, the Fed is able to control interest rates through open market operations. For instance, when it wants to reduce interest rates, it carries out open market purchases, buying bonds and raising their price. Since the Fed can control the level of interest rates, and since interest rates provide a guide to the effects of monetary policy on the economy, it seems perfectly sensible for the Fed to carry out monetary policy by controlling interest rates. When the Fed judges aggregate demand should be expanded, it lowers interest rates, and when it judges aggregate demand should be reduced, it raises interest rates. Through the 1950s and most of the 1960s the Fed did carry out its monetary policy by attempting to set the level of interest rates.

Friedman and monetarism brought two serious criticisms of the Fed procedure of attempting to set interest rates as the basis for the conduct of monetary policy. The first is that the behavior of *nominal* interest rates is not a good guide to the direction—whether expansionary or contractionary—of monetary policy. The *real* interest rate, the nominal interest rate minus the expected rate of inflation, is the rate relevant to determining the level of investment, as we saw in Chap. 6. But a high nominal interest rate, together with a high expected rate of inflation, means a low real rate of interest. Thus monetary policy might be quite expansionary in its effects on investment spending even when nominal interest rates are high. Accordingly, Friedman and other monetarists argued, the Fed should not concentrate on the behavior of nominal interest rates in the conduct of monetary policy.

The second criticism is that Fed attempts to control nominal interest rates might be destabilizing. Suppose that the Fed decides that monetary policy should be expansionary and the interest rate should be lowered. To do so, the Fed buys bonds in the open market, increasing the money supply. The expansionary monetary policy itself tends to raise the inflation rate. It thus tends to raise the nominal interest rate as investors adjust their expectation of inflation in response to the behavior of the actual inflation rate. But then the Fed would have to engage in a further open market purchase, in an attempt to keep the nominal interest rate low. And that would lead to further inflation, further increases in nominal interest rates, and further open market purchases. The end result is that an attempt to keep nominal interest rates low may lead to increasing inflation. Therefore, Friedman argues that the Fed should not pay attention to the behavior of nominal interest rates in the conduct of monetary policy,[7] and should rather keep the money supply growing at a constant rate.

Each of these arguments on the dangers of conducting monetary policy by reference to nominal interest rates is important. It is indeed correct that real, and not nominal, interest rates provide the appropriate measure of the effects of monetary policy on aggregate demand. It is also true that the Fed

---

[7]The details of the argument are spelled out in Friedman's "The Role of Monetary Policy," *American Economic Review*, March 1968.

could, by attempting to keep nominal interest rates low forever, destabilize the economy. However, once the latter danger has been pointed out, the probability that the Fed will destabilize the economy by operating with reference to interest rates is reduced. The use of interest rates as a guide to the direction of monetary policy does not mean that the Fed has to attempt to keep the interest rate fixed forever at some level. Instead, it may aim each month or quarter for an interest rate target that it regards as appropriate for the current and predicted economic situation.

The monetarist case for concentrating on the behavior of the money stock in the conduct of monetary policy is a strong, but not conclusive, one. The major weakness in the argument is that the demand for real balances may change over time and indeed has done so, as in 1975. A simple numerical example should help make the point. Suppose that real income is constant, and that the nominal interest rate is constant. Suppose also that the demand for real balances is constant. Then if the money supply grows at, say, the rate of 5 percent, the price level, too, will grow at 5 percent, so that the stock of real balances remains constant. Now suppose instead that the demand for real balances is falling by 2 percent per year. Then if the nominal money supply increases at 5 percent per year, the price level has to increase at 7 percent per year to keep the supply of real balances equal to the demand. Thus shifts in the demand for money affect the rate of inflation, given the growth rate of money. In this example, if the demand for real balances grew at 5 percent per year, 5 percent money growth would not be inflationary at all. These shifts in demand raise the possibility that concentration on the behavior of the nominal money stock may be seriously misleading and inappropriate for the conduct of monetary policy.

The possibility is not purely hypothetical. For instance, in late 1975, the money stock was growing very slowly, at about 2 percent, although nominal interest rates were low and real income was rising. Given rising real income and constant interest rates, the demand for real balances should, according to the demand for money function of Chap. 7, have been increasing. However, real balances were actually falling at the time, despite the rising real income. This suggests that the demand for money was shifting—that people were reducing their demand for real balances at given levels of interest rates and income. The question then was whether the Fed should attempt to increase the growth rate of the money stock, despite the low level of interest rates. Given the low nominal interest rates, real interest rates were assuredly low, since inflationary expectations at the end of 1975 cannot have been for less than 5 percent inflation over the coming two years. The low level of interest rates suggested that monetary policy was expansionary, and the low rate of growth of the money stock suggested on the contrary that monetary policy was contractionary. In the event, the Fed argued that monetary policy was expansionary despite the low growth rate of the nominal money stock, and that faster growth of the money stock was not needed for the recovery to continue. And the

Fed was right. In that case, concentration on the behavior of the money stock as a guide to monetary policy would have been inappropriate and inflationary.

Given the possibility, and the actual experience, of shifts in the demand for money, we see that the behavior of the money stock is not a perfect guide to the conduct of monetary policy. Neither is the behavior of nominal interest rates. However, the behavior of the nominal money stock and the behavior of nominal interest rates both provide some information about the direction in which monetary policy is pushing the economy, imperfect as each measure is. Accordingly, the Fed should pay attention to the behavior of both interest rates and the supply of money in the conduct of its monetary policy.[8]

The Importance of Fiscal Policy

Friedman has frequently, if tongue in cheek, said that fiscal policy is very important. Although we noted above that he argues fiscal policy itself is not important for the behavior of GNP, he does argue that it is of vital importance in setting the size of government and the role of government in the economy. Friedman is an opponent of big government. He has made the interesting argument that government spending increases to match the revenues available. The government will spend the full tax collection— and some more. Accordingly, he is in favor of tax cuts as a way of reducing government spending.

In the shorter run, Friedman has pointed to the size of the government deficit as one of the variables that does affect the growth rate of the money stock. That is in part due to the Fed's concern over the behavior of interest rates. When the deficit is large, interest rates tend to rise unless the Fed monetizes the debt, as we saw in Chap. 14. Large deficits, therefore, tend to be associated with rapid monetary expansion, and for that reason have an expansionary effect on the economy. But since there is no inherent reason why a deficit has to be financed by money creation, the link between deficits and expansion is not an immutable one, but rather a result of the way the Fed behaves. Friedman stands out in arguing that fiscal policy does not have strong effects on the economy except to the extent that it affects the behavior of money. Thus he has remarked:[9]

> To have a significant impact on the economy, a tax increase must somehow affect monetary policy—the quantity of money and its rate of growth. . . .
> The level of taxes is important—because it affects how much of our resources we use through the government and how much we use as individuals.

[8]The argument is worked out in Benjamin M. Friedman, "Targets, Instruments, and Indicators of Monetary Policy," *Journal of Monetary Economics*, October 1975.

[9]Milton Friedman, "Higher Taxes? No." *Newsweek*, Jan. 23, 1967. Reprinted in *There's No Such Thing as A Free Lunch*, op. cit., p. 89.

It is not important as a sensitive and powerful device to control the short-run course of income and prices.

Summary: We Are All Monetarists

From the viewpoint of the conduct of economic policy, the major monetarist themes are (1) the emphasis on the growth rate of the money stock (2) the arguments against fine tuning and in favor of a monetary rule, and (3) the greater weight that monetarists, as compared, say, with New Economists, place on the costs of inflation relative to those of unemployment.

Although we describe these as the major monetarist propositions relating to policy,[10] it is not true that macroeconomists can be neatly divided into two groups, some subscribing to the monetarist religion and the others to a less fundamentalist faith called neokeynesianism. Most of the arguments advanced by Friedman and his associates are technical arguments, susceptible of economic analysis and the application of empirical evidence. Many of those propositions are now widely accepted and are no longer particularly associated with monetarism. As Franco Modigliani has remarked, "We are all monetarists now." He adds that we are monetarists in the sense that all (or most) macroeconomists believe in the importance of money.

There is a further aspect of monetarism—the *inherent stability of the private sector*—that we have not emphasized, but that is implicit in most of this section. Monetarists believe that the economy, left to itself, is more stable than when the government manages it with discretionary policy, and that the major cause of economic fluctuations is inappropriate government actions. This view is not generally accepted, and may be the litmus test for distinguishing monetarists from other macroeconomists.

Much of the analysis of this book would, a few years ago, have been considered monetarist. For instance, we have assumed the Phillips curve is vertical, a proposition that was originally associated with monetarism. We have laid considerable stress on the behavior of the money stock and less stress on the behavior of interest rates. We have stressed that fiscal policy has little long-run effect on inflation. Older readers will doubtless detect other places at which we appear monetarist to their eyes. That is all to the good. If economists did not modify their analyses in the light of new theories and evidence, the field would be barren.

Friedman and his associates have indeed changed macroeconomics.

---

[10]For a range of views on monetarism, see Karl Brunner, "The Monetarist Revolution in Monetary Theory," *Weltwirtschaftliches Archiv*, 1970; Jerry Stein (ed.), *Monetarism*, North-Holland, 1976; Franco Modigliani and Lucas Papademos, "Monetary Policy for the Coming Quarters: The Conflcting Views," *New England Economic Review*, March/April 1976; and Franco Modigliani, "The Monetarist Controversy." *American Economic Review*, March 1977.

The forceful and persuasive way in which Friedman has emphasized the role of money has changed the views of most economists on the importance of monetary policy. It is always possible that those views would have changed anyway, in the light of the increasing inflation of the last decade. The fact remains, however, that it was Friedman, and not someone else, who hammered away at the importance of money. Fortunately, we are beyond the stage at which it is useful to think in terms of monetarists versus keynesians.

16-3 GRADUALISM, 1969–1971

The major economic problem confronting the new Nixon administration in 1969 was inflation. The low unemployment rate of 3.5 percent allowed policy to shift entirely to a fight against inflation. It was decided that the fight should be a slow one. In his review of the period, Cagan notes:[11]

> The concept of a "tradeoff" between inflation and unemployment had been widely discussed and was very much in the minds of policymakers. There was general agreement that any success in slowing inflation would produce a higher rate of unemployment. The unemployment would reflect a gap between potential and actual output, and this pressure of excess capacity in commodity and labor markets would bring down the rate of inflation. The policymakers thus had a choice: Larger excess capacity would bring inflation under control faster, but would also require a higher peak level of unemployment. The challenge to policy was to follow a thin line, bringing about reasonable if not spectacular reductions in inflation at the cost of moderate unemployment in the short run.

The plan was thus to reduce the inflation rate gradually in order to avoid excessive increases in the unemployment rate. This is precisely the type of choice that was discussed at the end of Chap. 15.

Policy Actions

Both fiscal and monetary policy became more restrictive in 1969. Chart 16-2 shows the increase in the high employment surplus for 1969 over 1968, and Chart 16-3 shows the growth rate of the money stock declining from 1968 to 1969. The actual course of money growth was one of increasing tightness through the first three quarters of the year.

The data for the growth rate of M_1 from the fourth quarter of 1968 through the third quarter of 1971 are presented in Table 16-2, as are Treasury bill rates. The tightness of monetary policy—the large reduction in the growth rate of money from 1968 to 1969—was excessive, given the ad-

---

[11]Phillip Cagan, "Monetary Policy," in Cagan et al., *Economic Policy and Inflation in the Sixties*, American Enterprise Institute, 1972, p. 104.

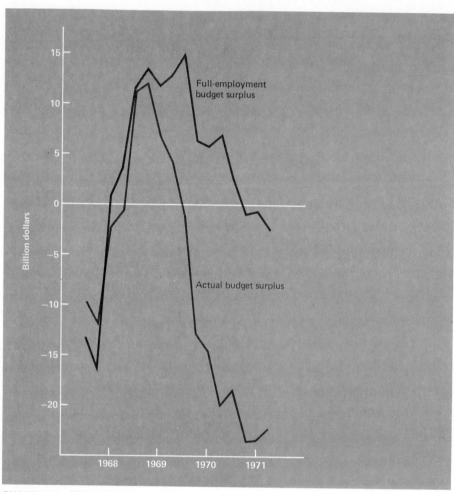

CHART 16-2 FISCAL POLICY. (Source: *Federal Budget Trends,* November 1976)

ministration's goal of avoiding large-scale unemployment. In August 1969, Friedman noted:[12]

> The Federal Reserve System has done it again. Once more it is overreacting as it has so often done in the past. . . . Some retardation in growth and some increase in unemployment is an inevitable, if unwelcome, by-product of stopping inflation. But there is no need—and every reason to avoid—a retardation of

[12]Milton Friedman, *An Economist's Protest,* Horton, 1972, p. 54. In his analysis, reprinted from one of his *Newsweek* columns, Friedman blames the Fed's behavior on its attention to interest rates.

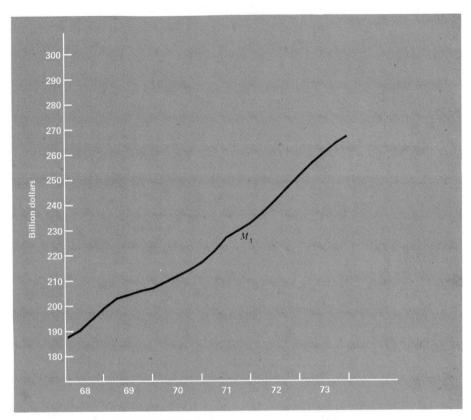

CHART 16-3 THE MONEY STOCK 1968–1973. (Source: Federal Reserve Bank of St. Louis)

TABLE 16-2 GROWTH RATE OF MONEY, AND TREASURY BILL RATE, 1968–1971

	1968	1969				1970				1971		
	IV	I	II	III	IV	I	II	III	IV	I	II	III
Growth rate of M_1*	8.1	6.8	3.9	2.3	2.3	3.6	5.1	5.1	5.4	6.8	10.0	6.6
Treasury bill rate†	5.6	6.1	6.2	7.1	7.3	7.3	6.8	6.4	5.4	3.9	4.2	5.1

*Based on quarter average seasonally adjusted stock.

†Average of monthly figures.

Source: Federal Reserve Bulletin, and *Federal Reserve Bank of St. Louis.*

the severity that will be produced by a continuation of the Fed's present monetary overkill.

The tightness of monetary policy in 1969 is visible also in the rise in the Treasury bill rate during the year. From the beginning of 1970, the Fed increased the growth rate of the money stock, although the increase in growth was not smooth. The rate of increase was rapid through August 1970, and then slow from August 1970 to early 1971. Monetary growth in the first half of 1971 was at an annual rate of 10 percent. It then slowed down in the third quarter of 1971.

Results of Policy

The restrictive policy measures of 1969, operating with a lag, produced the recession of 1970, during which unemployment rose to 6 percent. The reversal of the restrictive monetary policy started in 1970 and ensured that the recession did not last long, and that it was not very deep. By early 1971, real GNP was growing again, although not very rapidly.

The problem with gradualism was that the policy seemed to have no effect on inflation. The recession made no dent in the inflation rate; the rate of change of the consumer price index was even higher in 1970 than in 1969. There were some signs that the inflation rate was falling in early 1971, but then there was a slight increase in the rate of inflation in mid-1971. The costs of unemployment had indeed been borne by the economy, but the benefits in the form of a reduction in the inflation rate had not occurred.

*What Went Wrong?

In terms of our analysis of Chap. 13, the failure of restrictive monetary and fiscal policies to reduce the inflation rate must be placed on the behavior of expectations of inflation. Figure 16-1 reproduces the standard diagram of Chap. 13. The aggregate supply curve in 1968 is depicted by the AS_0 line. The late 1968 aggregate demand curve is represented by the AD_0 line, with 1968 short-run equilibrium being at point E.

The restrictive policies inaugurated in 1969 shifted the aggregate demand curve to the left, to AD'. These policies by themselves should have caused a decline in both the growth rate of output and the rate of inflation. However, at that time, expectations of inflation were probably still increasing in response to the rising inflation of the previous few years. There is nothing surprising in the lagged adjustment of inflationary expectations if we recall that throughout the second half of the sixties actual inflation had been creeping upward. Inflation increased from 1.5 percent in 1964–1965 to around 5 percent in 1968–1969. With actual inflation thus rising, we would expect expectations to be still catching up. The AS curve was thus shifting up over time, toward a position like AS'.

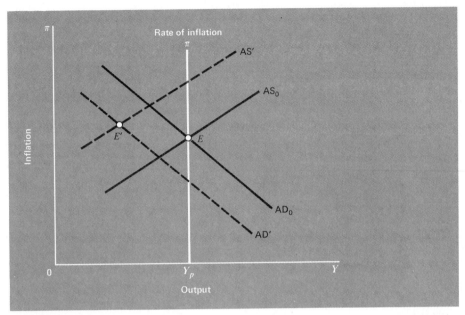

FIGURE 16-1 MONETARY AND FISCAL
POLICY, 1969–1970

The combination of the policy actions and expectations adjustment would have reduced the growth rate of output, while perhaps leaving the inflation rate roughly unchanged, or else—depending on the extent of the shifts in the curves—either increasing or decreasing the inflation rate. In the event, there seem to have been substantial shifts in the aggregate supply curve leading to an increase in the inflation rate along with the reduction in the growth rate of output. At E' the inflation rate is higher than it is at E, the level of output is below potential, and unemployment is increasing. This is precisely what happened over the period 1969–1970.

Why did expectations not react more rapidly, particularly when the administration had announced its intention of reducing the inflation rate? There are two reasons. The first is that the inflation from 1965 to 1969 was quite protracted and had undoubtedly persuaded people that inflation was a phenomenon that was here to stay. Second, the administration itself, perhaps unintentionally, encouraged the belief that the anti-inflationary policies were less than wholehearted. Frequently, administration economists referred to the economic recovery that was ahead, once the economy was through the valley of the small recession that was needed to get rid of inflation. Such statements suggested that the administration would not allow any period of unemployment to be protracted, and that expansionary policies should be expected to follow fairly soon after unemployment began to increase. And the growth rate of money was increased in early 1970, validating such expectations. At that time the aggregate demand curve shifted out to the right.

It is true, though, that the slowness of the inflation rate to respond to changes in aggregate demand and increases in unemployment during the 1969–1971 period was a surprise to many economists. For instance, Milton Friedman, despite his usual emphasis on the long lags of monetary policy, wrote in May 1969:[13]

> If the Fed continues its present policy of moderate growth in the money supply, we should start seeing results in the near future. By summer or early fall, the rise in income should start slackening. The effect will first be on output. However, by fall at the latest, the pace of price rise should start coming down.

The difficulties of reducing the inflation rate through restrictive aggregate demand policies were greater than had been predicted. Those predictions were, however, based on only scanty evidence, since the economy had not had a long period of inflation other than that of 1965–1969 in the years since 1946.

There are three major lessons from the 1969–1971 experience. The first is the pervasiveness of lags. It took some quarters for each change in policy to have its effects on nominal GNP. Thus the restrictive policies starting in 1969 had their major impact on nominal GNP only in 1970. Similarly, the increase in the growth rate of money in 1970 began to affect the behavior of GNP only in 1971. Indeed, there is also a lag between changes in real GNP and unemployment. It can be seen from Chart 16-1 that increases in the growth rate of real GNP began to affect unemployment only with a lag. The growth rate of GNP was less than that of potential output in 1969, but unemployment began to rise only in 1970. The growth rate of real GNP during parts of 1971 was greater than that of potential output, but unemployment barely changed during 1971. Thus the theory behind Fig. 16-1 is a useful guide to thinking about the operation of policy, but it inevitably tells too simple a story about the exact timing with which policy affects the economy.

Second, it can be very difficult to influence inflationary expectations. Despite the repeated statements of the policy makers that inflation was going to be reduced, and that anti-inflationary policies would be followed, there is little evidence that expectations of inflation were much reduced during 1969. And then when it became apparent in 1970 that the administration was *not* going to allow substantial unemployment to develop to kill inflation, those expectations turned out to be justified.

Third is a lesson that you have no doubt already learned. There is substantial uncertainty about the effects of policy on the economy, and

---

[13]In *An Economist's Protest*, op. cit., pp. 51–52.

particularly about the timing of those effects. Those uncertainties stem largely from the factors analyzed above—lags and expectations formation.

The 1970 Credit Crunch and Crisis Averted

One very interesting episode in the middle of the 1969–1971 period warrants special attention. As a result of the slow monetary growth of late 1969, interest rates rose sharply toward the end of 1969, and stayed high through the first half of 1970. The behavior of the commercial paper rate is shown in Chart 16-4. From 1968 on, the rate on commercial paper repeatedly exceeded the interest rate commercial banks and other financial intermediaries were allowed to pay on their deposits. The Fed sets maximum rates on time deposits under regulation Q. Thus Chart 16-4 shows the rate on four- to six-month commercial paper and the ceiling on time deposit rates. The dashed line refers to deposits of $100,000 or more, and the solid line indicates the ceiling on deposits of less than $100,000.[14] Regulation on large deposits (CDs) was actually suspended in May 1973.

Chart 16-4 reminds us of the adverse effect on financial intermediaries of market rates that exceed maximum deposit rates. Clearly when market rates rise above deposit rates, as happened in 1968–1970, there will be

[14]Interest rate ceilings are published in the *Federal Reserve Bulletin*.

CHART 16-4 THE COMMERCIAL PAPER RATE AND CEILINGS ON TIME DEPOSIT RATES. (Source: *Economic Trends* and *Federal Reserve Bulletin*, various issues)

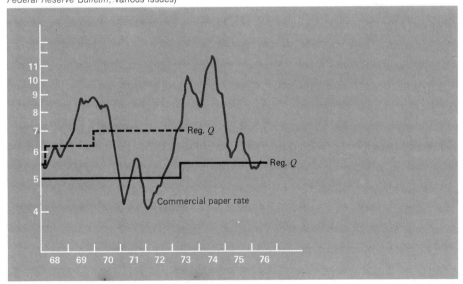

disintermediation. Financial institutions become uncompetitive in raising funds through deposits and accordingly they have to contract and cannot expand their loan business. As was noted in Chap. 10 in connection with the 1966 credit crunch, financial disintermediation is particularly harmful for mortgage lending. Accordingly, the construction industry was badly affected by these high market rates, *given* the interest rate ceilings that channelled funds away from institutions specializing in financing construction loans.

A specific episode we want to discuss is the bankruptcy of the Penn Central Railroad. Penn Central had been borrowing heavily in the commercial paper market. Then in June 1970, the company declared its bankruptcy. Holders of commercial paper issued by Penn Central thus suffered capital losses. More importantly, though, there was concern that other companies might be drawn into bankruptcy next, since Penn Central was one of the largest corporations in the country. Lenders were thus reluctant to buy commercial paper, which made it difficult for corporations which had been relying on borrowing in that market to obtain financing.

The situation had all the earmarks of a financial panic, in which a lack of confidence reduces the amount of lending lenders are willing to undertake, and thereby makes it difficult for borrowers to obtain funds, and can perhaps force them into bankruptcy. One of the original functions of a central bank is to act as *lender of last resort*. When a financial panic threatens, the panic can be prevented if the central bank steps in to ensure that funds are available to make loans to firms which are perfectly sound but, because of panic, are having trouble raising funds. In June 1970, the Fed did act as a lender of last resort. It encouraged banks to raise funds by removing the deposit ceiling rate for large-denomination and short-maturity deposits, and to lend the borrowed funds in the commercial paper market. It also made it clear to the banks that they would be able to borrow freely from the Fed in order to lend to firms needing to borrow.

The decisive action prevented a financial panic, and the money markets successfully weathered the Penn Central storm without major distress. Here was an instance of a successful Fed policy action that is little known outside the financial markets.

New Economic Policy and the 1971–1972 Boom

Pressures for a change in economic policy, and particularly *wage and price controls,* had been rising through 1970 and 1971 as the inflation rate remained high while the unemployment rate climbed to 6 percent. Wage and price controls are governmental measures to affect the prices firms charge and the wages labor earns *directly*, rather than through the slow roundabout route of affecting aggregate demand and expectations. The controls can vary from a wage-price freeze, in which no changes in prices or wages are allowed, to weak jawboning in which the administration uses its powers of persuasion to suggest to firms that they not raise prices or wages.

Wage-price controls had been used in the United States during World War II and the Korean war, and there had been periodic attempts at jawboning through the Kennedy administration. A related type of policy, incomes policy, has been widely used in Western European countries, usually to no great success over periods of more than a few years.[15]

The Nixon administration had emphatically rejected even the notion of jawboning, believing that it both interfered with the operation of free markets and had no effect on inflation. The Democrat-controlled Congress had fewer inhibitions, and in 1970 passed legislation authorizing the President to impose wage and price controls—a power the President did not then think he would ever want to use.

The slowing of inflation in early 1971, seen in Table 16-3, brought some hope to the administration that its stabilization policies were beginning to work. But then the inflation rate in the second quarter of 1971 increased, and the pressure for change became strong. The forthcoming 1972 election contributed to the pressure, since it would have been less than desirable to have to run on a record of an economic policy which had reduced the inflation rate by 1 percent at the cost of 2.5 percent unemployment. Something had to be done.

On August 15, 1971, the *New Economic Policy* was unveiled. The policy proposed fiscal measures to reduce both government spending and taxes. It also imposed a ninety-day wage and price freeze, that subsequently became known as phase I of the wage-price control program. The freeze meant just that: prices and wages were not allowed to be changed for ninety days. The 1972 *Economic Report of the President* makes the case for the freeze:[16]

> The chief virtues of the freeze were its decisiveness, comprehensiveness, and administrative simplicity. The President's announcement that practically all wage and price increases were prohibited left no doubt of a drastic change in the upward trend of prices and wages. Equally important, a freeze could be—and was—imposed immediately, precluding anticipatory price and wage

[15]See Lloyd Ulman and Robert Flanagan, *Wage Restraint: A Study of Incomes Policy in Western Europe*, University of California Press, Berkeley, 1971.

[16]P. 76.

TABLE 16-3 QUARTERLY INFLATION RATES, 1970–1973 *(Consumer price index, seasonally adjusted)*

	1970			1971				1972				1973	
	II	III	IV	I	II	III	IV	I	II	III	IV	I	II
Inflation rate*	6.2	4.9	5.3	2.8	4.9	2.8	2.8	3.7	2.4	4.5	3.2	8.7	7.4

*Based on last-month-of-quarter index.

Source: Economic Report of the President, various issues.

increases and providing time to prepare and set in motion more lasting and flexible measures.

Why would a freeze work in reducing inflation? Two points are to be recognized. First, we noted above that inflationary expectations accounted for much of the difficulty in reducing actual inflation. The imposition of wage-price controls in the form of a freeze solves that problem by the stroke of a pen. Secondly, the idea of a freeze, announced and imposed without prior warning, has the dramatic advantage of forestalling anticipatory price increases. If a long debate preceded the imposition of controls, then many firms would find the time to hike their (list) prices prior to the controls and thus frustrate the entire program by accelerating inflation rather than containing it.

The Controls Program

After the wage-price freeze came phase II, a more flexible program for control of wages and prices. Wages could now be increased at 5.5 percent per year, with special allowances for gross inequities and low-paid workers. Prices could be raised to pass along increases in costs. Some small firms and agricultural and imported commodities were exempt from wage-price controls.

Phase II ran from November 1971 to January 1973, when it was, logically enough, replaced by phase III, a yet more flexible set of controls. Phase III ran through June 1973, by which time the inflation rate had reached the vicinity of 10 percent. Another price freeze was imposed then, to be replaced by phase IV in August 1973. The controls ran out in April 1974. Details of the various phases are not vital,[17] beyond the facts that agricultural and imported commodities were exempt from price controls, and that phase III was more flexible than phase II.

Fiscal and Monetary Policy

Returning to Chart 16-2, we note again that there was little active use of fiscal policy during this period. The full-employment surplus was decreasing mildly from the end of 1971 through the first half of 1972. The surplus increased in the third quarter as a result of a fall in government spending, and then fell sharply in the fourth quarter of 1972 as a result both of increases in Social Securitiy payments and of tax reductions which were part of the New Economic Policy. The increase in the full-employment surplus at the beginning of 1973 was in turn the result of increases in Social Security taxes.

Table 16-4 shows the behavior of the growth rate of the money stock,

---

[17]See *Economic Report of the President*, 1974, p. 91, for a table listing details of the various phases.

TABLE 16-4 GROWTH RATE OF MONEY, AND TREASURY BILL RATE, 1971–1973

	1971		1972				1973		
	III	IV	I	II	III	IV	I	II	III
Growth rate of M_1*	6.6	2.6	7.2	8.1	8.4	8.9	7.3	6.4	5.6
Treasury bill rate†	5.1	4.2	3.4	3.8	4.2	4.9	5.6	6.6	8.4

*Based on quarter average seasonally adjusted money stock.

†Average of monthly figures.

Source: *Federal Reserve Bulletin*, various issues.

and the Treasury bill rate. The data in Table 16-4 should be considered in relation to the behavior of real GNP shown in Chart 16-1. Real GNP increased at a rate of more than 6 percent through this period. Monetary policy was expansionary, whether measured by the rapid growth of the money stock or by the low level of Treasury bill rates—although, admittedly, Treasury bill rates rose sharply during 1972. Through the end of 1972, there was no attempt to use monetary policy to moderate the pace of the boom of that year. That the boom was taking place was perfectly clear. We shall again have to ask why the Fed did it.

The Behavior of the Economy

The imposition of the wage-price freeze in August 1971 had an immediate effect on the inflation rate. The rate was less than 2 percent for the three months of the freeze. The inflation rate was not cut to zero by the freeze because some commodities were excluded. At the end of the freeze, there was a temporary bulge in the inflation rate as some catching up on price increases took place—with the permission of the Price Commission that was administering the price controls. Nonetheless, it is clear from Chart 16-1 and Table 16-2 that there was a definite reduction in the inflation rate after the imposition of wage and price controls. That reduction lasted through 1972.

As for the behavior of real GNP, we have already commented several times on the rapid rate of growth of output through the six quarters from 1971/IV through 1973/I. Housing investment expanded especially rapidly as interest rates fell, and consumption spending rose at a rapid rate. The unemployment rate was slow in responding to the growth rate of output, but it did eventually fall sharply toward the end of 1972, moving rapidly from 5.6 percent in October to 5.1 percent in December. It is clear once again that unemployment responds only with a lag to changes in real output.

On the surface, then, 1972 was, as President Nixon claimed,[18] "a very good year for the American economy." But the expansionary policy of the period, and the failure of monetary and fiscal policy to restrain the boom as it developed, stored up trouble for the next few years.

Did the Controls Work?

The rate of inflation did fall after the imposition of wage and price controls in 1971. The question we discuss in this section is whether the fall in the inflation rate was due to the imposition of controls, or whether, on the contrary, the inflation rate would have fallen anyway. The reason to believe the inflation rate might have fallen anyway is that the rate of inflation in the first half of 1971 was lower than in 1970, as can be seen in Table 16-2. If that improvement—and particularly that of the first quarter of 1971—had been maintained, the inflation rate might have fallen even without controls to the same level that it attained with them.[19]

Evidence on the effects of controls is difficult to interpret. Given monetary and fiscal policies, controls can have had an effect either indirectly through expectations, or directly, by preventing wage and price increases that would have taken place even after allowing for the effects on expectations. Now wages and prices did rise less rapidly after the imposition of controls than before. We cannot, however, be sure of the proportions in which the reduction was due to (1) the lagged effects of the high unemployment rate of 1971, (2) the effect of controls on expectations, and (3) the direct effects of controls in prohibiting wage and price increases that would, after allowing for the lower expectations of inflation, have taken place.

There is evidence, from surveys that directly asked people about their expectations, that inflation expectations were reduced by the imposition of controls.[20] Cagan estimates that about one-third of the reduction in inflation from 1971–1972 was due to expectations. There is also evidence that controls reduced the inflation rate by holding back prices by more than would normally have occurred given the rate of wage increase.[21] This evidence bears on point (3) above. If controls held back price increases

[18]*Economic Report of the President*, 1973, p. 3.

[19]A study by Edgar L. Feige and Douglas K. Pearce, of Wisconsin and the University of Houston respectively, suggests that the controls had no major effect on inflation other than during the freeze. See their article "Inflation and Incomes Policy: An Application of Time Series Models," in Karl Brunner and Allan Meltzer (eds.), *The Economics of Price and Wage Controls*, North-Holland, 1976.

[20]Phillip Cagan, "Controls and Monetary Policy," in Cagan et al., *A New Look at Inflation*, American Enterprise Institute, 1973.

[21]Robert J. Gordon, "Wage-Price Controls and the Shifting Phillips Curve," *Brookings Papers on Economic Activity*, 1972, 2.

TABLE 16-5   SOURCES OF REDUCTION IN INFLATION, 1971–1972

Source of reduction in inflation	Proportion
Reduction in expected inflation	$\frac{1}{3}$
Reduction in profit margins due to price controls	$\frac{1}{3}$
Reduction in aggregate demand (lagged effect)	$\frac{1}{3}$

relative to wage increases, then they reduced profit margins. Somewhat less than one-third of the 3 percent reduction in the inflation rate from 1971 to 1972 can be attributed to this effect of controls on inflation. As Table 16-5 shows, this leaves the lagged effects of low aggregate demand with about one-third of the credit for the falling inflation rate.

There is another reason that we know that not much of the effects of controls on inflation can be attributed to their direct effects on prices—that is, to source (3) above. If controls intervened directly in wage and price setting, then shortages should have developed. Contrary to what we would expect if controls had artificially kept down prices other than through expectations, there were very few shortages during 1972.

In contrast to the situation in which controls were introduced in 1971, one can think of trying to introduce wage and price controls in an economy at a high level of employment and inflation. In such an economy, the controls would soon lead to shortages and other microeconomic distortions. Any effects that controls would have on expectations in those circumstances would impose a heavier cost in terms of shortages than did controls in 1972.

In terms of Fig. 16-2, we can interpret the history of 1971–1972 fairly simply. The effects of controls on expectations moved the AS curve out and down from AS to AS'. Along with that downward shift of the AS curve in Fig. 16-2 went an expansion of current aggregate demand, mainly through the very rapid increases in the money supply of 1972. This shifted the AD curve to AD'. Together, the shifts of the curves were sufficient to produce rapid growth but a lower rate of inflation than had prevailed in 1971. By the end of the year, the unemployment rate had fallen to 5 percent, from its 6 percent level of a year earlier. At that stage, the economy was near full employment.

Why Did the Fed Do It?

The failure of the Fed to slow down the growth rate of money and run a tighter monetary policy toward the end of 1972 is difficult to explain fully. Two factors provide part of the explanation. First, as can be seen from

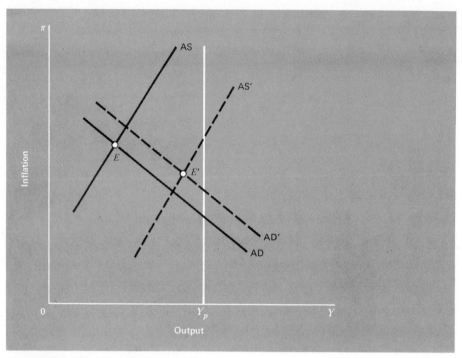

FIGURE 16-2 THE 1971–1972 EXPANSION

Table 16-4, the Treasury bill rate (and interest rates generally) were rising over the course of the year. Although the Fed had formally decided in early 1972 to pay more attention to the growth rate of money and less to interest rates than it had previously, it was still concerned over rising interest rates. It may have interpreted increases in interest rates as contractionary rather than as the reflection of the effects of increasing real output on money demand.[22] Second, the unemployment rate was slow in responding to the expansion of real output that began in 1971. It was only toward the end of 1972 that the unemployment rate began its fall from the 6 percent level down to 5 percent. The Fed may have waited to see more definite results of its policies on unemployment before it regarded the recovery from the earlier recession as truly under way.

Nonetheless, the monetary growth data of Table 16-4 reflect inappropriate Fed policy. In particular, the rapid growth in the fourth quarter was inappropriate for the stabilization of the economy.

---

[22]One reason for the Fed's attention to the behavior of interest rates in 1972 was that it was afraid Congress was about to impose controls on interest rates. To avoid such controls, the Fed may have wanted to act so as not to let interest rates rise to levels that would incur congressional wrath and action.

16-4 SLOWDOWN, RECESSION, AND INFLATION, 1973–1975

The period 1973–1975 is one of the most interesting from the viewpoint of economics of the post-World War II period—though, to be sure, "May you live in interesting times" is a curse and not a benediction.[23] The quarterly growth rates of GNP from the first quarter of 1973 through the second quarter of 1975 are shown in Table 16-6. The first quarter of 1973 was the last quarter of the boom, and the growth rate of real output was still an extraordinary 8.8 percent. The economy spent the next three quarters in a "growth recession" in which real GNP was growing, though at a rate below the growth rate of potential output. Interestingly enough, the original GNP data for the period showed a much less sharp deceleration of growth after the first quarter of the year than do the revised data of Table 16-6. The severity of the *growth recession* was not then recognized.[24]

At the end of 1973, the economy, already heading toward recession, was struck by the Arab oil embargo and oil price increase. Real GNP growth became sharply negative in the first two quarters of 1974 and moderated a little in the third quarter of 1974. Growth collapsed in the last quarter of 1974 and the first quarter of 1975, with spectacular negative growth rates for those quarters of minus 7.5 percent and minus 9.2 percent, respectively. The recovery began in the second quarter of 1975. The protracted period of slow and negative growth, and the sharpness of the recession at the end of 1974, are unprecedented in the post-World War II period.

Table 16-6 also shows the behavior of the unemployment rate over the period. Once more, we see the unemployment rate lagging behind the

---

[23]A lively analysis of policy in 1973 is presented by Franco Modigliani, "A Critique of Past and Prospective Economic Policies," *American Economic Review*, September 1973.

[24]In the *Economic Report of the President*, 1974, growth rates of real GNP for the last three quarters of 1973 are given as 2.4 percent, 3.4 percent, and 1.3 percent respectively.

TABLE 16-6   GROWTH RATES OF QUARTERLY REAL GNP, AND UNEMPLOYMENT RATE, 1973–1975

	1973				1974				1975	
	I	II	III	IV	I	II	III	IV	I	II
Growth rate of real GNP	8.8	0.2	2.7	1.4	−3.9	−3.7	−2.3	−7.5	−9.2	3.3
Unemployment rate*	4.9	4.8	4.8	4.9	5.0	5.3	5.9	7.2	8.5	8.7

*Last month of quarter.

Source: *Economic Report of the President*, 1976, 1975.

growth rate of GNP, not starting to increase seriously until the third quarter of 1974, at which time Chart 16-1 shows it rising precipitously.

The purpose of this section is to describe the events of the 1973–1975 period in somewhat more detail, paying particular attention to the effects of policy, and exogenous shocks such as the oil price increase, on the economy. We shall also be asking whether the recession had to be as bad as it was.

Inflation and Unemployment

It is difficult to understand the course of policy through 1973–1975 without realizing that for most of the period the prime goal of policy was to reduce the inflation rate. During this period, the inflation rate was at very high levels, and for most of the period, unemployment was below 6 percent. Only in 1974/III did the unemployment rate start to rise, and it then moved quickly to 8.9 percent by May 1975. Thus, although GNP started growing more slowly than potential output in the second quarter of 1973, the administration's attention did not shift away from reducing the inflation rate until the beginning of 1975. Quarterly unemployment and inflation data are presented in Table 16-7.

The inflation rate, as measured by the CPI (consumer price index), increased abruptly to a new higher level in 1973/I after the 3.2 percent in 1972/IV. It hovered close to 10 percent through 1973, and then moved into the double-digit range for each of the quarters of 1974. Thereafter it began to fall. The WPI (wholesale price index) behaves much more dramatically. The WPI reflects the prices of raw materials much more than does the CPI. The rapid rate of WPI inflation in early 1973 is in part the result of rapidly rising food prices. The rapid rise in early 1974 is the result of the increase in the price of oil, and the extraordinary inflation rate of the third quarter of 1974 again reflects increases in agricultural prices.

The major exogenous shocks—the increases in oil prices, and the increased demand from Russia and other countries for agricultural products,

TABLE 16-7 INFLATION AND UNEMPLOYMENT, 1973–1975

	1973				1974				1975	
	I	II	III	IV	I	II	III	IV	I	II
Inflation rate, CPI	8.7	7.4	10.0	8.7	13.6	10.9	13.1	10.9	5.7	7.4
Inflation rate, WPI	21.0	23.3	13.2	15.8	24.8	10.9	34.8	14.3	−5.8	7.4
Unemployment rate	4.9	4.8	4.8	4.9	5.0	5.3	5.9	7.2	8.5	8.7

Note: All calculations based on seasonally adjusted end-month-of-quarter data.

Source: *Economic Report of the President*, 1976.

which raised agricultural prices—were reflected first in the WPI.   Later
these price increases worked their way through to the CPI.

Economic Policy and Other Shocks

Table 16-8 shows the growth rate of money, the Treasury bill rate, and the
full-employment surplus, for the period.   The growth rate of money is
quite jerky.   Nonetheless, monetary growth during 1974 was at a very
moderate rate on average, compared with the extravagant monetary growth
in 1972.   There appears, from Table 16-8, to be a deceleration of monetary
growth in mid-1974.   The Treasury bill rate rose through 1973 to an extraordinary level of about 9 percent, then fell off, only to return to record
high levels in the summer of 1974.   Thereafter it fell again.

   The budget moved into surplus on the full-employment definition
early in 1973, and the surplus continued to increase thereafter until the
beginning of 1975.   Only the tax cut in March 1975 reduced the surplus
sharply.

   Despite the jerkiness of monetary growth, it is clear that the prime aim
of policy, both monetary and fiscal, through this period, was to reduce the
inflation rate.   Policy was thus quite restrictive until the second quarter of
1975.

   In addition to monetary and fiscal policy, wage-price controls were in
effect for part of the period.   Phase III was instituted in January 1973.   The
regime was more liberal than phase II, and was associated with the jump in
inflation from 1972/IV to 1973/I.   There was some catching up on price
increases following the move to phase III.   However, most of the extra
inflation of the first half of 1973 was a result of increases in food prices that
had nothing to do with the ending of phase II, because such prices were
exempt from controls.   The rapid inflation of early 1973 led, once again, to
pressures to do something.   In response, President Nixon imposed a
sixty-day price freeze in June.   The freeze, known as phase III½, was to

---

TABLE 16-8   MONETARY AND FISCAL POLICY, 1973–1975

	1973				1974				1975	
	I	II	III	IV	I	II	III	IV	I	II
Growth rate of M_1 (percent)	7.3	6.4	5.6	5.0	6.0	5.6	4.2	4.1	0.7	7.4
Treasury bill rate (percent)	5.6	6.6	8.4	7.5	7.6	8.3	8.3	7.3	5.9	5.4
Full-employment surplus (billion dollars)	−3.3	4.6	8.5	9.9	14.3	12.6	12.7	15.3	9.4	−37.6

Source: Money stock and Treasury bill rate: *Federal Reserve Bulletin*, and Federal Reserve Bank of St. Louis.   Full-employment
surplus: *Federal Budget Trends*, March 1976.

provide time for a new set of controls, phase IV, similar to those of phase II, to be prepared. However, there were more exceptions to phase IV than there had been to phase II, and the economic environment in late 1973 was very different from that in late 1971 when phase II had started. There is little evidence of the effects of phase IV on the inflation rate in the data of Table 16-5. Phase IV died an unlamented death in April 1974.

The experience of controls during the rapid inflation of 1973–1974 indicates that controls have difficulty containing inflation when the underlying inflation rate is high and there is no amount of slack (unemployment of resources) in the economy. Another view of the performance of controls is that there was no reason to expect the confirmed free-marketeers of the Nixon administration even to try to use controls effectively, and that their failure proves nothing. Nonetheless, it seems clear that controls are bound to have trouble operating in an environment like that of 1973–1974 in the United States.

One influence on the behavior of prices that has not so far been mentioned is the change in the dollar exchange rate that took place in 1973. Throughout most of 1973, the dollar was depreciating against foreign currencies, so that it cost more dollars to buy a unit of foreign currency at the end of the year than at the beginning. For instance, one deutschmark (the West German currency) cost 31.3 cents in January 1973 and 37.6 cents in December. These increases in the price of foreign currencies tended to increase the dollar price of imported goods,[25] thus contributing significantly to the increases in the consumer price index.

In summary, economic policy through the period until the end of 1974 was basically contractionary. The economy was affected by (1) the shortfall in world grain production in 1972, and consequent agricultural price increase early in 1973 (food prices in the CPI rose at an annual rate of nearly 36 percent from December 1972 to March 1973); (2) the depreciation of the dollar through 1973; (3) the quadrupling of oil prices at the end of 1973; and (4) the increase in agricultural prices in mid-1974. In addition, the operation of wage and price controls had effects on inflation.[26]

The Components of Aggregate Demand

In this section we review the behavior of the components of aggregate demand from 1973/I to 1975/I. The purpose is to identify the components of total spending which fell most heavily during the long-drawn-out recession.

The first dramatic fall in the growth rate of GNP, from 1973/I to 1973/II, stemmed from a decline in aggregate demand resulting from falls in con-

---

[25]See Chap. 18 below.

[26]See papers by Barry Bosworth, "The Current Inflation: Malign Neglect?" and William Poole, "Wage-Price Controls: Where Do We Go from Here?", in *Brookings Papers on Economic Activity*, 1973, 1.

sumer spending on goods and in real residential investment. As usual, the reduction in residential investment was a result of the high interest rates that can be seen in Table 16-8. Residential construction continued to fall through the year, as interest rates remained high. Consumption demand began to fall during 1973, with the biggest reduction coming in the fourth quarter.

Table 16-9 shows the components of aggregate demand from 1973/I to 1975/I. Over that period, real GNP fell by $68.6 billion (in 1972 dollars). The table shows the dollar change in real spending for each category of spending, and then calculates that change as a percentage of $68.6 billion, to produce the entries in the final column. For instance, the fall in investment of $75.3 billion is more than the total decline in GNP and thus "accounts for" 110 percent of the fall in GNP.

Before commenting further on Table 16-9, we note that the major sources of reduced demand in 1974 were, as in 1973, residential construction and consumption. The decline in consumption was largely a decline in durable spending, particularly on automobiles. Car buying fell as a result mainly of the increased price, and reduced availability, of gasoline. Nonresidential investment, i.e., business investment, did not fall for the first year after 1973/I, but thereafter began to fall rapidly.

The behavior of inventories over the period is shown in Chart 16-5. Inventories accumulate when output exceeds final sales and decumulate when sales exceed output. There appears to have been substantial unanticipated inventory accumulation toward the end of 1973, with little accumulation during 1974. Then at the end of 1974, and in the first quarter of 1975, there is rapid inventory decumulation, as firms cut production while maintaining their sales. This sharp cut in inventories—a classic feature of recessions—largely accounts for the rapid fall of GNP in the last quarter of 1974 and first quarter of 1975.

Table 16-9 shows that the entire fall in aggregate demand over the period can be attributed to three factors: first, the reduction in residential investment; second, the decline in consumer durable purchases, meaning mainly cars; and third, the decline in inventory accumulation. Business fixed investment, too, fell. Offsetting these reductions in aggregate demand was an increase in net exports, reflecting the results of the depreciation of the dollar.

*Diagrammatic Analysis

In this part we try to make some sense of the events of 1973–1975, using our familiar diagrammatic apparatus. By the beginning of 1973, the excessively expansionary policy in 1972 had left the aggregate demand curve in a position like AD in Fig. 16-3, p. 542. The aggregate supply curve is represented by the AS schedule, with the intersection at point E being close to potential output.

TABLE 16-9   COMPONENTS OF AGGREGATE DEMAND, 1973–1975 (billions of 1972 dollars)

	1973/I	1974/I	1975/I	(1975/I–1973/I)	Percent of total change in GNP
GNP	$1,227.2	$1,228.7	$1,158.6	−$68.6	100
1. Consumption	765.8	760.0	752.3	− 13.5	20
Durable goods	124.0	114.7	104.0	− 20.0	29
Nondurable goods and services	641.8	645.3	648.3	6.5	− 9
2. Investment	205.0	195.9	129.7	− 75.3	110
Residential	64.5	49.1	33.6	− 30.9	45
Change in inventory	11.9	12.4	− 19.0	− 30.9	45
Nonresidential	128.6	134.5	115.2	− 13.4	20
3. Government (spending on goods and services)	254.7	254.0	255.1	0.4	0
Federal government	100.4	94.7	93.7	− 6.7	10
State and local	154.3	159.3	161.4	7.1	− 10
4. Net exports	2.1	18.7	21.5	19.4	− 28

Note: Details may not add to totals because of rounding.
Source: *Economic Report of the President*, 1976.

The crop shortage and high agricultural prices of early 1973 move the AS curve up to the left, to AS', as does an increase in the expected rate of inflation that probably occurred in early 1973. At the same time, the aggregate demand curve moved in to the left because government spending was cut and the full-employment budget surplus increased. Further, the effects of regulation Q on housing investment are best represented in the diagram as shifting the aggregate demand curve to the left. We thus have the AD curve shifting to AD', with a new short-run equilibrium at E', where the growth rate of output is lower than it was at E, but the inflation rate only slightly higher than at E.

The slackening in food price increases may have moved the AS' curve down a little toward the end of 1973. The next big disturbance is the oil price increase, which shifts the aggregate supply curve out to a position like AS", with a new short-run equilibrium at E", where output has been reduced from that at E' and the inflation rate is higher than at E'. The shift from AS' to AS" reflects also the very high inflation of the first three quarters of 1973. The direction of the effects of monetary and fiscal policy on the AD' curve at the end of 1973 are hard to evaluate. Fiscal policy was undoubtedly tightening, as the full-employment surplus increased. But monetary policy had been so variable in the previous few quarters, that the overall effect on aggregate demand is not clear. The 6 percent growth rate of money for 1973 was less than the more than 8 percent of 1972, so on balance monetary policy might have been moving the AD' curve slightly leftwards (not drawn).

There were no further nonpolicy shocks through the first two quarters of 1974. The full-employment budget surplus was growing, while monetary growth on balance was unchanged, suggesting a slight leftward shift of the AD' curve. It would have been reasonable for expectations of inflation to be increasing, shifting the AS curve further to the left and up, as did increasing food prices. During the rest of the year we should expect the AS curve to have been moving up to the left, increasing the inflation rate and reducing the growth rate of output. Aggregate demand policies were not vigorously used, although monetary policy was somewhat contractionary while the full-employment surplus stayed about constant.

Our analysis is not sufficiently detailed for us to be able to include the dynamics of the change in inventory investment as part of our model. Treating that change as given, it is, from our viewpoint, a reduction in aggregate demand, so that in 1974/IV and 1975/I the aggregate demand curve shifts to a position like AD". The AS" curve in Fig. 16-3 moves to AS''' as the expected inflation rate and the unemployment rate moved during 1974, but we again want to avoid cluttering the diagram. The period ends with a sharp decline in output and a fall in the inflation rate, at point E'''.

CHART 16-5 REAL GNP AND FINAL SALES. (Source: *Economic Report of the President*, 1976)

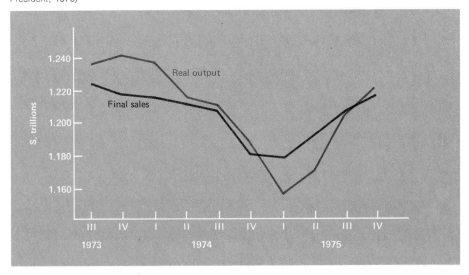

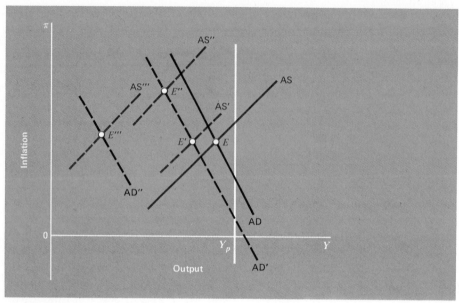

FIGURE 16-3 THE 1973–1975 PERIOD
(Note: E: 1973/I; E': 1973/II–III; E'': 1973–1974;
E''': 1974–1975)

Was It Necessary?

We argued at some length in Chap. 13 that the oil price increase could have been handled differently. We suggested there that monetary policy could have accommodated the oil price shock by increasing the growth rate of money as the AS curve shifted to the left. This would have prevented the sharp fall in income that took place during 1974, at the cost of a higher rate of inflation in the transition.

It appears from our examination of the period, that there were two distinct subperiods. The first, through the end of 1973, was a more or less standard beginning of a recession, with the complications of wage-price controls and the sharp rise in agricultural prices. The agricultural price rise shifted the aggregate supply curve to the left, tending both to reduce the growth rate of output and to increase the inflation rate.

While it appears from Table 16-4 that the growth recession began in the second quarter of 1973, that was not quite so obvious at the time. In the first place, the GNP data for that quarter have been revised down since 1973. Second, the behavior of variables other than GNP were not at the time suggestive of a recession. The unemployment rate remained steady through 1973, investment spending by business remained high, and industrial output did not fall during the period. Given the low unemployment and the high inflation of the time, it is again not clear what policies, other than aggregate supply policies, could have been used to stop the recession while not increasing the inflation rate.

The growth recession at the end of 1973 was exacerbated by the oil price increase, which led quickly to a deepening and worsening of the recession. Given the large cost in terms of output forgone, and the high levels of unemployment that resulted, the cost in inflation of accommodating the oil price increase would, in our judgment, have been worth bearing. In particular, there is little justification for the reduction of monetary growth in mid-1974. However, there is no policy that could have been used that would not have implied a reduction in real GNP to reflect the lower real standard of living that Americans could achieve with the new higher price of oil.[27]

It is much easier to decide what policy should have been than to decide what it will be. Unfortunate as the economic experience of the last few years has been, it should be realized that policy makers did not make colossal blunders. They were making policy in a difficult environment, with less than perfect knowledge. In the first place, no one knew how long the oil cartel would last. Second, there was not then a good body of economic theory to help them analyze the way to deal with supply shocks. Economists had largely concentrated on demand shocks for the past thirty years.

Third, as we have noted several times, the data the policy makers were receiving were quite poor. The money stock data are revised frequently, and the growth rates of money changed with each revision. We also mentioned above that the real GNP data available in 1973 considerably overestimated the growth of real GNP in the middle two quarters of the year. Thus the Fed was not alerted as early as it might have been to the slowdown in GNP growth that was then taking place.

Indeed, data problems were so bad that, in December 1974, Geoffrey H. Moore,[28] a respected business cycle expert and former Commissioner of Labor Statistics, said, "I can't help thinking how ironic it would be if by overdeflating the current dollar figures in a well-intentioned effort to get rid of the effects of inflation, we should have talked ourselves into a recession." Moore was saying that the real GNP data, even then, were subject to so much uncertainty that it was doubtful whether the economy was in a recession at all.

Making policy under such circumstances is difficult. Since there is no point in not using hindsight when it is available, we can now argue that policy was excessively expansionary in 1972, and that it should have accommodated the oil price increase in 1974. The first argument is probably widely accepted, while the second is controversial, and reflects our judg-

---

[27]We leave a question on why the oil price increase meant a reduction in American living standards for the problem set.

[28]*New York Times*, Dec. 8, 1974, Business & Finance section.

ment of the costs of inflation and unemployment. It is in any event clear that the economy would have shown some fluctuations in output and prices under the best of policies, given the disturbances that occurred in the 1973–1975 period.

16-5 RECOVERY, 1975–1976

The inventory decumulation of the second quarter of 1975 marked the end of the bloodletting of the 1973–1975 recession. Unemployment reached its peak level of 8.9 percent in May 1975, and thereafter declined slowly to 8.3 percent at the end of the year, down to 7.8 percent at the end of 1976. Unemployment, growth, and inflation rate data for 1975–1976 are presented in Table 16-10. The CPI inflation rate for each year as a whole was well below the inflation rate for the previous year, and the same applies for the WPI. The growth rate of real GNP makes a spectacular recovery in the third and fourth quarters of 1975 and the first quarter of 1976, largely as a result of the end of the period of inventory decumulation. Thereafter it slowed down substantially, falling below the growth rate of potential output in the last quarter of 1976.

The main policy variables are shown in Table 16-11. The Fed made a basic policy decision to try to come out of this recession without appreciably increasing the inflation rate. It also undertook, by congressional order, to announce to the public what growth rates of money it was aiming for over the next year. After the rapid monetary growth of the middle quarters of 1975, which was accompanied by a fall in the Treasury bill rate, monetary growth became low, and stayed there. Given that the Treasury bill rate was low relative to the rates of the previous two years, monetary policy at the time seemed quite expansionary, in the light of the interest rate measure of the thrust of monetary policy. We were thus in the situation previously described, in which the slow growth rate of money suggests a contractionary policy while the behavior of interest rates suggests a mildly expansionary policy. It did appear in those two quarters (1975/III and IV) that

TABLE 16-10 INFLATION, GROWTH, AND UNEMPLOYMENT, 1975–1976

	1975				1976			
	I	II	III	IV	I	II	III	IV
Unemployment rate	8.5	8.7	8.6	8.3	7.6	7.4	7.8	7.9
Inflation rate (CPI)	5.7	7.4	7.9	7.9	4.6	4.6	6.0	4.7
Inflation rate (WPI)	−5.8	7.4	10.9	5.7	−0.7	4.9	3.9	7.9
Growth rate of real GNP	−9.2	3.3	12.0	5.4	9.2	4.5	3.9	3.0

Note: All data seasonally adjusted at annual rates.
Source: *Economic Report of the President*, 1977.

TABLE 16-11   MONETARY AND FISCAL POLICY, 1975–1976

	1975				1976			
	I	II	III	IV	I	II	III	IV
Growth rate of money (percent per annum)	0.7	7.4	7.0	2.3	2.7	8.4	4.0	6.2
Treasury bill rate (percent)	5.9	5.4	6.3	5.7	4.9	5.2	5.2	4.8
Full-employment surplus (billions of dollars)	9.4	−37.6	−11.5	−12.7	−8.7	1.4	−1.1	
Actual budget surplus	−1.0	−49.7	−22.9	−25.8	−25.0	−15.2	−20.2	−24.0

Note: All data seasonally adjusted at annual rates.
Sources: Treasury bill rate: *Federal Reserve Bulletin*. The full-employment surplus is calculated on the basis of the new measure of potential output. Full-employment surplus: *Federal Budget Trends*, May 1977. Money stock: *Monetary Trends*, December 1976, and *United States Financial Data*, January 1977.

the money demand function was shifting, as discussed earlier in the chapter. The growth rate of real output of the third and fourth quarters of the year were adequate to make progress toward full employment, in that they exceeded the growth rate of potential output. The Treasury bill rate continued to decline into 1976, and real output growth was also sustained into 1976. That implies that monetary policy was about right in not trying to increase the growth rate of money merely because the growth rate of money was low. We have attributed the low interest rates combined with a low growth rate of money to a shift in the demand for money.

Fiscal policy in 1975 was largely the creation of Congress. The President recommended a tax cut early in 1975, and the Congress, acting with unusual speed, had the cuts in place by March. Some of the tax cuts were retroactive, so that the full-employment budget of 1975/II was substantially in deficit. The full-employment deficit for the rest of the year was lower, because the retroactive tax cuts were not paid in those quarters. Fiscal policy in 1976 was little changed from that of 1975.

What judgments can be made at this time about policy in 1975 and 1976? It does seem that the Fed, despite the objections of those who wanted faster monetary growth, came close to finding a path for the money stock that succeeded in financing the recovery, without putting pressure on the price level. And the fiscal stimulus of the tax cut occurred right when the recession was at its worst point, and helped turn the economy around.[29] Early 1976 showed a continuation of increasing real output, falling unemployment, and falling inflation. The Fed's careful steering of an anti-inflationary course seemed to be taking the economy slowly onto a desirable path. The slowdown in economic activity in the second half of

[29]The administration's policy of a moderate recovery was questioned by James Tobin in "For a Faster Recovery," *Economic Outlook USA*, University of Michigan Survey Research Center, 3, Summer 1976.

1976—the "pause" as it was called—led to a reconsideration of fiscal policy. The Carter administration in early 1977 proposed a new round of fiscal expansion including a rebate of about $12 billion, a cut in permanent taxes but also tax advantages for investment. Monetary policy remained conservative. Monetary growth targets for the period 1976/IV to 1977/IV were reduced to 4.5 to 6.5 percent for M_1 and to 7.0 to 10 percent for M_2.[30] One of the important questions for 1977 would be whether money demand would still be declining (given income and interest rates) so that the monetary growth would be adequate to support a continuing recovery.

By late spring 1977 there was a reorientation in fiscal policy. While monetary policy remained firm in its anti-inflation orientation, the administration drew back on its expansionary fiscal policy. The rebate proposal was withdrawn partly because growth in early 1977 had been satisfactory—7.5 percent for the first quarter of 1977—and partly because inflation showed an upturn. There was also the question of whether transitory tax cuts or rebates are really effective in stimulating aggregate demand. Many argued that the tax rebate was merely a give-away with little impact on spending and with undesirable budgetary effects, although that contention remains to be established.[31]

PROBLEMS

1 Most Americans felt economists had failed in their job of controlling the economy during the 1970s. Economists responded by claiming that policy making in the 1970s was simply harder than in the 1960s. Evaluate these arguments, and give your view of who is right.

2 During the 1960s there were no real recessions, whereas during the 1970–1975 period there was one minor and one major recession. Is this the fault of policy, bad luck, or what? Could the 1969–1970 recession have been avoided? The 1974–1975 recession? At what cost?

3 How would monetarists look at a policy whereby the Fed used *real* interest rates as a guide to monetary growth? How about unemployment rates? Evaluate the pluses and minuses of a monetary "rule."

4 It was the stated policy of the Nixon administration in 1969 to reduce inflation *without* creating a recession. Was this possible? Why did gradualism cause a recession despite their plans? Would you say it failed? Why or why not?

*5 Evaluate the wage-price control experiment in terms of its short-run and long-run effects on inflation and unemployment. What does the apparatus of Chap. 13 suggest would have happened in 1971–1972 in the absence of controls?

6 How can the rise of interest rates in 1972 despite the rapid growth of money in that year be explained? What were the consequences for Federal Reserve policy?

*7 Explain why the oil price increase necessarily reduced the purchasing power of

[30]See *Federal Reserve Bulletin*, April 1977.

[31]For a review of the fiscal policy options, see Robert Solow, "Requiem for a Rebate," *The New Republic*, May 7, 1977.

Americans' incomes.   Would this reduction have been inevitable if oil were not essential to our economy?   Demonstrate the effects of the oil shock using the familiar AS-AD diagrams of Chap. 13.

*8   In view of the data presented in this chapter, formulate a projection for growth rates of real GNP through 1980, and the monetary and fiscal policies appropriate for this goal.   Explain your plan carefully.

17

Long-Term Growth

This chapter discusses long-term growth. In earlier chapters we were concerned with the maintenance of full employment and the behavior of output relative to the full-employment or potential level of output. Now we turn to the path of full-employment output over time. We shall be asking what determines the growth rate of potential output. Over long periods, actual output on average stays close to potential output despite short-run fluctuations, so that we will also be discussing the long-run behavior of actual output.

The question we are asking is brought out by Chart 17-1, which shows the evolution of real output (in 1958 dollars) in the United States economy from 1890 to 1970. Over that period, real output grew more than tenfold, or at an annual rate of about 3.3 percent. Growth theory asks what factors account for the increase in output over time, and what behavior an economic system will show along the *growth path* of full-employment output.

In discussing these questions, we go to fundamentals. We step back from the aggregate demand and supply framework and ask how the economy would behave over time if there were always full employment. With full employment, output would be determined by *factor supplies*—by the availability of capital and labor to produce goods. Over time, output would be determined by the growth in factor supplies, and by changes in the productivity of factors of production.

CHART 17-1 REAL GNP IN THE UNITED STATES, 1880–1970. (Source: *Long-term Economic Growth*, U.S. Department of Commerce, 1973)

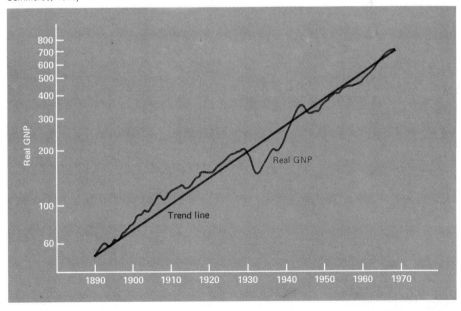

This in turn raises the question of what determines the growth of factor supplies, and how the growth in factor supplies translates into income and output growth. The simple theory we present emphasizes two elements: (1) the production function that relates factor inputs—capital and labor—and the state of technology to output or GNP and (2) the savings rate.

The production function relates growth in factor supplies to growth in output. And the savings rate determines what part of current output is saved and invested (added to the capital stock), and thus results in an increase in the input of capital. Because we assume that output is continuously at the full-employment level, we also assume that any output that is saved is automatically added to the capital stock, and we do not separately discuss the determinants of the rate of investment.

Chart 17-1 has already introduced the major questions raised in this chapter: What determines the growth rate of output in the long run? In particular, what made real output in the United States grow at the average annual growth rate of 3.3 percent over the last eighty years? For many purposes, though, we are interested not in the level of total real output, but rather in the level of output in relation to population, or in real *per capita* output. The difference between output and *output per head* is brought out by Chart 17-2, where we show the evolution of output per head for the 1890–1970 period.

The average growth rate of per capita income has been about 1.8 percent per year over that period. Output per head has increased fourfold over the last eighty years. The average person in 1970 had four times the amount of output or income at her command that the average person in 1890 had.

CHART 17-2 REAL PER CAPITA OUTPUT
THE UNITED STATES, 1890–1970. (Source:
Long-term Economic Growth, U.S.
Department of Commerce, 1973)

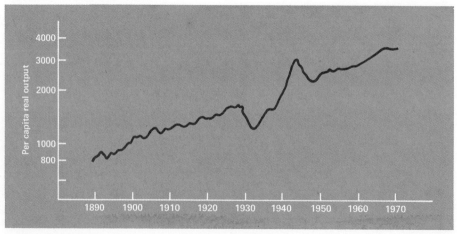

TABLE 17-1   AVERAGE ANNUAL GROWTH RATES, 1890–1970

Average growth of output	3.3%
Less: Average growth of population	1.5%
Equals: Average growth of output per head	1.8%

Source: Long-term Economic Growth, 1860-1970, U.S. Department of Commerce, 1973.

The relationship between Charts 17-1 and 17-2 is brought out by the numbers in Table 17-1. The table brings out the simple relationship: growth of output per head equals growth of output less growth of population. Most of our analysis below concentrates on the determinants of output growth per capita. We want to know why per capita output grew to produce the extraordinary fourfold increase over the last eighty years.

There are two central messages from the simple growth theory we study here. (1) The savings rate determines the rate of growth of output in the short and medium terms. The larger the fraction of output saved and invested, the larger the growth rate of full-employment output. (2) In the long run, the growth rate of output per head depends on the rate of technological change (improvements in methods of production). Total output growth depends on the rate of technological change and the growth rate of the population. In the long run, the savings rate determines only the *level* and not the *growth rate* of the capital stock and output per capita. The higher the saving rate, the higher the amount of capital.

This preview has laid out both the questions and some of the answers. We turn now to a more detailed analysis. In Sec. 17-1, we introduce the production function, which provides the framework for our analysis. In Sec. 17-2, we look at the empirical evidence on sources of growth in the United States. Here we allocate the responsibility for the growth in output shown in Table 17-1 among growth in the capital stock, growth in the input of labor, and improvements in technology. Section 17-3 turns to growth theory and formalizes the relationships among saving, population growth, and growth in capital. Section 17-4 briefly discusses the question of *limits of growth* that has become an important issue of public concern.

17-1 SOURCES OF GROWTH IN REAL INCOME: THEORY

In this section we ask the question: What are the sources of growth in real output over time? The simple answer is: First, growth in the availability of factors of production and, second, improvements in technology. If output is at the full-employment level, then there are only two ways of obtaining an increase in output: (1) have more factors of production and/or (2) be able to use existing factor supplies more effectively. The latter possibility means that we are producing more effectively either because of a more efficient allocation of resources or because of more effective technology.

The Production Function

The preceding remarks can be formalized by writing down a *production function*. A production function tells us how much output or real GNP is produced by given amounts of factor inputs. Denoting real output by Y, capital or machines by K, and the labor force by N, we have

$$Y = AF(K, N) \tag{1}$$

where we treat A as a constant.[1] Equation (1) states that output Y is a function of the inputs of capital and labor. An increase in either input will raise output. We impose a particular property on the production function, namely, *constant returns to scale*. Constant returns to scale means that if all inputs increase in some proportion, then output will increase in that proportion. For example, if both capital and labor were to increase by 10 percent, then output would increase by 10 percent. With constant returns to scale, the productivity of factors is independent of the scale of production. Constant returns to scale imply that output per head, Y/N, is independent of the scale of operation. Output per head or labor productivity depends on the amount of capital per worker, $k \equiv K/N$. The higher the amount of capital cooperating with each laborer, the more productive the laborer, or the higher is output per person.

Constant returns imply a simple relationship between labor productivity or output per worker, Y/N, and capital per worker, $k \equiv K/N$. The more capital per head we have, or the more capital-intensive the economy, the larger is output per head. We can write this relationship as

$$x = Af(k) \tag{1a}$$

where $x \equiv Y/N$ denotes output per head. We have already noted that in Eq. (1a) an increase in the amount of capital per head k will make labor more productive and therefore raise output per worker. We add now the further assumption of diminishing returns *not* to scale but to capital intensity. As we keep raising the amount of capital per head k, labor becomes more productive and therefore output rises. However, the increase in output becomes progressively less. Additional capital cooperating with a given labor force is invariably productive but at a diminishing rate.

In Fig. 17-1 we illustrate the properties of the production function that we have discussed so far. In particular we note that (1) output per head x is an increasing function of capital per head k, which is called the capital-labor ratio, and (2) the contribution to output of progressive increases in the capital-labor ratio diminishes. The latter aspect is captured in Fig. 17-1 in the flattening out of the production function.

---

[1] The term A used here has no connection with aggregate demand, which was denoted by that letter in other chapters.

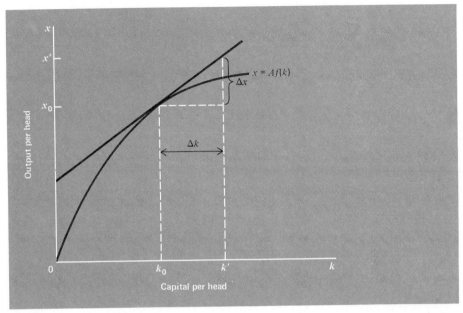

FIGURE 17-1 THE PRODUCTION
FUNCTION

The contribution of an increase in capital per head to the amount of output per head is called the marginal productivity of capital. We note from Fig. 17-1 that an increase in the capital-labor ratio from k_0 to k' raises output by $\Delta x = \text{MPK } \Delta k$. The term MPK denotes the marginal product of capital which is given in Fig. 17-1 by the slope of the production function.

The idea of the marginal product of capital is best understood in the following manner. We start off from a capital-labor ratio k_0, where we produce an amount of output per head x_0. Next we have an increase in the capital-labor ratio to k'. Obviously output per head will increase, and we can read off from the production function that it rises to x'. Now we have an increase in output of $\Delta x = x' - x_0$ that is brought about by an increase in capital per man of $\Delta k = k' - k_0$. Forming the ratio $\Delta x / \Delta k \equiv \text{MPK}$, we are looking at the increase in output due to the increase in capital or at the marginal product of capital. For sufficiently small changes in the capital-labor ratio we can use the slope of the production function to translate a change in capital into the corresponding change in output. Thus the marginal product of capital is given by the slope of the production function.

Sources of Growth

This exercise has prepared us for a discussion of a first source of growth. We have seen that growth in the amount of capital per head increases output per head. Therefore, one of the sources of long-term growth in output per head is that capital has grown faster than labor and therefore has caused the capital-labor ratio to rise.

A second source of growth is reflected in the constant term A in Eq. ($1a$). Let this term represent the state of technology. An improvement in technology would mean that we can produce with the same amount of capital per head a larger quantity of output per head. Given capital and labor, improved technology raises factor productivity and therefore output. In terms of Fig. 17-2 an improvement in technology is shown by an upward shift of the production function and thus a higher amount of output associated with each capital-labor ratio. Our second source of growth in output per head is therefore improvement in technology, or *technical progress*.[2]

We have now seen that there are two sources of growth in output per head: (1) increases in the amount of capital per head, which contribute to output by an amount $\Delta x = \text{MPK } \Delta k$, and (2) technical progress, which contributes to output an amount $\Delta x = f(k) \Delta A$. We can therefore write the

---

[2]*Warning*: Technical progress in general implies only that more output can be produced with the same inputs. The particular form of technical progress represented by increases in the constant term A in Eq. ($1a$) implies that the marginal products of both capital and labor increase by the same ratio. Other forms of technical progress imply changes in the *relative* productivities of capital and labor. We choose the form in which A increases for expositional convenience. For more details on technical progress see R. M. Solow, *Growth Theory*, Oxford University Press, 1970, pp. 33–38, and the very readable treatment in Daniel Hamberg, *Models of Economic Growth*, Harper and Row, 1971, and Philip A. Neher, *Economic Growth and Development*, John Wiley, 1971.

FIGURE 17-2 TECHNOLOGICAL PROGRESS

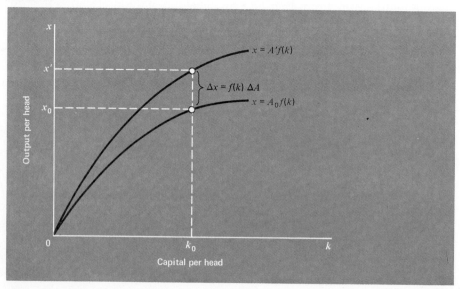

total change in output per head as

$$\Delta x = \text{MPK } \Delta k + f(k) \, \Delta A \tag{2}$$

If we divide both sides by the level of output per head x, we obtain a much more convenient expression:

$$\frac{\Delta x}{x} = \theta \frac{\Delta k}{k} + \frac{\Delta A}{A} \tag{3}$$

where the term $\theta \equiv (\text{MPK})k/x$ is capital's share in income.[3] It is capital's share in income because in a competitive economy the owners of capital are paid for the services of capital an amount equal to capital's marginal product. Accordingly, the marginal product—the return per unit of capital—times the stock of capital divided by total income, $(\text{MPK})k/x$, is the fraction of income that accrues to capital.

Equation (3) tells us that growth in output per head is equal to growth in capital per head times the share of capital in income plus the rate of technical progress, $\Delta A/A$. To take an example, assume that capital per head grows at the rate of 2 percent. Assume capital's share in income, quite realistically for the United States, is $\theta = 0.35$. Then, if the rate of technical progress is 1.1 percent, the growth rate of output is 0.35(2 percent) + 1.1 percent = 1.8 percent. In fact, this is the long-term growth rate in output per capita in the United States, as we noted earlier in commenting on Chart 17-2.

Growth in capital per head and technology are the only sources of growth in output per head. However, if we are interested in growth of total output—as opposed to output per head—we have to take account of increases in the size of the labor force. If we hold technology constant and hold constant the amount of capital per person but increase the size of the labor force, then we expect output to increase. We can simply use Eq. (3) to make this point by recognizing that the growth rate of ouput per head is equal to the growth rate of output less the growth rate of the labor force, $\Delta x/x \equiv \Delta Y/Y - \Delta N/N$. Similarly, the growth rate in the capital-labor ratio is the growth rate of capital less the growth rate of labor, $\Delta k/k \equiv \Delta K/K - \Delta N/N$. Using these substitutions in Eq. (3) yields

$$\frac{\Delta Y}{Y} = \frac{(1 - \theta)\Delta N}{N} + \frac{\theta \Delta K}{K} + \frac{\Delta A}{A} \tag{4}$$

Equation (4) conveniently summarizes the three sources of growth.

[3]In more detail, dividing the term $\text{MPK} \cdot \Delta k$ in Eq. (2) by x, we have $(\text{MPK} \cdot \Delta k)/x$. Now multiply and divide by k to obtain $[(\text{MPK} \cdot k)/x](\Delta k/k)$. Now $\text{MPK} \cdot k$ is the marginal product of capital times the amount of capital per head, or the amount of income received by capital divided by the number of workers. The derivation of the $\Delta A/A$ term in Eq. (3) is left for the problem set at the end of the chapter.

The growth contributions of capital and labor are weighted by their respective shares in income. Equation (4) implies, as we assumed at the outset, constant return to scale. This is apparent from the fact that a, say, 10 percent increase in both capital and labor will increase output in the same proportion.

17-2 EMPIRICAL ESTIMATES OF THE SOURCES OF GROWTH

The previous section prepares us for an analysis of empirical studies that deal with sources of growth. Equation (4) suggests that the growth in output can be explained by growth in factor inputs, weighted by their shares in income, and by technical progress. An early and famous study by Robert Solow of MIT dealt with the period 1909–1949 in the United States.[4] Solow's surprising conclusion was that over 80 percent of the growth in output per man hour over that period was due to technical progress, that is, to factors other than growth in the input of capital per man hour. Specifically, Solow estimates for the United States an equation similar to our Eq. (4) that identifies capital and labor growth along with technical progress as the sources of output growth. Of the average annual growth of total GNP of 2.9 percent per year over that period, he concluded that 0.32 percent was attributable to capital accumulation, 1.09 percent per annum was due to increases in the input of labor, and the remaining 1.49 percent was due to technical progress. Per capita output grew at 1.81 percent, with 1.49 percent of that increase resulting from technical progress.

The very large part of the growth contribution that is taken up by "technical progress" makes that term really a catchall for omitted factors and poor measurement of the capital and labor inputs. Further work therefore turned quite naturally to explore this residual, that is, growth not explained by capital accumulation or increased labor input.

Perhaps the most comprehensive of the subsequent studies is that by Edward Denison.[5] Using data for the period 1929–1969, Denison attributed 1.8 percent of the 3.4 percent annual rate of increase in real output to increased factor inputs. Output per man hour grew at the rate of 2.09 percent, of which 1.59 percent was due to technical progress. Denison's findings thus support Solow's estimate that most of the growth in output per man hour is due to technical progress. Table 17-2 shows a breakdown of the increased factor input into its various components.

Technical progress explains almost half the growth in output, with growth in total factor inputs accounting for the other half of growth. Consider now the breakdown between the various components of increased factor use. Here increases in the labor force get a very large credit for their contribution to growth. Why? Because labor grows very fast?

[4]"Technical Change and the Aggregate Production Function," *Review of Economics and Statistics*, August 1957.

[5]*Accounting for United States Economic Growth 1929–1969*, Brookings Institution, 1974.

TABLE 17-2 SOURCES OF GROWTH OF TOTAL NATIONAL INCOME, 1929–1969

Source of growth	Growth rate (percent per annum)
Total factor input	1.82
Labor: 1.32	
Capital: 0.50	
Output per unit of input	1.59
Knowledge: 0.92	
Resource allocation: 0.30	
Economies of scale: 0.36	
Other: 0.01	
National income:	3.41

Source: E. Denison, Accounting for United States Economic Growth 1929–1969, Brookings Institution, 1974, p. 127.

The answer is provided by Eq. (4), which suggests that labor's growth rate has a relatively large weight because labor's share in income is relatively large. The counterpart is obviously the relatively low share of capital. Thus, even if capital and labor grew at the same rate, the fact that they have different shares in income—labor having a share of about 65 percent and capital having a share of about 35 percent—implies that labor would be credited with a larger contribution toward growth.

Next we look at the various sources of increased factor productivity or increased output per unit factor input. Here the striking fact is the importance of advances in knowledge that account for almost two-thirds of the contribution of technical progress toward growth. Two other sources of increased factor productivity are worth recording. One is the increase in productivity that stems from improved resource allocation. Here we can think of people leaving low-pay jobs or low-income areas and moving to better jobs or locations, thus contributing to increased output or income growth. An important element here is relocation from farms to cities.

The remaining significant part of technical progress is *economies of scale*. This is a bit troublesome because we assumed away economies of scale in deriving Eq. (4). In deriving that equation, we explicitly assumed constant returns to scale, but we find now that more than 10 percent of the average annual growth in income is due to an expanding scale of operation. As the scale of operation of the economy expands, fewer inputs are required per unit output presumably because we can avail ourselves of techniques that are economically inefficient at a small-scale level but yield factor savings at a larger scale of production.

The major significance of Denison's work, and the work in this area of others, including Simon Kuznets and J. W. Kendrick, is to point out that there is no single critical source of real income growth. The early suggestion by Solow that growth in the capital stock makes a minor, though not negligible, contribution to growth stands up well to the test of new research. Capital investment is certainly necessary—particularly because some technological improvements require the use of new types of machines—but it is clear that there are other sources of growth that can make an important contribution. Furthermore, since for most purposes we are interested in output per head, we have to recognize that we are left with only technical progress and growth in capital to achieve increased output per head. Here it pays to ask what are the components of technical progress or growth in total factor productivity. Advances in knowledge stand out as a major source and point to the role of research, education, and training as important sources of growth.[6]

*17-3 GROWTH THEORY

In this section we will be concerned with growth of output from a theoretical point of view rather than in terms of the historical record. We will ask the question: What determines output growth in the short and long runs? You will see that we have already answered that question when we recognized in Eq. (4) that factor growth and technical progress are the sources of output growth. The next step therefore is to ask what determines the growth of factor inputs. We take a rather simple formulation here by (1) assuming a given and constant rate of labor force growth, $\Delta N/N \equiv n$, and (2) assuming that there is no technical progress, $\Delta A/A = 0$. With these assumptions we are left with the growth rate of capital. Capital growth is determined by saving, which in turn depends on income. Income or output in turn depends on capital. We are thus set with an interdependent system in which capital growth depends via saving and income on the capital stock. We now study the short-run behavior, the adjustment process, and the long-run equilibrium of that interdependent system.

Steady State

We start by discussing the steady-state of the economy. Here we ask whether in an economy with population growth and saving, and therefore growth in the capital stock, we reach a point where output per head and capital per head become constant. In such a steady state current saving and additions to the capital stock would be just enough to equip new entrants into the labor force with the same amount of capital as the average worker uses.

These ideas can be made more concrete by returning to Eq. (3), recognizing that we assume zero productivity growth. We therefore have

[6]A collection of important papers on the sources of growth are contained in Edmund Phelps (ed.), The Goal of Economic Growth, Norton, 1969.

$$\frac{\Delta x}{x} = \frac{\theta \, \Delta k}{k} \qquad\qquad (3a)$$

Equation ($3a$) states that growth in output per head is proportional to growth in the stock of capital per head, $\Delta k/k$. Clearly to reach a steady state where output per head is constant, we would have to reach zero growth in the stock of capital per head. Our focus is therefore on the determinants of the growth rate of capital per head.

Capital per head, $k \equiv K/N$, grows to the extent that current saving provides resources to be invested and added to the capital stock. Capital per head declines to the extent that population growth reduces the amount of capital the average worker has at her disposal.

More precisely the rate of growth of capital per head is equal to the difference between the growth rate of capital, $\Delta K/K$, and the growth rate of population, $n \equiv \Delta N/N$:

$$\frac{\Delta k}{k} = \frac{\Delta K}{K} - n \qquad\qquad (5)$$

where we use the shorthand notation n for the given rate of growth of the labor force. Equation (5) shows that capital per head grows if the capital stock grows faster than the labor force. Combining this with Eq. ($3a$), we realize that output per head grows if capital grows faster than the labor force:

$$\frac{\Delta x}{x} = \theta \left(\frac{\Delta K}{K} - n \right) \qquad\qquad (6)$$

where we have substituted Eq. (5) in Eq. ($3a$).

Equation (6) implies that output per head will be constant when capital and labor grow at the same rate. In other words, we will be in the steady state when output per head is constant because $n = \Delta K/K$. The next step in the analysis is to link growth in the capital stock to income and saving.

The growth rate of the capital stock $\Delta K/K$ is determined by additions to the capital stock, that is, by investment and thus by saving. Additions to the capital stock are equal to investment, which in turn is equal to saving, less depreciation:

$$\Delta K = \text{saving} - \text{depreciation} \qquad\qquad (7)$$

We will take particularly simple formulations of saving and depreciation. We assume that a constant fraction s of income or output is saved. Accordingly, saving is equal to sY. We assume that the depreciation rate of capital is d percent per year, so that total depreciation is at the rate of dK per year. Substituting for saving and depreciation in Eq. (7) yields

$$\Delta K = sY - dK \tag{7a}$$

We have to do some more work on Eq. (7a) before we arrive at a final equation that describes the growth process. The further modifications of Eq. (7a) are (1) to turn it into percentage change form by dividing both sides by the capital stock and (2) to get it into per capita form by subtracting the growth rate of labor from both sides. Undertaking these two operations, we have

$$\frac{\Delta K}{K} - n = \frac{sY}{K} - n - d \tag{7b}$$

We note that the left-hand side is the growth rate of the capital-labor ratio. The right-hand side is made up of three terms. First, we have saving per unit of capital which is equal to total investment per unit of capital. However, to get to the growth of capital per person, we have to subtract both depreciation and growth of the labor force, which are the remaining two terms in Eq. (7b). A final simplification of Eq. (7b) is obtained by multiplying and dividing the saving term (sY/K) by the labor force N to obtain $s(Y/N)(N/K)$. This allows us to replace that term by sx/k, using the production function in per capita terms:

$$\frac{\Delta k}{k} = \frac{sx}{k} - (n + d) \tag{8}$$

or

$$\Delta k = sx - (n + d)k \tag{8a}$$

Equation (8) is the final form of our growth model. It describes the growth rate of the capital stock in terms of saving behavior, population growth and depreciation.

The growth process can be studied in terms of Fig. 17-3. Here we reproduce the production function in per capita terms from Fig. 17-1. We have added the savings function, which, for each capital-labor ratio, is simply the fraction s of output. Thus, for any capital-labor ratio, say k_0, the corresponding point on the saving schedule tells us the amount of saving per head $sx(k_0)$ that will be forthcoming at that capital-labor ratio.

We know that all saving is invested so that gross investment or gross additions to the capital stock, in per capita terms, are equal to sx_0, given a capital-labor ratio of k_0. We know, too, that the increase in the capital-labor ratio falls short of that gross addition for two reasons:

1 Depreciation reduces the capital-labor ratio, and part of gross investment must be devoted to offsetting depreciation. In particular if the depreciation rate is d, then an amount dk is required as a depreciation

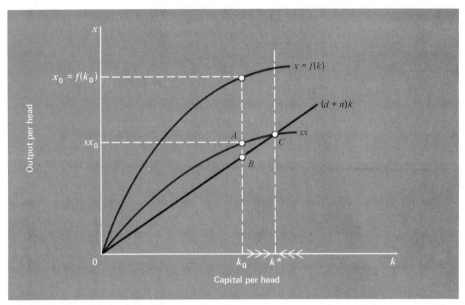

FIGURE 17-3 SAVING, INVESTMENT,
AND CAPITAL ACCUMULATION

allowance. For example, if the depreciation rate was 10 percent and the capital-labor ratio was ten machines per person, then each year the equivalent of one machine would depreciate and would have to be replaced, that is, 10 percent times ten machines equals one machine.

2 Growth in the labor force implies that with a given stock of capital the capital-labor ratio would be declining. To maintain the amount of capital per head constant, we have to add enough machines to the stock of capital to make up for the growth in population. Specifically if the capital-labor ratio were again ten machines (or units of capital) per person, and population growth were 1 percent, then we would have to add one-tenth of one machine each year to the stock of machines to maintain constant the capital-labor ratio.

It follows that we can write the investment required to maintain constant the capital-labor ratio in the face of depreciation and labor force growth as $(d + n)k$. That amount of investment is required to maintain constant the capital-labor ratio. If saving and hence gross investment are larger than $(d + n)k$, then the stock of capital per head is increasing. If saving and gross investment are less, then we are not making up for depreciation and population growth, and accordingly capital per head is falling. We can therefore think of the term $(d + n)k$ as the *investment requirement* that will maintain constant capital per head and therefore, from Eq. (1a), output per head.

In Fig. 17-3 we show this investment requirement as a positively sloped schedule. It tells us how much investment we would require at each capital-labor ratio just in order to keep the capital-labor ratio constant. It is positively sloped because the higher the capital-labor ratio, the larger the amount of investment that is required to maintain that capital-labor ratio. Thus with the depreciation rate of 10 percent and a growth rate of population of 1 percent, we would require an investment of 1.1 machines per head per year at a capital-labor ratio of 10 machines per head to maintain the capital-labor ratio constant. If the capital-labor ratio were 100 machines per head, the required investment would be 11 machines (= 100 machines per head times 11 percent). In summary, the investment requirement schedule tells us the amount of capital per head we need to invest merely to maintain constant the capital-labor ratio.

We saw above that the saving schedule tells us the amount of saving and gross investment associated with each capital-labor ratio. Thus at a capital-labor ratio of k_0 in Fig. 17-3, saving is sx_0 at point A. The investment requirement to maintain constant the capital-labor ratio at k_0 is equal to $(d + n)k_0$ at point B. Clearly saving exceeds the investment requirement. More is added to the capital stock than is required to maintain constant the capital-labor ratio. Accordingly, the capital-labor ratio grows. Not surprisingly, the increase in the capital-labor ratio is equal to actual saving or investment less the investment requirement and is thus given by the vertical distance AB. The excess of saving and investment over the investment requirement determines the change in the capital-labor ratio.

It is apparent from Fig. 17-3 that with a capital-labor ratio of k_0 we have a situation where saving and investment exceed the investment requirement. Saving and investment are sufficiently large not only to make up for population growth and depreciation but also to raise capital per head or the capital-labor ratio. This suggests that next period capital per head will be higher. You immediately recognize the line of argument we are taking. From Fig. 17-3 it is clear that with a somewhat higher capital-labor ratio, the discrepancy between saving and the investment requirement becomes smaller. Therefore the increase in the capital-labor ratio becomes smaller. However, the capital-labor ratio still increases as indicated by the arrows.

The adjustment process comes to a halt at point C. Here we have reached a capital-labor ratio k^* such that saving and investment associated with that capital-labor ratio exactly match the investment requirement. Given the exact matching of actual and required investment, the capital-labor ratio neither rises nor falls. We have reached the *steady state*. We can make the same argument by starting with an initial capital-labor ratio in excess of k^*. From Fig. 17-3 we note that for high capital-labor ratios the investment requirement is in excess of saving and investment. Accordingly, not enough is added to the capital stock to maintain the capital-labor ratio constant in the face of population growth and depreciation. Thus, the capital-labor ratio falls until we get to k^*, the steady-state capital-labor ratio.

To review our progress so far:

1 Capital and labor are used to produce output according to a production function assumed to have constant returns to scale.
2 To maintain the capital-labor ratio constant, saving and investment have to be sufficient to make up for the reduction in capital per head that arises from population growth and depreciation.
3 With saving a constant fraction s of output, we established that the capital-labor ratio moves to a steady-state level k^* at which output and therefore saving (investment) are just sufficient to maintain constant the capital-labor ratio.
4 The convergence to a steady-state capital-labor ratio k^* is ensured by the fact that at low levels of the capital-labor ratio saving (investment) exceeds the investment required to maintain capital per head and therefore causes the capital-labor ratio to rise. Conversely, at high capital-labor ratios saving (investment) falls short of the investment requirement, and thus the capital-labor ratio declines.

Now we can turn to a more detailed study of the characteristics of steady-state equilibrium and the adjustment process. First, we recognize what a steady-state equilibrium actually means. We note that the steady-state level of capital per head is constant, and thus from the production function that the steady-state level of output per head is also constant. The steady state is reached when all variables, in per capita terms, are constant. It is important to recognize the constancy of per capita variables because this implies that total output is growing at precisely the rate of population growth. In fact, in the steady state, output, capital, and labor all grow at the same rate. They all grow at a rate equal to the rate of population growth, and therefore output and capital remain constant in per capita terms. Note particularly that the steady-state growth rate is equal to the rate of population growth and therefore is not influenced by the saving rate. (Recall that we are assuming no technical progress.) To explore this property of the steady state in more detail, we turn now to an investigation of the effects of a change in the saving rate.

A Change in the Saving Rate

In this subsection we address the puzzling question of why the long-run growth rate should be independent of the saving rate. If people save 10 percent of their income as opposed to 5 percent, should we not expect this to make a difference to the growth rate of output? Is it not true that an economy in which 10 percent of income is set aside for additions to the capital stock is one in which capital and therefore output grow faster than in an economy saving only 5 percent of income?

We show here that an increase in the saving rate does the following: (1) in the short run it raises the growth rate of output, (2) it does not affect the long-run growth rate of output, and (3) it raises the long-run level of capital and output per head.

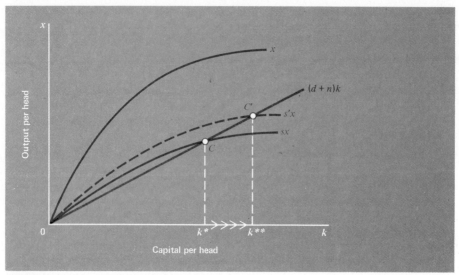

FIGURE 17-4 AN INCREASE IN THE
SAVING RATE

Consider now Fig. 17-4 with an initial steady-state equilibrium at point C, where saving precisely matches the investment requirement. At point C exactly enough output is saved to maintain the stock of capital per head constant in the face of depreciation and labor force growth. Next consider an increase in the saving rate. For some reason people want to save a larger fraction of income. The increased saving rate is reflected in an upward shift of the saving schedule. At each level of the capital-labor ratio and hence at each level of output saving is larger.

At point C where we initially had a steady-state equilibrium, saving has now risen relative to the investment requirement and accordingly more is saved than is required to maintain capital per head constant. Enough is saved to allow the capital stock per head to increase.

It is apparent from Fig. 17-4 that the capital stock per head will keep rising until we reach point C'. At point C' the higher amount of saving is just enough to maintain the higher stock of capital. At point C' both capital per head and output per head have risen. Saving has increased, as has the investment requirement. We have seen, therefore, that an increase in the saving rate will in the long run only raise the *level* of output and capital per head, as shown in Fig. 17-4, but not the *growth rate* of output per head.

The transition process, however, involves an effect of the saving rate on the growth rate of output and the growth rate of output per head. In the transition from k^* to k^{**} the increase in the saving rate raises the growth rate of output. This follows simply from the fact that the capital-labor ratio rises from k^* in the initial steady state to k^{**} in the new steady state. The only way to achieve an increase in the capital-labor ratio is for the capital stock to grow faster than the labor force (and depreciation). This is precisely what happens in the transition process where increased saving per head, due to the higher saving rate, raises investment and capital growth over and above the investment requirement and thus allows the capital-labor ratio to rise.

In summary, the long-run effect of an increase in the saving rate is to raise the level of output and capital per head but to leave the growth rate of output and capital unaffected. In the transition period the rates of growth of output and capital increase relative to the steady state. In the short run, therefore, an increase in the saving rate means faster growth, as we would expect.

Figure 17-5 summarizes these two results. Figure 17-5a shows the level of per capita output. Starting from an initial long-run equilibrium at

FIGURE 17-5a THE TIME PATH OF PER CAPITA INCOME

FIGURE 17-5b THE TIME PATH OF THE GROWTH RATE OF OUTPUT

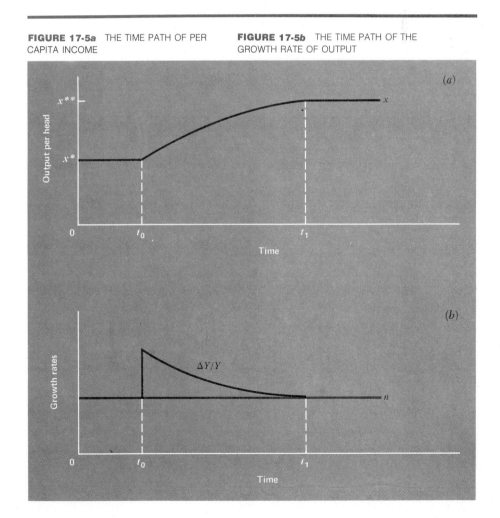

point t_0, the increase in the saving rate causes saving and investment to increase, the stock of capital per head grows, and so does output per head. The process will continue at a diminishing rate. In Fig. 17-5b we focus on the growth rate of output and capital. The growth rate of output is equal to the growth rate of population in the initial steady state. The increase in the saving rate immediately raises the growth rate of output because it implies a faster growth in capital and therefore in output. As capital accumulates, the growth rate decreases, falling back towards the level of population growth.

Population Growth

The preceding discussion of saving and the influence of the saving rate on steady-state capital and output makes it easy to discuss the effects of increased population growth. The question we ask is what happens when the population growth rate increases from n to n' and remains at that higher level indefinitely. We will show that such an increase in the rate of population growth will raise the growth rate of output and lower the level of output per head.

The argument can be conveniently followed in Fig. 17-6. Here we show the initial steady-state equilibrium at point C. The increase in the growth rate of population means that at each level of the capital-labor ratio

FIGURE 17-6 AN INCREASE IN THE RATE OF POPULATION GROWTH REDUCES PER CAPITA INCOME

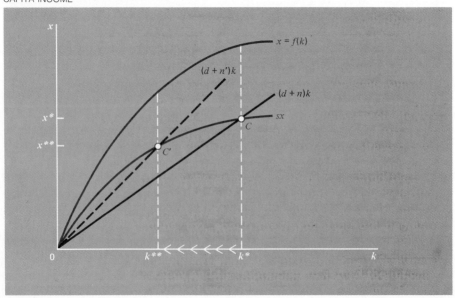

it takes a larger investment just in order to maintain the capital-labor ratio constant. Suppose we had ten machines per head. Initially the growth rate of population is 1 percent and depreciation is 10 percent so that we require per year 11 percent times ten machines, or 1.1 machine, just to offset population growth and depreciation and thus maintain capital per head constant. To maintain the capital-labor ratio constant in the face of a higher growth rate of population, say 2%, requires a higher level of investment, namely, 12 percent as opposed to 11 percent. This is reflected in Fig. 17-6 by an upward rotation of the investment requirement schedule.

It is clear from the preceding argument that we are no longer in steady-state equilibrium at point C. The investment that was initially just sufficient to keep the capital-labor ratio constant will no longer be sufficient in the face of higher population growth. At the initial equilibrium the higher population growth with unchanged saving and investment means that capital does not grow fast enough to keep up with labor force growth and depreciation. Capital per head declines. In fact, capital per head will keep declining until we reach the new steady-state equilibrium at point C'. Here the capital-labor ratio has declined sufficiently for saving to match the investment requirement. It is true, too, that corresponding to the lower capital-labor ratio we have a decline in output per head. Output per head declines from x^* to x^{**}.

The decline in output per head as a consequence of increased population growth points to the problem faced by many developing countries. Fast growth in population, given the saving rate, means low levels of income per head. Indeed, in poor countries one can trace poverty or low income per head to the very high rate of population growth. With population growth, saving will typically be too small to allow capital to rise relative to labor and thus to build up the capital-labor ratio to achieve a satisfactory level of income per head. In those circumstances, and barring other considerations, a reduction in the rate of population growth appears to be a way of achieving higher levels of steady state per capita income and thus an escape from poverty.

Maximum Consumption and the Golden Rule

In concluding the previous section, we noted that reduced growth in population would raise steady-state income per head. This is *not* the same, however, as increasing steady-state consumption per head. This point is quite important because it implies that there is a level of the capital-labor ratio that maximizes consumption per head.

Why is it that an increase in income per head, in the steady state, does not automatically imply an increase in consumption per head? The reason is that as we increase steady-state capital per head and therefore steady-state output per head, we raise, too, the investment requirement. Part of the increased output will have to be devoted to maintaining constant the higher capital-labor ratio. The question therefore must be whether an increase in the capital-labor ratio contributes more to consumption in terms of increased output than it takes away from consumption in the form of increased investment requirements. If so, then the remainder, the increased output per head less the increased investment requirement, is available for increased consumption per head. If not, then the increase in the capital-labor ratio, by taking more in terms of investment requirement than it contributes in terms of additional output, actually cuts into consumption. The question we have to ask therefore concerns the relation between the contribution of increased capital per head to output—the marginal product of capital, MPK, as we called it before—and the marginal investment requirement. The investment requirement, as we saw before, increases in proportion to the increase in the capital-labor ratio. The marginal investment requirement is simply the growth rate of population plus the rate of depreciation, $d + n$. From the preceding remarks it follows that an increase in the capital-labor ratio will raise consumption if the marginal product of capital is higher than the investment requirement, that is, if capital is sufficiently productive to add to output per head more than is required in terms of increased investment requirement.

Figure 17-7 will help get a further grasp of these issues. We show in the upper panel the production function that relates output per head to the capital-labor ratio. We show, too, the investment requirement. The vertical distance between the production function or output and the investment requirement shows the level of consumption that could be sustained at each capital-labor ratio. We say the "level of consumption that could be sustained" because we are subtracting from output just enough to maintain the capital-labor ratio constant. This vertical distance between output and the investment requirement at each capital-labor ratio shows, therefore, the levels of steady-state consumption that are possible given technology, the rate of population growth, and the rate of depreciation. In the lower panel of Fig. 17-7 we have drawn this vertical distance for each capital-labor ratio and therefore show all possible steady-state levels of consumption per head. We note from that schedule that for low levels of capital, capital is sufficiently productive to more than cover the increased investment requirement. Up to the capital-labor ratio $k^*_{\max}$, an increase in capital per head will raise consumption per head or, alternatively, raise output per head by more than the increased investment requirement.

The capital-labor ratio $k^*_{\max}$ has the special property that it maximizes steady-state consumption per head. At that capital-labor ratio the marginal product of capital is precisely equal to the marginal investment requirement. If we went slightly to the right of $k^*_{\max}$ in Fig. 17-7, the marginal product of capital would fall short of the marginal investment requirement and consumption would therefore be reduced. By contrast, starting from a point slightly to the left, an increase in the capital-labor ratio would raise consumption per head. The same point can be noted from the upper

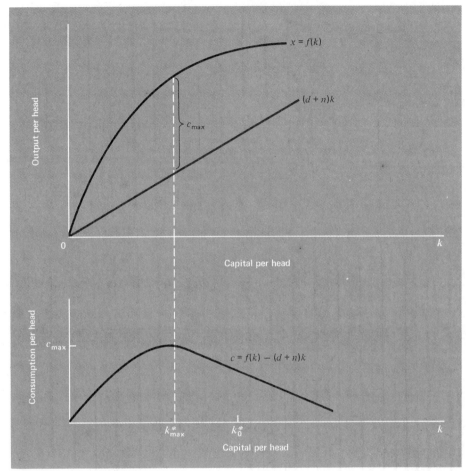

FIGURE 17-7 THE GOLDEN RULE

panel, where again k_{max} is the capital-labor ratio that maximizes the discrepancy between output and investment requirement. Remember that consumption in the steady state is exactly equal to output less the investment requirement, or

$$c = f(k^*) - (d + n)k^* \tag{9}$$

From the upper panel of Fig. 17-7 it is apparent that the level of consumption is maximized when the slope of the production function is equal to the slope of the investment requirement schedule. But the slope of the production function is the marginal product of capital, MPK. The slope of the investment requirement schedule is the rate of population growth plus the rate of depreciation. Thus at the maximum consumption level we have

$$\text{MPK} = d + n \qquad (10)$$

What relevance does the concept of a maximum sustainable consumption level have? Should society try to reach the level of capital per head $k_{\max}$ by influencing saving decisions? This is a very hard question because this *golden rule* only maximizes the level of consumption in the steady state. If initially the capital stock per head were below $k_{\max}$, then society would have to increase the saving rate and forgo consumption in order to build up enough capital per head to enjoy permanently the higher level of consumption. This involves an intertemporal consumption choice that our model cannot assess. Nor can we assess the question of how fast the society should try to get from the initial condition to the steady state. These issues involve a tradeoff between current and future consumption that has to be assessed in terms of individual preferences.

There is, however, one interesting implication of the model which concerns an initial capital-labor ratio above $k_{\max}$. Suppose society were, because of a high saving rate in the past, in an initial position with a level of capital per head k_0^* in Fig. 17-7. Does it pay to remain in the steady-state position even though it is not a position of maximum steady-state consumption? The answer is no. With an initial steady-state equilibrium at a capital-labor ratio k_0^*, too much of output has to be sacrificed just to maintain the capital stock per head intact. If society increased its rate of consumption and reduced the saving rate just sufficiently to achieve a steady state at $k_{\max}$, consumption per head would be higher although output per head and the investment requirement would be lower.

We noted before that one cannot say whether a society with an initial capital-labor ratio below the steady state should make the necessary current consumption sacrifice to invest in an increase in capital per head that will raise the permanent consumption level. By contrast one can say that a society with too much capital per head should reduce saving and raise consumption. Why? Because in the latter case society can have more now and more later. Society can raise its level of consumption both in the adjustment process and in the steady state.

In thinking of the consumption possibilities, it is well to start off with the startling recognition that a society that had a steady-state capital-labor ratio k_0^* could throw away some of its capital, $k_0^* - k_{\max}$, *and* be better off in the sense of raising consumption per head. Now there are clearly better ways of using this excess capital. In particular we can use it to finance consumption. We can for some time consume more than the permanent level $c_{\max}$ by simply using current output that previously was saved to maintain the capital-labor ratio and that now can be consumed. Only when the capital-labor ratio has fallen to $k_{\max}$ do we have to start maintaining it to guarantee the level of consumption $c_{\max}$. We are not equipped at this stage to analyze the precise rate at which society should reduce its capital stock under these circumstances.[7]

We must now ask about the relevance of this discussion. In the previous section we suggested that, given saving behavior, poor countries might want to cut down the growth rate of population and thus raise capital per head. Here it is argued, by contrast, that with a very high capital-labor ratio, given the growth rate of population, there is inefficiency, and a reduction in the capital-labor ratio is appropriate. The main lesson we can draw is that it is possible for a country to have too much capital, though one cannot really think of a particular example. Obviously, though, the problem for underdeveloped and poor countries is certainly not an excess of capital. In those countries per capita income is so small and saving rates at that low level of income per head are so low that capital is inadequately low. There is little prospect of raising the saving rate because of poverty. Accordingly, the major adjustment is likely to be on the population growth side.

Technical Progress[8]

The review of the empirical sources of growth showed that technical progress contributed almost one-half of the average annual growth in real income between 1929 and 1969. So far we have omitted technical progress from our growth model and simply studied the economy on the assumption of a given rate of population growth and given saving behavior. In such an economy we saw that the growth rate of output converges to a steady-state growth rate exactly equal to the growth rate of population. As a consequence, in the steady state output per head is constant. In the steady state, saving, investment, and capital accumulation are just sufficient to maintain the capital-labor ratio constant and thereby ensure that output grows at the rate of population growth.

What happens, though, once we allow for technical progress which, after all, has historically been so important? The historical record shows that for the period 1929–1969 real income per head grew at the rate of 2.13 percent (= 3.41 − 1.28).[9] Three-quarters of that increase in real income per head was due to technical progress.

How do we incorporate technical progress in the analysis? First we note that with technical progress we have an additional source of growth. We would therefore expect that, even with a constant capital-labor ratio,

[7]See R. M. Solow, *Growth Theory*, op. cit., chap. 5; and Avinash Dixit, *Equilibrium Growth Theory*, Oxford University Press, 1976.

[8]The treatment is deliberately brief since technical progress in growth theory is a somewhat technical and taxonomic matter. The reader is referred to Robert Solow, *Growth Theory*, op. cit., for an exposition of these issues.

[9]The average growth rate of total population from 1929 to 1969 was 1.28 percent. This is slightly less than the growth rate of labor hours of 1.32 percent in Table 17-2.

output per head can be growing. In this sense we would expect technical progress—that is, a continuously shifting production function—to add to real growth per head. The next question is whether the economy would actually settle down to steady-state growth. Here the answer depends on the precise form technical progress takes. If technical progress takes the form of a uniform increase in the productivity of factors so that at a given capital-labor ratio output increases in the proportion of technical progress, then a steady state will not exist. The economy keeps growing at a rate faster than the rate of population growth and at a rate that is *not* constant.

By contrast, if technical progress were *labor-augmenting*, a steady state would exist. Here the idea is that technical progress renders a given labor force more effective. Technical progress of this variety operates as if it increased the growth rate of the labor force. With this special type of technical progress the economy will actually settle down to a steady state where output per head grows at a constant rate equal to the rate of technical progress. Thus, technical progress is in fact compatible with steady-state analysis; more importantly, we see how it contributes to long-run growth in real income per head.

17-4 THE LIMITS OF GROWTH

This section briefly introduces the important and necessarily speculative question of where the economy is heading. Here the discussion becomes more general and concrete and raises the question of whether limited resources and the pressure of population on scarce land and food will ultimately bring the growth process to a dramatic halt. Are growing economies heading toward disaster?

We have first to raise the question of population and space. The world being of finite size it cannot accommodate an ever-growing population. It is accordingly quite apparent that, unless other planets can be colonized, population growth has to decline. In fact, one of the serious problems of our time is that this is recognized and indeed happening in rich countries that can still cope relatively well with growing populations while population growth has not been significantly reduced in poor countries. Although space is not yet clearly a problem in these countries, food shortages and poverty are certainly major problems.

The second preliminary point we have to raise concerns food. Even though we recognize that there is still a lot of space in the world to accommodate the physically growing world population, the question of food is a very serious one. Will there be enough food for the 5.17 billion people who are expected to be in the world by 1990? Experts agree to a significant extent that the food problem is largely a matter of distribution and income inequality, not a problem of the inability of the globe to produce enough food. With the right incentives, food can be produced, but there is the obvious problem that the poor may not be able to afford the costly food that could be produced. These issues are sufficiently important to warrant detailed study, and we refer to the reader to an article by Lance Taylor and the references contained in it.[10]

There is a related question that we want to raise here. There is the question of whether, abstracting from food considerations, we expect real income per head to keep growing. The question is whether the world will progressively encounter factors of production in limited supply that prevent continued growth. Factors that are essential to the production process, such as oil and minerals, are *exhaustible resources*, the available stocks of which appear to limit the growth process. This was clearly as true 100 years ago as today and a question that could have been, and was, raised at that time.[11] With the benefit of hindsight we would argue that new deposits of these resources have been discovered in the past at a rate much in excess of that at which we have used up resources. If anything, in the last 100 years the supplies of *known* resources have grown. This is the standard retort of the growth-oriented economist. The argument is perfectly valid as a matter of historical record though it obviously is true, too, that the more we discover, the less there is to be discovered in the future.

A more important challenge to the limits set by exhaustible resources is technical progress. There is no doubt that much technical progress takes the form of inventions and processes that dispense with or save on scarce resources used up in production. The expectation or hope then is that the same technical progress that in the last century has proved an important source of real growth will continue to keep up real growth in per capita income in the face of limitational factors and exhaustible resources. More particularly, it is hoped and expected that economic incentives will divert resources to inventions and innovations precisely in the field of exhaustible and limited resources and ensure that they will not prove a bottleneck to the growth process.

There is no assurance that the right technical progress will come along and bail us out when coal, oil, and copper run short in supply. Perhaps one should not bank on technological progress, innovation, and ingenuity to help us out. At the same time it would be irresponsible to dismiss entirely the extraordinary record of technical progress which has contributed around one-half of the average growth in real income. There will surely continue to be technical progress. The major problem of social policy then becomes to channel resources in the right direction to ensure that research and effort are devoted to solving society's bottleneck problems. The market mechanism itself is a powerful instrument to achieve precisely that purpose, but may in some instances need a helping hand.

There is one further potential contributor to real growth in the face of

[10]Lance Taylor, "The Misconstrued Crisis; Lester Brown and World Food," *World Development*, 1975.

[11]See W. S. Jevons, *The Coal Question*, 1865. Reprinted by Augustus M. Kelley, New York, 1965.

limited resources. That is *economies of scale*. We have assumed in the previous section that production is subject to constant returns to scale, and that productivity of factors is independent of the scale of operation of the economy. What this implies is that as capital and labor expand, output expands at the same rate without any gains in growth from the fact that the economy has become as it were a larger plant. Now the historical record reviewed above showed that returns to scale accounted for 10 percent of the annual average growth rate in real income in the United States economy from 1929 to 1969. As the economy expanded its use of capital and labor, output expanded more than proportionately, even holding the state of technology constant. Like technical progress, economies of scale are a potential counterweight against exhaustible resources. While exhaustible resources tend to put limits to growth, technical progress and economies of scale are sources of growth that help overcome or offset these limitational factors. Again, the only thing one can do is point to their important role in history and argue that, while nobody can or will guarantee their continued benefit, there will surely be some contribution to growth we should expect from economies of scale.

The subject of this section is one that cannot have a definite conclusion. This is a controversial question and an important one.[12] The only message we can convey is that historically there have been important counterweights to the role of exhaustible resources, and that these will continue to make an important contribution toward growth in real per capita income. That balance is important to bear in mind and indeed to stimulate by the right social policies toward research and invention.

7-5 SUMMARY

1 A production function links factor inputs and technology to the level of output. Growth of output, changes in technology aside, is a weighted average of input growth with the weights equal to income shares. The production function directs attention to factor inputs and technological change as sources of output growth.

2 Growth theory studies the determinants of intermediate-run and long-run growth in output. Growth in factor supplies—labor and capital—and productivity growth or technological progress are the sources of growth. Saving behavior determines capital accumulation.

3 In United States history over the 1929–1969 period, growth in factor inputs and productivity growth accounted each for roughly one-half of the average growth rate of 3.4 percent of output. Growth in the stock of knowledge along with growth in labor input were the most important sources of growth.

---

[12]William Nordhaus, "World Dynamics: Measurement without Data," *Economic Journal*, December 1973.

4 The per capita output grows faster the more rapidly the capital stock increases and the faster is technical progress. In United States history since 1890 output per head has grown at an average rate of 1.8 percent.

5 The concept of steady-state equilibrium points (in the absence of technical change) to the conditions required for output per head to be constant. With a growing population saving must be just sufficient to provide new members of the population with the economy-wide amount of capital per head.

6 The steady-state level of income is determined by the saving rate. In the absence of technical change, the steady-state growth rate of output is equal to the rate of population growth.

7 An increase in the growth rate of population raises the steady-state growth rate of total output and lowers the level of steady-state output per head.

8 An increase in the saving rate transitorily raises the growth rate of output. In the new steady state the growth rate remains unchanged, but the level of output per head is increased.

9 There is a steady-state level of capital that maximizes consumption per head. If capital is initially beyond that golden rule, the economy is devoting too much resources to maintaining the excessively large capital stock and could be better off eating up the capital.

10 With technical change, per capita output in the steady state grows at the rate of technical progress. Total output grows at the sum of the rates of technical progress and population growth.

11 Limits of growth pose a serious question for continued increases in real per capita income or even the maintenance of current consumption standards. The historical record is one of technological progress that offsets limitational factors and scarce resources. There is no certainty that this offset will continue, but public policy can make a contribution in that direction.

PROBLEMS

1 Which of the following government activities have effects on long-term growth of output? Explain how they can do so.
   a Monetary policy
   b Labor market policies
   c Educational and research programs
   d Fiscal policy
   e Population control programs

*2 The assumption of constant returns to scale in the production function Eq. (1) can be summarized as

$$F(bK, bN) = bF(K,N) \quad \text{for any } b > 0$$

Using this fact, derive Eq. (1a) from Eq. (1) and explain why k is the only determinant of x.

*3   a   Use the fact from microeconomics that capital is paid its marginal product to show that θ is the fraction of total income which is paid to capital.

       b   Derive the $\Delta A/A$ term in Eq. (3) from Eqs. (2) and (1a). Explain why, if $\Delta A/A = 0$, real output does not grow as rapidly as the capital-labor ratio.

*4   Present and explain the step-by-step derivation of Eq. (4) using Eq. (3) and the formulas leading up to Eq. (4).

5   Draw a figure like Fig. 17-3 which indicates the adjustment process when $k_0 > k^*$. How does the adjustment process work? Explain Fig. 17-3 in terms of the saving = investment identity (first consider the case when $n = 0$).

6   a   In the absence of technical progress, what happens to output per head and total output over time? Why?

       b   What is the long-run effect of the saving rate on the *level* of output per capita? On *growth* of output per capita?

7   Evaluate this statement: "The saving rate cannot affect the growth of output in the economy. That is determined by the growth of labor input and by technical progress."

8   Discuss why increases in capital per head do not necessarily increase consumption per head in the long run. How about output per head?

*9   Suppose we assume a production function of the form

$$Y = AF(K,N,Z)$$

where Z is a measure of the natural resources going into production. Assume this production function obeys constant returns to scale and diminishing returns to each factor [like Eq. (1)].

       a   What would happen to output per head if capital and labor grow together but resources are fixed?

       b   What if Z is fixed but there is technical progress?

       c   Interpret these results in terms of the limits to growth.

*10   Use the model of long-run growth to incorporate the government. Assume that an income tax at the rate t is levied and that accordingly saving per head is equal to $s(1 - t)x$. The government spends the tax revenue on public consumption.

       a   Use Fig. 17-3 to explore the impact of an increase in the tax rate on the steady-state output level and capital per head.

       b   Draw now a chart of the time path of capital per head, output per head, and the growth rate of output.

    *c   Discuss the statement: "To raise the growth rate of output, the public sector has to run a budget surplus to free resources for investment."

11   Use Fig. 17-3 to explore the impact of a *once-and-for-all* improvement in technology.

       a   How does technical progress affect the level of output per head as of a given capital-labor ratio?

       b   Show the new steady-state equilibrium. Has saving changed? Is income per head higher? Has the capital stock per head increased?

       c   Show now the time path of the adjustment to the new steady state. Does technical progress transitorily raise the ratio of investment to capital?

12 Consider an economy where a baby boom *transitorily* raises the growth rate of population from n to n'. After a few years the growth rate of population falls back to the rate n.

    a What is the impact of the baby boom on steady-state output per head?

    b Show the adjustment process of the economy as the growth rate of population increases and then falls back to the initial level. Draw the time path of the variables shown in Fig. 17-5.

13 Discuss the statement: "The lower the level of income, the higher the growth rate of output."

IV

PART

18

Macroeconomics in the Open Economy: Trade and Capital Flows with Fixed Exchange Rates

T his is the first of two chapters analyzing foreign trade and its effects on the economy. It extends the macroeconomics we have learned to open economies—economies that trade with others. Trade between economies takes place in both goods and services—Americans buy German cars and Europeans buy American brokers' services—and in assets—Americans buy Japanese stocks and Arabs buy American real estate. Since all economies engage in international trade, all economies are open.

The degree of openness, as measured by the ratio of imports to GNP, varies widely. For the United States the import-GNP ratio rose from about 3.5 percent in 1946 to more than 10 percent after the oil price increase in 1973. Britain imports an amount equal to about 40 percent of GNP, and the Netherlands about 60 percent. Trade is more important for most other economies than for the United States. Nonetheless, even for the United States, events connected with trade, such as the increase in oil prices in 1973–1974, can have serious effects on the economy.

This chapter begins with a brief description of the balance of payments accounts—the record of the country's transactions with other economies. We also describe the two basic exchange rate systems—*fixed* and *flexible rate* systems. In the fixed exchange rate system, central banks fix the dollar price of foreign currencies and stand ready to buy and sell foreign currencies at that price. The world was essentially on a fixed rate system from 1946 to 1973, though there were occasional adjustments of exchange rates during that period. In the flexible exchange rate system, the exchange rate is determined in the foreign exchange market and can change from moment to moment. After 1973, exchange rates between the dollar and other currencies were allowed to float, to be determined by the supply and demand for foreign exchange.

The remainder of this chapter analyzes trade in goods and assets in a fixed exchange rate system. Section 18-2 abstracts from trade in assets and examines the way in which foreign trade affects goods market equilibrium, and the determinants of the balance of trade in good and services. Section 18-3 examines the effects of devaluation and looks at the financing of deficits. Trade in assets is studied in Sec. 18-4, as are the implications of such trade for the conduct of monetary and fiscal policy. Chapter 19 presents an analysis of international trade under flexible exchange rates.

18-1 THE BALANCE OF PAYMENTS AND EXCHANGE RATE REGIMES

The *balance of payments* is the record of the transactions of the economy with the rest of the world. There are two main accounts in the balance of payments: the *current account* and the *capital account*. The current account records trade in goods and services, as well as transfer payments. Services include freight, royalty payments, and interest payments. Transfer payments consist of remittances, gifts, and grants. We talk of a current account surplus if exports exceed imports plus net transfers to foreigners, that is, if receipts from trade in goods and services and transfers exceed payments on this account.

The capital account records purchases and sales of assets, such as stocks, bonds, land, etc. There is a capital account surplus, or a net capital *in*flow, if our receipts from the sale of stocks, bonds, land, bank deposits, and other assets exceed our payments for our own purchases of foreign assets.

Closely related to the current account are certain subaccounts that we mention here for completeness. The *trade balance* simply records trade in goods. Adding trade in services to the trade balance, we arrive at the *balance on goods and services*. Finally, adding net transfers, we arrive at the current account balance.

The simple rule for balance of payments accounting is that any transaction that gives rise to a payment by United States residents is a deficit item. Thus, imports of cars, use of foreign shipping, gifts to foreigners, purchase of land in Spain, or making deposits in a bank in Geneva are all deficit items. Surplus items by contrast would be United States sales of airplanes abroad, payments for United States licensing of foreign firms to use American technology, pensions received by United States residents from abroad, or foreign purchases of GM stocks.

The overall *balance of payments* is the sum of the current and capital accounts. If both the current account and the capital account are in deficit, then the overall balance of payments is in deficit. If one account is in surplus, and the other is in deficit to precisely the same extent, then the overall balance of payments is zero—neither in surplus nor in deficit.

Table 18-1 shows the United States balance of payments accounts for selected years. In each of the years, the current account was in surplus. Receipts from the sale of exports, plus net transfers from abroad, exceeded payments to foreigners for imports. By contrast, the capital account was consistently in deficit in these years. Purchases of foreign assets by United States residents consistently exceeded foreigners' purchase of United

---

TABLE 18-1   THE UNITED STATES BALANCE OF PAYMENTS ACCOUNTS *(Billions of dollars)*

	1961	1970	1975
Current account	3.9	2.2	17.9
Capital account	−4.1	−12.5	−25.0
Errors and omissions	−1.0	− 0.5	4.6
Official reserve transactions*	$1.3	$10.7	$2.5

Note: Sum of components may not equal total, owing to rounding error.   Minus sign denotes deficit.

*Includes allocation of SDRs in 1970.

Source: International Financial Statistics, August 1976, p. 41.

States assets. In each year, the capital account deficit exceeded the current account surplus.

Since any transaction which gives rise to a payment by United States residents to foreigners is a deficit item, an overall deficit in the balance of payments—the sum of the current and capital accounts—means that United States residents make more payments to foreigners than they receive from foreigners. Since foreigners want to be paid in their own currencies,[1] the question arises of how these payments are to be made.

In Table 18-1, the "Official reserve transactions" entry measures the overall balance of payments deficit.[2] When the overall balance of payments is in deficit[3]—when the sum of the current and capital accounts is negative—Americans have to pay more foreign currency to foreigners than is received. The Fed and foreign central banks provide the foreign currency to make payments to foreigners, and the net amount supplied is "official reserve transactions." When the United States balance of payments is in surplus, foreigners have to get the dollars with which to pay for their excess of payments to the United States over their receipts from sales to the United States. The dollars are provided by the central banks.

Before proceeding, we should dispose of the "Errors and omissions" entry. That entry arises because not all transactions between United States residents and foreigners are recorded. The federal government collects data on current and capital account payments, and also has data on official reserve transactions. If all transactions were recorded, the official reserve transactions would exactly balance the recorded current and capital account transactions. However, in practice the numbers do not add up, and the errors and omissions entry is included to reconcile the recorded sum of current and capital accounts with the entry "Official reserve transactions."

Fixed Exchange Rates

We now return to the way in which central banks, through their official transactions, *finance* balance of payments surpluses and deficits. At this point we want to distinguish between fixed and floating exchange rate systems.

[1]An exception occurs if foreigners want to be paid in dollars to add to their assets. In that case we conceptually separate out, first, our demand for imports, which gives rise to payments in foreign currency that appears in the current account from, second, foreigners' demand for dollars, which appears in the capital account as an inflow.

[2]The presentation of balance of payments statistics as in Table 18-1 was stopped in mid-1976 after a review committee suggested that official reserve transactions are not a full measure of foreign exchange intervention. See "Report of the Advisory Committee on the Presentation of Balance of Payments Statistics," *Survey of Current Business*, June 1976.

[3]For the moment we ignore the "errors and omissions" entry and talk as if it were zero. If it were zero, official reserve transactions would be precisely equal to the sum of current and capital account deficits.

In a fixed rate system, foreign central banks stand ready to buy and sell their currencies at a fixed price in terms of dollars. In Germany, for example, the central bank, the Bundesbank, would buy or sell any amount of dollars in the 1960s at 4 deutschmarks (DM) per United States dollar. The French central bank, the Banque de France, stook ready to buy or sell any amount of dollars at 4.90 French francs (FF) per United States dollar. The fact that the central banks were prepared to buy or sell *any* amount of dollars at these fixed prices or exchange rates meant that market prices would, indeed, be equal to the fixed rates. Why? Because nobody who wanted to buy United States dollars with French francs would pay more than 4.90 francs per dollar if she could get dollars at that price from the Banque de France. Conversely, nobody would part with dollars in exchange for francs for less than 4.90 francs per dollar if the Banque de France, through the commercial banking system, was prepared to buy dollars at that price.

In a fixed rate system, the central banks have to finance any balance of payments surplus or deficit that arises at the official exchange rate. They do that simply by buying or selling all the foreign currency that is not supplied in private transactions. If the United States were running a deficit in the balance of payments vis-a-vis Germany so that the demand for marks in exchange for dollars exceeded the supply of dollars in exchange for marks from Germans, the Bundesbank would buy the excess dollars, paying for them with marks.

Fixed exchange rates thus operate like any other price support scheme, such as in agricultural markets. Given market demand and supply, the price fixer has to make up the excess demand or take up the excess supply. In order to be able to ensure that the price (exchange rate) stays fixed, it is obviously necessary to hold an inventory of foreign exchange that can be sold in exchange for domestic currency. Thus, foreign central banks held *reserve* inventories—of dollars, and gold that could be sold for dollars—that they would sell in the market when there was an excess demand for dollars. Conversely, when there was an excess supply of dollars, they would buy up the dollars, as in our example of a United States balance of payments deficit vis-a-vis Germany.

What determines the amount of foreign exchange intervention—buying or selling of dollars in the foreign exchange market—that a central bank would have to do in the fixed exchange rate system? We already have the answer to that question. The balance of payments measures the amount of foreign exchange intervention needed from the central banks. So long as the foreign central bank has the necessary reserves, it can continue to intervene in the foreign exchange markets to keep the exchange rate constant. However, if a country persistently runs deficits in the balance of payments, the central bank eventually will run out of foreign exchange, and be unable to continue its intervention.

Before that point is reached, the central bank is likely to decide that it can no longer maintain the exchange rate, and *devalue* the currency. In 1967, for instance, the British devalued the pound from $2.80 per pound to $2.40 per pound. That meant it became cheaper for Americans and other foreigners to buy British pounds, and thus affected the balance of payments. We shall study the way in which devaluation affects the balance of payments in Sec. 18-3.

We have so far avoided being specific on exactly which central banks did the intervening in the foreign exchange market in the fixed rate system. It is clear that, if there were an excess supply of dollars and an excess demand for marks, either the Bundesbank could buy the dollars in exchange for marks, or the Fed could sell marks in exchange for dollars. In practice, during the fixed rate period, each foreign central bank undertook to *peg* (fix) its exchange rate vis-a-vis the dollar, and most foreign exchange intervention was undertaken by the foreign central banks. The Fed was nonetheless involved in the management of the exchange rate system, since it frequently made dollar loans to foreign central banks which were in danger of running out of dollars.

Flexible Exchange Rates

We have seen that the central banks have to provide whatever amounts of foreign currency are needed to finance payments imbalances under fixed exchange rates. In flexible rate systems, by contrast, the central banks allow the exchange rate to adjust to equate the supply and demand for foreign currency. If today's exchange rate against the mark were 40 cents per mark, and German exports to the United States increased, thus increasing the demand for marks by Americans, the Bundesbank could simply stand aside and let the exchange rate adjust. In this particular case the exchange rate could move from 40 cents per mark to a level like 42 cents per mark, making German goods more expensive in terms of dollars and thus reducing the demand for them by Americans. We shall in Chap. 19 examine the way in which exchange rate changes under floating rates affect the balance of payments. The terms flexible rates and floating rates are used interchangeably.

Indeed, in a system of *clean floating*, central banks stand aside completely and allow exchange rates to be freely determined in the foreign exchange markets. The central banks do not intervene in the foreign exchange markets in a system of clean floating, and official reserve transactions would, accordingly, be zero in such a situation. That means the balance of payments would be zero in a system of clean floating: the exchange rate would adjust to make the sum of the current and capital accounts zero.

In practice, the flexible rate system, since 1973, has not been one of clean floating. Instead, the system has been one of *managed* or *dirty floating*. Central banks have intervened to buy and sell foreign currencies, in attempts to influence exchange rates, and official reserve transactions have, accordingly, not been zero. Table 18-1 shows that there were official reserve transactions in 1975, for instance. The reasons for this central bank intervention under floating rates are discussed in Chap. 19.

Terminology

The use of language with respect to exchange rates can be very confusing. In particular, the terms *depreciation* and *appreciation*, and *devaluation* and *revaluation*, will recur throughout this chapter and the next.

A *depreciation* of the exchange rate is an increase in the domestic currency price of foreign exchange. Thus, if the dollar price of marks moves from $0.25 per mark to $0.40 per mark, we talk of a depreciation of the dollar, or an appreciation of the mark. When our currency depreciates, we pay more units of domestic money per unit of foreign money. Conversely, an appreciation means that the domestic currency price of foreign money falls—we pay fewer dollars per unit of foreign money.

A further clarification concerns the difference between devaluation (revaluation) and depreciation (appreciation). The term *devaluation* is used to refer to the adjustment of a fixed exchange rate such as the sterling devaluation of 1967 from $2.80 per pound to $2.40 per pound. A depreciation by contrast refers to an increase in the dollar price of foreign exchange under a flexible exchange rate system. There is no substantial economic difference between depreciation and devaluation.

Summary

1 The balance of payments accounts are a record of the transactions of the economy with other economies. The capital account describes transactions in assets, while the current account covers transactions in goods and services and transfers.

2 Any payment to foreigners is a deficit item in the balance of payments. Any payment from foreigners is a surplus item. The balance of payments deficit (or surplus) is the sum of the deficits (or surpluses) on current and capital accounts.

3 Under fixed exchange rates, central banks stand ready to meet all demands for foreign currencies arising from balance of payments deficits or surpluses at a fixed price in terms of the domestic currency. They have to *finance* the excess demands for, or supplies of, foreign currency (that is, the balance of payments deficits or surpluses, respectively), at the pegged (fixed) exchange rate by running down or adding to their reserves of foreign currency.

4 Under flexible exchange rates, the demands for, and supplies of, foreign currency can be made equal through movements in exchange rates. Under clean floating, there is no central bank intervention and the balance of payments is zero. But central banks sometimes intervene in a floating rate system, engaging in so-called dirty floating.

The remainder of this chapter is concerned with the operation of a system of fixed exchange rates. We begin in Sec. 18-2 by abstracting from the capital account and dealing only with trade in goods. Section 18-3 examines the reasons for, and effects of, devaluation. Section 18-4 introduces the capital account and discusses the impact of trade in assets on the conduct of monetary and fiscal policy.

18-2 TRADE IN GOODS, MARKET EQUILIBRIUM, AND THE BALANCE OF TRADE

This section is concerned with the effects of trade in goods on the level of income, and the effects of various disturbances on both income and the trade balance—which, from now on, we use as shorthand for the current account. We also examine policy problems which arise when the balance of trade and the level of income require different corrective actions. The section concludes by introducing the important notion of the *policy mix*.

In this section we shall be fitting foreign trade into the IS-LM framework, which is the basic income determination model of Chap. 4, and which continues to underlie the aggregate demand function used in later chapters. As in Chap. 3 and 4, we assume that the price level is given, and that output that is demanded will be supplied. As you no doubt appreciate by now, this assumption enables us to develop the details of the analysis most simply. It is both conceptually and technically easy to relax the assumption, and we shall do so briefly later. But it is important to be clear on how the introduction of trade modifies the analysis of aggregate demand, and for that reason we start from a familiar and basic level.

A word of warning is in order before you start working through the following sections. The exposition here assumes you are thoroughly at home with the IS-LM analysis, and thus proceeds quite rapidly. However, the material is not inherently more difficult than that of earlier chapters and should, with careful and active reading, be totally accessible.

Domestic Spending and Spending on Domestic Goods

In this part we want to establish how foreign trade fits into the IS-LM income determination model of Chap. 4. With foreign trade, part of domestic output is sold to foreigners (exports) and part of spending by domestic residents falls on foreign goods (imports). If we go back to income determination as studied in Chaps. 3 and 4, it is apparent that the foreign trade complication will require some modification of our analysis.

The most important change is that it is no longer true that domestic spending determines domestic output. What is true now is that spending on domestic goods determines domestic output. Spending by domestic residents falls in part on domestic goods but in part on imports. Part of the typical American's spending is for imported beer, for instance. Demand for domestic goods which determines output, by contrast, includes exports or foreign demand along with part of spending by domestic residents.

The way in which external transactions affect the demand for domestic output was examined in Chap 2. We provide a reminder by looking at the definitions:

$$\text{Spending by domestic residents} \equiv A \equiv C + I + G \tag{1}$$

$$\text{Spending on domestic goods} \equiv A + NX \equiv (C + I + G) + NX \tag{2}$$

where NX is the trade balance (goods and services) surplus. The definition of spending by domestic residents $(C + I + G)$ remains that of the earlier chapters. Spending on domestic goods is total spending by domestic residents, *less* their spending on imports *plus* foreign demand or exports. Since exports minus imports is the trade surplus, or net exports, NX, spending on domestic goods is spending by domestic residents plus the trade surplus.

With this clarification we can return to our models of income determination. We will continue to assume, as in Chap. 4, that domestic spending depends on the interest rate and income, so that we can write

$$A = A(Y,i) \tag{3}$$

Further, we assume for the present that foreign demand for our goods or exports X is given and equal to $\overline{X}$. Domestic demand for foreign goods or imports Q is assumed to depend only on the level of income, so that $Q = Q(Y)$. As income rises, part of the increase in income is spent on imports, while the rest is spent on domestic goods, or saved.

Now the trade balance is

$$NX \equiv X - Q = \overline{X} - Q(Y) \tag{4}$$

With our assumptions, the trade balance NX is a function only of the level of income. The trade balance is shown as a function of income in Fig. 18-1. Imports are small at low levels of income so that, given the fixed level of exports, there is a trade surplus, $NX > 0$. As income rises, import spending increases until we reach income level Y_B, where imports match exports so that trade is balanced. A further increase in income gives rise to a trade deficit. We can thus write

$$NX = NX(Y,\overline{X}, \dots) \tag{4a}$$

where $\overline{X}$ denotes the given level of exports and the dots denote the other variables such as exchange rates and prices which we hold constant for now. We repeat that, as in Chap. 3 and 4, we assume that domestic prices

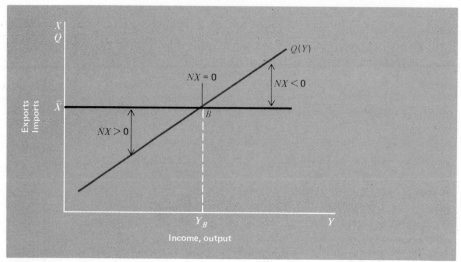

FIGURE 18-1 THE TRADE BALANCE AS A
FUNCTION OF INCOME

are given. Here we shall also assume that foreign prices are fixed. These
assumptions are relaxed below.

Goods Market Equilibrium

There is equilibrium in the domestic goods market when the amount of
output produced is equal to the demand for that output. The value of
output produced continues to be equal to income.[4] The equilibrium here
is different from that in Chap. 3 in that the demand for domestically produced goods includes net exports:

$$Y = A(Y,i) + NX(Y,\overline{X}, \ldots) \tag{5}$$

Figure 18-2 illustrates the goods market equilibrium condition (5).
We still refer to it as a goods market equilibrium schedule, or IS curve,
though it is important to recognize that now the trade surplus, or net exports, NX, appears as a component of demand for output. The schedule is
downward-sloping because an increase in output gives rise to an excess
supply of goods: the increase in income is only partly spent on domestic
goods, the rest being saved or spent on imports. To compensate for the

[4]We are thus implicitly assuming that all factors of production are owned by domestic residents, who in turn own no factors of production abroad. If foreigners owned some of the
factors of production located in our country, part of the value of output produced would be
paid to foreigners and the value of output produced would exceed the income of domestic
residents.

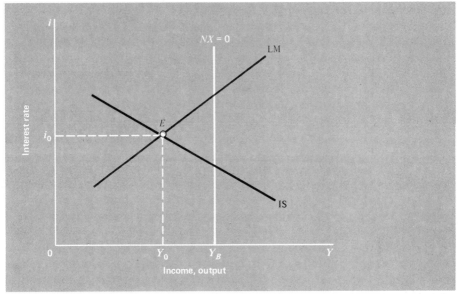

FIGURE 18-2 GOODS AND MONEY
MARKET EQUILIBRIUM

excess supply, interest rates would have to decline to induce an increase in aggregate demand. The IS schedule is drawn for the given level of foreign demand $\overline{X}$.

We have shown, too, in Fig. 18-2 the trade balance equilibrium schedule $NX = 0$. Given exports, we see from Fig. 18-1 and Eq. (4) that there is some level of income, Y_B, at which import spending exactly matches export revenue so that trade is balanced. Points to the left of the $NX = 0$ schedule are points of trade surplus. Here income and hence import spending are low relative to exports. Exports, accordingly, exceed imports. Points to the right of the $NX = 0$ schedule, by contrast, are deficit points. Here income and hence import spending are too high relative to exports for trade to be balanced. Finally, we have drawn, too, the LM schedule, which is precisely the same as in our study of the closed economy.

Equilibrium Income and the Balance of Trade

The next question to address, using Fig. 18-2, is where the short-run equilibrium of the economy will be. It will be at point E, the intersection of the IS and LM curves. The reason short-run equilibrium is at E is the following. Trade need not be balanced. In the short run a trade balance deficit can be financed by running down foreign exchange reserves and a surplus can be financed by building up reserves. The assumption then is that the central bank finances the trade deficit by selling foreign exchange and thus maintains the exchange rate at its pegged level in the face of a trade and balance of payments deficit, or that the bank purchases foreign exchange if there is a surplus.[5] We assume the goods and money markets clear sufficiently quickly so that equilibrium is determined at point E in Fig. 18-2. As we have drawn the equilibrium, the trade balance is in surplus.

Disturbances

How do internal and external disturbances—shifts in the level or composition of spending, or changes in exports—affect equilibrium income and the balance of trade? To answer that question, it is important to remember that both the IS and the trade balance schedules are drawn for a given level of exports, $\overline{X}$.

We can think of three types of disturbances, the effects of which we will briefly analyze in turn: (1) an increase in autonomous domestic spending that falls on our own goods, (2) an increase in exports, and (3) a shift in demand from domestic goods to imports. Before going through the exercises we want to indicate the results we expect to find. There are two results that we should expect. First, any increase (decrease) in spending on our goods should result in an increase (decrease) in equilibrium income. Second, we would expect the trade balance to worsen if domestic income expands, but we should expect it to improve if exports rise or if there is an autonomous decline in imports. It is not so clear how an increase in exports affects the trade balance. Say exports increase and, as a consequence, domestic income rises. This income increase, in turn, raises import spending, and we are not certain whether the net effect on the trade balance is an improvement or worsening. What we can show is that the net effect is actually an improvement—induced import spending dampens but does not offset the trade balance improvement resulting from an increase in exports.

The Effects of an Increase in Autonomous Spending

With these preliminary remarks we can proceed to our analysis. First, consider an autonomous increase in our spending on domestic goods, perhaps because of expansionary fiscal policy. In Fig. 18-3 we show the effect to be a shift in the IS curve. At the initial equilibrium E there is an

---

[5]We are abstracting here from a complication that is suggested by our study of the money supply process in Chap. 8. We saw there that foreign exchange transactions have an effect on high-powered money and thus on the money supply. Thus, a trade deficit would cause the central bank to lose foreign exchange and, as a counterpart, would cause the monetary base and the money supply to fall. We assume that the central bank automatically engages in offsetting open market operations that keep the money supply constant. In the case of a deficit such a "sterilization operation" would require a purchase of debt in the open market to offset the reduction in the monetary base due to the trade deficit, as we saw in Chap. 8.

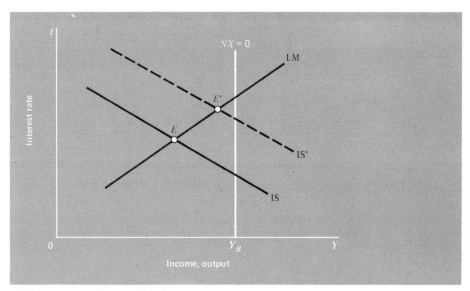

FIGURE 18-3 THE EFFECTS OF AN
INCREASE IN DOMESTIC SPENDING

excess demand for goods and, accordingly, the equilibrium income level will increase. The new equilibrium is at point E' where output and interest rates have risen and where we have a reduction in the trade surplus. The expansion in output will have increased import spending, and thus at E' the trade surplus is less than at E. The first lesson is, therefore, that expansionary domestic policies or autonomous increases in spending will raise income but will, too, cause a worsening of the trade balance.

There is a second point worth making, and that concerns the size of the income expansion induced by an expansionary policy. By comparison with a closed economy, we have less of an expansion in an open economy. Multipliers are smaller because induced spending on domestic goods is less. Induced spending is less than in a closed economy because part of an increase in income is now spent on imports rather than domestic goods. Imports are a leakage from the domestic multiplier process—because the spending on imports induced by income increases does not increase demand for domestic output—and thus reduce the size of the multipliers. Indeed, the larger the fraction of an increase in income that is spent on imports, the smaller the multiplier, because there is relatively little induced spending on domestic goods.

The Effects of an Increase in Exports

The next disturbance we consider is an increase in exports. An increase in exports raises the demand for domestic goods and thus shifts the IS curve to

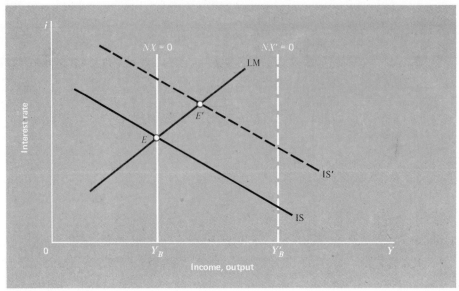

FIGURE 18-4 THE EFFECT OF AN
INCREASE IN EXPORTS

the right (to IS'), as shown in Fig. 18-4. At the same time, the increase in exports implies that at each level of income the trade balance is improved and that, therefore, the trade balance equilibrium schedule shifts out and to the right. It takes a higher level of income to generate the import spending to match the higher level of exports. Thus, the trade balance schedule shifts to $NX' = 0$. Starting from a position of balanced trade at point E, we find that the increase in exports raises equilibrium income and improves the balance of trade at point E'. The first part is quite intuitive. Higher demand for our goods leads to an increase in equilibrium output. The trade balance improvement, though, is less intuitive. Clearly the increase in exports by itself improves the trade balance, but the increase in income leads to increased import spending which, it seems, could perhaps offset the direct improvement from the export increase. This is in fact not the case, and we leave the demonstration of that result as a problem.[6]

A Shift in the Composition of Demand

The last disturbance we consider is a shift in demand from imports to domestic goods. You will recognize that this has the same effects as an increase in exports. It means increased demand for domestic goods and means also an improvement in the trade balance.

[6]See prob. 3 at the end of this chapter.

Internal and External Balance

We have now constructed and used, in Figs. 18-2 through 18-4, our basic diagrammatic apparatus for embodying trade in the IS-LM model. We can draw on the analysis of income and trade balance determination to ask about economic policy making. From a policy perspective we would want to be able to achieve both *internal* and *external* balance. Internal balance means that output is at the full-employment level Y_p. External balance is interpreted here as trade balance equilibrium.

It is clear enough why internal balance should be an aim of policy. But why is external balance desirable? In a fixed exchange rate world, balance of payments deficits cannot be maintained indefinitely, as the financing of the deficits requires the country to use its reserves of foreign currency. Such reserves will run out in the face of continual deficits. Hence, a country on a fixed exchange rate cannot aim to run a balance of payments deficit[7] indefinitely. On the other side, a country on fixed rates wants to avoid running a permanent surplus because that causes it to acquire foreign currencies to add to its reserves indefinitely. Since the foreign exchange could be used to buy and consume foreign goods, the country is permanently forgoing some consumption it could otherwise have had, when it chooses to run permanent balance of payments surpluses.

The policy problem is illustrated in Fig. 18-5. The problem is that for a given level of exports we may not be able to achieve *both* internal and external balance. In Fig. 18-5, we have drawn the trade balance schedule, $NX = 0$, for the given level of exports. We have drawn, too, the full-employment level of output Y_p, and the two lines do not coincide.

We can break up Fig. 18-5 into three regions, as shown in Table 18-2. To the left of the trade balance schedule, as we saw before, we have a trade surplus and to the right we have a deficit. To the left of the Y_p schedule we have underemployment and to the right we have overemployment.

From a policy viewpoint, regions I and III present no problem. In region I we want to pursue an expansionary policy so as to raise employment *and* reduce the trade surplus. Until we get to trade balance equilibrium, there is no issue since both the internal and external targets call for expansionary policies. Similarly, in region III we want to pursue restrictive policies to reduce overemployment and the trade deficit. Until we get to full employment, there is no issue. The dilemma area is region II. Here we have to choose whether we want to use tight policies to achieve trade balance equilibrium, or expansionary policies to achieve full employment. Not only are we unable to reach both targets simultaneously by manipulating aggregate demand, but any attempt to reach one target gets us further away from the other. Such a situation is called a *policy dilemma*, and it can always arise when one has more targets of policy than instru-

---

[7]In the absence of capital movements, and grants, remittances, etc., the balance of payments is equal to the balance of trade.

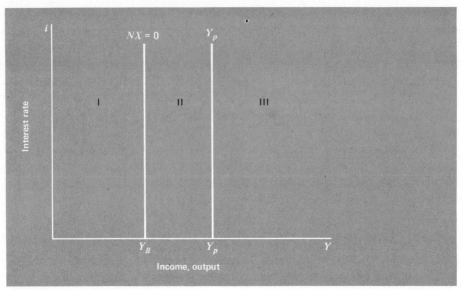

FIGURE 18-5 INTERNAL AND EXTERNAL
BALANCE AND THE POLICY DILEMMA

ments with which to move the economy toward its targets. In our case we
have only one policy instrument—aggregate demand policies—but we
have two independent targets—external and internal balance.

The policy dilemma that is pointed out by Fig. 18-5 can be solved by
finding another policy instrument to cope with the multiple targets. It is
quite apparent that what is needed is some policy that shifts the trade
balance schedule to the right until it overlaps with the full-employment
level of output line, Y_p. An obvious policy would be to cut down on
imports at each level of income. Such a policy would reduce import
spending at each level of income and thus shift the trade balance schedule
to the right.

How can we cut import spending? We can use any of a number of
tools, among them tariffs and exchange rate changes. Tariffs are excise
taxes on imported goods. A tariff would raise the cost of imports to domestic residents and thereby divert demand away from imports to domestic
goods. A 10 percent tariff on imported shoes, for instance, makes imported

TABLE 18-2 EXTERNAL AND INTERNAL BALANCE CONFLICT

	I	II	III
Employment	Under	Under	Over
Trade balance	Surplus	Deficit	Deficit

shoes more expensive relative to domestically made shoes, and shifts demand to locally made shoes. A devaluation, as we shall see below, would achieve the same effect by raising import prices relative to the prices of domestically made goods. In summary, the point is that if we have a trade deficit at full employment—as is the case in Fig. 18-5—then we require a policy that directly affects the trade balance so as to give us trade balance equilibrium at full employment.

The Use of Expenditure Switching and Expenditure Reducing Policies

The argument of the previous part needs to be spelled out in more detail to focus attention on a subtle and important point: policies to shift spending from imports to domestic goods generally also affect aggregate demand in the goods market. Accordingly, policies to shift the $NX = 0$ line generally have to be accompanied by policies which adjust aggregate demand.

Figure 18-6 shows a situation in which the level of output in the economy is at Y_p, but the balance of payments is in deficit, since the $NX = 0$ line is to the left of Y_p. As we saw earlier in this chapter, aggregate demand policies cannot, in this case, both keep us at full employment and reduce the trade deficit. Consider using a tariff which shifts demand from imports to domestic goods. By using the tariff, we reduce import spending and shift the trade balance line to the right until it coincides with the full-employment line.

FIGURE 18-6 THE POLICY DILEMMA
WITH A BALANCE OF TRADE DEFICIT

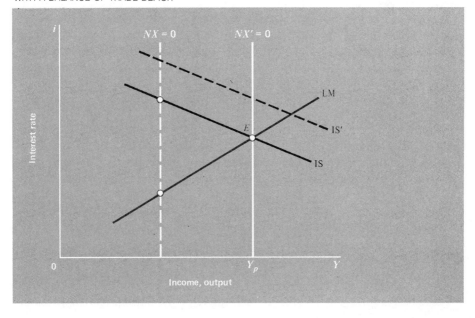

But the tariff will also affect the demand for domestic goods. The spending which at a given level of income no longer goes to imports goes to domestic goods instead. We are simply *switching* expenditures from imports to domestic goods. Accordingly, the tariff shifts the IS curve out to the right to IS'. We therefore have to use a further policy to offset the expansionary effect of the tariff in the domestic goods market. We could use either monetary or fiscal policy to shift the economy's equilibrium back to the full-employment level Y_p.

The important point, then, is that, in general, it is necessary to combine both *expenditure switching* policies which shift demand between domestic and imported goods and *expenditure reducing* (or *expenditure increasing*) policies, to cope with the targets of internal and external balance. This point is of general importance and continues to apply when we take account of capital flows and other phenomena abstracted from in this section.

Interdependence and Repercussion Effects

The next topic to be taken up in this section is the interdependence of income determination in the world economy. An increase in income in one country (country A), by spilling over into imports, will affect demand for output abroad and thus will lead, in turn, to a foreign expansion in imports from country A. These *spillover effects* in the income determination process have two implications: (1) Countries can, in general, *not* decide on appropriate stabilization policies without knowing what policies or income levels will prevail abroad and hence what the world demand for their exports will be. This suggests that coordination of stabilization policy between countries is desirable. (2) One country's income and import expansion spills over to increases in income abroad. But, in addition, the foreign income increase which the spillover induces leads to increased foreign import demand. There is thus a *repercussion effect* that we have so far ignored by assuming that export demand is autonomous. The repercussion effect is the additional effect on country A's income caused by the reaction of foreign countries' income to an initial increase in aggregate demand in country A.

We consider first the problem posed by spillover effects. The problem is actually a very important one. For instance, during the 1975 world recession, some countries, like Germany, were relying on the United States recovery to pull them out of their own recession. How? It was expected that United States monetary and fiscal policies would stimulate the United States level of income and therefore United States imports. With part of United States imports coming from Germany, this would have led to increased German exports. Increased exports, in turn, mean increased income and employment. Thus a recovery in Germany could clearly have been started off by an increase in exports. For obvious reasons, such a recovery is called an *export-led recovery*.

A critical question in the policy decision to wait for an increase in foreign demand rather than to undertake domestic action must be the size of the impacts of one country's income growth on another country's exports and thus on the latter's income. In the specific context of Germany, the question would be by how much a, say, 1 percent increase in United States income would increase German income. If the number were of the order of 0.5 percent, then United States growth could make an important contribution to German recovery, and disregard of United States policy could lead to serious policy errors. Table 18-3 sets out estimates of the international transmission of aggregate demand disturbances. The table addresses the question of how much a 1 percent increase in real spending in one country affects real income in another within one year.

We examine first domestic multiplier effects, where we find that a 1 percent increase in real spending in the United States has a one-year impact of raising real income within the United States—through the multiplier process—by 1.18 percent. Similarly, the impact of a 1 percent increase in spending in Canada is to raise Canadian real income by 1.15 percent.

However, we are more interested in the cross-country effects. Returning to an expansion in the United States, we can read the impact on other countries along the first row. Thus, 1 percent United States growth in spending raises German GNP by only 0.04 percent, while the impact on Canada is as high as 0.31 percent. Even for Japan the cross-country effect of a United States expansion is quite large, being of the order of 0.13 percent.

The difference in the cross-country effects reflects, first, differences in economic integration. Canada is very open to the United States in that the United States is its main trading partner and it thus experiences a large impact as a consequence of United States expansion. The same is true for Japan, which is a large exporter to the United States market. The second point to note about the table is the role of relative size. Looking at the last column, which shows the impact of a Japanese expansion, we observe that a

TABLE 18-3 THE INTERNATIONAL TRANSMISSION OF AGGREGATE DEMAND DISTURBANCES

Initiating country (1 percent increase in autonomous spending)	Affected country (percentage change in income)			
	United States	Germany	Canada	Japan
United States	1.18	0.04	0.31	0.13
Germany	0.04	0.98	0.05	0.04
Canada	0.08	0.02	1.15	0.02
Japan	0.02	0.01	0.02	1.18

Source: Bert Hickman, "International Transmission of Economic Fluctuations and Inflation," in Albert Ando et al., *International Aspects of Stabilization Policies*, Federal Reserve Bank of Boston, 1975, p. 211.

1 percent increase in Japanese aggregate demand yields an impact of only 0.02 percent in the United States. This reflects the fact that the Japanese economy is very small, relative to that of the United States, so that even a large expansion in Japan and, hence in Japanese imports, amounts to only a small (percentage) increase in United States exports and income. The point is important because it shows the role of large countries in setting the pattern for world economic activity through their aggregate demand policies.

We can now return to the question of export-led recoveries and ask what contribution United States real growth could have made to Germany. That answer from Table 18-3 is that the impact is quite minor. In the short run, United States real growth would have to increase by more than 20 percent to raise German income by only one percentage point. The transmission effect in this instance is quite small, although for a case like Canada, United States growth is a critically important determinant of Canada's short-run growth performance.

External Balance, Money, and Prices

The analysis has been developed so far on the assumption that domestic prices do not respond at all to changes in demand. This is a convenient assumption for expository purposes, but we know it is not realistic. We therefore show briefly how a more complete model—parallel to the aggregate demand and supply analysis of Chap. 12—would look in an open economy.

We start by reviewing the main points of Chap. 12. Aggregate demand depends on the level of prices. A higher level of prices implies lower real balances, higher interest rates, and lower spending. In an open economy, the relation is slightly more complicated because now an increase in our prices reduces demand for our goods for two reasons. The first is the familiar higher interest rate channel summarized above. The second reason arises because an increase in our prices makes our goods less competitive with foreign-produced goods. When the prices of goods produced at home rise, and given the exchange rate, our goods become more expensive for foreigners to buy, and their goods become *relatively* cheaper for us to buy. An increase in our prices is thus an increase in the *relative price* of the goods we produce, and shifts demand away from our goods toward imports, as well as reducing exports.

In summary, then, an increase in our price level reduces the demand for our goods both by increasing the interest rate (and reducing investment demand) and by reducing net exports—by making the goods we produce relatively more expensive than foreign-produced goods. In Fig. 18-7 we show the downward-sloping demand schedule for our goods D. Demand is equal, as before, to aggregate spending by domestic residents A, plus net exports NX:

$$D \equiv A + NX \tag{6}$$

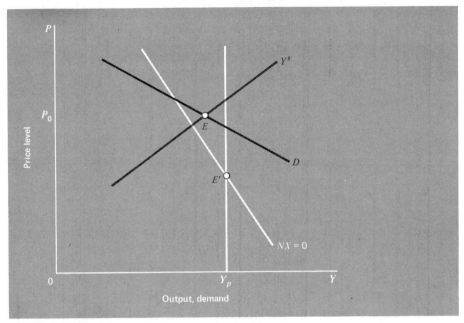

FIGURE 18-7 OPEN ECONOMY
MACROECONOMIC
EQUILIBRIUM WITH PRICE
ADJUSTMENT

The demand for domestic goods D is drawn for a given level of foreign prices, a given nominal money supply, and given fiscal policy. Remember, too, that the exchange rate is fixed. An increase in the nominal money stock shifts the schedule upward, as does expansionary fiscal policy. We have shown, too, the short-run aggregate supply schedule Y^s and the full-employment level of output, Y_p. Initial equilibrium is at point E, where we have unemployment.

Next we look at the trade balance equilibrium schedule, $NX = 0$. An increase in our income raises imports and worsens the trade balance. To restore trade balance equilibrium, domestic prices would have to be lower. This would make the home country more competitive, raise exports, and reduce imports. Thus, we show the trade balance equilibrium schedule as downward-sloping.[8] We assume that it is steeper than the demand schedule for domestic goods. The schedule is drawn for a given level of prices abroad. The short-run equilibrium at point E is one where

---

[8]We assume that a decline in prices improves the trade balance. This requires that exports and imports are sufficiently responsive to prices. There is a possibility that a reduction in our price lowers our revenue from exports—because the increased sales are not sufficient to compensate for the lower prices. We shall assume that this possibility does not occur. We assume, too, that import spending does not depend on the interest rate.

the home country has a trade deficit. Our prices are too high or our income is too high to have exports balance imports. To achieve trade balance equilibrium, we would have to become more competitive, thus exporting more and importing less. Alternatively, we could reduce our level of income in order to reduce import spending.

The Adjustment Process

Consider next the policy options from an external and internal balance point of view. At point E there is unemployment and a deficit. To restore full employment, we could expand aggregate demand, or else wait for wages and prices to fall sufficiently to raise the demand for our goods through the interest rate and increased net exports channels. From an external point of view we have to achieve a decline in income or in prices to restore balance.

Point E' is a point at which we have both internal and external balance. At E', we have full employment and balanced trade. But we cannot get to that point except through a protracted recession that cuts domestic prices sufficiently to shift the aggregate supply schedule down. This adjustment process would indeed occur if the government did not pursue any stabilization policy and simply pegged the exchange rate. The process is sufficiently important to deserve more attention.

First we look at the aggregate demand side. We remember that there is a link between the central bank's holdings of foreign exchange and the domestic money supply, assuming now no sterilization, as defined in footnote 5, p. 592. When the central bank pegs the exchange rate, selling foreign exchange, it reduces domestic high-powered money and therefore the money stock. This is exactly what happens in the case of a deficit. Thus the trade deficit at point E implies that the central bank is pegging the exchange rate, selling foreign exchange to keep the exchange rate from depreciating, and reducing the domestic money stock. It follows immediately that over time the aggregate demand schedule (which is drawn for a given money supply) will be shifting down and to the left. On the aggregate supply side we remember that unemployment leads to a decline in wages and costs which is reflected in a downward-shifting aggregate supply schedule. Over time, therefore, the short-run equilibrium point E moves down as both demand and supply schedules shift. The points of short-run equilibrium move in the direction of point E', and the process will continue until that point is reached. (The approach may be cyclical, but that is not of major interest here.)

Once point E' is reached, we have achieved long-run equilibrium. Because the trade balance is in equilibrium, there is no pressure on the exchange rate and therefore no need for exchange market intervention. Accordingly, there is no influence from the trade balance on the money supply and thereby on aggregate demand. On the supply side we have reached full employment. Therefore wages and costs are constant, so that the supply schedule is not shifting. At point E' we have a combination of relative prices, demand, and employment that gives both internal and external balance. The adjustment of the level of prices ensures that we can have—in the long run—both full employment and trade balance equilibrium.

The adjustment process we have just described is called the *classical* adjustment process. It relies critically on price adjustments and an adjustment in the money supply based on the trade balance. The adjustment process "works" in the sense that it moves the economy to a long-run equilibrium of internal and external balance. However, the mechanism is far from attractive. There is no good case for a protracted recession simply to achieve a cut in prices. A much preferable policy is to resort to expenditure switching policies, or to exchange rate changes, as means of achieving internal and external balance.[9]

The Monetary Approach to the Balance of Payments

How important are monetary considerations in explaining balance of payment problems? Is it true that balance of payments deficits are a reflection of an excessive money supply? These questions must be raised because it is frequently suggested that external balance problems are monetary in nature.

There is a simple first answer. It is obviously true that for any given balance of payments deficit, a sufficient contraction of the money stock will restore external balance. The reason is that a monetary contraction, by raising interest rates and reducing spending, generates a contraction in economic activity, a decline in income, and therefore a decline in imports. It is equally true that this result could be achieved by tight fiscal policy, and accordingly there is nothing especially monetary about this interpretation of remedies for external imbalance.

A more sophisticated interpretation of the problem recognizes the link we examined in the previous section between the balance of payments deficit, foreign exchange market intervention, and the money supply. The automatic mechanism is for a sale of foreign exchange—as arises in the case of deficits—to be reflected in an equal reduction in the stock of high-powered money. The central bank merely sells one asset (foreign exchange) and buys another (high-powered money). This process will automatically lead to a decline in the stock of money in deficit countries and an increase in the money stock in surplus countries. Given that the money supply is thus linked to the external balance, it is obvious that this adjustment process must ultimately lead to the right money stock so that external payments are in balance. This process was shown in Fig. 18-7.

The only way the adjustment process can be suspended is through

---

[9]Both exchange rate depreciation and shifts in demand from imports to domestic goods would shift both the net export schedule and the aggregate demand schedule up and to the right.

sterilization operations. We discussed this in the chapter on the money supply. There we noted that central banks frequently offset the impact of foreign exchange market intervention on the money supply through open market operations. Thus a deficit country that is selling foreign exchange and correspondingly reducing its money supply may offset this reduction by open market purchases of bonds that restore the money supply. Clearly, with such a practice, the automatic adjustment mechanism is suspended. Persistent external deficits are possible because the link between the external imbalance and the equilibrating changes in the money stock is broken. It is in this sense that persistent external deficits are a monetary phenomenon: the central bank actively maintains the stock of money too high for external balance.

The emphasis on monetary considerations in the interpretation of external balance problems is called the *monetary approach* to the balance of payments.[10] It has become important in the discussion of exchange rate questions. In that context, the argument has been advanced that depreciation of the exchange rate cannot improve a country's competitive position and external balance except in the short run. The argument is that in the short run, the depreciation does improve a country's competitive position and that this very fact gives rise to a trade surplus and therefore to an increase in the money stock. Over the course of time, the rising money supply raises aggregate demand and therefore prices until the economy returns to full employment and external balance. Devaluation thus exerts only a transitory effect on the economy, which lasts as long as prices and the money supply have not yet increased to match fully the higher import prices.

The analysis of the monetary approach is entirely correct in its insistence on a longer-run perspective in which prices and the money stock adjust and the economy achieves internal and external balance. The view is misdirected when it suggests that exchange rate policy cannot, even in the short run, affect a country's competitive position. More importantly, exchange rate changes frequently occur from a position of deficit and unemployment. In that case a depreciation moves the economy toward equilibrium. It eases the adjustment mechanism by achieving an increase in competitiveness through an increase in import prices rather than through a recession-induced decline in domestic prices.

Summary

We have covered a lot of ground at a hard pace, and it is worthwhile seeing where we have been and where we are going. In this section we amended

---

[10]For a collection of essays on this topic see Jacob Frenkel and Harry G. Johnson (eds.), *The Monetary Approach to the Balance of Payments*, Allen and Unwin, 1976. See also Marina Whitman, "Global Monetarism," *Brookings Papers on Economic Activity*, 3, 1975.

our previous analysis to allow for trade in goods. As yet, we have not taken into account trade in assets. We were assuming that the exchange rate was fixed, and that the central bank had enough reserves to meet any demands for foreign currency that might occur as a result of balance of payments deficits. Through most of the section we assumed that domestic and foreign price levels were fixed. This assumption was relaxed at the end.

The major points were:

1   The introduction of trade in goods means that spending by domestic residents is no longer equal to the demand for domestically produced goods. Some of the demand for goods of our residents goes for imports, and some of the demand for our goods comes from foreigners, to whom we export.

2   There is equilibrium in the goods market when the demand for our goods, consisting of spending by domestic residents, plus net exports, is equal to the output of domestic goods, which is equal to the income of domestic residents under specified conditions.

3   In short-run equilibrium, there is no guarantee that trade balances. In our simplest model, there is a unique level of income at which trade balances, and that is not necessarily the income level at which the economy comes into short-run equilibrium.

4   An increase in autonomous demand for domestic goods increases domestic output and worsens the trade balance. An increase in imports reduces domestic output and worsens the trade balance. An increase in exports increases domestic income and reduces the trade deficit. A shift in demand toward domestically produced goods increases the level of income and reduces the trade deficit, or increases the trade surplus.

5   Because trade does not necessarily balance in short-run equilibrium, there may be a *policy dilemma* in attempting both to move income to the potential output level and to balance trade. An increase in the level of income, to move it closer to potential, may well worsen the trade balance.

6   The use of *expenditure switching* policies, which change the relative prices of domestic and imported goods, combined with *expenditure reducing* policies, can move the economy to full employment with balanced trade.

7   Because foreigners' demands for our goods—our exports—are their imports, and because their imports depend on their level of income, the demand for our goods depends on the foreign level of income. Further, because an increase in their income increases our exports, and increases our level of income and therefore our imports, there are *repercussion effects* by which a change in foreign income eventually induces an increase in the demand for their goods through exports. The size of these interdependence and repercussion effects depends on the relative

size and openness of the economy. A small economy may be very dependent on a larger one, but a large economy's level of income does not depend much on the income level in small foreign economies.

8   Once we allow for price flexibility with fixed exchange rates, we use the analytical apparatus of Chap. 12. We see that price flexibility ultimately leads an economy to full employment with balanced trade. The mechanism involves changes in the domestic money supply which occur as the central bank keeps selling foreign exchange to domestic residents in exchange for domestic currency (essentially an open market sale of foreign currency). The falling money stock reduces our prices and therefore improves the balance of trade. Policy can be used actively to bring about adjustments without relying on this automatic and slow-moving mechanism.

So much for where we have been. In the next section we compare the alternatives of *financing* a trade deficit by the central bank drawing down its reserves (or by borrowing) with adjustment through *devaluation*. Then in Sec. 18-4 we introduce trade in assets, so-called *capital mobility*, and analyze its implications for stabilization policy.

18-3 FINANCING OF DEFICITS AND DEVALUATION

In a fixed exchange rate system, it is possible for the central bank to use its reserves to finance temporary imbalances of payments—that is, to meet the excess demand for foreign currency at the existing exchange rate arising from balance of payments deficits. Other ways of *financing* temporary payments imbalances are also available. A country experiencing balance of payments difficulties can borrow foreign currencies abroad. The borrowing may be undertaken either by the government (usually the central bank) or by private individuals. Although borrowing may be undertaken to finance both current and capital account deficits, we concentrate in this section on the current account.

A current account deficit cannot be financed by borrowing from abroad without raising the question of how the borrowing will be repaid. Clearly, if the counterpart of the current account deficit is productive domestic investment, there need be little concern about paying back the interest and capital borrowed. The investment will pay off in terms of increased output, some of which may be exported, or which may replace goods that previously were imported. The investment would thus yield the foreign exchange earnings with which to *service* (make payments on) the debt. However, problems may well arise in repaying the foreign debt if borrowing is used to finance consumption spending.

Maintaining and financing a current account deficit indefinitely or for very long periods of time is impossible. The alternative to financing of deficits is *adjustment* of the current account through policy measures to reduce the deficit. We examined in Sec. 18-2 one method of adjusting a current account deficit, through the imposition of tariffs. However, tariffs cannot be freely used to adjust the balance of trade, partly because there are international organizations and agreements such as GATT (General Agreement on Tariffs and Trade) and the IMF (International Monetary Fund) that outlaw, or at least frown on, the use of tariffs. Tariffs have generally fallen in the post-World War II period, as the industrialized world has moved to desirably freer trade between countries.

Another way of adjusting a current account deficit is to use restrictive domestic policy. In this regard, it is worth repeating that a trade deficit reflects an excess of expenditure by domestic residents and the government over income. In Chap. 2 we showed that

$$NX \equiv Y - (C + I^a + G) \tag{7}$$

where NX is the trade surplus, and I^a is actual investment. Thus, a balance of trade deficit can be reduced by reducing spending $(C + I + G)$ relative to income (Y). The trade deficit can, accordingly, be eliminated by reducing aggregate demand, by reducing G, or C, or I. In terms of Fig. 18-6, the trade deficit can be eliminated by using restrictive monetary and/or fiscal policy to shift the intersection of the IS and LM curves to the level of income at which trade balances. The costs of such a policy, in terms of unemployment, are obvious.

The unemployment that typically accompanies adjustment through recession, and the desirability of free trade, which argues against the use of tariffs, both suggest that an alternative policy for reconciling internal and external balance be considered. The major policy instrument for dealing with payments deficits in the dilemma situation is *devaluation*—which usually has to be combined with restrictive monetary and/or fiscal policy. A devaluation, as we noted in Sec. 18-1, is an increase in the domestic currency price of foreign exchange. Given the nominal prices in the two countries, devaluation increases the relative price of imported goods in the devaluing country and reduces the relative price of exports from the devaluing country.

Table 18-4 shows the effects of an exchange rate change on relative

TABLE 18-4 THE EFFECT OF EXCHANGE RATE CHANGES ON RELATIVE PRICES

	VW	Nova
Dollar price:		
(a) $0.25/DM	$2,500	$4,000
(b) $0.50/DM	$5,000	$4,000
DM price:		
(a) $0.25/DM	DM10,000	DM16,000
(b) $0.50/DM	DM10,000	DM 8,000

prices. Recall that we are assuming nominal prices in the home currency in each country are fixed. We assume that we (Americans) produce and export Novas and they (Germans) produce and export VWs. A Nova is priced at $4,000 and a VW at DM10,000. These prices, in terms of the respective producer's currencies, are assumed to remain constant. Now at an exchange rate of $0.25 per mark the relative price of VWs, in terms of Novas, is $2,500/$4,000 = 0.625, meaning that a VW costs 62.5 percent as much as a Nova. Next, consider a devaluation of the dollar by 100 percent. The table shows that the dollar price of VWs doubles and that the mark price of Novas declines to one-half. Both in the United States and in Germany, Novas become *relatively* cheaper, or VWs become relatively more expensive. The dollar devaluation lowers the mark price of United States goods and raises the dollar price of German goods. The exchange ratio between German and United States cars now becomes $5,000/$4,000 = 1.25, so that a VW now costs 25 percent more than a Nova. Clearly, the increase in the relative price of German goods will affect the pattern of demand, increasing both United States and German demands for Novas, at the expense of the demand for VWs.

How does a devaluation assist in achieving internal and external balance? Let us take first a special case of a country that was in full employment with balance of trade equilibrium, as shown by point E in Fig. 18-8. Now let there be an exogenous decline in export earnings, so that the NX =

FIGURE 18-8 THE EFFECTS OF A DE-CLINE IN EXPORTS ON INCOME AND THE TRADE BALANCE

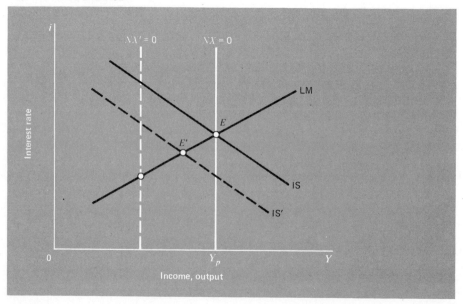

0 schedule shifts to the left to $NX' = 0$. At the given exchange rate and relative prices—that is, prices of domestic goods relative to world prices— the foreign demand for domestic goods is assumed to decline. In the absence of domestic policy intervention, and with fixed rates, the short-run and intermediate-run adjustment would be one of a decline in output and income. The IS schedule moves to the left as a result of the fall in exports and the resultant income decline at the point E' lowers imports, but not enough to make up for the loss of export revenue. The net effect is therefore unemployment and a trade deficit.

Next we ask how the home country can adjust to the loss of export markets. One possibility is for the home country to go through an adjustment process of declining domestic wages and prices as the high unemployment slowly reduces wages, or slows down their rate of increase. Such an adjustment would, over time, lower domestic costs and prices as compared to the prices of foreign goods. The home country would gain in competitiveness in world markets and thus restore export earnings and employment. There is no doubt that this is a feasible adjustment process, and, indeed, is the process that would occur by itself given enough time.

An alternative solution is to recognize that in order to restore full employment and export earnings, the home country must become more competitive in the prices charged for exports and imports. To restore competitiveness, domestic costs and prices have to decline *relative* to foreign prices. That adjustment can occur in two ways: (1) through a decline in domestic costs and prices at a given exchange rate and (2) through a depreciation of the exchange rate with unchanged domestic costs and prices.

The latter strategy has the obvious advantage that it does not require a protracted recession to reduce domestic costs. The adjustment is done by a stroke of the pen—a devaluation of the currency. Why would a devaluation achieve the adjustment? *Given* prices of foreign goods in terms of foreign currency (e.g., the mark prices of German goods), a devaluation, as shown in Table 18-4, raises the relative price of foreign goods. The effect is to induce an increased demand for American goods and a reduction in demand for imports in the United States

The case we have just considered is special, however, in one important respect. The economy was initially in balance of trade equilibrium at full employment. The disturbance to the economy took place in the trade account. Accordingly, if we could move the $NX = 0$ locus back to the full-employment level of income—as we could with a devaluation—both internal and external balance would be attained. Put differently, the reason there was an internal balance problem of unemployment in Fig. 18-8 was the reduction in exports and consequent external balance problem. Both problems could thus be cured through devaluation.

In general, we cannot cure *both* internal and external problems by a simple devaluation. The general case will require expenditure shifting through, say, a devaluation and a policy affecting the level of spending. To make that point, we look at the case of an increase in domestic spending

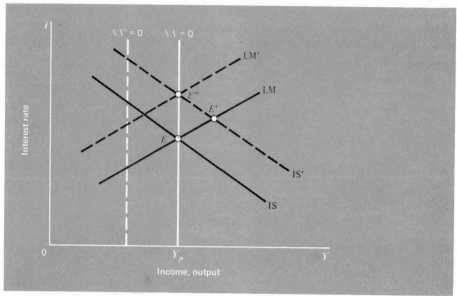

FIGURE 18-9 A DEVALUATION AND
TIGHT MONEY TO RESTORE INTERNAL AND
EXTERNAL BALANCE

that falls entirely on imports. This is studied in Fig. 18-9, where we start
from a full equilibrium at point E. The increase in import spending comes
entirely at the expense of saving and, accordingly, there is no change in
demand for domestic goods and thus no shift in the IS curve. The trade
balance schedule, however, shifts to the left. Since people now spend
more on imports at each level of income, a lower income level is required to
achieve trade balance. Thus, the trade balance schedule shifts to $NX' = 0$.
Now it is apparent that the only effect of the disturbance is to create a trade
deficit. There is no counterpart to that disturbance in the domestic goods
market.

Suppose next we corrected the trade deficit by devaluation, thus shifting the trade balance schedule back to the full-employment level of output.
This does not solve the entire problem because the devaluation now diverts demand from foreign to domestic goods, and thus the IS curve shifts
out and to the right to IS'. The devaluation thus gives rise to overemployment and a deficit at E'. Clearly we need a further instrument. We need
tight monetary or fiscal policy to accompany the devaluation.

We show, in Fig. 18-9, the use of a tight monetary policy. The monetary tightening shifts the LM curve to LM', and restores full equilibrium at
point E''. The point that we have made is that, in general, we need two
instruments—affecting expenditure *level* and *composition*–to achieve

internal and external balance. A devaluation shifts spending away from foreign goods and toward domestic goods and thus is an important ingredient of the policy mix. A further instrument is required to achieve the proper level of aggregate spending. In Fig. 18-9 the level of spending at E' is excessive and, accordingly, either tight money or tight fiscal policy is required to complete the policy mix.

We should not fool ourselves into believing that just because full employment can be maintained, current account adjustment with a devaluation is costless. Current account adjustment not only involves a cut in spending to the level of income, but it involves, in many instances, too, a worsening of the *terms of trade*—the price of exports relative to imports. Foreign goods become more expensive, thus reducing the purchasing power of the goods we produce. Therefore our standard of living falls.

Finally, a comment on the role of the exchange rate in a fixed rate system. In the fixed rate system, the exchange rate is an *instrument of policy*. The central bank can change the exchange rate for policy purposes, devaluing when the current account looks as if it will be in for a prolonged deficit. In a system of clean floating, by contrast, the exchange rate moves freely to equilibrate the balance of payments. In a system of dirty floating, the central bank attempts to manipulate the exchange rate while not committing itself to any given rate. The dirty floating system is thus intermediate between a fixed rate system and a clean floating system.

*18-4 CAPITAL MOBILITY AND THE POLICY MIX

So far we have been assuming that trade is confined to goods and services, and does not include assets. Now we allow for trade in assets and see the effects of such trade on the equilibrium of the economy and its desired policy mix.

One of the striking facts about the international economy is the high degree of integration or linkage among financial or capital markets—the markets in which bonds and stocks are traded. In particular, the capital markets are very fully integrated among the main industrial countries. Yields on assets in New York and yields on comparable assets in Canada, for example, move closely together. If rates in New York rose relative to those in Canada, investors would turn to lending in New York, while borrowers would turn to Toronto. With lending up in New York and borrowing up in Toronto, yields would quickly fall into line. Chart 18-1 shows the yields on United States short-term securities and their Canadian counterpart.[11] It is quite apparent that the yield differential is consistently small. There is impressive evidence in Chart 18-1 of the linkage of international capital markets which ensures consistency among interest rates in different

---

[11]The yield on Canadian securities in Chart 18-1 is "covered," which means that it is without exchange risk. Any yield differential in Chart 18-1 is *not* a reflection of exchange risk.

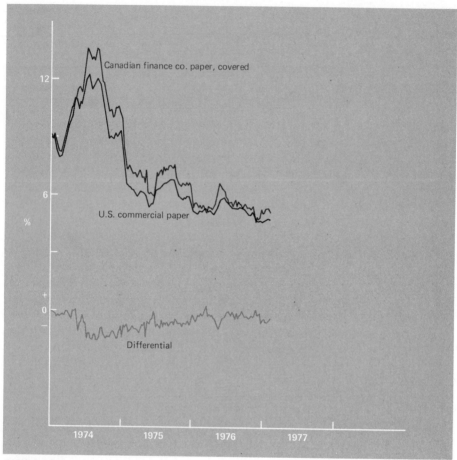

CHART 18-1 INTERNATIONAL INTEREST
RATE LINKAGES. (Source: *Selected Interest
Rates and Exchange Rates*, February 1977)

countries. That consistency arises because capital flows—lending to and
by foreigners—to countries with higher interest rates soon equalizes such
rates.

The high degree of capital market integration that is reflected in Chart
18-1 suggests that any one country's interest rates cannot get too far out of
line from those in the rest of the world without bringing about capital flows
that tend to restore yields to the world level. As we noted above, if Canadian yields fell, relative to United States yields, there would be a capital
outflow from Canada because lenders would take their funds out of Canada
and borrowers would try to raise funds in Canada. From a point of view of
the balance of payments, this implies that a decline in relative interest

rates—a decline in our rates relative to those abroad—will worsen the balance of payments because of the capital outflow—lending abroad by United States residents.

The recognition that changes in our interest rates affect capital flows and the balance of payments has important implications for stabilization policy. First monetary and fiscal policies, because they affect interest rates, have an effect on the capital account and, therefore, on the balance of payments. The effects of monetary and fiscal policy on the balance of payments are *not* limited to the trade balance effects discussed in Sec. 18-2 above, but extend to the capital account. The second implication is that the way in which monetary and fiscal policies work in affecting the domestic economy and the balance of payments changes when there are international capital flows. We will examine the monetary-fiscal policy mix that can be used to achieve internal and external balances, and see that capital flows can be used to *finance* the trade balance and thus help in achieving overall balance of payments equilibrium.

The Balance of Payments and Capital Flows

We can introduce the role of capital flows in a framework in which we assume that the home country faces a given price of imports and a given export demand. In addition, we assume that the world rate of interest is given and that capital flows into the home country at a rate that is higher, the higher the home country's rate of interest. That is, foreign investors purchase more of our assets, the higher the interest rate our assets pay, relative to the world interest rate. In Fig. 18-10 we show the rate of capital

FIGURE 18-10 INTEREST-RESPONSIVE CAPITAL FLOWS

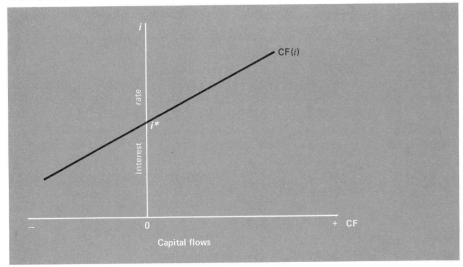

inflow CF, or the capital account surplus as an increasing function of the rate of interest. At the world interest rate, i^*, there are no capital flows. If the domestic interest rate is higher, there will be an inflow, and conversely, if the domestic interest rate is lower, there will be a capital outflow.

Next we look at the balance of payments. The balance of payments surplus BP is equal to the trade surplus NX, plus the capital account surplus CF:

$$BP = NX(Y, \overline{X}, \ldots) + CF(i) \tag{8}$$

In Eq. (8) we have shown the trade balance as a function of income, and the capital account as a function of the domestic interest rate. We remember from Sec. 18-2 that an increase in income worsens the trade balance. We have just learned that an increase in the interest rate raises capital inflows and thus improves the capital account. It follows that when income increases, an increase in interest rates could maintain overall balance of payments equilibrium. The trade deficit would be offset by a capital inflow. That idea is extremely important because it suggests that in the short run we can get out of the internal-external balance dilemma of Sec. 18-2.

The policy, we remember, was to achieve simultaneously internal and external balance from a position of deficit and unemployment or surplus and boom. The presence of interest-sensitive capital flows suggests that we can run an expansionary domestic policy without necessarily running into balance of payments problems. We can afford an increase in domestic income and import spending, provided we accompany it by an increase in interest rates so as to attract a capital inflow. But how can we achieve an expansion in domestic income at the same time interest rates are increased? The answer is that we use fiscal policy to increase aggregate demand to the full-employment level and monetary policy to get the right amount of capital flows.[12]

Internal and External Balance

In Fig. 18-11 we show the positively sloped schedule $BP = 0$, derived from Eq. (8), along which we have balance of payments equilibrium. To derive the slope of the $BP = 0$ line, start with an income expansion, which raises imports and worsens the balance of payments. To restore balance of payments equilibrium, interest rates have to be higher to attract the

[12]The idea of the policy mix for internal and external balance was suggested by Robert Mundell in an important paper. See "The Appropriate Use of Monetary and Fiscal policy under Fixed Exchange Rates," *I.M.F. Staff Papers*, March 1962. Mundell's work on international macroeconomics has been extraordinarily important, and the adventurous student should certainly consult his two books: *International Economics*, Macmillan, 1967 and *Monetary Theory*, Goodyear, 1971.

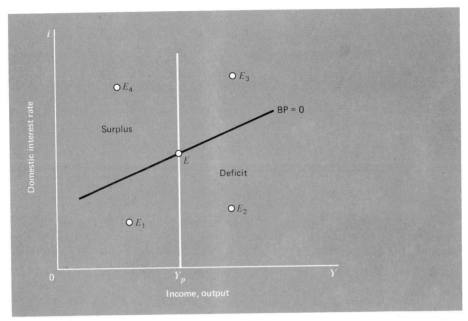

FIGURE 18-11 INTERNAL AND
EXTERNAL BALANCE

capital flows that finance the trade deficit. Thus to maintain payments balance an income increase has to be matched by a higher interest rate, and the $BP = 0$ line is therefore upward-sloping.

The schedule is drawn for given exports and a given foreign interest rate. The higher the degree of capital mobility, the flatter the schedule. If capital is very highly responsive to interest rates, then a small increase in the interest rate will bring about very large capital flows and thus allow the financing of large trade deficits. The larger the marginal propensity to import, the steeper the schedule. An increase in income worsens the trade balance by the increase in income times the marginal propensity to import. Thus, a high propensity to import means that a given increase in income produces a large deficit and thus requires a large increase in interest rates to bring about the right amount of capital flows to offset the trade deficit. Points above and to the left of the $BP = 0$ schedule correspond to a surplus, and points below and to the right to a deficit. We have also drawn, in Fig. 18-11, full-employment output Y_p. The full equilibrium with both internal and external balance is at point E.

We can talk about policy problems in terms of points in the four quadrants of Fig. 18-11. Each such point would be an intersection of an IS and LM curve and the question is how to use monetary and fiscal policy—shifting the IS and LM curves—to get to full equilibrium. Thus point E_1, for example, corresponds to a case of unemployment and deficit. Point E_2, by contrast, is a case of deficit and overemployment. What are points E_3 and E_4?

The Policy Mix

Suppose that the economy were at point E_1. The appropriate policy to produce internal and external balance requires a higher level of employment for internal balance and higher interest rates and/or a lower level of income for external balance.

In terms of the analysis of Sec. 18-2, there is a policy dilemma at E_1 because employment considerations suggest income should be raised and balance of payments considerations suggest it should be reduced. However, now there is a way out of the dilemma. Suppose we reduce the money supply and thus raise interest rates. To offset the effects of the higher interest rates on income, we could use expansionary fiscal policy. Clearly we could keep income constant and reach balance of payments equilibrium by getting interest rates high enough. However, we can do better. We can use fiscal policy to get us all the way to full employment and use tight money, in the form of higher interest rates, to achieve balance of payments equilibrium. Thus we can get to point E with both internal and external balance.

The lesson we have just derived is that we should expand income, through fiscal policy, whenever there is unemployment and use tight money whenever there is a deficit. The combination of policies moves us to both internal and external balance. With a situation like point E_4 we want to use the same principle, but the economic conditions are different. Here we have a surplus and unemployment. Accordingly, we need expansionary fiscal policy to achieve full employment and expansionary monetary policy to reduce interest rates. Point E_4 is actually *not* a dilemma situation, since any form of expansionary policy moves us in the right direction with respect to both targets.

We leave it to you to work through the remaining cases and simply note here the principle: Under fixed exchange rates and with capital mobility, we use monetary policy to achieve external balance and fiscal policy to achieve full employment. What is the experience with such a rule? There is little doubt that tight money, for balance of payments reasons, is the oldest remedy in the central bank's medicine chest. Since monetary policy is a flexible tool, attainment of external balance in the short run through tight money is relatively easy.

Limitations of the Policy Mix

The argument for a policy mix is persuasive, but it overlooks three important limitations. The first problem is that fiscal policy may not be sufficiently flexible to implement the needed policy mix. The discussion of lags in Chap. 9 made the point that the inside lag for fiscal policy is quite long. If fiscal policy cannot be modified readily, then all the policy maker can do is control the balance of payments, *or* employment, through monetary policy. We are back in a dilemma situation, because there are two targets—internal and external balance—but only one instrument—namely monetary policy. The second point is that a country will typically not be indifferent to the level of domestic interest rates. Even if fiscal policy were sufficiently flexible to implement the policy mix, it would still be true that the composition of domestic output would depend on the mix. Thus a country that attempts an expansion in aggregate demand together with tight money, effectively restricts the construction sector and investment spending in general. The notion of a policy mix with monetary policy devoted to the balance of payments, therefore, overlooks the fact that the interest rate determines the composition as well as the level of aggregate spending.

The final consideration concerns the composition of the balance of payments. Countries are not indifferent about the makeup of their balance of payments between the current account deficit and the capital account surplus. Even if the overall balance is in equilibrium so that one target is satisfied, there is still the problem that a capital account surplus or capital inflow means net external borrowing: our country's debts to foreigners are increasing. Those debts will eventually have to be repaid.

Under a system of fixed exchange rates, there are circumstances under which a country—much like an individual—will find it useful to borrow in order to finance, say, a current shortfall of export earnings. However, continued large-scale borrowing from abroad is not consistent with a fixed exchange rate over long periods. Large-scale borrowing eventually places the country in a position where the interest payments it has to make to foreigners become a major burden for the economy. Faced with the prospect of continued foreign borrowing on a large scale in order to maintain its exchange rate fixed, a country would be well advised to implement adjustment policies which improve the current account balance. Such policies would typically be a devaluation accompanied by restrictive monetary and/or fiscal policy to reduce domestic demand pressures.

18-5 SUMMARY

1 The balance of payments accounts are a record of the international transactions of the economy. The current account records trade in goods and services, as well as transfer payments. The capital account records purchases and sales of assets. Any transaction that gives rise to a payment by United States residents is a deficit item for the U.S.
2 The overall balance of payments is the sum of the current and capital accounts. If the overall balance is in deficit, we have to make more

payments to foreigners than they make to us. The foreign currency for making these payments is supplied by central banks.

3 Under fixed exchange rates, the central bank maintains constant the price of foreign currencies in terms of the domestic currency. It does this by buying and selling foreign exchange at that fixed exchange rate. For that purpose it has to keep reserves of foreign currency.

4 Under floating or flexible exchange rates, the exchange rate may change from moment to moment. In a system of clean floating, the exchange rate is determined by supply and demand without central bank intervention to affect the rate. Under dirty floating, the central bank intervenes by buying and selling foreign exchange in an attempt to influence the exchange rate.

The remainder of the chapter studies the role of international trade in goods and assets under fixed exchange rates:

5 The introduction of trade in goods means that some of the demand for our output comes from abroad, and that some spending by our residents is on foreign goods. There is equilibrium in the goods market when the demand for domestically produced goods is equal to the output of those goods.

6 In short-run equilibrium the balance of trade may be in deficit. If there is no trade in assets, there may be a policy dilemma in that balanced trade and full employment cannot be attained merely through the manipulation of aggregate demand by fiscal and monetary policy. Expenditure switching policies that change the allocation of spending between imports and domestic goods are needed to solve the problem.

7 Over longer periods, there is an automatic adjustment mechanism in the economy which eventually leads to full employment at balanced trade under fixed exchange rates. A balance of trade deficit leads to a reduction in the domestic money stock which eventually leads to falling domestic prices that, given the foreign price level, switch spending away from imports and increase foreign demand for our goods. In the long run, domestic wages will also adjust to ensure full employment.

8 However, there are alternative mechanisms for achieving balanced trade, without going through an adjustment process involving falling domestic prices. A devaluation, combined with restrictive aggregate demand policies, can lead to balance of payments equilibrium from a situation of trade deficit at more than full employment.

9 The introduction of capital flows points to the effects of monetary and fiscal policy on the balance of payments through interest rate effects on capital flows. An increase in the domestic interest rate, relative to the world interest rate, leads to a capital inflow that can finance a balance of trade deficit.

10 Policy dilemmas can then be handled by combining restrictive monetary policies to improve the balance of payments through higher interest rates and capital inflows, with expansionary fiscal policy to increase domestic employment.

11 However, such policies cannot be used in the long run to maintain balanced payments at the fixed exchange rate. The interest burden of the policies would, in the long run, be excessive, and the exchange rate could not be maintained. If balance of payments deficits are not temporary, then adjustment policies, such as devaluation, with accompanying monetary and fiscal changes, have to be undertaken to correct the imbalance.

PROBLEMS

1 This problem formalizes some of the questions about income and trade balance determination in the open economy. We assume, as a simplification, that the interest rate is given and equal to $i = i_0$. In terms of Figs. 18-1 and 18-2, the monetary authorities hold constant the interest rate so that the LM curve is flat at the level $i = i_0$.

We assume aggregate spending by domestic residents is

$$A = \bar{A} + cY - hi \tag{1}$$

Import spending is given by

$$Q = \bar{Q} - mY \tag{2}$$

where $\bar{Q}$ is autonomous import spending. Exports are given and equal to

$$X = \bar{X} \tag{3}$$

You are asked to work out the following problems:
a What is the total demand for domestic goods? The balance of trade?
b What is the *equilibrium* level of income?
c What is the balance of trade at that equilibrium level of income?
d What is the effect of an increase in exports on the equilibrium level of income? What is the multiplier?
e What is the effect of increased exports on the trade balance?

2 Suppose the marginal propensity to save is 0.1 and the marginal propensity to import is 0.2.
a What is the open economy multiplier?
b Assume there is a reduction in export demand of $\Delta \bar{X} = \$1$ billion. By how much does income change? By how much does the trade balance worsen?
c What policies can the country pursue to offset the impact of reduced exports on domestic income and employment as well as the trade balance?

3 It has been suggested that, the smaller the marginal propensity to import, the larger the cost of adjustment to external imbalance. What is the rationale for this argument? Do you agree?

4 It has been argued that a central bank is a necessary condition for a balance of payments deficit. What is the explanation for this argument?

5 Consider a country that is in a position of full employment and balanced trade. You are asked to discuss which type of disturbances lead to a policy dilemma and which disturbances can be remedied with standard aggregate demand tools of stabilization:

 a A loss of export markets

 b A reduction in saving and a corresponding increase in demand for domestic goods

 c An increase in government spending

 d A shift in demand from imports to domestic goods

 e A reduction in imports with a corresponding increase in saving

 Indicate in each case the impact on external and internal balance as well as the appropriate policy response.

*6 Derive the formula $1/(m + s)$ for the foreign trade multiplier, assuming the demand for imports is $Q = \bar{Q} - mY$. Use the formula to discuss the impact on the trade balance of an increase in autonomous domestic spending. In your discussion comment on the proposition that, the more open the economy, the smaller the domestic income expansion. Comment, also, on the counterpart proposition that, the more open the economy, the more the trade balance worsens. What measures openness?

*7 Consider a world with some capital mobility: The home country's capital account improves as domestic interest rates rise relative to the world rate of interest. Initially the home country is in internal and external balance. (Draw the IS, LM, and BP = 0 schedules).

 Assume now an increase in the world rate of interest.

 a Show the effect of the foreign interest rate increase on the BP schedule.

 b What policy response would immediately restore internal and external balance?

 c If the authorities took no action, what would be the adjustment process along the lines described by the "monetary approach to the balance of payments"?

*8 Consider again the case of a country that faces some capital mobility. Here we ask what monetary fiscal policy mix should be pursued to offset the following disturbances:

 a A transitory gain in exports

 b A permanent gain in exports

 c A decline in autonomous spending

 d An increased rate of capital outflow (at each level of domestic interest rates)

*9 This question is concerned with the repercussion effects of a domestic expansion once we recognize that as a consequence output abroad will expand. Suppose that at home there is an increase in autonomous spending, $\Delta \bar{A}$, that falls entirely on domestic goods. (Assume constant interest rates throughout this problem.)

 a What is the resulting effect on income, disregarding repercussion effects? What is the impact on our imports, ΔQ?

 b Using the result for the increase in imports, we can now ask what happens abroad. Our increase in imports appears abroad as an increase in their exports and therefore as an increase in demand for their goods. Accordingly, their output expands. Assuming the foreign marginal propensity to save is s^* and the foreign propensity to import is m^*, by how much will foreign income expand as a result of an increase in their exports?

 c Now combine the pieces by writing the familiar equation for equilibrium in the domestic goods market: Change in supply, ΔY, equals the total change in demand: $\Delta \bar{A} + \Delta X - m\ \Delta Y + (1 - s)\ \Delta Y$, or

$$\Delta Y = \frac{1}{s + m}(\Delta \bar{A} + \Delta X)$$

Noting that foreign demand ΔX depends on our increased imports, we can replace ΔX with the answer to 9b to obtain a general expression for the multiplier with repercussions.

d   Substitute your answer for 9b in the formula for the change in foreign demand, $\Delta X = m^*\ \Delta Y^*$.

e   Calculate the complete change in our income, including repercussion effects. Now compare your result with the small-country case. What difference do repercussion effects make? Is our income expansion larger or smaller with repercussion effects?

f   Consider the trade balance effect of a domestic expansion with and without repercussion effects. Is the trade deficit larger or smaller once repercussion effects are taken into account?

10   Use the central bank balance sheet to show how a balance of payments deficit affects the stock of high-powered money under fixed exchange rates. Show, too, how sterilization operations work.

11   Discuss the manner in which income, price adjustments, and money supply adjustments interact in leading the economy ultimately to full employment and external balance. Choose as an example the case where a country experiences a permanent increase in exports.

12   In relation to external imbalance a distinction is frequently made between imbalances that should be "financed" and those that should be "adjusted." Can you think of a classification of disturbances that give rise respectively to imbalances requiring adjustment and those that should more appropriately be financed?

19

Trade and Capital
Flows under
Flexible Exchange
Rates

This chapter is concerned with flexible exchange rates and events in the world economy since 1973. The world moved to a flexible exchange rate system in 1973 as the fixed exchange rate system that had existed since 1945 collapsed. The fundamental cause of the collapse of the fixed rate system—also called the Bretton Woods system, after the town in New Hampshire in which the conference setting up the system was held—was the incompatibility of macroeconomic targets among countries.

During the sixties, and again in 1971–1973, some countries, including Britain and the United States, pursued expansionary policies. Other countries—the hard-currency countries, particularly Germany—wanted lower inflation rates than the world economy was experiencing and followed less expansionary policies. With fixed exchange rates, the lower rate of inflation in Germany than in the United States meant that German goods were becoming progressively cheaper relative to United States goods. As a result, Germany ran increasingly large balance of payments surpluses, while the United States (and Britain) had large deficits. Under such circumstances, the countries with large surpluses have to revalue their currencies, or the deficit countries have to devalue, to correct the payments imbalances.

A fixed exchange rate system with free capital flows between countries is badly equipped to deal with revaluations or devaluations that are widely anticipated. To understand that point, we turn to the case of Germany in 1973. There were recurrent rumors in 1973 that the deutschmark would be revalued once more.[1] The rumors arose because the exchange rate adjustment of 1971 had not appreciably reduced the United States balance of payments deficit. The belief in an imminent deutschmark revaluation led to large capital outflows from the United States and inflows into Germany.

Why would the belief that the mark was about to be revalued lead to a capital inflow into Germany? Suppose people expect the mark will be revalued from 30 cents per mark to 40 cents per mark. A holder of $1 million today could buy DM3.33 million for his dollars at the price of 30 cents each. Then, after the devaluation, he could exchange his DM3.33 million for $1.33 million, receiving 40 cents for each mark. The operation nets a profit of 33 percent. Since there is no risk that the mark will be devalued, there is very little risk in buying it, and hence the belief in impending revaluation leads to large purchases of marks by holders of other currencies. If there is no revaluation, there is hardly any loss, and if there is a revaluation, there is a large profit.

As a result of the expected revaluation, the German Bundesbank had to buy about $10 billion in foreign exchange to meet foreign demands for marks at the existing exchange rate, in the five weeks from the end of January to the first of March 1973. Recall from Chap. 8 and 18 that central bank purchases of foreign exchange increase the domestic money supply.

---

[1]The deutschmark had been revalued in 1961, 1969, and 1971. In 1971 a number of other currencies also had their exchange rates adjusted.

Now the $10 billion that the Bundesbank purchased by selling marks amounted to almost 20 percent of the German money supply at that time. Thus, in order to defend the exchange rate, the Bundesbank was being forced to expand the German money supply at an extraordinary rate. The large increase in the money supply in turn created the fear—indeed the certainty—that the capital inflow would have substantial inflationary effects. The way out was to stop intervening in the foreign exchange market and thus to gain control of monetary policy for purposes of domestic stabilization. But once the Bundesbank decided to stop intervening in the foreign exchange market, it left the exchange rate to be determined by supply and demand in that market. That is, it chose to allow a flexible exchange rate regime.

A country which is expected to devalue also faces an intractable problem under fixed exchange rates. In that case, the expected devaluation produces an outflow of capital from the currency. Suppose that the pound was expected to be devalued. Then holders of pounds would buy other currencies in exchange for their pounds.[2] With the Bank of England committed to supporting the exchange rate, it would have to buy the pounds that others were selling. In so doing, it would rapidly reduce its reserves of other currencies, and eventually run out of reserves to exchange for the pounds. Thus it would be forced to devalue.

The general point is that a fixed exchange rate system is not viable if countries pursue policies which lead to different rates of inflation and there is free mobility of capital. The countries with lower inflation rates will eventually have to revalue or those with higher inflation rates will have to devalue. It is thus always clear in which direction there will be a revaluation or devaluation. Capital can flow with little risk and with the promise of large gains in anticipation of exchange rate changes. And as the capital starts flowing, surplus countries are forced to accept increases in their money supplies they do not want, and deficit countries face the risk of running out of reserves.

There were, in the early seventies, increasingly large-scale flows of capital in anticipation of exchange rate changes. The German decision to float the exchange rate in 1973 was merely the particular event which marked the end of the fixed rate system, rather than the fundamental cause of the change of system. The fundamental cause was the incompatibility of the economic policies being followed by different countries.

What is the system that has emerged since 1973? There are three chief characteristics. The first is the formation of *currency areas*. For instance, in 1973, some countries in the European Economic Community (EEC) joined Germany in a currency area with fixed exchange rates that is called the *snake*. The snake is an arrangement, shown in Chart 19-1, whereby exchange rates between partner countries can fluctuate only within narrow

---

[2]To see why expected devaluation produces a flight of capital, reverse the example of the expected mark appreciation above.

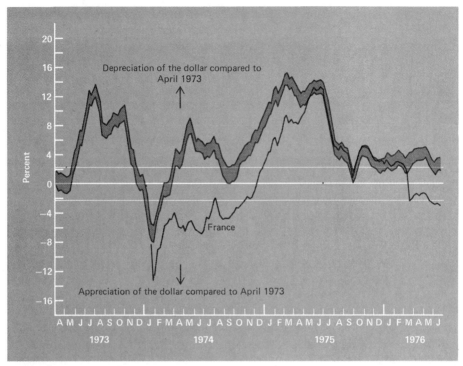

CHART 19-1 THE EEC SNAKE AND THE
FRENCH FRANC VIS-A-VIS THE DOLLAR.
(Source: OECD, *Economic Outlook*, July
1976)

limits. However, the exchange rates of all the currencies in the currency
area fluctuate relative to the United States dollar. If the small margin of
fluctuation within the snake were eliminated, the shaded band in Chart
19-1 would collapse to a fixed rate within the snake—a fixed rate between
Dutch guilders and marks, for instance—and a floating rate of the mark-
guilder relative to the United States dollar.

The second fact is apparent, too, from Chart 19-1. That is the large
fluctuations in exchange rates that have taken place since 1973. The snake
currencies have appreciated and depreciated relative to the dollar in a
fashion that some have called "wild gyrations." The question arises of
where these movements come from and whether central banks should intervene in the market to smooth exchange rate movements.

This leads us to the third fact—*dirty floating*. Rates have in practice
not been determined by the free interplay of private demand and supply
but have on the contrary been significantly affected by official intervention.
Central banks have intervened almost on a daily basis in the foreign exchange markets to smooth out short-run fluctuations. They may well also
have attempted and succeeded in fighting longer-run exchange rate move-

ments. Thus the Banque de France in 1976 intervened on a large scale to try to keep the franc from depreciating, and it has been suggested that the Bank of Japan did the same to keep the yen from appreciating. From November 1975 to June 1976 the Bank of Japan acquired fully 3 billion dollars' worth of foreign exchange in an attempt to moderate the appreciation of the yen relative to the dollar. These practices, known as dirty floating, raise the questions of why central banks would want to intervene in the market to affect exchange rates, and of what benefits they gain from maintaining rates rather than suffering appreciation or depreciation.

A final question that is raised by the new regime concerns world trade and capital flows. Prior to 1973, a flexible rate system was viewed with suspicion. The argument was that flexible rates create uncertainty and thus reduce trade and lending in the world economy. The question is important because such an effect, if it occurred, would obviously have repercussions at the macro level by forcing countries to be in trade balance. It turns out, though, that world trade did not decline after the move to flexible exchange rates and large payments imbalances continue to be financed through capital flows.

The plan of this chapter is to start by considering the behavior of a flexible rate system without capital flows, just as we started the theoretical part of Chap. 18 by ignoring capital flows. Next we introduce interest rates and capital flows. The complete framework allows a realistic discussion of monetary and fiscal policy under flexible rates. In the following section we look at financing of trade imbalances under the impact of the oil price increase of 1973–1974 and the subsequent recession. Section 19-4 considers the determinants of exchange rates in the intermediate run. Section 19-5 contains a discussion of central bank intervention in the foreign exchange markets.

19-1 FLEXIBLE EXCHANGE RATES AND TRADE BALANCE EQUILIBRIUM

In discussing the effects of expansionary policies under fixed rates, we noted the spillover of aggregate demand into a trade deficit. An expansion in income, brought about by, say, an increase in government spending, leads to increased imports and thus to a trade deficit. Part of the expansion in aggregate demand leaks abroad and thus reduces the expansionary impact of policies by comparison with a closed economy. In this section, we ask how that conclusion is modified in a flexible exchange rate regime.

As a preliminary remark, we have to clarify how exchange rates are determined in a flexible rate system. In a fixed rate system, central banks set the rates and maintain them by buying or selling any amount of foreign exchange at the set price. In a flexible rate system without intervention, the exchange rate adjusts to equate external payments in foreign currencies for imports and capital outflows, to receipts of foreign currencies from export sales and capital inflows. In other words, the exchange rate adjusts to achieve balance of payments equilibrium. In this chapter we shall see how exchange rate changes make it possible for balance of payments equilibrium to be attained.

Equilibrium Output and Exchange Rates

We start with the simple model of an open economy studied in Sec. 18-2, and ask how it is modified by a flexible rate system. We assume that the interest rate is fixed and that wages and prices do not adjust very quickly to produce full employment. Then, the goods market equilibrium condition is

$$Y = A(Y) + NX(Y,e) \tag{1}$$

where NX denotes the home country's trade surplus and e is the exchange rate, measured in cents per unit of foreign currency, e.g., 40 cents per mark.

In Eq. (1) the trade surplus NX is written as a function of income and the exchange rate. In Chap. 18 we assumed a fixed exchange rate, but now our focus is on exchange rate adjustments as an equilibrating mechanism for the balance of payments. Accordingly the exchange rate has to be introduced explicitly as a determinant of the trade balance. Specifically, a depreciation of the exchange rate or an increase in the dollar price of foreign exchange improves the balance of trade by raising exports and reducing import spending.[3] An increase in income worsens the trade balance by raising imports.

Under flexible rates without capital flows, a second condition of equilibrium is that trade be balanced. That condition is stated in Eq. (2):

$$NX(Y,e) = 0 \tag{2}$$

Our simple model of the economy with a fixed interest rate and domestic price level is summarized in the equilibrium conditions for the goods market and for the balance of trade. In the absence of capital flows, trade balance equilibrium and balance of payments equilibrium are equivalent. Accordingly, we can think of Eq. (2) as the condition of equilibrium in the balance of payments or, on still another interpretation, as the equilibrium condition in the foreign exchange market. That latter interpretation is appropriate because the balance of payments surplus—in this case export

---

[3]We are glossing over one difficulty here. The depreciation raises the relative price of imports in terms of domestic goods. Can we be sure that the value of imports will fall? It is true that in response to the relative price increase, imports will fall in quantity but their price is higher. Import spending—price times quantity—need not necessarily fall. We shall simply assume that a devaluation improves the trade balance by raising export revenue and reducing import spending. Students of trade theory will recognize that we are discussing here the famous "elasticity condition" for a successful devaluation.

revenue less import spending—measures the excess supply of foreign exchange.

To gain an understanding of how a flexible rate world works, we go through the effects of an increase in aggregate spending, A, in the home country. With the increase in spending assumed to fall entirely on domestic goods, the effect is to raise output and—if the exchange rate stayed fixed—to worsen the trade balance. The next step is to ask what happens to the exchange rate as a consequence of the potential trade deficit. Clearly, the trade deficit would produce an excess demand for foreign exchange. The exchange rate depreciates, or the domestic currency price of foreign exchange rises. The depreciation in turn reduces the deficit. The exchange rate continues depreciating until trade is balanced.

We have so far overlooked the feedback effect from the exchange rate and trade balance adjustment to the domestic goods market. It is true that the exchange rate depreciation restores trade balance equilibrium. It does so by raising exports and reducing import spending. In other words, the depreciation improves the trade balance by shifting demand away from foreign goods toward domestic output. There is thus an exchange-rate-induced increase in demand for domestic goods that further raises income. The increase in income in turn gives rise to increased import spending, which creates the need for further depreciation in order to restore trade balance equilibrium. Will that process come to an end? Or is it possible that the depreciation will continue to raise output demand, income, and imports thus creating the need for even more depreciation?

To answer these questions and to see how a flexible exchange rate economy works, we turn to Fig. 19-1. There we show two schedules that represent goods market and trade balance equilibrium.[4] The goods market equilibrium schedule YY is derived from Eq. (1), and the trade balance equilibrium schedule NX represents Eq. (2).

Consider first the schedule NX along which trade is balanced. We want to ask why that schedule is positively sloped. An increase in income, as we know, raises import spending and thus worsens the trade balance. To restore balanced trade, the exchange rate would have to depreciate—e would have to increase—and thus allow exports to expand and import spending to decline. Along the NX schedule we therefore have combinations of the exchange rate and income that assure balanced trade. To be quite certain to understand what happens along the schedule, ask yourself whether exports rise or fall as you go up and to the right along the schedule.

Next we look at the goods market equilibrium schedule YY. We want to know why it should be positively sloped as we have shown it. Say we were at point A_0, where the exchange rate and income are such that the goods market clears. What would happen in the goods market if the ex-

---

[4]The diagram was developed by Robert Mundell in his article "Flexible Exchange Rates and Employment Policy," *Canadian Journal of Economics and Political Science,* November 1961.

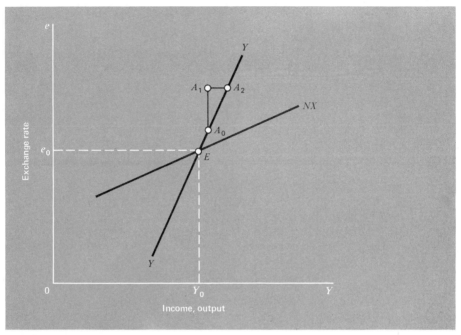

FIGURE 19-1 THE EQUILIBRIUM
EXCHANGE RATE AND LEVEL OF OUTPUT
IN A FLEXIBLE EXCHANGE RATE SYSTEM

change rate depreciated to a level indicated by point A_1? With income unchanged at point A_1 the depreciation in the exchange rate moves demand toward domestic goods because it lowers the relative price of our output. With demand for our goods increased, we clearly have an excess demand for goods and we can ask how output should adjust to restore balance. The answer is that output should increase. Although some of that increased output is absorbed by induced expenditures, the remainder goes to meet the excess demand generated by the exchange rate movement and thus serves to restore goods market equilibrium. This argument shows that the goods market equilibrium schedule must be positively sloped; a depreciation increases the demand for domestic goods which must then be met by an expansion in output.

The final question we want to ask concerns the relative slopes of the YY and NX schedules. We shall take the answer in Fig. 19-1—that the YY curve has the steeper slope—as given for a moment and go ahead to see what the model and graph do for us. The graph shows that point E is the full equilibrium point. At that point *both* the trade balance and the goods market clear. Associated with that equilibrium are the level of income Y_0 and the equilibrium exchange rate e_0.

Expansionary Fiscal Policy

We can use the diagrammatic apparatus of Fig. 19-1 to study the effects of expansionary fiscal policy on income and the exchange rate. In terms of Eq. (1), an increase in government spending or reduction in taxes increases aggregate demand $A(Y)$ at any given level of income. The expansionary fiscal policy accordingly shifts the YY curve in Fig. 19-2 to the right to Y'Y'. The result is an increase in the equilibrium level of income and an increase in e—or depreciation of the exchange rate.

Why? The fiscal policy change increases aggregate spending, and so increases the level of income. Part of the increase in aggregate demand is spent on imported goods, and the exchange rate has to depreciate (e has to increase) to maintain trade balance; exports increase and imports are cut back somewhat by the increase in e. We recognize from Fig. 19-2 that the effects of the expansionary policy on the exchange rate depend on the relative slopes of the YY and NX schedules. We will soon be able to confirm that the slopes shown are indeed implied by the model.

*Dynamics

In Fig. 19-3 we show the equilibrium of the economy at point E, and we want to ask now how and whether the economy would actually reach that

FIGURE 19-2 EFFECTS OF EXPANSION-
ARY FISCAL POLICY ON INCOME AND THE
EXCHANGE RATE

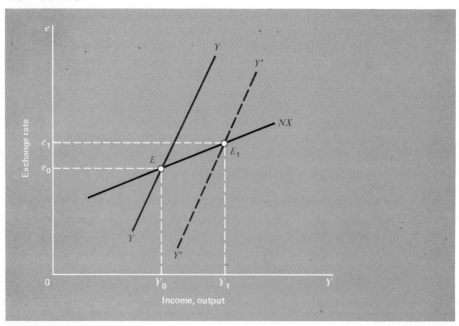

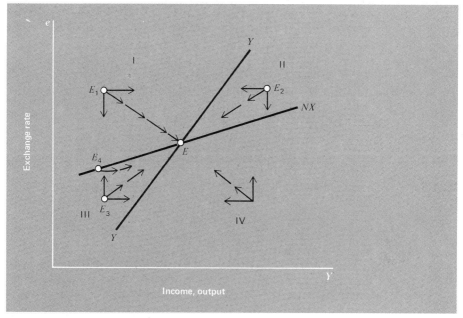

FIGURE 19-3 EXCHANGE RATE AND
OUTPUT ADJUSTMENT

equilibrium. Can we be certain, starting at some point like E_1, that the economy will reach the equilibrium at E where both the goods and foreign exchange markets are in equilibrium?

It will be helpful first to identify the various *disequilibrium* regions in Fig. 19-3, and then to discuss what income and exchange rate adjustments would be brought about by these disequilibria. We look first at a point like E_1. That point is one of an excess demand for goods and an excess supply of foreign exchange or a trade surplus. How do we establish that? Simply think of starting at point E and reduce output and raise the exchange rate in a move to E_1. What happens in the goods market? The exchange rate depreciation would raise the demand for domestic goods, while the output contraction would reduce supply. Clearly the move from E to E_1 produces an excess demand for goods. Exactly the same argument applies to the trade balance. Starting from E and moving to E_1, we reduce output and income, which improves the trade balance by reducing imports. At the same time, we depreciate the exchange rate, which raises exports and further reduces imports. Thus, we unambiguously move to a trade surplus. This argument establishes that any point in region I is a point of trade surplus and excess demand for goods. By symmetry of the argument, points in region IV are points of deficit and excess supply. This leaves us with regions II and III, which are not as easy.

We can use a direct argument to identify the disequilibrium at, say, point E_2. Starting vertically below that point, on the trade balance equilibrium schedule, we depreciate the exchange rate to point E_2. What happens to the trade balance? It clearly improves as a consequence of the depreciation. Alternatively starting vertically above point E_2, on the YY schedule, we can ask what happens to excess supply or demand in the goods market if we appreciate the rate to point E_2. The appreciation reduces the demand for domestic goods and thus creates an excess supply of goods. The argument establishes that point E_2 is a point of trade surplus and excess supply of goods. You should establish the corresponding argument for point E_3.

We summarize the various disequilibria in Table 19-1.

The next question we ask is whether equilibrium will be reached. Is a flexible rate system stable? We go about answering that question by considering a plausible adjustment mechanism for output and the exchange rate. In particular, we will assume that (1) output increases whenever there is an excess demand for domestic goods and (2) the exchange rate depreciates—e rises—whenever there is a trade deficit and appreciates whenever there is a trade surplus. We explore the implied dynamics in Fig. 19-3.

We use the information on the disequilibrium in each zone and the assumed adjustment processes in each market to establish in which direction output and the exchange rate will adjust. Start with a point like E_4. Here we have trade balance equilibrium but an excess demand for goods. Accordingly, output will expand. That output expansion in turn generates a trade deficit which causes the exchange rate to depreciate. That puts us in region III, where both adjustments in the level of income and the exchange rate move us toward the equilibrium point E.

Take another case, point E_2. Here we have a trade surplus causing e to fall (appreciate) and an excess supply of goods causing firms to reduce production. Both adjustments move us directly toward point E. Finally, consider a point like E_1, where we have a trade surplus and an excess demand for goods. The excess demand for goods causes output to be increased as firms respond to the running down of their inventories. The trade surplus causes the exchange rate to appreciate because export revenue exceeds import spending so that there is an excess supply of foreign exchange.

TABLE 19-1   DISEQUILIBRIA IN THE GOODS MARKET AND THE BALANCE OF PAYMENTS

Balance of payments	Goods market	
	Excess demand	Excess supply
Deficit	III	IV
Surplus	I	II

The arrows in Fig. 19-3 indicate the direction in which output and the exchange rate adjust. There is, as we see in the next paragraph, some ambiguity about the exact path along which we move from, say, point E_4 to E. The important thing, though, is that we do move to equilibrium or, in other words, that the system is stable.

The exact path is a question of the relative speeds of adjustment of the goods market and the foreign exchange market. One interesting possibility occurs when the exchange rate moves very fast to maintain trade balance equilibrium all the time. In that case the adjustment path is always along the NX schedule, because trade is by assumption always balanced. Such an assumption about the relative speeds of adjustment of output and the exchange rate is well in line with current thinking. Alternatively, the exchange rate might move more slowly—perhaps because the government intervenes in the foreign exchange market to slow down exchange rate movements—and adjustment would follow paths like those shown by the arrows in Fig. 19-3.

We have now shown in our discussion of dynamics using Fig. 19-3 that an economy with a flexible exchange rate will settle down to an equilibrium level of output and an exchange rate such that the goods market and the foreign exchange market clear. We have discussed the dynamics of that adjustment and found that the adjustment path depends both on the initial disequilibrium *and* on the relative speeds of adjustment of goods and foreign exchange markets. We have found the system to be stable. Have we cheated? What if we drew the schedules with the NX curve steeper? We would immediately find that instability is possible.[5] Clearly, then, the relative slopes are important, and we want to be satisfied that there is a good reason for the slopes we have shown in Fig. 19-3.

To solve the question of stability and establish that the slopes we have drawn are indeed correct, we return to Fig. 19-1. Assume we move from point E to point A_0 or A_2. We maintain goods market equilibrium, but output is higher. Now who buys the increased output? In part, the output expansion provides its own demand through induced spending. But, as we know, that is not enough. To sell the increased output, the relative price of domestic goods will have to fall or the exchange rate has to depreciate. A decline in the relative price of domestic goods creates the necessary demand to maintain goods market equilibrium at higher output levels. That additional demand comes from increased exports and a switch from imports to domestic goods—in short, it comes from an improvement in the trade balance. Thus, at a point like A_0 the trade balance is in surplus, and at a point like A_2 the trade surplus is even larger. High output levels are sustained by high net sales abroad or trade surpluses. For goods market equilibrium to be maintained at income levels higher than Y_0, a trade surplus must provide the additional demand. Thus points on YY to the right of E are points of trade surplus and therefore are above the NX

[5]Be sure you can show this by experimenting with the arrows in the diagram.

schedule. But since points A_0 and A_2 are to the right of E, the YY schedule must be steeper than the NX schedule.

Accordingly, the flexible rate system is indeed stable. In addition, our earlier analysis of the effect of expansionary fiscal policy on the exchange rate is validated.

Beggar Thy Neighbor Policies

Discussion of flexible or managed exchange rate systems invariably involves arguments about *beggar thy neighbor policies*. The problem is that exchange rates can be manipulated to give one country employment benefits at the expense of reduced output and employment abroad. This point is illustrated in Fig. 19-4. Assume the equilibrium was initially at point E with trade balance and goods market equilibrium. We have indicated, too, the full-employment level of output Y_p in Fig. 19-4. The policy problem posed by the equilibrium at point E is one of unemployment. We cannot achieve full employment because in the short run we have downward rigidity of wages and prices. If enough time passed, we would no doubt see falling wages and prices and thus increased demand for domestic goods. The alternative to waiting is to pursue an active stabilization policy.

Given underemployment, as at point E, the government could create extra demand for domestic goods and move to a position like E', if it could

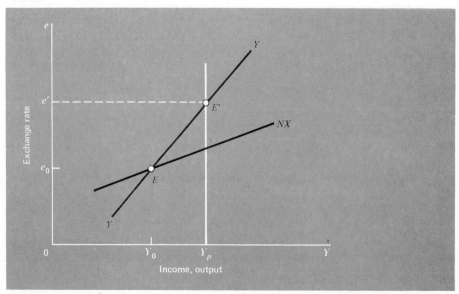

FIGURE 19-4 BEGGAR THY NEIGHBOR POLICIES

force the exchange rate to depreciate enough. That extra demand would come from increased exports and a shift of domestic spending from imports to domestic goods. A depreciation would—at the going domestic prices— lower the relative price of domestic goods and give the home country a competitive advantage which results in an increase in demand. That part is easy. The next question is how to get the exchange rate to depreciate.

In Fig. 19-4 we show that to get to full employment and goods market equilibrium the exchange rate would have to be e'. The depreciation would have to be equal to $(e' - e_0)/e_0$ percent. One way to get the exchange rate to depreciate to that level is to intervene in the foreign exchange market. The central bank would have to peg the rate at the level e'. At point E' there is a trade surplus—since that is after all the way we increased the demand for domestic goods. The surplus would cause the exchange rate to appreciate (e to fall), and the central bank has to prevent that appreciation by buying up the excess supply of foreign exchange arising from the trade surplus. Thus at point E', an *undervalued* exchange rate is sustained by intervention for the benefit of employment. Exchange rate undervaluation is one of the most common employment policies and one of the most feared ones, too.

The fear of exchange rate manipulation for employment purposes has its roots in the 1930s. In the thirties, given massive unemployment in most countries, there were attempts at *competitive depreciation*. Each country in turn tried to shift demand toward its own goods and away from the rest of the world. With each country trying depreciation in turn, all that happened was that world demand was moved around, but there was no net creation of demand in the world. What should have been done (obviously?) was to undertake very expansionary monetary and fiscal policies in each country to produce a coordinated recovery. In a world recession, everybody should expand aggregate demand by expansionary policies, not by expenditure switching that attempts to increase the demand for domestic goods at the expense of the demand for foreign goods.

The Multiplier under Flexible and Fixed Rates

The question we turn to now is the impact of aggregate demand expansion on output and employment under fixed and flexible rates. Assume we increased government spending on domestic goods. In Fig. 19-5 we see that, at a fixed exchange rate, the equilibrium shifts from E to E'. The expansion in demand creates an excess demand at the initial equilibrium point E. To maintain goods market equilibrium, output would have to be higher, increasing by the amount $Y' - Y_0$. Now at point E', the goods market clears and output has increased to meet the increase in autonomous spending and induced spending as well. Part of the induced spending, though, will fall on imports and, accordingly, at point E' there is a trade deficit. That trade deficit will cause the exchange rate to depreciate.

It is immediately apparent from Fig. 19-5 that the new equilibrium

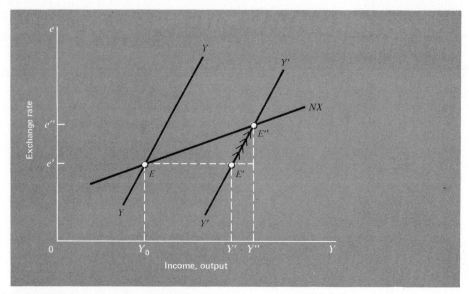

FIGURE 19-5 THE EXPANSIONARY
EFFECTS OF FISCAL POLICY UNDER FIXED
AND FLEXIBLE EXCHANGE RATES

under flexible rates will be at point E''. Only at point E'' will we have *both* internal and external balance. To get to point E'', the exchange rate has to depreciate, and that depreciation in turn adds further to the output expansion. While under fixed rates part of the expansion leaks into increased imports and a trade deficit, the effect of the exchange rate depreciation is to recover that leakage and restore trade balance. What is the implication? Looking at Fig. 19-5, we recognize that under flexible rates, the expansion is larger than it would be under fixed rates. Output rises to Y'' rather than only Y'. The requirement of trade balance equilibrium means that there is no net leakage of spending and, accordingly, the multiplier effects of expansionary fiscal policy are larger with flexible than with fixed exchange rates, in the absence of capital flows.

Employment and the Terms of Trade

Although the trade balance is kept in equilibrium under flexible rates, it is apparent from Fig. 19-5 that the exchange rate depreciates as a result of expansionary policies. The change in the exchange rate has welfare implications for domestic residents. Given domestic prices, the depreciation means that the purchasing power of our goods is reduced. Output and employment are increased by the expansion, but the standard of living of those who had already been employed (at point E) is reduced. Because the prices of imports have increased, those who were already employed prior to the expansion will find that the purchasing power of their incomes has fallen in terms of imports and that they are worse off. There is an offsetting benefit to this loss of purchasing power, in the form of increased employment and output.

*19-2 FLEXIBLE RATES AND CAPITAL MOBILITY

The discussion of equilibrium and stability in the previous section hinged on the fact that without capital flows the exchange rate adjusts to close the trade gap opened up by an expansion in income and therefore imports. Now we ask what happens if capital flows can arise in the adjustment process. There is an important difference from the previous section because now only the overall balance of payments has to be in equilibrium. Capital flows can be used to finance trade deficits or surpluses, and they thus greatly alter the adjustment process.

Fiscal Policy and Capital Mobility

Say we expand government demand and as a consequence increase income. In Sec. 19-1, we assumed a constant interest rate and no capital flows. Now, what would have happened if, throughout, the nominal quantity of money—rather than interest rates—had been held constant? We know from the IS–LM analysis that the increase in income would have been dampened. The increase in income would have raised money demand, and that would have caused interest rates to increase, thus dampening the income expansion. We are left now with the question whether, with higher income and higher interest rates, the analysis of the previous section continues to hold. Clearly not. If interest rates have risen, then there will be capital inflows that cause the exchange rate to appreciate and thereby induce a substitution away from domestic goods, a worsening of the trade balance, and a dampening of the income expansion. With capital mobility, the expansionary impact of fiscal policy must fall short of that of a flexible rate system without capital mobility.

Perfect capital mobility implies that small changes in the domestic interest rate bring about unlimited flows of capital. The balance of payments can only be in equilibrium when the domestic interest rate is at the level of the world rate. If the domestic rate were lower, capital outflows would be so large as to totally swamp the trade balance and produce a large depreciation, and conversely if the interest rate was above the world level.

What does perfect capital mobility imply for fiscal policy? If a fiscal expansion takes place, it tends to raise income and therefore interest rates. The increase in interest rates immediately triggers off a large capital inflow and thus a balance of payments surplus. The surplus causes the exchange rate to appreciate and the appreciation in turn reduces the demand for domestic output. How long will that process of appreciation continue? As long as the domestic interest rate is above the world level, capital flows will be keeping pressure on the exchange rate, keeping the rate appreciating, and thus continue reducing the demand for domestic goods. Only when the demand for goods has declined precisely to offset the fiscal expansion will the process stop. At that point income is back to its original level and so are interest rates. Thus, the end result is an appreciation in the exchange rate that reduces demand and worsens the trade balance by exactly the size of the fiscal expansion. Fiscal policy has no effect on income when there is perfect capital mobility.[6]

We have just shown a quite striking implication of flexible rates. Fiscal policy will not work with perfect capital mobility.[7] It cannot work because the domestic interest rate cannot diverge from the world rate without inducing large capital flows that move the exchange rate and thus offset the expansionary impact of fiscal policies. Indeed, under perfect capital mobility and flexible rates, an expansion in government spending will be one-for-one reflected in an increase in the trade deficit—the government absorbs more domestic output and the appreciation diverts (crowds?) the private sector toward foreign goods.

Monetary Policy and Capital Mobility

If fiscal policy does not work, how about monetary policy? As we might expect, monetary policy is particularly powerful under flexible rates with perfect capital mobility. To see this, let us look at an expansion in the money supply. The short-run impact would be to lower interest rates and cause an income expansion. But the moment interest rates fall, capital flows out. The capital outflow induced by the lower domestic interest rate gives rise to a balance of payments deficit and depreciates the exchange rate. That in turn causes demand for domestic goods to expand and output and income to increase. How far will the rate depreciate? The rate will keep depreciating until it has fallen so low that it raises demand and income enough for people to hold the higher money supply at the world rate of interest. Thus monetary policy works very powerfully. It works by inducing a depreciation in the exchange rate which in turn stimulates demand for domestic output. The more mobile capital, the more powerful monetary policy.[8]

---

[6]We can think of this result from a slightly different perspective. If fiscal policy cannot affect the interest rate, it cannot affect velocity, given the level of income. With velocity given, there is a unique level of income that can be sustained by the money supply.

[7]The argument is due to Robert Mundell in his article "Capital Mobility and Stabilization Policy under Fixed and Flexible Exchange Rates," *Canadian Journal of Economics and Political Science*, November 1963. See, too, Marcus Fleming, "Domestic Financial Policies under Fixed and Floating Exchange Rates," *I.M.F. Staff Papers*, 1962.

[8]Or, working through velocity, an increase in the money stock has no effect on the interest rate and, thus, on velocity. Expansion in the nominal money supply accordingly increases nominal income without having an effect on velocity.

A Graphical Treatment of Policy with Capital Mobility

We can review the discussion of monetary and fiscal policy under perfect capital mobility using Figs. 19-6 and 19-7. Here we have shown the LM curve for a given quantity of money, and the BP schedule, which reflects the fact that capital mobility is perfect. There is only one interest rate at which the balance of payments is in equilibrium, for at any other interest rate we are swamped with capital inflows or outflows. Now we have to remember that the IS curve is drawn for a given fiscal policy *and* a given exchange rate. A depreciation of the exchange rate will shift the IS curve up and to the right because it increases demand for domestic goods. An appreciation, by contrast, will reduce demand for domestic goods and shift the IS curve down and to the left.

Let us first look at an attempt to expand the economy through fiscal policy. Starting at point E, an increase in government spending or a tax cut would *at the initial exchange rate* shift the IS curve in Fig. 19-6 to IS'. With a given quantity of money, domestic equilibrium would be at point E_1, where we have an increase in interest rates and income. But clearly we have forgotten the external constraint. At E_1 we have a balance of payments surplus, which means that the exchange rate will start appreciating. The appreciation will shift demand away from domestic goods and thus will start shifting the IS curve backward. In other words, the appreciation exerts a deflationary effect on the economy. How long will the process continue? As long as we are above the BP schedule, the exchange rate will

FIGURE 19-6 FISCAL POLICY UNDER FLEXIBLE RATES AND PERFECT CAPITAL MOBILITY

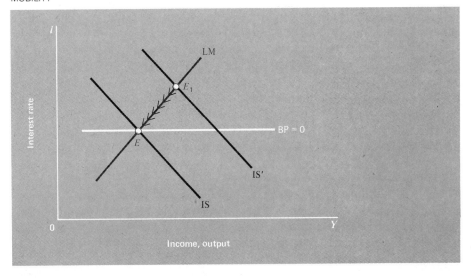

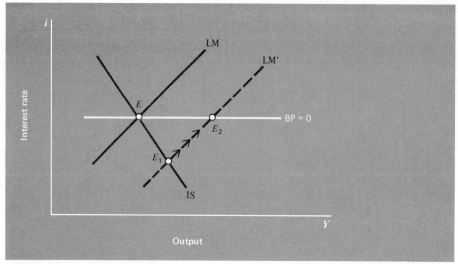

FIGURE 19-7 EXPANSIONARY
MONETARY POLICY UNDER FLEXIBLE
RATES AND PERFECT CAPITAL MOBILITY

keep appreciating and the IS curve will keep shifting back. The process, therefore, continues until we reach point E again. At that point total demand is back where it was initially. That means the fiscal expansion is precisely offset by a trade deficit.

When we have returned to E, the increase in the trade deficit is equal to the fiscal expansion—say, the increase in the government budget deficit. Since the balance of payments is in balance, there is an inflow of capital equal to the trade deficit and therefore equal to the budget deficit. The budget deficit is being *financed* with a capital inflow, or, more prosaically, by borrowing from abroad.

Next we look at a monetary expansion to achieve an increase in output. That is done in Fig. 19-7. Starting from point E, the monetary expansion shifts the LM curve to LM'. This lowers interest rates and raises income, and moves us to a point like E_1. At that point the increase in income and decline in interest rates have worsened the balance of payments. The deficit gives rise to a depreciation of the exchange rate. That depreciation acts in an expansionary way on goods demand and thus shifts the IS curve (not drawn) up and to the right. The process continues as long as we have a balance of payments deficit and therefore moves us all the way to point E_2. At that point income and hence money demand have risen enough for people to hold the increased money supply at an interest rate equal to the world rate.

What has happened to the trade balance? The trade balance will improve because the depreciation raises exports and reduces import spending. It is true that the income expansion raises imports, but that effect is more than offset by the trade balance improvement due to the depreciation.

We conclude this section with an assignment. You should go through the case of less than perfect capital mobility and show which (if any) results are modified.

19-3 FINANCING CURRENT ACCOUNT BALANCES AND THE OIL SHOCK

The discussion of capital mobility in the preceding section points up sharply the fact that *trade* need not be balanced just because the exchange rate is flexible. All a flexible rate implies is that the balance of payments will balance, which means that capital flows precisely finance the trade deficit. That point was of importance in the aftermath of the oil shock and world recession of 1973–1975. The role of capital mobility in that period was to ease the adjustment process to the change in the relative price of oil and to assist those countries that chose to react to the shock with continued high demand rather than a recession.

This section is concerned with the adjustment of the world economy to the fourfold increase in the price of oil which occurred at the end of 1973. For most countries the oil price increase implied a deterioration in their terms of trade (the ratio of their export to import prices), a reduction in their standard of living, and a trade deficit.[9] The oil-exporting (OPEC) countries, by contrast, enjoyed an improvement in their terms of trade and a trade surplus. The questions which concern us are how the deficits were financed and what other adjustment processes were at work.

What would a particular country do when faced with a substantial price increase for indispensable imports? There are basically two possible strategies. One is to create a recession and thus reduce aggregate demand and therefore import demand for *all* commodities, including those whose prices increased. Clearly a recession would reduce oil imports because the decline in industrial output would bring about a corresponding decline in the demand for oil and material inputs. Even on the consumption side a sufficiently large recession might make a dent in oil and gasoline consumption.

The other short-run strategy is to maintain aggregate demand in the face of the terms of trade deterioration. There might be an attempt to reduce oil imports by a variety of measures, including speed limits and heating regulations. There is no attempt, though, to reduce other imports significantly by broad macroeconomic measures. The clear implication of such a strategy may well be a current account deficit if the import price

---

[9]For a comprehensive study of the oil shock see Edward Fried and Charles Schultze (eds.), *Higher Oil Prices and the World Economy: The Adjustment Problem*, Brookings, 1975.

increase is not offset by a significant reduction in imports. The total import bill therefore might increase.[10]

Most oil-importing countries faced the choice between these two strategies. They had to decide whether to accommodate the oil price increase by a policy that maintained aggregate demand or internal balance, or a policy that maintained external balance by a reduction in imports through a domestic recession. The actual choices made were somewhat mixed. Many less developed countries maintained aggregate demand and, as a consequence, ran huge deficits. Industrial countries, in 1974, did not pursue highly restrictive policies and thus also incurred deficits. By 1975, though, most had moved into recession and showed corresponding reductions in their deficits.

Table 19-2 shows the current account balances of developed countries, including the United States, as well as the current account of developing non-oil-producing countries and OPEC countries. The striking fact is the enormous increase in the surplus of oil producers in 1974–1975 matched by the increased deficit in developing countries and reduced surplus in the developed countries in 1974.[11]

There is an important difference between developing and developed countries. Most industrial countries—the United States, Japan, Germany, to name some—went into a recession in order to fight the high inflation of 1973–1974. As they moved into recession in 1974, their import demand declined. The decline in import demand was in part at the expense of each other, but also partly at the expense of OPEC and developing countries. The sharp increase in developed countries' surpluses in 1975 reflects a reduced import bill from developing countries, increased exports to OPEC countries, and a fall in oil import spending.

Developing countries faced a second shock in 1975. Having already experienced the oil price increase, they were now struck by a recession-induced decline in world demand for their imports. In addition to an

[10]You should refer at this point to footnote 3 above.

[11]For the world as a whole, the sum of all current accounts should be zero. The reason is that the surplus of any one country has to be matched by deficits of countries with which it trades. Table 19-2 omits the current accounts of Eastern European and some other countries. Also, these data are not very good. For both reasons, the sum of the surpluses in the table is not equal to the sum of the deficits.

TABLE 19-2   CURRENT ACCOUNT BALANCES (*Exclusive of transfers; billions of dollars*)

	1973	1974	1975
Industrial countries	25.0	2.3	25.3
Oil-exporting countries	5.2	60.1	31.8
Developing countries	−10.6	−32.5	−42.9

Note: Minus sign denotes deficit.

Source: International Financial Statistics, August 1976, p.54.

increase in their import bill, they now faced a reduction in their export earnings. Furthermore, they had little prospect of significantly expanding their exports to OPEC countries, because they were not producers of investment goods that would suit the investment programs in OPEC countries. As a consequence of the world recession, the developing countries' current account further worsened in 1975 as compared with 1974.

The next question to ask is how their current account balances were financed. An individual who spends more than her income has to decumulate assets in order to finance the excess. The same is true for an aggregate of individuals or a country. Thus, a counterpart of the current account deficits of developed and developing countries is the extraordinary buildup of OPEC wealth. OPEC countries spent only a fraction of their increased income on goods and services, and chose to accumulate the rest in claims on the outside world. Developing countries and developed countries by contrast were running deficits or reduced surpluses—they were decumulating assets. In the world at large deficits and dissaving of one group are matched by surpluses and saving of another.

Table 19-3 summarizes how developing countries financed their deficits from 1973 to 1975. Financing was through external aid, loans on concessional (low) interest rate terms, and grants, as well as private borrowing. The official development assistance represents aid from foreign governments and international institutions. Perhaps the most interesting aspect of Table 19-3 is the strongly growing amount of financing that is privately provided. The world capital market channeled these private flows—$21 billion in 1975—from surplus countries toward deficit countries and thus from lenders to borrowers. Nevertheless, almost half the external financing is still made up of aid or concessional loans.

There is one striking omission from our discussion of the world economy's adjustment to the effects of the oil price increase. We have not discussed exchange rate changes as part of the adjustment process, even though the oil shock occurred shortly after the flexible rate system began operating. The reason for that omission is that exchange rate adjustments were not an important part of the adjustment process between the OPEC

TABLE 19-3 FINANCING DEVELOPING COUNTRIES' CURRENT ACCOUNT (*Billions of dollars*)

	1973	1974	1975
Official development assistance	9.4	11.3	13.6
Other official flows	2.5	2.2	2.7
Private flows	11.5	13.3	21.2
Grants by private agencies	1.4	1.2	1.4
Total: Net inflow of capital and aid	24.7	28.0	38.8

Source: International Monetary Fund, *Survey,* July 19, 1976, p. 216.

countries and other countries. Effectively, the OPEC countries, by setting the price of oil in dollars, were operating under fixed exchange rates vis-a-vis the developed countries.

19-4 LONG-RUN TRENDS IN EXCHANGE RATES

The emphasis so far has been on short-run questions of financing. It is appropriate now, as we complete our discussion of international trade in this book, to ask what determines the behavior of an exchange rate over a longer period of, say, three to five years.

It is useful for this purpose to look at the economy as essentially in full employment with the movement of prices reflecting both trend growth in real output and the growth rate of the nominal quantity of money. As we saw in Chap. 13, the long-term rate of inflation is higher, the higher the growth rate of the nominal quantity of money. This tight relation between money and inflation holds strictly only in the steady state, but over a period of three to five years it is a reasonable approximation. Thus, if we increased monetary growth, say, from 5 to 15 percent, and maintained it at the higher level, we would soon expect inflation to start increasing and eventually to reflect the faster monetary growth. The question of this section is how such inflation will be reflected in the exchange rate.

Other things equal, the trend behavior of exchange rates is a reflection of differences in inflation rates. If one country has a trend rate of inflation of 20 percent and another country has a rate of inflation of 10 percent, then the exchange rate should be depreciating at the rate of 10 percent. The country with the higher rate of inflation has an exchange rate that depreciates at a rate equal to the differences in inflation rates. That is because we expect the relative prices of goods in different countries to be little affected by steady inflation. Can such exchange rate behavior ever be observed? There are obvious examples during periods of hyperinflation. And, during such periods, when inflation is the main influence on the economy, the rate of depreciation closely matches the internal rate of inflation.

What about less dramatic episodes? We look at the behavior of the United States–United Kingdom exchange rate, that is, the dollar price of the pound sterling from 1970 to 1976. Britain had quite high inflation compared to the United States in that period. Accordingly, we would expect sterling to have depreciated, or the dollar price of pounds to have fallen. The question, though, is how closely the depreciation matches the behavior of the relative rates of inflation. We look at that question in Chart 19-2. The ratio of the United States to the United Kingdom consumer price index is shown by the line $P^{\text{U.S.}}/P^{\text{U.K.}}$. The line reflects the fact that prices have been rising faster in Britain than in the United States. The second line shows the behavior of the exchange rate. Clearly, the dollar price of pounds has fallen over the time period although both the timing and magnitude of the exchange rate movements only loosely match those of the

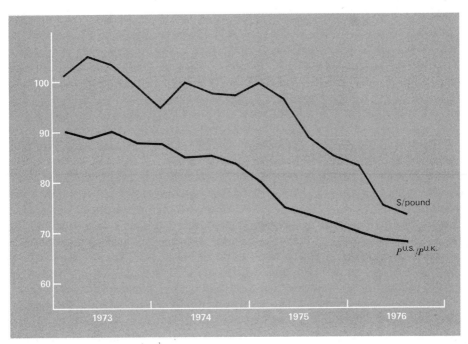

CHART 19-2 RELATIVE PRICE LEVELS
AND EXCHANGE RATE MOVEMENTS:
UNITED STATES AND UNITED KINGDOM
(INDEX 1970 = 100). (Source: *International
Financial Statistics*, January 1977)

price movements. The chart shows that British price inflation has been running ahead of inflation in the United States for quite some time (equivalently, the United States price level has been falling relative to the United Kingdom price level) with a pronounced acceleration since 1974. The exchange rate movement is concentrated in 1975 and only then catches up with the accumulated differences in price behavior.

Chart 19-2 reflects rather well what we expect of *purchasing-power-parity* theory, or PPP for short.[12] That theory suggests that the exchange rate mirrors the behavior of the purchasing power of money—an increase in prices is reflected in a depreciation of the currency. For instance, suppose United States dollar prices are moving at 5 percent per year and United Kingdom sterling prices are rising at 10 percent per year. PPP says that the exchange rate, expressed as dollars/pound, should be appreciating by 5 percent per year. That way, the ratio of prices of British goods, measured in *dollars*, to prices of American goods in dollars, remains constant.

The chart shows that the "truth" of PPP holds only approximately and

[12]An assessment of PPP can be found in Lawrence Officer, "The Purchasing-Power-Parity Theory of Exchange Rates: A Review Article," *I.M.F. Staff Papers*, March 1976.

that it is not exact either in respect to timing or magnitude of the exchange rate movements. In the short run and over time, many factors impinge on the exchange rate, and prices are only one of them. Along with prices and price expectations, there are output disturbances, shifts in demand, and capital flows. All these exert an effect on the exchange rate and can cause it to diverge from a path dictated by differences in inflation rates.

Looking at the depreciation of the pound sterling shown in Chart 19-2, we should ask what the real effects are. Does that depreciation lower the relative price of British goods, and therefore make Britain more competitive? The point of PPP and of movements in exchange rates that reflect differences in inflation rates is that there are no real effects. The exchange rate movement serves the purpose of offsetting the differential rates of price and cost inflation between the two countries and thus leaves relative prices unchanged. To the extent, however, that the exchange rate does not precisely move to offset differences in cost and price inflation, there will indeed be real effects. If the depreciation of the exchange rate is held back by intervention, then there is insufficient offset and the country with the higher inflation rate loses in competitive power. For example, if Britain is inflating at 10 percent and the United States at 5 percent, and the Bank of England intervenes to keep the exchange rate constant, the dollar prices of British goods rise at 5 percent per annum relative to American prices. By contrast, if the United Kingdom exchange rate were to depreciate faster than the difference in inflation rates, then the United Kingdom effectively gains in competitive position.

Chart 19-3 is designed to illustrate these points. We show there the sterling price of British exports. It is a reflection of the high inflation rate in Britain that these export prices are sharply increasing from 1973 to 1976. We show, too, the dollar export prices of the United Kingdom[13] and, for comparison, the dollar export prices of the United States. It is quite apparent that in dollars the United Kingdom does not nearly experience the same price increase as in sterling. The sterling depreciation offsets a large part of the British inflation and thus maintains the external competitiveness of British goods. Now we see from Chart 19-3 that this is not uniformly true. Until the second quarter of 1975 the exchange rate moved very little and, accordingly, the high British inflation was translated into a correspondingly high inflation of British export prices in dollar terms. In that period British goods lost competitiveness with exports of other countries.

Next comes the period from the second quarter of 1975 until the fourth quarter of that year. Then, sterling depreciated sufficiently, not only to offset the domestic inflation, but also partially to make up for the failure to depreciate earlier. British competitiveness was improved in that period.

---

[13]The dollar export prices of the United Kingdom are the sterling prices times the exchange rate. If the sterling price of a typewriter is 100 pounds and the dollar/pound exchange rate is $1.50 per pound, the dollar price of the typewriter is $150.

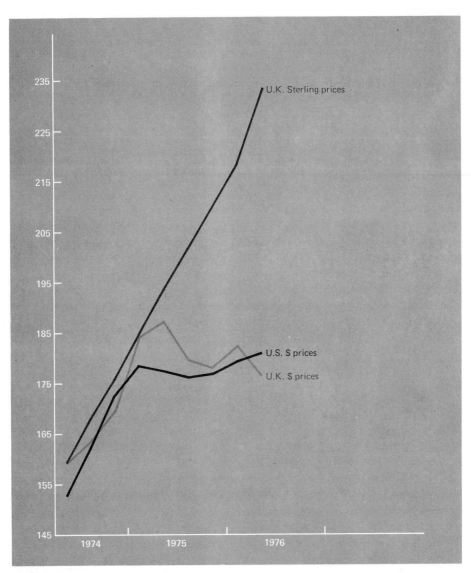

CHART 19-3 THE UNITED KINGDOM
COMPETITIVE POSITION (INDEX 1970 =
100). (Source: *International Financial
Statistics*, January 1977)

In the first quarter of 1976 there is again very little depreciation and competitiveness is lost. Finally, in the remainder of 1976, the dramatic depreciation brings about a forceful move to competitiveness.

19-5 EXCHANGE RATE VOLATILITY AND CENTRAL BANK INTERVENTION

Differential rates of inflation provide a good explanation for the medium-term trend behavior of the exchange rate. There remains, however, the big issue of short-term fluctuations. Returning to Chart 19-1 for a moment, we recognize the extraordinary volatility in exchange rates. There even appear to be cycles. Thus, in 1973–1974 there appear to be half-year cycles of appreciation and depreciation with swings in the exchange rate between the dollar and the snake of up to 20 percent. It is these recurrent, seemingly arbitrary, but sizable, movements in exchange rates that worry policy makers, and have led to reconsideration of the benefits of flexible exchange rates.

Before we briefly examine the substantive point about the volatility of exchange rates since the flexible rate system emerged, we should warn that the discerning eye appears to detect cycles where statistical techniques cannot. It is difficult to establish from the short experience we have had with flexible rates that exchange rates under a flexible rate system will indeed cycle in the future. All we can say is that in the last few years, exchange rates have made large movements which were subsequently reversed.

It can well be argued that if the exchange rate fluctuates greatly, as in Chart 19-1, then it moves production in the economy in an unnecessarily erratic fashion. When the rate depreciates, imports decline and exports rise. Next, the rate appreciates and the trade changes are reversed. These rate movements are not clearly understood, but the fact that they seem transitory and are frequently reversed suggests the potential for intervention. Perhaps, then, the Federal Reserve should intervene in the foreign exchange market to smooth out exchange rates?

The argument that the central bank can smooth out fluctuations in exchange rates is the basic argument for central bank intervention in the foreign exchange markets. At one extreme, the argument would assert that any movements in exchange rates produce unnecessary fluctuations in the domestic economy and that exchange rates therefore ought to be fixed. This is the basic argument for dirty floating. The only—and overwhelming—objection to the argument that the central bank should smooth out fluctuations is that there is no simple way of telling an erratic movement from a trend movement. How can we tell whether a current appreciation in the exchange rate is merely the result of a disturbance which will soon reverse itself rather than the beginning of a trend movement in the exchange rate? There is no way of telling at the time a change occurs, though with the benefit of hindsight one can easily look at diagrams like Chart 19-1 to tell which exchange rate movements were later reversed.

The history of the fixed exchange rate regimes of the sixties is full of examples of central banks which fought hard against devaluations on the grounds that balance of payments pressures were merely temporary. The

British delayed devaluing from 1964 to 1967 in the belief that they were fighting speculators rather than facing a deterioration of their competitive position. There is no guarantee that central banks know when they should intervene and when they should allow the exchange rate to move. The argument that it would be desirable to avoid unnecessary fluctuations in exchange rates is not proof that central banks should intervene in the foreign exchange markets.

You will notice a difference between our views on domestic stabilization policy and on exchange market intervention. On the domestic front we argued that policy should respond, in a cautious way, to aggregate demand disturbances. Thus an increase in the unemployment rate would call for expansionary policy, even though the authorities would not be certain whether the disturbance causing the unemployment rate to increase is permanent or temporary. We do not argue for similar policies to attempt to stabilize exchange rates. We feel that private capital flows potentially provide a sufficient stabilizing element in the foreign exchange markets. There is, and can be, very little such speculation to stabilize the behavior of aggregate output.

19-6 SUMMARY

1   Under flexible exchange rates, without government intervention, the exchange rate adjusts to ensure equilibrium in the overall balance of payments. The sum of the current and capital account deficits is zero with floating rates and no intervention.

2   The demand for our goods depends on the exchange rate which, given foreign and domestic prices, affects the relative price of imports versus exports. An increase in the exchange rate—a depreciation—increases the demand for domestically produced goods by reducing imports and increasing exports.

3   In the absence of capital flows and government intervention, the exchange rate adjusts to keep the current account in balance. Under these assumptions, expansive fiscal policy increases the level of income and leads to a depreciation of the exchange rate.

4   On the assumption that the exchange rate appreciates when there is a trade surplus and the level of output rises when there is an excess demand for goods, the simple floating exchange rate system without capital flows that we studied is stable. The economy moves toward balanced trade.

5   If an economy finds itself with unemployment, the central bank can intervene to depreciate the exchange rate and increase net exports and thus aggregate demand. Such policies are known as beggar thy neighbor policies, because the increase in demand for domestic output comes at the expense of demand for foreign output.

6 The multiplier is larger with flexible than with fixed rates. The reason is that under flexible rates, the increase in income caused by the policy change also causes the exchange rate to depreciate, thus providing a further stimulus to demand for domestic output.

7 When capital is very mobile, so that the interest rate essentially cannot differ from the world rate, fiscal policy becomes totally ineffective in changing the level of income. An increase in government spending merely reduces net exports, with the trade deficit being financed by a capital inflow.

8 Monetary policy retains its effectiveness when capital is very mobile. An increase in the money stock leads to a depreciation of the exchange rate and an improved foreign balance, which increases demand for domestic output.

9 In the long run, exchange rate movements between two currencies in a flexible rate system reflect changes in the price levels in the two countries. A country with a more rapid rate of inflation will find its exchange rate depreciating against the currency of a country which is inflating less rapidly. The exchange rate movements induced by the price level changes merely keep the relative prices of goods produced in the two countries constant.

10 Since the 1973 beginning of the flexible rate system, there have been substantial fluctuations in exchange rates. These movements are hard to explain and affect the allocation of resources. A central bank which wants to intervene to smooth out the fluctuations has to know when an exchange rate change is going to be reversed, and when it is permanent. For this reason, foreign exchange intervention to smooth out exchange rate fluctuations is extremely difficult.

PROBLEMS

1 Explain why the belief that a devaluation is imminent makes a devaluation more likely in a fixed exchange rate system.

2 Why do you think countries were reluctant to move away from the system of fixed exchange rates during the late sixties and early seventies, even though it was by then not operating very well? Also explain what "not operating very well" means.

*3 Assuming there are no capital movements, and that the interest rate is fixed, explain how a tariff affects the level of income and the exchange rate in a flexible rate system. (Note: A tariff is a tax on imported goods.)

4 Explain why an expansionary fiscal policy beggars our neighbors less than direct intervention by the central bank in the foreign exchange markets.

5 Still assuming there are no capital flows, explain how an increase in the domestic interest rate (which we have assumed fixed so far) affects the level of income and the exchange rate. How could the domestic interest rate be changed?

6 a What are the terms of trade?
  b Why does expansionary domestic policy affect the terms of trade in a floating exchange rate system?

*7 Assume now that there is perfect mobility of capital. How does the imposition of a tariff affect the exchange rate, output, and the current account?

*8 Explain how and why monetary policy retains its effectiveness when there is perfect mobility of capital.

9 Consult the *Wall Street Journal* or some other newspaper which has foreign exchange rates listed on the financial pages. For some countries, such as Britain and Germany, you should find future prices listed. This is the price to be paid today to receive one unit of the foreign currency in the future. A thirty-day future price for the pound sterling, say, is the price paid today to receive £1 thirty days from now. Explain why the future prices are not generally equal to the spot prices—the price paid today to receive the foreign currency today. See if you can explain the difference between the relationship of spot and future prices for the pound and deutschmark, respectively.

*10 Assume you expect the pound to depreciate by 6 percent over the next year. Assume that the United States interest rate is 4 percent. What interest rate would be needed on pound securities—such as government bonds—for you to be willing to buy those securities with your dollars today, and then sell them in a year in exchange for dollars? Can you relate your answer to this question to your answer to problem 9?

11 What considerations are relevant for a country deciding whether to borrow abroad to finance a balance of trade deficit, or to adjust?

12 Explain the purchasing-power-parity theory of the long-run behavior of the exchange rate. Indicate whether there are any circumstances under which you would not expect the PPP relationship to hold.

Index